Rent Reviews
and Variable Rents

To Judith, Johanna, Elizabeth and Naomi.
With all my love and gratitude

Rent Reviews
and Variable Rents

Third Edition

D N Clarke

Solicitor, Senior Lecturer in Law
University of Bristol

J E Adams

Solicitor, Emeritus Professor of Law,
Queen Mary and Westfield College, London

LONGMAN

© Longman Group UK Ltd 1990

ISBN 0 85121 3863

Published by

Longman Law, Tax and Finance
Longman Group UK Limited
21–27 Lamb's Conduit Street, London WC1N 3NJ

Associated Offices
Australia, Hong Kong, Malaysia, Singapore, USA

A CIP catalogue record for this book is available from the British
Library

Printed and bound by
Mackays of Chatham PLC, Chatham, Kent

Contents

Part Four: Special Situations and the Impact of Statute

Part Five: Variable rents other than Rent Review Clauses 557

Preface
to the Third Edition

It is nearly a decade since the first publication of this book — the first substantial treatise on the topic of rent reviews — and exactly six years since we penned the preface to the second edition. It is perhaps appropriate to have a 'review date' for the text on such a topic, though like many reviews of a rent, the submission of the text of this edition, due a year ago, has been delayed. In retrospect, this has been advantageous since it has meant that decisions such as *Ipswich Borough Council* v *Fisons plc, Jones* v *Sherwood Computer Services, Arnold* v *National Westminster Bank* and *Glofield Properties* v *Morley (no 2)* have been fully assimilated into the text.

Just as the standard rent review clause of a decade ago has often been transformed into a very different creature today, so too the text of this edition (most of which has been completely or substantially rewritten) and it is presented so as to reflect the developments in the ten years. The book is now divided into five parts. After the initial discussion of the issue of variable rents generally, Part Two (Chapters 4–9) deals chronologically with the machinery of rent review — from the drafting considerations through to all aspects of the operation of the standard review clause. Though the section on the issue of time limits, delay and notices reveals consolidation of the law since the last edition rather than radical change, the chapters on arbitration and valuation (now chapter 6) and evidential issues (chapter 7) are in a completely new guise as befits the substantial developments on these matters as they relate to rent review. Part Three draws together all aspects relating to the construction and interpretation of the review clause and the hypothetical lease which is to be valued. Chapter 10 is completely new and sets out the principles adopted by the courts when called upon to declare the true meaning of a clause and suggests that new canons of construction are being formulated which apply principally to the rent review clause.

The trend to emphasise the 'reality' may be welcomed, though the authors wonder if some of the decisions truly accord with the reality between the parties. Nevertheless, it is no coincidence that the discussion of the valuation framework of review is divided between the actualities (chapter 11) and the wholly notional aspects constructed solely for the purpose of review (chapter 12). A separate chapter is now devoted to ground rents and other shared development leases. Part Four draws together the impact of various statutory provisions and other special situations while the book continues to cover variable rents in their wider aspects by concluding with an updated discussion of index linked, turnover and equity rents.

Though the book remains an attempt to produce a scholarly exposition of the law of England and Wales, the growing jurisprudence in Scotland, New Zealand and Australia is also incorporated and we hope that the attempt to maintain a practical emphasis will continue to assist practitioners in all these jurisdictions.

Apart from chapter 15 and a large part of chapter 12, the task of research, rewriting and updating the text for this edition has fallen upon David Clarke. However, the resultant text has been the subject of detailed discussion by both of us and to that extent the book remains a work of joint authorship for which we accept joint reponsibility.

Our thanks are extended to Pat Hammond and Liz Young at the University of Bristol who transferred much of the existing but relevant text from the last edition into word processed form; to Steven Fogel of Titmuss Sainer and Webb for his informed and pertinent comment on a number of issues; to colleagues at the University of Bristol especially Keith Stanton and Christine Willmore who read and commented upon the sections on Professional Negligence and Evidence respectively; and David Clarke's Opus PCIII without which the task would remain unaccomplished.

More than ever, the lawyer or surveyor practising in the field of rent review needs to be versed in many and varied legal rules and be aware of how they operate in the review context. We hope that this book will continue to provide the framework to enable that to be done.

August Bank Holiday
(27th August 1990)

D N Clarke
Solicitor, Senior Lecturer in Law,
University of Bristol.
Consultant, Osborne Clarke, Solicitors, Bristol.

J E Adams
Solicitor, Emeritus Professor of Law,
Queen Mary and Westfield College,
University of London.
Director of Training, Titmuss Sainer and Webb,
Solicitors, Serjeant's Inn, London.

Preface
to the Second Edition

The warm reception afforded to the first edition of this book and the continuing developments in the case law allow us to present a second edition less than four years later. Our aim and approach remain the same—to produce a book which, while being scholarly in its handling of the difficult and controversial points of the law, yet maintains a practical emphasis useful to lawyers, surveyors, valuers and others in the property field. Since the first edition we have tried to keep abreast of, and take into account, both the opinions of other commentators and what we perceive as current thinking and practice in the property world.

The spate of litigation on rent review clauses continues unabated and there is every expectation that it will continue. Lord Diplock, in 1977 in *United Scientific Holdings Ltd* v *Burnley Borough Council* (the *Burnley* case) expressed the hope that the decisions 'in these appeals will reduce the number of occasions on which it will be necessary to have recourse to the courts in order to ascertain whether delay has deprived the landlord of his reight to have the rent reviewed'. One may ruefully observe that this prophecy has unhappily remained unfulfilled—both in relation to delay—where recent case law has necessitated the complete rewriting of Section 2 to Chapter 6—and more generally across the spectrum of rent review. On the other hand, it is also perhaps true to say that no one single decision has had the same landmark qualities as that case.

Apart from the general rewriting and incorporation of new material that such developments entail, we have, in the present edition, added a separate chapter on the treatment of inadequate rent review clauses and the remedy of rectification as applied to aspects of rent review in leases (Chapter 8). Chapter 7 has been much expanded to cover the position not only of the guarantor but also the original lessee; and what is now Chapter 10 there is much new material on the judicial control of arbitrations. Various statutory developments necessitated an expanded treatment of the topic of payment of interest in Chapter 5, and we hope that the drafting checklist at the end of that Chapter will provide assistance and serve as a pointer to discussion of topics elsewhere in the book. The enactment of the Agricultural Holdings Act 1984 took place after the manuscript had been delivered to the printers but we have been able to incorporate the main features of that Act, as it impinges on rent review and variable rent provisions, into Chapter 4. New material in the Appendices includes the Royal Institution of Chartered Surveyors 'Guidance notes for surveyors acting as arbitrators or as independent valuers'. We hope their inclusion will give the work even greater utility for the busy practitioner and we are grateful to the Royal Institution for their permission to print them.

We did consider deleting, or reducing, our discussion of 'Rent Freezes' (Chapter 13) on the ground that the present political climate would suggest that another freeze of commercial rents is remote. Yet it seemed to us that perhaps the vararies of the British political climate are as unpredictable as the national weather patterns and the material in that chapter may yet be of use on future reviews—as well as giving continuing guidance to the draftsmen who is as cautious in this context as ourselves.

Once again, we acknowledge the assistance and encouragement of professional colleagues. Combining as we both do, the life of an academic with that of a practising solicitor, such acknowledgement extends to all those who have helped use in both those fields. We are particularly indebted to Mr Stephen Fogel whose detailed comments on our first edition were invaluable, if we have not felt able to adopt all his helpful suggestions—and those of other readers and reviewers—we are none the less grateful for the stimulation given. We were gratified to receive correspondence from readers and trust that any who can further impart their wisdom to deal with any imperfections which undoubtedly remain will not hesitate to write and enlighten us.

Especial thanks go to both old and new friends at Oyez Longman Publishing who continue collectively to demonstrate those qualities to which we paid tribute when this work first saw light of day. Our own secretarial assistance, as generous as ever, has been accompanied and aided by the benefit of word processors. The contribution of modern technology, however, has gone further, for the availability of a LEXIS terminal at Bristol University (a service of Butterworth (Telepublishing) Ltd) has enabled us to include many recent cases as yet unreported, most of which will, no doubt, surface in law reports in due course.

In endeavouring to state the law as at the August Bank Holiday 1984, we took advantage of the fact that it ensured us of 3 day respite from the onslaught of new material.

August Bank Holiday
(27 August) 1984

D N Clarke
University of Bristol

J E Adams
Queen Mary College
London

Preface
to the First Edition

Rent review clauses and other forms of variable rents are not, as some might think, a 'new found holiday' (*Malpus' Case* (1455) Year Book 33, Hen 6, Trin F26 pl 12). Forms of variable rent existed at the time of Elizabeth I; and, while we cannot trace rent reviews from this early date, there are certainly some examples from the reign of Queen Victoria. It is, though, largely in the reign of Elizabeth II that rent reviews have become a standard feature of leasehold transactions and have increasingly made appearances as the subject of disputes before the courts.

This book attempts an exposition of the law relating to variable rents in general and rent reviews in particular. We have tried to produce a book that is scholarly in its discussion of difficult and controversial points of law yet at the same time maintains a practical emphasis that will make it useful to practitionerrs dealing with rent review clauses on a day-to-day basis. To the latter end, we have included in an Appendix some published precedents most commonly adopted in practice, including both variants of the Model Forms of Rent Review Clause, published by the Joint Working Party of the Royal Institution of Chartered Surveyors and the Law Society. Accordingly, the reader can refer to the relevant precedent when it is discussed in the text.

We have attempted to state the law as at 5 November 1980, the date on which the galley proofs were returned to the printers. However, the fervent desire of any author that developments prior to publication should be minor were not realised in our case. In recent weeks there have been no less than seven important cases reported and it has not been possible to add substantially to the standing type at this late stage. A summary of the effect of these judgements is given in the section 'Recent Developments in the Case Law', which follows this Preface.

This book was conceived and begun by the first-named author, but at an early stage it evolved into a joint project. Individual chapters were initially drafted separately; however, the book as a whole has been perused and considered by both of us. The result can truly be said to be work of joint authorship.

In preparing a work of this nature, the assistance of professional colleagues is invaluable. We would particularly mention the assistance received from Mr Norman Harker, who kindly gave permission for his valuation checklist to be included in an Appendix; J S Colyer QC, who generously proferred advice to the first-named author at an early stage in the preparation of the manuscript; and Philip Pettit, Harold Wilkinson and Tony Dugdale at the University of Bristol, who willingly offered advice and commented upon sections of the manuscript.

We would also wish to thank our secretaries in the Faculties of Law at Bristol University and Queen Mary College who have cheerfully typed and re-typed the manuscripts thrust upon them.

Finally, a particular tribute is due to the staff of Oyez Publishing Limited who have displayed patience, enthusiasm and encouragement at all stages, and speed and skill in preparing the book for publication once the completed manuscript was in their hands.

1 January, 1981

D N Clarke
J E Adams

Table of Cases

Table of Statutes

Abbreviations
and
Bibliography

'Aldridge'
T Aldridge and T Johnson, *Managing Business Property* 3rd ed (Oyez Longman Publishing Ltd, 1978)

'Barnsley'
D G Barnsley, *Land Options* (Oyez Longman Publishing Ltd, 1978)

'Bernstein and Reynolds'
R Bernstein and K Reynolds, *Handbook of Rent Review* (Sweet and Maxwell Ltd, in collaboration with the Royal Institution of Chartered Surveyors, 1981) as updated to 1989

'Blundell Lectures'
The Blundell Memorial Lecturers, Current Problems in Property Law, Royal Institution of Chartered Surveyors in collaboration with The Senate of the Inns of Court and The Bar, Annual Lecturers published April-May 1977, and annually therafter.

'CSW'
Chartered Surveyor Weekly

'Chitty'
Chitty on Contracts, A G Guest (Ed), 26th ed (Sweet and Maxwell Ltd, 1989)

'Conveyancer Precedents'
The Conveyancer and Property Lawyer; Precedents for the Conveyancer, E H Scamell (General Editor), J E Adams (Second General Editor) (Sweet and Maxwell Ltd, 1970, and as updated)

'Crowe'
W R Crowe, *Index Numbers: Theory and Application* (Macdonald and Evans Ltd, 1965)

'Dugdale and Stanton'
Professional Negligence, A M Dugdale and K M Stanton, 2nd ed, 1989
(Butterworths)

'EFP, 4th'
The Encyclopaedia of Forms and Precedents (in 24 volumes) 4th ed
(Butterworths, 1964–83)

'EFP 5th'
The Encylopeadia of Forms and Precedents (in 42 volumes) 5th ed
(Butterworths 1985 to date)

'Emmet'
Emmet's Notes on Perusing Titles and on Practical Conveyancing, J T
Farrand, 19th ed (Longman Publishing Ltd, 1986 as updated to 1990)

'Farrand'
J T Farrand, *Contract and Conveyance*, 4th ed (Oyez Longman
Publishing Ltd, 1983)

'Hallett'
V G H Hallett, *Hallett's Conveyancing Precedents* (Sweet and Maxwell
Ltd, 1965)

'Halsbury's Laws'
Halsbury's Laws of England, 4th ed, and 4th ed Reissue Lord Hailsham
of St Marylebone LC (Butterworths, 1973—1990)

'Hill and Redman'
Hill and Redman's Law of Landlord and Tenant, M Barnes *et al* (Eds)
18th ed (Butterworths, 1983, as updated to 1990)

'Holdsworth'
Sir W Holdsworth, *A History of English Law* (in 16 volumes) (Methuen
and Co Ltd, Sweet and Maxwell Ltd, 1903—1972)

'Kelly'
Kelly's Draftsman, R W Ramage (Ed) 15th ed (Butterworths, 1986)

'Lang'
A G Lang, *Inflation as it Affects Commercial and Legal Transactions*
(West Publishing Corporation Limited, Australia, 1974)

'Leach'
W A Leach, *Practical Points on Conveyancing* (Sweet and Maxwell Ltd,
1961) (with 1964 Supplement)

'*Kim Lewison*'
The Interpretation of Contracts (Sweet and Maxwell Ltd, 1989)

'*Monroe and Nock*'
J G Monroe and R S Nock, *The Law of Stamp Duties*, 6th ed (Sweet
and Maxwell Ltd, 1986)

'*Muir Watt*'
J Muir Watt, *Agricultural Holdings*, 13th ed (Sweet and Maxwell Ltd,
1987)

'*Mustill and Boyd*'
Sir Michael J Mustill and S C Boyd, *The Law and Practice of
Commercial Arbitration in England* 2nd ed (Butterworths, 1989)

'*Norton*'
Norton on Deeds, 2nd ed, 1928

'*Ross*'
Drafting and Negotiating Commercial Leases, Murray J Ross, 3rd Ed
(Butterworths 1989)

'*Russell*'
Russell on Arbitration, A Walton and M Vitoria (Eds) 20th ed (Stevens
and Sons Ltd, 1982)

'*Scammell and Densham*'
Scammell and Densham's Law of Agricultural Holdings H A C
Densham (7th ed (Butterworths, 1989)

'*Sergeant and Sims*'
Sergeant and Sims on Stamp Duties and Capital Duties, B J Sims and A
K Tavaré (Eds) 7th ed (Butterworths, 1977)

'*Sheriff*'
Service Charges in Leases–A Practical Guide, Gerald Sheriff, (Waterlow
Publishers, 1989)

'*Snell*'
Snell's Principles of Equity, P V Baker and P St J Langan, 28th ed
(Sweet and Maxwell)

'*Spencer-Bower and Turner*'

Estoppel by Representation, G Spencer-Bower and Sir A K Turner, 3rd
ed (Butterworths, 1977)

'United Scientific'
United Scientific Holdings Ltd v *Burnley Borough Council; Cheapside
Land Development Co Ltd* v *Messels Service Co Ltd* [1978] AC 904
(HL)

'Woodfall'
Woodfall's Law of Landlord and Tenant, V G Wellings (Ed), 28th ed
(Sweet and Maxwell Ltd, Stevens and Sons Ltd, 1978, as updated to
1990)

Part 1

General Considerations

In the first Part, the general considerations relating to all forms of variable rent are covered. *Chapter 1* discusses the objectives of reviewing a rent and includes a brief summary of the history of variable rents. *Chapter 2* traces how the concept of review and variation was accepted and established within the framework of property and contractual principles. *Chapter 3* summarises the differing methods of variation of the quantum of rent payable during the currency of the term of the lease.

Chapter 1

The Object of Reviewing a Rent

'We are all of us familiar with variable rents; I have seen a vast number of them.' No doubt such words express the sentiment of many solicitors and valuers in commercial practice today. Rent review clauses are now an invariable feature of every commercial lease, but the quotation is from a judgment of Jessel MR as long ago as 1882 (*Ex parte Voisey* (1882) 21 ChD 442 at 455). In other words not only are variable rents not new but the problems at which rent review clauses are directed are deep-rooted.

1 Securing the 'true value'

Rent is usually viewed in money terms, and then expresses the economic value of the interest conferred by the lessor on the lessee. Since the value of that interest can later fluctuate—the rent as fixed will no longer reflect the true value of the interest—the object of a rent review can be seen as a way to secure that 'true value'.

Fluctuations in the value of property interests can arise in one of two ways. First, the inherent nature of an interest might mean that it is impossible for a fixed rent to reflect its value accurately. This is particularly true, for example, of the tenant who has the right to extract minerals from the land demised. The removal of the minerals will reduce the value of the land and the speed and amount of extraction will determine the amount of the reduction. The desire of both parties will be for a rent to be set that will adequately cope with these sorts of problems.

Secondly, even if the 'true value' of the interest remains constant the expression of the value in monetary terms might change with 'a rise in the general price level or a decline in the purchasing power of money', phrases that have been used as popular definitions of inflation. Inflation has the effect of transferring real wealth from persons on fixed incomes to those whose position is flexible and it benefits debtors by reducing the real value of the debt owed. Thus, a tenant of a property with a fixed rent will progressively benefit as property values experience an

3

inflationary rise and the landlord will find that the real income from his investment, and hence its immediate re-sale value, has tumbled. The converse is true if there is a fall in the value of money. While an end to nation-wide inflation may be inconceivable in the short term a downward turn in property values can occur notwithstanding continuing inflation—as businessmen who took leasehold properties at the high rents of 1972 or even 1988 know only too well.

2   Earlier experiences with variable rents

In preceding periods of price fluctuations attempts were made to cope with the resulting hardship; and in these attempts, the origin of our present rent review structure can be found.

(a) Produce and corn rents

The simplest method of varying a rent was to make the adjustment in accordance with the value of the goods manufactured or the crops yielded from the land demised—the 'produce rents'. In earlier times this idea was particularly suited to lease of brick fields. Thus, one lease provided for payment of 8d for each cubic yard of solid marl got from the land and 1s 8d for every 1,000 bricks made therefrom (*Daniel v Gracie* (1844) 115 ER 56); in another the rent of £20 pa was a 'trifle' when compared with £300 paid in year as additional rent for 2,200,000 bricks produced at 1s 6d per 1,000 (*R v Westbrook* (1847) 116 ER 69). Similarly, the agreement for a lease in the well-known case of *Walsh v Lonsdale* (1882) 21 ChD 9 contained a variable rent of 30s a year for each loom run in a weaving mill. The lessee was to run a minimum of 540 looms and the rent would increase with every additional loom to reflect the value of the consequent increase in output, though the lessor could only distrain for the minimum or dead rent payable in advance on the 540 looms. The mining lease in *Mitchell v Mosley* [1914] 1 Ch 483 reserved one rent at a sum per acre worked and another related to the number of miners engaged; it was granted in 1740. The rents in these examples are the forerunners of today's 'turnover rents'.

'Corn rents' might well have been utilised at an earlier date than the produce rents: instead of the rent varying with the value of the produce of land demised the variation was linked to the national average price of the product. In a largely agricultural society that was much affected by the incidence of a good or a bad harvest the national average price was a crude barometer of the state of the economy. Statutory provision for 'corn rents' was made as early as the time of Elizabeth I (18 Eliz 1 c 6) and it appears that it was not uncommon for leases outside the ambit of the statute to utilise the device (for example, *Roskruge v Caddy* (1852) 155 ER 1190). A fixed rent would be stated in the lease but a provision would be made for a reduction or increase in this sum 'according to the average price of wheat in any one year of the term' (*Kendall v Baker* (1852) 138 ER 706). Examples of the linking of rentals to the current value of a standard commodity can be found in other jurisdictions and the same principle applies to rents today that are drafted to vary with cost of living or other indices.

Another ancient method of achieving a variable rent was an ingenious idea that found currency near Brighton in the early nineteenth century where, apparently, land had 'of late considerably increased, and [was] still increasing in value' and the invariable custom in leases for a term of years was for landowners to insert a clause that authorised them to take back (subject to compensation for growing crops etc) any part of the land demised at any time during the term (see *Gregory v Mighell* (1811) 34 ER 341).

(b) Valuation, arbitration and early rent review clauses

The insertion of valuation and arbitration clauses in leases has been a common practice for many years. The earliest examples provided for the independent valuation of the fair annual rental for the whole term (for example, *Chichester v M'Intire* (1830) 6 ER 597) and for matters incidental to the lease (for example, valuation of compensation for quitting, *Re Hopper* (1867) LR 2 QB 367) rather than for revision of rent during the term. However, the step to a rent review clause proper is by no means as recent as one might think. In New Zealand, at least, there is a reported instance of a demise for 50 years dated 1886 that provided for reviews of the ground rent every 10 years by the award of two arbitrators or their umpire (*Re Lund's Lease* [1926] NZLR 547). The latter were to determine the 'fair ground rent'; and the lease even contained 'disregards'. Even the issue in the case has an uncannily recent flavour. The principle of review was not called into question but rather it was the basis of valuation that was before the court, which held that a 'fair' ground rent must have regard to the terms and conditions of the tenancy and that the buildings and improvements undertaken by the tenant were to be ignored. This case is but one example of a number of early New Zealand decisions dealing with the fairly wide-spread practice of reviewing ground rents.

Of the many leases with review clauses to be considered in the English courts in the last three decades, the earliest appears to be that dated 10 August 1953 in Coventry (*Coventry City Council v J Hepworth & Son Ltd* (1982) 265 EG 608). Even so, the intrinsic validity of variation of an initial rent by arbitration could be questioned as recently as 1963 (see (1963) 107 SJ 924). Such doubts were by no means new (indeed, a similar question apparently exercised the minds of Roman lawyers (see (1964) 108 SJ 247)) and may have been the reason for the hesitation in adopting what is now, in England, the principal means of varying a rent. Once such doubts had been assuaged, the use of rent review clauses proceeded apace.

3   The modern objective: maintaining the original bargain

(a)   Inflation and property values

The original ideas of variable rents have been refined and developed into the now familiar rent review clause. In a period of acute inflation prices not only rise but rise at an unpredictable rate. As Lord Salmon observed in *United Scientific Holdings Ltd v Burnley Borough Council* [1978] AC 904 at 948 (referred to hereafter as *'United Scientific'*), this results in a fair market rent at the grant of a lease becoming wholly uneconomic within a few years. It is, however, too simple to view the use of forms of rent review as just the product of inflation. Certainly it is the alarming pace of inflation that provided the stimulus for their use, but it is also necessary to understand the effect of inflation on the basic assumptions underlying the commercial leasehold property market.

A lessor of leasehold premises is likely to be a finance or investment company whose motive in acquiring the freehold of the property is to secure a good financial return on the capital investment. Other lessors might be pension or insurance funds whose requirements and wide perspectives are more than *just* an adequate monetary return. Such bodies have a regular and large income that needs to be turned into capital investment yielding an income return over a substantial period of time sufficient to produce the pensions or insurance payments that will be of the appropriate value when paid. The capital value of the investment portfolio also must be maintained. Inflation, in reducing the true value of the monetary yield, ensures that a fixed rent for a period of time cannot achieve these goals. Accordingly, a remedy is sought by a rent review.

Lessees of commercial leasehold property, on the other hand, are businessmen who need the security of tenure that a long term of years can provide; and to achieve that security they must accept, and are usually willing to accept, a periodic variation of the rent through the machinery of a rent revision clause. To them rent is simply another cost to be absorbed and recouped in the price of their goods or services; a 'profit rental' is normally just a stroke of luck or good fortune (although obviously a measure of stability over a year or so is an attraction).

(b)   Maintaining the original bargain

The objective of variable rents can be more precisely identified as a method to maintain so far as possible the original bargain struck between the parties, a bargain that would otherwise be radically transformed by the impact of inflation. Messrs Colyer and Brewer suggested (Blundell Memorial Lectures 1977) that it is because a grant of a lease involves a division of ownership that inflation so seriously affects the agreement of the parties; in enhancing the value of the lessee's interest the bargain may be effectively destroyed. (The authors of that lecture consequently adopted the term 'inflation-proofing' to describe the process of utilising variable rent devices in the terms of the lease to combat the problem.) The provision for payment of a periodically reviewable rent in a lease thus becomes one term of the contract between the parties.

If a periodic attempt is made to maintain and restore the original bargain between lessor and lessee it is not only the fall in the value of money by inflation that can be taken into account, for the bargain was made in relation to a particular property, the intrinsic value of which might also have altered and fluctuations in its market value may differ from the rate of inflation. For example, there may be a general increase in property values that is considerably greater than the rate of inflation or property levels overall might fall while inflation continues. Similarly, local issues might modify property values: for example, the attractiveness, say, of a new shopping precinct will have a spin-off effect on adjoining premises. (Consideration of just such an event and of the exact time at which it started to affect rent levels in near-by shopping streets formed a significant issue in *Ratners (Jewellers) Ltd v Lemnoll Ltd* (1980) 255 EG 987.) The older forms of variable rents are unable properly to account for such fluctuations in the market value of particular premises. This is particularly true of indexation. Only a sophisticated, complex and detailed property index could provide an index that could truly allow for fluctuations in property market values—such an index appears not to exist at the present time. A well-drawn rent review clause can cope with all such changes in that it can allow the substitution of a rent that will most closely accord with the parties' original bargain, a rent that might well have been agreed if the parties were concluding their bargain at the later date.

The objective of a rent review clause may be viewed as the means of restoring the position of the parties in the light of changes in money values and in the property market. In theory, such a review clause ought to allow the rent to be adjusted up or down. This argument was accepted by Cross J in *Stylo Shoes Ltd v Manchester Royal Exchange Ltd* (1967) 204 EG 803 where in an application for a new tenancy under Landlord and Tenant Act 1954, Part II, the plaintiff tenants successfully argued for the inclusion of a clause giving them a right to apply for a reduction of the rent in the review after 7 years if conditions then warranted, such application balancing the landlords' right to apply for an increase at that time. Provision for an upwards or downwards review on statutory renewal was also made in *Janes (Gowns) Ltd v Harlow Development Corporation* (1979) 253 EG 799, but an 'upwards only' clause was authorised in *Charles Follett Ltd v Cabtell Investments Co Ltd* [1986]

2 EGLR 76. This decision reflects the practice whereby clauses in new leases usually allow a rent to move upwards only, a trend that results from the stronger bargaining powers of lessors and their desire to protect their investment in every way they can—a trend in which tenants tend to acquiesce since the prospect of a downwards review proving appropriate has, so far, been slight. However, 'upwards only' clauses limit the objective of rent review clauses to one that essentially benefits only the landlord, namely, to counter the effect of inflation on the monetary value of the rent or on the value of the property rather than in every case restoring the true value of the lessor's and lessee's interests under the lease.

(c) The modern commercial purpose

The purpose of the modern review clause has been expressed judicially by Sir Nicholas Browne-Wilkinson V-C in *British Gas Corporation v Universities Superannuation Scheme Ltd* [1986] 1 WLR 398 at 401:

There is really no dispute that the general purpose of a provision for rent review is to enable the landlord to obtain from time to time the market rental which the premises would command if let on the same terms in the open market at the review dates. The purpose is to reflect the changes in the value of money and real increases in the value of the property during a long term.

To the same effect was Dillon LJ in *Equity & Law Life Assurance Society plc v Bodfield Ltd* [1987] 1 EGLR 124 at 125:

. . . the general object of a review clause, which provides that the rent cannot be reduced on review, is to provide the landlord with some measure of relief where, by increases in property values or falls in the value of money in an inflationary period, a fixed rent has become out of date and unduly favourable to the tenant. The exact measure of relief depends on the true construction of the review clause.

These views, quoted with approval in *Basingstoke & Deane Borough Council v Host Group Ltd* [1988] 1 WLR 348 at 353, emphasise not only the dual purpose of a rent review clause—minimising inflation and coping with changes in property values—but also point to the reality that a review clause, emanating from the landlord's advisers, will be directed to maximising the rental return rather than adjusting the rent within the context of the original bargain made. The hypothetical or notional lease which falls to be valued may depart from the reality of the position of the parties in vital respects. The judicial perception of the commercial purpose of the modern rent review clause is more fully discussed in chapter 10 (see p 297).

The modern rent review clause in commercial leases will be more complex and more far-reaching in its implications than its nineteenth century forerunners but the overall objective is not dissimilar. Its flexibility has enabled lessors to reduce the impact of inflation and other external factors on the value of their investment. Yet that very flexibility has contributed to the problems facing the draftsman of the review clause and the parties who, some years later, set the prescribed review machinery in motion.

Chapter 2

The Acceptability of Variable Rents

The contractual freedom of a lessor and a lessee to provide for a variable rent—be it by a rent review clause or any other form—is a freedom that must be exercised within any restrictions imposed by law. In theory, the penalty for failure might result in the lease being held void for uncertainty and the bargain made thereby defeated. Fortunately, the limits have proved to be very flexible. The courts have been loath to strike down a contract that has been embodied in a lease freely entered into by the parties. Indeed, the rent review cases have upheld reservations of rent which, if found in other contexts, eg options, might well have failed. This trend is based on the desire to recognise and uphold the continuing nature of the relationship between the lessor and the lessee and is stated in a growing number of recent decisions.

1 The nature of rent

The concept of rent is one of the most ancient of English common law. Rent was originally regarded as

a thing issuing from the land, recoverable by the real actions and treated . . . very much like an estate in land. (Holdsworth, Vol VII, p 262)

It was seen to have an independent existence as a profit arising from the land itself. The rent would be due on a particular day and, if not paid, the remedy of distress was available to secure payment, the lessor seizing goods and chattels found on the premises in respect of which the rent was due. Rent was never understood solely as a money payment and this can be explained, said Holdsworth, by the wide variety of arrangements creating the relationship of landlord and tenant. Rent could be taken as 'hens, spurs, horses or other profits' as well as in money, but in whatever way it was reserved it had to be certain. This was a direct consequence of the concept of rent as a profit that can be distrained for—it was necessary that the amount due be known on the day when payment was due.

The concept of rent has gradually been modified. The requirement that a rent be certain has in theory remained but it is now clear that the principle is weaker than it was and, for rent review clauses at least, of limited significance. The modern understanding of rent is a payment that a tenant is bound by his contract to make to his landlord for the use of the land. It is, therefore, a retribution or compensation for the land demised (Woodfall, p 276, para 1–0679). The evolution of the contractual theme was traced as long ago as 1925 by Sir William Holdsworth (*loc cit*); and Lord Denning declined to apply what he termed 'outdated relics of medieval law' (*C H Bailey Ltd v Memorial Enterprises* [1974] 1 WLR 728 at 732). He stressed rent was a contractual term and a rent review clause was to be given its natural meaning as a term of the contract.

Thus the modern view of rent is 'the periodical monetary compensation payable by the tenant in consideration for the grant, however it be described or allocated': Megarry V-C, *Bradshaw v Pawley* [1980] 1 WLR 10 at 16. Just as in that case, the tenant had validly entered into an obligation to pay rent in respect of occupation prior to the grant of the lease, so too a tenant can validly agree to pay rent as subsequently reviewed—even if when the review takes place, all or part of the review period is past. What matters is that it is clear what payments are due rather than how or when the payments are made and calculated.

2   Requirement of certainty

(a)   The traditional analysis

The rent reserved in a lease must be certain: both parties must know the time when payment is due and the amount that will then become payable. At an early date it was clear that it was sufficient if the rent could be calculated at the time when payment was due—it was not necessary to be certain at the date of the lease. It was Coke who coined the well-known maxim to express this: *Id certum est quod certum reddi potest*. It was in this way that the oldest variable rents were established: the royalty rent calculated on the amount of brick clay worked and bricks manufactured was a certain rent (*Daniel v Gracie* (1844) 115 ER 56); the Court of Appeal upheld a rent that would fluctuate on the happening of particular events (*Ex parte Voisey* (1883) 21 ChD 442); and in an early decision a revised rent was sufficiently certain notwithstanding that the amount was determined by an independent third party (*Daly v Duggan* (1839) 1 Ir Eq R 311). This principle was summarised by Lord Diplock: 'A contract is complete as a contract as soon as the parties have reached agreement as to what each of its essential terms is or can with certainty be ascertained' (*Sudbrook Trading Estate Ltd v Eggleton* [1983] 1 AC 444 at 478C).

The concept has been made more flexible by recent decisions. These indicate that the above maxim enables leases to be valid even though they appear uncertain not only at the time of the demise but also as to the total sum payable during the currency of the lease. All that is necessary is that the sum due and payable at any one time can be calculated with certainty. Thus, a rent that was liable to increase or decrease on notice being given is valid (*GLC v Connolly* [1970] 2 QB 100) notwithstanding a dictum to the contrary in *Dresden Estates Ltd v Collinson* [1987] 1 EGLR 45 at 47G (see further p 30 below). A similar view was taken of a rent charge that was to be 2s in the £ of the gross rateable assessment of the premises (*Beachway Management Ltd v Wisewell* [1970] 3 WLR 1118).

A well-drawn rent review clause will ensure that the rent payable at a particular time can be calculated with certainty; but it was for some time thought that inadequate drafting meant a risk of the lease being void for uncertainty. On the traditional view, for a contract or lease not to be void for uncertainty there had to be a concluded bargain. 'Of course, it may leave something which has to be determined, but then the determination must be a determination which does not depend on agreement between the parties' (per Viscount Dunedin, in *May and Butcher Ltd v The King* [1934] 2 KB 21). It is a well settled principle of contract law that an agreement to agree is not a good contract (*Foley v Classique Coaches Ltd* [1934] 2 KB 1 at 13). For example, an option in a lease to renew at such rent as might be agreed between the parties was held void for uncertainty (*King's Motors (Oxford) Ltd v Lax* [1970] 1 WLR 426; though even in the field of options, this case has recently been distinguished by the Court of Appeal: *Corson v Rhuddlan Borough Council* [1990] 1 EGLR 255). An agreement to negotiate a price or other monetary consideration is not a contract known to law, and consequently unenforceable, for a vital matter is left to agreement between the parties themselves in the future (*Courtney & Fairbairn Ltd v Tolaini Brothers (Hotels) Ltd* [1975] 1 WLR 297), rather than to an independent third person such as an arbitrator, which would be valid (*Courtney* case at 301B). A court will strive to avoid a conclusion that negatives a bargain made for they are loath to hold a condition bad for uncertainty (*GLC v Connolly* [1970] 2 QB 100 at 108). On the basis of these authorities, it was once open to argue that where the contract or lease fixes a price or rent to be calculated in due course, then the method the parties have agreed upon must be sufficiently clear to enable the calculation to be made with certainty. A few older authorities indicated that if this cannot be done the lease will be void (for example, *Orby v Mohun* (1706) 23 ER 944, 951, where a lease at 'ancient and accustomed rents' was held invalid).

This traditional approach would suggest that a rent review clause should ideally contain two elements. Firstly, there should be a *formula* by which the variation can be measured—for example, the full market value of the premises in a rent review clause or indexation to a cost of living index in an index-linked rent. Secondly, there ought to be some *machinery* for calculation of the rent in accordance with the given formula—for example, by an independent arbitrator in a rent review clause or by reference to the particular index at the date of reference, in indexation. What is now clear is that while an adequate formula and rent review machinery are undoubtedly desirable, neither is essential and their absence will not necessarily make a rent review clause void for uncertainty.

(b) The certainty principle in leases

In *Sudbrook Trading Estate Ltd v Eggleton* [1983] 1 AC 444, the House of Lords considered the validity of the purported exercise in a lease of an option to purchase the reversion 'at such a price not being less than £12,000 as may be agreed upon by two valuers one to be nominated by the lessor and the other by the lessees or in default of such agreement by an umpire appointed by the said valuers'. The lessors refused to appoint their valuer; it was held (overruling older authorities to the contrary effect) that where the 'machinery' devised by the parties breaks down, the court will substitute its own machinery, since on the true construction of the agreement, the machinery in the lease was a subsidiary and non-essential part of the contract. Though the lease contained no formula by which the valuer was to determine the price of the reversion, the option was construed as an agreement for sale at a fair and reasonable price and consequently capable of objective ascertainment. An inquiry as to the fair valuation was ordered with a subsequent conveyance of the reversion to the lessees. In the *Sudbrook Estate* case, the machinery specified broke down; it was already clear that if the parties fail to provide for any machinery to determine the price, the court will if necessary determine the matter itself (*Brown v Gould* [1972] Ch 53)—even where there is a dispute between the parties as to the application of a proper formula to the facts of the case.

The logical consequence is that a review or option to renew a lease at 'a rent to be agreed' is valid and enforceable—and this is indeed the case (*Beer v Bowden* (Note) [1981] 1 WLR 522, see below). Yet this does not mean that the certainty principle is weakened or overturned— indeed the *Sudbrook Estate* case affirmed the doctrine. It is rather that an option in a lease, once exercised, becomes a synallagmatic or bilateral contract creating mutual legal rights and obligations on the part of both lessors and lessees (per Lord Diplock at 476-7); it is not a mere agreement to make an agreement. This is even more true of a review clause or other variable rent, which falls to be exercised in the context of a continuing landlord and tenant relationship.

The retreat from the certainty principle is further illustrated by the option case of *Trustees of National Deposit Friendly Society v Beatties of London Ltd* [1985] 2 EGLR 59. There a tenant of business premises agreed to withdraw an application for a new lease under the 1954 Act where the landlords wished to demolish and reconstruct the premises.

An agreement was reached embodied in correspondence whereby the landlords granted an option for a new lease to part of the new development. The landlords later tried to resile from the agreement alleging various matters in the relevant letter which made the agreement purportedly reached uncertain and unenforceable. Goulding J upheld the agreement and applied the *Sudbrook Estate* and *Beer v Bowden* cases. Though this was an option for and prior to the grant of a lease, the agreement was now part performed (the tenant could not now pursue its statutory rights). The *King's Motors* case (frequently distinguished in the latest cases) was not followed and the judge recognised that it is now hard to reconcile the result in the *King's Motors* case with the more recent statements of principle. The *Beattie* case may be contrasted with *Ashburn Anstalt v Arnold* [1989] Ch 1 where the tenant failed to enforce its option; not because of uncertainty but because the option was conditional and could not, as an overriding interest, extend beyond the physical extent of the premises currently occupied.

The fact that the tenant had performed its obligations weighed with the judge, and that is a factor absent from the lease context where the tenant's acts may be ascribed to its obligations under the lease, not the alleged binding agreement.

(c)   Rent reviews and the certainty principle

As far as rent review clauses are concerned, the approach in the *Sudbrook Estate* case confirmed the trend that was already apparent. The idea of rent review clauses was accepted as sufficiently certain first by practitioners and the courts and then by statutory recognition (Law of Property Act 1969). In one early decision the provision in a 14–year lease was for a review after 7 years, reserving a rent for the first 7 years only (*Accuba Ltd v Allied Shoe Repairs Ltd* [1975] 1 WLR 1559). For the remainder of the term the reviewed rent was to be the higher of either the reserved rent or the open market rental on the review date. It was held that delay in initiating the review left a gap since the covenant was to pay the higher of something specific and something that was unascertainable (because of the delay). Nevertheless, the clause was upheld with retrospective effect, and the result received the approval of the House of Lords in the *United Scientific* case [1978] AC 904 at 936G (the disapproval of the judges' reasoning not affecting this point).

A similar weakening of the need for certainty resulted from the decision in *C H Bailey Ltd v Memorial Enterprises Ltd* [1974] 1 WLR 728 where it was decided that a reviewed rent ascertained in accordance with the machinery provided by a rent review clause after the review date was payable retrospectively to that time (overruling *Re Essoldo (Bingo) Ltd's Underlease, Essoldo Ltd v Elcresta Ltd* (1971) 23 P & CR 1, where Pennycuick V-C decided that a reviewed rent was only effective for periods after the new figure had been determined). The decision effectively means that rent need not be certain at the date when it is payable provided it remains capable of being rendered certain in due course in accordance with the provisions of the lease. Such rent that remains unascertained cannot be sued for or distrained for: once determined the additional sum can be recovered on the rent day following the determination of a new rent (*United Scientific* at 935B-F, approving on this point the *C H Bailey* case).

The absence of a formula likewise does not render a rent review clause uncertain. In *Kenilworth Industrial Sites Ltd v E C Little & Co Ltd* [1974] 1 WLR 1069 a rent review clause that provided for a notice to agree the new rent and arbitration in default of agreement but failed to state the formula on which such an arbitrator was to act was upheld. The lack of a formula does not appear to have been challenged by counsel in the case and the dispute concerned the time-limits for service of the notice. Neither the judgment at first instance nor the judgment affirming the decision in the Court of Appeal [1975] 1 WLR 143 raised the issue. However, the point did arise for decision in the unreported case of *Store Property and General Investments Ltd v Darrington (Rustington) Ltd* on 3 February 1978 (Mr Leonard Caplan, QC, sitting as a Deputy Judge of the Queen's Bench Division). He rejected the argument that the clause in that case was too uncertain (it merely provided that the question 'of what rent shall be payable' should be referred to a single arbitrator) since it allowed the arbitrator to fix the rent according to his discretion untroubled by any formula. In other words, the provision of the arbitration machinery cured the lack of a formula (see (1978) 118 SJ 885). If he was wrong, the learned Deputy Judge provided an alternative basis for upholding the clause—namely, that a term could be implied to give business efficacy to the agreement within the doctrine of *The Moorcock* (1889) 14 PD 64 (ie that the rent should be 'reasonable' or 'fair' which the judge viewed as interchangeable terms).

It was the second basis of decision in the *Store Property* case that found favour with the Court of Appeal when faced with leases containing clauses baldly providing for payment on review of 'such rents as shall have been agreed' between the parties. In *Beer v Bowden* ((1976) but only reported at [1981] 1 WLR 552) it was held proper to imply that the lease should be read as 'such *fair* rent as shall thereupon be agreed' applying the principles of *The Moorcock*. A 'fair rent' was, therefore, a basis, and an adequate basis, for the calculation of the rent for the demised premises. It should be noted that the tenant in *Beer v Bowden* was not contending that the lease was void but rather that the amount of rent originally reserved continued unchanged. The Court of Appeal indicated, however, that such an argument would be difficult to sustain, and Geoffrey Lane LJ drew a distinction between a contract of sale or ordinary commercial contract and a rent review. In the former case, there would be a great deal to be said for holding the contract void for uncertainty, but where there is an existing estate some rent must be paid and it follows that the court must imply something enabling a rent to be fixed. *Beer v Bowden* was cited with approval in the *Sudbrook Estate* case (per Lord Fraser at 484H) and implication of a fair rent was the alternative basis for the decision in *Thomas Bates & Son Ltd v Wyndham's (Lingerie) Ltd* [1981] 1 WLR 505. For a full discussion of the way the courts have dealt with inadequately drafted rent review clauses see Chapter 9 p 273.

In conclusion, it is apparent that issues of certainty have little part to play in resolution of rent review disputes. In the continuing relationship of landlord and tenant, an argument of uncertainty is no escape from mutual rights and obligations, some of which will already be 'part performed' (see *Sudbrook Estate* case at 484E-H). A review clause, like all provisions in the lease, was intended by the parties to have legal effect; the courts will strive to give effect to that intent; or, in the words of Buckley LJ, 'the court must endeavour to fill any gap in the terms of the lease by means of a fair and reasonable implication as to what the parties must have intended their bargain to be' (*Bates v Wyndham's* at 519F).

Arguments of voidness for uncertainty are still occasionally, and very tentatively, raised (eg in *Jeffries v O'Neill* (1983) 46 P & CR 376 at 387); but to have any chance of success it will be necessary to show that the review clause is, for example, devoid of meaning, impossible to perform or it is impossible to divine the true intent of the parties— all of which are inherently improbable. There remains one caveat: it is open for the parties in their review clause to treat their chosen mode of ascertaining the rent as being of the essence of the contract (cf Lord Scarman in the *Sudbrook Estate* case at 487H). In such circumstances the review can be lost; but even then it is unlikely the lease will be void. Thus in *Weller v Akehurst* [1981] 3 All ER 411 a notice activating a rent review was served late; time for service was expressed to be of the essence. The review was to be set in motion by a landlord's activating notice (see Proviso 3(a) of EFP (4th ed) Form 7:1 (set out in Part Seven)) but this was served 1 month out of time. The landlord sought to escape the consequential loss of the review (it was conceded the notice was bad) by arguing that, since the review clause provided that the rent for the review period was to be the 'open market rental value' for the demised premises, and the machinery for determining that sum had broken down, the court should determine the quantum of the rent, and *Brown v Gould* was cited to the court. The judge had no hesitation in rejecting this argument; not only did the *United Scientific* case make it clear that the parties may provide expressly for time to be of the essence (and in that case the court will give effect to that intent) but also the parties had provided machinery for working out the formula for ascertaining the rent. When it was rendered inoperative by a time of the essence provision, no other mode of working out the formula was permissible. The lease was silent as to what should happen in the event of the review being lost; the judge held it was a reasonable and necessary inference that the old rent continued since that was the result the parties would have intended on the review being rendered inoperable.

An interesting example of the application of *Weller v Akehurst*, and the approval of that case by the Court of Appeal, is *McLeod Russel (Property Holding) Ltd v Emerson* (1985) 51 P & CR 176. A review clause in a residential lease was inoperable because the delay (it was held) meant the machinery set out could no longer be operated. The landlord argued that the *Sudbrook Estate* case meant the court could assess the fair rent; but the tenant's submission that the *Weller* case applied was upheld. Here time was of the essence, even though not made so expressly, which meant that the review mechanisms had to be operated timeously or not at all.

3   Rent as a return for an interest in land

Since rent was originally conceived as issuing from the land itself and as being similar to an estate in land, it not only had to be certain but also had to be connected with the interest in the land granted. At an early date it was held that an agreement to increase the 'rent' after the date of the lease was not effective to create a payment that had the quality of rent. Thus, when a landlord who had leased (by deed) premises at £50 pa orally agreed to improve those premises in consideration of a £5 increase to £55 pa, the rent of the property remained £50; the additional £5 could not be considered as rent and was only recoverable as a contractual sum due (*Donellan v Read* (1832) 110 ER 330).

If this principle had remained good law the implications for rent review clauses would have been far-reaching. After a review, for example, the agreed additional sum payable, though recoverable as a debt, would not be 'rent' and if the increase was not paid the tenant would not be liable on the covenant to pay rent. However, it is now widely accepted that, notwithstanding cases and dicta that might appear to be to the contrary, an agreement to increase the rent payable is effective and enables the new payment to be treated as rent without the necessity for any new lease. Authority for this appears from two decisions that are themselves founded on earlier cases. In *Gable Construction Co Ltd v IRC* [1968] 1 WLR 1426 it was held that it was possible in law to create additional rent without surrender of the old tenancy: there was no need to grant a new lease. However, the agreement for new rent according to this decision must be done in the appropriate manner, that is, it must be evidenced by deed (except in cases where a tenancy can be created at law orally where the new agreement can also be made in the same way). The decision was applied in the Court of Appeal (*Jenkin R Lewis & Son Ltd v Kerman* [1971] Ch 477) where it was held that a memorandum of agreement (to increase the rent of an agricultural tenancy) that showed an intention to continue the existing tenancy was effective both to increase the sum and preserve the original term. In *Torminster Properties v Green* [1983] 1 WLR 676 the surrender of the lease before the amount of the increased rent had been fixed did not prevent recovery after the determination; the landlord had an accrued right to the increased rent when the period in respect of which it was payable had started to run. There was a present right, not yet actionable, to a future payment. Accrued arrears of rent after a much delayed review were also treated as having the quality of rent in *Parry v Robinson-Wyllie Ltd* [1987] 2 EGLR 133; so the Apportionment Act 1870 applied, and rent review arrears were treated like ordinary arrears and therefore accruing from day to day in the period for which they fell due. Consequently, arrears were not recoverable by action from an assignee even when the rent review determination occurred after the date of the assignment (the decision has no bearing on the rules relating to forfeiture).

The result of these decisions is clear: an agreement to increase the rent payable is valid and effective and the rent as reviewed has the quality of rent. A review will not lead to a surrender of the old term and the grant of a new lease unless the parties clearly so intend. One problem that arises from this basic analysis is that it presupposes that any variation in rent is evidenced in the appropriate manner, usually by deed. This would lead to a charge to stamp duty under the Stamp Act 1891, s 77(5). Fortunately this may be avoided, as explained below.

The cases that might appear to contradict the proposition outlined above, founded on *Donellan v Read*—for example, *Duke of Westminster v Store Properties Ltd* [1944] Ch 129 and *Brecker Grossmith & Co v Canworth Group Ltd* [1974] 3 All ER 561—apply the old strict meaning of rent. In both of these decisions there was a question of interpretation of a statute or contract at issue. In each case the court decided that the term 'rent reserved' meant the sum actually being paid. However, neither case was concerned with a review of the rent: the former excluded an increase granted by a licence and the latter disregarded a reduction consequent upon counter-inflation legislation. Nor did either decision prevent a rent agreed on review from having the quality of rent. Indeed, in *T & E Homes Ltd v Robinson* [1979] 1 WLR 452 the Court of Appeal held that royalties taken under a licence to remove sand and gravel granted contemporaneously with a lease of the land concerned had the quality of rent. The judge at first instance had held that the payments could not be rent because the sum due could not be distrained for and had applied the technical meaning of rent. The Court of Appeal preferred to apply the idea of rent as a contractual term and the royalties, being part of one transaction and receipts for enjoyment of the land, were rents.

Even if it were correct that rent in its strict meaning only arises upon the occasion of the grant of a lease, then most forms of variable rent clauses should still qualify to make the rent, as altered, true rent. This will be because all well-drawn forms of variable rent clauses will contain both the machinery and the formula to achieve the revised rent. In a rent review clause the lease will set out the procedure to be taken. No new agreement is made to pay the increased rent: it is rather the result of the covenant to pay rent in the original lease, which envisaged that the review would occur. This analysis results in the original lessee having liability to pay the rent as reviewed, even where the sum was determined after an assignment, provided, as is usual, the rent covenant is drawn widely enough to cover this liability: see *Centrovincial Estates plc v Bulk Storage Ltd* (1983) 268 EG 59 and *Selous Street v Oronel Fabrics Ltd* (1984) 270 EG 643, discussed in Chapter 14, p 486, below.

This analysis might not be true of the form of clauses in *Beer v Bowden* (Note) [1981] 1 WLR 522 and *Thomas Bates & Son Ltd v Wyndham's (Lingerie) Ltd* [1981] 1 WLR 505 but no modern review clause is likely to be so ill-drafted. It is preferable to take this view because the necessity to execute an instrument to establish the new rent, as in *Gable Construction Co Ltd v IRC*, is avoided and no charge to stamp duty will arise.

4 Capacity to grant a rent review clause

In most situations an intending lessor will be granting the lease in his capacity as absolute owner and will consequently be free to include such variation of rent in the lease as he wishes subject only to the limited constraints already mentioned and the statutory provisions discussed below (p 477). For some time, it seems to have been merely assumed that limited owners of land, though subject to statutory limitation as to the length of the term of a lease that may be validly granted (eg Settled Land Act 1925, s 41), were not subject to any constraint on the form of rent reserved in the lease. However, in paras 8.3 and 8.4 of the Law Reform Committee 23rd Report (Cmnd 8733) entitled *Powers and Duties of Trustees* (1982) the suggestion is made that statutory powers of leasing given to limited owners of land should be brought up to date by authorising rent review clauses. It has been pointed out (Dockray [1979] Conv 258) that the implication of this suggestion, first made in para 32 of the Law Reform Committee consultative paper (1978), is that some limited owners do not at present have power to include a rent review clause or other variable rent in a lease granted by them in their limited capacity. Such leases would include not only leases by a tenant for life subject to the Settled Land Act 1925 but, perhaps more significantly, statutory trustees for sale and personal representatives who are given the powers of a tenant for life (Law of Property Act 1925, s 28(1); Administration of Estates Act 1925, s 39).

Though the 1978 consultative document gave no reason for its view that a statutory power to vary a rent needed to be promulgated, the contention was fully explored in the article cited and is based on the necessity for a rent in a lease by a limited owner to be at the 'best rent' that can reasonably be obtained (Settled Land Act 1925, s 42(1)). The authorisation of fluctuating rent for forestry and mining leases (Settled Land Act 1925, s 45(1)) might suggest that in other cases a 'best rent' must be a fixed rent at the start of the term but, as Dockray points out, this deduction is hardly conclusive. In the 1982 Report, the Committee gave two reasons for their doubts. First, that a rent review clause might reduce the starting rent below the best rent that would be obtained without it, relying on a dictum in *Hallett v Martin* (1883) 24 ChD 624 at 632 that a progressive rent was not a best rent; secondly, that under a review clause the future rent would be fixed by independent arbitration, not by the lease itself—something a tenant for life cannot do (*Re Wilton's Settled Estates* [1907] 1 Ch 50) as it involves delegation of the power to lease.

Thus it is only the wealth of old case law interpreting express powers given to a tenant for life that appears to cause misgivings, for this 'older learning' concerns standard or express powers later utilised in the wording of the Settled Land Act 1925 and this case law has been adopted as authoritative (see, for example, the examples given by Dockray [1979] Conv 258 at 259). It is not thought necessary to detail in full the technical objections to a variable rent that might be raised on the basis of the old cases as these are admirably discussed in the Dockray article (which concluded that none were insuperable). It would appear that s 117(1)(xxii) of the Settled Land Act 1925 (defining rent as including 'reservation by the acre, ton or otherwise') ought to be wide enough to allow the inclusion of all types of variation in a rent (see *Lonsdale v Lowther* [1900] 2 Ch 687), and it is probably that a court would strive to avoid a conclusion that prevented a tenant for life or other limited owner from reserving a reviewable rent—just as rent review clauses were included in business tenancy renewals without express power then being given (*Re No 88 High Road, Kilburn* [1959] 1 WLR 279). Thus, *Re Wilton's Settled Estates*, referred to by the Law Reform Committee, concerned an agreement to lease at a price fixed by someone else, and it is by no means clear why this should extend to the classic review provision for agreement on the new rent, with independent determination in default. In one of the few recent cases dealing with the meaning of 'best rent' in s 42(1) it was assumed that, had rent review provisions been usual at the date of the lease, a 'best rent' would have been one providing for review, although it does not appear that any argument was raised on the issue (*Re Morgan's Lease* [1972] Ch 1 at 10–11, per Ungoed-Thomas J). None of the arguments appears to be decisive. However, in the light of the decision that the 'highest rent' obtainable is no different from an open market rent (*Daejan Investments v Cornwall Coast Country Club* (1984) 50 P & CR 157) the better view is that a 'best rent' is the best rent in the open market; if, as is invariably the case, that market rent is one subject to review, then the provisions of s 42 are satisfied.

Certainly a declaratory enactment would remove doubts. Until that occurs it is thought that those doubts are not of sufficient weight to prevent a tenant for life or other limited owner reserving a reviewable or other variable rent.

Moreover, the uncertainty is not limited to leases by limited owners in the various categories discussed. The leasing powers given to mortgagors and mortgagees when respectively in possession are also subject to a 'best rent' constraint—see s 99(6) of the Law of Property Act 1925. Whilst it is almost universal to oust these powers so far as mortgagors are concerned the same is not true for mortgagees. The impact of the old cases relating to limited owners may be even less significant in respect of mortgagees' statutory leasing powers, but the risks of the limitation applying cannot be wholly discounted.

5   Growth of rent review clauses

The rent review clause is the most versatile and most frequently encountered form of variable rent; indeed, it would be difficult to find a recent commercial lease (at least, one for more than 5 years) that did not include a rent review clause in one form or another. Before the late 1950s, such a clause would have had a novelty value, so the growth in the adoption of rent review clauses in the 1960s can only be described as phenomenal (though in the circumstances not surprising). This contrasts with other forms of variable rent that have longer histories of both use and acceptance: there is a traditional use of variable rents in mining leases, culminating in recognition in the Settled Land Act legislation (see Settled Land Act 1925, s 45). A valuer recorded that certain pre-1914 leases contained rising rent provisions (1979) 251 EG 1054). It was only as inflation began to bite that commercial conveyancers sought to provide for a variable rent that would cope more adequately with the economic conditions.

(a)   Early tentative ideas

A provision that appeared at an early date was the taking, as additional rent, of sums equal to the amount of insurance premiums (or rates, or whatever) expended by the lessor (see, for example, Form 1 in (1938–39) Conv (NS) 450). This prevented increased expenditure by the lessor in these areas from reducing his income from the property. (This did not, of course, allow for an increase in income if the value of money fell.) The idea is now a standard practice. Since the additional payment is rent, the sums expended by the lessor and reimbursed by the tenant will be for the benefit of the tenant, or for the joint benefit of the parties. In *Mumford Hotels v Wheler* [1964] Ch 117 this was a major factor in the decision that the landlord must use the insurance moneys towards reinstating the property, despite the absence of a reinstatement covenant in the lease. Unfortunately, the Court of Appeal had earlier decided (by a majority only) in *Re King* [1963] Ch 459 that the tenant had no claim to even a share in insurance moneys under a policy in joint names but paid for by the tenant where there was a reinstatement covenant that had become impossible to perform. However, the scope of the decision in *Re King*, has been curtailed by the Court of Appeal in *Mark Rowlands Ltd v Berni Inns Ltd* [1985] QB 211 where it was held that a tenant who had paid an insurance rent and who was to be relieved of his repairing obligations in the event of damage by fire could not be sued by the landlord or its insurers for negligence in causing the blaze. The tenants had an insurable interest in the policy which included cover caused by negligence; the payment of the insurance rent also amounted to a full indemnity under the lease.

Later, during World War II, it was necessary to provide for variable rents in leases of new or previously unlet premises to avoid the depressed rentals obtainable in wartime becoming the 'standard rent' for the Rent Restriction Acts then in force. The devices adopted included a progressive rent idea (1940–41) 5 Conv (NS) 34, 329).

With the onset of inflation after the war further thought was given to the problem of the consequent decline in the value of rents. The point was made that the fall in the value of money affected landlords more than ever. Previously, a lessor who suffered loss as a result of money values falling could recoup that loss at the end of the term because of the development value of the land, but this was no longer possible for two reasons. First, unhindered development was prevented by the advent of the 1947 planning legislation: (1947–48) 12 Conv (NS) 2. Secondly, recovery of the premises was to be limited by legislation giving security of tenure or the right to a grant of a new lease (eg Landlord and Tenant Act 1954, Part II), which replaced the very limited security of tenure given in particular cases in the Landlord and Tenant Act 1927 and the temporary protection given to tenants of retail businesses in the Leasehold Property (Temporary Provisions) Act 1951.

A quite different stimulus to the adoption of rent review and variation was a new attitude to the ownership, holding and utilisation of land in the commercial environment. No longer was land purchased or leases taken solely when required for occupation or business use: land was increasingly recognised as a commodity in its own right—and potentially the most valuable one.

(b)   *Experiments with indexation*

In this immediate post-war period two stratagems were adopted. Both were a form of indexation. The most common was the one still sometimes used today, namely, varying the rent with changes in the indices of retail prices. An early form was a precedent using the newly published Interim Index of Retail Prices (1947–48) 12 Conv (NS) 322). For some years the use of such indexation progressed steadily and it received direct judicial approval in the High Court of Australia in 1952 where it was held that there was no principle of law to prevent a variation of liability by providing that more or less money must actually be paid as index numbers evidenced a variation of price levels (*Stanwell Park Hotel Co v Leslie* (1952) 26 ALJ 35). It was recognised that indexation is only a method of measuring the actual liability contracted for and was therefore acceptable. The following year the principle was tested and approved in England in *Griffiths and Diggens v Great Universal Stores* [1953] CPL 657 (noted in (1953) 17 Conv (NS) 437) where Vaisey J upheld an option to renew a lease at a rent adjusted to any increase in the cost of living: accordingly, the court fixed the new rent at 213 per cent of the original rent. The most significant feature of the decision is that the indexation provision, though crude, was incorporated in a lease entered into in 1932. This shows that the idea of indexation had some currency at this early date— and, it might be noted, in the aftermath of the great economic crash. The application of a provision providing for indexation linked to the Index of Retail Prices was made in *Blumenthal v Gallery Five Ltd* (1971) 220 EG 31 where the rental figure so produced was (in that case) substantially less than would have been obtained by a review clause.

The second form of indexation utilised was the 'gold clause' whereby the rent payable was linked to the price of gold—that price being used to evaluate the amount payable in sterling rather than requiring payment in gold (which became impossible with the abolition of the gold standard). Although the use of gold clauses in international contracts was sanctioned (*Feist v Société Intercommunale Belge D'Electricité* [1934] AC 161), the use of the device in domestic contracts was never extensive. It was, however, one of the ideas that was experimented with in the post-war years to combat inflation and some precedents appeared in print (see, for example, *Estates Gazette* of 12 July and 2 and 16 August 1947). What little currency the idea enjoyed was abruptly terminated by the decision in *Treseder-Griffin v Co-operative Insurance Society Ltd* [1956] 2 QB 127 where a 1938 lease required payment 'either in gold sterling or Bank of England notes to the equivalent value in gold sterling the rent of £1,900 . . . by equal quarterly payments'. By a majority the Court of Appeal held the obligation was to pay only £1,900 in notes and not the value of gold sovereigns of that amount. In a later chapter (Chapter 20, p 566, below) it is argued that this decision can be understood in the light of the particularly unfortunate drafting of the clause in question and did not, and does not, mean that a variable rent in a lease indexing the amount of rent payable to the price of gold would be void ab initio (see the judgments of Harman J, who dissented, and Morris LJ, who based his judgment on his analysis of the terms of the lease). This conclusion is supported by the analogous decision in *Multiservice Bookbinding Ltd v Marden* [1979] Ch 84.

At the time, it was the trenchant words of Lord Denning in *Treseder-*

Griffin that attracted most attention. He was clearly of the opinion that he who stipulated for a pound must take a pound when payment was made. He doubted if a gold clause in a domestic transaction was lawful and he was prepared to hold it was contrary to public policy and therefore void. Though neither of his brethren adopted this basis for the decision there is no doubt that the future of the gold clause in all types of leases was thereby jeopardised (recognised by Hargrove (1957) 21 Conv (NS) 265 at 271) and draftsmen sought to find other means to counter fluctuating economic patterns. The acceptance of other types of variable rent was an encouragement (for example, differential rents charged by local authorities—*Smith v Cardiff Corporation* (No 2) [1955] Ch 159). One idea, still utilised in some circumstances today, was the turnover lease (or percentage rent), though it is hardly suited to every form of commercial lease. An early instance occurred in *Bramhall Tudor Cinemas Properties v Brennans Cinemas* (1955) *The Times*, 19 October, and it was even described in 1957 (by Hargrove, above) as one of the 'few practical ways of dealing with the problems . . . of variations in the economic position'.

Indexation to the Index of Retail Prices was not affected by the *Treseder-Griffin* decision and for a time was adopted in a variety of situations. Precedents appeared providing for variation according to fluctuations in the Index (see, for example, the 1958 Supplement to the EFP, and (1959) 23 Conv (NS) 707). The disadvantages of indexation, however, became apparent (discussed more fully in Chapter 20 below), the practice never became widespread and an alternative was sought.

(c) The establishment of the rent review clause

The idea of varying rent by arbitration in a form of review clause had, as pointed out above, an early origin in some Commonwealth jurisdictions where a true rent review clause featured in *Re Lund's Lease* (1926) NZLR 541 (50–year lease of 1882 with 10–year reviews) and *Incorporated Synod of Huron Diocese v Ferguson* (1924) 56 Ont LR 161 (a 999–year lease dated 1863 with rent revision by arbitration every 15 years). Other New Zealand decisions (see p 463 below) would suggest that reviews of ground rents was an accepted practice in the early years of the twentieth century. In *The Scotsman* it was reported in 1882, 'An important and novel condition in agricultural leases has been introduced by Sir Patrick Keith Murray on his Auchtertyre estate. It provides for a re-adjustment of rent by arbitration at every period of five years' (see E D Buchanan, 'Rent review clauses in commercial leases' *The Journal of the Law Society of Scotland* (1983) W349 and 350). Some leases entered into in England in the nineteenth century included review clauses. The authors have seen a copy of a 999–year lease dated 1887 of land demised by the Church Commissioners. Reviews were to be every 100 years and the formula to measure the new rent was linked to the Tithe Act 1836 (which in view of the repeal of the relevant sections would almost certainly have rendered the review inoperable). A very similar lease was obviously the basis of a newspaper comment that the ground rents of terraced houses in Bradford 'had just been increased according to the formula set down 100 years ago—a combination of bushels of wheat, barley and oats. At today's prices, the lessees could not afford it. Fortunately, the landlord was realistic . . . ' *Daily Telegraph*, 7 March, 1987). It seems likely that other forms of review clause were included at this time but the idea does not seem to appear in any reported decision of the English courts prior to the 1950s. Indeed, the concept of rent reviews 'at decent intervals' to counteract the effects of depreciation in the value of money was suggested almost as if it was a novel idea in 1958 (by 'RB' in (1958) 102 SJ 52). It was seen as a provision 'preceded by headaches and followed by heartaches' and careful indexation was advised as the preferable alternative!

Yet it is probable that the correspondents in legal publications and draftsmen of precedents lagged behind their brethren in practice who were already providing that rents in longer leases (7 years or more) should be reviewed periodically during the term. This is demonstrated by some leases entered into during the 1950s which contain the earliest clauses and are only considered by the courts some decades later because of the long review periods they contain. Thus in a lease in the then new Coventry City Centre dated 10 August 1953 there was to be a review initiated by notice, with arbitration in default of agreement, after 21 years in a 42½-year term (*Coventry City Council v J Hepworth & Son Ltd* (1982) 265 EG 608). The practice was stimulated by early judicial recognition in the case of *In Re No 88 High Road, Kilburn* [1959] 1 WLR 279. The case is particularly significant because:

(1) a rent review clause was inserted by the judge into a new tenancy granted under the 1954 Act notwithstanding the fact that there was then no express power in the Act so to do;
(2) it was unlikely that the validity of rent review clauses then appearing in the leases of that period would be tested judicially until the time for review (then occasionally 7 but usually 10, 14 or 21 years) occurred.

Although there is no indication that the validity of rent review clauses was raised in either counsel's argument in the *Kilburn* case, the unhesitating adoption of the proposal by the judge enabled the development of the review concept. A precedent was published the following year (see (1960) 24 Conv (NS) 665) and rent review clauses became not just a fashionable feature of a commercial lease but almost an essential one. Many of the clauses later to receive judicial analysis were drafted and incorporated in leases in the early 1960s. The one that was later to achieve the most lasting fame happened to be contained in a lease made between Burnley Corporation and a company later called

United Scientific Holdings (see [1978] AC 904). The lease was dated 31 August 1962 and was one of the earliest of those later to come before the courts. Over a year later, however, it was still possible for a writer to doubt the validity of rent review clauses as too uncertain ((1963) 107 SJ 924 at 926–7), resulting in no little anxiety to practitioners. Though there was a firm rebutter to the idea ((1964) 108 SJ 247), such was the concern at the 'dangerous position postulated' by the contributor of the 1963 article that the Law Society took the opinion of leading counsel and reported the advice to the profession to the effect that a rent would be sufficiently certain provided that there is sufficient machinery for determining the amount of each periodical payment due ((1964) 61 *Law Society's Gazette* 674).

Chartered surveyors were less concerned with legal quibbles and saw periodic re-assessment of rents in the light of rental values prevailing at the time of the review as the most logical method of coping with inflation. Consequently, they were in the forefront of the movement to adopt rent review clauses (see Leach, pp 111–20). Fuller precedents in legal publications followed (for example EFP (4th ed), Vol 12, Form 8:1, p 828; (1964) Conv (NS) 662, 663; (1965) 29 Conv (NS) 722; and Hallett, pp 441–9, largely adopting the precedents of Leach). A profusion of types of clause followed, some of which will be discussed more fully in due course.

Statutory recognition of the usage of review clauses was given by the Law of Property Act 1969, which added s 34(3) to the Landlord and Tenant Act 1954. This enabled the court to make provision for varying the rent. The section was incorporating a recommendation of the Law Commission (Report No 17, January 1969) and in effect confirmed the power exercised in *In Re No 88 High Road, Kilburn*, thus removing doubts that had been expressed as to the correctness of the decision in that case.

The 1970s witnessed a spate of litigation on review clauses drafted in the 1960s which matured and bred disagreement, a process that culminated in the decision in the *United Scientific* case [1978] AC 904. The same period saw an increase both in the rate of inflation and in awareness of its effects. The result has been an adjustment of the periods between reviews. The earliest clauses envisaged reviews every 7, 10 or 14 years and in 1965 7 years (or possibly 5) were considered to be the shortest reasonable intervals (see (1965) 29 Conv (NS) 722). The practice now is to stipulate for reviews at least (and normally) every 5 years and 3-year reviews are not infrequently found. Clauses have been adopted for a wide variety of situations, and the effect on other provisions in the lease (and vice versa) is still being worked out. Developments and innovations continue, including ever more detailed elucidation of the terms of the hypothetical lease to be valued, reviewing the periodicity of the review and making provision for overriding indexation in addition to reviews to the market rent.

The disparate nature of the clauses that have been used, which is the result of draftsmen adopting their own favourite mode of approach to different circumstances, led to the joint publication by the Law Society and the Royal Institution of Chartered Surveyors of *Model Forms of Rent Review Clauses* (see (1979) 76 *Law Society's Gazette* 564), published as Conveyancer Precedent 5-61, p 2937, in the Conveyancer Precedents. These forms were the outcome of a working party set up after a suggestion made in the first series of Blundell Memorial Lectures (by Bernstein and Wheeler). The revised Model Forms, amended to take account of comments and criticisms, were published in (1980) 76 *Law Society's Gazette* 326 and as Conveyancer Precedent 5-61A; the Model Forms were further revised and republished in 1985 (see Conveyancer Precedent 5-61B); all three sets of forms are set out in full in Part Seven (p 653).

So in the space of just 20 years before the first edition of this work rent review clauses had moved from relative obscurity to a position of great commercial and legal significance. There had already been one period of statutory regulation (1972-74), which was part of the then government's counter-inflation programme, that prevented increases in rent from taking effect after reviews and further statutory interference, though unlikely at the time of writing, cannot be ruled out (see Chapter 19). Unless that does come, however, it is unlikely that the pre-eminence of the review clause will be challenged as the most effective method of varying a rent to counter inflation. One caveat can be entered. The 'percentage lease', or turnover rent, is now well established in leases of units in shopping malls in Australia and New Zealand and has long been favoured in North America. There are indications that such forms of rent are finding increasing currency in shopping centres in the United Kingdom and such developments may challenge the hegemony of the review clause in this part of the retail lease sector.

The widespread use of rent review clauses and other variable rents have confirmed the modern view of envisaging rent 'as a payment which a tenant is bound by his contract to make to his landlord for the use of his land' (Evershed LJ in *Property Holding Co Ltd v Clark* [1948] 1 KB 630, 648). It might be that there remains a distinction between 'rent protected by the remedy of distress' and 'rent as a mere contractual payment' (recognised by Templeman J in *T & E Homes v Robinson* [1979] 1 WLR 452, 458); but any such distinction that does exist will not affect the enforceability of variable rents, whether in the form of rent review clauses or otherwise.

Chapter 3

The Methods of Varying Rents

The methods available for varying a rent during the currency of a lease fall into the following categories:

(1) statutory methods for public sector landlords;
(2) variation by notice given by the lessor;
(3) alteration of the rent in stages and amounts, both agreed upon at the time the lease takes effect (which can be termed a 'progressive rent');
(4) adoption of the traditional methods of rent in kind or royalties;
(5) provision for the rent to vary with the amount of income from the premises, either by linking the rent to the turnover achieved by the business concern that occupies the property (a 'turnover rent') or by stipulating that the rent shall be a proportion of the rents the tenant himself receives or could receive from sub-lessees (an 'equity rent');
(6) provision for the rent to fluctuate by reference to an independent monetary index ('indexation');
(7) periodic reviews of the rent to restore it to a certain value ('rent review clauses'); and
(8) where a rent includes an element of reimbursement for services provided by the landlord or for rates or other outgoings paid by him, provision for the rent element representing those services and costs to increase accordingly.

An outline of each category is given below. The first four categories have very limited commercial application and are not considered in any great detail.

1 Statutory provision for public sector landlords

Statutory power for increases in the rent payable to a local authority for a council house let on a periodic tenancy was given by the Prices and Incomes Act 1968, s 12(1), a power which is now contained in the

Housing Act 1985 s 25. Such increases can be made without termination of the tenancy by a written notice of the increase being given by the local authority to the tenant not less than 4 weeks before the beginning of the period for which the increased rent is to apply. On receipt of such notice a tenant has a right to terminate the tenancy, and the notice of increase of rent must inform the tenant of his right of termination and the steps he must take to take advantage of his rights (s 25(3).

The scope of the power was narrowed in 1980 so that it does not apply to a secure tenancy within the meaning of s 79 of the 1985 Act. However, the rent of a periodic secure tenancy can be varied by a notice of variation served by a local authority in accordance with the provisions of s 102 of the 1985 Act, such a notice must specify the variation effected and the date on which it takes effect, and the period of the notice must not be shorter than the rental period of the tenancy nor shorter than 4 weeks s 103(5)). The variation of rent will not take effect if the tenant gives a prior valid notice to quit (s 103(6)). It is worth mentioning that housing associations enjoy similar powers of variation by notice (Rent Act 1977, s 93, as amended by the Housing Act 1980, s 77 and Sched 10 and the Housing Act 1988, s 140 and Sched 17).

The power in s 25 is given only to a local authority; and ss 102–103 (and s 93 of the 1977 Act) only apply to public sector tenancies. They are additional rights and do not replace or reduce any contractual rights to vary the rent that public sector landlords might have by virtue of the conditions in their contracts of tenancy (see *Greater London Council v Connolly* [1970] 2 QB 100, referred to below).

These statutory provisions only regulate the manner in which the public sector landlords may increase their rents. The amount by which they may make such increases has been subject to a number of different statutory provisions over the years. The law is now relatively straightforward and contained in s 24 of the 1985 Act. It empowers a local authority to make such reasonable charges for the tenancy as they may determine; s 24(2) provides for the authority to review rents from time to time and make such charges, either of rents generally or of particular rents, as circumstances may require.

2   Variation by notice

(a)   By express provision for notice by the lessor

A condition in a lease for an increase (or decrease) in the rent payable in such amount as the landlord will determine and upon reasonable notice being given is a valid method of varying a rent notwithstanding that the amount and timing of the increase is dependent on the whim of the landlord. This appears from *Greater London Council v Connolly* [1970] 2 QB 100. In that case a contractual term in a council rent book that the rent was 'liable to be increased or decreased on notice being given' was upheld, the Court of Appeal stating that it should be implied into the condition that the notice be reasonable. Though the case concerned the tenancy of a council house there is nothing in the judgments to limit the principle to that type of case; and there is no doubt that, provided the rent is sufficiently certain in that it can be calculated with certainty at the time when payment comes to be made, the same idea could be incorporated into any type of lease.

The power to vary a rent by unilateral notice was denied by Glidewell LJ in *Dresden Estates Ltd v Collinson* [1987] 1 EGLR 45 where he said (at 47) 'The tenancy agreement itself cannot give a landlord power to alter a rent unilaterally'. Though this view was one basis for the decision that an agreement to occupy was a licence not a tenancy, no authority for such a view was cited and it was not a ground that was relied upon by the other judge who sat in the case. The dictum would appear to be directly contrary to the *Connolly* decision and to the views of the Privy Council in *A-G for Alberta v Huggard Assets Ltd* [1953] AC 420 at 440.

If such a notice to vary is incorporated into the lease, it will be necessary to ensure that the length of the period of notice given by the landlord is reasonable. In the *Connolly* decision the court decided that the term in the rent book implied that the notice given should be reasonable and that 5 or 6 weeks was reasonable in the circumstances of that case. The court calculated the length of the notice by reference to the period necessary to determine a periodic tenancy (4 weeks) plus 1 or 2 weeks to allow a tenant to decide whether or not to give a counter-notice (to quit) if he wished to leave rather than pay an increased rent. Reasonable notice for a commercial lease could undoubtedly be longer, perhaps 6 months or so. The lease itself might provide for such period of notice in specific terms and if it does so that will be the minimum period required. However, unless the period stipulated is itself a reasonable time such a notice may well be ineffective (*Re Barr's Contract* [1956] Ch 551— so far as that case survives the criticisms of it in *British and Commonwealth Holdings plc v Quadrex Holdings Inc* [1989] QB 842). Consequently, a draftsman of a lease that stipulated such a period would have to ensure that the period stated in the lease was adequate for the circumstances when the notice was given, circumstances he might not be able to forecast with accuracy.

Thought would have to be given as to whether to include provision for a tenant to determine the lease if he was dissatisfied with the new rent, a very necessary safeguard for a tenant but likely to prove highly inconvenient to one or both of the parties. Not only would the term of the lease cease, with consequent difficulties, but the time-limits and procedure laid down for the service and receipt of such a notice would have to be observed strictly since the break-clause will probably result in time being of the essence, see, eg *Al Saloom v Shirley James Travel Service Ltd* (1981) 259 EG 420 and p 106 below). Clearly, the whole concept, though perhaps attractive to certain lessors, ought to be quite inappropriate for commercial leases of any sort. Most lessees would not accept a position where the amount of rent can be changed at the whim of the lessor, unless of course it is important to get a lease for the premises in question whatever the cost. However, there may be scope for use of notice reviews in residential leases, see Chapter 17 p 523.

A modification of this system is found as part of a common type of rent review clause. This occurs in cases where there is provision for the review to be initiated by the lessor proposing a figure for the new rent; unless the lessee responds with counter proposals, which bring arbitration or expert valuation machinery into play, the proposed figure of the lessor takes effect automatically whether or not it is a fair market rent. Sometimes, normally after failure by the landlord to act in time, the tenant may take a similar step. This aspect is further discussed in the context of rent review clauses (see Chapter 4 p 51).

There are situations where this form of variable rent may be used at the first stage of a lease as part of a stamp duty saving scheme. Thus, wherever there is a position of mutual trust between the parties (for example, as exists in the case of two group companies or the trustees of a pension fund and one of the companies for whose employees it caters) the reddendum of a lease can be such rent as the lessor specifies in a notice at a later date specified in the lease or such rent as the parties agree represents the market value of the premises (see Conveyancer Precedents 5–55 and 5–55A). Such a lease would attract duty of £2 rather than ad valorem duty. A more complex version of the same principle can be adopted where there is not the same mutual trust. In the latter case the rent could be a percentage of the construction costs of the premises as subsequently calculated by a qualified accountant. The possible risks of such a scheme are considered in the notes to the precedents referred to; in particular, there will be no stamp duty saving if a calculation can be made of the maximum rent payable—*Coventry City Council v Inland Revenue Commissioners* [1979] Ch 142.

(b) By a tenant utilising statutory renewal rights

A suggestion has been made that where a lease contains an option to determine that coincides with a rent review date a tenant may use the right to give notice under the break-clause to achieve a more favourable rent review. The idea would be to terminate the contractual term and then apply to the court for a new tenancy under the Landlord and Tenant Act 1954, Part II; perhaps, trying to avoid any provision for an 'upwards only' review (if there is one in the lease) or hoping that the court sets a rent that is more favourable to the tenant than one fixed by a valuer on review (see (1979) 252 EG 244). However, this idea would appear to be unsound since a notice exercising an option to determine will rank as a notice to quit for the purposes of the 1954

Act, and the tenant will have lost his rights under the Act (ss 24(2) and 69(1); (1979) 252 EG 707 and 888).

A similar idea, which might appear to have greater prospects of success, is that wherever there is an option to determine the lease a tenant might, under s 26 of the 1954 Act, request a new tenancy without, however, actually exercising the option to determine. For such request can be made 'whether or not the tenancy is one continued by section twenty-four of this Act' (s 26(1)) and the request can be made where, apart from the Act, the tenancy '*could* be brought to an end by notice to quit' (our emphasis) (s 26(2)) which as noted above is defined to include any notice to terminate a tenancy in accordance with the provisions of the lease (s 69). The contractual tenancy will terminate on a valid request being made (s 26(5)). The aim of the procedure, as in the first suggestion, would be to attempt to secure more favourable rent terms from a court than from the contractual provisions in the lease. This ingenious idea is contrary to the spirit both of the agreement embodied in the lease and that of the 1954 Act, though on a strict literal reading of the Act it might appear to be possible. The difficulty a tenant would face would be twofold: first, the court may apply the 'mischief' rule of statutory interpretation and hold the request for a new tenancy to be a nullity as contrary to the intent of the statutory provision (see also *Biondi v Kirklington & Piccadilly Estates Ltd* [1947] 2 All ER 59); and secondly, even if the request was valid, a landlord might well oppose the consequent application to the court for a new tenancy under s 30(3) of the Act (ie that the tenant ought to be denied the new tenancy 'in view of . . . substantial breaches by him of his obligation under the current tenancy'), for the tenant is seeking to avoid his agreement to hold the property for the agreed term, subject to periodic reviews and subject to his right to determine the term completely. Moreover, the tenant might (contrary to his expectations) end up with a new tenancy under the Act much shorter and on more onerous terms than under the option itself.

3   Progressive rents

It is quite common to provide for a rent to vary by pre-determined amounts—for example, to provide that a rent shall be £1,000 per annum for the first 2 years of a 4–year term and £1,200 thereafter. There are two quite separate reasons for the adoption of this approach.

(a)   Functional progressive rents

Such rents, also known as 'differential' rents, are used for purposes unconnected with inflation. The lower amount, or amounts, payable at the start of the term reflect, say, the cost of repairs to the property or the cost of fitting out premises, and such necessary work would be agreed upon by the parties in advance and will be undertaken by the tenant. In this instance the differential rent figures would reflect the fact of the lower income (or absence of income) received by the tenant initially. Similarly, the business conducted from the premises might have been run down and the rent could be adjusted accordingly to take account of the extra work required in the first few years to enable the business to be restored. An analogous situation occurs in building leases: in the first few years of the term, while the tenant is executing the works agreed upon, the rent is only a peppercorn or other nominal rent; on completion of the building work the lease provides for a larger sum.

The idea can take also the form of a 'pioneering' rent. This will be appropriate, for example, where a tenant retailer is starting a business in a new shopping centre or parade and the letting of units is sluggish. To attract tenants the lessor will offer initial rent-free periods and the market rent will be applied at a later date. Such differential rents can be very sophisticated and could give added protection to both parties by providing that the rent differential varies according to the number of units occupied, with the open market rent only to be applied when all, or a pre-determined number, of the units are let.

A functional progressive rent was included in a case that concerned a renewal of a tenancy under the 1954 Act, Part II. In *Fawke v Viscount Chelsea* [1980] QB 441 the Court of Appeal held it had the power to provide for a differential rent, which would reflect the serious state of disrepair of premises that were subject to lessor's repairing covenants, when fixing both an interim rent payable under s 24A and the new rent for the new tenancy under s 34. The lower figure would be payable until completion of the repairs to eradicate extensive dry rot and the full open market rent would be payable thereafter. The court has refused to allow an arbitrator in a rent review similar powers to fix a differential rent. All these aspects are more fully discussed in Chapter 16.

(b) Anti-inflationary progressive rents

When express provision is made for such functional differential rent, incidental provision can be made to combat inflation by increasing the figures otherwise agreed for the later period or periods in the term by such amount as will be equivalent to the annual rate of inflation. It is, therefore, quite feasible to adopt the procedure solely for the purpose of reducing the impact of inflation. Indeed, when inflation was of the order of 1 per cent (or so) per annum it became quite usual for certain long leases to provide for a progressive rent for this purpose. The idea can be used for a shorter lease. Thus, in a 3–year lease of a property where the current rental value is £1,000 per annum the projected rate of inflation is taken as 10 per cent, the lease could be drafted to provide for a rental of £1,000 in the first year of the term, £1,100 in the second and £1,210 in the final period. An example of a commercial lease that adopted this idea is the lease featured in *Horford Investments v Lambert* [1976] Ch 39 where 21–year leases of houses converted for multiple occupation provided for staged increases; in one case, for example, the rent was £1,300 in the first 7–year period, £1,600 for the second and £2,000 in the last. Such a procedure is an exceptionally crude method of adjusting a rent. It presumes that the rate of inflation remains constant and takes no account of the effect of inflation on the intrinsic value of the premises. Consequently, if the annual rate of inflation suddenly increases the lessor will experience a fall in real terms in the value of the return from his investment—albeit a smaller fall than if no provision is made at all! If a cut in the annual rate is achieved after the lease is concluded it will be the lessee who will suffer accordingly.

Yet the adoption of a progressive rent by increasing the rent in set annual amounts should not be dismissed out of hand. For the idea has three points in its favour:

(1) *simplicity*: because it is a straightforward concept that does not need complex drafting, all that is required is the addition of the necessary words to the reddendum;
(2) *economy*: the cost of a later rent review and the professional fees of valuation and arbitration are avoided and disagreement as to the amount of rent cannot occur—a particularly important consideration as the expenses of rent review may become disproportionately large (while the fees of an arbitrator or expert, or even the parties professional advisers, are often fixed as a percentage of the new rent, there will often be a minimum fee which will operate when rents are low), especially when valuation difficulties occur (eg the lack of comparables); and
(3) *predictability*: from the outset both parties to the lease know exactly where they stand and can plan accordingly.

These advantages may be attractive in the following instances:

(a)   The annual rental value of the premises is relatively small
In such cases (eg a lease of a small amount of storage space) the complexity, trouble and cost of a rent review clause is undesirable and a fixed proportionate rise in the annual rent can have a modest effect in reducing the impact of inflation on the bargain struck between the parties; and/or

(b)   The term of the lease is short
The longer the term the more inappropriate will it be to provide for a fixed rise in the rent payable (as it will be unable to take account of later unforeseen monetary or property fluctuations). Yet, the mere fact of an agreement for a short term will not necessarily indicate that a progressive rent is desirable—because of the impact of legislation. Such a procedure may be inappropriate for residential tenancies (see Chapter

17, below) and in a business letting a tenant may apply to the court for a new tenancy (Landlord and Tenant Act 1954, s 24), thereby extending the duration of the term. Subject to particular exceptions, the right is given to all tenancies of a duration exceeding 6 months (s 43). It would be quite in order for the parties on such renewal to agree a similar pattern of rent, which is to rise periodically, but in default of agreement the rent would be fixed by the court. It would be usual for the court to fix one rent for the whole of such short term, though by s 34(3) of the Landlord and Tenant Act 1954 (as amended) a court has power 'to include such provision for varying the rent as may be specified'. It is submitted that this provision is wide enough to allow the inclusion, if the court thinks fit, of periodic progressive increases. This would not appear, however, to be the view of Goff LJ in *Fawke v Viscount Chelsea* [1980] QB 441 at 453B where he said: 'I am satisfied that s 34(3) authorises nothing more than the inclusion of a rent review clause' so apparently excluding a differential rent. However, a differential rent was ordered since the court held that if evidence indicated that the open market rent would be a rent increasing by fixed amount at fixed times then that is the rent the court should determine under s 34(1). (The case is more fully discussed in Chapter 16, p 508.) Nevertheless, even though a court might provide for a differential rent in this way in a situation where the parties are unable to agree, the court in the *Fawke* case emphasised that the power so to provide will not be exercised frequently and it is by no means clear that it would so provide at all where the purpose is to counter inflation. For, since evidence of rents in the market will be required, and progressive rents are unusual, the court is unlikely to include such a provision in the absence of such positive evidence (cf *National Westminster Bank Ltd v BSC Footwear* (1980) 42 P & CR 90, an option case, (see p 516) where the court declined to insert a rent review clause on the exercise of an option to renew where none existed before). Therefore, even in short leases, which are likely to be periodically renewed under the statute, a progressive rent is unlikely to be preferred to a normal review clause, for the latter will not only provide a more accurate revision of the rent but also encourage a court, on renewal under the Act, to incorporate into the tenancy the review provision from the original lease. If both parties wish to exclude the operation of Part II of the 1954 Act, joint application may be made to the court under s 38(4) of the 1954 Act (as amended by the Law of Property Act 1969, s 5). A progressive rent might be more attractive in such circumstances; the landlord would now be free to select the method of varying the rent of his choice with the knowledge that on the expiry of the excluded tenancy, if it was to be followed by a further lease, he will be free to propose a rent, and review procedure or further progressive rent, of his choice and control the terms of any new lease. (See Chapter 16 for further discussion on these points.)

(c)   Where the progressive rent is to be used as a device to encourage a tenant to honour his bargain and avoid statutory provisions that hinder the agreement

For example, a progressive rent might provide for a moderate increase in the first part of a term and a massive progression in the latter part. The increase would be linked to an option to determine and would, therefore, encourage and embody the intention of the parties that the tenant would break the lease at that point. The machinery for the break-clause could be based on Conveyancer Precedent 5–70. (For the possibility that such a tenant might break the lease and then apply for a new tenancy under the provisions of the 1954 Act, see the discussion at p 31 above.) In agricultural tenancies a penal rent ('a higher rent or other liquidated damages') is irrecoverable if the liability is to arise on breach of a term of the contract—Agricultural Holdings Act 1986, s 24—but would not apply to a provision of this nature. Similarly, a progressive rent can be used to discourage assignment or sub-letting by providing for a lower level of rents whilst the original tenant remains the tenant and a higher level of rents in the case of the original tenant assigning or otherwise ceasing to be the effective occupier, and Conveyancer Precedent 5–17 is to this effect. In order not to fall foul of the Law of Property Act 1925, s 144, or the Landlord and Tenant Act 1927, s 19(1), the clause is drafted to give a reduced rent so long as the original tenant remains the tenant and effective occupier, rather than stipulate for an increase on assignment. Such arrangements are frequently provided for in 'side letters'.

Thus, a progressive rent will be worthy of consideration in tenancies of a few years' duration of the smaller type of premises, particularly in instances where no renewal of such tenancy is envisaged by either party and where simplicity and economy are at a premium. A form of reservation of a progressive rent appeared in EFP (4th ed), Vol 11, p 299 (Form 2:11) and, though it is unlikely now to be suitable for the term of 21 years it envisages, the form may be adapted for shorter leases. It is perhaps significant that the fifth edition of EFP (Vol 22) does not bother to include such a form.

In most cases, the advantages, such as they are, of this type of variable rent will not be of sufficient weight to justify their use. The rigidity of the fixed rise in the rent payable, with the consequent inability to cope with changes in the rate of inflation, will mean that the inclusion of a rent review clause in the lease or tenancy agreement will be preferred.

4   Royalties and other traditional methods

The time-honoured method of varying rent by linking it to the value or quantity of the produce of the land may still be utilised and remains a standard practice in mining leases. In such it is usual, and indeed desirable, for a minimum rent to be reserved (known as a 'dead rent') and to stipulate for payment of an additional rent (or 'royalty') on each ton of coal, stone, etc worked from the mine. Statutory approval of this method was given by the Settled Land Acts. The 1925 Act, s 45(1), gives power for a rent in a mining lease of settled land to be ascertained or to vary according to the acreage worked, the quantities of mineral or substance mined, or to the price of these. If linked to the price, such price may be calculated by the sale price, by reference to a trade list, or fixed by any other agreed manner, including arbitration. Power is given to take a fixed minimum rent in addition to such variable rent.

Provision of royalty rents in mining leases calls for care in drafting. It is necessary not only to make provisions for careful accounting of the quantity of substance worked and for a covenant that the tenant will diligently work to win the minerals but thought must also be given to the speed of extraction with provision for the event of the mine being worked out before the end of the term of the lease. If a minimum rent has been stipulated this will remain payable whether the mine is worked or not, even if calculated by reference to a minimum amount of coal (*Marquis of Bute v Thompson* (1844) 153 ER 202), which may result in a considerable loss to a lessee of a mine that is prematurely worked out. On the other hand, without any minimum payment or dead rent the landlord's income by way of royalty may cease in the same situation (*Clifford v Watts* (1870) LR 5 CP 577). Thus, a lessor will invariably wish to stipulate for such minimum payment.

In *Mitchell v Mosley* [1914] 1 Ch 438, the court had to consider a lease granted in 1740 creating a 200 year term and reserving (a) an annual rent of £4 per acre worked and (b) an annual rent of £50 for such coal or cannel as should be raised by ten getters (ie hewers of coal) and proportionately after that rate for any additional number of getters. There was further provision for suspending the rents if mining was interrupted by accidents or the like, the sum to be made up in later years, without charging additional rent.

The other traditional variable rent—that of taking the rent by reference to the price of corn rather than by reference to money—is now obsolete. It is still perfectly valid, but even if used in agricultural leases it will not be a practical alternative. Even if a situation arose where it could be utilised, the taking of rent in kind would be disadvantageous: (1) the price of the commodity taken would not only fluctuate with inflation, but would be subject to market pressures etc and, therefore, as an anti-inflationary device it would be unpredictable; and (2) statutory intervention, whether by price-fixing or the giving of subsidies, might adversely affect the result (as in *Re Scremby Corn Rents* [1960] 1 WLR 1227).

Though the taking of rent in kind in agricultural leases is obsolete, the royalty rent idea, long used in mining leases, may be adopted with advantage. Thus, a lease of an agricultural holding might provide for a basic rent and stipulate for an additional royalty rent calculated as a percentage of the gross turnover of the farm or as a percentage of the revenue (gross or net) obtained from the sale of crops or milk (see *Bolesworth Estate Co v Cook* (1966) 116 NLJ 1218). In all leases of agricultural holdings, however, the impact of the 1986 Act must be considered, a topic discussed in Chapter 18 (see p 532).

It has been suggested that the taking of services as rent is possible if they are sufficiently certain (*Montagu v Browning* [1954] 1 WLR 1039) but another view is that it is necessary that the services must be quantifiable in money terms to give the certainty a lease required (see Chapter 2) otherwise a mere licence will be created (*Barnes v Barratt* [1970] 2 QB 657). If that is so, it is not theoretically feasible to take services as rent to counter inflation.

5   Turnover and equity rents

A turnover rent has similarities with both the ancient 'produce' rent and an index-linked rent. Like the former, the amount payable is closely allied to the business of the demised premises, but may have the effect of a 'local' index (eg of the price of items sold from demised retail premises). A basic (or 'dead') rent may be stipulated and the turnover rent is an additional payment calculated as a percentage of gross takings or sales (as in *Tucker v Granada Motorway Services* [1979] 1 WLR 683). Such a provision necessarily entails as a consequence an obligation on the lessee to produce detailed accounts so that the turnover can be calculated. The turnover rent is particularly attractive in so-called speciality shopping complexes and some major shopping centres have been let on a similar basis, partly to boost the 'collective image' aspect of promoting the centre.

An equity rent is an example of the same principle as a turnover rent but applied to an investment property rather than to retail or industrial premises. The rent payable will, as before, provide for a basic rent and the additional rent will vary with the rents that the tenant himself receives or should receive from subtenants. An equity rent is particularly appropriate for a large property, let as a whole on a long lease, that the lessee intends to sub-let as smaller units. In such cases the lease can provide for the additional rent to vary with either the income the lessee actually receives or the income he should receive. There are difficulties with either alternative (see *British Railways Board v Elgar House Ltd* (1969) 209 EG 1313). These options are more fully set out in Chapter 21.

6 Indexation

Index-linked rents attempt to tackle inflation in a fundamentally different way from that of rent review clauses. In particular:

(1) The rent is linked to an index and rises proportionately to the index chosen. Superficially the idea is attractive, producing a simple counter to inflation by ensuring that the rent payable moves steadily upward alongside the index. Unlike a rent review clause, the adjustment can be made annually, quarterly or even monthly, and not just at relatively infrequent intervals. In practice, however, indexation has not proved to be an effective method of combating inflation.

(2) Index-linked rents suffer from the particular disadvantages of not reflecting property market fluctuations (whether those of general effect or those of more limited application in a particular area) that may be independent of inflationary tendencies. More than anything else, this has been the reason for the reluctance of both lessors and lessees to accept the idea, for one or the other will suffer. In the last two decades the property market has generally moved ahead of inflation and the lessors have been the party more fearful of indexation. There have been periods when rents lagged behind the Retail Price Index (as in 1974–77)—at such times lessors can benefit. By way of contrast, an index-linked rent at the more modest inflation rates of the mid to late 1980s would have given a landlord a very poor return when compared to a rent review in the then buoyant property market.

(3) If adjustments are made at frequent intervals index-linked rents are the most unpredictable variable rent in that neither party will be able accurately to forecast the rent payable in the next few years because forecasts of the forward rate of inflation are difficult. This uncertainty occurs for rent review clauses only as a review date approaches, whereas for indexation the extent of predictability will depend on the frequency of adjustment.

A rent that varies by reference to an index has been accepted and applied judicially (eg *Blumenthal v Gallery Five* (1971) 220 EG 31: a rent linked to the Retail Price Index). The decision in *Multi-service Bookbinding v Marden* [1979] Ch 84, which upheld the validity of mortgage payments index-linked to the exchange rate of the Swiss franc and the pound sterling, indicates the wide ranging possibilities of the idea. Moreover, it is quite possible to mix indexation with rent reviews. On the one hand, a lease may provide for a rent to vary, say, annually by indexation in conjunction with an overriding rent review clause having effect periodically, say, every 7 years; alternatively, there could be more regular reviews with overriding indexation. Index-linked rents are fully discussed in Chapter 20.

7 Rent review clauses

Although not of as recent an origin as might be supposed (see, for example, *Re Lund's Lease* [1926] NZLR 541 and *Incorporated Synod of Huron Diocese v Ferguson* (1924) 56 Ont LR 161), the concept of periodically amending a rent during the currency of a term, not by agreeing a figure in advance but by provision of machinery for the independent determination of the figure at a particular time in the light of circumstances then prevailing, has certainly been the subject of rapid development and utilisation. This is an indication of its ability to deal adequately with both permanent inflationary trends and also with an increasingly volatile property market. At the heart of each rent review clause is the same idea—the object of restoring the rent payable to a figure that will take account of any fall in the value of money and fluctuations in the market value of the property. Such fluctuations will rarely mirror the exact rate of inflation. Thus, under the now traditional rent review, the new rent will be determined by reference to the current open market rent; but it can also take account of, or disregard, any factor which the parties consider appropriate provided directions to that effect are set out in the lease. This may be a great advantage, but also poses problems in drafting and valuation.

It might be that the greatest asset a rent review clause can confer is to allow a fresh independent determination at an interval, but this can only be done within the framework provided by the parties and their advisers. The exact layout of the machinery is, therefore, vital. Moreover, the fresh look only comes periodically; while an inflation rate can rise in a straight line, a reviewed rent will go up by stages. Consequently, much will depend on the periods between reviews and the exact circumstances prevailing at the date of the review. The period between reviews has dropped from 14, 10 or 7 years in the earlier leases and settled to the now 'normal' review pattern of 5 years and occasionally less. This reduces the disparity between current rents and present market values. Frequent reviews have their disadvantages, particularly in that they are more costly to operate, make forward financial planning more difficult and may sour the landlord/tenant relationship. (It is not unknown for one review only to be settled as the next falls due.) Review can be made of whatever type of rent—whether it be a full rack rent, a ground rent or whatever—and the detailed formulations will vary according to the type of property, the length of term and the different circumstances that are met. The main portion of this book is devoted to detailed consideration of rent review clauses.

8 Variable service charges

A well-drawn lease will make provision for recovery by the landlord of insurance premiums paid by him and in many cases (particularly where a building is leased to two or more lessees) there will be a further provision for reimbursement of the cost of services provided by the lessor to the lessees as a whole and for repayment of those costs paid by the lessor that are the ultimate responsibility of the lessee (eg rates). It is well settled that: (a) a lease may provide that a lessee shall pay sums equal to the amount of insurance or service charges that have been paid by the lessor; and (b) such sums may be taken and reserved in the reddendum of the lease in the form of additional rent or included in the basic rent payable (for example, *Property Holding Co Ltd v Clark* [1948] 1 KB 630). If these measures are taken the normal remedies for non-payment of rent can be exercised in default, and inasmuch as the insurance premiums or service charges increase, so also the amount of rent will increase by the same sum. The alternative to reserving service charges as rent is to insert a covenant to pay the service charges and not reserve them as rent, a method that has its own attractions (discussed at [1979] Conv 320–2). For a decision concerning the construction of a variable service charge in a residential block of flats see *Adelphi (Estates Ltd v Christie* (1983) 269 EG 221.

The form of service charges in leases has altered radically in recent years. It has been pointed out that they began as little more than a few lines requiring the tenant to pay a fair proportion of the costs of maintenance of the common parts of the premises but now the usual form is a covenant to pay charges as detailed in a Schedule to the lease where the landlord seeks to impose on the tenant the costs of everything that could possibly be for the tenant's benefit (see Pryor, 1978 Blundell Memorial Lectures (1978) 247 EG 707, 799). This trend is largely the result of increases and fluctuations in the costs of servicing commercial premises, and consequently it is difficult to forecast the sums that will have to be expended upon maintenance, repair, insurance and management services. Where the burden of these items is borne by a landlord, this will often mean a fluctuation in his net income. Since pension funds or property investment companies, regarded as the most willing purchasers of commercial and office premises, prefer a steady and predictable income, modern leases tend to seek to throw responsibility for all variable outgoings on the tenant or tenants rather than just provide for reimbursement of a number of times. Leases that seek to attain this result are known as 'clear leases'.

Clear leases may be sought by landlord on three possible occasions:

(1) On the grant of a new lease

In some situations it might be that both parties to the proposed agreement will be content so to provide. Where a tenant is opposed to the idea, perhaps disliking the burden of estimating and budgeting for future uncertainties, the outcome will depend on the relative bargaining strengths of the parties.

(2)   On a statutory renewal of a tenancy under Part II of the Landlord and Tenant Act 1954

In *O'May v City of London Real Property Co Ltd* [1983] 2 AC 726, the House of Lords held that, on renewal under the Act, the landlords could not insist on alteration on the terms of the original tenancy so as to transform it into a clear lease. Section 35 of the 1954 Act places an onus on the party seeking to introduce new or modified terms to justify the change, which had to be fair and reasonable. The landlords' desire for a clear lease, to enable them to command a readier market should they decide to sell the reversion, could not be imposed on the tenant against his will since he could not be adequately compensated by a downward adjustment in the open market rent. The House of Lords affirmed the decision of the Court of Appeal [1981] Ch 216 which had reversed an earlier judgment of Goulding J to the opposite effect ((1978) 247 EG 1065). However, this earlier judgment contains some useful guidelines to test whether the introduction of clear lease terms is proper in any given case and these were applied by the House of Lords (though with reservations) and by the Court of Appeal, though both reached a different result. The *O'May* decision is more fully discussed below at pp 329 and 514.

(3)   On the occasion of contractual rent review

A landlord may well not be able to insist on altered terms on review of the rent so as to give him a clear lease. He can certainly seek an agreement with the tenant to this effect and offer a lower rent on review to encourage agreement on those lines. However, a tenant can insist on review on the original terms and where he does so the rent will be valued on that basis. If the market has moved to a clear lease concept, and new lettings are on a full recoupment of service charge basis, then a rent review on the original terms has to take account of the fact that comparables, whether derived from new lettings or from reviews on a full recoupment basis, will be grounded on different circumstances and cannot be directly applied.

The importance of comprehensive service charges from the variable rent aspect are as follows:

(a) The principal rent reserved in the lease will be adjusted in favour of the tenant as compensation for the additional rent payable for, and the uncertainties and risks associated with, the comprehensive service charge. On any review of that principal rent there will be a similar diminution of the open market rent as reviewed to reflect the impact of the service charge on the tenant. In the *O'May* case, the parties' valuation experts had agreed that, in so far as the transfer of contingent liabilities from the landlord to the tenant could be translated into monetary terms, then a reduction in rent by 50p per square foot was the right figure to reflect the additional liability cast on the tenants. Had the court agreed to the change to a clear lease (and the House of Lords upheld the Court of Appeal's rejection of an enforced change to a clear lease, focusing on the contingency risk thus imposed on the tenant), then the rent reduction would have been one of £4,950 to a figure of £100,700 (ie not far short of 5 per cent). In return for such a reduction the landlord under a clear lease enjoys the security of a more certain net income largely free from worries about variable expenditure on the demised premises.

(b) The drafting of comprehensive service charges requires careful attention to detail—see, for example, the service charge reserved in Form 29 of EFP (5th ed) Vol 22, p 356. If, as is now standard practice, it is taken as additional rent, it will be a rent that will vary in accordance with the cost of the services in any given period. Funding provisions, by including annual sums towards periodic expenses such as repairs, external redecoration and replacement of plants (boilers, lifts etc), attempt to avoid the prospect of an exclusively large payment in any one year. Nevertheless, the tenant or tenants remain subject to the risk inherent in the uncertainty of management of the premises, and the amount payable by way of additional rent will always be difficult to calculate in advance and with the addition (very often) of management expenses, auditors' fees and VAT, this will be a not inconsiderable sum.

(c) The insurance costs will normally be recovered as additional rent also, but separately from the service charge. This enables early recoupment of premiums paid, perhaps on the rent day following disbursement or as demanded by the landlord in advance of the policy renewal date (see Form 22, clause 74 in EFP (5th ed) Vol 22). Such separate recovery was authorised in the new tenancy approved in the *O'May* case.

In the context of 'inflation-proofing', variable service charges must be seen as a neutral, if nonetheless important, device. They ensure that inflationary increases in the cost of services and the burden of repair, maintenance and re-equipment of leasehold premises do not reduce a landlord's net income. Variation in the basic or principal rent reserved, by periodic review or otherwise, is needed to cope with any fall in the value of that net income.

The authors have encountered an indexed-linked service charge in a lease drafted before the emergence of the clear lease concept where the 'index' was those services provided on a regular basis. An overall service charge was fixed with speculative items being covered by a formula reflecting the then relationship to the actual cost of recurring items. However, the inclusion of fuel oil in the index base of recurring items

led to an imbalance once the price of oil escalated dramatically so that
the landlords had accumulated a reserve far in excess of actual
expenditure. The landlord's offer to abandon the existing formula in
return for a clear lease on the usual reimbursement of actual costs incurred
basis was met with hesitancy by the tenants. They argued that the
overprovision so far resulting from the existing formula should be
reflected in a downwards adjustment in the rent obtained at review as
tenants in the market would share their reluctance to overfund reserves.

For more specialist treatment of this topic, the reader is referred to
Sherriff, *Service Charges in Leases.*

Part 2

Drafting and Operating the Machinery of Rent Review

Part Two contains a detailed analysis of the machinery of rent review clauses. *Chapter 4* considers the various possible forms of the clause and the drafting considerations and concludes with a drafting check-list. *Chapter 5* takes the reader through the operation of the review machinery and covers the issues of time-limits, notices and delay. *Chapter 6* covers the topic of independent determination of the rent in default of agreement, the distinction and choice between arbitrator and valuer acting as an expert and the basis of a challenge to the determination once made. *Chapter 7* is concerned with the procedural aspects, particularly relating to evidence and valuation. *Chapter 8* deals with the various matters subsequent to a review while *Chapter 9* draws together the aspects relating to erroneous and inadequate review clauses including obtaining a decree of rectification, the basis of implication of terms into the rent review clause and remedies in an action for professional negligence.

Chapter 4

The Format of Rent Review Clauses and Drafting Considerations

The essential purpose of a rent review clause is, in the words of Lord Diplock, to 'specify a procedure for the determination of the revised rent by agreement between the parties or, failing that, by an independent valuer or arbitrator' (*United Scientific Holdings Ltd v Burnley Borough Council* [1978] AC 904 at 922H). This feature, though the basis of the numerous varied clauses found in published precedents, can appear in significantly different guises at each stage of the process. Decisions will be required on questions such as these:

— What type of review clause should be adopted?
— How will the review mechanism be initiated?
— How can one ensure that an adequate attempt is made to agree the revised rent by the parties themselves?
— In the absence of agreement, will the revised rent be fixed by valuation or arbitration?
— What criteria of value shall be adopted by which the rent to be revised can be measured?
— What assumptions and disregards should be stated to qualify and explain those criteria of value?
— How often shall a review take place?

In many situations, these questions are distilled into a more general issue. If acting for the landlord, the matter becomes one of the extent to which (if at all) the firm's or client's current preferred rent review clause needs to be altered for the particular circumstances of this property. If acting for a tenant, then the issue will resolve into the amendments which need to be made to the draft presented. On the other hand, a particular tenant, or its advisers, may have standard provisions to be included in every review clause if the relevant bargaining strength exists to achieve such amendment. This might exist, for example, in the case of a sought after 'anchor tenant', one of the usual household names, for a new shopping centre.

It is not the purpose of this chapter to attempt to draw together all the advice that may be appropriate for the draftsman of a rent review clause since all that is said in later chapters of this book will have implications and lessons for drafting. Thus, the inherent dangers in operating rent review machinery (see Chapter 5) will usually now lead to the conclusion that the whole paraphernalia of notices and time-limits are best avoided; the construction and modification of the notional lease constructed for valuation purposes will take account of the ever growing jurisprudence considered in Part Three (Chapters 10–13) and the meaning given to various assumptions and disregards (and the extent to which their presence leads to a departure from the reality for the parties to the lease) will have to be borne in mind when deciding whether their inclusion in particular clauses is appropriate. It will be unusual to draft a rent review clause from scratch—a corporate client may insist on the fundamentals of its standard form and the draftsman is likely to have his favoured precedent. In those circumstances, this chapter attempts to review the essential elements of any review clause, with discussion of the various alternatives; appropriate cross-references are provided to later chapters where many issues are explored in greater depth. The text makes reference to various standard published precedents, including the RICS/Law Society *Model Forms of Rent Review Clauses*. These are reproduced in full, with annotations, in Part Seven, to which the reader is referred. Assistance may also be had from the drafting check-list at the end of this chapter (p 89 below).

1   Types of clause

The limitations within which rent review clauses operate (such as they are) have been outlined in Chapter 2. The revised rent, which clearly cannot be known until the review procedure is complete, should be able to be determined with certainty by the review procedure. Thus, while the concept of a rent review clause is itself not too uncertain, an individual clause could possibly be challenged if so ill-drafted that it does not allow the rent to be ascertained with certainty, and the consequence might be that at worst the clause was void or, at least, that disputes arise on the meaning and effect of the words used. Whatever type of clause is chosen, therefore, it should be clear, certain and comprehensive. Hill and Redman state: 'The varieties of rent review clauses found in practice are enormous' (18th ed, para 1491). Nevertheless, on analysis a number of basic patterns emerge.

(a)   Basic rent with additional rent at review

Some clauses presuppose the rent reserved by the lease is 'basic rent' and is recoverable throughout the term. The rent review clause provides machinery for the determination of a revised open market rental to take effect from the review date and if, as is probable, this exceeds the basic rent, then the difference between the basic rent and the open market rent is payable as an additional rent. This formula ensures: (a) that the basic rent is due and recoverable throughout the term whether or not the review machinery is initiated and whether or not the determination of the reviewed rent, initiated or not, is delayed; and (b) that the rent cannot be less than the basic rent reserved, thus precluding any downwards revision below this figure. This is the traditional pattern of royalty leases although in those the dead rent is rarely the full market rent as is the case with this type of review clause.

(b) Reservation of reviewed rent

More usually now, leases provide for the reservation of a rent for a period of the term only (eg for the first 7 years of a 14–year term or the first 5 years of a 15–year term); this may be designated the 'initial rent'. The rent review machinery then supplies the method for substituting an entirely new figure for the remainder of the term, or for the next period of the term as the case may be. The rent reserved by the lease for each review period is the rent, as yet unascertained, as agreed or determined at the review. This is the pattern used in the Model Forms (in both the original and the revised versions) and in the majority of modern precedents.

A possible advantage of the second type of clause is that a stamp duty saving can occur when the lease is stamped at the commencement of the term—but only when the rent for the subsequent review periods is completely at large and the rent can go up as well as down. In such a case, instead of ad valorem duty being payable on the basic rent payable throughout the term (as in the first pattern above, applying the principle approved in *Independent Television Authority v IRC* [1961] AC 427, ignoring the possibility of an increase or decrease), the term is treated for stamp duty purposes as if it were two leases, resulting in ad valorem duty only being payable for the period until the first review. The unascertained rent for the remainder of the term attracts the fixed duty of only £2 (see Monroe and Nock, para 5–17, p 110 and (1963) 60 *Law Society's Gazette* 175). (The saving thus made may be lost if additional duty is levied on additional rent payable on review but this result can and should be avoided—see p 271). However, a vast majority of commercial leases contain 'upward only' clauses so the stamp duty is assessed, on the contingency principle, on the rent initially reserved over the full term of the lease. Stamp duty is further considered in Chapter 8, p 270 below.)

A well-drafted clause of the second type will make express provision, as in the Model Forms clause 2(B), for the initial rent to continue to be paid and be recoverable in the event of a delay occurring in the revision procedure. Such delays may be of some length and occur without fault of either party, as in the situation where the duly appointed arbitrator falls ill or dies. To omit provision for the initial rent to continue might lead to a situation where no rent was payable at all for the period from the review date to the time that the revised rent is ascertained. This result was envisaged in *Kenilworth Industrial Sites Ltd v EC Little and Co Ltd* [1974] 1 WLR 1069, per Megarry J at 1071F and [1975] 1 WLR per Megaw LJ at 146A but in subsequent cases judges have been prepared, as a matter of construction of such leases, to imply a term that the original rent continues to be payable pending later ascertainment or if the review for whatever reason is lost: *Weller v Akehurst* [1981] 3 All ER 411; *Henniker-Major v Smith* [1990] 1 EGLR 180. With inclusion of the provision to continue the initial rent, the practical result is the same as with clauses of the basic rent pattern.

The substitution of an entirely new rent that is to be determined in accordance with a given formula (eg the open market rental value) means that, unless the lease provides otherwise, the revised rent could be a lower figure than the initial rent, a result that cannot occur with a basic rent pattern. Though often unlikely, such occurrence is not impossible; the danger is not so much that of a national recession or downturn in rental values (though these occur) but that local circumstances or economic factors that affect the particular property in question may reduce the open market rental value of that area or of that particular property. Consequently, the vast majority of clauses, and almost all of the published precedents of this type, are what is commonly termed 'upwards only' clauses, and provide that if the revised rent, as eventually determined, is lower than the initial rent (or the rent as last reviewed), then the initial rent or the current rent arising from the last review shall continue to be payable, again preventing a fall in the rent. EFP (5th ed) Form 22 is a modern example.

In Chapter 1 it is suggested that to achieve an equitable balance between the parties and always allow restoration to their original bargain, a rent review clause should make allowance for downwards revision if this is demanded by the then open market rental value. Certainly, tenants should always attempt to ensure in the light of whatever bargaining power they have that this is so in order that they do not suffer in a period of economic recession and falling rents (as sometimes occurs either because of national trends or local factors); though in many fields the 'upwards only' review is so entrenched as a practice that tenants may find great difficulty in insisting upon a review clause allowing for downwards revision. The particular problem is the investment market in property; the 'upwards only' review ensures the return on the investment can never decrease. Yet without the protection of a possible downwards review, a lessee may be bound to a rent greater than the market value and may find difficulty in assigning the lease, or at least be forced to pay a reverse premium. Where tenants are unable to secure provision for downwards revision in the lease, an alternative but less complete method of protection would be to include the right to underlet at the current market rent— even if this is lower than the rent payable under the head lease. This will, at least, allow for a partial recoupment of losses. Where lessors in the stronger bargaining position refuse to allow a lessee to have protection against deflationary pressures to match their own protection against inflation, the consolation might be in the thought that on renewal of the lease under the 1954 Act, Part II, the lessee can argue for, in some circumstances at least, the inclusion of provision for a reduction on review if this will be the appropriate market rent formula. (See Chapter 16, p 511, for a full discussion of these issues.)

The Model Forms (Clause 2 in the current version, but the previous versions were the same) include alternative provisions that allow for either 'upwards only' review or 'upwards/downwards', thereby either acknowledging (in effect) that there is a demand for both versions or perhaps attempting to be 'all things to all men' and being understandably reluctant to lend, as it were, quasi-official backing to 'upwards only' reviews.

(c) Reviews at unspecified intervals

It is possible to include a review clause that, unlike the above, does not provide for review at intervals pre-determined by the lease. As the rate of inflation has increased and fluctuated, the period between reviews customary in new leases has narrowed; where once 10 and 7–year reviews were the norm, 5 years is now the standard pattern but 4 and 3–year periods are also found—illustrating that what appears to be a satisfactory interval between reviews at the commencement of a term may not be so in later years. Consequently, attempts have been made to avoid fixed periods either by allowing a review at any time at the option of the landlord between stipulated dates (eg 'once in each of the first second and third periods of five years') or even by enabling a landlord to have a review at any time he should care to choose or after such period as he might decide. Such clauses are highly undesirable for a tenant, and, fortunately, have not become widespread. A variation of this theme, which finds expression in some long leases, is to provide for periodic review and possible revision of the future length of the review periods in otherwise standard review clauses (see p 81).

Whatever type of review machinery is chosen the time will come when it has to be put into operation. Such initiation of the machinery is closely related to the time scales adopted and is discussed more fully in the next chapter. At this stage, it will suffice to outline the methods of initiating the procedure, which fall into two broad categories: notice and automatic reviews.

2   Reviews by notice

The majority of the early rent review clauses adopted a 'notice' format to commence the review. Over the years, the mechanisms were honed and refined into the still familiar 'trigger-notice and counter-notice' formula before being largely abandoned in new leases (though a few devotees of the notice procedure remain). Reviews by notice will remain for some time—not only in existing leases but often in new leases agreed or granted under the 1954 Act.

It is important to appreciate that notice clauses themselves can take differing forms.

(a) Form of the notice

(i) 'Desire to review' notices.

In its older and simpler form, the notice merely 'sets the ball rolling' so that one party acquaints the other of his desire to review: such notice is only really a 'call for a review' (*Drebbond Ltd v Horsham District Council* (1978) 37 P & CR 237). A clause stating that the 'landlords shall be entitled to require the rent to be revised' implied that such desire could only be shown by written notice of the fact (*Stylo Shoes Ltd v Wetherall Bond St W1 Ltd* (1974) 237 EG 343). In a slightly more developed form, the notice is to 'state the suggested new rent'—this idea was a forerunner of the true 'trigger-notice'. Such a notice can be valid even if the notice omits any suggested rent—*Dean and Chapter of Chichester Cathedral v Lennards Ltd* (1978) 35 P & CR 309. A feature of notices calling for review is that they presuppose that negotiation for the new rent has to follow, with a valuation mechanism in default of agreement. It was rapidly appreciated that clauses providing notices of a desire to review the rent, without suggesting the proposed new rent, have little to commend them and few clauses of this type are now found. Certainly, the form does nothing to encourage a rapid conclusion to the review process for the tenant is much more likely to respond when an actual figure is presented to him.

(ii) 'Trigger-notice' reviews.

The more sophisticated and more common form of notice is the classic trigger-notice format. The notice, which is usually to be given by the landlord only, not only initiates the review but specifies the revised rent in respect of the ensuing review period, which takes effect unless the tenant serves a valid counter-notice electing for arbitration or independent determination. A number of precedents adopt this approach EFP (4th ed) Form 8:1 (revised as Additional Form 76) is the basis of many clauses in leases featured in the reported cases; there is also Conveyancer Precedent 5–57 and EFP (5th ed) Form 127 is a modern simplified version of the old Form 8:1.

At first glance, this procedure fails to balance the interests of the parties, putting a tenant at a disadvantage. Thus, if the tenant fails to serve a counter-notice on the landlord, then the sum specified in the landlord's notice stands and in view of the clutch of cases ruling that tenants' counter-notices purportedly given were inadequate, the trigger-notice procedure is a trap for the unwary (see Chapter 5, p 128). A tenant is usually further disadvantaged by express provision that time is to be of the essence for service of the counter-notice—in contrast to the landlord's trigger-notice which is often permitted to be served at any time, or for which time-limits are not made of the essence.

The trigger-notice procedure may be disadvantageous for the landlord in those minority of cases where time is of the essence for service (see eg EFP (4th ed) Form 7:1). He too may omit to serve in time or fail to serve an adequate notice; see further Chapter 5, p 121).

The earlier widespread use of this form of notice reflects not only the strong bargaining position of lessors but the benefits it may bring. The most obvious of these is the element of timetabling that is introduced. Once the landlord has served his notice there will be a period of, say, 3 months (or such period as stipulated in the lease) during which the parties may agree a figure or the tenant by notice may elect for valuation or for arbitration, but if neither occurs the rent specified in the landlord's notice takes effect. A time-limit is set and the new rent will be fixed within a reasonable time. On this view, making time of the essence for the tenant's counter-notice is justified as part of the mechanism ensuring that there is no undue delay and introducing an element of certainty about when reference to arbitration can be made.

One case which illustrates the advantages of the 'notice' clause is the Scottish unreported case of *Skirt N' Slack Centre of London Ltd v Buchanan* (1986) more fully noted at p 217 below. The tenant in that case both refused to agree a proposed rent and declined to enter into meaningful negotiations. In such circumstances the trigger-notice procedures specifying a new rent, and the subsequent timetable set out, is of real value in ensuring that the eventual determination of a revised rent is not too protracted.

Where arbitration is the chosen method of resolving the dispute, however, failure to meet a strict time-limit may not be fatal to the tenant's chances of opposing the imposition of an excessive increase in rent. Section 27 of the Arbitration Act 1950 permits a court to extend a time-limit for commencement of an arbitration where the court is of the opinion that undue hardship would result from exact adherence to the strict timetable (see Chapter 5, p 113 for a full consideration of s 27).

Advantages may also accrue to tenants by the procedure. This will occur if the rent specified in the landlord's notice is too low—for a lessor may, for example, be ignorant of rental comparisons known to the tenant or of imminent changes that may affect the market. In such circumstances tenants will be happy to accept the rent suggested.

(b) Competency to commence reviews by notice

It is quite usual for a lease to provide that only the landlord may initiate the review by notice. In all cases where the procedure allows for a downwards revision then the tenant should be given the right to serve the notice; it is better in all cases that either party should be able to do so but much will depend on the bargaining strength of the parties. It is true that in many instances the tenant will not wish to initiate a review that will result in a higher rent: for though, after a late determination, arrears of the revised rent will normally have to be paid in full to the review date (*C H Bailey Ltd v Memorial Enterprises Ltd* [1974] 1 WLR 728, affirmed in the *United Scientific* case), the tenant will have enjoyed interest on the money in the meantime (provided there is no provision in the lease whereby the landlord can ask for interest).

On the other hand, a tenant may wish to get a review on time; he may wish to know the amount he has to pay to assist his financial planning; he may wish to assign the lease and find this is difficult or impossible until the review is complete; or he may fear that a higher rent might result in a later determination by reason of changed circumstances or new comparables (for evidence of rents settled after a review date are relevant and probably admissible in evidence and can, in any event be legitimately used to corroborate an opinion as to the way the market was moving—see Chapter 7 p 238). The point was made succinctly by Buckley LJ:

The importance of discovering in good time what the rent of leasehold property is to be after a date from which the rate of that rent is liable to change is, in my opinion, self-evident. The tenant will want to now what his liability will be. He may want to know whether and at what price he is likely to be able to dispose of it and will in any event want to know what the effect of any change in the rent will be on his financial position generally.

These remarks, made in the Court of Appeal judgments in the *United Scientific* case ([1976] Ch 128 at 142–3) and echoed by Roskill LJ (at 150), were expressed in the context of their arguments, now overruled, that time-schedules in such clauses should be strictly adhered to, thereby preventing prejudice to a tenant. In view of the House of Lords decision that time-schedules will usually not have to be observed, these arguments, paradoxically, carry even greater weight and make it more important that a tenant is able to initiate the review process.

Even in a case where the notice is to specify a new rent to take effect in default of a counter-notice, there is no reason why either party should not initiate by notice and allow for counter-notice by the other. Certainly, the landlord ought not to be allowed to reserve the right of initiation to himself in a case where the lease allows a downward review unless there is some other way the tenant can secure a review (eg by making reference to arbitration unilaterally if the landlord fails to initiate). Thus, the Model Forms Variation C, clause F (see clauses 4E and 3(6) of the older versions) makes provision for a tenant to give an activating notice if the landlord fails to proceed to arbitration before the review date. Variations A and B allow the tenant to refer to arbitration or valuation. Likewise, Conveyancer Precedent 5–57 contains subclause (b)(iv) allowing the tenant, once the review date has arrived, to serve notice specifying a substituted rent. The provision differs from the Model Forms in that it operates on a landlord's failure to proceed at all rather than on his failure to refer to arbitration or independent valuation, though once operated the effect of each is similar. These clauses are more than adequate to protect the interests of the tenant and the inclusion of provision on these lines is recommended in all such cases.

For these reasons, a tenant should attempt to provide in a lease containing a trigger-notice review clause that he is competent to set the review in motion by giving the activating notice or at least a notice to operate if the lessor defaults. In a lease where no such right is given the only remedy will be to serve a separate notice on the landlord requiring him to set the review machinery into motion within a reasonable time (for which see Chapter 5, p 165) and this will only be possible where the review date has passed and if the lease does not preclude such action (eg by expressly or impliedly stating that review is at the discretion of the landlord).

(c) Time for activating a notice review

The lease should specify the time at which the notice is to be served. It is important that sufficient time is given to allow the review machinery to operate, so it has been common practice to provide for the notice to be given at least 6 months before the review date (as in *Samuel Properties (Developments) Ltd v Hayek* [1972] 1 WLR 1296). However, unless expressly so provided, these limits will not be of the essence, though they will still be useful as guidance for the parties. It is more important that notice cannot be given at too early a date since in a falling market the landlord will then give notice as soon as possible, either with a view to having this figure take effect or to seek agreement to complete the review at the earliest possible date. (The significant difference in rentals can be appreciated by reference to *Lovely and Orchard Services Ltd v Daejan Investments (Grove Hall) Ltd* (1977) 246 EG 651 where a tenant, according to his pleadings and affidavits in an application under the 1954 Act, was seemingly prepared to pay £27,500 in August 1975 but only £15,300 in February 1977).

Consequently, provisions allowing for notice at any time before a certain date (as in EFP (4th ed) Form 8:1) are to be avoided; either a limited period should be specified (eg 'within the last 6 months before the expiration of seventh or fourteenth year' *Drebbond Ltd v Horsham District Council* (1978) 37 P & CR 237) or it will be sufficient to provide that the notice be served 'at any time not earlier than 6 months before the review date' (Conveyancer Precedent 5–57) or by stating a 'window of opportunity', eg 'not less than 3 and not more than 12 months'.

Prior to *United Scientific*, the danger that a review might be lost through the landlord inadvertently missing a time-limit resulted in a move to widen time-limits for the serving of notices. An example of this is Additional Form 76 (a revision of the old Form 8:1), clause [2](4) (reproduced in Part Seven) providing for notice at any time, with an optional provision to restrict this to a period of (say) 1 year from the commencement of the relevant review period. Such wide time-limits should now be avoided for reasons more fully discussed in Chapter 5, p 169, though there is no real need for concern *provided* the clause gives the tenant the right to activate the review if the landlord delays, (see above). However a clause like Additional Form 76, which gives a tenant no such remedy yet provides for wide or indeterminate time-limits, should be firmly resisted by a tenant's solicitor.

For an example of extended time-limits, see the review provisions in the leases in *Esso Petroleum Co Ltd v Anthony Gibbs Financial Services Ltd* (1983) 267 EG 351 which allowed a period of 12 months either side of a review date for service of a notice to initiate a review effective at that date and also provided for service of a later notice to take effect at a specified date not before 1 month after its service.

The need to define clearly the time when notice can be served and, from a tenant's point of view, to limit or prevent the lessor from serving a notice once the review date is passed, is graphically illustrated by the appellate judgments in *London & Manchester Assurance Co Ltd v GA Dunn & Co Ltd* (1982) 265 EG 33 and 131 where the wording allowed service of a notice 'at any time not earlier than twelve months prior to the expiration' of each review period. The three judgments are each based on different interpretations of these words and whether time was of the essence of the limits (if any) so found. Yet clear lessons emerge:

(1) If the lease clearly provides for service of a notice 'at any time' early or late in the review period then there is no obligation in the contractual terms to act earlier so no adverse consequences for the lessor can follow—see Chapter 5, p 117.

(2) If wide time-limits for service of notices are insisted upon (and there are no good reasons why they should), the tenant's advisers should ensure that the lessor cannot benefit by deliberately serving a late notice—in the *London & Manchester* case the provision that the surveyor was to determine the annual rental value *at any time of the determination* allowed just such an advantage to be taken (but see now *Glofield v Morley (No 2)* and the full discussion of this issue at p 75 below.)

(d) Should time-limits be made 'of the essence'?

If time-limits are incorporated into the review process, a decision must be made whether the time-limits are to be of the essence or not. It is advisable to state expressly whether or not such limits are of the essence, as advised by Lord Diplock in *United Scientific* at 936H. Problems about time becoming impliedly of the essence (see Chapter 5, p 105) will then be avoided.

If time is made expressly of the essence, then care must be taken to ensure that it is clear exactly which limits are, or are not, of the essence. In particular, it is pointless to make time of the essence for the first step or steps in the review process and not later ones since a party out of time can ignore those first stages and proceed to review *Laing Investment Co Ltd v G A Dunn and Co* (1981) 262 EG 879 (landlord could ignore earlier stages of process and apply for appointment of an arbitrator). If some time-limits are expressed to be of the essence, but not others then it follows, in all probability, that the latter are not intended to be of the essence (*Amherst v James Walker Goldsmith & Silversmith Ltd (No 1)* (1980) 254 EG 123, where it was held that a trigger-notice could be served late even though it meant that later time-limits, expressed to be of the essence, could not be observed).

Where time is made of the essence, care should be taken to ensure that the rules relating to service of the notice are known and observed. Diary dates for service of the relevant review notices become essential, if only (as far as the professional advisers are concerned) to avoid claims for professional negligence. (General principles relating to computation of the period of time are given in Chapter 5, p 141).

There has been a decline in popularity of reviews by notice. Making time of the essence provides for certainty, but only at the cost of risking loss of a review and disputes over time-limits, forms of notices, delay and so forth. If time-limits are *not* of the essence, there is no good reason why the now usual 'automatic review' should not be used.

(e) Providing for counter-notices

The lease will often make provision for a counter-notice by the tenant in response to the original activating notice. Most such counter-notices will be given by the tenant; though if the lease allows a tenant to give the first notice in some circumstances, then the landlord will be giving the counter-notice. Counter-notices are a necessary feature of the trigger-notice form of review which specifies a rent to take effect in default of such counter-notice.

The usual purpose of a counter-notice is to elect for independent determination of the rent and a counter-notice in these terms is often required by the terms of the lease. The risk is that the tenant makes known his disagreement with the rent specified in a trigger-notice but omits the necessary election. The procedure, and pitfalls, in serving counter-notices is fully discussed in Chapter 5, p 128. The problems discussed there suggest that tenants' advisers might wish to alter the procedure envisaged in the standard precedents. At present, an unequivocal election for arbitration must be made; letters merely disagreeing with the rent specified in the trigger-notice will be ineffective counter-notices. If deletion of the requirement of a counter-notice in time is resisted, a half way house may be to require the counter-notice only to indicate rejection of the rent suggested so leaving greater leeway for validly initiating the subsequent arbitration or valuation process. Another alternative suggestion for revision of the procedure is to state that failure to serve a counter-notice is to be construed as deemed rejection of the landlord's stated rent (rather than deemed acceptance as at present), with independent determination of the rent to follow forthwith. It must, however, be recognised that only a tenant in a strong bargaining position would be likely to persuade a landlord to agree to this.

If the period for service of counter-notice is to be made 'of the essence', as is often the case, the hallowed words should be used. It will not be sufficient merely to state a time-limit for the service of the counter-notice. Thus, in *Davstone (Holdings) Ltd v Al-Rifai* (1976) 32 P & CR 18 it was held that a tenant could make a later objection to the landlord's proposal as to the rent notwithstanding a proviso in the lease that 'if the lessee shall raise no objection to the increased rent proposed by the lessor within 28 days of receiving such notice the lessee shall be deemed to have accepted and agreed the same', and the decision in the *Davstone* case is reinforced by the principles enunciated in the *United Scientific* case.

3   Automatic reviews

In this type of clause the 'parties are contractually obliged to carry out a review or by the terms of the lease the review is an automatic operation' (per Buckley LJ in *United Scientific Holdings Ltd v Burnley Borough Council* [1976] Ch 128, CA). Such clauses do not provide for initiation by notice; instead, normally after providing for an initial rent only, the review is mandatory. It is mandatory because the lease reserves the initial rent only for the first review period and revised rents for the later specified periods. The usual method is to provide that in default of agreement the review shall be submitted to a valuer or arbitrator for assessment. There may be a contractual obligation to review in the sense, as Roskill LJ pointed out, of an 'obligation to submit the matter to arbitration in default of the parties agreeing' (*United Scientific* (CA) at 138A) but the contrary conclusion can be drawn from *Re Essoldo (Bingo) Ltd's Underlease* and *Wrenbridge Ltd v Harries* discussed below.

In the early cases these kinds of clauses were sharply distinguished from clauses whereby the review was initiated by notice, so that in the former type time-limits did not have to be strictly observed but in the latter they did. (See, for example, *Mount Charlotte Investments Ltd v Leek and Westbourne Building Society* [1976] 1 All ER 890.) While this distinction has been abandoned since the *United Scientific* decision there remains a difference in procedure. 'Notice clauses', by initiating the process at a point in time, encourage consultation with a view to agreement and time stipulations may introduce some limits and attendant problems to the process. 'Automatic' reviews are not so circumscribed.

The Model Forms and more modern precedents (eg EFP (5th ed) Form 22 and the ISVA forms) adopt this method. Thus, the revised rent to take effect for any review period is to be that which 'may be agreed at any time between the landlord and the tenant' and reference to an expert or arbitrator may be made in default of agreement by either party, such reference being possible not earlier than 6 months before the relevant review date or at any time after the commencement of the relevant review period (Model Forms, clause 3). Where only the landlord is to make a reference, and he is given a choice of arbitration or valuation, then the tenant is given a separate right not to refer the matter himself but to serve notice containing a proposal of a revised rent (clause F in Variation C) which is to be treated as agreed by the landlord unless he makes application for appointment of an arbitrator or valuer within 3 months.

The advantage of automatic reviews is that controversy over time-limits, notices and dates of referral are largely avoided and the procedure is more likely to produce an amicable result (or a figure reached by independent arbitration or valuation). Dangers of a unilateral imposition of a rent by failure to act or serve a notice are avoided. The disadvantage is a lack of certainty over the risk of late invocation of review with retrospective effect.

4 Agreement between the parties

If agreement can be reached between the parties for the revised rent, then clearly this will be the simplest, cheapest and the least acrimonious solution and the one incentive to agreement is the prospect of the cost of reference to valuation or arbitration. Consequently, provision for the parties to agree is an almost universal feature of rent review clauses and it would be most unusual to have a lease that was silent as to agreement. Moreover, it is undeniable that most reviews are resolved by agreement whether or not some stages of the reference to a third party have been reached.

(a) Requiring an attempt to agree

Some older clauses apparently seek to provide that an attempt to agree should be mandatory. Thus, there was specific provision that the parties 'shall review the rent and agree' (Davstone (Holdings) Ltd v Al-Rifai (1976) 32 P & CR 18) or 'shall agree a new rent' (Kenilworth Industrial Sites Ltd v E C Little and Co Ltd [1975] 1 WLR 143). While there is obviously no requirement that the parties must reach agreement, such clauses clearly envisage that a genuine attempt be made. A clause that envisaged the parties should 'use their best endeavours to agree' might suggest that the parties must do what they reasonably could in the circumstances (*Terrell v Mabie Todd & Co Ltd* [1952] 2 TLR 574) and thus introduce a requirement that the parties attempt to agree. However, such an argument failed in *Wrenbridge Ltd v Harries (Southern Properties) Ltd* (1981) 260 EG 1195, where the landlord respondents, having proposed a revised rent, which was not agreed, proceeded to apply to the President of the RICS to appoint an arbitrator. The tenants applied for revocation of his authority under s 1 of the Arbitration Act 1950, as there had been no attempt to agree the revised rent or the identity of the arbitrator, both steps envisaged in the lease as preliminaries to seeking a Presidential appointment. The application failed, the judge being unable to distinguish the effect of the wording of the relevant clauses in the lease from those in *Re Essoldo (Bingo) Ltd's Underlease; Essoldo Ltd v Elcresta Ltd* (1971) 23 P & CR 1 where Pennycuick VC had reached the same conclusion. A similar ruling resulted in *Laing Investment Co Ltd v G A Dunn & Co* (1981) 262 EG 879, also relying on the *Essoldo* case but without citation of the *Wrenbridge* case which had not then been reported. Any attempt, despite these cases, to show an obligation to negotiate from the wording of a particular review clause would face the difficulty of an appropriate remedy. An order to negotiate or the appointment of a nominee with plenipotentiary powers is virtually unthinkable; a claim for damages would br theoretically open but proof of loss would be difficult. These considerations demonstrate the unlikelihood of enforcement of any obligation to negotiate.

(b)   Providing for the possibility of agreement

More usually, clauses merely envisage the possibility of agreement on the revised rent—eg 'Such revised rent for any review period may be agreed at any time between the landlord and the tenant' (Model Forms) or merely provide for arbitration or determination by an independent valuer 'in default of agreement'. This discretionary approach is better suited in most cases, especially to forms where some time scale is stated and an element of certainty required.

There is a divergence of approach in identifying the party on whom the task of attempting to agree shall fall. The most usual reference is just to the 'parties', or alternatively referred to as 'the landlord' and 'the tenant' as in the Model Forms; while other clauses are more precise in referring to 'the landlord and the tenant or their respective surveyors in collaboration' (*Drebbond Ltd v Horsham District Council* (1978) 37 P & CR 237). This distinction is really one of drafting preference, as parties may and do delegate to their surveyors. In some instances, however, the clause may demonstrate a desire that the parties try first to agree without surveyors, as occurs in the now rather old Conveyancer

Precedent 5–31. The latter precedent provides for the landlord and tenant to agree and, in default, for a determination by two surveyors appointed by the parties respectively as a second stage in the review process. Such a two-stage process is unnecessary, except in exceptional circumstances: for such a procedure demands a 'third stage' of arbitration if the surveyors are also unable to agree, thus increasing costs and lengthening the process. Conversely, the lease may provide that the 'respective surveyors of the landlord and tenant' shall agree and thereby on its face it precludes the parties themselves from doing so (as in *Re Essoldo* above), though a court would almost certainly avoid such a construction since the parties are always free at any time to vary their bargain. It will usually be both sufficient and desirable in all cases to achieve maximum flexibility and leave the agreement to either 'the parties' (or, if the Model Form is preferred, 'the landlord and the tenant').

(c)   Limiting the time for agreement to be reached

Many earlier clauses set a limitation on the time allowed for negotiations and agreement, and, if agreement is not concluded within the limits, allow the machinery to be set in motion to determine the rental independently. The time-limits vary from 1 month (as in *Samuel Properties (Developments) Ltd v Hayek* [1972] 1 WLR 1296) to as long as 1 year prior to the review date (as in the *United Scientific* case). Clauses may be dated in one of two ways: either 'forwards' (that is, for example, *from* the date of the notice initiating the review) or 'backwards' (that is, at any time or for a set period *before* a fixed date; for example, 3 months or one quarter before the review date). The published precedents adopt the latter method, which is the better of the two since the review date should be known to both parties. Moreover, setting a time-limit 'from' a date of a notice could lead to a dispute as to whether the reference is to date of service of the notice or date of receipt of the notice sent by ordinary post (cf Landlord and Tenant Act 1927, s 23, and *Stylo Shoes Ltd v Price Tailors Ltd* [1960] 1 Ch 396 and see discussion in Chapter 5). Some time-limits are desirable to avoid prolonged negotiation and to provide certainty on initiating the machinery to resolve the dispute.

However, the approach of the Model Forms, which avoids any 'cut off' time-limit either for agreement *or* for reference to independent assessment in default of agreement (except for the optional 'longstop' time-limit in clause 3 of the Revised Model Forms), enables a balance to be struck. Each party is aware that reference to an arbitrator or an expert can be made at any time after a particular date (6 months before the review date), and this provides the limit (if required) to the period of negotiation.

(d) 'Subject to contract' agreement will not bind

Agreement between the parties on a revised rent will often be by exchange of letters between the parties or their advisers. In such a case, a binding agreement can only be reached by 'open' letters. In *Henderson Group plc v Superabbey Ltd* [1988] 2 EGLR 155 the landlord's proposals for the new rent was contained in a letter headed 'Subject to contract' and 'Without prejudice'. The tenant responded in an open letter that the new rent was acceptable but resiled from that position before signing a formal memorandum. It was held, applying well known propositions, that the tenants reply was governed by the 'subject to contract' condition so there was no binding agreement on the new rent. Similarly, in *J Schryer & Son Ltd v Lexington Securities Ltd* (1990) 20 February, there was an alleged oral agreement on the revised rent in a telephone conversation. Earlier correspondence had been headed 'subject to contract'. Harman J held that, though the telephone conversation did result in a complete consensus or agreement, it was still a consensus subject to contract. The earlier documentation created a condition that meant the matter continued to be subject to contract until it is mutually agreed that the suspensive condition should cease. The judge relied on the appellate decisions (not rent review cases) in *Munton v Greater London Council* [1976] 1 WLR 649 and *Sherbrook v Dipple* (1980) 41 P & CR 173.

(e) The choice in the precedents

Many clauses expressly provide that an agreement on a revised figure must be 'agreed upon in writing' (eg Conveyancer Precedent 5–57), though not all forms so provide; neither the ISVA Forms nor the latest revision of the Model Forms require the agreement to be in writing. This sensible provision should, it is submitted, be standard practice. No doubt, agreement reached under clauses that are silent on this point will almost invariably be in writing, eventually, but express provision will avoid any possibility of dispute as to whether a binding oral agreement was reached or as to the terms of an oral agreement alleged to have been made. If there had been a requirement of a written agreement in *J Schryer & Son Ltd v Lexington Securities Ltd* (above) then no dispute would have arisen in that case. A requirement of writing may allow one party to resile from an oral bargain on the revised rent but it is the authors' view that it is a risk more than balanced by the certainty a written record provides. Such a written agreement may, of course, be made by correspondence and should be distinguished from a memorandum usually drawn up and affixed to the lease, for this will merely record the prior agreement. The Model Forms do not insist on agreement in writing though the addition of the words 'in writing' in clause 3 may be made without difficulty if desired.

We have examined the majority of the published precedents and no particular pattern is discernible:

(i)   The four forms in the EFP (4th ed)

One provides for agreement in writing, with, in default, a written expert's award; one does not mention the possibility of agreement but provides for an arbitration award with no mention of writing and two provide for written notice, and written agreement, but only require the arbitrator's award to be 'communicated' which we submit does not necessarily imply in writing;

(ii)   The seven forms in the Conveyancer Precedents (ignoring the Model Forms, which are also reprinted there)

One does not mention writing in connection with either agreement or the expert's award; three require no writing for agreement but do require it for the expert's award; one request both agreement and expert's award to be in writing; one does not mention agreement nor require writing for the expert's award; and one provides for written notice, written agreement and a written award from the expert/arbitrator.

(iii)   The form in Kelly's Draftsman

This provides for an agreement in writing with, in default, a written award from an arbitrator.

(iv)   The Model Forms, in all versions

These do not require writing for either agreement or award, but a tenant's notice under the 'long stop' provision is required to be in writing.

(v)   EFP (5th ed) Form 22

Requires an agreement in writing (clause 2.2).

On this showing it is incumbent on anyone using a particular precedent or advising on the validity of an alleged oral agreement at a review to check which combination of possible approaches the precedent or lease employs; and to make any necessary adjustments at the drafting stage. To repeat, the authors strongly favour agreements in writing and an express obligation for a written award—and this reflects what most often happens in practice.

It may be noted that agreements on a new rent under a existing lease will not have to meet the requirements of s 2 of the Law of Property (Miscellaneous Provisions) Act 1989 since a rent so agreed is not a 'disposition of an interest in land' within the section.

(f)   Conclusions

(1) All clauses should specifically provide for an attempt to be made at agreement.
(2) The attempt should be by 'the parties to the lease' or 'the landlord and the tenant', unless it is desired to make specific reference to the parties' surveyors or agents.
(3) Adoption of the approach of the Model Forms is preferable and

no time-limit need be set as to when agreement should be reached. If time-limits are desired, a limit could be fixed from the notice initiating the review; if no notice is provided for, then the limit should be a period prior to a fixed date (usually calculated by reference to the date of review), which should itself be at a time to allow for a later independent determination in default of agreement.

(4) Clauses should provide for the agreement to be in writing.

5 Valuation or arbitration?

All clauses should provide for the eventuality of the parties failing to agree. This is the heart of a rent review clause: the independent assessment of the market rental value of the demised property. A considered choice must be made as to whether the final and binding determination is to be made by an independent surveyor (or by a valuer acting as an expert in his field) or, alternatively, by an appointment of an arbitrator who will act, subject to contrary provisions in the lease, in accordance with the rules relating to arbitration under the Arbitration Acts 1950–79. This basic 'expert valuation or arbitration' decision is not as straightforward as it once was; not only can the decision be postponed, but the relatively new 'flip flop' or 'baseball' methods of expert valuation are very different to valuation by the normal method.

The view is sometimes expressed that, in the context of disagreement over a revised rent, 'there is probably little or no practical difference' between use of an expert or an arbitrator (see Aldridge, *Managing Business Property*, p 94). This can only be said to be true (if at all) about the new rental figure eventually ascertained—for neither valuation nor arbitration will, of itself, tend to produce a higher or significantly different figure from the alternative method. The differences between the two are in approach, in procedure and in the available remedies and are not differences that can be ignored; so it is essential that the clause specifies which procedure is to be adopted. The importance of the distinction is fully discussed in Chapter 6 (p 174) where the procedure on arbitration and valuation is explored. Our suggestions as to the circumstances where arbitration or valuation are respectively appropriate are made (p 188); reference should also be made to Chapter 5 p 113 where we suggest that, in the light of s 27 of the Arbitration Act 1950, the choice of an arbitrator may be better (at least, from a tenant's point of view) where the review clause is of the 'notice' type with time expressly of the essence. At this point, it will be helpful to indicate how arbitration and valuation are used in rent review clauses and to outline the procedure of the new types of valuation.

(a) By arbitration

In default of agreement on the revised rent, the final determination is by a sole arbitrator. This is a common provision and is adopted in a number of precedents (eg in EFP (5th ed) Form 22 and Model Form, Variation A) and in many of the clauses at issue in reported cases. More than one arbitrator could be used at this stage (usually two, appointed by the respective parties, with umpirage if the arbitrators disagree) but it is not a method commonly adopted or to be recommended. Sometimes it is specified that the arbitrator shall be a surveyor but, unless so stated, (and some clauses do so state), the arbitrator need not be a surveyor or an expert in valuation. It has been and continues to be the practice for clauses to give the President for the time being of the Royal Institution of Chartered Surveyors the task of appointing the arbitrator in default of agreement on an appointee, and he almost invariably will appoint a surveyor. An argument exists for a clause that provides for appointment by the President for the time being of the Law Society since arbitrations may raise points of law better suited for determination by a legally qualified arbitrator. The point has gained in importance with the restrictions on appeal discussed in Chapter 6. The authors, however, prefer the more usual appointment by the President of the RICS if the choice is to be fixed at the drafting stage, for not only do the majority of arbitrations present no difficulty but, more significantly, it will not be possible to pin-point those leases raising legal issues at the drafting stage. However, it may be appropriate to provide for alternative appointees and thus achieve maximum flexibility. This may be done by allowing the parties to agree at the date for appointment of the arbitrator, whether it is to be the President of the RICS or the Law Society, who shall make the appointment, with additional provision that in default of agreement, the application is to be made to one or other President who himself decides whether he or the other appointor should make the appointment. An alternative approach is to insert the words 'or, at the option of the landlord, the President for the time being of the Law Society', so that one party can make a choice in the light of the nature of the dispute. It may also be desirable to state expressly that the President so appointed may act through his Vice- or Deputy President, (as is now commonly done (see para 1.5 of the Second Schedule to EFP (5th ed) Form 22) thus avoiding objection to the current practice of allowing the President to act through his deputy (although the clause is silent on the point) or avoiding delay should the President be indisposed or unavailable (and see the discussion in Chapter 6, p 219). It is also worth considering appointment through a local branch of the RICS, though a particular branch may not be in a position (or have the resources) to cope with appointments on a regular basis.

(b) By a valuer or surveyor acting as an expert

In default of agreement the final determination is by one independent and suitably qualified person acting as an expert. This person will almost invariably be a chartered surveyor because of the expertise required and the clause will sometimes also require him to be a Fellow or Associate of the RICS (as in Form 130). EFP (5th ed) Form 119 and Model Forms, Variation B are two modern examples. In both instances, in the absence of agreement on the person to act as arbitrator or valuer, the nomination is to be by the President for the time being of the Royal Institution of Chartered Surveyors. The valuer appointed under the ISVA Forms is, not surprisingly, to be appointed by the President of that Institution.

Since experts, unlike arbitrators, do not have to afford the opportunity for the parties to make representations, most modern clauses (reflecting common practice) expressly allow or require the expert to afford an opportunity to the parties to make representations and comment on the other parties' expressed views (see Model Form, Variation B, clause 4(a)(ii); Conveyancer Precedent 5–57 clause (e)).

The issue of the cost of valuation must also be addressed. Once again (unlike an arbitrator) there will be no power for the valuer to award costs unless the lease so provides. The Model Forms prefer the simple if potentially unjust provision that each side bear their own costs; Conveyancer Precedent 5–57 clause (f)(ii) embodies the alternative—giving power to the valuer to provide for payment of costs by one party to the other. However, that precedent gives the valuer an unfettered discretion (which will not be open to challenge) but to set down guide-lines for the exercise of any discretion on costs (perhaps by requiring final rental offers) introduces further drafting complications.

Consideration should be given as to whether the expert should have experience of the lettings of the type in question—EFP (5th ed) Form 131, para 1.6 is an example of such a stipulation. The better view is to avoid such limitations since however the definition is phrased, disputes are possible, initiated perhaps by one party unhappy with the valuation produced—and to define 'experience' with any certainty will be difficult.

(c) By landlord's choice at the review date

In the absence of agreement the revised rent is determined either by an arbitrator or by a valuer at the option of the landlord, the choice being made at the date of review. This option is contained in Model Form, Variation C, embodying an idea earlier outlined in Conveyancer Precedent 5–57, which in subclause (d), achieves a similar result by providing that the lessor may, within 1 month (time to be of the essence) of the service of the lessee's counter-notice, stipulate by notice in writing that the referee shall act as an arbitrator. If no such notice is served the referee shall act as an expert. Though Conveyancer Precedents 5–57 and Model Form, Variation C have a similar objective—namely, delaying the choice as to whether an arbitrator or valuer shall act—it is our view that the drafting procedure of Conveyancer Precedent 5–57 is to be preferred since a clear time-limit is introduced (time to be of the essence) during which the lessor may choose arbitration. Once this time-limit has expired the lessee is free to seek appointment of the referee to enable the new rent to be determined. Model Form, Variation C allows the landlord to choose between arbitration and valuation at any time before making application to the President for the time being of the RICS. The tenant is powerless if the landlord fails so to apply and must be content with his remedy under clause (F) (service of notice once the review date has passed). The idea behind both versions is to postpone the decision on whether to have an expert valuer or an arbitrator until the occasion of review and unforeseen factors can be taken into account and the choice may then become clear. The dispute may be a simple one of value and an expert valuer will be appropriate to decide the issue; whereas, if the dispute revolves around the meanings of terms in a lease a referral to arbitration can be chosen. For example, in *F R Evans (Leeds) Ltd v English Electric Co Ltd* (1977) 36 P & CR 185 (discussed at p 393) there were problems raised that involved the interpretation of certain key phrases in the rent review clause. It is unlikely that such issues would be apparent at the drafting stage—indeed, if they had been, an attempt to resolve them could have been appropriate— but they may well have been perceived at the date when reference was made to adjudication. Moreover, the particular surveyor whom the parties wish to decide the dispute may be willing to act only in a particular capacity, and the clause allows his wishes to be accommodated. An objection to giving a landlord a choice is that it may put a further weapon into the armoury of the landlord by enabling him to choose the method of assessment which he perceives to be more favourable to his cause.

(d) Obsolete variants of expert valuation

There are two (at least) variations of expert valuation which introduce greater complexity:

(1) In default of agreement between the parties the rent is to be determined by two surveyors (or other suitably qualified experts), one appointed by each party. They attempt to determine the rental as expert valuers, and, if they fail to agree, a third independently appointed surveyor, also acting as an expert, determines the issue. An example is Conveyancer Precedent 5–8 at p 2571, but this old 'three-tier' structure is not often used. This approach does, however, mirror in formal terms what very often happens informally; namely, that both parties instruct or take advice from their surveyors in an attempt to agree, before invoking the rent review machinery; and indeed those surveyors almost invariably attempt to negotiate agreement of the rent. To formalise this procedure is however an unnecessary complication.

(2) Whether in default of agreement between the parties, or as the initial

step, two surveyors are appointed to fix the revised rent and act as in (c) above; but if agreement is not reached, then the matter is finally referred to arbitration. This pattern was common in the nineteenth century when the two appointees, often labelled 'arbitrators' acted as protagonists of one party's point of view. For a modern variant of this idea used in an option clause, see *Sudbrook Trading Estate Ltd v Eggleton* [1983] 1 AC 444.

(e) 'Flip flop' valuation

This method of valuation, which involves giving a valuer a very restricted discretion, is slowly growing in popularity for use in leases of the smaller or less valuable premises or in residential lettings. The aim is to encourage parties to be reasonable in their proposals for a new rent and thereby encourage agreement without the expense of independent valuation. This is done by providing for each side to submit a written valuation of the open market rent—time-limits, made of the essence, attempt to ensure that this will be done. The expert then decides which valuation is correct or more correct and that valuation then becomes the revised rent. The expert cannot chose a 'midway' position or substitute his own view; he must decide which of the two is closer to the figure which, in his unfettered view, is the market rent—hence the term 'flip flop'. The method was recommended (instead of reviews by trigger-notice with 'deemed market rents—see p 99) by Sir John Donaldson in *Henry Smith's Charity Trustees v AWADA Trading and Promotion Services* (1983) 269 EG 729 at 731, and as the judge noted, each party is 'forced to put forward a highly realistic figure'. Therein lies its advantage—realism encouraging agreement, with a swift settlement of any dispute. These advantages are bought at the expense of a clause introducing strict time-limits—with consequent disadvantage if they are missed since the revised rent becomes that figure submitted in the other party's valuation. The idea also lacks sophistication and is unlikely to appeal where the premises are large or unusual. EFP (5th ed) Form 130 is a precedent of this type and a simplified form for use in residential tenancies has been published as Conveyancer Precedent 5–100.

(f) 'Baseball' valuation

This American import is a variation of the 'flip-flop' method and (apparently) was first used in baseball contract disputes. It also has affinities with the obsolete forms of valuation referred to in (d) above. In this version, and EFP (5th ed) Form 131 is a modern precedent of this type, the revised rent is determined by averaging the two closest of three valuations—two submitted by the parties, the third prepared by the independent expert (the 'third valuer'). As with 'flip flop', the form is designed to encourage agreement without invoking the machinery. Where agreement does not occur, each party appoints a valuer; those valuers prepare the first two valuations and unless they agree at this stage in the process, the 'third valuer' is appointed (either by agreement or by the President of the RICS) who prepares his own valuation. The revised rent is then the average of whichever two of the three valuations are closest in rental value. Once again, it is necessary to impose strict time-limits for the preparation and delivery of the parties' two valuations.

The notes to EFP (5th ed) Form 131 suggest that, since the third valuer's figure is likely to be between those of the parties (in the ballpark?) there is (again) the incentive to the parties' two valuers to 'pitch' their figures close to the market rent, but the procedure avoids any feeling of injustice about either a 'robust' award (which may sometimes be perceived to occur in the standard rent review valuation when the award is half way between the parties contentions) or the unusual but unfortunate case where the market rent is less than the tenant's figure or more than the landlords (outside the ballpark?).

The draftsman of EFP (5th ed) Form 131 contends that the sophistication of the idea allows for wider use than that of 'flip flop'; but there are the disadvantages of the strict time-limits and the (unnecessary?) cost of three valuers producing formal reports. There is also the difficult choice of whether the third (independent) valuer should see the valuations of the parties before preparing his own valuation (EFP (5th ed) Form 131 provides that he should).

6   Constructing the valuation framework

A rent review clause should specify the basis on which the reviewed rent is to be assessed. No clear consensus has emerged in the precedents as to the detailed wording of the criteria of value though they are all directed in one way or another to determining the open market rent. Since a careful and appropriate definition of the criteria adopted is desirable, all review clauses except a few early examples will contain a detailed limitation of the criteria, with many assumptions and disregards some of which may be 'usual' phrases commonly occurring and others may be specially formulated. These are fully discussed in Part Three, Chapter 12.

(a)   The modern notional or hypothetical framework

A modern review clause will have a full elaboration of the valuation criteria which should be appropriate to the property in question. Where this occurs the differences in meaning (if any) between 'market rents' and 'best rents' (see p 382) and so forth will cease to have relevance.

The aim, ideally, of the valuation directions should be to provide a framework within which a valuer can carry out his appointed task so that the rental so fixed at review should reflect not only the open market rent of the property at the review date but also take account

of all those factors which were relevant to the original bargain made
between the original parties to the lease and the relevant factors occurring
since the grant of the lease (such as improvements voluntarily undertaken
by the tenant). Consequently, for example, the reviewed rent will usually
take account of all the terms of the original lease (which incorporate
the terms of the original bargain) including provisions for rent review
but excluding the original sum agreed as rent.

In order to achieve a correct balance between the parties, review clauses
have, from the outset, contained certain 'assumptions' and 'disregards',
namely directions to a valuer or arbitrator to make certain factual
assumptions, or to disregard a particular state of affairs. Many of these
reflect simple justice, such as a direction to ignore any goodwill which
attaches to the premises arising by reason of the tenant's business, or
to ignore improvements voluntarily undertaken by the tenant and paid
for by him, for otherwise the tenant will have to pay rent on the goodwill
he has generated or on the capital works which he has financed. From
the landlord's point of view, there will need to be an assumption that
all the tenant's covenants have been performed so that the tenant cannot
claim a reduction in the rent a willing tenant would pay as a result
of his, the actual tenant's, own default.

The inevitable result of such assumptions or disregards is that the
valuer is directed not to value the actual premises let by the actual landlord
to this particular tenant on the basis of the terms of the lease as they
stand. Rather, the valuation is of a *notional* or *hypothetical* letting which
will shift the terms of the letting away from the actual position. It is
submitted that the key to drafting a rent review clause which will fairly
balance the interests of the parties is to have the terms of the hypothetical
letting as close as possible to the terms actually existing between the
parties to the lease so far as consistent with the determination of an
open market rent.

(b)   Notional or willing parties

There will invariably be *notional parties*. The parties to the hypothetical
letting will be abstractions—willing persons in the market place and
not the actual parties to the lease. This is inherent in the concept of
a letting in an open market for if the parties to the lease are identified
with the actual parties then the rent will not be that arrived at in an
open market. So most review clauses will expressly postulate a letting
by a *willing lessor* to a *willing lessee* and if this basis is not expressly
set out then it is likely to be implied (*Dennis & Robinson Ltd v Kiossos
Establishment* [1987] 1 EGLR 133); for the 'notion of a letting in the
open market between an unwilling lessor and an unwilling lessee . . .
makes no sense' (per Fox LJ at 134). There may then be express
assumptions about the nature of such a willing lessee, for example, that
he is registered for valued added tax (VAT) purposes and can make

full recovery of any VAT paid on the rent—whether or not this is true of the actual tenant.

(c)   Notional premises

There will usually be *notional premises*. Certainly, the starting point will be the premises as they stand but then the terms of the review clause will demand that certain adjustments are to be made for the purposes of the valuation. An assumption of *vacant possession* is common; even if the premises are actually sub-let there may be a direction to value *as a whole*. Premises not actually subdivided may have to be assumed to be available for sub-letting. *Improvements* voluntarily undertaken by the tenant which exist on the ground will almost invariably fall to be ignored or rather their effect on the rental value must be ignored. The premises may be in disrepair and, for example, have peeling paintwork; the valuation will be on the assumption that any painting covenant has been observed and performed. These and other matters mean that the premises and the use to which they are notionally to be put in the eye of the valuer may bear little relation to the actual state at the review date.

(d)   A notional lease

There will often be a *notional lease*. Certainly, there may well be (and often should be) the express common assumption that the terms of the lease apply and if not so express, it may well be implied: *Basingstoke & Deane District Council v Host Group Ltd* [1988] 1 WLR 348. Yet the parties may expressly, and sometimes inadvertently, direct a valuation on terms different, and perhaps substantially different, to the terms which actually govern their on-going relationship. The infamous '*Arthur Young* saga' (fully discussed in Chapter 11 at p 333) concerned just this issue: was the hypothetical letting to contain, in the notional lease, provisions for rent review? Rent reviews existed in the actual lease of course. Again, the current *use* of the premises may be set aside in favour of a notional and more valuable user—even though the actual use under the lease will continue after the review date. *Planning permission* may be expressly deemed to exist for such or certain specified notional uses, or to be free of conditions or limitations which apply to the actual permission.

One aspect of the notional lease that is often present is an express statement of the length of the notional term different to the actual term. Though there may be good theoretical justification for this particular departure from actuality (see p 396), the real motivation from the landlord's point of view is that behind the creation of all 'artificial' assumptions and disregards—to protect and enhance the rental value at review and thereby the capital value of the reversion. Recognising that this can be an unjust burden on tenants, the courts have adopted construction guide-lines (discussed fully in Chapter 10); in applying the perceived commercial purpose of rent review and the 'presumption of reality' the hypothetical letting will be interpreted as far as possible to accord with the actual lease.

(e)   The impact of the actual on the notional

Paradoxically, the most significant valuation consequences in terms of the quantum of rent payable after a review may not arise from the notional assumptions in the hypothetical letting but from the terms of the actual lease incorporated therein. Thus:

(1) A clause restrictive of the use in the lease may reduce the open market rent if the market of willing lessees for such use is restricted: eg *Plinth Property Investments Ltd v Mott Hay & Anderson* (1978) 38 P & CR 361, an issue fully discussed in Chapter 11, p 342;

(2) An unusually oppressive repairing obligation can have a similar depressing effect at review: *Norwich Union Life Assurance Society v British Railways Board* [1987] 2 EGLR 137 and see p 371;

(3) Restrictions on alienation greater than those normal in the market will reduce the rental value at review.

There is a school of thought which argues that this approach fails to recognise that the clause(s) did not have a great impact on settling the rent at the date of the lease (a contention often finding support from empirical evidence of the bargaining process at that stage) so they should not have substantial effect at review. An answer lies in the hypothetical letting which is in the open market at the review date. The effect on the *actual* parties at the date of the lease is not relevant to the impact of these clauses on the *notional* willing parties at review who are accepting a letting on non-negotiable terms. One must have some sympathy with those who protest at the enforced unreality; the process now seems too well established and tolerated for any change to be expected. For this reason, the draftsman of the lease must always consider the valuation impact of the other terms of the lease and so should those advising the initial lessee or any later assignee.

A trend in modern review clauses is to ensure (in the landlord's favour) that the notional letting is not so strictly circumscribed, not only by creating perhaps unreal assumptions as to use but also by opening the (notional) letting to alternatives allowing the valuer to assess which produces the higher or highest rent for the particular property. Examples are:

'the best rent at which the property might reasonably be expected to be let *either as a whole or in parts*';

'for such term as would at the beginning of the review period in question command the best rent' (thus leaving the valuer to choose the notional term).

Such clauses give a greater discretion to the arbitrator or expert at review so that they select the most favourable terms and then determine the rent on that basis. Tenants and their advisers may, with some justification, object (say) that the tenant has a letting as a whole so a valuation in parts is departing from the actual.

(f) Drafting objectives

Thus it is that the modern review clause creates a hypothetical framework and a hypothetical letting as the basis of valuation. In itself, this is not to be criticised—for many of the usual assumptions and disregards are essential to achieve balance and justice and to ensure that it is the market rent which is to be determined. The modern problem is more subtle. In any attempt to ensure that the maximum rental value is attached to the reversion, the modern review clause may contain assumptions and disregards not only of great complexity but also designed solely to protect the rental return and often far removed from the reality which prevails in the real world between the actual parties.

It is suggested that the ideal aim should be to include within the valuation framework those directions, assumptions, and disregards which are commercially justified and relevant to the property in question. Those which merely impose a requirement on a tenant to pay for something which he does not get and to provide a financial advantage referable to a factor which has no actual existence between the parties must be seriously questioned—and not only by a tenant's solicitor when the lease is negotiated. For they are a source of potential future conflict, and will be closely scrutinised by the courts who will apply a strong presumption against either party obtaining an advantage which is referable to a factor which has no existence between them (*Railstore Ltd v Playdale Ltd* [1988] 2 EGLR 153 at 155 applying *Basingstoke & Deane Borough Council v Host Group Ltd* [1988] 1 WLR 348). Moreover, there is always the risk that the stated notional assumptions and disregards will, when read together, create a hypothetical letting which, like the mythical unicorn, have no counterpart in the real world of commerce. Valuation at rent review may be an art and not a science but it must not degenerate into the fictional.

This plea for restraint does not only stem from the tenant's standpoint. Too great a departure from reality may eventually backfire on a landlord, at least to the extent that the value of the reversion in the market will not reflect the calculation based on the optimum rent to be derived from the formula. Past examples include rents in shopping centres geared to the Retail Price Index which would produce a rent several times above both what could be obtained in the market and what tenants could afford to pay when the centre met competition from rivals in better locations and with more modern facilities. To insist on the full rent based on the formula in such cases invites tenant's default or collapse. Vacancies in a centre, once above a certain level, then have a depressive effect on the rents of the units still occupied and on rents obtainable on review or the reletting of vacant units (as witness the damages awarded in *Costain Property Developments Ltd v Finlay & Co Ltd* [1989] 1 EGLR 237). In turn, there is a loss of value in the reversion when sold.

The detailed consideration of commonly occurring assumptions and disregards and their meaning scope and impact is contained in Part Three. Readers are referred to:

> Chapter 10—for general principles of construction;
> Chapter 11—for the drafting consequences at the review of the existing terms of the lease;
> Chapter 12—for the meaning, scope and appropriateness of assumptions and disregards that define the hypothetical lease.

7 Review dates

To observe that the clause should specify the date or dates upon which the rent is to be reviewed may be stating the obvious; but it is important both to ensure that the dates are clear and that they accord with the client's instructions. Normally, that review date will be the date both for the valuation of the open market rent and for commencement of payment of the sum so determined and the review clause should so state. Any departure from this standard position will require justification.

(a) Specifying the review date

Much the best position is to have the actual date or dates clearly stated as in the current Model Forms. To state that the review dates are (for example) '24 June in the years 1995, 2000 and 2005' leaves no room for doubt. The common phrase '24 June in every fifth year' is often sufficient but may cause difficulty if the term is calculated from 24 June 1990 but the lease is granted from a later date.

Where the review date is calculated, as is still sometimes the case, from the 'commencement of the term' and the parties have agreed (say) a review every 5 years, it is vital to understand when the term does so commence (an issue fully explored in Chapter 5, p 143, below) and whether the review is to take place at the beginning, end of (or, indeed, any time during) the fifth year, and indeed, when that fifth year occurs. The dangers are illustrated by *Beaumont Property Trust Ltd v Tai* [1982] 265 EG 872 when the stated date for commencement of the lease was about three and three quarter years before the date when the lease took effect. On the construction of the review clause, the first 'five yearly' review was calculated from the commencement of the term, or just 15 months from the execution of the lease and the start of the tenant's actual enjoyment of the premises.

If the review dates are to be suspended or altered on the happening of specified events, then either the alternative dates must be set out or the period of delay must be unequivocally stated. In *Ladbroke Group plc v Bristol City Council* [1988] 1 EGLR 126 the review date was to be delayed by 1 year for each year that road improvements had not been carried out but the starting date from which the delay was to be measured was not clearly stated which proved costly when it was held that the 8 year delay ran from the first review date in 1980 and not from 1973 (the date of the grant of the lease).

(b) Review date as the valuation date

A good review clause will also specify that the open market rent payable at review is to be that obtainable at the relevant review date—as in the Model forms (all versions), Conveyancer Precedent 5–57 and EFP (5th ed) Form 22, clause 2.3. Since these express review dates are invariably stated to be the dates when payment falls due, then if the lease is silent on the valuation date there will be an implication that it is the review date: *MFI Properties Ltd v BICC Group Pension Trust Ltd* [1986] 1 EGLR 115. The commercial purpose of a rent review clause points to this prima facie assumption but express provision to the contrary can be made so care is required to ensure that a different valuation date is not introduced inadvertently: *Parkside Knightsbridge Ltd v The German Food Centre Ltd* (1987) 8 RRLR 131 (review initiated by a trigger-notice to 'the then exclusive rack rental value'—valuation date was date of the notice).

(c) Review date as 'liability for payment' date

It is usual to intend that the specified review date is not only the valuation date but also the date from which the reviewed rent takes effect. If some different date or dates are required, this must be clearly set out. The settlement of the review may be some time later in which case payment only falls due after such settlement but will normally be calculated retrospectively to the review date. The actual time when payment falls due is considered in Chapter 8, p 262.

(d) Review assessed 'at the time of such determination'

What must normally be avoided is to provide for the reviewed rent to be that obtainable 'at the time of the determination' of the reviewed rent which may be many months, or longer, after the review date. Unfortunately, this is a relatively common wording in older leases because it is found in the now obsolete EFP (4th ed) Form 8:1 and its revision as Additional Form 76. These forms were apparently the basis of review clauses in many early leases. No difficulty would arise if the reviewed rent was only payable from the date of the determination—since the dates of valuation and for calculation of the reviewed liability would again coincide. However, the old precedents do not so provide and payment retrospectively under the normal rule to the review date is invariably found in leases with this formula. The potential injustice that a review 'at the date of such determination' can cause when a late review occurs was illustrated in *London and Manchester Assurance Co Ltd v G A Dunn & Co* [1982] 265 EG 39. In that case, a trigger-notice 4 years late was upheld (see p 160 below) and by the time the reviewed rent could be determined, following the court's judgment, the whole review period would have expired. Yet the reviewed rent was to be fixed 'at the date of determination'; if this was read literally then a 1982 market rent was payable retrospectively for the whole of the 1977–82 review period. The Court of Appeal assumed that this result was correct but the point was not in issue before them in the *London and Manchester* case (although it was apparently decided in favour of the landlords at first instance—(1982) 262 EG 143). Similar appellate assumptions were made in *Accuba Ltd v Allied Shoe Repairs Ltd* [1975] 1 WLR 1559 and *Touche Ross & Co v Secretary of State for the Environment* (1982) 265 EG 982.

If there is a delay in concluding the review in a time of rising rents the tenant may find himself bound to pay retrospectively for the whole period a rent much in excess of that which could actually have been commanded in the market in the period for which it is payable. Faced with this result, it now appears that the courts will strive so to construe the lease to avoid the literal but potentially unjust result. In *Webber v Halifax Building Society* [1985] 1 EGLR 58 the drafting of the review clause, described as 'slipshod', incorporated much of clause 3(1) of EFP (4th ed) Form 8:1 including the words 'at the date of such determination'. Notwithstanding the assumption in the *London and Manchester* case that these words meant the rent was to be fixed at values prevailing at the time of the determination, the deputy judge construed the clause as providing for the review date to be the beginning of the review period. He found himself able to do this because of the way he viewed an earlier clause in the reddendum of the lease, and because clause 3(2) of EFP (4th ed) Form 8:1 was omitted from the lease. There was therefore no express guidance as to initiation of review or how the valuation was to proceed; 'at the time of such determination' was therefore said to relate to the subject matter of the determination not its timing. *Glofield Properties v Morley (No 2)* [1989] 2 EGLR 118 concerned a lease with a review clause closely modelled on Form 8:1. After prolonged litigation on the validity of the rent review notices, the rent was now to be fixed for 5 year periods commencing in 1982 and 1987. The first instance judge felt he could not construe the clause to produce a realistic commercial result ([1988] 2 EGLR 149, applying dicta in the *London & Manchester* case) but the Court of Appeal overruled him and rejected the natural and obvious meaning of the words 'at the time of such determination' because:

(1) the parties had not clearly and unequivocally expressed their intention in that way so it was open to the court to construe the clause to produce the more sensible and realistic commercial result; and
(2) the more sensible and realistic result was to read the words as meaning 'at the time *for* such determination'.

This enabled the rent for the 1982 and 1987 review periods to be calculated by reference to values then prevailing, not at 1989 values.

It is submitted that the decision in *Glofield v Morley (No 2)* ought to be decisive where the point arises in other leases modelled on the same precedent. Yet the actual wording used will be vital in any particular case. *Prudential Assurance Co Ltd v Gray* [1987] 2 EGLR 134 concerned an unusual review clause in a reversionary lease which allowed a review by notice within 1 year of the commencement of the term. The valuer was directed to fix a rent in the open market 'at the date of the review'. The deputy judge considered the words were too clear to admit any other construction than the date of actual determination of the rent.

Consequently, EFP (4th ed) Form 8:1 and Additional Form 76 should never be adopted today (as noted in Part Seven, p 703). Any new lease should adopt a more modern precedent (for this and other reasons) and it will be prudent when leases which are based on the old precedent are renewed under the 1954 Act to make an adjustment in the terms of any new lease agreed to ensure that the review date is the valuation date.

8   Review periods

(a)   *Frequency of review periods*

The parties are at liberty to specify such periods between reviews as they consider and agree to be most appropriate. The periods between reviews may be 'unequal', though set periods are far more usual. Once the periods were every 14, 10, or 7 years; now 5 years is normal and 4 or 3 yearly reviews are not unusual. The biennial review has been recorded; and the only limitations on the brevity of the period appear to be practical and commercial. It is fair to say that at the present time a 5-year rent review pattern is most commonly encountered; and this has been judicially recognised as the normal term, for shop lettings at least, in *Ratners (Jewellers) Ltd v Lemnoll Ltd* [1980] 255 EG 987 at 989. If a local practice for a shorter period can be established, then that will be the period in the new lease at a statutory renewal: *W H Smith v Bath City Council* (1986) unreported but see 277 EG 822.

Rent reviews can be costly and time consuming (particularly if agreement on the new rent is not forthcoming) and the more frequent the review the more difficult forward financial planning becomes. The mere cost of the review can, therefore, become a factor. A speedy and inexpensive procedure, always desirable, is particularly important when review periods are short. One possible advantage, however, of a frequent review pattern, perhaps at 3 years, is that a tenant is not faced with quite such a large increase each time; but the main benefactor of frequent reviews would appear to be the lessor.

(b) Initial review periods

As noted above, a lease whose term is calculated from a date prior to the grant may result in the first review period being shorter than the others. This may be required, perhaps, to ensure that the review coincides with that in the head lease or with reviews on adjoining properties. If these factors are not present, a tenant's solicitor may wish to adjust the review periods to run from the date the lease is granted.

(c) 'Eleventh hour' rent reviews

Modern leases emanating from institutional lessors may contain express provision for a rent review in the last year, or even the last month of the contractual term. These 'eleventh hour' reviews are designed to be effective when the contractual term is likely to be extended under the Landlord and Tenant Act 1954, part II.

(i) Arguments in favour
Last minute reviews offer several potential advantages for a landlord:

(1) The tenant begins the period of statutory continuation at a freshly determined open market rent.
(2) There is no monetary incentive for a tenant to delay the statutory renewal procedure.
(3) The landlord will probably not need to bother with the notices for an interim rent under the Act.
(4) The rent determined contractually will avoid the valuation formula for an interim rent (s 24A of the Act) which lessors, probably correctly, consider is likely to result in a rent less than the open market level.
(5) The contractual rent review will take effect as soon as it is complete whereas interim rent applications are often combined with the hearing for the new tenancy which may be delayed in the event of a dispute over terms.

(ii) Disadvantages for a tenant
The obvious disadvantages for a tenant are the reverse of the arguments for a landlord in the previous paragraph. There are additionally:

(1) A tenant loses the statutory protection of the interim rent procedure judicially described as a 'cushion against the shock' of a large increase

at renewal (*Charles Follett Ltd v Cabtell Investments Ltd* [1987] 2 EGLR 88).

(2) There is the possibility of a series of rent negotiations in quick succession, first for the last review, then, perhaps, for an interim rent if for any reason the contractual review is unacceptable to the landlord and finally for the rent in the new lease.

(3) The 'end of the term' or 'eleventh hour' rent review will be on the basis of a notional term as set out in the review clause. This may specify a period equal to the original term or a set period of years (either deliberately stated to be greater than the residue). The reality is, however, that the tenant only has an uncertain period and the value of the occupation will depend very much on whether the lessor has grounds to oppose.

(4) If the landlord secures a favourable rent at the end of term review, it will place him in a stronger bargaining position for the negotiations for the terms of the new tenancy. He may be tempted himself to delay the negotiations for a new lease.

(iii) Some possible problems

An end of term rent review may face problems:

(1) In existing leases there may be review clauses which are early examples of an attempt to state a notional term equivalent to the original term. However, in the light of the cases of *Norwich Union Life Assurance Society v Trustee Savings Banks Central Board* [1986] 1 EGLR 136 and *Ritz Hotel (London) Ltd v Ritz Casino Ltd* [1989] 2 EGLR 135 (see p 398) the notional period may be found to be either the residue of the lease or a term of years equal in length to the original term but dated from the grant of the lease—resulting in either case in a notional term of a month or so. The market rent in such an instance is not likely to be realistic! The effect may be mitigated if the lease contains the provision for a minimum level of rent or is an 'upwards only' clause and by the ability to take account of the prospects of statutory renewal (see the *Pivot Properties* case discussed at p 403). By the review date, it may be a matter of fact not speculation whether the landlord is opposing a new lease. Nevertheless, the result will often be not only a rent below the usual market rent but one below the interim rent. If there is a problem with the notional term at eleventh hour rent reviews, then the landlord should still apply for an interim rent. If 'eleventh hour' reviews are included in new leases, the notional term must be set out with absolute clarity.

(2) Though there is apparently nothing in the 1954 Act to prevent an end of term review, it should be noted that the Law Commission have proposed that a tenant have the right to apply for an interim rent. If this change were to be introduced, it would be a nice question

whether the court could or would determine an interim rent less than that settled by a last minute contractual rent review or even, perhaps, still to be settled, as there is no reason to suppose that such reviews will be speedily concluded.

At the time of writing, 'eleventh hour' rent reviews are not an established feature in commercial leases and tend only to be included by those landlords convinced of their merits.

(d) Contractual reviews in any statutory continuation?

It has been suggested, by Ross *Drafting and Negotiating Commercial Leases* para 6.4:3, that a lease which provides for rent review on 'every fifth anniversary of the term' could import a review into the period of statutory continuation if a relevant anniversary date fell in that period. This may well be true, notwithstanding that the contractual term, a fixed period, is a different concept to a statutory continuation of the term (*A Plesser & Co Ltd v Davis* (1983) 267 EG 1039) particularly if the 'term' is expressly defined as including any continuation of the tenancy. If not so defined, the issue remains one of speculation which may turn on the construction of the lease in question.

(e) Obsolete review patterns

Where reviews are infrequent different problems arise, not least of which are long-term leases that were entered into some years ago and whose rent review patterns are now obsolete (ie reviews (say) every 14 years, where in today's market the maximum period would be every 5). A valuation difficulty is thus created: should the reviewed rent (which will be in force for the next 14 years) be increased to reflect the fact that most rents in the market are only fixed for 5–year periods (ie be set at a higher figure than would otherwise be the case)? One suggested method of combating this problem is the 'Constant Rent Tables' and these are discussed in Chapter 7, p 252. Even if these are rejected, the prevailing sentiment is to 'uplift' the rent to reflect the abnormal rent review pattern. Certainly, the longer the review period the more important it is that each party has the opportunity to make representations, and therefore an arbitration process may be more appropriate.

Neither party will have cause to seek in a new lease review periods at longer intervals than those currently prevailing in the market. Any departure from the market standard may be ill-advised. The landlord may find that the value of the reversion is reduced quite apart from being kept out of a market rent for a longer period; a tenant may suffer a 'notional uplift' added at the eventual review which will penalise in the first few years of the period and which may or may not even out over the whole period; and both parties may struggle to unearth suitable comparable lettings.

(f)   Review of review periods

The experience of obsolete rent review patterns or changes in the usual pattern has led lessors to insert into long term leases a provision to review the frequency of review. A relatively simple option is to provide for a single review of the rent review dates once during the term at the option of the landlord by notice and a precedent to this effect is EFP (5th ed) Form 133. It is however, relatively improbable that newly negotiated rent review periods will ever be much more frequent than 4 or 5 years for practical reasons and Form 133 does not give the tenant a right to operate the mechanism if the periods between reviews in the market are greater than those in the lease. A later change in the whole basis of review is perhaps more likely than a significant shift in the intervals between reviews. It is possible to have a clause providing for a review of the whole rent review clause but it must be questionable whether the complexity of such a provision justifies the possible benefits. The problems of settling the criteria by which the new clause is to be selected probably matches the difficulties of showing that any postulated replacement meets the criteria laid down.

9   Provision for interest

(a)   No provision for interest implied

In *Trust House Forte Albany Hotels Ltd v Daejan Investments Ltd* [1980] 256 EG 915 Walton J held that an obligation to pay interest on a delayed review could not be implied on the 'business efficacy' principle, although it would have been commercially reasonable and not inconsistent with any other provision in the lease. The judge was of the opinion that, while the landlord may thus be disadvantaged, it was certainly not *necessary* to imply the term.

(b)   Arguments for express provision for interest

Thought must therefore be given to the question of whether to provide for interest payments on arrears of increased rents. (The issue of when such increases have to be paid is discussed later at p 262.) The question assumes a greater significance after the *United Scientific* decision since in most circumstances a late review of rent can be made, perhaps after a delay of a considerable time. In premises enjoying a high rental value on the open market, the amount of interest that might be payable on increased rent retrospectively due to the review date could be a not inconsiderable sum. Lessors may wish to include some provision for interest on the basis that the tenant has had use of the money representing the difference between the former rent and the new rent the lease envisages he should pay from the review date. Indeed, this was recognised a an 'economic benefit' to the tenant in the *United Scientific* case (per Lord

Diplock at 932A). From the tenant's point of view, however, provision for interest can impose a significant burden in the event of delay (particularly if he has not put aside sums to meet such interest payments), nullify the principal benefit he has from a delay which may not be of his making and impose a greater degree of uncertainty in the event of a delayed review (see Chapter 5). Moreover, one incentive for a landlord to proceed to a review expeditiously is removed.

It is significant that the Model Forms in 1979 and 1980 did not provide for payment of interest on arrears of increased rents, and the Background Notes acknowledged that provision for interest depended on market practice at the time when the lease was granted. It was then thought that provision for interest was a matter better dealt with in a general provision for interest on all unpaid rent in a lease. This was and is a sound approach, but it does require such general provision to be drafted and considered in the light of the rent review clause as a whole. The attitude of the Joint Working Party has changed and accordingly the 1985 Revision of the Model Forms includes (optional) provisions for interest on rent ascertained after the review date. The current practice reflects this change in the Model Forms and some provision for interest is now very common.

(c) Appropriate rate of interest

The Model Forms suggest the 7–day deposit rate of a named bank, although Background Note 13 does not argue the case for the choice. The 1984 ISVA Forms plump for a base rate. What is vital is to ensure that the rate is not the 'penal' rate applicable to default and really should not exceed the rate which could be obtained by investment. Therefore, those leases which stipulate a rate some percentage points over a bank base rate (perhaps equating twice that chosen in the latest Model Forms) are unfair to the tenant. In *Chartered Trust plc v Maylands Green Estate Co Ltd* (1984) 270 EG 845 (see p 115) a condition was imposed, on a grant of an order under s 27 of the Arbitration Act 1950, that interest be paid on the rent ascertained late. The rate chosen was left to counsel to determine and is not stated in the report.

An attempt was made in Conveyancer Precedent 5–57 to provide a safeguard against delay but to avoid a provision whereby the tenant is faced with payment of interest in all circumstances. It provides that rent retrospectively due shall not bear interest unless the referee in his award (determining the reviewed rent) provides for the payment of interest because of delay by the lessee in or about the determination of the substituted rent. Such provision for interest may be for such period and at such rate as the referee may specify. In this way, a landlord has a remedy for delay when the tenant has caused or contributed to the delay but otherwise interest is not payable. This may be a fair provision but the market sentiment is against it.

(d)   Calculation of the interest

If there is to be express provision for interest, then it is important to ensure that it applies to give interest from the review date. In *Shield Properties & Investments Ltd v Anglo Overseas Transport Co Ltd (No 2)* (1986) 279 EG 1089, the lease only stated that interest was to be payable if the lessee ' . . . shall make default in effecting payment to the lessor forthwith on demand of any monies becoming payable by the lessee . . . '. The review date was 25 December 1982; an arbitrator made an award on 24 May 1983; before the next rent day, the tenants issued a notice of motion to set aside the award; on 3 April 1984, the award, though not set aside, was remitted to the arbitrator for further consideration (see [1985] 1 EGLR 7 and p 206 below); and on 20 November 1984 he made a substituted, and lower, award. The lessors claimed interest from the date of the original award but it was held that the tenants were not 'in default' under the lease. The original award had been annulled by the remission; under the revised award, the reviewed rent was not due until the next quarter day following the award (applying the *South Tottenham* case—see p 262); that had been paid by the due date so no interest was payable. If the clause had provided for interest as in the 1985 Model Forms, a substantial sum would have been payable as interest. The judge, Michael Wheeler QC, suggested that one remedy for the lessors, given that the lease did not make provision for interest, would have been for them to request that the tenants be put on terms as to interest when the motion to set aside the arbitrator's original award was issued.

On the other hand, if the interest clause provides for interest on *all* the shortfall from the review date until payment, the tenant will suffer if more than one rent day elapses. The interest must be paid in respect of *each instalment of rent* so that interest is paid on the shortfall from the date each such instalment fell due. Interest is not awarded as a punishment but because the landlord has been deprived of the use of his money (see *Allied London Investments Ltd v Hambro Life Assurance plc* [1985] 1 EGLR 45) so should not be calculated from a date earlier that it is due.

10   Rent payments pending the review

(a)   Payment on account

Almost without exception, rent review precedents provide for the current rent to continue to be paid after the review date until determination of the review and if this has not been expressed it is likely to be implicit in the terms of the lease or implied—see *Weller v Akehurst* [1981] 3 All ER 411 and p 50 above. It is better to express such payments as being on account of the sum which eventually falls due (and this may be helpful if counter inflation restrictions on rent increases were ever to be reintroduced—see Chapter 19, p 551 below).

(b)   Interim 'without prejudice' rent

(i)   Nature of the concept

A device sometimes found permits the landlord on initiating the review process to nominate an interim rent, or provisional rent, to be paid by the tenant pending settlement of the revised rent and without prejudice to the sum eventually agreed or determined. Such a rent is paid from the review date to the date of ascertainment of the reviewed rent. Provided the interim rent becoming payable is not outrageously large, the result has obvious cash flow advantages for the landlord and may not always be unwelcome to the tenant, particularly if the review process is not concluded until well into a later accounting period. It is, of course, essential that the interim rent level is without prejudice to the revised rent and that express provision to that effect is included.

(ii)   How determined

This is the crucial issue and it is the lack of a procedure which is both simple yet safeguards the tenant which is the reason that the idea has not found widespread favour. Simplicity is essential; there is no point in duplicating the review process and it is unlikely that anyone will advocate an interim rent assessment based on the model in the 1954 Act!. The alternatives are:

(1)   The sum may be 'at large' and be the figure nominated by the landlord by written notice. This procedure is the most disadvantageous to a tenant and some limit to the sum specified is essential. Yet if a fixed limit is to be introduced, the alternatives suggested below are to be preferred. A requirement in the notice of a surveyor's certification introduces expense and opens the Pandora's box of the nature of the duty of care owed to the tenant.

(2)   It may be the rent currently payable increased by a stated and predetermined percentage. Clearly, there is a difficulty in choosing in advance what that percentage is to be but a figure to be nominated not exceeding the stated percentage would be possible.

(3)   The method which will at least be a simple inflationary counter is to refer to, say, the Retail Prices Index (RPI) so that the interim rent is an index-linked fraction bearing the same proportion to the original rent, or rent as last reviewed, as the current monthly or annual index bears to the index at the date of the lease or last review date as the case may be. This device will ensure some extra interim payments but a tenant should note the lack of flexibility if the open market rent is less than that currently payable. (The details of the RPI and the possible inequity of using that inflation index which may bear no relation to property values is discussed in Chapter 20).

An interim rent precedent has been published as EFP (5th ed) Form 132. The landlord must give notice indicating an interim rent based on the landlord's opinion of the open market rent. Tenants are advised to consider this form carefully. The landlord, for good negotiating reasons, is hardly likely to set a figure less than the 'opening shot' specified in the rent review trigger-notice or in the letter opening discussion of the revised rent. If this is right, and without further protection, then tenants would almost invariably end up paying an interim rent in excess of the rent finally agreed or determined. For this reason, Form 132 puts an upper limit on the interim rent and suggests those limits should be the higher of twice the passing rent or the passing rent plus 50 per cent of the amount by which the rent specified by the landlord in the interim rent notice exceeds the passing rent. These safeguards are essential and the tenant's solicitor should ensure that the upper limits specified are fair in the particular case.

(iii) Interest and overpayments

Some landlords still insist on retrospective interest on the excess of the revised rent over this interim rent. Form 132, referred to above, does so. It is largely a matter of the bargaining strength of the respective parties whether or not that has to be accepted. Treatment of any overpayment may be more controversial. It is perhaps not unreasonable for that excess to be carried forward and credited against future rent, rather than refunded, but the absence of any provision for an allowance of interest to compensate the tenant for overpayment is not reasonable, although it is not an uncommon situation. Form 132 states that any overpayment is refunded to the tenant without interest though there is a note that the tenant is likely to seek an interest provision on overpayments. The potential injustice is most marked where the landlord is free to state any figure he chooses as the interim rent, for just as the landlord is likely to ask for a greater review rent than he is prepared to settle for, so also an interim rent unilaterally imposed may be set at a high figure—if only because to set the interim rent below what the landlord seeks at review may weaken his bargaining position. Drafts giving landlords an unfettered discretion to set an interim rent should therefore be resisted by the tenant; if this objection fails, the tenant must, at the very least, ensure that he has power to initiate the review himself and try to include provision for interest on any adjusting figure as a deterrent against overstating the interim rent.

11 Drafting review clauses in sub-leases

The relationship between rent reviews in a superior lease and sub-leases, particularly of parts of the premises in the head lease, calls for particular alertness on the part of the draftsman and those later advising sub-lessees. A common approach is to keep the provisions of the head lease and those in the sub-lease separate as far as possible. Certainly, it will be sensible to mirror the head lease terms in the sub-lease and this applies to the rent review clause as much as to other terms, but the sub-lease rent review clause must be able to stand on its own and operate independently where required.

In many cases the only link between the two rent review clauses will be the date and timing of the review. In others, it may have been agreed that the quantum of rent payable in the sub-lease rent review is to be a specified proportion of the quantum of the head lease rent. The drafting then has to satisfy the different concerns of the parties. A subtenant is primarily concerned with his own review, but if the amount paid under the sub-lease is in some way dependent on the figure agreed in the head lease, then involvement in the head lease rent review is an essential protection. The intermediate lessor, on the other hand, will be looking both ways at two rent reviews seeking to protect the existing differential or any profit element.

(a) Timing of the sub-lease rent review

The issue of timing is one that requires careful consideration. The usual practice is to state rent review dates in the sub-lease which will coincide with those in the head lease. This will ensure that the reviewed rents are payable from the same review date but of itself will do nothing to assist the review process in the two leases.

Two alternative strategies present themselves. One is to pick review dates for the sub-lease(s) to follow by, say, a quarter the review dates in the head lease. Whilst he can have no guarantee of it, the mesne landlord can hope that, knowing the new head-rent, he can secure his profit sub-rental on agreeing or having a referee determine the sub-rent(s). The other approach is to have the sub-lease reviews precede those under the head lease, so that the mesne landlord enters upon the process of ascertaining the head-rent knowing the (aggregate) sub-rent(s). He may seek to secure his profit, as it were, from the other end. The choice has so far been presented from the point of view of the mesne landlord. However, both the head landlord and the subtenant(s) will also have a point of view which may or may not coincide with that of the party in the middle between them or with each other. Whatever choice has been made in settling the documentation, moreover, may turn out in particular circumstances to be unwelcome to one or other of the interested parties. Manipulation, not to put too fine a point upon it, of the available procedures for settling the two levels of rent, or having them settled, may enable the set order to be reversed in effect so that the order of settlement becomes that which best suits the party who is most skilful at reversing the stipulated sequence of events to serve his perceived commercial interests. Given these issues, it is not surprising that the parties tend to compromise and the dates in the sub-lease are made to coincide with those in the head lease.

(b) Mirroring the head lease rent review

It is obviously sensible to mirror the head lease provisions in the sub-lease rent review in the absence of circumstances producing obvious incompatibility. Apart from any other consideration, the involvement of the head lessee's surveyors in the review of the head rent and of the sub-rent(s), in whatever order this is settled (see above) will probably be more effective and even less costly if the verbal and valuation frameworks are identical or at least comparable. Of course, it may be necessary where sub-leases are only of part of larger premises contained in the head lease to add elements to the formula, to alter assumptions or disregards which would be neither appropriate nor necessary in the rent review provisions in the sub-lease, and untoward results may flow as much from failures to make such additions or amendments as from unthinking and slavish adherence to the handiwork of the draftsman of the head lease. Indeed, wherever problems exist for rent review generally, the problems may be magnified by the extra complication of the two leases. For example, if the head lease user clause in a lease of a public house in a shopping arcade contains a clause permitting retail user with consent, such consent not to be unreasonably withheld, then on review the head landlord may argue, possibly successfully, for a rent based on the more profitable retail use for the premises. If the sub-lease does not contain a similar provision, then the sub-lease rent review will be based on the actual and permitted licensed use which may result in a lower rent on review—and the mesne landlord suffers the consequent loss. The failure to mirror that particular head lease provision in the sub-lease means that the mesne lessor is the author of his own misfortune.

There may be some particular merit in consulting with the client's valuer to consider an agreed statement of the valuation aspects so as to ensure the same treatment in both reviews. In *Thomas Miller & Co v Richard Saunders & Partners* [1989] 1 EGLR 267 agreement at review to exclude corridors from the sub-lease rental valuation left surveyors resisting a negligence claim, (successfully in that case) when the head lease arbitrator included the rental value of the corridors.

Aspects of the problem of the inter-relationship can arise where, for example, the head lease calls for a review on the basis of a notional letting of the demised premises as a whole, or, even, merely with vacant possession of the whole (these are discussed respectively at p 406 and p 411) for it will then not be possible to parallel exactly these features in the sub-lease rent review formula. The valuation impact of the existence or otherwise of renewal rights under Part II of the Landlord and Tenant Act 1954 may affect the head lease in a different manner to the sub-lease on review.

(c) Linked sub-lease formulas

Particular problems arise when there is a rental formula linking the sub-lease rent review to that in the head lease. The cases chronicling the litigation that has ensued when such clauses fall to be operated are discussed in Chapter 14, p 489; the drafting lessons are:

(1) Ensure that the sub-lease rent review can still operate if the head lease rent review is lost or the head lease surrendered: *R & A Millett (Shops) Ltd v Leon Allan International Fashions Ltd* [1989] 1 EGLR 138.

(2) Make sure that there is no confusion in reference between one lease and the other particularly as to dates and timing of the reviews. In *Finger Lickin' Chicken Ltd v Ganton House Investments Ltd* [1989] EGCS 99 it was not clear whether the phrase 'the said term' referred to the head lease or that in the sub-lease.

(3) Wherever the quantum of the sub-lease rent primarily depends on the head lease rent as reviewed then the actual head lease rent base level must be known to ensure that the formula reflects the current rents in the market and the formula when operated will not unfairly disadvantage either party (consider the lessons from the *County Personnel* case discussed at p 290).

(4) Formulas may be better expressed algebraically as well as, or instead of, by verbal description: *London Regional Transport v Wimpey Group Services Ltd* [1986] 2 EGLR 41.

(5) Whenever there is an aspect of the head lease rent review that could adversely affect the subtenant then consideration should be given as to the best way to involve or protect the subtenant.

(d) Involving a subtenant in a head lease rent review

There are various approaches that might be adopted either separately or in tandem:

(1) A subtenant could bargain for a notice to be served on him before any head lease rent review and for a provision requiring his agreement to any settlement.

(2) A right to insist on notice being given of a proposed settlement of the head lease review with a consequent right to insist on independent determination if dissatisfied with the proposals (perhaps with an indemnity and security for the mesne lessor's costs).

(3) A right to make submissions either independently or through the intermediate lessor to the head lease arbitrator.

The importance of all or any of these steps will depend on the impact of the head lease review on the subtenant. They will assume significance, for example, if the sub-lease rent is a substantial percentage of the head lease rent as determined or if the underlease rent is that payable under the head lease from time to time. In either case, the intermediate lessor will have little or no incentive to resist the rent proposed by the head lessor. When the reviews take place, the surveyors will need some skill to ensure that their client's interests are fully protected as the head lease and sub-lease rent reviews progress together—see the discussion in Chapter 14, p 490.

The guide-lines suggested above may be counsels of perfection in that the terms of the head lease may already be fixed and the mesne lessor, however willing to accommodate the sub-lessee, may be unable to do what is ideally required.

(e) Conclusions

Given the imponderables, the authors do not feel able to indicate any general preference or guide-lines except those already indicated. A tactical decision has to be made in each separate set of circumstances. Other considerations beyond those identified may be relevant—even mere matters of cashflow can be taken into account. (Indeed, where the head-rent is payable on the usual quarter-days, the rent days under the sub-lease(s) should ideally be the corresponding day in the same 4 months, whatever the relative timing of the reviews). It is not clear whether or not there is a predominant view on all these aspects in the property world.

12 Drafting check-list

A drafting check-list is probably a misnomer since the solicitor for the landlord is likely to commence with the client or office standard draft and the tenant's solicitor will be perusing the draft proposed. It may nevertheless be helpful to summarise the main issues for the adviser faced with a proposed rent review precedent or schedule and seeking to adapt it for the case in hand. We raise issues briefly arising either from the discussion above, or by pointing the reader to fuller argument later in this book:

Page references in text

(1) What form of rent review clause is most appropriate, an automatic review (perhaps based on the Model Forms or EFP (5th ed) Form 22) or a review initiated by notice (eg Conveyancer Precedent 5–57 or EFP (5th ed) Form 127)? See ss 1–3 above. pp 47–59

(2) If the review is to be initiated by notice, are time-limits specified? Is it clear whether they are, or are not, of the essence? Is an option to determine associated with the review clause which may make time impliedly of the essence? See Chapter 5. pp 92–111

(3) Is suitable provision made for agreement between the parties? Is that agreement only enforceable if made or evidenced in writing? See section 4 of this chapter, above.   pp 59–64

(4) Does the tenant have to serve a counter-notice? If so, is the procedure acceptable, or should an expression of disagreement suffice to bring the third party reference into operation in default of agreement? Better still, can the format of the review be changed so that an automatic review is substituted?   pp 128–131

(5) In default of agreement, is the rent to be fixed by arbitration or valuation? Is it clear which is chosen? See section 5 of this chapter, above and Chapter 6. Is it appropriate to allow a choice between the two at a later date? If so, to which party and at what stage?   pp 64–69 and pp 188–194

(6) What criterion of value is used to describe the reviewed rent? Is there a good reason to depart from an open market rent? See Chapter 12, section 1.   pp 382–393

(7) What are to be the terms of the notional letting? (see generally Chapters 11 and 12):

  (i) Is it clear that any inappropriate matters are omitted or stated to be disregarded (eg current rent payable, option to renew)?   p 318 ff

  (ii) Is it clear that all appropriate terms are included (especially the full rent review machinery)?   p 333

  (iii) Is the notional period of letting expressly stated with absolute clarity as to the date from which the notional term is to be calculated?   pp 396–406

(8) Check the assumptions and disregards. Are any which are usual omitted? Are any included in the draft inappropriate? Do any appear inconsistent with another? Consider the following:

  (i) Is it to be a letting 'as a whole'?   p 411

  (ii) 'Without a premium'?

  (iii) Is the usual 'vacant possession' appropriate in the particular case?   p 406

  (iv) Consider the assumption of fitness for occupation and its relationship with any assumption of vacant possession or allowance for fitting out.   p 418

  (v) It is usual to assume the hypothetical 'willing

lessor'. Check that it also presupposes a willing
lessee.   pp 393–396

(vi) Check carefully the disregard on improvements if this is included. How far is the
disregard to extend?   pp 427–449

See generally section 6 of this chapter above and
Chapter 12.

(9) What effect will provisions and restrictions in the
lease have on valuation if incorporated into the
notional letting? (See generally chapter 11.)
Consider:

  (i) Any restriction on user.   pp 342–362

  (ii) Any restriction on alienation.   pp 365–371

  (iii) Any restriction on alteration.   pp 376–377

  (iv) The extent of the tenant's repairing obligation.   pp 371–376

  (v) Service charge provisions.

(10)   (i) Are the review dates clearly specified? If not,
can they be calculated with certainty?   p 74

  (ii) Is it clear that the rent payable at review is
to be that obtainable at the review date (and
not at the date of determination)?   pp 75–77

  (iii) Has the date on which the reviewed rent is
to be paid been clearly stated?   p 262

  (iv) Is there any reason why it should not be the
review date? Is that date the rent date?   p 75

(11)   (i) Are the parties happy that, in the event of
delay in the review, all eventualities are
covered?   p 162

  (ii) Can the tenant initiate the review in default?   pp 53–55

  (iii) Is it appropriate for the review to be backdated to the review date, or, in the event of
a long delay, only to the date of the trigger-
notice?   p 239

  (iv) Consider providing for interest to be paid on
backdated payments and check the specified
rate to ensure (from the tenant's point of view)
that it is a fair figure and not at a penal rate.   p 81 and p 263

  (v) Is an interim without prejudice rent appropriate? Consider treatment of under or over
payments. See section 9 of this chapter, above.   pp 81–83

  (vi) Once the reviewed rent is determined, is it
clear on which date any arrears fall due to
be paid?   p 261

(12) How is the reviewed rent to be evidenced? See
Chapter 8.   p 266

Chapter 5

Operating the Review Machinery

When negotiating and drafting the lease the parties are free to choose the type of mechanism they prefer and believe to be most suitable for reviewing the rent. Once incorporated into the lease the review machinery is part of the contractual bargain and, in the absence of subsequent agreement to vary the lease, these terms regulate the review process.

Since the review machinery agreed upon will govern the later process at the time of review, an awareness of the issues and problems is necessary when drafting the review clause.

1 Time-limits in the machinery

Many older review clauses, and most of those appearing in leases executed in the 1960s, still include time-limits of one sort or another. Some of these are precise in detailing a timetable for each stage of the process (eg Conveyancer Precedent 5–57); whereas others may state a time-limit at one particular stage of the process only (eg for appointment of the arbitrator or for the conclusion of the arbitration—see *Fousset v Twenty Seven Welbeck Street Ltd* (1973) 25 P & CR 277) for an early example. The approach that avoids, wherever possible, the strict adherence to time-limits appeared after the *United Scientific* case and is now currently the dominant school of thought (see EFP (5th ed) Form 22 and the Model Forms). However, there will always be instances, even in such clauses, where some time-limits will be necessary. On the other hand, the alternative approach—that is, to provide clearly stated periods of time for review notices at each stage of the process expressly making these of the essence—attempts to ensure that the operation of the review machinery is not unduly protracted.

(a) The United Scientific decision

The decision in *United Scientific Holdings Ltd v Burnley Borough Council* [1978] AC 904 (the '*United Scientific* case') was a watershed for all stipulations as to time. Prior to that case a sharp distinction had been drawn. It was said that all review clauses would fall into one of two categories for the purpose of determining the impact of failing to observe strictly the time-limits prescribed by the lease (though there was often grave difficulty in deciding on which side of the fence a particular case fell: see, for example, *Mount Charlotte Investments Ltd v Leek & Westbourne Building Society* [1976] 1 All ER 890 at 896F). On the one hand, in those clauses either framed or construed as conferring on the landlord an option or unilateral privilege to exact additional rent, the time-limit in which the review was to occur, or notice to be served, was taken (applying the established rules relating to options) as a condition that had to be strictly complied with if the benefit of the option or privilege was to be taken (*Samuel Properties (Developments) Ltd v Hayek* [1972] 1 WLR 1296 at 1302). Time-limits in such clauses were thereby 'of the essence'. On the other hand, there were clauses that envisaged a contractual obligation on the parties to undertake the review of the rent payable after the review date. In these cases the time-limits were part and parcel of the prescribed machinery for the performance of this obligation. Failure to adhere to the requirements of time might lead to a breakdown in the mechanics, but it was not fatal to a later determination of the reviewed rent beyond the period envisaged by the review clause (*Accuba Ltd v Allied Shoe Repairs Ltd* [1975] 1 WLR 1559). This distinction produced the unhappy consequence that the question whether a time-limit had to be observed depended on whether the review clause could be categorised as conferring an option or not. The analysis of the rent review clause as an option was recognised as 'a triumph for theory over realism' (per Templeman J in the *Mount Charlotte Investments Ltd* case at 892G). In the *United Scientific* case, however, both the Court of Appeal and the House of Lords abandoned the option analysis.

This abandonment made it essential to decide a new basis for stipulations as to time. The view of the Court of Appeal in *United Scientific Holdings Ltd v Burnley Borough Council* [1976] Ch 128 and in *Cheapside Land Development Co Ltd v Messels Service Co* (1976) 120 SJ 554 was that time-limits were prima facie of the essence since this was the presumed intention of the parties and that equity would not give relief in commercial contracts. As is well known, their Lordships reversed both decisions, preferring the view that there is a presumption that the timetable specified in a review clause for the completion of the various steps for determining the rent payable in respect of the period following the review date is not of the essence of the contract (per Lord Diplock [1978] AC 904 at 930G). The result of the *United Scientific* decision is that wherever a time-limit is specified in the context of a rent review clause, the timetable need not be strictly adhered to, except in those instances where time is expressly made of the essence or is impliedly so, or where the review is interrelated with a break-clause. This rule does not only apply to the situation that arose in the *United Scientific* and *Cheapside* cases— namely to delays in timetables relating to the operation of the review machinery (eg failure to observe the deadline for appointment of an arbitrator in default of agreement). It will also apply to all time stipulations in review clauses and in particular to trigger-notices, default clauses and to the commencement or completion of an arbitration.

(i) Time-limits for the service of a 'trigger-notice', which is a pre-requisite to initiation of the review process

Strictly speaking, the expressions of opinion in the *United Scientific* case that time was not of the essence in the service of such trigger-notices were obiter, since they were not relevant to the decision in either case before the House. Indeed, Viscount Dilhorne was clearly of the view that time should be of the essence in this one respect. However, the majority views of Lords Diplock, Salmon and Fraser were adopted in *Amherst v James Walker Goldsmith Ltd (No 1)* (1980) 254 EG 123 CA, where the *United Scientific* case was said to show the general bias against treating time of the essence.

(ii) Time-limits provided in 'default clauses'

For example, in *Phipps-Faire Ltd v Malbern Construction Ltd* [1987] 1 EGLR 129 the review clause was in the form of the original 1979 draft version of the Model Forms and gave the lessee the right to serve a notice, after a particular date, proposing the new rent and this amount was to be the revised rent unless the lessor applied within 3 months for a valuer to be appointed. The *United Scientific* presumption applied to this time-limit as much as to any other (but see the section on default clauses below).

(iii) Time-limits for the commencement or completion of an arbitration process in the context of a rent review

A late submission to arbitration can be made and, if the arbitrator is to be appointed by the President for the time being of the RICS or other person, a valid appointment may be made in such circumstances (*United Scientific* at 940A-D and 955-6). Where the clause states that the award should be made by a certain date an omission to complete the award in the time-limit will not invalidate the process, for the general presumption that time is not of the essence, enunciated in the *United Scientific* case, will apply. In other words, the presumption applies to the determination of the reviewed rent as well as to a step in the process towards such determination—*Power Securities (Manchester) Ltd v Prudential Assurance Co Ltd* [1987] 1 EGLR 121. In the event of time-limits relating to appointment of an arbitrator being expressly made of the essence, a remedy may still be available by virtue of s 27 of the Arbitration Act 1950 (discussed in (*e*) below).

In *Scotland*, the applicability of the *United Scientific* presumption has been doubted as not accurately reflecting the law of Scotland (*Yates, Petitioner* [1987] SLT 86) but Lord Davidson referred with approval to the *United Scientific* case in *Scottish Development Agency v Morrison Holdings Ltd* [1986] SLT 59 and in *Legal and Commercial Properties Ltd v Lothian Regional Council* [1988] SLT 463 Lord Jauncey considered that it was to be treated as laying down principles which are applicable equally to Scotland as to England.

In *New Zealand*, the *United Scientific* presumption has been expressly applied to time-limits in a rent review clause: *Wing Crawford Holdings Ltd v Lion Corporation Ltd* [1989] 1 NZLR 562.

The formulation in the *United Scientific* case involved a prima facie assumption of the parties presumed intention, and it was recognised that in cases where the contrary intention was shown time could and would be of the essence. Thus, Lord Diplock observed that the presumption applied 'in the absence of any contra-indications in the express words of the lease or in the inter-relation of the rent review clause itself and other clauses or in the surrounding circumstances . . .' (at 930G).

(b) Expressly making time of the essence

The simplest and safest way to make time of the essence is to use those very words—a well-established formula and the clearest possible 'contra-indication in the express words of the lease'. Indeed, Lord Diplock urged that whenever a time-limit was stated in the lease, it should be stated explicitly whether *or not* time was of the essence (at 936H). The parties can then be sure that uncertainty is eliminated.

If an express term that time is of the essence is not in the lease particular care must be taken in drafting to ensure that words that have a similar effect are not introduced inadvertently and, on review, to check that the form of the review clause or other clear words have not made time of the essence. In *Kenilworth Industrial Sites Ltd v E C Little and Co Ltd* [1975] 1 WLR 143 it was held that the mere use of the verb 'shall serve' was not sufficient to make time of the essence but 'shall' has an ambiguous meaning and does not always appear in an imperative context. It was used in the clauses in both the *United Scientific* and *Cheapside* leases: 'shall agree or failing agreement shall determine by arbitration' (*United Scientific*); and 'shall be specified in a notice in writing' and in default of agreement 'shall be valued by' a Fellow of the RICS (*Cheapside*). In neither case, of course, was time held to be of the essence. While it is clear that there is no magic formula which alone achieves the result of making time of the essence in a lease, subsequent decisions reveal that very clear words or provisions are required to rebut the presumption that it is not. The lease must show that a time-limit is obligatory and means what it says. On this basis there is a marked reluctance to hold that time is of the essence on the strength of one phrase in a review clause. Thus (and perhaps somewhat surprisingly) the formula that, failing agreement, there should be reference to a surveyor 'as soon as practicable but in any event not later than three months' was held not to require strict compliance by the Court of Appeal in *Touche Ross & Co v Secretary of State for the Environment* (1982) 46 P & CR 187. Neither 'as soon as practicable' nor the 3–month period, standing alone, would, in the light of the *United Scientific* case, involve strict compliance and their being linked by 'in any event' did not persuade the court to the contrary. In *Thorn EMI Pension Trust Ltd v Quinton Hazell plc* (1983) 269 EG 414, an identical phrase fell to be considered; notwithstanding some minor differences of phraseology, it was also held that time had not been made of the essence. In both these cases, the time-limit at issue involved the complex transaction of reference to a surveyor (to be mutually agreed or, failing that, appointed by the President of the RICS): the difficulty of complying with a fairly tight timetable was relied upon to support the conclusion reached. These cases were accepted as decisive on the interpretation of a similar phrase in *Factory Holdings Group Ltd v Leboff International Ltd* [1987] 1 EGLR 135. Similarly and not surprisingly, in *Metrolands Investments Ltd v J H Dewhurst Ltd* [1985] 3 All ER 206 it was held that the words 'but such yearly rent shall not in any event be less than £1,800', even when they followed a time-limit, was not a sufficient contra-indication to displace the presumption (and this part of the decision was not challenged on appeal—[1986] 3 All ER 659).

These decisions must be contrasted with *Drebbond Ltd v Horsham District Council* (1978) 37 P & CR 237 where the landlord was able to refer the determination of a reviewed rent to an arbitrator by notice in writing given to the tenant within 3–months of a certain date 'but not otherwise'. Megarry V-C, applying the *United Scientific* principles, held that these words made time of the essence for service of this notice and a notice given out of time was therefore ineffective and the right to review was lost. In the *Touche Ross* case, the Court of Appeal declined to express a view on whether the *Drebbond* case was rightly decided on the terms of the lease, contenting itself with the observation that there were differences in the scheme of the clause in the two cases. Dillon LJ observed that 'Obviously it is undesirable that questions of whether time is of the essence of a rent review clause should depend on minute differences of language'; regretfully it seems that small differences of language can lead to opposite conclusions. The *Drebbond* decision has been applied by two first instance judges; in each case the words 'but not otherwise' have been held to make time of the essence for review in two cases involving the same parade of shops and similar (but not identical) review clauses: *Norwich Union Life Insurance Society v Tony Waller Ltd* (1984) 270 EG 42 and *Norwich Union Life Assurance Society v Sketchley plc* [1986] 2 EGLR 126. In *Scotland*, the presence of a deeming provision in one case was held to make the whole review machinery mandatory so that a 'requirement of three months written notice' meant precisely or substantially three months notice (*Yates, Petitioner*; see p 102 below)—a conclusion unlikely to be followed in any jurisdiction.

The result is that a degree of uncertainty remains about the effect of other words and phrases that import a degree of compulsion; in each case the context of the clause, the overall scheme of review and the ability of the party concerned to comply with the time-limit will be factors in deciding an issue which is essentially one of construction. Thus, a clause that provided that a party 'must serve' a notice might appear to be sufficiently strong to make time of the essence; where the word 'must' appears in a statute it is usually construed as imposing a mandatory requirement as in *Chapman v Earl* [1968] 1 WLR 1315, (where it was held that, since an application for a fair rent 'must be in the prescribed form and contain the prescribed particulars in addition to the rent it is sought to register', an omission to specify such a rent was a fatal defect rendering the application a nullity). Yet in the *Henry Smith's Charity Trustees v AWADA Trading* case (see below), Griffiths LJ opined that a provision that 'a tenant must serve a notice', would, standing alone, be insufficient to displace the general rule that time was not of the essence.

By way of contrast, in *Staines Warehousing Co Ltd v Montague Executor and Trustee Co Ltd* [1987] 2 EGLR 130 it was common ground between the parties that a provision which made a landlord's trigger-notice 'void and of no effect' if the landlord failed to apply for the appointment of an independent surveyor by a certain date had the effect of making time of the essence. As Fox LJ remarked 'the procedure for rent review would be brought to a halt and extinguished'.

In earlier editions of this book, we speculated on the impact other phrases might have and made reference to cases in other fields of law other than that of rent review. It is now clear that such speculation is unlikely to assist; not only does the nature of rent review give rise to different considerations from (eg) completion dates for the sale of land but, more particularly, 'the *United Scientific* presumption that time is not of the essence in a rent review is strong and will not be rebutted by any contra indication in the express terms of the lease unless it is a compelling one' (per Millett J in *Power Securities (Manchester) Ltd v Prudential Assurance Co Ltd* [1987] 1 EGLR 121).

(c) Ambiguous or limited time of the essence provisions

(i) Making time of the essence for only some stages of the process

An express provision for time to be of the essence for one time-limit in a lease will, if anything, be an indication that it was intended that time was not of the essence for any other time provisions, and thereby the *United Scientific* presumption is strengthened (*Accuba Ltd v Allied Shoe Repairs Ltd* [1975] 1 WLR 1559 at 1564C; compare also the arguments advanced in *Johnson v Moreton* [1980] AC 37. In *Amherst v James Walker (Goldsmith and Silversmith) Ltd (No 1)* (1980) 254 EG 123 the review clause specified a time for doing three things, two of which had a time-limit that was stated to be 'of the essence'. It followed that the time that was not stated to be of the essence (for the trigger-notice) was not intended to be of the essence. The lease in question in *Laing Investment Co Ltd v G A Dunn & Co* (1981) 262 EG 879 repeated the pattern of that in *Amherst v James Walker (Goldsmith and Silversmith) Ltd* whereby time was made of the essence in relation to agreeing a rent and, on failure so to agree, to agreeing on an arbitrator, but not for the third step of applying for appointment of an arbitrator. The Court of Appeal's decision in the *Amherst* case was followed, notwithstanding that no attempt had been made to attempt to perform either of the first two steps.

The judgment of Slade LJ in *London & Manchester Assurance Co Ltd v G A Dunn & Co* (1982) 265 EG 33 and 131 at 134 provides further judicial support for the proposition that an express statement that time is to be of the essence for one step is a quite powerful indication that time is not to be regarded as of the essence for other purposes. The position therefore seems to be:

(1) If time is of the essence of the commencing or first step(s) in the review process, but not the later ones, a party out of time can ignore those first stages and proceed to review (*Laing Investment* case); but
(2) If time is of the essence of the last stage of the process, failure to observe that limit will be fatal.

(ii)   Ambiguity

Where there is an express time of the essence provision but it is unclear whether it relates to every aspect of the review process, it will be a question of construction as to how it applies. Thus in *C Bradley & Sons Ltd v Telefusion Ltd* (1981) 259 EG 337 the phrase occurred in the middle of a review clause, in brackets, after reference to absence of agreement but before provision for arbitration. Though it was held not to apply to the whole clause (if that had been intended, it was said that the words would naturally have appeared at the end) they could not sensibly relate to what had gone before since to make time of the essence for agreement was meaningless. The strict time-limit therefore related to the application of the arbitrator and the landlord was out of time. In *Panavia Air Cargo Ltd v Southend-on-Sea BC* [1988] 1 EGLR 124 para 13 of a review clause stated that periods of time in the Schedule were not to be of the essence; para 14 went on to provide for an automatic 25 per cent increase in the rent if the review was not completed within 12 months. As a matter of construction, the Court of Appeal held para 13 applied to the whole Schedule and was decisive. By way of contrast, in *Wrenbridge Ltd v Harries (Southern Properties) Ltd* (1981) 260 EG 1195, time was twice stated to be of the essence but in each case it was to be 'in respect of' failing to agree a rent or failing to agree on the appointment of an arbitrator. No such limit was said to apply to appointment by the

President. It was held that the clause effectively provided three ways for the rent to be assessed and only two were subject to strict time-limits. The landlord could proceed to review through the arbitrator appointed by the President. The moral for drafting is to make any strict time-limits unambiguously clear; at review, to heed all limits in cases of possible ambiguity.

(iii) Time not of the essence for some stages

If time is expressly made *not* of the essence for one stage in the review process, but not others, an argument might be raised that, by implication, time *is* of the essence for those other time-limits. The authors' view is that such an argument would not find immediate favour since the *United Scientific* presumption would still have to be overcome. Consequently, it could only be where a statement that time is not of the essence unquestionably applies only to some time-limits that the argument of implication (that it was for others) could apply. To avoid the difficulties, it is advised that if time is to be made not of the essence, it must be clearly applied to all time-limits—not just for some. If the parties wish to have some strict time stipulations, but make time not of the essence for others, then this should also be made very clear.

(d) Deeming clauses

There have been a series of cases litigating the effect of what may be termed 'deeming' or 'default' clauses'. This is a convenient shorthand phrase for clauses which expressly provide for what is to happen in the event of a non-compliance with a time-limit or which, when taken as a whole, evince the concept of finality to the review process. In such cases, the lease will not only set out a timetable but in terms purport conclusively to provide what is to happen in the absence of strict compliance. For example, such a clause may provide for the existing rent to continue for the next review period; or may deem the market rent to be the figure stated in the lessor's trigger-notice; or may apply a mathematical or other formula to fix what may be quite an arbitrary figure as the new rent.

The state of the law in this area can only be described as a tangled web of cases where it is difficult to propound the law with any degree of confidence. This is only partly due to cases coming before the courts by way of construction summons (where the emphasis will be on the particular words of the lease); it is also the result of disagreement among the judges as to whether there is any general principle to apply and if so, what the basis of any such principle should be.

(i) Some early decisions

The earliest authority is that of Goulding J in *Davstone (Holdings) Ltd v Al Rifai* (1976) 32 P & CR 18 where the review clause provided for a trigger-notice stating the new rent; if the lessee did not object within 28 days of receipt 'the lessee shall be deemed to have accepted' the proposed increase. In a judgment that foreshadowed the *United Scientific* decision (and which was cited in argument but not referred to in the speeches of that case) the judge applied a presumption that time was not of the essence and held that the deeming provision was not an express statement to the contrary. The Court of Appeal reached the opposite conclusion in *Lewis v Barnett* (1981) 264 EG 1079 where the lease provided for a notice of intention to review; in default of agreement, the landlord was to make application for appointment of a surveyor within a stated time-limit. In default of such application, the original notice to review 'shall be void and of no effect'. The Court of Appeal found that time was of the essence; default in adhering to the timetable avoided the whole process, the default mechanism being a sufficient 'contra indication' within the *United Scientific* principle. In *Staines Warehousing Co Ltd v Montagu Executor and Trustee Company Ltd* [1986] 1 EGLR 101 the review clause was virtually identical to that in *Lewis v Barnett* and undoubtedly was based on the same precedent: it was common ground between the parties at first instance that the default clause provided a time-limit which was of the essence.

(ii)   The conflicting approaches in the Court of Appeal

In *Henry Smith's Charity Trustees v AWADA Trading and Promotion Services Ltd* (1983) 47 P & CR 607, a clause which made elaborate provision for exactly what was to happen on failure to observe a time-limit, by automatically resolving the dispute in a draconian way, led to the conclusion that time was of the essence. The clause provided that the rent specified in the landlord's trigger-notice 'shall be deemed to be a market rent' in default of a tenant's counter-notice. The amount stated in such counter-notice 'shall be deemed to be the market rent' in default of application by a landlord for a surveyor. It was made clear in the case (at 617 and 623) that the mere presence of a deeming provision will not, in all cases, be sufficient to make time of the essence but if in the context of the lease in question they denote finality, effect must be given to such words. The majority (Slade and Griffiths LJJ) emphasised the particularly specific and detailed provisions on what was to happen in default of action by either party so that in the instant context 'shall be deemed to be market rent' could only mean 'conclusively presumed to be the market rent'. The *Henry Smith's* case was distinguished by a majority of the Court of Appeal in *Mecca Leisure Ltd v Renown Investments (Holdings) Ltd* (1984) 271 EG 989, where a deeming provision was held not to make time of the essence. The lease in that case was of the trigger-notice type, requiring a counter-notice by the tenant. Although time was not expressly made of the essence for service of the counter-notice, it was provided that on failure to serve such a notice, the tenant 'shall be deemed to have agreed to pay the increased rent specified in the Rent Notice'. Eveleigh LJ, noting in *Henry Smith's* case that it was said that not all deeming provisions make time of the essence, held that, reading the clause as a whole, time was not of the essence—largely because, it seems, he felt that to hold otherwise would make 'the clause a trap and the chosen machinery dangerous'. The authors respectfully observe that this is, sadly, true of all time of the essence clauses, but it hardly seems a sound basis for the construction of an agreement. The judgment of May LJ also dwelt heavily on the 'expectation of the landlord and tenant that a fair market rent will be paid throughout the lease' and the 'potential detriment to the tenant if time is held to be of the essence'. The warning of Browne-Wilkinson LJ, who dissented, that to fail to follow the decision in *Henry Smith's* case would lead to doubt about every lease containing a deeming provision, or default rent, was not heeded.

(iii) The conflicting approaches applied

The complexity grew worse with two first instance decisions decided within 1 month of each other, the judge in the second being, forgivably, in ignorance of the decision in the first. Each case considered both the *Henry Smith's* and *Mecca Leisure* decisions—but came to different, if not opposite, conclusions.

In *Greenhaven Securities Ltd v Compton* [1985] 2 EGLR 117 a review clause provided for the rack rent to be agreed between the parties, or by an arbitrator appointed by the President of the RICS on the application of either party before a period expiring 12 months after the review date. It then provided (para 3) that, in default of agreement on an arbitrator within that time-limit, or application to the President, the rent was to be 'a sum equal to the rent payable immediately before the review date'. On the face of it, this was a relatively 'simple' deeming provision; yet considering the matter apart from authority but in the light of the *United Scientific* case, the judge (Goulding J) was clear in his own mind that the contractual provisions were clear and to allow a late application to the President would in effect be making a new bargain for the parties. To put it in the language of time-limits, para 3 of the clause had made time of the essence. Of course, analysis of the cases showed that *Lewis v Barnett* and the *Henry Smith's* case supported the judge's view. The contrary views in the *Mecca Leisure* case 'created some difficulty' but the judge felt that the deeming provision before him was 'stronger' than that in *Mecca Leisure*, not in the words used but rather because the deeming provision there only applied to a counter-notice with no such provision applying as regards the later appointment of the arbitrator. The judge felt that the case before him was stronger by embracing every point. He concluded therefore that time was of the essence.

Taylor Woodrow Property Co Ltd v Lonrho Textiles Ltd [1985] 2 EGLR 120 was a decision of B A Hytner QC sitting as a deputy judge, and he was called upon to construe a review clause in very similar terms to that in the *Mecca Leisure* case. In other words, the machinery called for a counter-notice by the tenant and on failure to serve such counter-notice the tenant 'shall be deemed to have agreed to pay the increased rent' as specified in the landlord's notice. The tenants served a late counter-notice but the landlords claimed the increased rent alleging that the counter-notice was invalid because of the deeming provision. The judge considered both the *Henry Smith's* case and that of *Mecca Leisure* and preferred to follow the latter for two reasons:

(1) With reluctance, he accepted the submission of counsel for the tenants that there was a vital distinction between the two cases, namely:
— if there is 'one-way' deeming provision applying only to one party and one stage in the process, then time is not of the essence (*Mecca Leisure*);
— if there is a 'two-way' deeming provision applicable to both parties, time was of the essence.
(2) If the two cases were in conflict, he should apply the approach of *Mecca Leisure* as the later decision reached after full consideration of the first (applying *Minister of Pensions v Higham* [1948] 2 KB 153 and *Colchester Estates (Cardiff) v Carlton Industries plc* [1984] 2 All ER 601).

(iv) The conflict in Scotland
The conflicting judicial attitudes are also revealed in the Scottish authority. In *Yates, Petitioner* [1987] STL 86 Lord Davidson applied the dissenting opinion in the *Mecca Leisure* case and the decision in *Henry Smith's* and held time was of the essence where the 'deeming' clause provided that 'failing such intimation, the rent payable under this lease . . . .shall be the rent specified in the said notice'. (He also held, as a consequence of the mandatory timetable for a counter-notice, that 'the parties attached importance to time' so that the timetable for the trigger-notice was also obligatory; the landlord had to give 'precisely, or in any event, substantially' three months notice and the alleged trigger-notice was too early. This construction, it is submitted, is wrong). By way of contrast, in *Legal and Commercial Properties Ltd v Lothian Regional Council* [1988] SLT 463 Lord Jauncey chose to construe almost identical words in the opposite way, giving greater emphasis to the *United Scientific* presumption and the fact that the landlord (unlike the tenant) had an express right to review at a later date if he missed the review date. It is just possible to view the *Yates* case as involving a 'two-way' deeming provision and the *Legal and Commercial Properties* decision as a 'one-way' provision but a close examination of the judgments, as in the English cases, suggests the distinctions are tenuous. In *Leeds Permament Pension Scheme Trustees Ltd v William Timpson Ltd* [1987] SCLR 571 the landlord was three weeks late in serving the trigger-notice but it was held that time was not of the essence and the review could proceed.

(v) A trend towards avoiding finality

Three subsequent English decisions all resulted in a deeming or default provision being construed as not 'evincing finality' so that time was not of the essence and the review, or relevant step in the review process, could proceed. *Power Securities (Manchester) Ltd v Prudential Assurance Co Ltd* [1987] 1 EGLR 121 concerned a complex review mechanism which (inter alia) required an agreement between the parties of the total income received from the demised premises, which 'if not so agreed shall be £225,000'. Millett J held that 'agreement' in this context meant the acceptance of facts capable of being objectively established; the express default provision and the time-limit which preceded it were necessary because otherwise the lessee would have had an indeterminate length of time to satisfy the landlord of the true figure. The judge saw this default clause as one which would be implied if not expressed, and therefore consistent with time being not of the essence. That being so, the presence of the default clause was not sufficient to displace the *United Scientific* presumption.

In *Phipps Faire Ltd v Malbern Construction Ltd* [1987] 1 EGLR 129 the lease provided for the lessor to apply for independent valuation of the rent; on his failure to do so, the tenant could serve a notice proposing the revised rent; if the lessor then failed to apply within 3 months 'the amount so proposed shall be the revised rent'. The clause was closely modelled on Clause 3(6) of the 1979 Model Forms. Unlike Variation C, clause 4(F) of the current 1985 Model Forms, time was not expressly made of the essence. The tenant duly served a proper notice and the lessors missed the time-limit specified for applying. Warner J held that there were insufficient 'contra-indications' to displace the usual presumption. Time was not of the essence notwithstanding the argument that the whole purpose of the clause was to achieve finality.

Finally, in *Panavia Air Cargo v Southend-on-Sea BC* [1988] 1 EGLR 124 a default provision was in para 14 of the rent review Schedule which followed a provision in para 13 expressly making time *not* of the essence for the 'periods of time in this Schedule'. Paragraph 13 was (surely correctly) construed as applying to the whole Schedule, including the (rather weakly drafted) default provision.

By way of contrast, in *Mammoth Greeting Cards Ltd v Agra Ltd* [1990] 29 EG 45 a lease providing that the rent shall be 'conclusively fixed' at the amount in the lessor's notice in default of a tenant's counter-notice did make time of the essence. *Henry Smith's Charity Trustees v AWADA Trading* (above) was applied.

(vi) Some possible solutions

Can one glean any principle from the cases? Should one attempt to do so? It is, perhaps significant that other writers in the field of rent reviews have not attempted either to reconcile the above decisions, nor (if reconciliation is not possible) to indicate which of the conflicting

approaches they prefer (see the article by D W Williams (1985) 275
EG 624 and Bernstein and Reynolds para 3.24(c)).

It is submitted that there are three possible solutions to default or
deeming clauses:

(1) One could have an approach that the existence of a default rent
    or deeming clause is not, by itself, a contra indication sufficient
    to displace the presumption that time is not of the essence. Although,
    as Browne Wilkinson LJ pointed out in the *Mecca Leisure* case,
    this approach is supported by justice, common sense and fairness
    in that the machinery of review can continue to operate, only Eveleigh
    LJ in the same case has based a decision on this ground.
(2) A more logical and compelling argument is to view an express
    provision for a default rent as necessarily showing time is of the
    essence for the prior step or action that must be taken. Such a result
    (as Browne-Wilkinson LJ observed) can be reached by viewing the
    default rent as the clearest possible indication that time for service
    of the notice (or prior step in the process) should be of the essence.
(3) A better view, and one espoused by the authors in the last edition,
    is to see deeming provisions as not involving the time of the essence
    doctrine at all. The default rent is part of the substantive term of
    the contract; to say time is not of the essence in such circumstances
    is not simply to extend the time-limits within which the parties bargain
    could be performed but to alter the parties bargain itself. Logic
    and precedent (cf *Raineri v Miles* [1981] AC 1050) and the judgments
    of Sir John Donaldson MR in *Henry Smiths* and Browne-Wilkinson
    LJ, dissenting, in *Mecca Leisure* proposed this view, which has the
    abiding merit of giving a specific meaning to the deeming clause.
    If it does not operate according to its terms, its only conceivable
    purpose is as a basis for service of a notice making time of the
    essence.

Had any of the above approaches received widespread judicial
approval, there would have been, at least, superficial consistency allowing
a greater degree of certainty in operating review clauses containing a
default rent or deeming provision. Absolute rules would, naturally, be
impossible since the first would have to admit the case where there were
other contra indications making time of the essence; the second and
third would have to accommodate the lease where there was doubt if
there was a true default provision at all (as in the *Panavia Air Cargo*
case at first instance—[1988] 1 EGLR 124).

The dominant judicial sentiment currently appears to be one which
emphasises the construction of the lease before the court. In the words
of May LJ in *Mecca Leisure* the only *principle* is that against time being
of the essence; a contention that a particular deeming provision makes
time of the essence is only *argument*.

(vii)   Analysis of the present position

In the light of the above, it will be appreciated that a logical and comprehensive analysis is not possible, but with some diffidence the authors suggest that:

(1) The streams of authority cannot be reconciled without recourse to 'meticulous semantic and syntactical analysis' so derided by Lord Diplock in *The Antaios* [1985] AC 191. In particular, the attempt to do so in the *Taylor Woodrow* case cannot be supported. The deputy judge's differentiation of the approaches by reference to 'one-way' or 'two-way' deeming provisions cannot, with respect, be justified by reference to the judgments in *Henry Smith's* and *Mecca Leisure*; nor by logic, because surely a deeming provision is intended to operate at whichever stage in the process it is stated to occur and whether it applies to one party's actions or both. Similar criticism can be levelled at the way the *Mecca* case was distinguished in the *Greenhaven* case.

(2) Each case will have to be decided on the true construction of the lease, this being the majority view in *Mecca Leisure*, and operating the *United Scientific* presumption as a starting point.

(3) The mere presence of a default rent or deeming clause will not of itself be a decisive contra-indication (*Phipps-Faire* case), but may be an important factor in evincing a contrary intent from the lease as a whole. This will depend on all the circumstances, including the context and wording of the provision, the degree of emphasis and the purpose and effect of the default clause.

(4) The decisions detailed above would indicate that where the clause makes a step in the review process 'void and of no effect' (*Lewis v Barnett*) or can apply to either party to the lease (*Henry Smith's*) the courts will be more ready to find that contrary intent and allow the default clause to operate.

(5) 'In the end the matter is one of impression to be derived from a consideration of the rent review clause as a whole, together with any other relevant considerations, avoiding fine distinctions but giving effect to every provision in the lease' (per Millett J in the *Power Securities* case).

So until a definitive ruling from the House of Lords is obtained, the question of whether the presence of a default rent or deeming provision in effect makes time of the essence can only be answered by careful consideration of the exact wording of the lease.

(e)   When time is made impliedly of the essence

The *United Scientific* case postulated two ways in which time might be impliedly of the essence, thereby preventing a retrospective review out of time.

(i)   In the inter-relation of the rent review clause itself and other clauses'

The only reported example is where a lease contains an option to determine (a 'break clause') the operation of which is dependent in some way on the review clause. In the *United Scientific* decision, all the speeches (see eg Lords Diplock and Fraser at 936, 962) make it clear that interrelationship of a review clause and a break clause may have the effect of making time impliedly of the essence; they express approval of the result (but not the reasoning) in the earlier decision of *C Richards & Son Ltd v Karenita* (1971) 221 EG 25. In that case the review notice had to be given in the first 3 months of the seventh year of the term; the break clause was to be exercised by 3 months notice to determine at the end of the seventh year when the reviewed rent would otherwise become payable. Though the clauses were not (it appears) directly linked in the lease it was 'sufficient by necessary implication' to make time of the essence; the later date to operate the break clause gave the tenant time to know and assess the amount of increase in the rent before making his decision on whether to exercise his option to determine. This rationale of the principle is that the parties must have intended that the tenant should have this knowledge, and to allow a late review notice would frustrate that intent.

However, later cases show that is not necessary for this feature to be present; if, on the construction of the lease, the review clause and break clause are interrelated or interlocked, time will be of the essence for any rent review notice. Thus in *Al Saloom v Shirley James Travel Service Ltd* (1981) 42 P & CR 181 the lease contained both provision for rent review and for a break (option to determine) and the last date on which the lessor could serve his trigger-notice coincided with the last date on which the lessee could give notice to determine the underlease. It was held that there was a 'perfectly clear interrelation' between the two that was sufficient to make time of the essence. Indeed, the review and break provisions were contained in one continuous integrated clause so there was more than mere interrelation and the implication that both time-limits were of the essence was overwhelming. It followed that the review notice, which was out of time, was ineffective. In a series of subsequent cases, in each of which the rent review procedure began with a trigger-notice and the break clause either followed or operated at the same time, it was held that it was to be inferred that the parties did intend time to be of the essence—*Coventry City Council v J Hepworth Ltd* (1982) 261 EG 566; even when the consequence is, as a result of inept drafting, to permit service of the review trigger-notice on one day only in each 7 year period (*Rahman v Kenshire* (1981) 259 EG 1074). In *Legal and General Assurance (Pension Management) Ltd v Cheshire County Council* (1983) 269 EG 40, the argument that, because the last date for service of the review notice was identical to the last date for service of the break notice time was not of the essence, was expressly rejected. Though these cases must now be read in the light of the *Metrolands* decision (see below), in those cases where the review clause involves a time scale and a triggering process by the landlord, it is likely time will be of the essence. Thus in *Stephenson & Son v Orca Properties Ltd* [1989] 2 EGLR 129 the appellate decisions in the *Amherst* and *Legal and General* cases were treated as binding authority requiring time to be held impliedly of the essence in that case of interrelation between a triggering notice and a break-clause. It appears therefore that the *Metrolands* decision has not weakened the application of the rule, probably even in cases like *Rahman v Kenshire* or *Legal and General v Cheshire CC*, where the correlation of the two clauses were not so obvious. Neither case, nor that of *Al Saloom*, was mentioned in the *Metrolands* judgment.

Even in the early decisions it was stressed that time will not be of the essence of the rent review clause in every case where it is associated with a tenant's option to break; the presumption that time is not of the essence is only displaced by evidence that there is an interrelation, with perhaps some opportunity for the tenant to know or assess the financial consequences of review before the time comes to serve his own notice. Time will not be of the essence for the review clause, even where there is an associated option to determine, in the following cases.

(1) *If there is no time to become of the essence*

Where the review clause is not one that is initiated by notice to which time-limits apply and has no stated limit as to when application for independent determination in default of agreement may be made, there is no time that can become of the essence. In *Edwin Woodhouse Trustee Co Ltd v Sheffield Brick Co plc* (1983) 270 EG 548 a 21–year lease with 7–yearly reviews also contained an option for the tenant to determine at the end of 7 and 14 years on giving 6 months' prior notice. The review was of the 'automatic' type, and there was no mention of notices, merely the provision for a valuer to be appointed by either party in default of agreement. The tenant's contention that a trigger-notice should be implied and time was of the essence for such notice (not surprisingly) failed. The result was that the tenant had missed the opportunity to break at the end of 14 years some months before the landlords indicated their intention to review the rent. In *Scotland*, a similar result was reached in *Scottish Development Agency v Morrison Holdings Ltd* [1986] SLT 59; the review clause there was not initiated by notice and this was one reason for not implying a time limiation.

(2) *If the time-limit is not within one party's control*

In the absence of a trigger mechanism, even an element of

timetabling, for example, for the conclusion of the arbitration, linked
to an option to determine, will not necessarily make time of the
essence. Thus in *Metrolands Investments Ltd v J H Dewhurst Ltd*
(Court of Appeal [1986] 3 All ER 659 overruling Peter Gibson J
[1985] 3 All ER 206) as in the *Woodhouse* case, there was no trigger-
notice of which time could be of the essence. There was, however,
a clear requirement to obtain the decision of an arbitrator by a
particular date and this date was correlated with the timetable in
the break clause in the 'clearest possible' way. Notwithstanding this
correlation, time was held not to be impliedly of the essence for
two reasons, which the court said must be considered in conjunction
with one another:

(i)   the date of the relevant event (the obtaining of an arbitrator's
      award) was to a substantial degree outside the lessor's
      control; and

(ii) any potential hardship to a tenant was mitigated since the
      tenant could initiate the process of arbitration himself.

In *Scotland*, where a valuation was to be obtained from the Valuation
Department of Scotland, a body not subject to the landlord's control,
an argument that time was impliedly of the essence was rejected: *Scottish
Development Agency v Morrison Holdings Ltd* (above). In such a case,
the landlords could not be sure that the valutaion could be produced
in time. This was one of four factors referred to in justifying the
conclusion; the tenants ability to make his own inquiries in advance
as to the likely amount of the rent was another.

Whether or not time will be impliedly of the essence where the relevant
event is outside the landlord's control but the tenant cannot act to resolve
the issue remains to be seen; the court stressed its task in each case
of determining the parties' intentions from the words they actually use.

The *Metrolands* decision must be contrasted with *William Hill
(Southern) Ltd v Govier* (1984) 269 EG 1168 where a Deputy Judge found
time was of the essence for an 'automatic' review linked to a break
clause, time being of the essence for the reference to and appointment
of an arbitrator. This time schedule was linked to the option to determine
in the same clause and showed an intention by the parties to the lease
that time should be of the essence. Counsel in *Metrolands* argued the
William Hill case was wrongly decided but the Court of Appeal did
not find it necessary to rule on this submission. The judgment in
Metrolands can be considered in its reasoning as difficult to reconcile
with the earlier Court of Appeal decisions in the *Amherst* and *Legal
& General* cases (which were not referred to) and further litigation may
be needed before one can decide whether *Metrolands* heralds a shift of
emphasis or whether it is confined to the particular facts of the case.
Consequently where there is an interrelated timetabling of review and

break-clause this may still operate as a contra indication to rebut the *United Scientific* presumption even in the absence of a trigger-notice mechanism particularly if the relevant event is within the landlord's control.

(3) *Extended time-limits for exercise of the option*
      Time will not be of the essence if the lease itself contains a provision under which the period during which the tenant could exercise his right to determine would be extended in the event of the renewed rent not having been ascertained within the time stipulated in the rent review clause. This is clear from the comment upon the over-ruled case of *Samuel Properties (Developments) Ltd v Hayek* [1972] 1 WLR 1296 in *United Scientific*, where it was said that time would not be of the essence in the circumstances of that case (at 936D, 963A).

(4) *Where there is no correlation between the clauses*
      Time will not be of the essence in any case where, on the proper construction of the lease, there is no correlation between the review and the break-clause—for example, they operate independently and at different dates.

In all these cases, it is possible that the tenant may have to decide whether to operate the break-clause without the advantage of knowing the quantum of the reviewed rent, but he may avoid this by setting the review machinery in motion himself in good time if this is permitted by the terms of the lease, or obtaining from his valuer some idea of what quantum of rent might be settled at review.

It seems no case has yet been reported where a break-clause is associated with only one of a number of review dates. It would be a difficult issue to decide, if the break clause made time impliedly of the essence for the associated date, whether time was also of the essence for the other review dates. Certainly, when drafting such a lease, it will be particularly advisable expressly to specify whether time is or is not of the essence.

There is no other obvious clause which by interrelating with the review clause, will have the effect of displacing the presumption that time is not of the essence. An option to purchase the reversion at a date interrelated with a rent review might be an example. Though such a situation may be rare, the amount of rent determined at review will have an impact on the value of the reversion so similar principles could apply.

(ii) *'In the surrounding circumstances'*
      Time may be impliedly of the essence if the 'surrounding circumstances' are sufficient to rebut the normal presumption (per Lord Diplock at

930G). Unfortunately, the meaning of the concept was not explored in the speeches of their Lordships, and in particular it was not differentiated from the opinions expressed on the possibility that unreasonable delay on the part of the landlords in initiating the review would result in a forfeiture of their rights (a topic discussed at pp 158–161 below).

The main issue is whether circumstances before or during the review process can make time impliedly of the essence or whether it will be limited to circumstances at the time the lease was granted and which appear from the lease itself. Arguments may be advanced for both points of view. The better view is that only circumstances at the date of the lease are relevant and this view is based on the principle that subsequent events ought not to affect the construction of contractual terms embodied in a lease. On the other hand, at least one speech in the *United Scientific* case appears to suggest that conditions implying that time shall be of the essence can be introduced by events subsequent to the lease (per Lord Salmon at 955F-H). Support for the view that circumstances subsequent to the date of the lease may assist in construction of its terms may be found in a number of decisions. The most striking example is *West Layton Ltd v Ford* [1979] QB 593 concerning the reasonableness of the landlord's refusal to consent to a sub-letting on a furnished basis of the residential part of business premises demised in 1971. One factor that weighed heavily with the court in deciding that the refusal was indeed reasonable was the change of circumstance caused by the passing of the Rent Act 1974, which altered the law relating to security of tenure for furnished residential tenancies.

The issue is finely balanced, but the authors' view is that 'surrounding circumstances' sufficient to make time impliedly of the essence will be limited to those existing at the time the lease was granted and these will probably have to be reflected in the terms of the lease or the review clause. For if time is to be of the essence of a contract, it should be from the outset or not at all. For this purpose, however, the lease will be construed in the light of the law then prevailing; leases entered into prior to the *United Scientific* decision cannot be construed in the light of what the law was then thought to be: *Henry Smith's Charity Trustees v AWADA Trading and Promotion Services* (1983) 269 EG 729. In either event, 'surrounding circumstances' will only assist in the construction of otherwise ambiguous phraseology and cannot negative express provisions in the lease.

The only litigation on the meaning of 'surrounding circumstances' has been concerning matters appearing in the review clause itself. In *Touche Ross & Co Ltd v Secretary of State for the Environment* (1982) 265 EG 983 an attempt to argue that, where the reviewed rent was to be fixed as 'at the date of determination', time was of the essence because of potentially greater hardship for the lessor was not surprisingly rejected. An obiter dictum to the contrary by Lawton LJ in *London & Manchester Assurance Co Ltd v G A Dunn & Co* (1982) 265 EG 39 at 40 was not referred to but is, with respect, of doubtful validity. In exceptional circumstances, the overall structure of the review clause may make time of the essence impliedly. So in *Kirkland Properties v GRA Developments Ltd* (1978) 4 May, unreported, the date of first rent review in a building lease was to depend on a landlord's notice; the time for service of such notice (there were five alternatives) depended on the date of practical completion. The alternatives were mutually exclusive, it was held, so the parties must, in those circumstances, have intended time to be of the essence for the landlord's notice on each of the postulated occasions.

Finally reference may be made to *McLeod Russel (Property Holdings) Ltd v Emerson* (1985) 51 P & CR 176 where the Court of Appeal found a review clause in a residential tenancy made time of the essence, even where the lease did not so stipulate, because such a finding was necessary in order to make the machinery in the review clause work. The review clause provided that from the review date the rent should be: 'the fair rent as at August 1 1978, to be ascertained in accordance with the provisions of the Rent Act . . . ' The Court noted that a rent officer can only assess a fair rent at the time of the application; consequently, unless an application was made before 1 August 1978 the rent officer could not assess a fair rent. Time was therefore of the essence and the review was lost. The decision appears, with respect, to be an unusually strict application of construction of a lease and might be thought to run counter to the approach to the time-limit issues which the courts have faced in commercial leases and which are discussed above. It would have been open for the Court, applying the principles of the *Sudbrook* case (as counsel for the landlord urged), to have found that the machinery supplied by the parties was not of the essence of the contract; for there can be little doubt that a residential fair rent at the relevant date could have been assessed—indeed the parties had agreed the rent of the property to be between £1,055 and £1,100 at 1 August 1978.

(f)   No relief for default

In a case where there is a failure to observe a review time-limit that is of the essence, the right to review is lost. This was made abundantly clear in *Weller v Akehurst* [1981] 3 All ER 411 where the lessor failed to comply with a time-limit for service of a rent review trigger-notice; it was held it was not open to him to seek an inquiry as to the open market rent as defined in the lease by any other method even though the formula adopted in the review clause was otherwise certain enough for this to be done. A similar argument failed in *Darlington Borough Council v Waring and Gillow (Holdings) plc* [1988] 2 EGLR 159. It was contended that the landlord could still have its review after missing a time-limit which was of the essence since otherwise there was no express provision for the current rent to continue. This was rejected so, by necessary implication, the current rent remained payable.

Any existence of a general power to relieve against contractual stipulations was denied in *Hill v Barclay* (1811) 34 ER 238 and it remains true today that 'equity expects men to carry out their bargains' (per Lord Wilberforce in *Shiloh Spinners Ltd v Harding* [1973] AC 691 at 723, affirming the general principle). An attempt made in *Samuel Properties (Developments) Ltd v Hayek* [1972] 1 WLR 1296 to obtain relief in equity from strict compliance with the contractual time-limit was rejected on two grounds:

(1) that the special jurisdiction of equity to relieve against forfeiture on the grounds of fraud, accident, mistake or surprise were not relevant to the rent review situation at all (at 1303C, 1305C, 1305G-H); and

(2) that even if the jurisdiction did apply, the power to relieve for mistake was, on the authority of *Barrow v Isaacs and Son* [1891] 1 QB 417, not applicable to unilateral forgetfulness (at 1307F-G).

However, it is just possible, but increasingly unlikely, that, in the light of the *United Scientific* decision, a court might act in limited circumstances to relieve a party in the context of a rent review clause; for the *Hayek* case was overruled by the House of Lords, and though there was no reference to those parts of the speeches dealing with the power to grant relief, it is clear that the option analysis on which they were based (see *Hayek* at 1305C, 1307H-1308A) was firmly rejected. In doing so, and in placing the review clause firmly in the context of the 'inseverable part of the whole consideration of [sic] the landlord's grant' (*United Scientific* at 930D), it may now be open for argument to be raised again that equity has jurisdiction to grant relief. This may be on the basis of Lord Wilberforce's reaffirmation in *Shiloh Spinners Ltd v Harding* of 'the right of courts of equity in appropriate and limited cases to relieve . . . where the primary object of the bargain is to secure a stated result which can effectively be attained when the matter comes before a court . . . ' Though applied to forfeiture for breach of covenant or condition, the remaining words appear particularly apposite to a rent review. The argument would, however, have to overcome the same objections that proved decisive in *Hayek*, particularly the view that the power to relieve in cases of forfeiture for breach of covenant, in the context of which Lord Wilberforce's statement was made, cannot be extended to review clauses. A lessor or lessee facing a large financial loss as a result of failing to observe a limit where time was of the essence might just consider that, notwithstanding the *Hayek* decision, it is an argument worthy of revival. The authors are not aware of any case where the argument proposed in the text has been put forward but it seems highly unlikely to be successful in the (usual) case of one party omitting to observe time-limits and it is submitted that this aspect of the *Hayek* decision remains good. Parties to a lease would do well to continue to act on the basis that no relief can be given for failure to observe a time-limit that is of the essence where such failure arises from forgetfulness, negligence or unilateral mistake.

The discretionary power to extend mandatory time-limits for references to arbitration conferred by s 27 of the Arbitration Act 1950 is an exception to this rule.

(g) Relief under the Arbitration Act 1950, s 27

This section gives power to the High Court to extend time for commencing arbitration proceedings. It provides:

Where the terms of an agreement to refer future disputes to arbitration provide that any claims to which the agreement applies shall be barred unless notice to appoint an arbitrator is given or an arbitrator is appointed or some other step to commence arbitration proceedings is taken within a time fixed by the agreement, and a dispute arises to which the agreement applies, the High Court, if it is of opinion that in the circumstances of the case undue hardship would otherwise be caused, and notwithstanding that the time so fixed has expired, may, on such terms, if any, as the justice of the case may require, but without prejudice to the provisions of any enactment limiting the time for the commencement of arbitration proceedings, extend the time for such period as it thinks proper.

(i) Applicability of the section to rent review arbitrations

It has been held that s 27 applies to arbitration pursuant to a rent review clause, though it is a power that, since the *United Scientific* case, need only be exercised where time is expressly or impliedly made of the essence. The importance and applicability of s 27 was assumed in *Amalgamated Estates Ltd v Joystretch Manufacturing Ltd* (1980) 257 EG 489 and in an early first instance decision it was held to be sufficient for s 27 if the effect of the clause was to bar one party's right to arbitration (*SI Pension Trustees Ltd v William Hudson Ltd* (1977) 242 EG 689). The section will apply to any time-limit in a contract relating to the appointment of the arbitrator or any step to commence arbitration proceedings but not to other time-limits: *Babanaft International SA v Avant Petroleum Inc* [1982] 1 WLR 871. Where a review clause on its true construction can be said to bar arbitration if notice is not given in the time allowed, then the clause must be read as being subject to the court's power to extend the time (*SI Pension* at 693).

Clarification of the applicability of s 27 to rent review clauses has been given by the Court of Appeal in *Pittalis v Sherefettin* [1986] QB 868. Earlier, in *Tote Bookmakers Ltd v The Development and Property Holding Co Ltd* [1985] Ch 261 Peter Gibson J had held that provision for a counter-notice electing for arbitration lacked the essential element of an arbitration agreement since the right of reference was unilateral and not bilateral, relying on *Baron v Sunderland Corporation* [1966] 2 QB 56 a case which had not been cited in the earlier decisions. If the *Tote Bookmakers* decision had stood it would have denied the use of s 27 in many rent review situations as well as denying the applicability of all the other sections of the Act. *Pittalis v Sherefettin* overruled this decision and it is now clear that s 27 applies to any contract—and thereby to a lease—which gives rights of reference to arbitration, whether bilateral or unilateral. The court also stressed that an agreement to arbitrate in the future, if a party so elects (eg by a notice), can correctly be described as an agreement to refer a 'future dispute to arbitration' within the section. Moreover, since s 27 is mandatory and cannot be excluded by the parties, it applies notwithstanding the express provision in the lease that time shall be of the essence.

(ii) Exercise of discretion under s 27

The procedure is for the party seeking an extension of time to apply to the High Court by way of summons or originating summons and the jurisdiction is exercisable by a judge in chambers or a master (RSC Ord 73, r 3). The restriction previously contained in RSC Ord 73, r 1, on assigning the matter to the Chancery Division has been revoked. The court may, if it is of the opinion that in the circumstances of the case undue hardship would be caused by adherence to the time-limits fixed by the agreement, extend the time as it thinks proper and as the justice of the case requires. The discretion will not be exercised in all cases but only where there is 'undue hardship', defined in one case as 'greater hardship than the circumstances warrant' *(Liberian Shipping Corporation ('Pegasus') v A King and Sons Ltd* [1967] 2 QB 86 at 98G and see further Russell (20th ed) pp 72–82 and Mustill and Boyd (2nd ed) pp 209–15). Undue hardship, though not to be construed too narrowly, does mean excessive hardship; where the hardship is the fault of the claimant, it means hardship the consequences of which are out of proportion to such fault.

The second lesson from the *Pittalis* case is that the onus of proving undue hardship within s 27 is on the tenant or other applicant; and in any event, whatever the hardship, a long delay in making application to the court will make it very unlikely that the court will exercise its discretion in favour of the applicant. So, in the *Pittalis* case, a failure to adduce evidence as to the true market rent and a 3–year delay in making a s 27 application were fatal to the claim. In the *SI Pension* case, by way of contrast, a delay of about 4 months, in the context of 'considerable activity' which left the other party under no misapprehension about the determination to pursue the right of review, did not prevent the court extending time under s 27.

In *Edlingham Ltd v MFI Furniture Centres Ltd* (1981) 259 EG 42, where a counter-notice was ineffective and the tenant out of time, the court granted, for a short period, a stay of proceedings issued for arrears of rent arising from the sum specified in the trigger-notice to enable a s 27 application to be dealt with. The court stressed the need for a prompt application under the section.

A useful example of the operation of s 27 is *Chartered Trust plc v Maylands Green Estate Co Ltd* (1984) 270 EG 845. In that case a lessee's agent failed to serve a counter-notice electing for arbitration (time being of the essence). It was later alleged that the lessor's trigger-notice was bad because it failed to specify if it was given just under the original lease between the parties or included notice under a supplemental lease of a further part of the building. Consequently, the lessor served a second trigger-notice, without prejudice to its contention that the first notice was good. As a result of a misunderstanding between the tenant's solicitor and the tenant's (new) surveyor, once again no valid counter-notice was served by the tenants! The court granted relief in respect of the second, later, trigger-notice but declined to do so in respect of the original notice. In deciding whether undue hardship would be caused by refusing to extend the time-limit, Vinelott J applied the 'factors which have to be weighed' summarised in *Moscow V/O Exportkhleb v Helmville Ltd ('The Jocelyn')* [1977] 2 Lloyd's Rep 121, and applied and approved in the rent review context in the *Pittalis* case, namely the length of the delay; the amount at stake; whether the delay was due to the fault of the claimant; the degree of such fault (if any); whether the claimant was misled by the other party; and whether the other party had been prejudiced by the delay. Relief was refused in respect of the first notice both because of the length of delay and because the tenant originally chose to accept tacitly the first trigger-notice and sue its surveyor in negligence. In granting relief in respect of the second notice, the judge stressed the fact the lessor would not be prejudiced but relief was only given on the basis that interest would be payable by the tenant on any arrears of rent. Jurisdiction for the imposition of such conditions is given by the section itself for extension of time is to be subject to 'such terms . . . as the justice of the case may require'.

As was observed in the *Chartered Trust* case (at 847), it is anomalous that such relief is available when the independent referee is to fix the reviewed rent as an arbitrator, but not when he is directed to act as an expert. Yet it is so, and therefore there is a strong case, at least for a tenant's advisers, to ensure that arbitration is the chosen method when the review clause provides for a tenant's counter-notice, time to be of the essence. What is not clear is whether the section would apply if the status of the referee was either arbitrator or expert and the choice was only to be made on appointment (or application for appointment) which ex hypothesi, had not been made. If an application under s 27 is permissible in such circumstances, the principle of estoppel should then preclude an election for the referee to be treated as an expert.

(h) Extension of time-limits

It is open for the parties or their agents either to agree to extend the strict time-limits provided for the lease or for the party with the benefit of the time-limit expressly to waive his right to insist on the limit being observed. Whichever course is adopted, the agreement or waiver should be clear and recorded in writing. If this is not forthcoming, the requisite notices should be given or applications made notwithstanding the prospect of an agreement on the new rent (as in *Staines Warehousing Co Ltd v Montague Executor and Trustee Co Ltd* [1987] 2 EGLR 130), for without such clear evidence the strict time-limit may be enforced (cf *Kammins Ballrooms Co Ltd v Zenith Investments (Torquay) Ltd* [1971] AC 850). A party who fails to observe a time-limit that is of the essence cannot argue that the other party waived the strictness of the timetable by continuing negotiations on the issue (as in *Drebbond Ltd v Horsham District Council* (1978) 37 P & CR 237). Such a claim can only be made if the party with the benefit of the time-limit expressly and unreservedly agrees to extend the limit applicable. It does appear that the rules relating to waiver are more strictly applied in rent reviews than elsewhere. In contracts for the sale of land, for example, waiver by conduct will be found if the parties delay 'and go on negotiating for the completion of the purchase' (per Malins VC in *Webb v Hughes* (1870) LR 10 Eq 281 at 286). Yet in *Oldschool v Johns* (1980) 256 EG 381 it was held that continuation of negotiations for a new rent after the date for the service of a tenant's counter-notice had passed did not amount to waiver of the landlord's right to insist that the rent specified in his notice should take effect, though a Court of Appeal dictum suggests that 'in a case of protracted negotiations the facts might well show that the tenant had waived the landlord's duty to comply strictly with the timetable' (per Griffiths LJ in *Henry Smith's Charity Trustees v AWADA Trading and Promotion Services Ltd* (1983) 47 P & CR 607 at 618–19). In *Darlington Borough Council v Waring and Gillow (Holdings) plc* [1988] 2 EGLR 159 an unsuccessful attempt was made to validate an out-of-time appointment of a surveyor by reference to correspondence between the parties. It was not alleged that the time-limit had been waived and the proposition that the tenant had entered into a subsequent agreement to appoint a surveyor foundered because all the correspondence was marked 'subject to board approval'.

It will not be open to argue that the other party to the lease failed to warn of the imminence of the time-bar. There is no duty on a party or his solicitor to do this, notwithstanding judicial expressions of disapproval of the morality of 'standing by' (see *Wallis Cayton Bay Holiday Camp Ltd v Shell Mex and BP Ltd* [1975] QB 94 at 104; and, particularly, *Cooke v Talbot* [1977] 243 EG 831, discussed at (1977) 41 Conv (NS) 373). On the other hand, where a notice to review the rent has been received there is a duty to disclose this fact to any proposed assignee of the tenant's interest as a latent defect in title (*F & B Entertainments Ltd v Leisure Enterprises Ltd* (1976) 240 EG 455).

(i) Delay still a breach of contract

Though the *United Scientific* principle—that stipulations as to time are not generally of the essence—permits a late operation of the review machinery, a prudent landlord will always observe the time-limits provided for in the lease. Not only will any possibility of arguments about time being 'impliedly' of the essence be stifled, but the problems of delay discussed below will be avoided. There may be a further advantage. In *Raineri v Miles* [1981] AC 1050, in a contract for the sale of land, it was held that damages could be obtained for loss resulting from a failure to complete the contract on the dates fixed by the parties notwithstanding that the contract did not provide this time-limit was to be of the essence. The principle propounded was that a breach of a contractual stipulation as to time which was not of the essence, though not allowing the innocent party to terminate the contract, was still a breach of contract (at 857H and 869C). Reference was made to the *United Scientific* case by both Lords Edmund Davies and Fraser (with whom Lords Russell and Keith concurred) and they decided it was not inconsistent with their conclusions since 'No question of damage was involved' in that case. The irresistible conclusion is that if a tenant can show that a delay by the landlord in operating the review causes loss that directly results from the delay, he may obtain damages on the basis of breach of contract (*Amherst v James Walker Goldsmith & Silversmith (No 2)* [1983] Ch 305 at 315C). One example of such loss might occur when a tenant has allowed the last date for a tax election to slip by and is then faced with a notice for a late rent review in circumstances in which the increased rent that results would have indicated such a tax election was desirable. Similarly, uncertainty about the level of rent after a delayed review could dampen or even destroy an advantageous sale of a business carried on at the premises and the tenant's position is exacerbated if he cannot take the initiative. Postulating examples such as these might show that the arguments advanced in the *United Scientific* case—that no harm results to the tenant from a delayed rent review— might not always be valid. When loss does ensue, the tenant may well be able to claim damages for the resultant loss, and this possibility will be particularly important if (as is likely) he is unable to resist a claim to a late review. An interesting example of damages awarded in comparable circumstances of delay caused by a landlord's breach of repair covenants will be found in *City and Metropolitan Properties Ltd v Greycroft Ltd* [1987] 1 WLR 1085.

(j) Drafting advice

Conflicting views have been expressed on the benefits (or otherwise) flowing as a consequence of the *United Scientific* decision. On the one hand, an argument can be made that the benevolent treatment of time-limits in review clauses created as many problems as it has solved—

and these are discussed in section 4, p 147 below. On the other hand, the bargain reached by the parties when negotiating the lease is less likely to be frustrated and there are fewer pitfalls, though the hope of Lord Diplock (*United Scientific* at 936G) that the need to have recourse to the courts over time-limits would be reduced appears to have been unfulfilled. Nevertheless, Lord Diplock's advice to draftsmen incorporating time-limits in review clauses (at 936H) deserves to be heeded:

The best way of eliminating all uncertainty in future rent clauses is to state expressly whether or not stipulation as to the time by which any step provided for by the clause is to be taken shall be treated as being of the essence.

Mecca Leisure Ltd v Renown Investments (Holdings) Ltd, discussed at p 100 above, amply demonstrates the wisdom of Lord Diplock's advice. If a deeming provision, as in that case, can be held to be inoperative, then a draftsman cannot rely on anything less than the hallowed words.

The authors would respectfully stress the 'whether or not' formulation of his Lordship. It is far more usual to say time is of the essence than to say it is not but including the negative provision precludes problems over the implication that time is of the essence. The clauses in *Kelly's Draftsman*, Forms 14 and 15, reproduced in Part Seven (p 687) contain, optionally, such a negative provision (see para 6). However, there is an understandable reluctance for a draftsman to say, in effect, 'here are my time-limits but you don't need to take them seriously'. An express relaxation of observing time-limits could also weaken any claim for damages for delay though not necessarily destroy it.

Most modern precedents, both those published and those used as standard drafts by large firms or organisations, tend to avoid all time-limits for the basic review process and certainly eschew strict time-limits. This is true of the Law Society/RICS Model Forms, the ISVA Forms and Form 22 in EFP (5th ed) Vol 22. Even in such 'automatic' review clauses, some time-limits may appear, for example, allowing a landlord to give notice to alter the frequency of review. More commonly, as in the current Model Form, Variation C, clause 4 (F), there is provision for a tenant to require the landlord to apply for appointment of an arbitrator or valuer and to propose a new deemed rent in default of such action. Time is rightly expressly made of the essence for such a notice: if it is not, it is likely that the landlord can make a late application (see the *Phipps Faire* case discussed at p 103 above). The two earlier (1979, 1980) versions of the Model Forms did not make time of the essence for similar clauses.

Precedents with strict time of the essence clauses, and the once common 'trigger-notice' and 'counter-notice' provisions may still be found in Conveyancer Precedent 5–57 and Form 127 of EFP (5th ed), and references to older precedents (eg the widely used forms from the EFP (4th ed)) may be found in previous editions of this book and some are still printed in Part Seven below. Leases based on such forms will be operative for many years to come, and the clauses may also be carried over into new leases of the same property under the 1954 Act (a change in the form of review clause may be agreed at a renewal but probably cannot be imposed by the landlord—see *Charles Follett v Cabtell* (1987) 2 EGLR 88 and the discussion in Chapter 16, p 514).

The Model Forms in both the 1980 and 1985 versions include one further time-limit. It is optional and occurs in clause 3 of each variation and allows a landlord (in Variation C) or either party (Variations A and B) to make application to the President 'not earlier than 6 months before the relevant Review Date *but not later than the end of the relevant Review Period*' (emphasis added). The italicised words presuppose a late review at any time in the review period and a consequent payment of the increased rent retrospectively to the review date. Such a provision leaves a prospect of a late review open for perhaps many years and may produce uncertainty. However, a tenant, by either serving a Clause F notice or (where Variations A and B are employed) by seeking the appointment of a referee directly, may terminate the uncertainty. This may involve a difficult tactical decision between opting for a review with a resultant rent increase and maintaining the status quo. Where both parties lose sight of the review but the landlord eventually gives the late notice envisaged by the lease, a tenant will, in the absence of an estoppel, have no right to resist a late review. Consequently, a tenant might be wise to seek the elimination of the additional words from a draft lease. Alternatively, thought should be given to making the limit expressly of the essence. Such a 'longstop' provision might well be held to be impliedly of the essence, but on the present state of the cases this could not be guaranteed.

Finally, it should be noted that all provisions whereby time becomes of the essence may have the effect of transferring disputes between the parties from the real issue (ie what is the rental value of the premises for the ensuing review period in accordance with our agreement for review) to narrow legal points of whether a notice was properly served, whether a letter in the post was sufficient communication and so forth (see section 2 of this chapter, below). Such situations, where they have occurred already, might give rise to claims for professional negligence and this may be another reason for the current reluctance to agree to the inclusion of strict time-limits.

2 The giving of notices

A notice should always contain all that is envisaged by the lease in question. Subject to what is said below, no particular formality will be necessary beyond that required by the lease. Though failure to observe such requirements will rarely be fatal since a fresh notice will often be possible, the care that should be taken to conform will be well worthwhile. Where, of course, time is of the essence for service of any notice, a mistake can be very serious and may lead to a loss of the review; or, where a tenant fails to serve an adequate counter-notice, he may be saddled with the rent stated in the landlord's trigger-notice, whatever its relationship to the true market rent.

Rent review notices take many forms. The case-law is littered with cases on trigger-notices initiating a review and tenants' counter-notices to elect for arbitration. Such a format has become increasingly unpopular though leases with such clauses will be with us for many decades. In more modern leases, these may be absent but there may still be other notices envisaged, for example, to alter the frequency of review.

(a) Requirement of written notice

A review clause that provides that notices shall be a feature of the review machinery should always stipulate that such notices shall be in writing, and the published precedents invariably so provide. An oral notice is consequently invalid in such cases (*Legg d Scot v Benion* (1738) 125 ER 1047). A suggestion has been made (obiter) in the Court of Appeal that even a provision in a review clause that notice should be 'in writing' was not 'of the essence' since a review clause is part of a bargain whereby the parties treat one another fairly and they should not insist upon strict measures upon which their attempts to vary the rent should be dependent (per Eveleigh LJ in *Dean and Chapter of Chichester Cathedral v Lennards Ltd* (1977) 35 P & CR 309 at 314–5). However, in the same case Lord Russell agreed with the traditional view that a requirement of written notice is to be regarded as essential (at 314) and it is submitted that this is the better view but the point is probably an open one and the force of the *United Scientific* presumption in relation to time stipulations might result in Eveleigh LJ's view prevailing. If the lease provides for written notice to be served then the force of the argument that written notice is essential is much stronger. Even in a case where the lease fails to prescribe the mode of exercise and an oral notice may suffice, the prudent party will still give written notice, thereby avoiding argument on the issue and providing evidence of the giving of the notice.

There is an additional reason for always giving notices in writing because, where the lease refers to the service of a notice, there is an argument that the Law of Property Act 1925, s 196(1) (discussed more fully below) will always import the necessity for writing.

The effect of absence of writing for notice where it is requisite under the statute or the express terms of the lease has not been tested in relation to a rent review notice to our knowledge apart from the observations noted above. In relation to a notice exercising an option it proved fatal in *New Hart Builders Ltd v Brindley* [1975] Ch 342, but in relation to a notice of defects under the NHBC scheme the express need for writing was brushed aside in *Marchant v Caswell and Redgrave Ltd* (1976) 240 EG 127. One line of cases prior to the *United Scientific* and *Cheapside* decisions likened one category of review provision to options, which might make the *Brindley* case the more apposite, but the accuracy of the parallel may not have survived the House of Lords' decision.

(b) Content of a notice

In simple terms, a notice should contain all that the lease requires it to contain and though this may be stating the obvious, a glance at the case law reveals that this truth is all too frequently ignored. Issues on content will only matter in a minority of cases not least because it is only if time is of the essence that a second more complete notice is not possible.

Moreover, many stated requirements are likely to be directory, not mandatory. So in *Taylor Woodrow Property Co Ltd v Lonrho Textiles Ltd* [1985] 2 EGLR 120, a landlord's trigger-notice was (in addition to specifying the new rent):

(1) to be based on the calculation formula to be adopted by an arbitrator;
(2) to inform the tenant of the right to serve a counter-notice; and
(3) to draw the tenant's attention to the consequences of the failure to serve a counter-notice.

Counsel for the landlord used the existence of these details as supporting his argument that a later deeming provision made time of the essence for a tenant's counter-notice (see p 101 above). However, the judge held, applying the *Chichester* case, that a trigger-notice under this lease would be valid even if it omitted or failed to observe the requirements set out above. In other words, such omissions are not sufficiently serious so as to invalidate the notice as noted below.

In an option case, *Multon v Cordell* [1986] 1 EGLR 44, it was held that a letter enclosing copies of earlier notices was not in itself a fresh request to exercise the option. A degree of formality, though not essential, may be desirable to avoid such difficulties.

(c) Dealing with allegedly defective notices

A defect in the form of a notice under a rent review clause will usually be of little significance, for two reasons:

(1) A defective notice may be ignored and the defect cured by a second notice in due form.
(2) A notice that is defective in some way may often be relied upon, notwithstanding the defect, by the party serving the notice even in those instances where service of a further notice is precluded.

It has been argued that the decision in the *United Scientific* case on time stipulations in leases applies equally to other terms of the contract and particularly to provisions as to the form of notices (Colyer (1977) 242 EG 943). This is because the arguments in that case were based, at least in part, upon s 41 of the Law of Property Act 1925, which refers to 'stipulations in contracts as to time *or otherwise* which are not deemed to be or to have become of the essence of the contract'. If therefore time stipulations are prima facie not of the essence, neither, it is argued, are stipulations as to form. This argument proved to be correct for it was the basis of the main judgment in the *Chichester* case ((1977) 35 P & CR 309 per Lord Denning MR at 311). On the basis of s 41, and applying the decision in the *United Scientific* case, it was held that a provision in a lease requiring that the notice of the lessor initiating the review should 'state the suggested new rent to be recovered' was not essential. Consequently, a notice omitting any suggested new rent was valid.

Thus, stipulations as to form need not normally be strictly adhered to by the party giving notice unless the defect in the notice is such that the alleged notice cannot be said to be sufficient or, to put it another way, it is apparent from the provision in the lease and from the circumstances that the notice had to contain certain provisions and this it failed to do.

(d) Principles applicable to all notices

In earlier editions of this work, we discussed at some length cases on option notices and notices under the 1954 Act—on the basis that rules on rent review notices were analogous to them. The growing jurisprudence on rent review notices makes such a detailed comparison unnecessary, however illuminating. However, it is helpful to remember that reference to such cases may be of relevance.

The general principles applicable to all such notices can be summarised as follows (though the cases dealing with notices under the 1954 Act may not provide exact parallels):

(i)   The notice will normally be valid if it meets the requirements of informing the other party with sufficient precision of the server's intention (*Bolton's (House Furnishers) Ltd v Oppenheim* [1959 1 WLR 913 at 917. The test the 'court really has to consider is whether the statement or notice given by the landlord has given the proper information to the tenant which will enable the tenant to deal in a proper way with the situation, whatever it may be, referred to in the notice' (per Barry J in *Barclays Bank Ltd v Ascott* [1961] 1 WLR 717 at 722). In other words, 'there is no magic formula, but . . . the tenant must make it clear' (per Templeman LJ in *Amalgamated Estates v Joystretch Manufacturing Ltd* (1980) 257 EG

489). Sufficient clarity is what is required. Thus where a rent review clause provided that a landlord might 'require' an independent surveyor to be appointed (to act as an expert) within a specified time-limit, it was said that the landlord had to disclose his requirement to the tenant. A 'suggestion' in a 'without prejudice' letter that the matter go to 'arbitration' did not bring home to the tenant with sufficient clarity the fact that the landlord was invoking the review mechanism: *Darlington Borough Council v Waring and Gillow (Holdings) plc* [1988] 2 EGLR 159.

(ii) Defects or omissions will not invalidate a notice if the notice is otherwise clear (*Sunrose Ltd v Gould* [1962] 1 WLR 20). If the recipient 'must have known' the intent of the notice, it will still be valid (*Nunes v Davies Laing & Dick Ltd* [1986] 1 EGLR 106; and see *Durham City Estates Ltd v Felicetti*, below.

(iii) Even a positive error in a notice will not render it invalid providing (once again) that the notice is clear in the message it conveys to the recipient and that he would not be misled by it: *Germax Securities Ltd v Spiegal* (1978) 37 P & CR 204 CA (a mistake in a notice under the 1954 Act did not invalidate it) applying the test propounded by Goulding J in *Carradine Properties Ltd v Aslam* [1976] 1 WLR 442 where an error, which was nonsensical (a notice given in 1974 purporting to terminate in 1973—a slip for 1975) was ignored since it was clear what was meant. Though this test has been criticised as being too uncertain since it will never be clear exactly what is or is not misleading to a reasonable tenant (see Smith (1979) 251 EG 653) it is submitted that the test should be applied to rent review. Thus, if a notice specified the wrong date from which the reviewed rent was to come into effect, it is probable that this error should be discounted if the recipient knew the effect of the notice and could ascertain the correct date from the lease. On the other hand, a notice that misled the other party (eg specified an incorrect time for the tenant's counter-notice, upon which the tenant relied to his detriment) is likely to be held invalid as in *Barclays Bank Ltd v Ascott*, where the landlord purported to give a notice under the 1954 Act stating that he would not oppose the grant of a new tenancy but that non-opposition was conditional upon the provision of a guarantor. This was construed as stating that the landlord would oppose the new tenancy in certain circumstances that did not fall within any of the statutory ground of opposition and the notice was consequently ineffective. This sort of approach to errors which mislead is similar to that in *Shirlcar Properties Ltd v Heinitz* (1983) 263 EG 383, discussed below.

(e) Rent review trigger-notices—early forms

The earliest leases sometimes contain unsophisticated trigger-notices. In its simplest form, the notice merely 'sets the ball rolling' so that one party acquaints the other of his desire for a review. Such a notice is a 'call for review' only *Drebbond Ltd v Horsham District Council* (1978) 37 P & CR 237. A similar pattern also makes the notice calling for review the first stage of a negotiating process but requires the party giving notice to 'state the suggested new rent to be reserved'. In such an event the party giving notice must operate the review machinery and cannot rely on the figure proposed if the tenant does nothing. Consequently, the inclusion of the suggested figures is not a vital part of the review mechanism and it has been held that a notice that omits to state a figure as a new rent will still be a valid notice, the requirement being merely directory and not mandatory (*Dean and Chapter of Chichester Cathedral v Lennards Ltd* (1978) 35 P & CR 309). If, however, time is of the essence for the service of such a trigger-notice, a requirement that the notice 'shall specify' the proposed new rent may be construed as being a mandatory requirement, even in the absence of any counter-notice mechanism and notwithstanding that the sum so stated is merely a proposal to give the 'negotiations a good start': *Commission for the New Towns v R Levy & Co Ltd* (1990) 28 EG 119 (the *Chichester* case was distinguished both on the wording of the clause and because there time was not of the essence). These early forms of initiating notice are now very rare in new leases but may still be found in current older leases (the two *Norwich Union* cases (discussed below) are of this type).

(f) The 'classic' rent review trigger-notice

The classic style of trigger-notice, found in a number of reported cases and common in older leases, is based on precedents in EFP (4th ed) Form 8:1 (revised as Additional Form 76) and Conveyancer Precedent 5-57. The lessor's notice does more than just initiate the review; for the open market rent is defined as 'such sum as shall be specified in a notice in writing'. The figure so specified takes effect automatically unless agreement is reached in writing for an alternative figure or unless the tenant gives a written counter-notice to require independent adjudication either by valuation or arbitration, depending on which is specified in the lease.

A tenant is usually disadvantaged by express provision in the lease that makes 'time of the essence' for the period in which he may serve the counter-notice. This is in contrast to the landlord's notice that initiates the review, which often will not be so circumscribed by the lease, thus enabling a valid notice to be served beyond the limits prescribed. (Only a minority of precedents (eg EFP (4th ed) Form 7:1 made time of the essence expressly for the trigger-notice as well as the counter-notice.) The tenant is thus put in a 'time-trap' if the time for service of his counter-notice is stated to be of the essence. Any delay in serving his counter-notice, even if reasonable, leaves him to pay a rent determined unilaterally by the landlord.

The following points can be made:

(1) A statement of the proposed new rent would appear to be an essential requirement for the operation of the review machinery where the review clause is of this type. This is because the rent so specified is to take effect unless altered by agreement between the parties or a tenant's counter-notice electing for arbitration (see EFP (4th ed) Forms 7:1 and 8:1; EFP (5th ed) Form 127; Conveyancer Precedent 5–57. Without a specified rent, there is nothing on which the tenant can agree and no basis for a counter-notice. Consequently it is submitted that a notice that omitted to specify the rent would be invalid and if time is of the essence and the relevant period has expired the review is lost. The authors are aware of instances where landlords have accepted this submission without litigating the issue. The decision in *Commission for the New Towns v R Levy & Co Ltd* (1990) 28 EG 119 lends support for this view since in that case the requirement to specify a new rent was held to be mandatory even though the sum so specified could not take effect in the absence of agreement. The *Chichester* case, distinguished in the *Levy* decision, was of a different type—the rent merely being a 'suggested' figure by way of opening negotiations which could never take effect in default.

(2) An error in the rent so specified will not invalidate the notice provided the meaning is clear. Thus in *Durham City Estates Ltd v Felicetti* [1990] 1 EGLR 143 a notice which required the rent to be increased to '£8,850 (Eight thousand seven hundred and fifty pounds)' was a good notice. It was said that a recipient would look to the words and it would have been obvious that there had been a typographical error. The tenant's argument that two sums had been specified was rejected by the Court of Appeal. One can only speculate if the result would be different if the amount in words had been the larger figure or if the discrepancy had been greater, though the court expressly stated that it did not rely on the de minimis principle.

(3) There is, of course, no duty on the lessor's solicitor to warn the lessee or his solicitor of the imminence of a time-limit.

(4) Though it is possible that express agreement between the parties will extend the period, the mere fact of continuing negotiations is insufficient to prevent the figure specified in the lessor's notice taking effect in the absence of a counter-notice in time (*Oldschool v Johns* (1980) 256 EG 381).

(5) In the most common form of trigger-notice, which merely requires

a new rent 'to be specified', it is not necessary that the sum so specified is capable of qualifying as the 'full yearly market rental' in accordance with the formula in the lease for there is no room for a necessary implication into the lease that the landlord can only propose a rent that will be a market rent as defined: *Davstone Holdings v Al-Rifai* (1976) 32 P & CR 18 at 26, a ruling applied in the Court of Appeal in *Amalgamated Estates Ltd v Joystretch Manufacturing Ltd* (1980) 257 EG 489. In such circumstances, it is now accepted practice and wisdom that the figure stated is likely to be higher than the true market rent and no more than an opening shot in negotiations (cf *Cordon Bleu Freezer Centres Ltd v Marbleace Ltd* [1987] 2 EGLR 142 where two agents each served a trigger-notice for the same lease—one chose £30,000 as the specified rent; the other £45,000). The trap is laid, and failure to serve a counter-notice can leave the tenant saddled with the sum so specified, whether or not it is in excess of the true market rent. In *Taylor Woodrow Property Co Ltd v Lonrho Textiles Ltd* [1985] 2 EGLR 120 the amount specified in the trigger-notice was to be based upon the valuation formula which would apply on reference to an arbitrator. The judge was of the opinion that such a method of calculation was a 'little bit of machinery' and so a notice using a different basis of calculation would still be valid. Nevertheless, there may be forms of clause to which this principle will not apply. Thus if a clause required a rent which 'in the opinion of the landlord' was the market rent, it might be open for the tenant to challenge the notice if he could prove (which might be difficult) that the figure specified was known to the landlord (or, in practice, those advising the landlord, to be clearly excessive.

(6) A rent review trigger-notice must be clear in the message it conveys to the tenant; the (seemingly gratuitous) addition of 'subject to contract' under the signature to an otherwise good trigger-notice robbed it of efficacy in *Shirlcar Properties Ltd v Heinitz* (1983) 268 EG 362. The test is whether the notice is such as to leave the recipient in no doubt as to what the landlord is up to; in that case, it was said, the words 'subject to contract' meant that the tenant would be led to believe the landlord was only taking a preliminary step before the rent review machinery was put in motion. A similar approach was adopted in *Norwich Union Life Assurance Society v Tony Waller Ltd* (1984) 270 EG 42 where a trigger-notice from a chartered surveyor marked 'without prejudice', though not privileged and therefore admissible evidence, was equivocal and ineffective as a rent review notice. In *Sheridan v Blaircourt Investments Ltd* (1984) 270 EG 1290 the tenant's agent was doubly cautious, heading his letter, later alleged to be a valid counter-notice, 'without prejudice and subject to contract'. Predictably, the tenant's claim that the notice was valid failed. These cases must now be compared to *British Rail*

Pension Trustees Co Ltd v Cardshops Ltd (below) where a 'subject to contract' counter-notice was upheld and *Royal Life Insurance v Phillips* [1990] EGCS 32 where Nolan J was prepared to uphold a trigger-notice headed both 'subject to contract' and 'without prejudice' and sent by recorded delivery 4 days before the relevant time-limit—apparently on the basis that the headings made no sense in a document intended to have legal effect and that since the tenant responded to the notice this was strong evidence that she knew and understood it as a trigger-notice. It is submitted that the *Royal Life* decision is difficult to reconcile with Dillon LJ's opinion in the *Shirlcar* case and that the appellate decision remains sound—the words 'subject to contract' are 'wholly inapposite' to a trigger-notice. It is significant that, in all these cases, the purported notices were served by surveyors or valuers within the prescribed time-limits (indeed in the *Shirlcar* case, 2 months early, a point noted by the first instance judge (at 266 EG 126 at 128) as supporting the conclusion that it was not a good trigger-notice) and otherwise meeting the requirements of the lease. It may therefore be prudent for legal advisers to undertake the service of such notices.

By way of contrast, in *Norwich Union Life Assurance Society v Sketchley plc* [1986] 2 EGLR 126, a surveyors' letter indicating that they had instructions to negotiate a rent review was treated as sufficient 'notice in writing' of a 'call for review'. Consequently, the letter set the next review timetable, (which was held to be of the essence) in motion. The landlord, by failing to refer the valuation to a referee within 6 months, lost the opportunity to revise a rent of £1,650 which, after 14 years, was to be £11,500 if the landlord's figure had been accepted. The *Tony Waller* case involved a lease of a unit in the same parade of shops as the *Sketchley* case. The leases appeared to follow the same precedent, but the *Sketchley* lease only allowed a trigger-notice at 'any one time', whereas the *Waller* case omitted the word 'one'. This allowed Harman J to permit a second trigger-notice to restart the cycle but in the *Sketchley* case Scott J held the additional words ruled out the possibility of a second notice and the review was lost. (It is perhaps right to point out that the slight but significant difference in wording was not explicitly alluded to, but it is submitted that it forms the best rationale to distinguish the opposing constructions of otherwise identical wording in identical situations.)

(7) In *Scotland*, in *Yates, Petitioner* [1987] SLT 86 the alleged letter constituting a rent review trigger-notice was written by the lessor personally to the Managing Director of the tenant company, who was a close friend. It was argued that the inclusion of (considerable) social pleasantries, personal matters and greetings in the letter meant that the letter did not constitute a good trigger-notice within the terms of the lease. This argument was not ruled upon, the judge

preferring to argue that the notice had been served too early and
had to be served on a specific date three months before the review
date—a construction which the authors consider highly questionable
if not obviously wrong.

(g) Tenant's counter-notices

A rent review clause initiated by a trigger-notice specifying a new
rent which is to take effect in default of any action by a tenant almost
invariably requires (often after a period of time for negotiation and
agreement) a counter-notice by the tenant electing for arbitration or
reference to an expert in default of such agreement. In the absence of
such agreement or counter-notice, the rent specified by the landlord
stands. Published precedents adopting variants of such a procedure
include EFP (5th ed) Form 127, Conveyancer Precedent 5–57 and EFP
(4th ed) Forms 8:1, Additional Form 76 and 7:1. Since time is often
expressly 'of the essence' for the service of such a counter-notice, the
form of such a notice is important. If the sequence of cases, many holding
that a counter-notice was insufficient on the facts, is indicative of a
trend, it appears that many tenants have fallen in to the trap laid in
such review clauses by failing to serve a proper counter-notice.

(i) The form of counter-notice

There is no magic formula or form of notice required. A simple
precedent such as EFP (5th ed) Form 129 will suffice. The test for such
counter-notice is that 'the tenant must make it clear to the landlord
that he proposed to have the rent decided by arbitration in accordance
with the provision of the lease' (per Templeman LJ in *Amalgamated
Estates Ltd v Joystretch Manufacturing Ltd* (1980) 257 EG 489). Applying
this test, McNeill J opined that, though a reference to the relevant clause
of the lease was an unnecessary formality, nevertheless the notice must
identify the form of relief unequivocally: *Edlingham Ltd v MFI Furniture
Centres Ltd* (1981) 259 EG 421 at 424. This approach did not find favour
with the Vice-Chancellor in *Nunes v Davies Laing & Dick Ltd* [1986]
1 EGLR 106 where a 1973 lease contained a rent review clause
substantially in the form of EFP (4th ed) Form 7:1. In response to a
landlord's trigger-notice, the tenant's agent sent a letter to 'give you
hereby formal notice that the open market rental is £12,000 per annum
and call on you under the terms of the above lease to agree to this.
Please confirm it is accepted as notice'. In holding this to be a valid
counter-notice, Browne-Wilkinson V-C quoted and applied the test of
Templeman LJ in the *Joystretch* case quoted in the text. However, that
test had been paraphrased in the *Edlingham* case to mean that the notice
must be unequivocal. Notwithstanding the fact that McNeill J in
Edlingham, and the later decisions in the *Horserace Totalisator* and
Sheridan cases, treated the concept of a 'clear' notice and an 'unequivocal'
notice as meaning the same thing, here the Vice- Chancellor was of

the view that the test of a 'clear notice' and one of 'equivocal' notice were different. The letter in the *Nunes* case, it was held, was equivocal (in the sense that it could bear more than one meaning) but it was still 'clear' since it stated it was a 'formal notice' and the landlord 'must have known' that the only provision for a notice was a counter-notice electing for arbitration.

While the relaxation of harshness of the rule (for tenants) resulting from the *Joystretch* test is to be welcomed, the authors doubt if the distinction between a 'clear' notice on the one hand and an 'unequivocal' notice on the other can be sustained. As it is, we are left with two possibly conflicting first instance decisions (*Edlingham* and *Nunes*) purporting to apply the same Court of Appeal test (*Joystretch* case) a situation which can only lead to uncertainty in the operation of this commonly occurring type of review clause based on a popular 1970s' precedent. In the *Glofield v Morley* case (see below) Hutchinson J was of the view that the decisions did not conflict; if they did, he chose to follow the *Nunes* decision.

(ii) The problem of counter-notices

The problem in practice appears to be that the trigger-notices are (correctly) received by the tenants themselves, the specified rent is one that cannot be agreed and the natural reaction is to dispatch a letter disagreeing with the sum stated. Such letter of objection will invariably fail the *Joystretch* test. Examples of letters which failed to give a clear counter-notice vary from a mere statement of disagreement (*Bellinger v South London Stationers Ltd* (1979) 252 EG 699), through those which disagree and request further evidence (*Joystretch* case) to those which refer to the right to proceed to arbitration but fail to elect for such action (*Horserace Totalisator Board v Reliance Mutual Insurance Society* (1983) 266 EG 218). In *Sheridan v Blaircourt* (above) a letter which 'suggested that it would be appropriate' to apply to the RICS was insufficient to elect for such action even without the further consideration that it was marked 'without prejudice and subject to contract'. Nor can the tenant escape the consequences of failing to serve the proper counter-notice by arguing that inconclusive negotiations to agree a new rent continued after the last day for service of a counter-notice (*Oldschool v Johns* (1980) 256 EG 381); or by showing or contending that the rent proposed in the trigger-notice is more than would have been properly fixed as the open market rent (see the discussion at p 126 above on the *Davstone* case).

Though it was said in the *Edlingham* case (where a letter was sent stating that the rent was excessive and inquiring about any comparable properties relied on) that it did not assist the tenant that the letter calls itself a counter-notice if it is in fact equivocal, the more liberal approach exemplified in the *Nunes* decision was applied in *Glofield Properties Ltd v Morley* [1988] 1 EGLR 113 where a letter which described itself as a 'formal objection and counter-notice' without electing for arbitration was upheld. The reference to 'formal' and 'counter-notice' meant that the notice was sufficiently clear in conveying its intention.

Where there are counter-notices which do not have to elect for arbitration or reference to an expert, it is less likely that invalidity will be found. In *British Rail Pension Trustees Co Ltd v Cardshops Ltd* [1987] 1 EGLR 127 the counter-notice envisaged merely had to state what was, in the opinion of the tenant, the open market rent. A letter from a director of the tenant company, headed 'subject to contract' and which was 'prepared to agree a rental of £24,000', was upheld since a sensible businessman would find the notice clear. The 'subject to contract' heading could be taken as designed to ensure it was not an offer capable of acceptance. By way of contrast, a counter-notice requiring election and headed 'Without prejudice and subject to contract' did not suffice (*Sheridan v Blaircourt*, above).

(iii)   Remedies if counter-notice is defective

There are two possible avenues open to a tenant who has failed to get his counter-notice in on time. If the review clause involves a reference to arbitration, a timeous application for discretionary relief will be available under the Arbitration Act 1950, s 27 (*Joystretch* case; and see discussion at p 113). Such application will require evidence of the undue hardship the tenant will otherwise suffer (*Edlingham* case). A second, albeit faint, possibility is that the tenant may establish a waiver or estoppel by the landlord (defences more fully discussed at p 147 above). The failure of these defences in *Oldschool v Johns*, notwithstanding the fact that a letter by the landlords said 'the issue will have to go to arbitration' and that there were negotiations subsequent to the last date for a valid counter-notice, shows that the burden of proof on a tenant is an onerous one. A defence of a waiver has also failed in the context of notices under the Law of Property Act 1925, s 146, as amended (*B L Holdings Ltd v Marcolt Investments Ltd* (1979) 249 EG 849).

It hardly need be emphasised that, in the light of the above, counter-notices should be drafted with great care. More significantly, legal advisers should ensure that clients, and their agents, are aware of the dangers if they choose to handle the operation of the rent review machinery themselves. (It is pertinent to observe that in *Chartered Trust plc v Maylands Green Estate Co Ltd* (1984) 270 EG 845 an action for professional negligence against a firm of surveyors is referred to. The defence to that action was that it was not within the scope of their instructions to give a counter-notice. In the same case a later notice was not given because a solicitor and an agent each believed the other was undertaking the task. The lessons are obvious.) It must also be borne in mind that the failure to serve adequate counter-notices in so many cases may be because the tenant readily accepts that the rent must increase and so wishes to negotiate with his landlord in a temperate and amicable way. He may well fear that a notice invoking the third party reference in a formal and inevitably somewhat contentious manner could sour the atmosphere and so the tenant is reluctant to take a step which could be interpreted, or misinterpreted, as hostile. Leases requiring counter-notices strictly within a specified time thus present tenants with a dilemma and do little or nothing to encourage amicable agreement on review. On the other hand, of course, some ill will may result in the absence of time-limits as where prolonged negotiations break down without agreement.

The lessons to be drawn from the cases are:

(1) A notice electing for arbitration, or reference to a valuer if that is stipulated, must be timeously served.
(2) A degree of formality is appropriate, with the notice clearly electing for the step required within the terms of the lease.
(3) Professional advisers should warn tenants of the dangers of inadequate responses to trigger-notices, or of delay in passing them to property departments in large organisations where they may have been, quite properly, served on an operational 'out-station'.

(h) Mode of service of notices

It is the interrelationship of the express provisions in the lease and s 196 of the Law of Property Act 1925, if it applies, which will govern the mode of service of rent review notices. Ideally, the best mode is that prescribed in the lease. The provisions and, particularly, the presumptions, in s 196 will apply if the section is expressly incorporated or, impliedly, if s 196(5) applies to rent review notices.

(i) Time for service

Our earlier discussion shows the importance of serving a notice in time—late service where time is of the essence will usually lead to a loss of the review. It is possible that a notice can be given too early (*Biondi v Kirklington and Piccadilly Estates* [1947] 2 All ER 59). In *Multon v Cordell* [1986] 1 EGLR 44 it was held that a notice to be given '3 months before' a date had to be made a reasonable time before the 3 month period began to run. A request 3 years before such a date was too early but it was said, obiter, that 7 months before was probably reasonable. It is unlikely this problem will be relevant to many rent review notices and if the situation does arise it may be possible to distinguish these option cases since an option normally requires due, or sometimes substantial, performance of the tenant's covenants at the date of its exercise.

If the time for service of a notice falls due when the landlord is in the process of selling the reversion, there are risks both in missing any relevant time-limit or in specifying a figure in a trigger-notice or agreeing a rent with which the assignee does not agree. The risks are illustrated by *Cordon Bleu Freezer Food Centres Ltd v Marbleace Ltd* [1987] 2 EGLR 143, referred to at p 126 above.

(ii)   Contractual requirements as to service

Proper service will need to accord with any express stipulation in the lease and this will be a question of construction of the relevant provisions. Guidance as to the meaning of common phrases is given below.

The giving of a notice means causing a notice to be received. Actual receipt is required unless a contractual or statutory presumption otherwise provides: *Sun Alliance Assurance Co Ltd v Hayman* [1975] 1 WLR 177 at 185. If, as is the usual case, it is stated that there must be *notice* in writing *to* the other party then that notice must be so communicated to the other party (subject to various presumptions as discussed below): *Holwell Securities v Hughes* [1974] 1 WLR 155. It is not sufficient that the party be told that the notice is in the post. Thus, where a notice is sent by post, and in the absence of any presumption deeming or assuming receipt, evidence may be adduced by the addressee that the letter did not arrive, thus showing the intended recipient had no actual knowledge of its contents (*Holwell Securities v Hughes*, above, and at [1973] 1 WLR 757 at 760D). It may be significant that the case involved exercise of an option, where strict compliance with machinery is normally required.

Whether any contractually specified mode of service is mandatory or directory will be a matter of construction but it is likely that the specified method will be construed as non-exclusive. So, where the mode of service prescribed by the lease is by registered or recorded delivery post (as is frequently the case for rent review notices) a notice delivered personally or sent by ordinary post will still be valid provided it is actually received by the person to be served. The manner of service was construed as directory or permissive and not mandatory in *Yates Building Co Ltd v R J Pulleyn and Sons (York) Ltd* (1975) 237 EG 183 (where the relevant phrase was 'notice to be served'). This decision on an option notice was followed for rent review notices in another appellate decision, *Midland Oak Construction Ltd v BBA Group Ltd* (1983) 15 February, unreported, where a notice delivered by hand on a Sunday, the last day allowed by the lease, was not invalidated by the lease prescribing recorded delivery (in the form of EFP Form 7:1—see Part Seven). Thus, if the notice is to be posted when the relevant time-limit is about to expire, then it may even be prudent to serve two or three identical notices—one by recorded delivery (probably in accordance with the express provision or under s 196), one by first class post and/or fax and (perhaps) one personally and so avoid the risk that one or other method may fail to secure service in time. In *Stephenson & Son v Orca Properties Ltd* [1989] 2 EGLR 129 a recorded delivery letter was out of time since there was no available recipient to sign on the first day of delivery (see below p 135) but a normal first class letter posted at the same time, or personal delivery, would have sufficed in that case, subject to the necessity to establish service if challenged. The evidence in that case of what had happened to the recorded delivery letter would not necessarily have been available for a letter sent by ordinary post, of course.

(iii)   Law of Property Act 1925, s 196
This section provides that:

(1) Any notice required or authorised to be served by the Act shall be in writing (s 196(1)).
(2) Any such notice served on a lessee (but not a lessor) by that designation is sufficient even though the actual name is omitted (s 196(2)).
(3) A notice is sufficiently served if:
   Either: it is left at the last known place of abode (or business) in the United Kingdom of the lessee (or lessor or other person) to be served or affixed or left at the premises comprised in the lease (s 196(3));
   Or: it is sent by post in a registered letter addressed to the person to be served at the last known place of abode or business, provided it is not returned undelivered; service is then deemed to be made at the time when the registered letter would in the ordinary course be delivered (s 196(4)).
(4) Recorded delivery may be used in place of registered post (Recorded Delivery Service Act 1962, s 1).

The purpose of the section is to ensure a notice is given and received. Thus, where ordinary post is used, whilst it is not service by post within subsection (4), and the presumptions do not apply, such a letter which is actually received may nonetheless be good service under s 196(3) as it is left for the addressee through the medium of the post (*Stylo Shoes Ltd v Price Tailors Ltd* [1960] Ch 396, a case on the analogous provisions of s 23 of the Landlord and Tenant Act 1927 and applying *Sharpley v Manby* [1942] 1 KB 217). Section 196 is permissive as to the mode of service and not exhaustive so that a notice actually received may still be valid.

Consequently, s 196 is of greatest value for the presumptions it contains as to receipt. The section may apply by express incorporation in the lease (which is quite common), but, in the absence of such incorporation, does the section apply to rent review notices? The provisions of s 196 extend to notices 'required to be served' by any instrument affecting property (s 196(5)) 'unless a contrary intention appears'.

The difficulty is whether the words 'required to be served' are wide enough to embrace a standard form rent review notice. If a narrow construction of the subsection (5) was adopted (see Montgomerie (1952) 16 Conv (NS) 98 at 107 and Murdoch (1984) 269 EG 297) then it can be argued that a landlord's trigger-notice is not 'required', only permitted (though, on this view, a tenant's counter-notice in response to that trigger-notice may well be 'required'). A wider interpretation of 'required' is to say that the parties to the lease intended a review to take place and therefore all notices are 'required' in that sense. It is submitted that this is the view to be preferred and in *Davstone Holdings Ltd v Al Rifai* (1976) 32 P & CR 18 at 28 it was conceded by both parties that s 196 applied to rent review notices; the same assumption is made in the judgment of Templeman LJ in the *Joystretch* case (above). Doubt must remain, however, as to whether s 196 is always applicable and this may be the reason why some precedents, far from excluding operation of the section, expressly incorporate it, sometimes with amendments (eg EFP (4th ed) Form 8:1, p 847; EFP (5th ed) Form 22, para 9.8; Kelly, p 175, clause 16). If s 196 does apply, then its provisions will be read into the lease.

Though the section only applies 'unless a contrary intention appears', it is rare, in any context, for the section to be expressly excluded; neither of the authors can recall ever meeting such a provision. Some clauses, however, must surely show a contrary intention; provision that notices 'must be served' or 'shall be served' in a particular manner could be so construed, although there appears to be no reported case. The wording in other clauses—for example, that in EFP (4th ed) Form 7.1 of 'and posted by recorded delivery post'—have been held to be directory and not mandatory: *Midland Oak* case, above. Express provision for a 'notice address' specified in the lease, or later notified for the purpose, may have a similar effect of excluding at least the permitted place of service aspects of s 196. It will be a matter of construing the words used.

(iv) Notices 'left' at premises

Where a notice is 'left' at premises it must be left there in a manner which a reasonable person, minded to bring the notice to the attention of the person to whom it is addressed, would adopt (*Lord Newborough v Jones* [1975] Ch 90. A notice pushed under a door, where there was no-one at home and no letterbox, sufficed as good notice under the Agricultural Holdings Act 1948, s 92(1) ('left at the proper address'). The tenant's claim that it had lain under the linoleum and was only found 5 months later was disbelieved, but, even had it not been, it was said that would still have been good service. In *Emerson E Smith Ltd v Rapacioli* (1973) 231 EG 617, a rent review notice left on the counter of the defendant's sandwich shop sufficed. In *Henry Smith's Charity Trustees v Kyriakou* [1989] 2 EGLR 110 the Court of Appeal upheld the judge's finding that a notice had been properly served in accordance with s 196(3) when placed through the letter slot of the ground floor entrance door, although it did not meet the test of service specified in the tenancy agreement of being left at the demised premises—a room on the fourth floor. It was held to be sufficient to comply with s 196(3) or (4) if the document 'is left at a place which was the furthest a member of the public or postman can go to communicate to tenants residing there'. The reference to the postman is highly significant, even if arguably obiter.

(v) Place of abode

A place of abode for a person to be served will include a business address (*Price v West London Investment Building Society* [1964] 1 WLR 616). However, the last known address of a person is that which an ordinary person would so regard. Thus in *National Westminster Bank Ltd v Betchworth Investments Ltd* (1975) 234 EG 675 a registered office given in a lease remained the 'last known address', even when correspondence sent there prior to the notice in question elicited a reply from managing agents at a different address and later correspondence about the lease had been with them (except some on legal matters which had been with solicitors). The former registered office to which the notice was sent had been demolished but the plantiffs had not been informed of the consequent change in the registered office; the letter had been returned to the plaintiffs' solicitors who then sent it on to the correct registered office, but it was by then out of time. Nevertheless, the old demolished registered office remained the last known address and the notice had been properly served. The managing agents' address had not become that of the company nor were the plantiffs under a duty to check if the registered office had changed.

(vi) Presumptions as to service under s 196

Service is deemed to be made at the time the registered letter would in the ordinary course be delivered (s 196(4)) so that *posting* (as opposed to delivering by hand or faxing) on the last day for service will be insufficient. Where service of a notice is made on a businessman or solicitor or other professional person at an address where he does not reside, service can probably only be effected on a normal business day since a notice, whose function is to convey a fact to someone, cannot convey such information if there is no one to receive it (*Rightside Properties Ltd v Gray* [1975] Ch 72). Consequently, posting of a notice on a Friday may result in service on the following Monday, or even Tuesday should there be a bank holiday, unless the office is open on a Saturday. Even if it is open, a registered or recorded delivery letter will only be served under s 196(4) if there is a recipient to sign the receipt at the time of delivery of the post. In *Stephenson & Son v Orca Properties Ltd* [1989] 2 EGLR 129 it was held that a recorded delivery letter posted on a Friday was not served the following day since there was no recipient to sign (the post was delivered before the office opened) and there was no second delivery on a Saturday. The notice was retained by the Post Office until the Monday when it was delivered and signed for but since time expired on the Sunday the notice was served out of time. Where service is by delivery, the requirement may be not only on a normal business day but during normal business hours. Such a requirement was found to apply to a time of the essence completion in *Commodities and Services International SA v Clemence Properties (Grays Inn) Ltd* (14 July 1986, unreported, but noted at [1986] Conv 307) although in that case it was not necessary to make a finding what the hours were. In view of the extended working hours of some professional offices that could be a matter of some difficulty, and for some businesses with a 24–hour cycle the problems may be more acute. In commercial cases involving international transactions, communications up to midnight have been held to be in time. Perhaps a distinction can be drawn between 'after hours' delivery to start a period running, where delaying the effective service to the next working day, when action can first be taken, may be excusable and such delivery on the last day for taking a step (as in the cited case) where late service will not be forgiven. The likely outcome is not readily predictable; in the second instance just given, extending the limit to midnight has attractions in terms of fairness if not expediency. Completion, unlike serving a notice, is a bilateral act.

A notice may be duly served even if the recipient refuses to sign a receipt for a registered letter when it is offered to him at his place of abode causing the notice to be returned to the Post Office (*Van Grutten v Trevenen* [1902] 2 KB 82). It would depend on the making of a factual finding such as was made in that case. Such a finding would have been made in *New Hart Builders Ltd v Brindley* [1975] Ch 342 had it been necessary. Return of the letter is express proof of non-delivery: *Hewitt v Leicester Corporation* [1969] 1 WLR 855 (recorded delivery letter returned marked 'Gone away'); but mere absence of a receipt was not, where no evidence of non-delivery was given (*Towli v Fourth River Property Co Ltd* (1976) (*The Times* 23 November). Indeed, such 'proof' of non-delivery will not displace the statutory presumption, for that allows only for the return of the letter.

If 'unless the contrary is proved' is used as the means to overturn a presumption of service, the cases on that phrase in a statutory context give guidance on its meaning. Thus in *Lex Services plc v Johns* [1990] 1 EGLR 92 there was an illegible signature on the postman's sheet and a denial by the tenant of actual receipt, but service was found to have been effected. It was said that unless evidence is adduced that the document was signed for by a person other than the one on whom it was to be served and that it had not been brought to the latters attention, the statutory presumption applies. It is not enough to assert that it was not received by the correct person. The relevant provision in the *Lex Services* case was s 23 of the Landlord and Tenant Act 1927, as incorporated into the 1954 Act. The same section, as incorporated in the Leasehold Reform Act 1967, was litigated in *Galinski v McHugh* [1989] 1 EGLR 109 where the Court of Appeal held that service on solicitors instructed by the tenant was to be treated as service on him, applying the doctrine of ostensible authority. The wording of many private notice clauses will mirror the permissive wording of s 23, so the decision would be apposite there, subject to proof of actual or ostensible authority. That may more often exist for surveyors than for solicitors in rent review transactions.

Review clauses which expressly provide, as in the *Joystretch* case, that a notice shall be conclusively deemed to have been received in the due course of post were deprecated as an unfair burden for any tenant by Templeman LJ. The same criticism applies to deemed service at a stated time after posting and in respect of those *Carne v Debono* [1988] 1 WLR 1107 lays down that proof of actual service at an earlier time can be made, which may be important either to start a period running or to meet a strict time-limit.

(vii)   Service by telex, fax and other electronic methods

Notice provisions in leases most often cover all notices, not merely those associated with rent review. Increasingly they will cover the use of telex, fax and possibly document exchanges, none of which figure in s 196. They are acceptable alternatives to those dealt with in the section, because it is permissive; they may not be effective where the lease designates only one or more other methods of service. Presumptions of time of service and means of proof of service by proof of transmission or delivery to an exchange are commonly added. An example is EFP (5th ed) Form 22, para 9.8.3 providing for service by telex and fax if transmitted before 4 pm on a working day. Aspects of the use of telex are considered in *Entores v Miles Far East Corporation Ltd* [1955] 2 QB 327 and *Brinkibon Ltd v Stahag Stahl und Stahlwarenhaudelsgesellschaft mbH* [1983] 2 AC 34. The use of document exchanges between solicitors was dealt with in *John Wilmott Homes Ltd v Read* [1985] 51 P & CR 90.

(viii)   Mode of service—drafting considerations

Designation of one mandatory mode of service may prove a trap whenever strict time-limits apply since doubts over due compliance with the exclusively prescribed method cannot be stilled by use of any alternative measure. The facts of the *Midland Oak Construction* case aptly illustrate this state of affairs; only personal delivery could be effected on the final Sunday. Return of a registered or recorded delivery letter, sent a few days before a time-limit runs out, after expiry of the specified period creates an insuperable obstacle. This disadvantage would also affect a tenant in relation to a counter-notice.

The flexibility of s 196 of the Law of Property Act 1925 is thus to be preferred. The object of s 196(3) and (4) is to specify circumstances in which proof of absence of actual knowledge of the notice may be disregarded. It is, therefore, well worthwhile to ensure that notices comply with the section and are served either personally or (preferably) by registered or recorded delivery post. The intended recipient will not then be able to adduce evidence to show the notice was not actually received (as in *Holwell Securities v Hughes*). Thus in the *Emerson E Smith* case (above) there was valid service under s 196 even though there was no evidence it had come to the tenant's attention. Some of the problems of s 196, and in particular the problem, in modern circumstances, of deemed delivery in ordinary course, are discussed by one of the authors at (1980) Conv 246 and 323. The presumption of delivery in due course under s 196(4) does not extend to ordinary post, but if delivery is proved or conceded and only the question of time of service remains in issue, it is submitted that the same presumption would be made as a factual inference. The problem will often be just to establish what would be the ordinary course of post. Regular reports by the Post Office on the *average* time for delivery feature in the newspapers and amply demonstrate the difficulties of proof. EFP (5th ed) Form 22, para 9.8.1 avoids the problem by substituting deemed service on a specified working day after the registered letter has been posted which solves the problem at the expense of potential unfairness.

Incorporation of the section can prove a mixed blessing for recipients unless clear instructions for forwarding formal correspondence to a relevant department or person within a large organisation exist. Without such procedures, notices deemed properly served may only reach the person required to act on the notice after delay. Similarly, failure to collect mail regularly from premises no longer in regular use may create problems where those premises constitute a proper place of service.

(i) To whom notice should be given

The notice should be served upon the party concerned and, unless the lease expressly so authorises, service upon a solicitor, agent or subsidiary company may well be insufficient (*Holwell Securities v Hughes*; *Midland Oak v BBA Group*); although the agent or solicitor can, of course, be expressly authorised to receive it. Express provision allowing service upon a solicitor is increasingly common. An example is EFP (5th ed) Form 22, para 9.8.2 which provides that it will be sufficient service if served 'on solicitors who have acted for that party in relation to this lease at any time within the year preceding service of the notice'. Such provision gives the convenience of service on solicitors at the expense of possible argument as to whether the solicitors have indeed acted within the time-limit specified and at the risk that the party named in the notice will not actually receive it.

In the *Midland Oak* case (above) the lease required service upon 'the Tenant at its Registered Office' and the Court of Appeal regarded both the address and the addressee provisions as mandatory. However, the lease incorporated s 196 expressly. Consequently, a notice delivered by hand to the demised premises avoided the difficulties about the address (s 196(3)); but the notice was held bad because it was not addressed to the tenant but to a subsidiary company. Service on an agent will be sufficient where either or both of the parties have left the conduct of the business relating to their leasehold interest to an agent on their behalf and the actual lessor or lessee has stood by without interference. Notice will then be valid as if served on the principal for the other party has acted to his detriment in reliance upon the implied agency (*Townsends Carriers Ltd v Pfizer Ltd* (1977) 33 P & CR 361); compare *National Westminster Bank Ltd v Bletchworth Investments* (1975) 234 EG 675 (discussed at p 135, above).

Where one of the parties to a lease is a limited company, as is often the case, a mistake can easily be made. Where a notice is addressed to the directors of a company, the notice will be good provided it is clear that it is a notice to the company (*Hawtrey v Beaufront Ltd* [1946] KB 280). In *Dean and Chapter of Chichester Cathedral v Lennards Ltd* (1977) 35 P & CR 309 the letter that was held to be a good notice was in fact addressed to a director of the defendant company, Lennards Ltd, and made no direct reference to the company lessees (see the report of the first instance judgment in (1976) 241 EG 311); yet no challenge was made to the notice on this basis. The *Pfizer* case shows that the court will uphold notices given to associated companies of the party to be served or (indeed) by an associated company of the party giving the notice provided the circumstances show there was sufficient implicit authorisation by the party concerned. However, there must be evidence (with the burden of proof on the party propounding the notice) of ostensible authority or a clear course of dealing sufficient to found an estoppel if service on an associate company is to suffice—in the *Midland Oak* case, the plaintiff landlords failed to meet this test and lost their review.

(j) Can a notice be withdrawn?

This issue will only be of importance where it is a notice that specifies a rent. Once the period of notice has expired the notice cannot be withdrawn by the landlord because the rent so stated has, by the terms of the lease, taken effect as the rent payable: *Museprime Properties Ltd v Adhill Properties Ltd* [1990] EGCS 29 (landlord unable to negotiate higher rents once the time-limit had expired); *Nunes v Davies Laing & Dick Ltd* [1986] 1 EGLR 106. However, there is no clear authority as to whether such a rent review notice can be withdrawn before the expiry of the period or acceptance by the tenant. It would, of course, be possible to provide expressly whether or not a notice could be withdrawn in the relevant period but in the absence of such express provision it appears that the classic form of words in such a notice (in Form 5–57 'specify a substituted rent' and in Form 8:1 'such sum as may be specified') might prevent the party serving the notice from resiling from the figures proposed in that notice. This was the view of Lord Diplock since such a notice constitutes an 'irrevocable offer' (*United Scientific*, at 933). Though the classic analysis of an option is that it constitutes an irrevocable standing offer (*Helby v Matthews* [1895] AC 47) and a more modern view is as an irrevocable unilateral 'if' contract (*Harvela Investments Ltd v Royal Trust Co of Canada Ltd* [1985] AC 207), there is no obvious reason why an offer in a rent review trigger-notice should be treated as irrevocable—offers made under rights of pre-emption or first refusal clauses are not irrevocable. So in *Tuck v Baker* [1990] 32 EG 46 it was held that a purchase notice under a pre-emption clause could be withdrawn before acceptance. It can be argued that the rent review notice is more closely analogous to these types of clause rather than options, given the freedom of choice as to whether to serve such a notice and what figure to state in it. Departure from the view of Lord Diplock may also be justified on the grounds that exercise of an option requires action by only one party but rent review trigger-notices presuppose action by both parties. If that is right, a tenant should act promptly to accept a favourable specified rent which is not an obvious mistake. By way of contrast, where a tenant serves a notice under clause 4(F) of the Model Forms 'containing a proposal as to the amount of such rent', there seems little doubt that a later change of mind on the tenant's part would be possible since the figure is only a 'proposal'—at least until the figure is deemed to become the market rent.

If the notice contains an obvious mistake or clerical error, it follows from the principles applicable to defective notices that the recipient will not be able to take advantage of such mistakes. An example might be when a notice refers to an increase in rent, the review is upwards only, but the figure specified is lower than the existing rent. Similarly, the omission of an '0' in a figure which a tenant had 'snapped up' may prevent reliance on the mistaken figure. (For mistakes giving rise to a claim for rectification see p 281 below.) On the other hand, if the mistake or error is not obvious and the recipient relies upon it to his detriment, then the party giving the notice may be estopped from correcting the error (see p 148 ff, below).

In the light of the rent review cases, discussed at pp 124–128 above, the test may be whether the mistake or error made the notice unclear. A not dissimilar point arose in *Centrovincial Estates plc v Merchant Investors Assurance Company Ltd* (1983) *The Times*, 8 March, which involved an 'automatic' rent review clause, not activated or dependent upon notices, which provided for by an increase to the current market rent with a reference to an independent valuer if the parties failed to agree. The landlords' solicitor wrote to the tenants offering (by mistake) a new rent less than the rent originally reserved. The defendants promptly accepted the offer. The plaintiffs having then rapidly appraised the defendants of the error sought summary judgment on the writ claiming a declaration that no binding agreement had been reached. In rejecting that claim, the Court of Appeal held the tenants could plead the apparent agreement even on the basis that they knew, or ought to have known, of the error in the letter. (The circumstances in which such knowledge might bar a claim are discussed in Chapter 9, p 281 below.)

3 Computation of time-limits

(a) Ascertainment of the relevant period

Time periods in rent review clauses will, almost invariably, be prescribing a period within which an act may or must be done; thus a lessor's trigger-notice may be served 'at any time not earlier than 6 months before a review date' (Conveyancer Precedent 5–57 and EFP (5th ed) Form 127) or 'at any time before the beginning of two clear quarters of a year' (EFP (4th ed) Form 7:1). A tenant's counter-notice, which is particularly important in this connection because time for its service is frequently expressly of the essence, may be served 'not later than 3 months after the service of the (lessor's) notice' (Conveyancer Precedents 5–57) and EFP (4th ed) Forms 7:1 and 8:1 and EFP (5th ed) Form 127 are to similar effect. Indeed, the 'may' is effectively 'must' in so far as timely service alone will prevent the prescribed consequences following. Clause 3(6) of the first draft of the Model Forms provided for notice by a tenant where the landlord has failed to initiate the review 'at any time [there] after' the first day for payment of the revised rent. The 1985 and 1980 Forms avoid even that phrase though are to a similar effect by stating a tenant's notice may be served 'whenever a revised rent in respect of any Review Period has not been agreed between the Landlord and the Tenant *before the relevant Review Date* and the landlord has not made application to the President for the time being of the Royal Institution of Chartered Surveyors as hereinbefore provided' (emphasis added). In both cases, therefore, a tenant's notice may be given once the relevant review date is passed. (For the rules for ascertaining the duration of periods of time, which may be highly significant in this context, see p 144 below.)

When time is of the essence and it is essential the notice be given within the time-limits, ascertainment of the exact duration of the period may be of importance. The general rule for ascertaining periods within which a person must act is that the day of the act or event from which the period runs should not be counted against him (*Halsbury's Laws* (4th ed) Vol 45 para 1127, and *Lester v Garland* (1808) 33 ER 748); since there is an important choice to be made there is no case for narrowing the time allowed (see *Lester v Garland* at 752). So a notice under a rent review clause may normally be served up to and including the last day specified or envisaged by the lease. This general rule accords with the prima facie approach to calculation of a period of time—namely, that the first day of a period will be excluded and the last day will be included (confirmed in *Trow v Ind Coope (West Midlands) Ltd* [1967] 2 QB 899).

In all cases, however, regard must be had to the exact words of the clause in question. In cases of doubt the words will be interpreted to effectuate the intention of the parties (*Halsbury's Laws* (4th ed, Vol 45, para 1127). It is clear, however, that the presumption can be displaced by clear words. Thus (i) an 'inclusive' period will include both the first and last days of a period; and (ii) the insertion of the word 'clear' as in 'two clear quarters' (eg EFP (4th ed) Form 7:1) has the effect of excluding both the first and last days of the period: in the case of Form 7:1, if time was of the essence the effect would be to invalidate a notice given actually on the quarter day. Where periods are expressed to be 'from' or 'after' such a day the general presumption will apply and the time will be computed excluding the specified day (*Acland v Lutley* (1839) 112 ER 1446; *Cartwright v MacCormack* [1963] 1 WLR 18); but a period 'beginning with' a particular date will be inclusive of that date (*Trow v Ind Coope*). Moreover, a lease for a term 'from May 1st' was held to be a lease starting on 1 May and not 2 May contrary to the usual presumption, since this was clear from the context of the lese, which provided for payment of rent in advance and for the first instalment on 1 May (*Ladyman v Wirral Estates Ltd* [1968] 2 All ER 197). The decision might well apply to a review notice calculated by reference to the anniversary date of the term of the lease (as Conveyancer Precedent 5–57); though, in many cases, there may be sufficient other evidence from the terms of the lease to confirm that the general presumption still applies and the method of computation of, or payment dates for, the rent will not, as in the *Ladyman* case, be decisive. Common examples would be when the term of the lease precedes the rent commencement date, or when there is a rent free period. If a lease or notice requires an act 'within' a certain period, then the full amount of that period is available to complete the action since 'within' is capable of meaning 'during' or 'before the expiry of': *Manorlike Ltd v Le Vitas Travel Agency and Consultancy Services Ltd* [1986] 1 All ER 573 (lease required 'not less than 3 months' notice; notice requiring tenant to vacate 'within' 3 months was valid). In *Maraday Ltd v Sturt Properties Ltd* [1988] 2 EGLR 163 a trigger-notice had to be served 'at least 6 months before the expiration of the period in question'. These words were given their literal meaning of allowing a late notice and a retrospective review to within 6 months of the expiration of the review period.

(b)   'Clear periods'

The use of the term 'two clear quarters' raised difficulties in *East v Pantiles (Plant Hire) Ltd* (1981) 263 EG 61 which involved a lease running from 1 August and with a review date of 1 August 1979, provided notice was served two quarters prior to the review date. Rent was payable on 1 November, 1 February and 1 May and on 14 August. The Court of Appeal refused to follow the trial judge in amending 14 August to 1 August, but held a notice served on 26 January met the two quarters requirement which was to be calculated to 31 July, notwithstanding the postponement of the rent payment date. In *Rowe & Co, Cornwall (Properties) Ltd v Ganton House Investments Ltd* (1983), 12 December, unreported, a notice had to be served before the beginning of a clear period of two quarters of a year 'commencing on one of the usual quarter days hereinbefore mentioned'. Yet although the quarterly rent days in the lease were not the *usual* quarter days (Lady Day, Midsummer, Michaelmas, Christmas) the notice given by reference to the traditional dates was good; the alternative construction of reference to the specified quarterly rent days would have invalidated the notice.

(c) 'The commencement of the term'

Problems may be caused when the period of time is computed from 'the commencement of the term'. Conveyancer Precedent 5–57, prior to an amendment, defined the 'review date' as 'each fifth anniversary of the commencement of the term'. This phrase will prima facie mean the date of the lease and not the date from which the term was calculated (*Roberts v Church Commissioners for England* [1972] 1 QB 278); for a lease cannot vest a term in a tenant before it is executed. This general principle has been applied in *Henry Smith's Charity Trustees v Hemmings* (1983) 265 EG 383 and in *Keen v Holland* [1984] 1 WLR 251. However, much will depend on the construction of the lease and the parties may, if they so intend, make an obligation or liability enforceable in respect of an earlier date (*Bradshaw v Pawley* [1979] 3 All ER 273 and see *Alan Estates Ltd v WG Stores Ltd* [1982] Ch 511). So, an option to determine may be drafted to date the break from a date described (strictly inaccurately) as the beginning of the term in the document (*Bird v Baker* (1858) 120 ER 812; *Page v Mallow Investments* (1974) 29 P & CR 168). *Bradshaw v Pawley* was applied in *Beaumont Property Trust Ltd v Tai* (1982) 265 EG 872 where a lease dated December 1979 created a term of 25 years from March 1976. On construction of the wording used the first review was held to be on a date calculated by reference to the earlier date, a mere 15 months or so into the lease but the end of the first 5 years of the term. It may well be a matter of chance or coincidence but it is interesting to observe that the cases where the period was held to run from the date of the lease all relate to statutory provisions and those where it was held to run from the computation date all involve construction of private documents (we are indebted to Professor Jill Martin for this observation).

To avoid doubt, therefore, it is wise to avoid dating a time-limit from the 'commencement of the term', or at least to expand the phrase to add the dates to put the matter beyond doubt. Conveyancer Precedent

5–57 has been altered accordingly. Where leases incorporate the earlier wording of Conveyancer Precedent 5–57 it was argued by one of the authors that, on construction of the wording, the review date is calculated from the date of the lease (see [1980] Conv 10; though it has to be said that, in a rent review context, it would be open to argue that the construction to be placed on the words is to the contrary effect, ie from the date from which the term is calculated. This latter interpretation was assumed to be correct without argument in *Shirlcar Properties Ltd v Heinitz* (1983) 268 EG 362. Most of the other published precedents in common use do not adopt the definition 'from the commencement of the term' as the sole basis for calculating review dates and consequent time-limits but refer to a specified term of years in the habendum and provide for differing rents for each review period in the reddendum. In such circumstances, it is clear from *Bradshaw v Pawley* (at 276) that the timetable runs from the date specified for the commencement of the term in the habendum and not from the date of the lease. In EFP (4th ed) Form 8:1 and Additional Form 76, however, the review is initiated by 'a notice in writing by the lessor to the tenant at any time before the expiration of the period of [six and a half years] *after the commencement of the term hereby granted*' (emphasis added). This could, it is submitted, be held to relate to the date of the lease, if different; though fortunately the precedents do not make time of the essence for service of this notice. An addition to the clause of the words 'namely the . . . day of . . . 19 . . . ' may be prudent or consistency could be achieved by reference to the 'said term' rather than the 'term hereby granted'. Only if a review date upon which notices depend is defined 'from the commencement of the term hereby granted' will, it is submitted, the reference will be to the date of the lease.

(d)   General rules of computation

For the purpose of computation of time periods in a rent review clause, it should be noted that:

    (i)   Fractions of a day will always be ignored (*Lester v Garland*)— so that a period can be complete even though strictly short by a fraction of a day; or, conversely, be incomplete even when a computation that includes fractions would make it complete (see, for example, *Cartwright v MacCormack*).

   (ii) 'Months' will mean calendar months (Law of Property Act 1925, s 61 (a)) and this statutory provision applies to all post-1925 deeds and leases. It will be only displaced where it is clearly stated otherwise and the context requires that the word means a lunar month of 28 days—it is not sufficient that the context admits of a construction of a lunar month (*Re Figgis* [1969] 1 Ch 123).

(e) *The corresponding date rule*

The meaning of 'calendar months' was considered in the important case of *Dodds v Walker* [1981] 1 WLR 1027. It was held by a majority in the Court of Appeal, but unanimously in the House of Lords, that where the time within which a person was required to act was fixed by reference to a period of months or calendar months from a particular date, the specified period elapsed on the corresponding day of the month of expiry. The case concerned a tenant's application for a new tenancy under Part II of the Landlord and Tenant Act 1954 which must be given 'no more than four months after the giving of the landlord's notice'. As was pointed out, had the landlord's notice been given on the day between the first and twenty-seventh of any month the expiry of the 4–month period would clearly have been on the corresponding date in the fourth succeeding month. However, the landlord's notice was served on 30 September; it was held that the period expired on 30 January and a tenant's application on 31 January was out of time. No account can be taken of the fact that some calendar months are shorter than others. Thus, in a rent review, if a tenant has to give a counter-notice 'within three months' of the service of the landlord's notice then:

(i) the period will normally expire on 'the corresponding day' (ie for a notice served on 20 November, the period will expire on 20 February);

(ii) where the landlord's notice is served on the last day of a short month, the period still ends on the corresponding day (thus, for a notice served on 30 April, the 3–month period will expire on 30 July; counter-notice on 31 July is too late);

(iii) where the landlord's notice is served on the 29th, 30th or 31st of any month, the 3–month period will expire on the corresponding day; but if there is no corresponding day because the relevant month is too short, then the period expires at the end of the month. Thus, where a landlord's notice is served on 31 March, the period expires on 30 June; for one served on 30 November, the period expires on 28 February (or 29 February in a leap year).

Some adverse criticism was directed at *Dodds v Walker* but, whatever rule is adopted, anomalies remain because calendar months are unequal in length. Prudent parties and their solicitors will ensure that notices are given in good time.

The corresponding date rule in *Dodds v Walker* was applied in *Riley (EJ) Investments Ltd v Eurostile Holdings Ltd* [1985] 2 EGLR 124 where the Court of Appeal held that the statutory requirement for service of a notice 'not less than two months after the giving of the landlord's notice' was satisfied where the landlord's notice was given on 23 March and the tenant's notice on 23 May. Thus service on the exact anniversary

of a date suffices if the relevant time is 'not less than . . . ' the specified
period; it would not suffice if it was required 'more than' a specified
period. Service on the anniversary would then be too early. Similarly,
in *Hogg, Bullimore Co Ltd v Cooperative Insurance Society Ltd* (1984)
50 P & CR 105 notice was given on 2 April to terminate a tenancy
under the 1954 Act, and the notice specified 2 October as the date of
determination. The notice was held as validly given 'on a date less than
six months before the date specified as the date for determination'.

(f)   Application to the precedents

Applying these principles to some of the published precedents
(reproduced in Part Seven) it is suggested that:

(i)   Clause 3(6) of the original 1979 draft of the Model Forms

Where notice by a tenant may be given to a landlord in default of
agreement on the revised rent and in default of the landlord applying
for arbitration, the tenant's notice may only be given after midnight
of the first day for payment of the revised rent, since the tenant is able
to give such notice 'at any time thereafter'. This construction is reinforced
by the provision that the notice may be given where the landlord has
not 'before that day made application . . .'—which will allow the landlord
to make application on the day itself. In the 1980 and 1985 Model Forms,
both phrases referred to above from the earlier clause 3(6) have been
deleted. Nevertheless, a tenant will still be precluded from giving a notice
earlier than after midnight of the review date, since a tenant's notice
may only be given 'Whenever a revised rent in respect of any Review
Period has not been agreed between the Landlord and the Tenant before
the relevant Review Date . . . ' It is, consequently, open for agreement
to be reached up to and including the review date.

(ii)   Conveyancer Precedent 5–57 and EFP (5th ed) Form 127

(a) Where, as in these two precedents, the lessor may serve a notice
    specifying the substituted rent 'at any time not earlier than 6
    months before a review date' and a review date is, say, 25 March,
    notice should be given before the review date; but late notice
    will be allowed since time is not of the essence for this notice.
    In *London and Manchester Assurance Co Ltd v G A Dunn &
    Co* (1982) 265 EG 39, 131 the court had to construe the meaning
    of the phrase 'at any time not earlier than 12 months prior
    to Dec 25 1977'. The majority on this point (Slade and Lawton
    LJJ) agreed that the notice had to be given before the specified
    date, while Oliver LJ was in the minority in preferring the

view that notice could be given any time after 25 December 1976.

(b) The 3–month period in which the parties may agree in writing or the tenant's counter-notice may be given (time to be of the essence) will be calculated from midnight following the date of the service of the lessor's notice up to midnight of the date 3 calendar months hence (thus, where the lessor's notice is served on 26 September, the 3–month period will exclude that day and run until midnight of 26 December and see the discussion on *Dodds v Walker* (above).

(c) The lessee's default notice under clause (b)(iv) of Conveyancer Precedent 5–57, which may be given where the lessor fails to given notice 'by the review date', may only be served after that date.

(d) The periods of the review machinery specified as 'within one month' in clauses (c) and (d) of Conveyancer Precedent 5–57 will be calendar months exclusive of the day from which they are calculated and inclusive of the final corresponding day and, again, see *Dodds v Walker*.

(iii)   EFP (4th ed) Forms 7:1 and 8:1 and Additional Form 76 (which are similar in purpose and design but with differences in wording)

The overall effect will be analogous to that of Conveyance Precedent 5–57 save that: (a) the lessor's notice, which all the precedents state must be given 'before' a certain date, should be served within that time-limit and notice on the last day of that period will be good (but since only Form 7:1 makes time of the essence for such notice, delay will only be of consequence in that case (*United Scientific*); (b) the 3–month period, where time *is* of the essence, will be 3 calendar months as in (*ii*)(b) above, but in Form 7:1 will be calculated from midnight of the date of *posting* of the notice (clause 3(b) and (c)) not the date of service or presumed service on the lessee as in Form 8:1 and Additional Form 76.

4   Excessive delay

The *United Scientific* case made it clear that in a case where time is not originally of the essence, whether expressly or impliedly, mere delay on the part of a landlord in enforcing his right to a rent review will not of itself debar him from a review out of time, though other adverse consequences can befall a landlord, for example, relating to the value of his interest. Thus, on an assignment of the reversion, a purchaser may feel unsure about operating a late review and not be prepared to add to the purchase price until agreement has been reached or a court has ruled in the landlord's favour (*Gates v Southwark London Borough* (1980) 254 EG 617 (LT). The difficulty has been in resolving the consequences of a delay that is 'excessive' or 'unreasonable'. There has been a measure of unanimity that there are some circumstances where delay can result in a review being lost but the sequence of cases since the *United Scientific* decision reveals a chronicle of conflicting views. Even now, the law can only be stated with a degree of diffidence, though in practice one thing is abundantly clear—the defences raised by tenants to a claim for a review after a long delay rarely succeed—save to the extent that their resolution itself involves further delay.

There are various suggested ways that a delay in proceeding to a rent review might lead to a total or partial loss of increased rent for the next review period. Of these, only a delay which may be the foundation of an estoppel is an indubitably valid defence. Arguments based on the period of delay itself (eg unreasonable delay, or abandonment) have either been rejected or seriously doubted.

(a)   Estoppel in pais or estoppel by representation

The defence of estoppel by representation, also known as estoppel in pais or (confusingly) as equitable estoppel, may be available *(Amherst v James Walker Goldsmith and Silversmith Ltd* [1983] Ch 305 at 316F). The requirements are strict and are unlikely to be found in many rent review situations:

> (i)   *A representation of existing fact* must be made, either by statement or conduct, although the representation may include a representation of law;
>
> (ii) *The representation must have been made with the intent that it be acted upon,* or at least the person who makes it must so conduct himself that another, as a reasonable man, would understand that the representation was intended to be acted upon;
>
> (iii) *The representation must be acted upon* by the person to whom it is made; and
>
> (iv) *An alteration to his prejudice* of the position of the person to whom the representation was made must have occurred.

The last three requirements are not dissimilar to those of promissory estoppel fully discussed in the section (b) of this chapter; it is the requirement of a representation of existing fact which distinguishes the two.

In *Esso Petroleum Co Ltd v Anthony Gibbs Financial Services Ltd* (1982) 262 EG 661 an estoppel in pais plea failed. The alleged representation of fact ('Rent £197,225. Rent Review July 6 1984') was made by an intermediate lessor to his lessee when suggesting the lessee might acquire the intermediate reversion. Both parties believed the next rent review was in 1984; neither appreciated that the decision not to review in 1978 (when it was apprehended that the then current rent exceeded the market rent) did not prevent a later review during the review period under an express provision to that effect in the lease. There was a representation of fact, which happened to be incorrect, but there was no evidence, or insufficient evidence, that the lessee either acted upon the representation, or suffered detriment. On appeal, (1983) 267 EG 351, the lessee's estoppel allegation was dropped.

Taylor's Fashions Ltd v Liverpool Victoria Trustees Co Ltd [1982] QB 133, though not a rent review case, illustrates a successful defence of estoppel by representation. In that case, two leases to tenants gave options to renew which were dependent upon the exercise of an option to renew in another lease of adjoining premises. In fact, that other option was void for want of registration. It was held the representation in the leases founded an estoppel; the tenants took the lease in reliance upon the existence of the other option and incurred expenditure in expectation of its exercise. Though these facts dealt with an option, one can easily imagine a similar result if an underlease was to contain an incorrect representation about the state of rent review in a head lease upon which the review in the underlease depended. A successful plea of estoppel by representation has occurred in the Australian case of *Gollin & Co Ltd v Karenlee Nominees Pty Ltd* [1982] VR 493 but the difficulty of establishing it in the landlord and tenant context is shown by the case of *Stevens & Cutting Ltd v Anderson* [1990] 1 EGLR 95.

If an estoppel in pais is established, it will preclude the party estopped from asserting any fact to the contrary (*James v Heim Gallery (London) Ltd* (1980) 41 P & CR 269 at 275).

(b) Promissory estoppel

The doctrine revived by *Central London Property Trust v High Trees House Ltd* [1947] KB 130 affords a defence to the tenant when faced by a claim to a late review of the rent. The suggestion that the principle of estoppel might assist a tenant in such circumstances appears, obiter, in three early reported decisions: *Essoldo Ltd v Elcresta Ltd* (1971) 23 P & CR 1 at 6, *CH Bailey Ltd v Memorial Enterprises Ltd* [1974] 1 WLR 728 at 732F, and in *Accuba v Allied Shoe Repairs Ltd* [1975] 1 WLR 1559 at 1564E, and has been accepted as a valid defence in a number of appellate decisions since then, particularly in *Amherst v James Walker Goldsmith and Silversmith Ltd* [1983] 3 WLR 334. Strikingly, however, the defence has never, to the authors' knowledge, been ultimately successful in a reported rent review case. The difficulties faced by those who raise the defence are illustrated by *James v Heim Gallery (London Ltd* (1979) 39 P & CR 155 (first instance); (1980) 41 P & CR 269 (CA) where an initial success was overturned on appeal. In that case a rent review was to operate from 25 June 1972 and the lessors were to give written notice of their desire for a review not less than 6 months prior to that date. The lessors' notice was late and the lessee contended that the right to review had been lost. This appeared to be tacitly accepted by the lessors since the lessee's contention was understood to be the law at that time. Certainly, at a subsequent chance meeting between the parties, the lessor remarked that 'One can't always win'. For a period of 5 years rent at the original figure was demanded and paid without qualification. The tenants, subsequently assuming the right to review was lost, conducted their affairs, prepared accounts, paid tax, and generally acted on the basis that the existing rent would remain unchanged. Following the decision in the *United Scientific* case in 1977, the lessors sought to contend that their original notice in 1972 was valid and they were entitled retrospectively to a reviewed rent. At first instance it was held that the lessors' representations by words and conduct caused the lessee to assume a state of affairs from which the lessors were disentitled to depart by reasserting their rights. However, the Court of Appeal held that the tenant had failed to establish the basic requirements of promissory estoppel.

Unlike estoppel in pais, promissory estoppel involves a promise as to future conduct. *James v Heim Gallery* is not only illustrative of the difference of judicial opinion which can result when applying the law to a given set of facts, but also indicates that it will not be easy to ascertain when an estoppel can be raised in law. For the scope of promissory estoppel is notoriously uncertain 'raising problems of coherent exposition' (per Lord Hailsham in *Woodhouse AC Israel Cocoa Ltd SA v Nigerian Produce Marketing Co Ltd* [1972] AC 741 at 758). The problems are fully discussed in Spencer Bower and Turner, *Estoppel by Representation,* Chapter 14. Nevertheless, it is submitted that where a tenant raises the defence of promissory estoppel when faced with a late claim for rent review the following principles apply:

(i) It will be necessary for the tenant to show that the landlord made a promise or assurance either by his words or his conduct or both as to the future conduct of the rent review

The words or conduct should amount to 'a promise or representation' that is intended to be binding (per Lord Denning MR in *Brikom Investments Ltd v Carr* [1979] QB 467 at 482). A promise is thus at the heart of the principle and it will be difficult to spell out that promise from conduct alone: *Stevens & Cutting v Anderson* [1990] 1 EGLR 95. It is true that the principle has been stated in a wider form, reducing the emphasis on the positive representation as in *Crabb v Arun District Council* [1976] Ch 179 where it was stated as a principle preventing a person insisting on his strict legal rights whenever 'it would be inequitable for him to do so having regard to the dealings which have taken place between the parties' (per Lord Denning MR at 187–8). On the other hand, there is a strong body of opinion that would limit promissory estoppel to a course of negotiation that would have the effect of leading one of the parties to suppose that the strict rights arising under the contract will not be enforced *(Brikom Investments Ltd v Carr* per Roskill LJ at 486, adopting a passage from Spencer Bower and Turner, p 313, which quoted *Hughes v Metropolitan Railway* (1877) 2 AC 439,448).

It was the stricter view which was applied in *James v Heim Gallery*. The statement 'one can't always win' and the dropping of the words 'without prejudice' from the rent demands might have been sufficient within the wider formulation but the Court of Appeal held that there was no clear and unequivocal representation by words or conduct that the landlord would not reply on his strict contractual rights. The Court of Appeal took the view that the plaintiff landlords, following their notice to review being out of time, tacitly accepted the contention of the defendant tenant—that the review was lost—on a view of the law subsequently held in the *United Scientific* case to be incorrect. Such acceptance, it was held, involved nothing in the nature of a promise.

(ii) The representation made must be with the intention, or at least the knowledge, that it is to be acted upon by the other party

This was stated as a separate requirement by Oliver LJ in *James v Heim Gallery*, though it is inherent in the nature of the estoppel. Thus it was said that, even if the words in that case had been a promise, they were not made with the requisite intent or knowledge.

(iii) The tenant, in the light of the promise or assurance, must so act or abstain from acting in reliance thereon with the result that he would be prejudiced if the landlord was allowed to proceed with the review

There are two aspects to this requirement, namely reliance on the promise and consequent prejudice. Both aspects have been the subject of inconsistent judicial pronouncements.

(1) Reliance: In both the *Essoldo* and *Accuba* cases it was said that estoppel could only be raised by a tenant as a defence to a claim for review if he had altered his position, and that positive evidence to this effect must be led by the tenant. In *James v Heim Gallery*, the Deputy Judge held this requirement was satisfied but once again the Court of Appeal took a different view. It was true that the tenant had done various things, or abstained from acting, on the assumption that there would be no review: but the plaintiff landlord knew nothing of the tenant's financial affairs. It was because of the tenant's confidence in its solicitor's and accountant's advice that it acted as it did, rather than because of any promise or representation by the landlords. Similarly, in *Vince v Alps Hotels Ltd* (1980) 258 EG 330, the landlord failed to observe a time-limit in review machinery in 1975. Following the decision in the *United Scientific* case, the review was reopened over 2 years later. A defence, apparently of estoppel in pais, failed, it was being held that the tenants had relied

upon their solicitor's advice rather than any conduct of the landlords. A similar example is *Glofield Properties Ltd v E B Tobacco Ltd* (1985) 273 EG 74 where the tenants relied on their self-induced belief that they had given a valid counter-notice by letter, not on any act or promise of the landlord.

Thus, there must be an acting on the promise of representation, in the sense that the tenant has altered his position on the faith if it and acted differently to what he would otherwise have done, for the requirement to be satisfied *(WJ Alan & Co Ltd v El Nasr Export and Import Co* [1972] 2 QB 189). There is some authority suggesting that the principle extends wider than this: that it is sufficient to show that the representation was calculated to influence the judgment of a reasonable man; and, once shown, the presumption is that he is so influenced *(Brikom Investments v Carr,* per Lord Denning MR, at 483; *Stevens & Cutting v Anderson* [1990] 1 EGLR 95). This, if correct, would mean that reliance on the promise, as traditionally interpreted, need not be shown nor, consequently, need evidence be led. Since the majority of the court in *Brikom* did not rest their judgments on promissory estoppel the view may be regarded as obiter, and certainly this more liberal approach finds no support in the judgments on estoppel in rent review cases. It is submitted that a tenant seeking to found an estoppel will need to show he relied on the representation and bring evidence to that effect and this view is supported by the decision in *Oldschool v Johns*, discussed below.

(2) Prejudice: In addition to showing reliance on the representation, the tenant may have to show that by altering his position he was thereby prejudiced. In some cases, it is expressed as saying that he must have 'suffered a detriment' and this was the view of Judge Thomas (sitting as a High Court Judge) in *James v Heim Gallery* at first instance, adopting a passage from pp 110–11 of Spencer Bower and Turner (which is itself a citation from the judgment of Dixon J in the Australian case of *Grundt v Great Boulder Proprietary Gold Mines Ltd* (1948) 59 CLR 64). As previously noted, the Court of Appeal held that, on the facts, there had been no promise and, even assuming a promise, there was no acting upon it. In the course of his judgment, Buckley LJ (at 274) appeared to criticise the reference made by Judge Thomas; with respect, this is unfair since the better view must be that prejudice, or detriment, must be shown for promissory estoppel as well as an estoppel in pais (see Spencer Bower and Turner pp 101–11 and 391–4). This accords with the basis of the decision in *Fontana NV v Mautner* (1979) 254 EG 199 where the inability of the defendant tenant to show reliance, whether by action or inaction, on a representation that possession of demised premises would not be sought and the absence of detriment to him at the moment the plaintiff landlord sought to resile from the

representation and seek possession of the demised premises meant that estoppel could not be successfully raised as a defence. Lord Denning has repeatedly argued that it is not necessary to show 'detriment' both extra judicially ((1952) 15 MLR 1 at 5) and judicially in *Alan v El Nasr* where he pointed out that acting on the belief induced by the representation may not result in detriment to the party. Indeed, it may be a 'benefit to him to have an extension of time or pay less as the case may be'—a particularly apposite view for a rent review where a delay will give the tenant the benefit of the interest on the difference between the rent he is paying and the higher sum payable on review (a benefit which will however be reduced or nullified if the lease provides for interest to be paid retrospectively). This view, that there is no need for prejudice or detriment, appears to have been applied in *Ogilvy v Hope-Davies* [1986] 1 All ER 683. However, it may be that 'detriment' in this context only means injustice to the promisee that would result if the promisor were allowed to resile from his promise (Spencer Bower and Turner, pp 392–3). If this is so, once the representation and reliance are shown then 'detriment and prejudice to the defendant are bound to flow from the change of position when the rights are reasserted' *(James v Heim Gallery,* first instance decision at 162).

According to Viscount Simonds in *Tool Metal Manufacturing Co Ltd v Tungsten Electric Co Ltd* [1955] 1 WLR 761, 'the gist of the equity lies in the fact that one party has by his conduct led the other to alter his position' and that some prejudice must inevitably flow therefrom. Be that as it may, a tenant raising the defence of estoppel will be wise to bring evidence of the prejudice or detriment he would suffer should a late review be allowed to operate retrospectively. Though the length of delay will of itself be immaterial to establishment of an estoppel, delays of a substantial period (a year or more) will produce prejudice of an obvious or usual kind. 'The tenant will probably have done his costings, made up his accounts, paid his taxes and generally ordered his affairs on the footing that there would be no increase in rent' (Hague, 1979 Blundell Memorial Lectures, p 76). Indeed, this was exactly the position in *James v Heim Gallery*. Barnsley (p 269) suggests that a sub-lease on the basis of the unrevised rent, or expenditure on improvements in the belief that the rent would be unchanged, would be examples of prejudice, though the latter example could hardly apply if the lease states that such improvements are to be disregarded in assessing the new rent. The suggestion by Barnsley that hardship would be sufficiently established by the tenant having to find at short notice a large sum (by way of the difference between old and new rents) is more difficult to accept in view of the opinions in the *United Scientific* case that mere delay in determination of the rent works to the economic benefit of the tenant since he has the use of that money in the meantime (eg per Lord Diplock at 932A).

Nevertheless, proof of prejudice, however severe, will be of no avail unless the necessary pre-conditions—ie the promise and the reliance thereon (and not on someone else—eg solicitor's advice) are satisfied. Thus in *James v Heim Gallery* the tenant, who perhaps could not be said to have acted imprudently at any stage, faced a relatively large bill for rent retrospectively due over a 6–year period.

(c) Establishing an estoppel

When the defence of estoppel is raised the following practical points must be borne in mind:

(i) Each of the requirements of law outlined above must be satisfied: It should now be clear that an estoppel will be the exception rather than a common occurrence. Thus:

(1) There may be no clear words or conduct of the landlord but merely a period of delay and inaction until the landlord 'wakes up' and seeks a late review. The current rent, perhaps payable by bankers' standing order, may not even be the subject of a rent demand and receipt. Collecting the existing rent in such a fashion will be insufficient to found an estoppel.

(2) The only 'conduct' upon which the tenant can rely may be a demand and receipt for the rent currently payable for rent periods after the review date. This will be insufficient (of itself) to found an estoppel, especially where (as in Model Forms and many rent review clauses) there is express provision for rent to continue to be paid at the rate previously payable until the revised rent is ascertained (see eg *Glofield Properties Ltd v E B Tobacco Ltd* (1985) 273 EG 74). Moreover, the conduct must be acted upon by the tenant and since the tenant often has, in effect, the opportunity to initiate the review himself either under the express terms of the lease or by serving a notice making time of the essence, it becomes even less likely that a demand or receipt for rent can, of itself, found an estoppel.

(3) Where the tenant relies upon a series of acts or omissions, it is still essential to be able to point to words or conduct 'in the nature of a promise' (per Buckley LJ, *James v Heim Gallery* at 277) or a representation of existing fact (for an estoppel in pais). An oral or written assurance by a lessor to the effect, express or implied, that he had decided not to pursue a review ought to be sufficient. However, in *Esso Petroleum Co Ltd v Anthony Gibbs Financial Services Ltd* (1983) 267 EG 351 an informal preliminary agreement between the parties' surveyors did not amount to a concluded rent review so an express provision in the lease for a later notice of review could operate. The tenant did not plead estoppel. Where a lease called

for a counter-notice for the tenant to elect for independent determination of the rent, the fact that the parties entered into correspondence about a new lease was insufficient to found a estoppel, and the lessor could rely on the rent stated in his trigger-notice: *Glofield Properties Ltd v E B Tobacco* (above).

(ii)   An estoppel can only be established by clear evidence: Since a defence of estoppel (of whatever kind) may ultimately depend on detailed evidence as to what exactly happened, it is desirable that a case the decision of which depends upon an estoppel should be tried on pleadings with discovery and oral evidence, and not by originating summons (*James v Heim Gallery*, per Buckley LJ at 274).

(iii)   A tenant who successfully pleads promissory estoppel will normally only succeed in preventing a review of the rent for the period of delay from the review date until such time as the landlord reasserts his right to review: This is the consequence of estoppel being a defence to a legal claim rather than giving rise to a clause of action. The right to review is suspended by the estoppel but not extinguished, for the estoppel does not give rise to a permanent modification of rights of the parties (Spencer Bower and Turner, p 395). Thus in *James v Heim Gallery*, at first instance, when the estoppel defence initially succeeded, the right to review could be resumed from 31 October 1977 for approximately the last 2 years of the 7-year review period. It was noted that once the right to review had been reasserted in 1977 the tenant had budgeted for an increase in rent from that time. There was, therefore, no representation on which the tenant could continue to rely.

However, there may be exceptional circumstances where the right to review could not be automatically reasserted. For an estoppel modifies legal rights for as long as it is equitable to do so and, thus, a clear representation, on which the tenant relied, that the landlord would not seek a review for the whole of the period should prevent a reassertion of the right. It is true that there are dicta to the effect that a promissory estoppel may be applied 'not only so as to suspend strict legal rights but also preclude the enforcement of them' (*D & C Builders v Rees* [1966] 2 QB 617 at 624). However, this would appear to be inconsistent with the decision in the *Tool Metal* case, and in *Emmanuel Ayodeji v RT Briscoe (Nigeria) Ltd* [1964] 1 WLR 1326 (PC), their Lordships said 'that the promisor can resile from his promise on giving reasonable notice, which need not be formal notice, giving the promisee a reasonable opportunity of resuming his position' (at 1330). In *Brikom Investments Ltd v Carr*, where the lessors had made an oral representation that they would pay the cost of repairs to the roof of a block of flats, they were not allowed to go back to the strict rights under the lease. However, this case is really an example of a clear representation in respect of particular repairs: it was inequitable for them ever to seek to re-establish their rights to charge for those repairs; or alternatively, the promise became final and irrevocable because the tenant could not resume his position (*Ajayi v*

Briscoe at 1330). Their rights to charge for other matters under the covenant had not been extinguished.

Consequently, a successful plea of estoppel should normally result only in a loss of an increase in rent during the period of delay and the rent may still be reviewed for the part of the review period yet to come, though the rent would be valued at the rate appropriate to the review date. A result is thus produced that is fair, doing rough justice between the parties. It appeared cases were once settled on this basis (Hague 1979 Blundell Memorial Lectures, p 77), but it is less likely now given that a claim of estoppel is so difficult to establish.

(iv)   The benefit of an estoppel may be personal to the tenant to whom it is made and the benefit may not be claimed by an assignee of the tenant: In *Brikom Investments v Carr*, Lord Denning MR stated at 484–5 that such a benefit was not personal to the promisee. However, though an assignment on the strength of a representation would found a clear estoppel for the assignor, it is difficult to see how an assignee can claim the benefit of an estoppel founded on a promise made to somebody else. This was the clear view of Cumming-Bruce LJ in *Brikom* (at 490H). Perhaps one way of resolving these directly opposing views is to say that a representation or a promise made to the tenant qua tenant will 'run with the estate' to an assignee, whereas one which is personal to the tenant will not. The difficulty with such an analysis is one of evidence, for it may not be clear whether the representation was personal or not. It is submitted, therefore, that an assignee of a tenant cannot rely on an estoppel unless the representation is repeated to the assignee or (possibly) if the representation is clearly made to the tenant in his capacity as tenant.

(v)   Inaction on the part of the tenant: There is one further hurdle a tenant might face in establishing promissory estoppel. He may have to satisfy the court that it was not unreasonable to refrain from setting the review machinery in motion himself, either by using any right given to him by the lease or, if necessary, by serving a notice making time of the essence (a procedure canvassed in the *United Scientific* case and discussed in section 6 (*a*) of this chapter, below). It is submitted that, though this will be a factor disentitling him to equitable relief, it ought not to be decisive for the existence of the promise or representation on which the estoppel is founded is the very reason why a tenant may say he was led to believe such action or notice was unnecessary. Consequently, the defence of estoppel may be successfully pleaded even where the tenant has not set the review in motion himself.

Finally, it should be noted that estoppel may be raised in situations other than that of delay. Thus, in *Oldschool v Johns* (1980) 256 EG 381 a tenant who had failed to serve a proper counter-notice argued that the landlord was estopped by representations in a letter he had written, and by continuing negotiations, from imposing the quantum of rent specified in his activating notice. The defence failed because the representations made by the landlord were not clear and unambiguous and, in any event, there was insufficient evidence that the representations (such as they were) had been relied upon. An example of a successful pleading of an estoppel relating to an agricultural tenancy occurred in *Troop v Gibson* [1986] 1 EGLR 1. An agricultural rent arbitration was conducted on the basis that there was no written tenancy agreement. Later the tenant assigned the tenancy only for the landlords to claim possession on the basis of a 1923 written tenancy agreement which had come to light and which prohibited assignment. The arbitration proceedings estopped the claim but the prohibition on assignment applied for the future.

(d) Waiver

The concept of waiver of a contractual right may assist as a defence. The term 'waiver' is used with different meanings and it is not proposed to dwell on the difficulties here and the reader is referred to standard contract texts; see also Dugdale and Yates (1976) 39 MLR 680. Waiver has been described as 'the process whereby one party voluntarily grants a concession to the other party by not insisting upon the precise mode of performance provided in the contract' (*Halsbury's Laws* (4th ed) Vol 9, para 571.) As so described, it might be apposite in a rent review. For example, a landlord may 'waive his rights' to a rent review. In such a case, where there is no breach of the contractual terms of the lease, waiver in this context is substantially a variation of the terms of the contract and, as such, an agreement (not necessarily supported by consideration) between the parties must be shown for the waiver to be effective. On the other hand, as in the case of *Oldschool v Johns* (above) the tenant may allege that the landlord has waived his right to insist on the proper counter-notice in the form and time demanded by the lease. In this context, the idea of 'waiver' is analogous to promissory estoppel, for the tenant is alleging 'an unambiguous representation arising as a result of a positive and intentional act done by the party granting the concession with knowledge of all material circumstances', and must show he acted in reliance on the concession (*Halsbury's Laws* op cit, para 574). In this context waiver is not a consensual variation of terms, but close to promissory estoppel—indeed in *W J Alan & Co Ltd v El Nasr Export and Import Co* [1972] 2 QB 189 at 212, Lord Denning said waiver was an example of the same principle as promissory estoppel. It does not, though, require any 'acting to detriment' whereas promissory estoppel may do so; but it does have the additional feature of 'knowledge of all material circumstances'.

Significantly, waiver is sometimes spoken of as 'an abandonment of a right in such a way that the other party is entitled to plead the right by way of . . . avoidance if the right is thereafter reasserted' (*Halsbury's*

Laws (4th ed) Vol 16, para 1471)—and this may explain the source of the now discredited concept of abandonment of a rent review by delay.

Waiver as a defence was successfully pleaded by a tenant in the Scottish case of *Banks v Mecca Bookmakers (Scotland) Ltd* (1982) SLT 150 (one of the few reported Scottish rent review cases). Lord Grieve applied the *United Scientific* case in holding that the landlord was not in principle barred from a late review, but held that, by accepting rent at the pre-review level at the quarterly terms (for 2 years in one case and one in another), the landlord had waived his right to seek a rent review. For Lord Grieve, waiver was 'concerned with whether or not a right under contract has been abandoned'—and a tenant did not have to show that he was prejudiced. The *Banks* case was not referred to in *Amherst v James Walker* (see p 159, below) nor was the doctrine of waiver argued when that case rejected the defence of delay. Even Scottish commentators accept that it is unlikely the *Banks* case would have been decided in the same way in England. It may be possible to regard this case 'as reflecting a genuine difference in the law north of the border' (McAllister, Scottish Law of Leases) though it is not obvious that the principle of waiver is different in the two jurisdictions.

(e) Defences based on delay

In the first edition of this book (pp 106–10), we were able to suggest, on the basis of dicta in the *United Scientific* case and elsewhere, that in certain circumstances, a period of delay could result in the loss of the review though doubts were expressed as to the correctness of the concepts. Those doubts were justified and as far as the Court of Appeal are concerned, the defences have been rejected or seriously questioned. Those defences have been stated in three forms which will be considered in turn:

(i) A period of unreasonable delay

This idea found expression in the early case of *Accuba Ltd v Allied Shoe Repairs Ltd* [1975] 1 WLR 1559, where Goff J was of the view that where the delay has been unreasonable the tenant could treat the contract as broken. The concept was based on the principle enunciated in *Farrant v Olver* [1922] WN 47 but since that case was concerned with notices to complete a contract for the sale of land it was by no means certain that the principle extended to delay to proceed to rent review, though the linking of the principle to the two different factual situations was perhaps made by Lord Simon in the *United Scientific* case (at 942C-D ff). The one case where it was held a review was lost because the lessor company was guilty of such a delay (6 years in the context of a 7–year review period in a 14–year term) as to make it unreasonable for it to call on the lessee for a review was *Telegraph Properties (Securities) Ltd v Courtaulds* (1981) 257 EG 1153. This case has now been overruled by *Amherst v James Walker Goldsmith and*

Silversmith Ltd (No 2) [1983] Ch 305. The analogy with *Farrant v Olver* was rejected and it was held that there is no ground for saying that mere delay, however lengthy, destroys the contractual right to a review. The matter was seen as one of construction of the contract, so that, if it was construed with time of the essence, the review is lost; if not, then the right to review subsists and the tenant is not discharged from his obligation to submit to a review by mere passage of time.

In *New Zealand*, a number of cases (prior to the decision in *Amhurst* but partly founded on English decisions and dicta existing at the relevant time) held that a delay could lead to the loss of a rent review: *PTY Industries Ltd v Penrose Sawmilling Co Ltd* (1972) 7 New Zealand Recent Law 150, *Aetna Life of Australia & New Zealand Ltd v Grace Bros Ltd* [1975] 2 NZLR 577 and *Peter Fortzer v Ryan* (1983), unreported. However, in *Wing Crawford Holdings Ltd v Lion Corporation Ltd* [1989] 1 NZLR 562 applied the *Amherst* decision and held that, even though a 19 month delay in the context of 30 month review periods was unreasonable, the lessor was entitled to initiate the review since there was no evidence of an estoppel nor of a notice by the lessee requiring a review within a reasonable time. The case of *Barber v Barber* [1987] 1 NZLR 426 in the New Zealand Court of Appeal was distinguished (right to increase rate of interest in a mortgage deed carried the implication it would be exercised within a reasonable time).

(ii) Abandonment of the review

The idea of abandonment of a review as a separate legal concept appeared in *Kirkland Properties Limited v GRA Developments Ltd* (1978) 4 May, unreported, where Slade J was of the opinion that: 'The right to enforce a rent review clause on [sic] which time was not of the essence could in my judgment be lost, even in the absence of evidence of hardship to the tenant, if the delay in enforcing it was so great as to amount to evidence of abandonment of the right'. The concept was, understandably, approved in the judgment of Slade LJ in *London & Manchester Assurance Company Ltd v G A Dunn & Co* (1983) 265 EG 39 and 133 at 135 where his Lordship stated that a long and inexplicable delay could amount to sufficient evidence that a landlord has abandoned his right to review. The first instance decisions of *H West & Son Ltd v Brech* (1981) 261 EG 156, *Printing House Properties Ltd v J Winston & Company Ltd* (1982) 263 EG 725 and *Million Pigs v Parry* (No 2) (1983) 268 EG 809 also assume the existence of this defence. However, in the *Amherst* case (above), Oliver LJ (at 316—Lawton LJ agreed with what he said) opined that he could not see how a contractual right could be lost by abandonment or non-exercise of that right. This view though firmly expressed does appear to be strictly obiter since (see Ackner LJ at 318G) the tenant in that case did not seek to suggest that the landlord had abandoned his entitlement to invoke the review clause. It does, however, appear to accord with Lord Brandon's restricted interpretation of the circumstances in which a contract can be abandoned (*Paal Wilson & Co v Partenreedreei Hannah Blumenthal* [1983] 1 AC 854) which would limit abandonment to the inference of implied agreement from the conduct of both parties or estoppel.

(iii) Unreasonable delay causing hardship

The genesis of this formulation is the opinion of Lord Salmon (at 956C) in the *United Scientific* case:

'if the lessors had been guilty of unreasonable delay which caused prejudice or hardship to the lessees they would have forfeited their rights to be paid the market rent from April 8 1975 to April 8 1982'

ie for the whole of the review period—the dates were those appearing in the lease and perhaps should have read to 'April 7 1982']. This dictum raises a number of problems:

(1) It could provide a separate means by which delay may result in a rent review being lost. The dictum was so treated in *Kirkland Properties Ltd v GRA Developments Ltd* (above) where all three concepts (ie estoppel, abandonment by substantial delay, and unreasonable delay resulting in hardship) were stated as separate principles. Nevertheless, Lord Salmon quoted no authority for this view and began his dictum: 'I certainly would agree that . . . '. This means it is unlikely that a new principle was being propounded and it would be an unfortunate complication if it were so. Arguments on hardship without any express basis do not usually provide a base for sound legal principles. Moreover the idea of delay causing hardship as a separate defence has been doubted in the Court of Appeal by Slade LJ in the *London & Manchester* case, and by the majority in the *Amherst* case.

(2) Lord Salmon may have assimilated, intentionally or otherwise, two grounds (estoppel and abandonment by delay) previously outlined. In the authors' view, this is unlikely since such an uneasy alliance of ideas can only lead to confusion.

(3) A third possibility, preferred by the authors in the first edition, is that Lord Salmon's dictum is a statement of the principle outlined above that an inexplicable delay can lead to an abandonment of the right to review, but with the additional requirement that there must be prejudice or hardship to the lessees and this was assumed in some early first instance decisions (eg *H West v Brech* (above). Support for such a requirement might be deduced from Lord Diplock's speech in the same case, for he emphasised that absence of any serious detriment to the tenant in support of the general principle that time is not of the essence. If this is so then some evidence of prejudice or hardship may have to be shown; for as Lord Salmon remarked, no such evidence had been shown in the

United Scientific case. This approach has not found favour with the Court of Appeal, as noted above.

If all the above views are to be rejected, then Lord Salmon's dictum must be a reference to the principles of promissory estoppel. There is no suggestion of this in his speech, since his Lordship made no reference to promises or representations or to the disputed matters of reliance and detriment previously discussed and there are further clear references to 'unreasonable delays' causing prejudice earlier in his Lordship's speech (eg at 950G, 953G-H). Nevertheless, Oliver and Lawton LJJ in the *Amherst* case were forcefully of the view that estoppel was what Lord Salmon had in mind (at 316E).

(f) The present position

A tenant, who after a long delay receives a claim for a retrospective review out of time, may resist the claim if he can found an estoppel (or perhaps waiver). This will require evidentiary proof of:

(1) a promise or representation in conduct or words;
(2) reliance by the tenant on such promise and (probably) proof of detriment.

Additionally, an estoppel will not normally prevent the right to review being re-asserted for the rest of the review period. If an estoppel cannot be founded, it is now extremely unlikely that any other defence will be accepted, though until there is a definitive decision by the House of Lords some uncertainty remains. There may be a financial inducement for a tenant to seek that definitive resolution of the issue, for a defence based on delay, if ultimately successful would not require: (i) proof of any promise or representation as with an estoppel claim; nor (ii) need a tenant show he acted to his detriment though, on Lord Salmon's formulation, proof of prejudice or hardship would be required. Moreover, unlike estoppel, if the claim is made out, it seems that the right to review would be lost or 'forfeit' for the whole of the review period as reference to Lord Salmon's words quoted above makes clear, and it certainly is a logical consequence of 'forfeiting' or 'abandoning' a right.

Whether or not there should be a defence to a late review based on inordinate delay is an open question. Perhaps an elementary principle of justice is at the root of the claim for tenants that there must be some limit to scandalous delay, some period after which a landlord would forfeit his rights by idleness. Certainly despite the prevailing judicial opinion that delay is a prima facie advantage to the tenant, a late review with retrospective payments due can be a heavy burden on a tenant who has acted, perhaps not imprudently, on the basis the review was lost or abandoned. On the other hand, it is not easy to divine a sound juridical basis for any delay defence. The principle that recission of a contract may be implied where there is a long period of delay (see Chitty, para 1484) is hardly applicable to the continuing relationship of landlord and tenant. A more fruitful line of argument is to distinguish those review clauses which do impose time-limits, albeit not of the essence, and those which require or allow a review unhindered by any stated date. Such a distinction between 'express' and 'silent' clauses was made by Goulding J in *Million Pigs v Parry* (1983) 268 EG 809; and in the *London & Manchester Assurance* case (1983) 265 EG 39 where Oliver LJ stated:

Delay, can, as I see it, be relevant only where there can be deduced from the contract some obligation to act earlier. Where the contract itself, on its true construction, envisages that the landlord may exercise his right at any time, early or late in the period, he cannot be said to be guilty of unreasonable delay if he simply does what the contract entitles him to do.

On this basis it can be argued that, just as damages may be obtained for failure to comply with a fixed date for completion if damage can be shown even where time is not of the essence (*Raineri v Miles* [1981] AC 1050, see p 117, above), and the right to specific performance of a contract can be lost by extensive delay (*MEPC Ltd v Christian-Edwards* [1978] Ch 281), so also delay might lead to loss of a review. Yet notwithstanding his dictum in the *London & Manchester* case, Oliver LJ specifically rejected this line of reasoning in the *Amherst* decision already referred to. If this is right then it appears the early opinion of a distinguished advocate in the rent review field has prevailed: 'nothing short of an equitable estoppel will defeat a review' (Colyer, 1977 Blundell Memorial Lectures p 7). Tenants' advisers will have to rely on the remedies noted in section (g), below; or on better drafting to cope with future delays.

(g) Drafting response

Where time is not of the essence, the possibility and consequences of a delayed review should be borne in mind when considering the draft lease. One approach is to side-step the issue by making it clear that a late notice, or notice after the review date is valid. Thus, the Model Forms impose an optional 'longstop' time-period for application by the landlord to the President of the RICS in default of agreement, such application to be made 'not later than the relevant Review Period' (clause 3). This provision, criticised earlier (see p 119), will be sufficient to stifle any argument that there has been an abandonment or unreasonable delay. Clause F of Variation C also gives the tenant power to initiate a review himself, and this feature is an important balancing provision for a tenant. A different procedure, but one achieving a similar result, is to provide specifically for a (separate) right to review after the review date if the landlord fails to call for a review in time. Such 'second bites at the cherry' can work injustice to the tenant (*Esso Petroleum Company Ltd v Anthony Gibbs Financial Services Ltd* (1983) 267 EG 351; *London & Manchester Assurance Company Ltd v G A Dunn & Co* (1982) 265 EG 33 and 131; and see p 148, above) but may avoid the 'insult added to injury' effect of a late review plus interest on the retrospective increase.

Tenants' advisers may prefer to cope with delay by placing a limit, not on the time for initiating the review, but on the length of the period rent is payable retrospectively by ensuring that the revised rent is only payable from the date of the notice or (with 'automatic' reviews) by limiting the retrospectivity directly. Much of the sense of grievance felt by tenants faced with a delay will then be avoided. Indeed, a lot of the 'heat' might be taken out of disputes over late notices if the general rule that they should only apply prospectively had been promulgated (at least one large property expressly so provided in its standard lease—see the reference in Colyer, 1977 Blundell Mmeorial Lectures, p 9). Sadly, it seems that retrospective effect (plus, often, interest for the delay which may not be of the tenant's making) is too firmly established to be displaced, although it creates much of the acrimony in this area. (See further Chapter 8, p 261).

5 Remedies for a tenant faced with excessive delay

A tenant of property subject to review that is overdue because of a default by a landlord in observing the time-limits contained in the lease is, since the *United Scientific* case, faced with a dilemma. Though he may be tempted to remain quiet and continue to pay the unreviewed rent, the above discussions on time issues and excessive delay illustrate the complex issues involved and the likelihood, if not certainty, in the absence of time being of the essence, that a late review will be allowed. The tenant will rarely, if ever, be able to relax, for a demand for a late review may be made—with the possible prospect of a large bill for the increased rent payable retrospectively to the review date. This will be a daunting prospect if interest is to be charged on the lump sum retrospectively due, whether by the express words of the rent review clause or under some general provision elsewhere in the lease.

The judgments in *United Scientific* stress the advantage to a tenant of having the use of the money representing the difference between the former rent and the new rent pending the delayed review (at 932A). This may appear to be poor compensation for a businessman who wishes to produce a reliable costing of his products in a competitive market or to assess the continuing viability of a branch or business showing a modest profit (which could be swallowed up if a rent fixed (say) 7 years earlier were to be trebled or quadrupled, as past experience has shown to be quite feasible), not to mention the need to know the amount of profit for an accurate tax computation (and declaration of dividend) and to avoid notes of contingent liabilities in an audited account. In such a situation, where the tenant reckons that the advantage of knowing exactly how much higher his new rent will be outweighs the economic benefit of the use of the money, he has, it is said, 'the remedy in his own hand' (*United Scientific* at 933G). However, since there is more than one remedy such a tenant may be forced to make a difficult tactical choice from the following:

(i) *He can often get a pretty good idea of the market rent from his own surveyor and plan his business on that basis.* A prudent tenant might choose to put aside the estimated extra sum where it will be readily available if a review is requested, and a revised rent agreed and determined, and at least he can earn some interest in the meantime. This remedy may result in an added bonus if in fact the landlord never 'wakes up' to initiate the review. There is the risk, still, that the tenant or his surveyor may underestimate the revised rent (cf the facts of *Charles Follett Ltd v Cabtell Investments Ltd* [1987] 2 EGLR 88).

(ii) *The tenant may open the negotiations for review himself.* This might be well in advance of the review date if need be and in a majority of cases a satisfactory review will eventually result. Nevertheless, the problem may re-occur if the negotiations or review mechanisms stagnate.

(iii) *The tenant may activate the review in those increasingly common cases where the initiative and completion of the review mechanism can be done by a tenant.* For example, as in Model Forms Variations A and B (clause 4(E) or clause 3(6) of the earlier drafts).

(iv) *Where review is initiated by a landlord's trigger- notice, or where the landlord is in breach of some other obligation to act in a particular time, then the tenant may serve a notice making time of the essence.* This is the ultimate remedy in these cases, according to the *United Scientific* decision, and arises once the relevant time-limit has elapsed. A tenant can then 'give to the landlord notice specifying a period within which he requires the landlord to serve a lessor's notice' initiating the review: 'The period so specified, provided it is reasonable, will become of the essence of the contract' (per Lord Diplock at 934A). This concept of a tenant's notice making time of the essence was described as 'startling' (Colyer, 1977 Blundell Memorial Lectures, p 7); and it can certainly be argued that it raises more problems for a tenant than it solves.

6 Service of notice making time of the essence

(a) The concept

The concept of 'notice making time of the essence' was borrowed from the doctrine applicable to defaults in completion of a contract for sale and purchase of land (eg *Stickney v Keeble* [1915] AC 386) and the extension of the idea to rent review clauses can be criticised from a number of aspects (see, for example, Smith [1979] Conv 10 at 14–15; Colyer, 1977 Blundell Memorial Lectures, p 8). The principle has not escaped criticism in the primary field of its operation either—see Sydenham [1980] Conv 19. Lord Simon explained in the *United Scientific* case, however, that to speak of a notice by one party making time of the essence is misleading. It is not a method by which one party introduces a new term into a contract, but rather a notice giving reasonable time for the performance of a pre-existing obligation (ie to review). In his view the notice thus 'operates as evidence that a promisee [tenant] considers a reasonable time for performance has elapsed by the date of the notice and as evidence of the date by which the promisee [tenant] now considers it reasonable for the contractual obligation to be performed' (at 946G). To put it another way, the effect of the notice is that a landlord ignores it on pain of being treated as electing to abandon the right to review.

The only reported rent review case where the doctrine has been considered in detail is *Factory Holdings Group Ltd v Leboff International Ltd* [1987] 1 EGLR 135 where Warner J held that the validity and use of the device depends on the tenant needing such a remedy. Consequently, the right to serve a notice making time of the essence will not exist for every tenant; he must require it. It cannot be used to avoid, fortuitously, his obligations under the lease.

Viewed in this light, the idea can be seen as an inevitable, if now limited, consequence of the *United Scientific* decision that time-limits that appear to necessitate compliance do not necessarily bind the parties. The notice by the tenant allows him to escape from any uncertainty or difficulty caused by the presumption enunciated in that case. Yet, however attractive the idea may be (and some may dispute its attractiveness), it is doubtful whether tenants and their advisers have made much use of the concept. Despite the torrent of cases reported in the years since the *United Scientific* case, there is only the *Leboff* case reported (to the authors' knowledge) where such a notice was served—and this is notwithstanding the failure of the defences raised after a delayed review (noted above) and the endorsement of the concept expressed in some of the judgments in those cases (a useful list of appellate dicta referring to the concept with approval is contained in the *Leboff* judgment at 137F). Indeed in the *Amherst (No 2)* decision the ability of the tenant to bring matters to a head by serving a notice fixing a time for performance was stated as the reason why the tenant could not legitimately claim the landlord had lost his right to review.

So it may be a tenant will have to consider this remedy. There are, however, a number of difficult practical problems a tenant has to face when considering serving a notice to make time of the essence.

(b) Limitations to the use of such a notice

It is implicit in the concept itself, from the speeches in the *United Scientific* case and from the *Leboff* decision, that service of such a notice is not possible unless it relates to a specific obligation on the other party to act in some way—eg to serve a trigger-notice or apply for an arbitrator to be appointed. For an 'automatic' review clause, without notice and where independent determination of the rent is not dependent upon application by one party alone, such a notice will not be possible.

Secondly, the *Leboff* case held that even where there is an obligation to act, and a time-limit for so doing, not every such limit can be subject to a notice making time of the essence. In that case, the review was of the trigger-notice type—and the lessor had duly given such notice. In default of agreement, determination was to be by an arbitrator. The lease was silent as to whether either or both parties could apply. The tenant purported to give a 28 day notice for the landlord to apply for appointment, a limit which the landlord failed to observe. However, it was held that the tenant could not serve such a notice. It was open to him to apply for the arbitrator to be appointed. He did not need to resort to such a notice; therefore he could not do so. Consequently, and notwithstanding that some of the appellate dicta might be read more widely, a notice making time of the essence can only be served if the lease provides for the landlord to act in a particular way within a particular time-limit and this step is not one that the tenant himself can take. On the other hand an argument in the *Leboff* case that the doctrine was only applicable to the first step in the trigger-notice procedure and not to any subsequent step was specifically rejected. The right to serve a notice making time of the essence is a remedy against inaction by the landlord, provided that the right can be conferred without unfairness to the landlord.

(c) Time for service of the notice

The timing of a notice may be crucial. If it is served too early then time will not run against the landlord and he will still be able to reopen the review in the future—and the whole object of giving the notice in the first place will be lost. In making the decision as to when to give the notice, the tenant must: (i) take into account general principles and (ii) make reference to the terms of the lease.

(i) General principles

There are three periods of time which may have to elapse before the landlord loses his review. The tenant must *first* wait for the relevant time-limit to expire and that will be a question of construction of the lease (just such an issue was disputed in the *Leboff* case—see 136L). *Secondly*, the tenant may have to wait a reasonable time before serving his notice. *Thirdly*, the tenant will, in his notice, stipulate a reasonable period of time during which the landlord may begin the review or otherwise act as the lease obliges him to do. In other words, 'a party who has been subjected to unreasonable delay gives notice to the party in default making time of the essence' (*Halsbury's Laws* (4th ed), Vol 9, para 481). The issue that remains unclear is the extent to which there is the second intermediate requirement of waiting for a reasonable time before serving the notice.

The requirement of a period of unreasonable delay, followed by a notice which gives a further reasonable period for the performance of the obligation, appears in three of the judgments in the *United Scientific* decision. Lord Fraser (at 958B) and Viscount Dilhorne (at 937E) both referred to the passage from *Halsbury's Laws* (noted above) with approval, and Lord Simon stated that notice giving time for performance could only be given 'after the lapse of a reasonable time'. Lord Diplock, however, was of a contrary view, stating that the tenant could give his notice as soon as the time-limit for service of the landlord's notice has elapsed (at 933H-934A). Support for the view of the majority may be found in *Re Barr's Contract* [1956] 1 Ch 551 where, in the context of notice to complete the contract for the purchase of land, it was said that 'at the time when the vendor purports to make time of the essence, the purchaser must be guilty of such default as to entitle the vendor to rescind the contract subject to its being done by reasonable notice' (at 556). Ackner LJ in *Amherst v James Walker Goldsmith & Silversmith Ltd (No 2)* [1983] Ch 305 at 318E also stated the rule as one requiring reasonable time to have elapsed before notice can be given. However, these cases must now be read in the light of *British and Commonwealth Holdings plc v Quadrex Holdings Inc* [1989] QB 42 where *Re Barr's Contract* was disapproved in so far as it established a general principle, though its applicability to notices to complete was said to be too long established to be overturned. In the *Quadrex* case, it was held to be open for an immediate notice to be given requiring the completion of an agreement to purchase shares within a reasonable time. The facts are not closely analogous to that of a notice requiring a rent review to be commenced though one can conceive of circumstances in a volatile market or of a proposed assignment of a lease where there could be a similar need for urgency.

There is much to be said for the minority view of Lord Diplock in *United Scientific*, which now has the authority of the *Quadrex* decision in its favour, that a notice can be served immediately the relevant time-limit has elapsed notwithstanding the fact that the weight of earlier authority is against it. In particular:

(1) The analogy to principles applicable to a vendor and purchaser was rejected in the *Quadrex* case. There may be good reasons for requiring a period of unreasonable delay, or default, when serving notice to complete a contract for the sale of land, for the party served may have problems in deducing title or finalising the finance of the purchase. Moreover, the notice making time of the essence, if not acted upon, will terminate the contractual relationship. In a review, on the other hand, the notice merely requires the landlord to start the review process, or make the requisite application to the agreed referee, which will be a simple matter to accomplish. Since the parties are in, and will remain in, a continuing contractual relationship it seems hard if the tenant should have to wait for a 'reasonable time'— an indeterminate period that may vary according to the circumstances—before taking action himself.

(2) If Lord Diplock is correct, then this approach to service of a tenant's notice would accord with common form clauses expressly permitting notice on these lines, as in Model Form, Variation C, clause 4(F) or Conveyancer Precedent 5–57, clause (iv).

(3) It may be difficult for a tenant or his advisers to decide just what period of time must elapse before the notice can be given. On the face of it, the words used in both *Re Barr's Contract* and in the quotation from *Halsbury's Laws* (given above) resemble closely those employed to define a period of unreasonable delay whereby it was earlier suggested that a review might be lost (see p 158). Yet it would be strange if a tenant had to wait for such a long period before serving his notice. Consequently, a reasonable period in this context ought to be shorter, but how short may be difficult to quantify: 'What is a reasonable time is a question of fact to be determined in all the circumstances' (Lord Simon, *United Scientific*, at 946). Much may depend on the length of the review period, and if the tenant has already informally notified the landlord of his oversight without response, then a notice making time of the essence would surely be justified.

The authors have a preference for Lord Diplock's view that notice can be served immediately the relevant time-limit has elapsed and the decision in *British and Commonwealth Holdings plc v Quadrex Holdings Inc* [1989] QB 42 may suggest that judicial opinion is now leaning in favour of this view. Nevertheless, there is still clear statements to the contrary so a prudent tenant would be advised to wait for whatever period he adjudges to be reasonable. Yet, even then, the terms of the lease may prevent such a notice.

(ii)   The terms of the lease

The speeches in the *United Scientific* case did not envisage any problem in serving notices making time of the essence. It was thought that this could be done once a reasonable time had elapsed from the specified time-limit (per Lord Simon) or immediately thereafter (per Lord Diplock). Certainly, it does not appear that the leases their Lordships were then considering would have caused difficulty, but this will not be true in every case.

The leases in both the *United Scientific* and *Cheapside* disputes contained fixed time-limits (ie 1 year before the start of the review period and a 2–month period after the lessor's trigger-notice) and it was a failure to observe these that was, respectively, at issue. In such cases, the expiry of these time-limits provides an occasion when service of a notice making time of the essence is appropriate. However, it is significant that both leases were granted in the 1960s long before the flurry of cases, beginning with *Samuel Properties (Developments) Ltd v Hayek* [1972] 1 WLR 1296, which alerted lessors to the danger that even a slight delay might lead to loss of a review. The *United Scientific* case may have shown that the danger was illusory but it was real enough for 5 years (1972–77) for many new leases granted in this period to provide expressly that a trigger-notice could be served over a very long period of time (perhaps for 1 or 2 years, 1 year either side of a review date, or even 'at any time' after a certain date). In such a lease it appears that service of a notice 'making time of the essence' is not possible for a considerable period (at least), for the contractual date for serving the notice has not elapsed (Aldridge (1977) 121 SJ 246 at 247). In *Maraday Ltd v Sturt Properties Ltd* [1988] 2 EGLR 163 a trigger-notice had to be served 'at least 6 months before the expiration of the period in question'. These words were given their literal meaning of allowing a late notice (and, indeed, a very late notice) and a retrospective review to within 6 months of the expiration of the review period. The tenant could not have served a notice making time of the essence in such a case except, presumably, towards the end of the final 6 months.

It is suggested that in those cases where there is no contractual limit at all a notice giving a reasonable period after the review date would suffice. This construction may be consonant with Lord Simon's formulation. This still leaves no remedy by notice to a tenant who is faced with a long contractual limit; he will only be able to rely on informal negotiations, and the remedy of serving a notice making time of the essence will not be available for a very long time. Yet the longer the delay, the more harmful a lump sum of 'arrears' may be to the tenant's business.

The revised version of the Model Forms, in clause 3, (in all three Variations; it also appears in the 1980 forms) introduces just such extended time-limits by (optionally) providing that a reference to the referee may be applied for 'not later than the end of the relevant Review Period'.

There is, however, no difficulty since either party can initiate the review or, at least, the tenant has a remedy in clause F of Variation C. It is only where there are extended time-limits to initiate a review and the tenant has no right to act himself that the tenant may be in difficulties.

One answer to such problems lies in an approach that avoids the need for a tenant to consider this type of notice. The idea is that a lessor can *always* serve notice or otherwise initiate an overdue review *but* can only obtain the revised rent from the rent day following such notice (suggested by Colyer, 1977 Blundell Memorial Lectures, p 9). A tenant in such cases need only consider taking action himself where he is considering assignment of his term and requires completion of the review to assist the process of sale, since he is protected against a claim for a retrospective increase in his rent.

(d)   Reasonable period for compliance

Once a tenant is satisfied the time for service of the notice has arrived, he will need to state in the notice a period within which the landlord must take the necessary steps to activate the review. This period itself must be 'reasonable'. Lord Diplock suggested that a reasonable period might well be 'very short' in view of the ease with which the landlord can comply with the requirement of a notice to commence the review (at 934). It would also be relevant, he said, that the tenant had a pressing need for the rent to be determined or had been pressing informally for negotiations to start. Yet even with such guide-lines, it will be a decision on the particular facts of the case (cf *Re Barr's Contract* [1956] Ch 551 where a 28 day notice to complete under the National Conditions of Sale was held not to be reasonable while in the *Quadrex* case (above) the court had no doubt that a 32 day notice period was reasonable). Perhaps the best that can be said is that a notice specifying a further full period equal to the period utilised in the original machinery ought (at the very least) to be reasonable in most circumstances. In the *Leboff* case, the tenant specified 28 days for the landlord to act and no attack on, or criticism of, this period was made.

(e)   The need for clarity

As with all notices (see section 2, above) the notice must be clear. It should state:

— what the landlord must do to comply with it (explicit reference to the obligation in the lease would be preferable);
— make it plain that the tenant regards such action within the time-limit to be 'of the essence'; and
— state the consequences of default, ie the loss of review.

The notice in the *Leboff* case was possibly deficient in the latter two of these three requirements but it was not necessary for the judge to express a view on the arguments advanced.

(f) Coping with a prolonged determination of the review

The problem will occur when the response to a tenant's notice is a prompt initiation but then the review machinery is not vigorously pursued. It is doubtful if the original notice could properly limit the time for the conclusion of the review as well as for its initiation, since this will usually be outside the control of the parties. This point was likewise urged forcefully in the *Leboff* case (see 139D) but since the tenant conceded his notice did not require *appointment* of an arbitrator but only an *application* to appoint, there was no need for the judge to express a view. In a case where only the landlord can make a reference to arbitration (eg making the application to the President of the RICS), the tenant can give a further notice making time of the essence for such application to appoint (as was implicit in the *Leboff* decision); otherwise he will have to apply for such appointment himself or endeavour to encourage the review process to be concluded as soon as may be. As was said in *Bremer Vulkan Schiffbau und Maschinenfabrik v South India Shipping Corporation, Gregg v Raytheon Ltd* [1981] AC 909, if one party is dilatory in an arbitration then the other has a duty to keep it moving.

(g) Consequence of service of notice

The result of a valid notice by a tenant making time of the essence where there is no response by the landlord will be that the right to review will be lost for the whole of the ensuing review period. A similar notice requiring the reference to arbitration would not necessarily be final since the Arbitration Act 1950, s 27, would appear to apply (see p 113), giving a landlord the right to apply for an extension of time notwithstanding the expiry of the period of time specified in the tenant's notice, however reasonable such notice may have been. That application should be made promptly but the prior delay which eventually led to the tenant serving his notice should not affect the availability of the s 27 remedy.

7 Application for the appointment of a referee

The mode of application for the appointment of an independent expert or arbitrator is usually clearly defined in the lease.

A vast majority of the clauses in use today provide for the nomination or appointment of such arbitrator or expert by the President for the time being of the RICS and the RICS Guidance Notes give assistance to people making such application (see Part 6).

Some clauses (eg Conveyancer Precedent 5–57) provide that rents specified in either a landlord's or tenant's notice shall be the reviewed rent unless the mechanism for independent determination of the rent is set in motion by the application to the President of the RICS.

In *Staines Warehousing Co Ltd v Montagu Executor and Trustee Co Ltd* [1987] 2 EGLR 130 the question arose on the validity of an attempt to put in a 'holding' application to ensure such time-limits were met. The lease contained a 'deeming' provision that 'if the landlord neglected to make an application' to the President of the RICS then the landlord's trigger-notice was to be void and of no effect. While negotiations with the tenant continued, and 1 month before the time-limit the landlord wrote to the President making 'an in time only application' for the appointment of a surveyor. The landlord did not pay the requisite fee. The tenant's challenge to the validity of this notice failed; the judge held that neither the fact that the tenant was not told of the application, nor the failure at that stage to pay the prescribed fee, nor the fact that the application could not proceed further without the fee, rendered the application invalid. The Court of Appeal, in dismissing the appeal, held that it was a 'valid application' if it met the internal procedures of the RICS then in force. Since it is customary to apply by letter, and payment of a fee and a copy of the lease were not essential for the RICS to regard it as a valid application (as opposed to proceeding to process the application) this letter was sufficient to meet the time-limit in question.

The process of appointment by the President is an administrative act and he owes no duty to refrain from making an appointment if the parties are in dispute; injunctive relief to prevent appointment is not therefore available: *United Co-operatives Ltd v Sun Alliance & London Assurance Co Ltd* [1987] 1 EGLR 126. For a full discussion of the practical aspects of appointments by the President, see Chapter 6, section 8, p 219.

Chapter 6

Independent Determination—
Arbitration and Expert Valuation

The use of third party referees to settle disputes in leases, as in other legal documents, has a long history despite changes from time to time in the court's attitudes to such attempts to substitute private adjudication, by agreement, for resolution by the courts. In many instances, the substitution of private adjudication serves to discharge a function equally apt for the court to perform—to settle the interpretation of a disputed clause in the lease, the scope of a user restriction or the alleged unreasonableness of a refusal to consent to alienation, and so on. In other instances, however, the reference to third-party adjudication relates to matters less obviously, conveniently or readily justiciable by the traditional methods of common law litigation and these have always included many matters of valuation and compensation. This is not to say that the courts would not or could not deal with matters such as valuation and compensation. It is rather that the parties prefer to have individuals chosen or appointed by or for them. Such individuals can use their known skill or experience in deciding matters that were deliberately left uncertain at the time of the original transaction and on which the parties later find themselves (after all) unable to agree. Typically, they are used where ascertainment is to be effected in a context of circumstances that the parties had been unable to forecast at the time of their original bargain—and reviewing a rent is a classic example.

The neutral term 'referee' is deliberately used in the preceding paragraph to cover the status in law of the third party, whether in law he was to be treated on the one hand as an arbitrator or on the other hand as a valuer, an expert or an independent surveyor, all of which three terms we treat as synonymous. We shall use the term 'referee' later when we wish to include both types of decision maker. The distinction between the referee as arbitrator and as valuer emerges in cases back in the seventeenth century, before Parliament first intervened in any way in the arbitration process. It became of increased importance once Parliament passed legislation regulating aspects of arbitration, as it has continued to do till the present day. The appointment of valuers, or other experts, has by contrast never directly engaged the attention of the legislature, although the resolution of dispute by this means has been affected by general legislation affecting private contractual bargains, as will become apparent.

1   The distinction between an arbitrator and a valuer

An arbitration imports a judicial function and, if written, incorporates the provisions of the Arbitration Acts; the decision is primarily on the evidence submitted, whether oral or written. A decision by an expert is only subject to the restrictions imposed by the contract which appoints him (usually in the lease); though he may listen and have regard to the views of the parties, the conclusion is reached using his own expertise.

(a)   A different status and role

Lord Esher MR in *Re Carus-Wilson and Greene* (1886) 18 QBD 7 summarised the basic distinction established by the cases up to that time as being that where 'the intention of the parties was that [the third party] should hold an inquiry in the nature of a judicial inquiry and hear the respective cases of the parties and decide upon the evidence laid before him, the case is one of arbitration . . . [but] there are cases in which a person is appointed to ascertain some matter for the purpose of preventing differences from arising—not of settling them when they have arisen—and where the case is not one of arbitration but mere [sic] valuation'. He continued: 'There may be cases of an intermediate kind, where though a person is appointed to settle disputes that have arisen, still it is not intended that he shall be bound to hear evidence and arguments. In such cases, it may be difficult to say whether he is intended to be an arbitrator or to exercise some function other than that of an arbitrator . . . Such cases must be determined each according to its particular circumstances.'

Thus, the traditional and generally accepted view is that there is a clear separation between the role of a valuer (or independent surveyor), giving an opinion as an expert in his field, and the role of an arbitrator, although it may not be easy in a particular case to identify the status of the individual concerned. In Lord Salmon's opinion this distinction leads to:

the most striking differences between the roles of the valuer . . . and the role of a judge or arbitrator. Judges and arbitrators have disputes submitted to them for decision. The evidence and the contentions of the parties are put before them for their examination and consideration. Then they give their decision. None of this is true about the valuer or architect who were merely carrying out their ordinary business activities. Indeed, their functions do not seem to me even remotely to resemble those of a judge or arbitrator. (*Sutcliffe v Thackrah* [1974] AC 727 at 759F)

The different status results in a contrasting theoretical basis and very different practical consequences. In the rent review field at least, the sharp distinction may be blurred by express provision in the lease as to evidence, costs and oral hearings (for example). Even without express provision, rent review experts will usually accept submissions from both sides and often invite a second round of counter submissions; when that happens, the conduct of the review will look remarkably similar to the equally common rent review arbitration conducted without an oral hearing. Yet in all cases the consequences of the distinction remain clear cut.

Lord Wheatley in *Arenson v Arenson* [1977] AC 405 (at 428E-F) set out certain indicia of an arbitration to serve as guide-lines in deciding whether a person is clothed with an arbitral function. These guide-lines have been applied in later rent review decisions and are as follows:

(a) there is a dispute or a difference between the parties which has been formulated in some way or another;
(b) the dispute or difference has been remitted by the parties to the person to resolve in such a manner that he is called upon to exercise a judicial function;
(c) where appropriate, the parties must have been provided with the opportunity to present evidence and/or submissions in support of their respective claims in the dispute; and
(d) the parties have agreed to accept his decision.

The last indicia will invariably be present in the form of the review clause, but the first three merit examination; though it is worth stressing that any clear choice for an arbitrator or expert in a rent review clause is unlikely to be overturned—see p 180, below.

(b) Existence of a dispute or difference

Lord Wheatley's formulation starts with 'a dispute or difference' and the essence of an arbitration has been stated to be 'that some dispute is referred by the parties for settlement to a tribunal of their own choosing instead of to a court' (*Russell*, p 1); such a dispute, which will be one that has arisen or may arise in the future, is determined by the arbitrator. If it were still the case that there is this distinction and the existence of a 'dispute' was necessary for an arbitration, that might create a difficulty for a rent review clause unless 'dispute' is defined to include a mere failure to agree. However, dicta in *Arenson v Arenson* ([1977] AC 405) now show that it may no longer be regarded as essential to an arbitration that it follows from a dispute, and the resolution of conflicting interests of the parties may suffice (per Lord Kilbrandon at 430H). This must be the better view because the creation of 'disputes' can be rather artificial; but Lord Simon does not accept it (at 424E). Certainly, if the parties have made a clear choice in the lease, the ground for arguing that there can be no arbitration because there is no dispute must be non-existent.

When Lord Wheatley's indicia were applied in *Palacath v Flanagan* [1985] 2 All ER 161 (see below), the existence of a dispute or difference was readily found in a quite normal rent review situation, namely what the revised rent should be (at 165j). By way of contrast, in *North Eastern Cooperative Society Ltd v Newcastle upon Tyne City Council* [1987] 1 EGLR 142, Scott J held when, applying the guide-lines, that there was no dispute or difference in the sense Lord Wheatley had in mind. In that case, there was certainly a dispute in the sense that the parties could not agree the amount of the yearly rent but it was not a dispute in which each had formulated a view which had been or had to be placed for decision before the independent surveyor. The indicia of a dispute or difference were not therefore present and this was an indication that the surveyor acted as an expert.

(c)   The exercise of a judicial function

An arbitration is a legal proceeding to which the Arbitration Acts 1950–79 normally apply, but no such formality applies to a valuation. In some early cases, the referee was found to be a valuer even though there was apparently a judicial function. Thus, in *Bottomly v Ambler* (1877) 38 LT 545 the umpire settled a rent after hearing the two 'arbitrators', one appointed by each party, who had failed to reach agreement. The clause was construed as showing an intention to resolve issues by an expert, not an arbitrator. In *Re Dawdy and Hartcup* (1885) 15 QBD 426, the umpire settled a rent following failure of the two appointed valuers to agree, but despite having sat to hear witnesses he was found to be only an expert and not an arbitrator. This tripartite machinery, where the so-called 'arbitrators' might now be labelled 'conciliators', is not often used in modern leases (but occurred in the four leases, dating from 1949 to 1968, to fix the price for the exercise of an option, which were subject to the decision in *Sudbrook Trading Estate Ltd v Eggleton* [1983] 1 AC 444) though it is still found in shipping and commodity disputes. However, in lease cases today, each party's valuer acts, to a considerable extent, in the same way as the 'arbitrators' do in the tripartite system, that is they try to reach an agreed solution but, failing that, present the arguments of their respective principals to a third party—who is usually required to act as an arbitrator. Notwithstanding the older cases, the centrality of the judicial function for an arbitrator has been stressed in more recent rent review cases. In *Palacath v Flanagan* [1985] 2 All ER 161, Mars Jones J was required to determine the status of an independent surveyor. The judge, applying Lord Wheatley's indicia, said that though there was a dispute, with the opportunity to the parties to submit evidence the vital missing feature of an arbitration was that the surveyor did not exercise a judicial function. The ultimate test was: 'how was he to arrive at his decision?' If he was entitled to act solely on his own expert knowledge (as this lease made clear) then there was no element of judicial function and the surveyor had the status of an expert.

(d) The opportunity to present evidence

Although not conclusive, provisions for the reception of evidence and submissions on the merits are indications that the parties had intended an arbitration (*Re Hopper* (1986) LR 2 QB 367), which explains why this is Lord Wheatley's third criterion. An arbitrator will always take evidence from the parties to the dispute if they wish to tender it and the parties have the consequent right to present such evidence as they see fit. The decision of the arbitrator, it has been said on many occasions, will be reached on the evidence before him. On the other hand a valuer, proceeding in a normal professional manner, is not required to take evidence from the parties because the decision is based on his own knowledge and expertise. He may consult the parties, seek information and hear evidence if he wishes, but there is no right to present any facts to him unless the lease or agreed contract of appointment of the expert requires him to receive them; the decision will not necessarily be based on such facts or evidence but on his own expertise. Indeed, the decision may be at variance with such evidence as was presented.

Section 12 of the Arbitration Act 1950, which is imported into every written submission to arbitration (s 32), can only make sense on the basis that a hearing will take place unless the parties have otherwise agreed; though they might well be content to rely on written representations. Where an expert must permit representations, the authors do not regard that as necessarily requiring him to allow oral representations, neither need he show any submissions to the other party and invite comments. The award of an arbitrator who acted in that way would on the other hand be open to attack as improper. Background Note 8 to the 1980 Model Forms, which is cited in full at p 715 below, and Background Note 11 to the 1985 Forms (see p 668) show how the Working Party expresses these principles.

However, provision for at least written representations to experts are increasingly common and this may have weakened these indicia of arbitration, at least in the field of rent review. Such express clauses may or may not require the referee to 'have regard to' or 'consider' those representations. Yet, if he is to be an expert, he remains free to ignore them for this is inherent in his status, but at peril of a possible increase in accusations of negligence. The fear is sometimes expressed that in permitting an expert to receive representations, or even requiring him to do so, he is thereby turned into an arbitrator but this fear does not seem well founded and reception of evidence by an expert is now common practice. Such a provision now appears in the Model Forms (see Variation B, clause 4(A)(ii)) (it was an optional clause in the 1980 version), in Form 119 in EFP (5th ed), Vol 22, p 513, as well as in Conveyancer

Precedent 5–57. The ISVA forms are, surprisingly, silent on the point. The referee who was held to be an expert in *Palacath v Flanagan* (above) was obliged to invite the parties to submit a statement of reasons and a professional valuation. He was obliged to consider such submission, but was still expressly entitled to rely on his own judgment and opinion and had, it was held, the status of an expert. In short, the right to submit representations to an expert has become a normal feature of modern rent review clauses so that a tenant's solicitor would now look to insert it where a draft lease omitted it.

(e)   Use of own knowledge by an arbitrator

Notwithstanding the principle that an arbitrator decides on the evidence but an expert is appointed because of his expertise, there seems in fact no insuperable obstacle to an arbitrator using his own knowledge, whether or not evidence is given on a particular issue. The fact that an arbitrator may so act, and may even be expected so to act, is established by the cases relating to trade arbitrations. The authors think this principle derived from the trade cases would apply to rent review cases, even bearing in mind distinctions between a lease (containing a rent review provision) and a more obviously commercial contract as emphasised in the Court of Appeal in *Amherst v James Walker Goldsmith & Silversmith Ltd (No 1)* (1980) 254 EG 123. The special knowledge and experience of the surveyor seems obviously a major reason that such a professional is chosen to be the arbitrator. Similarly, the arbitrator is not inescapably bound in his award to stay within the limits suggested by the evidence brought forward by the parties, as is established by *Mediterranean & Eastern Export Co v Fortress Fabrics (Manchester) Ltd* [1948] 2 All ER 187. Moreover, in *Eads v Williams* (1854) 24 LJ Ch 531 the Lord Chancellor declined to treat an award of two valuers, appointed to arbitrate on the rent and other terms of a mining lease, as invalid on the ground they had not heard any witnesses. (Whether the two valuers were arbitrators in the strict sense may be doubted, and of course this weakens the authority of the decision.)

The authors are aware that this view is contrary to the espoused by the RICS in the Guidance Notes. In Note 1:1.5, point 1, the point is stated thus: 'His award must lie between the extremes contended for by the parties'. It is conceded both that the occasions for an arbitrator to go outside the limits contended for will be rare, or very rare, and that the arbitrator intending so to act would be unwise to do so without taking the parties into his confidence, as discussed below, but, subject to those two highly significant limitations, such an award would not, in the submission of the authors, be invalid. Moreover, as the courts have constantly stressed, it is not arbitral misconduct to be wrong, on law any more than on fact. However, the greater the degree to which the award departs from the range of rents suggested by the witnesses, the more scope there is to argue that the arbitrator must have misconducted himself and that his award should be set aside. (Perhaps a cynicism about arbitrators 'splitting the difference', notwithstanding their duty to decide on the evidence—see RICS Guidance Notes, Note 3.8.4., has played some part in the support for the 'flip flop' variant of arbitration, discussed in Chapter 4, p 68 above).

An arbitrator intending to rely on his own knowledge would be well advised, nevertheless, to tell the parties what exactly he has in mind to do and invite their comments, as in *Thomas Borthwick (Glasgow) Ltd v Faure Fairclough Ltd* [1968] 1 Lloyd's Rep 16. Failure so to do will be strong grounds for the award to be remitted or set aside (on which see below p 206).

Even in cases where the arbitrator does not use his own knowledge and experience to make good the absence or insufficiency of evidence brought before him on a particular issue, he should not put or try to put that knowledge and experience out of his mind. He should bring that expertise to bear in his assessment of the evidence and arguments before him. That, after all, is one of the major reasons why the parties chose to have their dispute or difference resolved by a person skilled in valuation matters rather than a judge. (The possible inability of a judge to deal with matters of valuation is fully recognised by the fact that he is given the power, under the County Courts Act 1984 to sit with assessors, although the power is very rarely exercised.)

We should mention the risks, alluded to in *Arenson v Arenson*, that an arbitrator who enters upon an investigatory role may thereby render himself at risk for negligence (per Lord Kilbrandon at 431A and Lord Salmon at 439H). This issue is discussed at p 216 below.

2 Distinguishing an arbitrator from an expert

A well-drafted rent review clause will make an explicit choice as to whether the referee is to act as an expert or as an arbitrator, or, at least, provide adequate machinery for the choice to be made later at the time of the review. There are two particular problems to be addressed:

(1) In what circumstances (if at all) can the choice so made be challenged?
(2) If the choice is unclear, on what principles can the true status of the referee be determined?

(a) The 'label' is not decisive

In *Re Taylor v Yielding* (1912) 56 SJ 253 the provision was for two valuers [sic] and an umpire to be appointed 'in pursuance of and in accordance with the Arbitration Act 1889' and the process was held to be an arbitration. In that case, nevertheless, Neville J stated: 'You cannot make a valuer an arbitrator by calling him so or vice versa'.

It may be noted that EFP (4th ed) Form 8:1, on which many early rent review clauses in leases were based, (and its revision in Additional Form 76) uses the formula of an 'independent surveyor' acting 'in accordance with the Arbitration Act'; but Form 22 in EFP (5th ed), Vol 22 p 30 rightly refers to an arbitrator. A similar formula was used in the leases in *London & Manchester Assurance Co Ltd v G A Dunn & Co* (1982) 265 EG 39 and *Chartered Trust plc v Maylands Green Estate Co Ltd* (1984) 270 EG 845 but the status was not in issue in either case (see also RICS Guidance Notes, Note 1.1.6). In *Re Evans, Davies v Caddick* (1870) 22 LT 507 the valuation of a partner's share and the validity of an alleged notice of dissolution was, if raised, to be referred to certain individuals and an umpire. The decision in that case was that the parties intended an arbitration on the wide dispute, going beyond a mere valuation. (One cannot avoid feeling that the consequences of that decision—namely that the court could appoint a new umpire to replace the one who had died—influenced the court in reaching the finding that it was an arbitration.) There are authorities showing that persons appointed as arbitrators may, nevertheless, have to determine the question using their own skill and knowledge (*Re An Arbitration between Hammond and Waterton* (1890) 62 LT 808); this has been applied to valuers who by the nature of their appointment were arbitrators under the Arbitration Acts (*Re Hopper* (1967) LR QB 367).

(b) A clear choice indicated in the lease is likely to be decisive

Where the relevant provisions of a rent review clause provide for an express choice to be made between an arbitrator and an expert, as in the Model Forms, the court would be unlikely to overturn such an election, whatever the indications might otherwise be. Nevertheless, the issue must not be regarded as a formality. In *Arenson v Arenson* [1977] AC 405 at 425 Lord Simon, in declaring that the respondent accountants (who were appointed to act 'as experts and not as arbitrators') could not as experts claim arbitral immunity, stated that 'it would be open to the Respondents to show that their role was a judicial one so that they were appointed arbitrators', naturally having to overcome the obstacle that the contract letters declared them to act as experts.

The issues were fully explored in *Palacath v Flanagan* [1985] 2 All ER 161 where Mars Jones J had to settle a preliminary issue in a negligence claim as to the status of the independent surveyor. The lease stated that the independent surveyor was to 'act as an expert and not as an arbitrator'. The significance of the case is that, notwithstanding that apparently clear wording, the judge was prepared to enter into a full investigation. The phrase was only a 'very potent factor' in indicating that the parties did not intend the reference to be to an arbitrator and the true status remained at issue, though the burden of proof was on the surveyor to show that he had arbitral immunity. By way of contrast, the Court of Appeal in *Pittalis v Sherefettin* [1986] QB 868 had no hesitation in rejecting a claim that where the lease provided for determination 'In accordance with the provisions of the Arbitration Act' the surveyor appointed acted in reality as an expert. Fox LJ said (at p 874F) 'I see no reason why the parties should expressly incorporate the provisions of the Arbitration Act . . . unless they were intending that the proceeding should be an arbitration'.

(c) Where the choice is unclear

Where no 'label' has been used, it may not be easy to decide the status of the referee. The wording used in *Leigh v English Property Corporation Ltd* [1976] 2 Lloyd's Rep 298 was that a 'fair value shall be as agreed and in default of agreement shall be as certified by the auditors . . . (whose decision shall be final and binding on the parties)'. The view that this constituted a reference to arbitration was held open to argument. In *Langham House Developments Ltd v Brompton Securities Ltd* (1980) 256 EG 719 the rent in default of agreement was to be determined by a chartered surveyor nominated by the President of the RICS. The preceding clause expressly stipulated that questions of cesser of rent were to be decided by an arbitrator, so that led to a conclusion that the rent review referee was to act as a valuer not an arbitrator. A similar distinction was drawn in *North Eastern Cooperative Society Ltd v Newcastle upon Tyne City Council* [1987] 1 EGLR 142. The lease provided that the reviewed rent, in default of agreement, was to be 'determined by an independent surveyor agreed between the [parties] or (in default of agreement) by an arbitrator to be nominated by the president of the Royal Institution of Chartered Surveyors on the application of either party and this lease shall be deemed for this purpose to be a submission to arbitration within the Arbitration Act'. The lessee was dissatisfied with the rent as fixed by the surveyor appointed by agreement—but to challenge the determination he needed to know whether he had acted as an arbitrator or as an expert. The correspondence appointing the surveyor left the issue at large; and the judge narrowly concluded that the independent surveyor was to act as an expert. The reference to arbitration only applied when the President appointed so the independent surveyor appointed by agreement acted as an expert. In the authors' judgment, the result, that the status of the referee depended on the mode of appointment, was unfortunate and could well have been a factor indicating an opposite conclusion.

In view of the substantial consequences of the distinction, such uncertainty should be avoided and the draftsman should designate the status intended. Uncertainty is something that a draftsman must also avoid because of the procedural differences and divergences in the areas of liability for negligence and costs (as noted below), which a dissatisfied party might be tempted to raise.

The RICS Guidance Notes state that reference to an 'umpire' simpliciter would require appointment of an arbitrator (Note 1.1.8.) and there seems no compelling reason to differ from that opinion. However in the context of a lease providing for the valuers for the parties to reach agreement, but, if they did not, to agree on an umpire to settle the question, Goulding J (with some hesitation over whether he ought to decide the outcome) held in *Safeway Food Stores Ltd v Banderway Ltd* (1983) 267 EG 850 that the umpire should do so as an expert, not an arbitrator. Not all the reasons given by the judge are convincing; one that is, however, was express reference in another clause to an arbitrator acting under the Arbitration Act, a similar approach to that in the *Langham House* and *North Eastern Cooperative* cases. While the authors do not regard the matter as beyond doubt, it is worth mentioning that the RICS apparently takes the view that a reference to an 'independent surveyor' in a lease without further elucidation is an indication that such referee is to act as an expert. The Guidance Notes do not mention this point; where there is any reference to arbitration, that is taken to over-ride concurrent references to 'valuer', independent valuer', 'expert' and so on (Note 1.1.6).

3   Consequences of the distinction

The consequences of the distinction do not only arise when, for example, issues of liability or challenge to the quantum of the reviewed rent arise; they also need to be clearly appreciated if an informed choice is to be made at the drafting stage.

(a)   Formalities and the incorporation of the Arbitration Acts

(i)   Arbitration

The advantage of providing for a reference to arbitration and not valuation by an expert is the incorporation of the machinery of the Arbitration Act 1950, as amended by the 1979 Act. An arbitrator is required to observe the rules of natural justice and the procedures laid down under the Arbitration Act. Thus, as to evidence, the parties must submit to examination (s 12(1)), produce all relevant documents (s 12(1)), and can be required to give evidence on oath (s 12(2) and (3)). Witnesses can be subpoenaed to give evidence or produce documents (s 12(4)) and orders made for discovery, affidavit evidence, the giving of security or the seizure of property (s 12(6)). All of these require the intervention of the court, which can also grant interim injunctions (s 12(6)), although the likelihood of one being needed in a rent review is small. In *The Vasso* [1983] 1 WLR 838 it was held, in relation to an arbitration over a claim for salvage of a ship, that an arbitrator had power under s 12(1) to order inspection of property belonging to one of the parties to an arbitration, and that application to the court under s 12(6) was not necessary. The application of the decision to rent review arbitrations is both obvious and salutary, for, without the statutory power and in the absence of any express provision in the lease, an unco-operative tenant could refuse access both to the landlord and his agents and the arbitrator himself. Instances of such intransigence on the part of tenants, especially where unrepresented, are not unknown. The existence of the court provides, as it were, a safeguard in support of the arbitrator whose directions are ignored. However, the House of Lords in *Bremer Vulkan Schiffbau und Maschinenfabrik v South India Shipping Corporation Ltd, Gregg v Raytheon Ltd* [1981] AC 909 denied an arbitrator a right of dismissal for want of prosecution, and refused an injunction to prevent the party grossly in delay from proceeding further with the arbitration. Moreover, the House of Lords showed in *Paal Wilson & Co A/S v Partenreederei Hannah Blumenthal, The Hannah Blumenthal* [1983] 1 AC 854 that delay where both parties are at fault will not necessarily terminate an arbitration and that the doctrine of frustration cannot easily be prayed in aid. In *Food Corporation of India v Antclizo Shipping Corporation, The Antclizo* [1988] 1 WLR 603 the House expressed virtual dismay at the situation while finding itself unable to overturn it. Lord Goff, in the leading speech, entered a fervent plea for legislative intervention. Fortunately, few rent reviews get quite as bogged down as the commercial arbitrations which led to these decisions.

If the party with power to appoint an arbitrator refuses to do so, as happened in *National Enterprises Ltd v Racal Communications Ltd* [1975] Ch 397, the court can now make an appointment under s 10 as amended by the 1979 Act, expressly to overcome the lack of such power as demonstrated by that case. Section 10 also allows the court to appoint a substitute arbitrator if the person appointed dies or cannot or refuses to act.

(ii) Expert

None of the statutory powers are available in a reference to an expert and, whilst some could be incorporated by express agreement, such detailed procedural provisions are virtually unheard of. Again, any possible problems, such as death or refusal to act, have to be expressly provided for in the case of a reference to an expert, as has been done in all versions of the Model Forms, which also provide for substitution because of delay or if the President of the RICS shall 'for any other reason . . . . think fit' (see Variation B, clause 4(iii)). Arbitrary exercise of power to replace would surely be restrained by the court, were it ever contemplated.

An expert is probably not even subject to the rules of natural justice. Even were it possible to require that the procedure he adopts be 'fair', it is difficult to envisage a challenge to the procedure adopted in any particular case unless it involved a substantial departure from accepted practice.

(b) Costs

(i) Arbitration

The costs of an arbitration are in the award of the arbitrator unless a contrary intention is expressed under s 18 of the Arbitration Act 1950. Moreover, a provision for each party to bear his own costs in any event is ineffective by reason of s 18(3), unless made after the dispute that is submitted to arbitration has arisen. 'Each party to bear own costs' in a rent review clause providing for arbitration is thus clearly inoperative, though not unknown. In *Windvale Ltd v Darlington Insulation Co Ltd* (1983), 20 December, unreported, a rent review clause provided that the review was to be at the expense of the lessee. An arbitrator, in his award, applied that provision but Walton J held that s 18 rendered the provision void as it related to the arbitration and an argument that s 18, on a literal construction, did not cover an agreement to pay the costs of both parties was rejected.

The statutory machinery provides for taxation of the costs of an arbitration (ss 18 and 19). The principles for the award of costs by arbitrators have been established by a series of decisions, largely following the principles laid down for litigation. The general principle is summarised in the maxim 'costs follow the event'. It is not always easy to apply to rent review in the absence of an open or sealed offer as the arbitrator does not award a sum of money but answers a question as to what the rent should be. Thus, whilst an award of costs should take account of an open offer, as in *Lewis v Haverfordwest Rural District Council* [1953] 1 WLR 1486, it should not be influenced by a without prejudice offer (*Stotesbury v Turner* [1943] KB 370). In other cases, there will, from the very nature of rent review, be contentions as to the proper rental figure but unless the arbitrator largely accepts the case of one party and determines close to the figure that party put forward, it may well be that there will be no order as to costs and the parties will each pay half the arbitrator's fees and expenses and bear their own costs.

Judicial acceptance of the 'sealed offer' technique—whereby a without prejudice offer is made expressly reserving a right to refer to such offer on any issue of costs—has meant it is now frequently adopted in a rent review arbitration. The suggested procedure will be found in *Tramountana Armadora SA v Atlantic Shipping Co SA* [1978] 2 All ER 870. The applicability of this process (known, outside the field of arbitrations, as a 'Calderbank letter' through its origin in the Court of Appeal in *Calderbank v Calderbank* [1976] Fam 93 to any dispute where payment in of a sum of money is not available) was vindicated in *Cutts v Head* [1984] Ch 290 and the use of the sealed offer process in arbitrations was referred to with approval. The procedure has subsequently been written into the rules of the Supreme Court and the County Court Rules: see RSC Ord 22, r 14; CCR Ord 11, r 10. It may be noted that the sealed offer technique may not be quite as effective in rent review arbitrations when compared to payments into court or its use in other fields; the more fluid nature of the issues might allow a valid argument on costs that an earlier sealed offer was justifiably refused. So, unless the sealed offer made is more generous than the award or at least extremely close to it, the party who refused it can argue that it was necessary to refuse and proceed with the arbitration to achieve the higher figure awarded. Despite this, it must always be worthwhile to frame a party's offer, or each one of a series of offers, on a sealed offer basis so as to impose whatever sanction it ultimately proves to have.

Where either or both parties have made sealed offers in the *Calderbank* form, the arbitrator should be specifically requested to reserve costs in his award to allow later argument or the issue of costs must be raised and argued at the end of the hearing. This is because an arbitrator, unlike a court, will not allow the question of costs to be raised after the award has been given. He has a duty to deal with costs in his award unless a specific request is made to reserve them. In *Harrison v Thompson* [1989] 1 WLR 1325 both parties had made *Calderbank* offers and both erroneously believed that the letters could be brought to the arbitrator's attention after the award. The deprivation of the opportunity to make submissions on costs was said to be a procedural mishap (even though the arbitrator was not at fault) so the award was remitted on the question of costs.

In the RICS Guidance Notes, Note 3.10.7 gives helpful advice the procedure to be adopted at the hearing when a 'without prejudice offer save as to costs' has been made. An alternative procedure is suggested in Note 3.10.8; that the parties agree at the preliminary meeting to seek an interim award on the subject matter of the dispute, with costs reserved for a supplementary award after a hearing at which inquiry is made into the conduct of the negotiations, including without prejudice communications. Whilst it is correct that the parties could so agree, it must be said that the wisdom of so acting, especially as a matter of routine, is somewhat suspect and an invitation so to agree must be most carefully considered and only acceded to with caution.

Finally, if it is thought that the fee of an arbitrator is excessive then it can be subject to taxation—Arbitration Act 1950, s 19.

(ii) Expert

An expert, by contrast, has only the power to award costs if this is given him by the agreement and there is no direct control over the level of his fee. In this regard the provision of the original (1979) draft of the Model Form that 'the costs of the reference shall be in the award of the valuer' or of the 1980 or 1985 versions that 'the fees and expenses of the valuer including the costs of his appointment shall be borne equally by the Landlord and the Tenant' only covers costs of the reference and not the costs of the parties. The 1980 and 1985 versions put this beyond doubt as they continue after the phrase in question 'who shall otherwise bear their own costs'. The approach of, say, Conveyancer Precedent 5-57 is different, for it reads:

The award of the referee shall also provide for the manner in which the costs of the determination shall be borne and may also provide for the payment of costs by one party to the other and in settling upon such matters the referee may have regard to the contents of any notice served, any offers made by either party to the other (whether 'without prejudice' or not) and the nature and content of any representation made to him by or on behalf of the parties.

The authors not only prefer this approach but must point out that it approximates, save for the reference to without prejudice offers simpliciter, to the position that will rise under the Model Forms (or any other similar clause) if arbitration ensues. The courts evolved their general rules whereby costs normally follow the event because that provided an incentive for the parties to settle. The courts have required arbitrators to follow the same principles so as to obtain a similar result. For that reason, the 'each party to pay own costs in any event' can work injustice. Nevertheless, it has been argued that the 'small' tenant who is in a dispute with a much bigger landlord may be deterred by the risks of paying two sides' expenses and prefers the certainty of just paying his own costs, which he can control closely, whatever the outcome of the reference.

In commercial cases, the costs of a reference, whilst not inconsiderable, have to be measured against sums by way of increased rent at stake and may thus be an acceptable burden for the loser to bear in the light of the differences between them. In residential leases, where the Housing Act 1980 has provided new opportunities for variable rents (see Chapter 17, p 523), the costs may be quite disproportionate to what is at stake. This may be a strong disincentive to invoking any reference machinery.

(c) Liability in tort or contract

The traditional position is that an arbitrator is immune from suit but an expert is liable. These assertions remain true but require qualification.

(i) Arbitration

Though the House of Lords have ruled that valuers can be sued for negligence in their valuation (*Sutcliffe v Thackrah* [1974] AC 727; *Arenson v Arenson* [1977] AC 405) and subsequent cases have extended the scope of the duty of care that is owed to the client (eg *Smith v Eric S Bush (a firm)* [1989] 2 All ER 514), the immunity from suit of arbitrators appears to remain, at least for the present. However, it was an issue which produced divided opinions in the House of Lords in the *Arenson* case so the future position cannot be guaranteed (see E A Marshall, 'Arbitral Immunity', (1976) JBL 313). There was, for a time, a possibility that liability for negligence had been imposed by ss 13 and 14 of the

Supply of Goods and Services Act 1982 with effect from 4 July 1983, at least in those instances where the arbitrator could be said to be acting under a contract. Any such liability was removed by the making of a statutory instrument, the Supply of Services (Exclusion of Implied Terms) Order 1985 (SI No 1) under powers contained in s 12(4) of the 1982 Act. The traditional view that arbitrators are immune was reasserted by Lord Denning in *Campbell v Edwards* [1976] 1 All ER 785 at 788.

For a party dissatisfied with an arbitrator's award, the remedy can only lie by way of appeal, remission or setting aside under the Arbitration Acts as discussed in section 6 of this chapter, below.

(ii) Expert

The liability of an expert in negligence is the principal remedy for a dissatisfied party. The rent as determined will remain binding as between the parties (*Campbell v Edwards*)—unless it is a determination on a wholly erroneous basis when there is a possibility that the court will act to set it aside, see below. If a case of negligence is proved, then the damages awarded will reflect the extra rent, or shortfall as the case may be. The remedies are considered in detail in section 7 of this chapter, p 216 below.

(d) Judicial control

(i) Arbitration

The remedies of remission of an award (Arbitration Act 1950, s 22), setting aside the award or removal of an arbitrator for misconduct (s 23) and appeal after leave has been given (s 1), give a variety of remedies for an aggrieved party and ensure judicial oversight of arbitrations. A substantial body of case law in the field of rent review now exists and this is discussed in section 6 p 195, below. A further distinction is that an arbitrator's award, unlike an expert's determination, can be enforced as a judgment of the court but this difference is rarely of consequence.

(ii) Expert

Since expert valuation is a matter of contract, none of the above procedures is available to a person wishing to challenge an expert's determination and *Campbell v Edwards* [1976] 1 WLR 403 held an expert's award to be unimpeachable for his negligence, although the aggrieved party may have a course of action against the expert personally. A differently constituted Court of Appeal reached the same conclusion in *Baber v Kenwood Manufacturing Co Ltd* [1978] 1 Lloyd's Rep 175. Whether or not this general principle admits the right of the court to intervene in an wholly erroneous reasoned determination is fully considered in section 7 p 211, below.

The point to stress is the stark contrast in remedies as against an arbitrator when compared to those against an expert.

4 Making the choice in the lease

(a) A specific choice initially

The initial choice of the status of the referee (or even the later exercise of any choice between the arbitrator and expert when allowed for in the lease) is largely governed by the incidental matters discussed above. There is no evidence that the use of, say, an expert will inevitably tend to produce a different result from that to be expected of an arbitrator. At one stage during the relatively recent growth in rent review provisions, the preference was for expert valuation and arbitration had fallen into disfavour but there has been a swing back to arbitration, and an element of personal preference persists. The 'built-in' option came with Conveyancer Precedent 5–57 and the Model Forms, as the respective merits of the alternatives were debated. The Introductory Note to the 1979 draft of the Model Forms did not advert to the issue of the choice, but the 1980 version does. The whole of Background Note 8 of the 1980 Revised Model Forms is worth quoting as it sets out most of the arguments, though perhaps a caveat may be entered that the remarks may be more applicable to the larger property than the smaller, where cost may be a decisive factor. It reads as follows:

Where the President of a professional or learned society is required to appoint an arbitrator, this method of appointment is specified because the person so appointed should have (and under arbitration law is expected to utilise) his specialised professional skills in adjudicating upon the matter in dispute, which includes in particular his ability to distinguish between the quality, relevance and the value of the evidence presented to him. In any RICS Presidential appointments, in order to ensure impartiality, enquiries are made of possible appointees to ensure that neither they nor their firm or partners have had any previous business or social connections with either of the parties to the dispute, or the subject property, or for any reason are likely to be held to be biased, are able to deal with the subject of the dispute expeditiously, and finally that the subject matter of the dispute falls within their normal sphere of everyday professional work.

Thus where a Presidential appointment or 'appointment by agreement between the parties' arises, any valuer so instructed would normally decline the appointment, unless he can satisfy these conditions. In an arbitration, the parties at least have the right to appearance and the valuer must adjudicate. The independent valuer, however appointed, is not bound by the rules and procedures laid down by the Arbitration Acts and may, unless the lease provides that he shall do so, properly decline to receive any statement of facts or evidence from either of the parties to the dispute. On balance the Joint Committee consider that reference to an arbitrator is more appropriate in most cases than reference to an independent valuer.

(b) Delaying the choice until review

It may be noted that Conveyancer Precedent 5–57 provides that the referee shall act as an expert unless the landlord within a strict time-limit requires him to act as arbitrator. It might have been expected, given its stated preference, that the Working Party would have drafted the Model Forms to provide a comparable (though opposite) choice (ie 'arbitrator unless changed to expert') but it did not do so. Instead, in both the 1980 and 1985 versions, an election has to be made by the landlord at a time that is somewhat uncertain but seemingly no later than application to the President of the RICS in every case (see, 1985 Model Forms, Variation C, clause 2). The ISVA forms both provide that the valuer acts as an arbitrator unless the parties agree otherwise before the nominee accepts appointment.

The matter of timing is not only of theoretical interest. In any situation where time is of the essence for an application to be made for appointment, it could be crucial to decide whether an application to the appointor at the last minute (saying, as it were, 'Please appoint a referee. I'll tell you (or him) later whether he is an arbitrator or an expert valuer') was a valid application or not. If it were not, then a rent stated in a trigger-notice might take effect (see, for example, 1985 Model Forms, Variation C, clause 4(F), 1980 Model Forms, clause 4(E), 1979 Model Forms, clause 3(6), or Conveyancer Precedent 5–57), or the opportunity for a third party decision could be lost for a whole review period. Whilst the date of application might be one to be strictly met, it does not follow that the choice between the two types of referee should be similarly construed, especially as the general attitude of English law is against making time stipulations of the essence (as in s 41 of the Law of Property Act 1925). There is the contrary argument that it is necessarily implied that the choice must be made at the latest when the request for appointment is made. It may be noted in passing that in *Amherst v James Walker Goldsmith & Silversmith Ltd (No 1)* (1980) 254 EG 123 the President of the RICS had not made an appointment because he had been informed that there was a dispute. It is possible and perhaps preferable to make express provision for a time-limit by which the choice must be made, and to provide a 'fall-back' indication of the status if no choice is made. In this context, reference should also be made to the *Staines Warehousing* case (see p 172 above) where it was held that an 'in-time only' application to the President was valid.

The draftsman of the lease in issue in *North Eastern Co-operative Society Ltd v Newcastle upon Tyne City Council* [1987] 1 EGLR 142 used wording that was held to require that the referee appointed by the parties would rank as an expert (or, at least, a non-arbitrator, as the judge declined to declare him an expert or quasi arbitrator so as not to pre-empt later decisions on liability); but if appointed by the President would be an arbitrator. The later status was expressly defined but the party appointment was of an 'independent surveyor'. For the present purposes, it is interesting to note the view expressed that the parties might well want a local practitioner known to them to be an expert, but would wish the President's nominee to act as an arbitrator, since he would not necessarily have either the attribute of local experience or that of the personal confidence of the parties.

(c) Assistance to the referee

A few other factors may be significant for the choice—whether at the initial bargaining stage or on the later exercise of an option—between arbitrator and expert. The issue of what evidence may be received is one (discussed later at p 228–23) and the possibility of giving evidence of comparable rents on a basis of keeping the information secret is another (discussed at p 243). A third is the freedom of the referee, if not a lawyer, to seek his own legal advice or, if not a valuer, to take his own valuation advice. An arbitrator may do so within established limits although the Privy Council indicated 50 years ago 'the precise length to which an arbitrator may go in seeking outside advice upon matters of law may be difficult to prescribe in general terms' *(Louis Dreyfus & Co Ltd v Arunachala Ayya* (1931) 58 LR Ind App 381 at 391). That case laid down that advice might be taken on general legal principles applicable to the matter referred to arbitration but not upon the specific issue. The latter would be tantamount to delegation of the arbitral function and this is improper unless authorised by the parties. The arbitrator would be well advised to inform the parties of his intention to seek legal advice or assistance, to seek their consent and to supply each with a copy of the instructions by which he submits the issue for legal advice. A case can even be argued for a legal assessor, agreed on by the parties, to be appointed at the outset, to be consulted if the need arises by the non-lawyer arbitrator and to have the power to appeal to the court excluded, but this is rarely done.

(d) Weighing up the costs of the determination

On the question of the arbitrator's own costs and expenses, a former practice of fixing fees by reference to the RICS scale is now discouraged by the RICS itself following abandonment of the scales on 1 March 1982 (but may still be found in some leases before that date), and the basis of charging is fully discussed (together with many aspects of costs) in Notes 3.9 and 3.10 of the RICS Guidance Notes, in relation to arbitrators, and Notes 4.4.1 to 4.4.4 for an independent expert. The latter section suggests, in Notes 4.4.1, that 'In view of his duty to assemble information and his potential liability in negligence the independent expert may be justified in charging a fee higher than if he were acting as arbitrator.' This comment, with respect, does not deal with the significant aspect of the costs of interlocutory and final hearings in which an arbitrator will almost certainly be involved, but an expert very rarely. The extra costs involved in assembling the evidence for himself by an expert might often be less than those conducting the adversarial proceedings. The incidental costs of a venue for the hearing and ancillary administrative back-up in a major arbitration must also be borne in mind.

As to the broader issue of costs of the parties, it is also the authors' view, where disputes 'go the full distance', that the greater formality of the arbitration process, as compared with valuation by an expert, may involve greater expense on the parties. This can be a significant factor, but if each side employs its own lawyers as well as valuers to make representations to an expert, the costs incurred may be not dissimilar. Nevertheless, for the relatively uncomplicated property at a modest rent, and in all residential cases, the costs factor may point strongly to valuation as the better choice. A party who has chosen to act for himself in any negotiations, without employing a surveyor, may also prefer to have a reference to the valuer as the arbitration procedure may seem a little daunting for the party acting in person (no matter what legitimate help the arbitrator may try to provide). It can be argued, somewhat paradoxically, that the potential expense of an arbitration may well serve to induce a greater willingness in the parties to settle or compromise. Whether that proves to be the case must depend on the amount of rent at stake over the relevant review period compared to the likely costs to fall on the loser.

(e) The nature of the dispute

Apart from these specific aspects, the major criterion for the choice must be the foreseeable nature of the dispute, a matter that will be far more speculative at the initial drafting stage than when the issues requiring adjudication have actually arisen. Moreover, if the parties could foresee the problems at the first stage they might well have so amended the drafting as to eliminate or side-step them. Nevertheless, there have emerged some recognisable categories of leases where the case for arbitration is particularly strong. One is the rare or unique property, which Messrs Bernstein and Hill so felicitously encapsulated in the title of their Blundell Memorial Lecture of 1979—'Valuing the Incomparable' (reprinted, slightly abridged in (1979) 76 *Law Society's Gazette* at 674 and 841). Their argument is that if the valuers for each side experience great difficulties in providing evidence of comparables or of accepted valuation techniques (and one sees letters in the professional press from valuers seeking assistance in valuing unusual properties) there is little reason to expect the selected expert valuer to be able himself to command superior knowledge in those areas either. Hence, it becomes wiser to allow the nominated surveyor to adjudicate as an arbitrator upon such evidence and arguments as are advanced before him. If he does possess the magic valuer's elixir that enables him to supply the deficiencies in the knowledge of the parties' advisers—that will be a most welcome bonus. He can still bring that special knowledge to bear as an arbitrator in the manner discussed above (p 178). Examples of properties with virtually unique attributes that have figured in reported cases are the massive office complex in *Pivot Properties Ltd v Secretary of State for the Environment* (1980) 253 EG 373 and the 60 acre factory in *F R Evans (Leeds) Ltd v English Electric Co Ltd* (1977) P & CR 185. It is easy to list others: chemical works, mediaeval castles used as museums, restaurants, leisure centres and the like, wind-mills, coal depots, private marshalling yards, a cattle market (as in *Naylor v Uttoxeter Urban District Council* (1974) 231 EG 619), dock undertakings, aerodromes, sports stadia, riding stables, marinas, motorway service stations (as, for another purpose, in *Tucker v Granada Motorway Services Ltd* [1979] 1 WLR 87 and 683), car parks *(National Car Parks Ltd v Colebrook Estates Ltd* (1983) 266 EG 810) and many others. Specialist uses with high rental returns, such as large hotels, will also benefit from arbitration; and the multitude of legal issues thrown up in the spate of cases on casinos vividly illustrate the problems.

The choice of arbitration as the machinery of settlement in the absence of agreement may well be wise in a new lease granted under the Landlord and Tenant Act 1954 where the determination of the rent at statutory renewal has already proved difficult, particularly if there is the prospect of comparable problems on review. In such cases, the issues of fact, of interpretation and of valuation can once more be fully ventilated, if that is what the parties desire.

On the other hand, the prospect of intense disagreement can be regarded as an argument for the choice of the expert decision, the intervention and binding pronouncement of some acceptable wise man. There is biblical precedent and the parties may well prefer a judgment of Solomon, and the finality of a decision from an expert is an attraction in itself to some clients, even though the chances of appeal from an arbitrator have now been curtailed. There is no doubt that the delay and uncertainties of litigation may prevent or depreciate dealings with the term or the reversion at a time when one or other of the parties is anxious so to act. That consideration lies behind the Working Party's decision to include power for a tenant's notice to fix a rent. Background Note 3 to the 1980 version of the Model Forms accordingly reads:

'A most important consideration was that the model clause should be able to reflect the market conditions prevailing at the time when the letting was negotiated. Thus, there are variations which cover 'upwards only' and 'upwards/downwards' rent reviews:

(a) There are provisions which might apply in a Landlord's market where the Landlord has the sole right to initiate the review process and to chose either arbitration or reference to a valuer acting as an expert. In this case, clause 4(E) was included to protect the tenant in the situation where he needs to avoid uncertainty or wants to assign after a rent review date and the Landlord has not applied for the appointment of an arbitrator or valuer.

(b) There is also provision which might apply in a Tenant's market for either party to be able to initiate the review procedure where the choice as to arbitration or reference to an independent valuer is fixed at the outset.'

Where a number of leases fall for review at the same time, say in a shopping centre, and the standard form lease provides for a choice between arbitration or valuation, there could be merit in a 'test case' procedure, whereby one selected review went to arbitration and the others were later referred to a valuer.

(f) Some guide-lines as to the choice

The following matters, or a combination of them, will point to an independent valuer being appropriate:

(1) Where the property leased is not large and the initial rent modest: In these cases, both parties may well agree that valuation will be appropriate as the simpler and cheaper method.
(2) Where the property leased is one of a comparable number of similar units: Where the relevant premises are, for example, a shop in a parade or shopping centre or small suite of offices in a block containing a number of similar units then this will enable comparisons to be made, and a valuation should be a straightforward matter. However, it may be worthwhile to see if a 'test case' could be taken to arbitration so ascertaining if there is any major problem and the others go to valuation, but such a common approach may not be easy to obtain.
(3) All simple cases: In all situations where the determination of the new rent is likely to be relatively simple, the property is not unusual and the criteria of value to be used do not raise difficulties, then there should be no problem in determination by an expert valuer.
(4) Cheapness and speed as factors: Valuation is likely to be the cheaper method in all cases (pace the RICS Guidance Notes section (d) above) and is less likely to cause delay in determining the new figures.
(5) Where parties have acted in person: Valuation is appropriate and desirable where the parties are not represented by their own surveyors prior to the final determination of the revised rent.

The following are circumstances where arbitration is appropriate:

(1) Whenever there is a clearly formulated dispute: Especially if the respective valuers have already used their expertise yet reached diverse results, arbitration has much to commend it, if only on the rather cynical view that the result may only leave one party dissatisfied rather than both. Reasons for this have been mentioned above but practical considerations may call for it in any event. Only an arbitration will ensure the *right* to representations at an oral hearing

if necessary; relevant documents can be produced and even orders for their discovery made and, most important of all, the parties' own surveyors may be witnesses, together with anyone else who the parties may wish to be called to give oral evidence. The procedure is laid down and it allows for a full ventilation of every aspect relating to the review of the rent.

(2) If the property is out of the ordinary or if difficulties are likely to arise: In such a case, the rental figure proposed by the respective parties may be widely separated or argument may arise as to the relevancy of different factors (as in *F R Evans (Leeds) Ltd v English Electric Co Ltd* (1977) 36 P & CR 185) and only an arbitration allows full consideration of these. Substantial points of law may arise and an arbitrator, if not legally qualified himself, can hear legal argument or refer the question to the court subject to the limitations now contained in the Arbitration Act 1979. Even without reference to the High Court by way of the new procedures, an arbitrator may seek legal professional advice, either of counsel or elsewhere, with the consent of the parties. If no such consent is forthcoming they may seek advice as to general principles of law but not the actual questions of law in the dispute. A surveyor acting as an expert will not have these options open to him, subject to the parties authorising such an approach.

In the end, the choice may be one of individual taste. Though the above analysis may represent a widely held view, the authors are aware of one institutional landlord which prefers to use an arbitrator for straightforward cases (on the basis that it can deluge the arbitrator with a large number of comparables from other properties it owns in the area) and an expert for the very unusual letting.

(g)　*Changing the choice at review*

The parties can, of course agree to alter the provisions of a lease. Thus an arbitration agreement can be entered into at a later stage and may be needed if a very difficult point of law arises. However, a guarantor or original lessee may not thereafter be bound unless the consent of such persons to the change of procedure is obtained.

5　Construction summons

If a dispute arises as to the true construction of a rent review clause, or even where there is likely to be a possible dispute in the hearing before or submissions to the arbitrator or expert, it will be wise to consider whether an originating summons to the court for a declaration as to the true construction is appropriate. If this is done prior to the award or determination, then the referee will be able to make his decision in the light of the construction as set out by the court. The principles of the process of construction of rent review clauses is considered in Part Three.

What is clear, as the principles set out in the next two sections demonstrate, is that it may be too late to remedy a alleged error of legal interpretation or construction once an arbitrator has made his award or an expert issued his determination.

6 Challenging an arbitral award

The right of appeal with leave (Arbitration Act 1979, s 1), the court's power to remit an award (Arbitration Act 1950, s 22) and to remove an arbitrator for misconduct or, on the same ground, to set aside an award (Arbitration Act 1950, s 23) provide alternative remedies and a measure of reassurance for parties to an arbitration in the event of dissatisfaction.

(a) The right of appeal

The right of appeal against an arbitral award is now contained in s 1(2) of the Arbitration Act 1979. It provides:

'An appeal shall lie to the High Court on any question of law arising out of an award made on an arbitration agreement; and on the determination of such an appeal the High Court may by order—

(a) confirm, vary or set aside the award; or
(b) remit the award to the reconsideration of the arbitrator or umpire together with the court's opinion on the question of law which was the subject of the appeal; . . .'

This right of appeal is hedged around with restrictions; in particular it is subject to s 1(3):

'(3) An appeal under this section may be brought by any of the parties to the reference -
(a) with the consent of all the other parties to the reference, or
(b) subject to section 3 below, with the leave of the court.'

Since consent is inherently improbable once the arbitrator has made his award, obtaining leave to appeal is invariably essential.

(i) Background to the Arbitration Act 1979, s 1

The right to appeal was restricted by s 1, primarily as a response to the alleged abuse of the former case stated procedure which the 1979 Act abolished. This former procedure allowed either party to ask the arbitrator to state a case for the court's consideration; which led, in effect, to all legal issues as to the meaning of the lease or contract being determined by the courts. The right resulted in high costs and long delays.

The legislative purpose of the 1979 Act was to restrict appeals; and in Lord Diplock's view in *Pioneer Shipping Ltd v BTP Tioxide Ltd, 'The Nema'* [1982] AC 724 it demonstrates

'a parliamentary intention to give effect to the turn of the tide in favour of finality in arbitral awards.'

The clear result is a 'presumption in favour of finality' and thus against granting leave to appeal; *Ipswich Borough Council v Fisons plc* [1990] 2 WLR 108—this latter case also illustrates, after a period of doubt, that rent review arbitrations fall within these guide-lines as much as any others.

(ii)   Requirements for an appeal

To launch an appeal, a party to the award must meet, fulfil or satisfy the related conditions contained on s 1(4) of the 1979 Act:

'(4) The High Court shall not grant leave under subsection (3)(b) above unless it considers that, having regard to all the circumstances, the determination of the question of law concerned could substantially affect the rights of one or more of the parties to the arbitration agreement; and the court may make any leave which it gives conditional upon the applicant complying with such conditions as it considers appropriate.'

From s 1(4) the following requirements can be extracted:

(1) The issue must be the determination of one or more questions of law.
(2) Those questions of law must substantially affect the rights of one or more of the parties to the arbitration agreement.
(3) The case must be a proper one for leave to be given, having regard to all the circumstances.

These requirements are cumulative; a question of law may substantially affect the rights of one or more of the parties to the arbitration agreement yet leave can be refused. No statutory guidance is given as to how the court's discretion in granting leave is to be exercised; the courts have thus been left free to supply their own guidance. The decade since the enactment of the 1979 Act has witnessed substantial controversy on the issue and though the judicial guide-lines on granting leave tend to overshadow the first two statutory requirements it is nevertheless useful to consider each in turn.

(iii)   A question of law

Unlike the position before 1979, when an error of fact on the face of the record could found the basis to set aside or remit an award, s 1(2) and (4) restrict an appeal to questions of law. The policy of the Act is to confine the determination of issues of fact to the arbitrator; moreover, the arbitral forum is also the place where most issues of law, intention of the parties and meaning of the terms of the lease are to be addressed. As Lord Diplock observed in *The Nema*, it is not self evident that an experienced arbitrator will be any less competent than a judge. Thus it follows that not all, or even most, issues of law can be appealed, but to appeal at all, a question of law there must be.

A finding of fact will rarely be categorisable as a question of law. To do so, the matter sought to be impugned must fall within the principles of *Edwards v Bairstow* [1956] AC 14 (approved in *The Nema*). The applicant must show that the only true and reasonable conclusion on the facts has been contradicted in the finding of the arbitrator, ie there was no evidence to justify his findings. In *Fine Fare Ltd v Kenmore Investments Ltd* [1989] 1 EGLR 143, it was alleged that the arbitrator had erroneously valued a comparable on a 'shell' basis when it was in fact fitted out—with a possible mistake in the reviewed rent of up to 10 per cent. The test in *Edwards v Bairstow* was not satisfied; no question of law arose and the attempt to construct an ingenious point of law failed. In *Warrington & Runcorn v Greggs plc* [1987] 2 EGLR 9 the disregard of a premium paid in respect of a comparable property was held to be a point of law—though some may share the authors' unease at this decision. It is no surprise therefore that the *Warrington* case was distinguished in *Tesco Holdings Ltd v Jackson* [1990] 1 EGLR 153 where it was held that the manner in which an arbitrator assessed and weighed valuation evidence disclosed no question of law.

(iv) Substantially affect the rights of the parties

This requirement was first discussed in the rent review context in *Segama NV v Penny Le Roy Ltd* (1983) 269 EG 322, a case which indicates that the court first determines whether the question of law could substantially affect the rights of one or more of the parties to the arbitration agreement; and then decides (if it does) whether it is a proper case to give leave. In deciding this point, the word 'could' means that the court considers if there is a possibility that the question will substantially affect the rights of one or more of the parties; it must be a real and not just a fanciful possibility: *Manders Property (Estates) Ltd v Magnet House Properties Ltd* [1989] 2 EGLR 126.

In the *Segama* case, there were two issues; the admissibility as evidence of rents agreed after the review date was clearly a question of law; that of the admissibility of comparable evidence of rents agreed between landlords and sitting tenants was treated as a question of law by the judge though not by the arbitrator. The former did not, however, substantially affect the parties' rights so leave to appeal was refused on the first ground, even though that might be 'advantageous to the public'. The second issue did substantially affect the rights of one or more of the parties, but, though there were possible different judicial schools of thought on the former issue, there was not on the latter. Since on both issues, Staughton J found the arbitrator was right, leave ought not to be granted on the second issue on the *The Nema* guide-lines (discussed in (*v* below) even though the question did substantially affect the rights of one or more of the parties to the arbitration agreement.

It is only matters arising directly from the arbitration that can have a bearing on substantiality; indirect effects on one of the parties may be disregarded. Thus, Staughton J ruled in the *Segama* case, that the wording of s 1(4) meant that he must leave out of account that fact that the landlords owned two adjoining properties, with reviews pending before the same arbitrator. The section is directed to a question the determination of which will directly affect the rights of one or more of the parties, and not one which will affect one of the parties if the determination is used as a precedent. Once over this hurdle, the court can look at wider considerations when addressing the issue of whether it is a proper case for leave to be granted (see below).

If more than one question of law is raised, then the statute indicates that the court must consider whether each individually satisfies the statutory test—they cannot be aggregated so as to make a substantial whole from parts which are themselves insubstantial—*Manders Property (Estates) Ltd v Magnet House Properties Ltd* [1989] 2 EGLR 126 at 128.

'Substantial' is not a word of precise meaning but it does indicate an error of law of real and major consequence, and more than merely not de minimis. In other words, the awards of arbitrators 'are not to be subject to fine tuning': *Manders Property* case at 128. In relation to rent review, this means that the economic effects for one of the parties will be the major consideration in showing substantiality. 'While the determination of the question of substantiality is not confined to the consideration of percentages, that plainly is a most relevant factor': *Manders Property* case at 129. In that case, 2.8 per cent of the total rent was at issue—that was insufficient to satisfy the test so there was no need to proceed to consider the question of leave. In *Segama*, the amount was 5.5 per cent; that, too, was insubstantial for s 1(4) and in *Beaconscross Ltd v Norris* (1989) 7 July, unreported, Morritt J was of the opinion that 10 per cent of the open market rent was too small where there would be no further reviews to be affected by the decision.

(v) Obtaining leave to appeal

The determination of the judges, who had played a prominent part in the move which culminated in the 1979 reforms, to give full effect to the new regime requiring leave was soon manifest, and in *Pioneer Shipping Ltd v BTP Tioxide Ltd, 'The Nema'* [1982] AC 724 the House of Lords seized the opportunity, on the first case to reach it, to lay down guide-lines. Lord Diplock's speech, which dealt with the issue, was concurred in by his four brethren. He distinguished disputes arising on 'one-off' clauses and disputes on standard terms. For the former:

'leave should not be normally given unless it is apparent to the judge on a mere perusal of the reasoned award itself without the benefit of adversarial argument, that the meaning ascribed to the clause by the arbitrator is obviously wrong. But if on such perusal it appears to the judge that it is possible that argument might persuade him, despite impression to the contrary, that the arbitrator might be right, he should not grant leave: the parties should be left to accept, for better or worse, the decision of the tribunal that they had chosen to decide the matter in the first instance (at 742H-743A).'

For a dispute centred on a the standard term in a contract 'rather less strict criteria' are imposed:

'If the decision of the question on construction . . . would add significantly to the clarity and certainty of English commercial law it would be proper to give leave in a case sufficiently substantial to escape the ban imposed by the first part of section 1(4) [viz that the appeal would substantially affect the rights of the parties] (at 743E).'

He continued that:

'leave should not be given, even in such a case, unless the judge considered that a strong prima facie case had been made out that the arbitrator had been wrong in his construction (at 743F).'

These *The Nema* guide-lines, imposing a very heavy burden on those seeking leave, were not accepted without further argument, either generally or especially in the field of rent review. Thus an attack on the *The Nema* guide-lines was mounted in *Italmare Shipping Co v Ocean Tanker Co Inc, The Rio Sun* [1982] 1 WLR 158 but failed in the Court of Appeal, save only to the extent that Lord Denning MR stated, at 162G:

'It must be remembered that they are only guide-lines. They are not barriers. You can step over guide-lines without causing any harm. You can move them, if need be, to suit the occasion.'

They have been referred to, and relied on, in a number of other cases. In *Antaios Cia Naviera SA v Salen Rederierna AB* [1983] 1 WLR 1362, what is to be noted is the gloss put upon the phrase that 'the arbitrator had been wrong'. In the House of Lords, Lord Diplock referred to his *The Nema* guide-lines and stressed that they 'are not intended to be all embracing or immutable, but subject to adaptation to match changes in practices when these occur or to refinement to meet problems of kinds not foreseen, and are not covered by, what was said in this House in *The Nema*' (at p 200). Brief mention may also be made of *Finelvet AG v Vinava Shipping Co Ltd, The Chrysalis* [1983] 1 WLR 1469 where Mustill J stressed the clear distinction to be made between the issue of leave to appeal, a filtering process to be effected by the exercise of discretion with reference to the *The Nema* principles, and the appeal itself, where discretion is not involved in the decision.

The Nema, and the other cases referred to above, were all cases on commercial contracts primarily in the field of shipping; and the statements in *The Nema* itself were expressly confined to 'English commercial law'.

To what extent did the guide-lines apply to rent review arbitrations? Criticism of their application to property arbitrations continued even after it had subsided in the commercial field. The absence of any 'spokesperson' for property interests on the Committee whose Report led to the 1979 Act was stressed; and the contrast between the relatively small cadre of maritime and commercial arbitrators and the larger number of property arbitrators was emphasised. The Master of the Rolls apparently showed himself, extrajudicially, sympathetic to these views (see [1987] 18 CSW 57)—though his judgment in *Ipswich v Fisons* (below) has a different emphasis; and the *Antaios* suggested the *The Nema* guide-lines might be modified in appropriate cases.

The reaction against rigidity surfaced in *Lucas Industries plc v Welsh Development Agency* [1986] Ch 500. The Vice-Chancellor, Sir Nicholas Browne-Wilkinson, found the *The Nema-Antaios* guide-lines 'difficult, if not impossible to apply to rent review arbitrations'. He gave three reasons:

(1) Those guide-lines dealt with standard commercial contracts but rent review clauses, though taken from the books, were frequently modified in practice and did not correspond with the commercial model.
(2) Points of law arose 'which apply generally to rent review clauses'; they should not therefore be treated as 'one-off' contracts.
(3) In all except final review situations, the construction placed on a review clause will bind the parties at future reviews under the doctrine of issue estoppel so the ascertainment of the true legal meaning was most desirable. (This reasoning remains sound notwithstanding the decision in *Arnold v National Westminster Bank*—see below p 209.)

Consequently, the Vice-Chancellor concluded that, at least in rent review cases, leave to appeal should be given whenever the judge is 'left in real doubt whether the arbitrator was right in law'—a lower hurdle than either of the *The Nema* guide-lines. The *Lucas* decision appeared to be welcomed and was followed in a series of first instance decisions: *Warrington & Runcorn v Greggs plc* [1987] 2 EGLR 9, *Triumph Securities Ltd v Reid Furniture Co Ltd* [1987] 2 EGLR 139 and *Railstore Ltd v Playdale Ltd* [1988] 2 EGLR 87. In short, the *Lucas* decision established a modus vivendi allowing a greater access to appeals than was permitted in other areas.

Any such greater freedom is now in jeopardy if not completely curtailed following the Court of Appeal decision in *Ipswich Borough Council v Fisons plc* [1990] 2 WLR 108, which disapproves the *Lucas* test and restores the applicability of the *The Nema* guide-lines to rent review cases.

The judgment of Lord Donaldson MR in *Ipswich v Fisons*, concurred in by his brethren, places rent review arbitrations firmly back within the second, less restrictive, *Nema* guide-line applicable to standard term contracts. His view was that rent review clauses are not so different from commercial contracts, with groups of clauses showing a family resemblance. The test for leave is therefore that a judge has:

'. . . to be satisfied that there was a more or less strong prima facie case for thinking that the arbitrator had erred on a question of law [1990] 2 WLR at p 116E).'

It is not sufficient, as the *Lucas* case had suggested, that the judge is left in real doubt whether the arbitrator is right, nor that his reasons were faulty. It is the arbitral conclusion that matters. To obtain leave to appeal in a case of a rent review arbitration, and within the confines of the brief argument allowed on an application for leave, counsel must demonstrate a strong prima facie case of error. 'Strong', opined Lord Donaldson, is an imprecise term to which no meter can be devised—it is a matter of relative values in the light of the presumption of finality. Thus the presumption of finality will be greater if the arbitrator is a lawyer chosen for his expertise. However, his Lordship gave three examples where less strength will be required and leave may more readily be given:

(1) If the arbitrator is not a lawyer and the whole dispute centres on a difficult question of law.
(2) If the clause in question is of a class commonly encountered so that others would benefit from a definite ruling.
(3) If the alleged arbitral error would have particularly serious consequences for the parties.

Some appeals from rent review arbitrators may have to satisfy the first *Nema* guide-line applicable to 'one-off' contracts—namely to show that the arbitrator is 'obviously wrong'. This may apply, said Lord Donaldson in *Ipswich v Fisons*, to the last rent review during the term, particularly if the remainder of the term is short. Whether or not the 'grades of persuasion' have distinct meanings was doubted by Hoffman J in *Norwich Union Life Assurance Society v Trustee Savings Banks Central Board* [1986] 1 EGLR 136. For him, it was the simple issue; 'one thinks either that the arbitrator was right or that he was wrong'.

It is too early to take a view as to whether *Ipswich v Fisons* will shut out appeals to which the *Lucas* test opened the door. It is probable that argument will centre on the three situations (above) to which a less strong case may be required. Indeed, in *Ipswich v Fisons* itself, at first instance ([1989 3 WLR 818 at 823A) the Vice-Chancellor doubted if there was a strong prima facie case that the arbitrator was wrong (the arbitrator had held that the terms of a lease which he had to settle pursuant to a 1982 agreement extending time under a 1955 contract should not contain provision for rent reviews); yet the Court of Appeal found just such a strong prima facie case (holding that there was no reason why the terms of the lease should not be those appropriate at the date the lease was offered, 1986, and not on 1955 market terms). Though it was not adverted to in the judgment, the terms fixed by the arbitrator would affect the legal relationship of the parties until 2054, and would thus seem to justify 'less strength' within exception 3 noted above.

It is at least clear after *Ipswich v Fisons* that, in considering whether leave should be granted, wider considerations can be taken into account than in judging 'substantiality'- here it may be vital in obtaining leave to show that others may benefit from the correction of the error and the seriousness of the consequences may extend beyond the immediate effect on the parties to the arbitration.

In the first edition of this book (1980), we expressed the hope that arbitral appeals which had elucidated and clarified some of the problems of rent review would not be shut out under the 1979 Act; 10 years on, we can only trust that such appeals will still be appropriate for leave in the light of *Ipswich v Fisons*.

(vi)   Reasons

The strict guide-lines for the granting of leave makes it essential that a party to an arbitration gives written notice to the arbitrator that a reasoned award is required. Without such reasons it will be difficult to know if and why he has erred and therefore fatal to an attempt to get leave to appeal.

There has been some discussion as to whether an arbitrator must comply with a request to give a reasoned award, whether from one party or both. The need to comply with a court order under s 1(5), discussed below, raises different issues and does not solve the problem. The authors' conclusion is that a failure to comply would be misconduct sufficient to justify setting aside the (non-reasoned) award and, possibly, to deprive the arbitrator of his fees. After all, he has failed to perform his contractual obligations to the parties. Two developments bear upon this issue. Some arbitrators include in their directions a statement that no reasoned award will be given. The parties should indicate their dissent to such a course of action, if they disagree with it, and invite the arbitrator to change his mind or resign, although the effect of putting pressure on the arbitrator to reverse his ruling on future good relations with him may influence the choice. With hindsight, a party later dissatisfied with the award may regret taking a stand on the issue, especially where the reasons have not proved to be contentious. In extreme cases, an arbitrator who will not provide reasons even when requested so to do might have to be removed, for his unyielding attitude may destroy the necessary confidence of the parties in him. A second trend has emerged when arbitrators cite one level of fees for an unreasoned award and a higher rate for one with reasons. This may not be intended to discourage a request for reasons but it may well have that effect. Some extra payment for the additional work in preparing a reasoned award may well be justified but the case for an ad valorem uplift is more dubious; to suggest it compensates for the extra responsibility is an unworthy attitude.

A party to an arbitration may, under s 1(5) of the Arbitration Act 1979, with consent of all parties or with leave of the court, ask for a court order requiring the arbitrator to state reasons for his award should an appeal be brought. However, this power is subject to the proviso that the court must be satisfied that either one of the parties gave notice to the arbitrator that reasons were required or that there is a special reason that such notice was not given. In *Leeds Permanent Building Society v Latchmere Properties Ltd* [1989] 1 EGLR 140, the arbitrator arrived at a figure close to the landlord's submission; that submission was based on an erroneous view of the law. However, neither party had requested a reasoned award; and carelessness by a professional adviser in not requesting a reasoned award is not a special reason, which must be a 'reason why it would be unjust to deny to the applicant an opportunity of appealing to the court despite the fact that he failed to require the arbitrator to give reasons for his award' (at p 143). In the absence of a request for reasons or a special reason that notice was not given, it has been held that the court has no jurisdiction to make an order that reasons be given, unless the arbitrator has set out to give some reasons: *Trave Schiffahrtsgesellschaft mbH v Ninemia Maritime Corp, The Niedersachsen* [1986] 1 Lloyd's Rep 393. That decision was in the context of confidential reasons, as rare in rent review cases as they are common in shipping cases, but there seems no doubt that it applies to any 'bare' award.

(vii) Determination of a difficult point of law

Under s 2 of the Arbitration Act 1979, either party can apply for the High Court to determine a point of law arising in the reference. Consent of either the arbitrator or all other parties is required (s 2(1)) and the application can only be entertained if the question of law is one in respect of which leave to appeal would be likely to be given *and* the determination might produce substantial savings in costs. In *Chapman v Charlwood Properties Ltd* (1981) 260 EG 1041, two points were brought before the court on a s 2(2) preliminary application, namely whether on the construction of a particular review clause the rent should reflect a rent for the residue of the term or not, and secondly, whether 'best rent' meant such a rent for the premises let as a whole or the aggregate of such rents for separate lettings or parts. The judge held the second to be a question of valuation not of law and so not within s 2 at all. On the first, Hodgson J reiterated the tests laid down in s 2(2) of the 1979 Act. The second test (that the point would be one likely to attract leave to appeal under s 1(3)(b)) was satisfied but not, it was found, the first (that the determination might produce substantial cost savings). Even had he been satisfied on that score, moreover, leave would have been refused because of the dangers of making decisions on construction points without full findings of fact, an element on which he laid great stress. This reflects the authors' view in the first edition of this book that the cases where preliminary rulings on points of law can be sought under s 2 of the 1979 Act will surely be rare in the context of rent review. However, even before the 1979 Act, in an increasing proportion of the reported cases, legal issues of construction were resolved by seeking declarations on points of construction in advance of the arbitration hearing and the restrictive impact of *Chapman v Charlwood* has ensured that approach became more wide-spread. Nevertheless, its continued availability was stressed in *Scottish & Newcastle Breweries plc v Sir Richard Sutton's Settled Estates* [1985] 2 EGLR 130.

In *The Vasso* [1983] 1 WLR 838 Lloyd J discussed some of the infelicities of s 2 and dropped a broad hint that some of them could perhaps be circumvented by procuring an interim award on the point of difficulty. Whether or not the device would work will fall to be tested against the guide-line principles just discussed. A preliminary issue succeeded in *Cornwall Coast Country Club Ltd v Cardgrange Ltd* [1987] 1 EGLR 146, one of a number of cases thrown up by the problems of reviewing rents for casinos. The arbitrator's refusal to order production of accounts, as he thought the profits method of valuation inappropriate, was reversed. Perhaps s 2 is most useful when both parties consent; in *Ritz Hotel (London) Ltd v Ritz Casino Ltd* [1989] 2 EGLR 135 six questions of law were determined under the procedure.

(viii) Contracting out of appeal rights

The freedom to contract out of the appeal rights for arbitration introduced by ss 3 and 4 of the 1979 Act is not of major significance in this field. Most leases will be 'domestic arbitration agreements', so that initial contracting out will be ineffective (s 3(6)) and only contracting out after the start of arbitration will be permitted. Where one party to a lease is a foreign national or resident or a corporate body incorporated or with its central management outside the United Kingdom, the agreement will not be a domestic one and there will be full freedom to contract out of these appeal procedures from the outset. Landlords in the United Kingdom have shown no readiness to permit such bargains; indeed it seems that contracting out is a dead letter in the context of leases.

(ix) Contracting in and facilitating an appeal

Far from contracting out, parties to a lease may wish to consider 'contracting in' to an appeal, for s 1(3) allows an appeal 'with the consent of all the other parties'. In an existing lease therefore, it would be open to the parties to agree this prior to the award, whether or not this agreement is made before or after the dispute arises (*Ipswich v Fisons*

[1990] 2 WLR at 113B). This course might be appropriate for a particularly complex question of law when both parties wish to have the opportunity to appeal. Indeed, there is no reason why, in a new lease, an express agreement to permit arbitral appeals should not be set out in the review clause. This 'would constitute either a sufficient consent to satisfy s 1(3) of the 1979 Act or a very powerful reason for giving leave, subject only to s 1(4)' (*Ipswich v Fisons* at 113B). However, if the problem can be foreseen at the drafting stage, it would be better dealt with by an appropriate provision to remove the problem rather than invite a dispute and an appeal therefrom. Draftsmen are rarely prone to modesty about the effectiveness of their own handiwork.

(x) Procedural points

It is settled law (*The Nema, Ipswich v Fisons*) that a decision on whether to grant leave to appeal to the High Court should be arrived at after only brief argument. It is not the function of the judge to hear the putative appeal.

Applications under s 1 of the 1979 Act, or Part I of the 1950 Act, are by originating motion within 21 days of the publication of the award. Since an award is published when the arbitrator tells the parties it is ready, a delay in paying the fee and taking up the award may sacrifice the right both of appeal and to apply for remission or setting aside (below): *The Archipelagos* [1979] 2 Lloyd's Rep 289, *South Tottenham Land Securities v Millett* (1983) 268 EG 703 at 706.

Applications for leave to appeal, or under s 2, are to a single judge (RSC Ord 73, r 2). Under RSC Ord 73, r 6, applications for leave to appeal are to a judge of the Commercial Court. In practice, the earlier assignment of cases to the Chancery or Queen's Bench judges has continued; see, generally, *Practice Note* [1985] 2 All ER 383.

(xi) Appeals to the Court of Appeal

An appeal to the Court of Appeal against the decision of the High Court on an arbitral appeal (s 1) or on the determination of a preliminary point of law (s 2) is only possible if the High Court gives leave and certifies that the question of law to which its decision relates is either one of general public importance or for some other special reason should be considered by the Court of Appeal (s 1(7) of the 1979 Act). The Court of Appeal may give leave if it is refused by the High Court; if the High Court refuses to certify the question of law, there is no jurisdiction enabling the Court of Appeal to review that refusal: *National Westminster Bank v Arthur Young McClelland Moores* [1975] 2 EGLR 13. In *The Antaios*, some further guidance was given on the criteria for the giving of leave for an appeal to the Court of Appeal from the decision of a High Court judge granting or refusing leave to appeal from the award under s 1(6)A where he has made the necessary certification; leave should only be granted where the decision calls for some amplification, elucidation or adaption to changing practices of existing guide-lines. The principles are also discussed in *Babanaft International Co SA v Avant Petroleum Inc* [1982] 1 WLR 871. That issue is too wide, in the authors' view, to call for further discussion in this book (but see Mustill and Boyd, pp 626–31).

(b) Remission or setting aside of an award

Sections 22 and 23 of the Arbitration Act 1950 provide alternative but related remedies; a power to remit an award, a power to set aside an award and a power to remove an arbitrator for misconduct. The relevant part of the sections provide:

s 22(1)—In all cases of reference to arbitration the High Court or a judge thereof may from time to time remit the matters referred, or any of them, to the reconsideration of the arbitrator or umpire.

s 23(1)—Where an arbitrator or umpire has misconducted himself or the proceedings, the High Court may remove him.

s 23(2)—Where an arbitrator or umpire has misconducted himself or the proceedings, or an arbitrator or award has been improperly procured, the High Court may set the award aside.

(i) The basis of the jurisdiction

The lesser remedy of remitting an award (under s 22) to the same or a different arbitrator was not altered by the 1979 Act. Though the power of remission is in the court's discretion, principles to guide and restrict the statutory discretion have been laid down in the substantial case law (see, eg *Re Montgomery Jones and Co and Liebenthal and Co* (1898) 78 LT 406). They include cases where fresh evidence has been acquired after the award, where a mistake is admitted by the arbitrator or the issue of costs has been inadequately dealt with or where the arbitrator has exceeded his jurisdiction. However, procedural irregularity or technical misconduct are the basis of most rent review cases which have led to remission. The basis of the jurisdiction to set aside an award or remove an arbitrator is very similar save that misconduct must be shown and to that extent remedies under s 23 are more stringently applied and limited to more serious cases. In *Windvale Ltd v Darlington Insulation Co Ltd* (1983) 20 December, unreported, an award was set aside. A series of errors was catalogued—indeed, 'on every point that he could go wrong the arbitrator has in this particular case gone wrong'. So a second arbitration before a new arbitrator was ordered.

In essence, what is required under both sections is a 'mishap or misunderstanding or error in procedure in the course of this arbitration which could lead, or might have led, to an unjust result' per Bingham J in *Shield Properties & Investments Ltd v Anglo-Overseas Transport Co Ltd* [1985] 1 EGLR 7 at 9, serious enough in the case of setting aside or removal to amount to misconduct. So the essence of the jurisdiction is *procedural* mistakes, akin to a breach of natural justice or procedural fairness—quite the opposite to a question of *law* which is the basis of an application for leave to appeal. A procedural error by one or both of the parties may suffice for remission even if the arbitrator is not at all at fault: *Harrison v Thompson* [1989] 1 WLR 1325 (question of costs remitted when both parties had wrongly assumed that they could make submissions on costs after the award—see discussion at p 185 above).

For detailed treatment of these topics reference may be made to the standard texts (Russell, pp 392–430 and Mustill and Boyd, pp 547–70). The discussion which follows centres on those principles as they have been applied in rent review cases.

(ii) 'Misconduct' in rent review

The term covers a wide range of situations from reprehensible malpractice through to procedural error where the courts are often anxious to express the view that the arbitrator cannot be held personally to blame notwithstanding the technical misconduct on which the remedy is based. So, while bias, fraud, acceptance of hospitality or acting for one of the parties during the reference would be obvious examples of misconduct, it is procedural irregularity which is the most likely basis on which a remedy will be sought.

Reliance on personal knowledge without proper disclosure to the parties (discussed in detail above at p 178) is a particular risk for a rent review arbitrator since most will be surveyors with their own expertise. The Court of Appeal discussed the extent to which an arbitrator might use his own knowledge and experience in a case which was not a commodity or informal arbitration, namely, *Fox v P G Wellfair Ltd* [1981] 2 Lloyd's Rep 514 where an arbitration proceeded in the absence of one party. The arbitrator, in his award, relied on his own knowledge and rejected much of the evidence, of necessity untested, laid before him by the only party who appeared. That was held to be misconduct and the award was set aside. Dunn LJ summed up the position thus: 'If the expert arbitrator forms a view of the facts different from that given in the evidence which might produce a contrary result . . . , then he should bring that view to the attention of the parties' (at 529). The judgment of Lord Denning MR was to like effect: 'he should not use his own knowledge to derogate from the evidence of the [parties'] experts without putting his own knowledge to them and giving them a chance of answering it and showing that his own view is wrong' (at 522). Reference may also be made in this context to a useful discussion by Callender in an article in (1982) 47 *Arbitration* 197.

The judgments in the Court of Appeal in *Fox v Wellfair* were cited and followed by the judge in the rent review case of *Top Shop Estates v Danino* [1985] 1 EGLR 9. The misconduct consisted of reliance on personal knowledge without disclosure to the parties. The personal knowledge consisted of inspections of cited comparable properties, where the directions issued had indicated only that the arbitrator would inspect the property in question, and pedestrian counts carried out on his own initiative. Furthermore, having directed that comparables be validated (ie established by direct evidence, see discussion at p 234 ff below) he had treated one as validated because he was involved in other arbitrations in which it figured. It may well be, in such a case as this, that an arbitrator will misconduct himself through an excess of zeal; indeed, had an expert valuer, acting in that capacity, conducted himself as did the arbitrator in the *Top Shop* case, he should have been commended for his conscientiousness.

The decision in *Zermalt Holdings SA v Nu-life Upholstery Repairs Ltd* [1985] 2 EGLR 14 is consistent with the above cases, although none of them were considered in it. The arbitrator's award was set aside on two grounds. First, he had treated the property as a developer's shell, a proposition for which neither party had argued. Secondly, he had rejected a valuation approach to comparables adopted by the valuers to both parties. The arbitrator should have put his views on both issues to the parties and invited their comments but he had not done so.

It is common in rent review arbitrations for the arbitrator to set out in advance to the parties the procedure he intends to adopt. No doubt these parameters normally assist the procedure but failure to observe such self imposed rulings can amount to procedural misconduct. Thus in *Shield Properties & Investments Ltd v Anglo-Overseas Transport Co Ltd* (above) the arbitrator failed to draw the attention of the tenant to a letter received from the landlord, a letter, moreover, referring to hearsay evidence which the arbitrator's directions, in a written submission proceeding, had forbidden the parties to submit. (In fact, the 'offending' letter offered to comply with the direction if required.) The error was held to constitute misconduct and the award remitted. (A second aspect of the case is discussed at p 227 below). The arbitrator was again the author of his own misfortunes in *Control Securities v Spencer* [1989] 1 EGLR 136. He laid down firm and fair guide-lines but departed from them in three respects: in not insisting that the tenant's surveyor verify his comparables so that some were hearsay with no evidence to suggest that they were excluded from consideration; an accidental error in not forwarding a letter to the other side; and a failure to observe his self imposed rule to discuss whether an oral hearing was required. In this case, the award was set aside on the basis that it was not fair to require the arbitrator to clear his mind of the view he had already formed.

Remission may be granted on a consent application (*Yorkshire Insurance Co v Eagle Star Insurance Ltd* (1983) unreported—some copy leases were not sent to the other side) but not every mishap will be sufficient. Thus the mere possibility of hearsay evidence having been incorrectly admitted is not a sufficient ground for remission: *Fine Fare Ltd v Kenmore Investments Ltd* [1989] 1 EGLR 143 at p 145.

The power under s 22 to remit must not be used as a back door method of circumventing the restrictions on obtaining leave to appeal. Possible errors of law categorised as procedural mishap will not be a successful basis for remission: *Fine Fare* case, above; *Manders Property (Estates) Ltd v Magnet House Properties Ltd* [1989] 2 EGLR 126, applying *Moran v Lloyds* [1983] QB 542, CA.

The effect of remission being granted is to suspend the original award; so that no increase in rent is payable until the revised award is published: *Shield Properties & Investments Ltd v Anglo-Overseas Transport Co Ltd (No 2)* [1986] 2 EGLR 112—in this case, since interest was only due under the lease once the award was published, it followed that no interest was payable. Where an award is remitted on a limited issue, the revived authority of the arbitrator is limited to that issue: *Interbulk Ltd v Aiden Shipping Co Ltd, 'The Vimeira' (No 3)* [1986] 2 Lloyd's Rep 75.

There is insufficient evidence to state whether the constraints on appeals led to an increase in applications under ss 22 and 23, but the attempts in the *Fine Fare* and *Manders Property* cases to combine application for leave under s 1 with applications to remit or set aside under ss 22 and 23 suggest both that this may be so but that the courts will ensure that the two remedies are kept distinct. The constraints on appeals will not be easily circumvented by alleging that errors of law constitute arbitral misconduct so as to allow remission or setting aside.

(c) Issue estoppel

The decision in *Fidelitas Shipping Co Ltd v V/O Exportchleb* [1966] 1 QB 630 indicated that an arbitrator's award created an issue estoppel between the parties. Serial arbitrations between the parties to, say, a shipping, commodity or construction arbitration are likely to be rare, but the very structure of a lease with rent reviews envisages the prospect of successive arbitrations between the parties, the landlord and tenant for the time being if not the original parties; and the possible problems of issue estoppel for rent review were highlighted by Mr Gaunt in his 1982 Blundell Memorial Lecture (see (1982) 79 *Law Society's Gazette* 541). It is now clear that issue estoppel probably does apply to rent review arbitral awards and certainly does so if the decision is that of a judge on appeal.

Just such a case arose in *Arnold v National Westminster Bank plc* [1990] 1 All ER 529, the latest stage in the long-running saga between the parties which began with the decision of Walton J [1985] 1 EGLR 61. There the judge decided that the hypothetical lease should contain no provision for rent review. He refused leave to appeal and refused a certificate that the question of law was of general public importance. The spate of decisions on similar points thereafter belied his view; though the guide-lines for construction were changed later (see p 333 ff), that did not assist the tenant in the instant case. The principle of issue estoppel suggested that the tenant was stuck with a ruling out of line with subsequent decisions and stymied on an appeal on a technicality—and with a long lease faced a loss running into millions of pounds. However, faced with this question, the Court of Appeal decided that issue estoppel does admit of exceptions for special circumstances and such special circumstances could include developments in the law. When combined with the continuing contractual relationship of the parties and the fact that the court considered that Walton J was plainly wrong, the court found special circumstances and the tenant could reopen the issue on the next review. (Rectification proceedings, to reverse, in effect, the judicial ruling on the first review are also in train.)

It is to be noted that the judges in *Arnold v National Westminster Bank*, though they agreed the plaintiffs were within the exception, differed on the exact circumstances which qualify as special. The majority thought, as in that case, that the decision had to be plainly wrong; a different majority emphasised the continuing contractual relationship; Mann LJ refused to define the meaning of special or exceptional circumstances. Whether it is open to argue that a decision was plainly wrong without further elucidation of the law was expressly left open by Staughton LJ; but it is clear that it will only be in a rare case that a decision can be reopened.

Several consequences flow from the applicability of issue estoppel. To establish the scope of any such estoppel, it would be essential to preserve evidence of the exact issues raised and decided in any arbitration, and a successor in title to either party ought to inquire about, and seek to have handed over, any such record. This factor would have to be weighed in the balance in deciding whether or not to request a reasoned award, a decision that has perforce to be taken when the likely reasons cannot be known but only guessed at. A party may prefer not to have a specific adverse ruling or finding on the record, so as to be free to argue the point anew in a further 5, 10 or more years' time; conversely, he may be happy to have a favourable decision recorded and so concluded for the residue of the term.

It should be noted that the exception for special circumstances is only applicable to issue estoppel and is only likely to apply to arbitral awards and appeals therefrom. Proceedings before the courts, for example for a declaration on a construction summons, give rise to cause of action estoppel which will bind absolutely for the duration of the lease. The only remedy is an appeal, if necessary getting leave to appeal out of time as in *Property & Reversionary Corporation v Templar* [1977] 1 WLR 1223.

7 Challenging an expert or his determination

There are three possible remedies for a party to a rent review by an expert who is aggrieved with the determination.

(1) Fraud or collusion

In the unlikely event that fraud or collusion with the other party could be proved, the binding nature of the award, as between the parties, could be challenged, for 'fraud unravels everything' (per Denning LJ in *Lazarus Estates Ltd v Beasley* [1956] 1 QB 702 at 712). This basis was affirmed in *Campbell v Edwards* [1976] 1 WLR 403.

(2) A Wholly Erroneous Basis

It appears that a determination can be declared a nullity if founded on a wholly erroneous principle: *Collier v Mason* (1858) 53 ER 613 at 614. The jurisdictional basis for the court's power so to act remains controversial; and after the recent decision in *Jones v Sherwood Computer Services* [1989] EGCS 172 it is likely that the jurisdiction will be more sparingly exercised. Its value to an aggrieved party, where it can be established, is that it is the only method, short of showing fraud or collusion, which will allow a setting aside of the determination. (It is not strictly an 'award' because the referee acts as an expert but the term is often used in this technically incorrect sense.)

(3) Action for negligence

An action for negligence, or possibly for breach of contract, against the expert personally for breach of his duty of care (or breach of contract) is the often the only option for a dissatisfied party. Though the determination will remain binding between the parties to the lease, a successful action will allow recovery of the loss in damages; the difficulty is that such actions require a high burden of proof.

Nothing more need be said about fraud or collusion but the other two remedies require detailed examination.

(a) Impugning an 'award' or determination

Until 1976, it could be said that the line of authorities based on *Collier v Mason* (above) established that a valuation based on a fundamental mistake would not be binding on the parties. Then in *Campbell v Edwards* (above) and *Baber v Kenwood Manufacturing Co Ltd* [1978] 1 Lloyd's Rep 175, a very much stricter rule applied so that it seemed that the determination could not be impugned if the expert was fulfilling his contractual duties honestly.

The width of the statements in *Campbell v Edwards* led to the view that, following *Arenson v Arenson*, there was no jurisdiction, short of fraud or collusion, to challenge the determination of any expert valuer acting within his instructions. The expert was now liable in tort in negligence which provided a remedy where it was required; he could hardly be so liable if the effect of his error was also that the certificate was not binding on the parties.

However, both *Campbell v Edwards* and *Baber v Kenwood* were concerned with a non-speaking valuation and in *Burgess v Purchase & Sons (Farms) Ltd* [1983] Ch 216 it was held that a 'speaking award' could be the subject of a challenge. The decision did not concern rent reviews but an accountancy valuation; the auditors concerned set out how they had arrived at their valuation. The plantiffs sought a declaration that the valuation was not binding and for a fresh valuation. In an action to strike out, it was held that a speaking valuation made pursuant to a contract to have a valuation made and which demonstrated on its face that it had been made on a fundamentally erroneous basis could be impugned by a party to a contract; a good cause of action had been established and the application to strike out failed. Nourse J applied three earlier decisions to the same effect and rejected the argument that they were no longer good law in the light of *Campbell v Edwards*. It was stressed that the impugned award had not been acted on (though it did not matter that it had been completed), and it must be said that Nourse J virtually invited an appeal from his decision. No such appeal was taken and there are subsequent rent review cases where expert's reasoned determinations were set aside.

In *Jones v Sherwood Computer Services*, the Court of Appeal has disapproved of *Burgess v Purchase & Sons* and the distinction between a speaking and non speaking determination. It is thought that the scope of the jurisdiction to set aside, though it will require elucidation in subsequent cases, has been restricted.

(i)   Basis of the jurisdiction

In *Burgess v Purchase & Sons* Nourse J justified the rule on the basis that a valuation on a fundamentally erroneous basis is not what the parties have contracted for and that it could be argued that there was an implied term to that effect. He recognised that it was something of an anomaly that a fundamental error could not be corrected in all valuations and in *Jones v Sherwood Computer Services* Dillon LJ agreed with his reservation but rejected his view that the authorities prior to *Campbell v Edwards* were still the basis of the law. Instead the jurisdiction to set aside has as its starting point the contractual principle laid down by Lord Denning in *Campbell v Edwards* at 407:

'If two persons agree that the price of the property should be fixed by a valuer on whom they agree and he gives that valuation honestly and in good faith, they are bound by it. The reason is because they have agreed to be bound by it.'

The difficulty after *Jones v Sherwood Computer Services* is to determine the extent of the jurisdiction that remains and the principle on which the court will intervene, if at all. The *Jones* case itself was one of pure valuation and the error alleged was a mistake in what was properly included in the valuation. This was alleged to be an error of law but was not obviously so. The approach, said Dillon LJ, with whom Balcombe LJ agreed, is to ascertain the extent of the contractual reference; and then to see the nature of the mistake. If the mistake involves a departure from the expert's instructions in a material respect then the determination is not binding because the expert has not done what he was appointed to do. In the *Jones* case the valuers did precisely what they were instructed to do and the determination could not be impugned.

On one view, *Jones v Sherwood Computer Services* can be read as admitting of no power to set aside the determination if the expert honestly seeks to fulfil his contractual duties. However, Dillon LJ in his judgment quotes the words of Romilly MR in *Collier v Mason* (above); namely that the valuation stands unless he 'had valued it on some wholly erroneous principle'. There was no such allegation in the *Jones* case but it is likely to be the claim made against a rent review valuation. Where there is a expert determination, clearly made on a view of the law which is wrong, it is submitted that the power to set aside remains and further support for this propsition can be gleaned from *Heyes v Earl of Derby* (1984) 272 EG 935, CA. The merit of this view is that it will accord closely with the power to give leave to appeal against an arbitrator's award, considered in the previous section. It is also justified on the ground referred to in *Burgess v Purchase & Sons* where Nourse J considered that the remedy in negligence against the valuer might not always be available—as in the case of a fundamentally erroneous construction of an agreement which it was not within the professional competence of the valuer to detect. The relevance of this last comment to rent review should be obvious (cf *JT Sydenham & Co Ltd v Enichem Elastomers Ltd*, below). If there is no basis for setting aside such a determination or for negligence, then a party will be left with no remedy.

In *A Hudson Pty Ltd v Legal and General Life of Australia* [1986] 2 EGLR 130, the Privy Council rejected an appeal from New South Wales which sought to set aside a rent review valuation. Neither *Campbell v Edwards* or *Burgess v Purchase & Sons* was mentioned; indeed no authorities were discussed at all. However, the better view of Lord Templeman's opinion (part of which is quoted below) is that he declined to upset the award on the basis that no fundamental error had been shown rather than that there was no jurisdiction to do so.

(ii) Requirements for the exercise of the jurisdiction

Until *Jones v Sherwood Computer Services*, it could be said that the valuation sought to be challenged must have been a 'speaking' determination. In other words, it must on its face, have explained how the valuation had been arrived at (*Burgess v Purchase & Sons*). The distinction between a speaking and non-speaking valuation was said not to be relevant in the *Jones* case; the real question is whether it is possible to say from all the evidence what the valuer has done and why he has done it. Thus, a reasoned award will still be of value as it will be the best evidence of the basis of the determination and avoid such issues as whether the valuer or certifier can be a defendant in proceedings for the purpose of discovering his reasons, a point expressly left open in the *Jones* case. If, as is common, the expert simply determines a figure, there is no way available to the parties to demonstrate that the sum determined is founded on a manifest error.

Consequently, in order to give the best opportunity to challenge, the parties may require a reasoned determination, either by terms in the lease or in the agreed appointment at review. Added point is thereby given to the admonition in the RICS Guidance Notes (Note 4.5.4) for an expert to eschew a reasoned award (unless bound to do so) but to keep his notes to hand against the risk of a negligence claim!

There must be shown to be a fundamental error. In the earlier cases, it was said that the error must be one of law or, perhaps, established valuation practice which amounts to 'a mistake of a substantial character' or a material misdirection: *Dean v Prince* [1954] Ch 409 at 418–19). *Jones v Sherwood Computer Services* now suggests that the error must be a mistake so wrong that it can be characterised as a breach of contract; the expert has not done what he was appointed to do. So, an error of fact or of valuation judgment which is not so substantial or material will not suffice nor, probably, a mistake due to professional negligence— because it is the fact of the greater extent of liability in negligence that has led to the narrower rules for setting aside which currently prevail. The error must 'go to the basis of the valuation such that the valuation was not conducted in accordance with the parties contract': *Apus Properties Ltd v Douglas Farrow & Co Ltd* [1989] 2 EGLR 265, adopting the submission of counsel. In *A Hudson Pty Ltd v Legal and General Life of Australia*, the valuers made no such mistake in fact or law to justify interference. The objection was that the valuers had attributed $7 per square foot to the whole of the ground floor notwithstanding that it included air space used in connection with the lower ground floor. This was a possible valuation approach and Lord Templeman spoke critically of the plantiff's case: 'It would be a disservice to the law and to litigants to encourage forensic attacks on valuations by experts where those attacks are based on textual criticisms more appropriate to the measured analysis of fiscal legislation'. This passage suggests that to show a fundamental error will not be easy. If the view taken by the valuer is one which can properly be held by a competent valuer, then the plantiff's case must fail: *Re Imperial Foods Ltd's Pension Scheme* [1986] 1 WLR 717.

The error must be apparent either on the face of the award or from the totality of the evidence. If there are two possible constructions of the alleged error, only one of which shows the valuer to be fundamentally wrong, it is submitted that the action will fail. In the *Apus Properties* case, the Deputy Judge held it was sufficient that he was satisfied of the misconstruction on the balance of probabilities. In the light of *Jones v Sherwood Computer Services*, the authors prefer to side with the submission of counsel that the error must be clear.

(iii) Some recent examples

Valuations have been set aside or declared a nullity in two rent review cases; but these decisions must be treated with caution and read in the light of *Jones v Sherwood Computer Services*. In *JT Sydenham & Co Ltd v Enichem Elastomers Ltd* [1989] 1 EGLR 257, but decided in 1986, the deputy judge decided that a surveyor acting as an expert who had interpreted a user clause restrictively with a consequent impact on the reviewed rent had fallen into error. He made a declaration, after a close analysis of the lease, that the restrictions on user were permissive or protective rather than imposing an obligation to use in that way so that the user clause did not have a limiting effect on the open market rent. The basis of the expert's determination was clear—the ambiguity of the user clause and the (erroneous) interpretation adopted by the valuer were set out in the determination. However, the deputy judge did not avert to the need that the error must be a fundamental one; having made the declaration as to the true construction of the lease, he set aside the valuer's certificate.

The other example is *Apus Properties Ltd v Douglas Henry Farrow Ltd* [1989] 2 EGLR 265, where, in a preliminary hearing of an action to recover arrears of rent from an original lessee and sureties, a 1982 expert's determination was declared a nullity. Once again it was an error of law relating to the correct assumption to make as to the use of the premises. The valuer had adopted the wider use permitted by a licence to assign given on the grant of an underlease whereas it was held that the rent review should have been on the assumption of the use clause in and at the date of the head lease. The modification by licence was, in any event, a variation personal to that subtenant.

The issue which the author's expect may be litigated after *Jones v Sherwood Computer Services* is the extent to which such an erroneous assumption of law can be categorised as a breach of contract; in the two examples cited, had the expert done what he was appointed to do? There is an argument that the parties will expect a determination according to law; if this is right, then there may still be room for challenges to rent review valuations. The issue may also be considered in drafting new leases or when making an agreed reference; an explicit direction requiring a determination according to the correct legal principles might persuade a court more easily that a mistake of law was a breach of contract.

(iv)   Effect of setting aside

It should be noted that if the plaintiff succeeds in setting aside a determination, the court has no jurisdiction to determine the true value itself. The valuation process must be recommenced in accordance with the terms of the lease; *Dean v Prince, Burgess v Purchase & Sons* (above). However, it is possible, if the court can discern from the determination what the true valuation should be, that it will make a declaration of the true valuation: *Smith v Gale* [1974] 1 WLR 9. This might be applicable if the valuer reveals, for example, what the open market rent would be but for the restrictive user clause that he erroneously takes into account. Secondly, a declaration of nullity may be made in favour of parties other than those for whom the rent review was commissioned. Thus in the *Apus Properties* decision, the determination was declared a nullity at the suit of an original lessee and his surety who were seeking to escape liability for rent arrears some 7 years after the event. However, the nullifying effect of the court order was restricted to the liability of the original lessee and his surety and the surety for the assignee was held to be bound by reason of his involvement in the review process. He had personally negotiated the relevant sub-lease and the modification of use, the misconstruing of which was the basis of the valuer's errors. Quite what measure of involvement will deny a remedy may need to be settled by later decisions.

(b)   Action for negligence or breach of contract

An action against the expert for damages is the principal remedy for a dissatisfied party to a determination.

(i)   The basis of the action

The aggrieved party will seek damages for negligence (or, perhaps, breach of contract) in a separate cause of action, though one set of proceedings could be used both to seek to set aside a determination and to claim damages for negligence in the alternative (as in *Burgess v Purchase & Sons*). He may have a choice of remedy, being able to sue in both contract and tort (*Midland Bank Trust Co Ltd v Hett, Stubbs and Kemp* [1979] Ch 384) and thereby taking advantage of the different rules for the measure of damages; though the trend against concurrent liability in both contract and tort should be noted: *Tai Hing Cotton Mill Ltd v Liu Chong Hing Bank Ltd* [1986] AC 80; *Lee v Thompson* [1989] 2 EGLR 151. The defendant surveyor in *Palacath v Flanagan* (above), appointed by the President of the RICS, challenged the contractual basis but conceded the tortious claim, so the point was left open. The different periods of limitation would rarely be significant in a rent review context and the obligations arising in tort are no different to those which would arise by reason of a contractual undertaking to act in a professionally competent manner. The other party to the determination will not be involved except that he might be called as a witness in support of the allegations.

(ii) Proof of negligence

The cases where negligence has been alleged indicate that the burden of proof will be a difficult one to sustain. It is not enough to show that another valuer would have reached a different conclusion. Thus in the Scottish case of *Skirt N' Slack Centre of London v Buchanan* (1986), unreported, Lord Cowie set out the conditions to be satisfied if a claim for negligence is to be established. He applied the test set out in *Hunter v Hanley* [1955] SC 200 and applied by the House of Lords in *Maynard v West Midlands Regional Health Authority* [1984] 1 WLR 634, namely, that it must be shown that:

(1) there is a usual and normal practice;
(2) the defendant departed from that practice;
(3) the course adopted was one that no competent surveyor acting in a rent review would have taken if he had been acting with ordinary care.

The classic statement of the degree of care necessary by persons exercising professional skills is found in *Bolam v Friern Hospital Management Committee* [1957] 1 WLR 582 at 586–7; see Dugdale and Stanton, *Professional Negligence*, paras 15–17. In many contexts, proof of an accepted practice is not as vital as the criteria stated above might suggest but in the rent review context, where the valuation exercise involves a matter of judgment in the light of a particular property, to prove negligence without proof of some accepted professional practice will be a very difficult task.

In the *Skirt N' Slack* case each allegation of negligence foundered on one or other of the points, particularly in failing to prove a normal practice. The need, in practice, to prove all three points places a heavy onus on the plaintiff. Moreover, the defendant in that case produced a valuation by an independent expert witness arriving at a rental figure which was for all practical purposes the same as the defendant had produced; and the judge indicated that was sufficient for the negligence claim to fail. Similarly, the defendant in *Belvedere Motors Ltd v King* (1981) 260 EG 813 might ruefully have reflected that fraud was about the only misdeed not alleged against him, but neither the general allegation of negligence in his decision as an expert nor the particular allegations were substantiated; the court concluded (at 819) 'Indeed . . . . he came fairly near to the true mark'. A substantial attack and negligence claim was mounted unsuccessfully against an expert's valuation in *Wallshire v Aarons* [1989] 1 EGLR 147, which gives a typical example of the criticisms which may be levelled by a dissatisfied party but which do not amount to proof of negligence. In particular, it may be that another valuer might well not have reached the same conclusion, 'but it does not follow that because another valuer might have reached a different conclusion that therefore the defendant is negligent' (at p 151). Finally, reference to claims against valuers in other aspects of their work may provide guidance and there is some authority that, since valuation cannot produce answers of absolute precision, there is a permissible 'margin of error' which operates before negligence can be established: see Dugdale and Stanton paras 17.43–44. Whether or not this margin is one not exceeding 10 per cent (*Singer and Friedlander Ltd v John D Wood & Co* (1977) 243 EG 212) or a permissible width to be decided upon on the evidence in the particular case (*McIntyre v Herring Son & Daw* [1988] 1 EGLR 231), it means there is a further hurdle before a claim can succeed.

An action for negligence therefore involves the difficult task of, in effect, arguing the issue at one remove as well as being rather distasteful to some disappointed clients. Even if successful with an assessment of damages, leaving the reviewed rent operative is a less satisfactory solution than an adjustment of the rent—an assignment of a lease at an inflated rent, perhaps with a reverse premium, will, for example, not be a straightforward transaction. The differing tax treatment of a lump sum award of damages and revenue payments of rent on a quarterly basis, the complications of assessing the award by discounting future rent payments and the problems of delay in obtaining the award all complicate the issue.

(iii) Disclaimer of liability

The possibility that the expert invited to take on the reference might decline to do so save under a disclaimer of liability is now subject to the constraint that under s 2 of the Unfair Contract Terms Act 1977 such an exclusion clause would have to be shown to be reasonable if it were to be relied on. A 'blanket' disclaimer might not meet that test, quite apart from the reluctance that the person invited to carry our the review would have in putting it forward. A partial disclaimer would be equally ill-judged psychologically and would present drafting problems too. Most expert valuers have simply accepted the added risks of liability for negligence and have not sought to contract out of it. It is to be expected that most of them are adequately covered by indemnity insurance in any event. Similar arguments apply to any attempt by an arbitrator to exclude or limit liability, if it now exists, and the issue is also discussed in an article by Professor Adams: (1984) 270 EG 27.

(iv) Quasi-arbitral immunity?

It is worth averting to the possibility that a valuer acting as an expert might claim immunity on the basis that he was acting as a quasi-arbitrator. The validity of the quasi-arbitrator status is questioned in dicta and is far from authoritatively established. In *Palacath v Flanagan* [1985]

2 All ER 161, considerable stress was laid on the proposition derived from *Arenson v Arenson* and the speech of Lord Simon [1977] AC 405 at 419 that the referee who claims immunity from liability as a quasi-arbitrator bears a heavy onus of proof because he is escaping the usual consequences of acting for the parties. The public policy element of imposing liability when so acting is the primary rule and any arbitral immunity is subsidiary to it. Consequently, it is not thought likely that an expert acting in a rent review could ever claim quasi-arbitral immunity.

(v) Negligence action against the party's own surveyor

This is an entirely distinct remedy founded upon usual principles in a case where there is a breach of a duty of care, more fully discussed at p 289 below. In *Rajdev v Becketts* [1989] 2 EGLR 144 a successful claim was made where a surveyor had failed to put representations to the independent expert and so lost the opportunity of influencing his determination. The measure of damages was the difference between the true market rent and the rent as determined which was agreed higher than was justified.

8 Practical points

(a) Selection or appointment of referee

Most precedents (including all those reproduced in Part Seven) and most other leases which provide for third party decision in the event of failure to agree the revised rent do so in two stages; namely joint appointment following agreement between the parties or failing such agreement (in some instances within a stated period, variously expressed, but in others merely, by implication, within a reasonable period) appointment by a named office-holder, overwhelmingly the President of the RICS. A full discussion of all the drafting options appears in Chapter 4, p 64 ff, above.

It has been made clear that the process of appointment by the President is an administrative act and he owes no duty to refrain from making an appointment if the parties are in dispute; injunctive relief to prevent appointment is not therefore available: *United Co-operatives Ltd v Sun Alliance & London Assurance Co Ltd* [1987] 1 EGLR 126. The remedy is an application to the court to determine the issue of construction and, if the arbitrator or expert appointed refuse to delay pending those proceedings, then to take proceedings for an injunction or otherwise in which the arbitrator or expert is a party.

Provisions for appointment by the President or other named office-holder may create problems if for any reason the named appointor is unable to act, if only to the extent of the need to apply to the court under s 10 of the Arbitration Act 1950 (as amended in 1979). Standard precedents thus provide for the eventuality. Conveyancer Precedent 5–

57 allows appointment by 'some other officer . . . if the President is unable to act'. The Model Forms in both the 1980 and 1985 revisions adopt the more general formula of appointment 'by or on behalf of the President', which side-steps the issue of establishing that the President is unable to act. The ISVA Forms include a person authorised to act on behalf of the President in the definition of President. The reason for precautions is that appointment by someone other than the President himself may offend against the maxim *delgatus non potest delegare*. The appointment is sometimes made by a person nominated by the President for that purpose following a request to the parties to agree to that procedure, although the lease in question lacks one or other of the form of words just discussed. This seems to be an established routine.

On the issue of who can initiate the procedure, the Model Forms have always provided a choice; in some of the variants only the landlord can apply to the President but in others either party may do so (as in the ISVA Forms). Where the landlord has a choice of status (arbitrator or expert), it is logical in the first instance to restrict the power of initiation to him, as in the Model Forms; provided that the tenant is given power to initiate at a later stage, in default of action by the landlord. One possible difficulty which has, to the authors' knowledge, arisen in one case is who has the right to apply where the clause is silent. The better view must be either party, so an appointment would be made on the application of the first to apply. In the (unlikely) event of both parties applying simultaneously or nearly so with the result that two appointments were made, there would be the question of which was to take precedence—the first to be appointed or the first to accept appointment; on which see *Tradex Export SA v Volkswagenwerk AG* [1970] 1 Lloyds Rep 62 and *University College, Oxford v Durdy* [1982] Ch 413.

Delayed reviews cause problems for tenants and, sometimes, for landlords; we have dealt with these in the discussion of time-limits (see Chapter 5, p 163 above). So there is a strong case for allowing a tenant power to initiate the process, at least after a certain period. It is essential if a downwards review is a possibility to ensure a review is commenced; few landlords will pay interest on refunding, or make an allowance for, overpaid rent in the interim period pending settlement of the lower rent. The various versions of the Model Forms allow application by the tenant but where there is a choice of referee to be made by the landlord, then a simple application by the tenant is not possible. So these forms (1985 Model Forms, Variation C, clause 4(F); 1980 Model Forms, clause 4(E); and 1979 Model Forms, clause 3(6)) produce a comparable result by the different route of allowing the tenant to serve a trigger-notice in the event of the landlord's delay, thereby placing the onus on the landlord to respond and apply for appointment within the set period, failing which the tenant's figure specified in his notice takes effect.

The RICS has a detailed procedure. Parts of it are described in Part

Two of the RICS Guidance Notes and there is no doubt that substantial efforts are made to select individuals, whether as arbitrators or independent experts, who have suitable experience in the type of property in question and are not disqualified by interest in the property, professional connection with either party or some other conflict of interests actual or potential. The form of application for appointment issued by the RICS is designed to elucidate these aspects of selection of an appropriate referee, and includes a section headed 'Surveyor Already Involved (names of any firms or individuals considered unsuitable for appointment on grounds of previous connection with either party)'.

Nevertheless, given the volume of appointments, some 8,000 a year of which about half become effective, there is a school of thought amongst some practitioners that the exclusion processes are not always sufficiently rigorous. No criticism is made of the standard RICS procedures, or of its statement of principle in the RICS Guidance Notes (see Note 2.1.4) but those of this frame of mind would wish if possible to eliminate more indirect influences than it is practical for the RICS to monitor, having regard to the scale of its operations. For example, they would want a potential referee to confirm that neither he nor his firm was currently involved in the letting or rent review of any broadly comparable property in the relevant vicinity. Of course, this desire to try to eliminate the risk of even unconscious bias may well run counter to the advisability of securing a referee fully conversant with the type of property and locality, but considerable efforts are sometimes made to secure by joint agreement an appointee as relatively detached, whilst as knowledgeable, as possible. Some may think such caution over-precise or unrealistic; but the problems are exemplified by the Scottish case of *Grahame House Investments Ltd v Secretary of State for the Environment* [1985] SLT 502. The arbitrator had settled the revised rent of another floor in the same building, acting as an expert and that provided an obvious comparable. The majority (Lord Dunpark and the Lord Justice Clerk) held that he was not disqualified. Avoiding discussion of the earlier Scottish authorities cited in the decision, the authors must say that they find, on general principles, the dissenting judgment of Lord Hunter more compelling. (Incidentally, no point was taken that the arbitrator in that case had been appointed by a surveyor acting for the Scottish President and not, as the lease required, by that office-holder personally).

Care in the procedures leading to appointment may reflect the possibility that the President owes a duty of care in selecting the arbitrator or expert. This was raised tentatively by Hoffman J in the *United Co-operatives* case (above) at 127G but the judge declined to express an opinion on the point.

In the light of the discussion over legal advice and the possible use of assessors at p 179 above, it is worth noting that in *My Kinda Town Ltd v Castlebrook Properties Ltd* [1986] 1 EGLR 121 co-arbitrators, a chartered surveyor and a Queen's Counsel, were appointed.

(b) RICS Guidance Notes

Part Three of the RICS Guidance Notes (see Part Six, below) sets out guidance on rent review arbitrations in some considerable and helpful detail (p 618). Whilst it was not thought appropriate to add a full apparatus of citation of authorities, most of the statements are solidly based on statute or case law. Occasional differences of opinion are raised in this book as they arise.

Part Four on 'The Independent Expert' (see pp 645 ff) is potentially contentious. In the first place, of course, there is virtually no statutory provision and little case law to provide a basis or background (as Note 4.1.1 itself states) and, in the second place, there is undoubtedly considerable value in providing guide-lines for surveyors acting as experts. The fact that what is offered consists only of guide-lines is fully stressed in the RICS Guidance Notes.

On the issue of representations, however, there were grounds to challenge some of the statements in Note 4.3.3 as it appeared in the 1983 publication. It stated that 'if one party only wishes to make representations or submit facts and other party refuses, the Independent Expert should make it plain that he will not receive statements or opinions or arguments'. The distinction between statements of fact (which could be received) and opinions or arguments (which should not) was quite deliberately drawn. In the second edition of this book, the authors ventured criticism of this guide-line and considered that an expert was free to receive facts and representations from one party and to make of them whatever use he considered appropriate. The revisions to the RICS Guidance Notes in 1987 changed the nature of the advice in Note 4.3.3, which is set out in full in Part 6, p 649 below. It now says that an expert should be prepared to receive representations from the only party who wishes to make them in response to his invitation but a copy should be sent to the other party for comment.

A tabular comparison in Note 1.1.5 seeks to summarise the views of the RICS on the difference between the duties and suggested procedures for arbitrators and independent (sic) experts in rent reviews. It will be seen from the preceding remarks, and other comments elsewhere in this book, that the authors do not quarrel with most of the points made though they do differ somewhat on point 1 (see p 178).

(c) Enforcement of the award

The awards of referees, whether arbitrators or experts, are almost invariably self-enforcing in that the structure of the lease will supply its recovery measures—distress, forfeiture or action in debt—to the adjusted rent following the award automatically. The existence of the direct enforceability for arbitrators' awards once registered with leave of the court under s 26 is thus not normally of great importance as a feature of distinction from experts' awards. For a discussion of when an arbitrator's award takes effect, see p 262.

However, enforcement following registration may be necessary where an award creates liabilities which do not pass to the assignee. One example would be an award of costs, both the arbitrator's fees and the costs of the other party. An arbitrator will not normally release his award without prior payment but where payment is made by one party and the award puts liability on the other the paying party will want to recover that amount as well as any costs awarded to him. The liable party, in this respect, may be a former lessee or lessor. A second example, which would only affect a former lessee, is where an award creates liability for a back payment of an increase retrospectively related to the review date plus, probably, interest. *Parry v Robinson-Wyllie* (1987) 54 P & CR 187 shows that a liability for that portion of a retrospective award covering the period before assignment will not pass to the assignee. The assignor, in that case, was in receivership so enforcement under the s 26 procedure was probably a theoretical remedy.

Chapter 7

Procedural Matters—Evidence and Valuation Techniques

The essence of the process embodied in most rent reviews is the periodical re-establishing of the open market rent for the property to reflect, as far as possible, the initial bargain between the parties. Rent reviews permit the parties to bargain for an adjustment as they bargained over the rent when the lease was first granted, and failing agreement to invoke the decision of a third party by reference to a set of criteria that mirror, with variable accuracy, the factors the parties assume or assert went into the original bargain. It is possible that the particular factors chosen, or the way they are expressed, may produce a wide measure of discrepancy between the formula and reality; the discussion in this chapter is of what evidence is admissible and what valuation techniques are to be adopted in that bargaining process between the parties or, if the dispute is not resolved, before the arbitrator or expert.

1 Evidence in negotiations

At the negotiation stage of a review, each party can rely on, and put forward for consideration by the other, whatever 'evidence' and opinions are thought to exist and be relevant. The more factual the evidence and the more obvious its relevance, the more convincing and compelling it may be but there are no formal legal constraints. Ideally, the evidence will strengthen and justify the opinions, and a party may demonstrate only the weakness of his side of the argument by putting forward poor and irrelevant material. This may encourage the other to break off negotiations and proceed to the reference to a third party in the belief that he has a strong case to argue. That is the only sanction, at this stage, against inadmissible evidence. Nevertheless, the collection and assessment of what will be legally acceptable evidence if the matter does have to go to a referee will make the advice at the negotiation stage the more confident and convincing.

The desire to reach a solution that is satisfactory to the client, to retain his confidence and future business and to maintain professional integrity, standing and good reputation with fellow practitioners—these are sufficient incentives not to rely on material that is weak or inadmissible. The ever present possibility that the matter will proceed to arbitration or determination will also act as a disincentive to open correspondence (see section 2 of this chapter, below) at this stage.

It is not easy to state what proportion of rent reviews go to third party decision as compared to settlement by negotiation but the preponderance of the latter is undoubted. The Civil Judicial Statistics give one set of statistics showing that of 17,326 county court applications in 1988 for statutory renewal, court orders were made only in 3,096, some or many of which will have been by consent. The figures for agricultural rents, to move into another area for comparison (where statutory arbitration exists), show that only a very minute number of the total rent adjustments went to arbitration. The Royal Institution of Chartered Surveyors receives approximately 8,000 requests per annum to appoint arbitrators or experts for rent reviews and makes appointments in a little over half of them (the figures for 1986 were 7,920 applications and 4,951 appointments, of which 2,165 were as an arbitrator and 2,651 as an expert). It is again not clear in how many of the 5,000 or so appointments there is a final award or decision. It is not possible even to guess what proportion awards bear to total settlements by agreement at some stage or other in the procedure, but we may safely suggest it will not be significant. Consequently, the number of rent reviews where the issue of legally admissible evidence has to be faced is a small proportion of the whole. The rules applicable in the minority of cases that do go to a formal hearing will now be examined.

2 Without prejudice negotiations

(a) Scope of the rule

The normal consequence of attaching the without prejudice label is privilege from disclosure of statements made during negotiations to settle a dispute. 'The 'without prejudice' rule is a rule governing the inadmissibility of evidence and is founded upon the public policy of encouraging litigants to settle their differences rather than litigate them to a finish'—per Lord Griffiths, *Rush & Tompkins Ltd v GLC* [1988] 3 WLR 939 at 942B. The idea is that parties 'should not be discouraged by the knowledge that anything that is said in the course of such negotiations . . . may be used to their prejudice in the course of the proceedings. They should . . . be encouraged freely and frankly to put their cards on the table'; per Oliver LJ in *Cutts v Head* [1984] Ch 290 at 306.

The rule applies to exclude all negotiations genuinely aimed at a settlement whether oral or in writing from being given in evidence. It must be stressed that attaching the label does not guarantee privilege— the document so marked must be part of an attempt to settle. A competent surveyor or solicitor will always head negotiating correspondence 'without prejudice' to make it clear beyond doubt that in the event of the negotiations on the new rent being unsuccessful they are not to be referred to in the subsequent arbitration. If done at the outset, the protection may well continue to apply throughout the negotiations: *Sherbrooke v Dipple* (1980) 41 P & CR 173. Protection can be implied from the nature of the negotiations for the application of the rule is not dependent upon the use of the phrase 'without prejudice' if it is clear that a compromise was being sought. In matrimonial or custody disputes, the courts are willing to find such an implication but it is hard to see it being done very often in the commercial context of a rent review unless it is a situation of a clear offer to compromise the dispute.

An opening 'shot' or offer in negotiations on a rent review can be privileged provided it is expressly marked 'without prejudice': *South Shropshire District Council v Amos* [1986] 1 WLR 1271, disapproving remarks to the contrary in *Norwich Union Life Assurance Society v Tony Waller Ltd* (1984) 270 EG 42. The need for a dispute was established in *Walker v Wilsher* (1889) 23 QBD 335 and *Re Daintrey* [1893] 2 QB 116 but since the purpose of the rule is to facilitate compromise it is important that an opening offer can be made under the cloak of protection (*Cutts v Head*, above at p 113). However, if an opening offer is not expressly made 'without prejudice' then the older cases would suggest that it is likely that it could not be implied. Care must be taken not to confuse a 'without prejudice' opening offer with service of a formal notice (where this is required) because attaching the label can be fatal to the validity of a trigger-notice: *Shirlcar Properties Ltd v Heinitz* (1983) 268 EG 362 (see p 126, above). Nevertheless, provided the efficacy of formal notices and like steps is not jeopardised, the protection of the cloak of privilege is a sensible precaution for the parties and their advisers to take. The need for a conscious decision needs to be emphasised.

(b)   When the protection can be waived or lost

The privilege can be waived by the mutual accord of the parties since the purpose of the rule is only to protect a party from being embarrassed by any admission made purely in an attempt to agree a settlement. So, where several issues are under negotiation and one is agreed, the protection no longer attaches to that issue, though it may continue for the others: *Tomlin v Standard Telephone and Cables Co Ltd* [1969] 1 WLR 1378. The danger can be averted by making agreement on one issue conditional on agreement of all. Documents do not lose their 'without prejudice' status once a compromise has been reached; so privilege still attaches in any subsequent litigation connected with the same subject matter whether between the same or different parties: *Rush & Tompkins Ltd v GLC*, above. This rule will protect privileged material which relates to one review being revealed at a later date, even if between different parties, unless both parties to the original correspondence consent. It is also thought that it will be applicable to the analogous situation of a common lessor dealing with a series of related rent reviews on adjoining properties; the settlement of one of those reviews will not permit 'without prejudice' documentation relating thereto being used in proceedings on the others unless, again, there is joint consent.

Once negotiations are initiated on a 'without prejudice' basis, there is no discretion in a court or arbitrator to admit them as evidence. If it is alleged that the nature of the negotiations were changed to an open basis, then this must be clearly proved. Thus, reference by an arbitrator to a without prejudice offer in deciding liability for costs was held to be misconduct on his part in *Stotesbury v Turner* [1943] KB 370. However, a party with clear evidence of such a step who does not protest but continues to proceed in the arbitration may forfeit his chance to attack the award later. This situation arose in an arbitration by written submission in *Shield Properties & Investments Ltd v Anglo-Overseas Transport Co Ltd* [1985] 1 EGLR 7 where, indeed, the arbitrator had directed the parties not to refer to without prejudice negotiations in their submissions, but one did. The other complained but carried on with the proceedings and Bingham J held that, not having made a stand, its challenge to the award on that ground failed. The result parallels that reached in relation to hearsay evidence discussed in section 6 of this chapter, below.

Offers 'without prejudice save as to costs' are discussed at p 184 above.

(c)   The wider rules of privilege

The rules on 'without prejudice' offers and documents are just one aspect of the legal privilege rules and the normal principles of legal professional privilege will apply. Advice from surveyors or other non-legal experts will be protected if obtained in contemplation of an arbitration or court action; if not so obtained, it will not attract privilege (though there remains a discretion not to admit such material). If the advice or report is obtained for more than one purpose, it will be privileged if the dominant purpose for obtaining it is in anticipation of the arbitration: *Waugh v British Railways Board* [1980] AC 521.

It follows that not all valuations made by the surveyor for a party to an arbitration will be privileged. For privilege to attach, it must have been commissioned primarily with a pending rent review in mind. Consequently, valuations for other purposes (eg sale, or in connection with the clients portfolio) are not privileged and could be made subject to an order for discovery or their production requested orally in cross-examination of an expert witness involved in making them. Where such valuations exist, they can be potentially very useful to the other party to test the veracity of the valuation argument being made in connection with the rent review. This is one of the areas, it appears, where many surveyors find the legal rules rather unreal and irksome; attitudes amongst lawyers and the vigour with which they pursue earlier and unprotected expressions of valuation opinion to the valuer's own client also vary. Certainly, the present situation is omewhat unseemly.

3 Admissible evidence in arbitration

(a) Normal rules of evidence apply

Although informality is often advanced as one of the benefits of arbitration in contrast to litigation, there is clear and substantial authority that the rules of evidence applicable in the latter should be applied in the former. *Russell* (p 273) puts it firmly thus: 'Arbitrators are bound by the same rules of evidence as the courts of law, unless the parties have otherwise agreed.' Citations from *East & West India Dock Co v Kirk* (1887) 12 App Cas 738, *Re Enoch and Zaretsky, Bock & Co* [1910] 1 KB 327 and *A-G v Davison* (1825) 148 ER 366 support this proposition which also appears in Mustill and Boyd, p 352).

(b) Relaxation of the technical rules

It would be unwise to act otherwise than on the basis that the rules of evidence apply in all respects. Certainly, cases from rent review arbitrations assume that this is so: see *Town Centre Securities Ltd v William Morrison Supermarkets Ltd, Duvan Estates Ltd v Rossette Sunshine Savouries Ltd* and *Shield Properties & Investments Ltd v Anglo-Overseas Transport Co Ltd* all discussed later in this chapter. Moreover, the general principle is that, save in relation to hearsay, the parties cannot waive the rules of evidence. Nevertheless, some of the strict rules may have to be taken to be relaxed in arbitrations by written submissions. Possibly, too, the parties are taken impliedly to have agreed on the departure from the strict rules where no objection to the introduction of inadmissible evidence is raised. Such implied assent may have been so much taken for granted as not to merit mention in any later proceedings by way of appeal. This aspect is discussed below at pp 237–8.

The extent to which any greater relaxation will ever be allowed remains an open issue. A certain relaxation is permitted in 'trade' arbitrations, which may include rent reviews by arbitrators where they are qualified surveyors, and the question is not only if any such relaxation applies but also how far it extends. The classic exposition had for long been taken to be that of Lush J in *Walford Baker & Co v MacFie & Sons* (1915) 84 LJKB 2221 at 2223 when he accepted that the rules of evidence may not be strictly enforced before a lay arbitrator and continued: 'but when [an umpire] acts upon evidence which is *absolutely* inadmissible and which goes to the very root of the question . . . this court has ample jurisdiction to set aside the award on grounds of legal misconduct'.

(The inadmissibility there was because of irrelevance of the evidence allowed to be given.) The fuller but less well-known report of the case at 113 LT 180 refers to evidence 'which is *obviously* inadmissible'—see Mustill and Boyd, p 352. If it survives, that rule would be appropriate, it is submitted, as a guide-line in rent review arbitrations. The whole concept of the use of comparables and the assessment of market values depends on drawing inferences of what would happen if the premises were being let, or re-let, although that is the very thing that is not taking place in fact. Accordingly, evidence of alleged comparables 'goes to the very root of the question'.

However, the continuing validity of the rule (against any relaxation) was brought into question in the Court of Appeal decision in *GKN Centrax Gears Ltd v Matbro Ltd* [1976] 2 Lloyd's Rep 555. Bridge LJ stated: 'For my part I do not regard the second paragraph of Mr Justice Lush's judgment [that cited above] as being good law. I do not think it can stand with the later decisions in the cases of *Gillespie, Terson* and subsequent decisions on that line' (at 583). *Gillespie Brothers v Thompson Bros & Co* (1922) 13 Lloyd's Rep 519 contains statements on the inability or unwillingness of the court to overthrow for error in law on the face of the award (a jurisdiction which no longer exists) an arbitrators findings if based on evidence, despite the view of the evidence the court itself might entertain. *Terson Ltd v Stevenage Development Corporation* [1965] 1 QB 37 was also concerned with whether or not there was evidence to support a finding of fact by the arbitrator. Consequently, the dismissal by Bridge LJ of the earlier ruling of Lush J was not directed at the specific issue of hearsay evidence nor other aspects of admissibility. As one of a series of reasons for dismissing a particular argument advanced in the appeal, the statement cannot be said to be a conclusion to any sustained line of reasoning. It is, nevertheless, a statement that cannot be disregarded or dismissed as *obiter dictum*. Moreover, Lord Denning MR, in the same case (*GKN Centrax Gears Ltd v Matbro Ltd*) stated matters even more broadly when he said at 575: 'One of the very reasons for going to arbitration is to get rid of technical rules of evidence and so forth'.

The extent to which this reversal of the traditional attitude has been followed is unclear. Thus, *Russell* unfortunately, cites the criticism of Bridge LJ at one place (p 419) but retains the statement of Lush J at another (p 275) without even there referring to the doubts cast upon it by the later judgments. (It also perpetuates the errors in the report of the 1976 cases of mis-stating the name and misciting the report of the 1915 case, so compounding the problems.) The discrepancy, and the post-1976 impact of the decision in *GKN Centrax Gears v Matbro Ltd*, are not discussed in either place and we have not found any further judicial pronouncement or commentary in a textbook or legal article on the issue, vital though it may be said to be. Sadly, Mustill and Boyd does not appear to discuss the issue nor cite the dicta in the 1976 case.

(c) Evidence must be relevant and convincing

Whatever the current position on reception of technically inadmissible evidence as a matter of law, the same comments as were made above on the low factual and extra-legal significance of hearsay or other inadmissible evidence in negotiations also applies in arbitrations. The evidence must be relevant to the issue. The experienced surveyor sitting as an arbitrator will pay scant regard, it is suggested, to unconvincing or uncertain evidence, and much of the rationale for excluding hearsay is that it will show one or other of those faults.

(d) Expert evidence

This is a vital part of any rent review arbitration. Once the status of the expert is established, then an opinion based on that expertise can be expressed—contrary to the general rule which confines evidence to matters of fact. Written proofs of such evidence must be presented and exchanged (see RSC Ord 38, r 36 and r 38, which apply to arbitrations with modifications—Civil Evidence Act 1972, ss 2 and 5, and Criminal Evidence Act 1968, s 18 and the RICS Guidance Notes, Note 3.7.7 which is a useful summary of the best procedure to adopt).

Particularly useful practical advice on the preparation and presentation of expert evidence is contained in the judgment of Garland J in *University of Warwick v Sir Robert McAlpine and Sons Ltd* (1988) 42 BLR 1 at 22–4. The judge stressed:

(i) The role of the expert witness is not to advocate their client's case; an adversarial approach may be largely avoided if experts who earlier held inconsistent views dealt with the issues in their reports.

(ii) If a number of experts are involved with overlapping expertise (eg, in a rent review dealing with improvements, a quantity surveyor and a valuation expert) then the contribution of each should be identified and be available for cross-examination.

(iii) Exchange of reports, a meeting of experts to identify and schedule points of difference and the furnishing of proofs of fact will reduce time and costs.

(e) Practical presentation

Whilst the courts are increasingly willing to accept photocopies even when the originals are available, evidence is most impressive when it conforms to the best evidence rule. Though originals of documents are better, photocopies will suffice if accuracy is agreed. Oral evidence by witnesses is another aspect of the best evidence rule thus enabling the evidence given to be tested by cross-examination.

The practice of preparing an agreed bundle of relevant documents, excluding any that are privileged, is now a standard procedure. Agreeing such a bundle is only an admission of authenticity and not of the veracity of what is contained therein.

4 Admissible evidence—the expert's position

There can be no room to argue that the expert, or independent valuer, is bound by the rules of evidence. He can, after all, reach a decision simply by use of his own knowledge and skill and can do so without taking any evidence from the parties at all—although most experts will, in practice, sensibly afford the parties the opportunity to put submissions and counter-submissions to him. This basic principle cannot and does not alter when the parties have a *right*, under the relevant clause in the lease, to make representations to the referee or are afforded that right by him. The purpose of any representations is to assist the chosen expert to arrive at a decision and to allow the parties to draw specific aspects of their side of the arguments to his attention. Even an express requirement that he shall 'have regard to' representation does not undermine the basic rule. Once again, the effect of (for example) hearsay evidence in this context may well be much weaker than that of evidence that would meet the criteria for admissibility imposed by law in relation to litigation. Moreover, if an expert were to demonstrate by his award that he had given undue weight to patently unreliable 'evidence' that might be adduced as proof of negligence on his part if the aggrieved party decided to sue him.

5 Discovery of documents and accounts

(a) Generally

In an arbitration, the duty to produce to the arbitrator all relevant documents is secured by s 12 of the Arbitration Act 1950. The requirements for discovery are consequently broadly similar to those in a court action.

If one party considers that documents are being withheld, then a order for discovery can be sought from the arbitrator, the granting of which is in his discretion and from which an appeal to the court may lie on the grounds that he misdirected himself. A request for general discovery can be made requiring the listing of all relevant documents; in practice an order for specific discovery of either a particular document or a class of documents will normally be more appropriate.

(b) Discovery of trading accounts

The basic tool used in rent review valuations are 'comparables'—evidence of the rental value of comparable property. If these do not exist or are inadequate, then an acceptable alternative tool is the profit earning capacity of the premises. To assess this, or the trade turnover, the question arises whether the trading accounts of the tenant are relevant and admissible to provide evidence to support a profits valuation and, if they are, whether an order for discovery can be made. The issue is complicated by the assumptions and disregards commonly found in rent review clauses and in particular that requiring a disregard of the fact of the actual tenant's occupation.

(i) No discovery of confidential accounts

In a case where the arbitrator is entitled to take into account the earning capacity of the premises, relevant evidence of this can be found in a tenants trading accounts. Statutory or published accounts are admissible accordingly; discovery will not normally be required. However, other trading accounts, being material confidential to the tenant, will not normally be admitted as evidence. Their discovery cannot be ordered unless they are not confidential but represent information available on the open market. These propositions were established in *Cornwall Coast Country Club v Cardgrange Ltd* [1987] 1 EGLR 146 where Scott J relied on and applied a decision of the House of Lords in *Lynall v IRC* [1972] AC 680 which decided that an estate duty share valuation could only take account of open market knowledge. Hypothetical bidders could not be treated as having access to confidential information. The *Cornwall Coast* decision was followed in *Electricity Supply Nominees Ltd v London Clubs Ltd* [1988] 2 EGLR 152.

A clause may expressly direct that the arbitrator is to take no account of the turnover and profits of the business of the actual tenant and in such a case even the published accounts must be left out of account. However, in such a case, this will not exclude evidence of profits or turnover of other companies in the same group as the tenant, though the arbitrator must put out of his mind anything he learns from those accounts about the profits or turnover of the tenant: *Ritz Hotel (London) Ltd v Ritz Casino Ltd* [1989] 2 EGLR 135.

The *Cornwall Coast* decision was made notwithstanding an earlier Court of Appeal authority, *Harewood Hotels v Harris* [1958] 1 WLR 108, where it was held that trading accounts were rightly admitted to assist in the indication of the earning capacity of an hotel and the determination of the open market rent on statutory renewal. The disregards contained in s 34 of the Landlord and Tenant Act 1954 mirror and often form the basis of rent review provisions so the authority was relevant. However, Scott J in *Cornwall Coast* considered that the point about confidentiality and availability in the market had not been argued; the trading accounts admitted in *Harewood Hotels* may have been the statutory accounts but, to the extent that that case purported to lay down a wider principle, the judge appeared to accept counsel's argument that it should be treated as decided on this point per incuriam the decision in *Lynall v IRC*.

(ii)   Effect of disregards

On the impact of a disregard of the tenant's occupation, the *Harewood Hotels* case decides that the presence of such a disregard does not require the exclusion of all evidence based upon or derived from the tenant's previous occupation (per Lord Evershed at 111). Thus if the trading accounts are not confidential but public knowledge, the disregard will not operate to exclude them. This aspect of the case was applied in the *Cornwall Coast* decision.

(iii) The need for relevance

Nevertheless, even where there exist trading accounts which are not confidential, the arbitrator may rightly decline to admit them or order discovery in a case where the evidence the accounts will provide is not still not relevant to the issue. So in the usual case where there are plenty of comparable premises on which a valuation can be based trading records will not assist for the best evidence is provided by what other traders are prepared to pay for premises of the type under consideration: *W J Barton Ltd v Long Acre Securities Ltd* [1982] 1 WLR 298. Trading accounts will be relevant, it was said, where ascertainment of the open market rent may depend on an assessment of profitability of the business for which the premises are adapted. Examples given in the *Barton* judgment include petrol stations, theatres and a race-course as well as hotels.

Finally, where accounts are relevant and admissible, the evidence they supply cannot be used to determine what the incoming lessee could afford to pay but only to assist in answering the question as to what rent might reasonably be expected to be obtained in the open market: *Harewood Hotels* case per Romer LJ at 115.

(iv)   Express contrary provision

These principles will yield to an express provision to the contrary in the lease. So in *Electricity Supply Nominees Ltd v London Clubs Ltd* (above) a proviso allowing the arbitrator to require production of the lessee's accounts was taken to include an agreed assumption that the hypothetical tenant was to be assumed to have the accounts available to him so that they could be admitted as evidence.

(v)   Is the result acceptable?

The principles relating to admissibility laid down in the *Cornwall Coast* case must be treated with some reserve if only because the *Harewood Hotels* decision was taken to be decided per incuriam. Moreover, the view has been expressed that the rules are exactly the opposite of what they should be (*Bernstein and Reynolds*, para 7–23).

It is our submission that the rules are correctly stated in the *Cornwall Coast* case.

(1) It is argued (by Bernstein and Reynolds para 7–23) that published accounts should not be admitted because of the standard disregard of the effect on rent of the occupation of the tenant. If, the argument goes, the tenant had not been in occupation there would be no published accounts so they must be ignored. In the view of the authors, the narrow interpretation of the disregard given in the *Harewood Hotels* decision provides the key: it is directed to the effect on the rent (so that the higher rent a sitting tenant would offer falls to be disregarded) not to the evidence of the profitability of the trade conducted from the premises that published trading accounts may provide to the open market. Moreover, the hypothetical tenant might surely look to the published accounts of any previous occupant— the premises are assumed to be vacant at the review date but not prior to it. As the *Cornwall Coast* case decided, the disregard did not require the arbitrator to assume the tenant had never been in occupation.

(2) It is further argued (again by Bernstein and Reynolds) that unpublished trading accounts should be admitted since they do not directly infringe the disregard and do have a direct bearing on the notional profits valuation. This would be a valid argument if the lease were to direct the rent to be assessed on a notional profits valuation (which is the express assumption made in their example) for the actual profits made would be relevant on the issue. In the relevant and reported cases before the courts and in all standard rent review clauses, however, the lease directs the valuation to be on the basis of an open market valuation between hypothetical parties who are not to be identified with the actual parties. In the open market, the evidence would not be available and so it is rightly inadmissible.

The lesson to be drawn is that in cases where valuation using comparables is likely to prove difficult, those drafting the lease should consider whether a notional profits valuation is likely to be important. If it is, then evidence of trading accounts should be declared in the lease to be admissible and thought should be given to identifying what types of trading accounts are to be covered.

6   Hearsay evidence

(a)   *The rule against hearsay*

The hearsay rule, that a witness cannot give evidence of what was said by another person out of court to establish the truth of the content of the statement asserted by that other person, applies in full measure to rent review arbitrations. The only relevant exception to the rule is an admission made by the opposing party or its advisers.

An independent expert, determining a rent review, is not directly affected as he bases his determination on his own expertise; he will be well advised, however, not to pay regard (or at least not be seen to pay regard) to hearsay evidence presented to him by one of the parties in case this is made a basis of a challenge by way of action for negligence or otherwise.

(b) Applicability to valuation evidence

The statements of Megarry J in *English Exporters (London) Ltd v Eldonwall Ltd* [1973] Ch 415 contain a salutary reminder of those rules rendering hearsay evidence inadmissible in regard to valuation evidence; though these were made in the context of renewal applications under the Landlord and Tenant Act 1954 they are of equal application to rent review as is shown by *Town Centre Securities Ltd v William Morrison Supermarkets Ltd* (1981) 263 EG 435. The judge stresses the distinction to be drawn between:

(1) the right of the expert witness to express opinions as to the significance of proved transactions in relation to the valuation with which he is concerned or opinions that he has formed as to values even though substantial contributions to the formation of those opinions have been made by matters of which he has no first hand knowledge; and

(2) the need to confine his evidence of fact to matters of which he can speak from personal knowledge.

The part that second-hand evidence may have played in the formation of the expert's opinion is readily acknowledged; it is recognised that hearsay objections to allegedly factual assertions may not be 'pressed to an extreme'. However, the basic rule is clear: a valuer is not entitled to state details of transactions in which he has no personal knowledge in order to establish them as matters of fact (though, when giving an opinion he must be prepared to state the facts he has assumed, not to prove their truth but to make clear his standpoint). So, at 422B Megarry J states quite firmly:

'Details of comparable transactions upon which a valuer intends to rely in his evidence must, if they have to be put before the court, be confined to those details which have been, or will be, proved by admissible evidence, given either by the valuer himself or in some other way.'

These principles received appellate approval in *Rogers v Rosedimond Investments (Blakes Market) Ltd* (1979) 247 EG 467.

(c)   Getting round the rule—lists of comparables

The rule can be circumvented by consent; an agreed list of comparables is now an acceptable practice. So in the *English Exporters* case, Megarry J dealt specifically with lists of comparables:

'If the parties exchange [such lists] at an early date, often much time and money can be saved by the experts on each side agreeing such of the transactions in each list as, after any necessary inquiry, they can accept as being reliably summarised (at 423G).'

Nevertheless, he does continue:

'. . . if the other side will not accept the facts, then either the transaction must be proved by admissible evidence or it must be omitted as a comparable.'

The scope for avoiding disputes over admissibility by prior agreement between the expert witnesses is obviously as great in rent review arbitration as it is in renewal applications under the 1954 Act. The pre-trial review (in the county court) or summons for directions (in the High Court) provide the occasion for such measures of agreement to be pressed upon the parties in litigation. The arbitrator's preliminary hearing can lead to similar directions in arbitrations, and the rigours of the hearsay rule of exclusion can be thus side-stepped. However, in a number of reported cases, the opposite has happened and arbitrators have made firm prohibitions on the use of hearsay evidence or strictly circumscribed the conditions of its use. It is clear that this approach commends itself to a number of regular practitioners in such arbitrations.

What the passages in the *English Exporters* judgment emphasises is the difference between opinion and fact. The tribunal, whether the court in a renewal or the arbitrator in a review, has greater freedom to reject the former than to ignore the latter. To put it in another way, it is much easier on appeal to upset the finding that departs from weighty evidence than the ruling that differs from the assertions of witnesses, however eminent, experienced and skilled, on opinion or belief. Incidentally, for reasons discussed below in relation to the date for assessment, caution is needed in applying too literally the exhortation for agreement 'at an early date' unless care is taken to continue to update the facts until as close to the hearing as possible.

(d)   Civil Evidence Acts 1968 and 1972

It must also be borne in mind that both the Civil Evidence Act 1968 and the Civil Evidence Act 1972 apply to arbitrations and constitute a statutory relaxation of the hearsay evidence rule. They permit the admission of hearsay evidence of, respectively, fact and opinion provided this is 'first hand', subject to compliance with the procedural requirements of the relevant sections. Trade and business records will normally be admissible, notwithstanding the fact that they might rank as 'multiple hearsay', if they comply with the conditions of s 4 of the Civil Evidence Act 1968. A system of subsidiary rules is to be found in the Rules of the Supreme Court (RSC Ord 38, rr 20–34 and 36–44) or the County Court Rules (CCR Ord 20, rr 20–30). These rules apply, subject to such modifications as may be appropriate, to an arbitration (ss 10(3) and 18(1) of the 1968 Act). However, modifications may not be entirely straightforward given the absence of detailed framework in the Rules and the lack of such a framework in an arbitration. The matter could be expressly provided for by agreement between the parties or by directions by the arbitrator.

7 Taking objections to hearsay evidence

(a) The need to object

When evidence is given, whether orally or in writing, which is hearsay or otherwise inadmissible, it is important that objection is made promptly and firmly. *Rogers v Rosedimond Investments (Blakes Market) Ltd* (1979) 247 EG 467 gives guidance on how objections to the introduction of hearsay evidence should be raised (in that case, in litigation under the Landlord and Tenant Act 1954). The appellant landlord complained that the deputy judge in the county court had wrongly taken into account and to some extent relied on the evidence given by two other tenants in the same market that they thought the rents they were paying for their units too high. This was contrasted with evidence they could be allowed to give of general trading conditions in the market. Secondly, the complaint was made that the tenants' expert had given evidence of comparables but had not himself seen any of the leases. Roskill LJ deals with the latter point at 469:

'. . . had this point been taken fairly and squarely at the trial—and here again we are told no question was raised until final speeches—the learned deputy judge might well have said to counsel, 'Now how real is your objection based on hearsay?' If [counsel for the landlords] had shown good reason for saying 'No, I really must be satisfied by admissible evidence that those are the true rents' the learned deputy judge might well have offered an adjournment, albeit at the landlords' risk. On the other hand, [counsel] under pressure as to costs, might well have felt it was reasonable to allow this evidence, albeit hearsay, to be admitted.'

Nevertheless, on the combined effort of the two objections a new trial was ordered.

(b) Some rent review examples

This approach was applied in two rent review cases. *Town Centre Securities Ltd v Morrison Supermarkets Ltd* (1981) 263 EG 435 concerned a failure to object to the hearsay status of evidence, the standing of

which should have been apparent when it was first disclosed before the
hearing; this failure excused the arbitrator's actions in receiving it and
assessing its weight. A similar need to elect between insisting on an
objection or waiving a right to challenge the award later arose in relation
to without prejudice matters in *Shield Properties & Investments Ltd. v
Anglo-Overseas Transport Co Ltd* [1985] 1 EGLR 7, discussed at p 206
above. A further ground, of improper admission of hearsay evidence,
relating to comparables which were not vouched for by a person with
first-hand knowledge, was categorised as a procedural irregularity and
one basis for remission of an award (see also Chapter 6, p 208, above).
Where an arbitrator imposes on himself restraints on adducing hearsay
evidence, then it may be less necessary to take objection because the
failure clearly to exclude hearsay thereafter will be grounds, again, for
remission or setting aside: *Control Securities v Spencer* [1989] 1 EGLR
137 (Award set aside; the other party had merely refused to comment
on hearsay evidence presented).

8   Post-review date evidence

(a)   Admissibility of pre-review date evidence

Any rent review clause will, either expressly or by implication, require
a valuation of the market rent; that valuation will be assisted by the
evidence of actual rents agreed whether by way of new lettings, on review
or at statutory renewal. Such evidence will give a guide to market trends
and pressures and so enable the particular property to be assessed.

Normally, there can be no general issue as to the relevance or
admissibility of any such evidence coming into existence prior to the
review date—though the weight to be given to any particular piece of
evidence will be a matter for the arbitrator. It is not uncommon, however,
for the lease to specify with some precision what exactly the arbitrator
is to look at. In *Segama NV v Penny Le Roy Ltd* (1984) 269 EG 332
the yearly value was to be determined 'having regard to rental values
current at the relevant time for similar property . . . let with vacant
possession'. It was argued that this meant that evidence of rents of
comparables premises agreed between existing landlords and tenant (eg
on review or renewal) were to be excluded. Staughton J rejected this
argument, and was surely right to do so; he was of the view that an
arbitrator was to have regard to the *worth* of comparable property and
that did not prevent him having regard to property which was not let
with vacant possession. Even if such evidence was not within the category
of evidence the lease *required* him to take into account, it was not expressly
or by implication to be excluded from his consideration. A lease
containing such a direction or implication to exclude is likely to be rare.
Nevertheless, the arbitrator might have to adjust evidence of property
not let with vacant possession to reflect his own determination of any

difference in the rent likely to be agreed with a sitting tenant and that obtainable from an intending tenant of empty premises.

(b)   The problem with post review date evidence

The problem of the use to be made of evidence of rents (established by properly admissible evidence) arrived at in the market by new lettings, statutory renewals or reviews effected after the relevant date for the rent review in question is one of a clash of principle with practicalities.

In the overwhelming proportion of cases, negotiation or determination of the new rent will be completed after the date by reference to which the new rent is to take effect. It will be rarely possible to achieve a determination even close to the review date.

There are dangers for a party to a lease in agreeing rents in advance of the relevant date at a time of rapidly rising or falling rent as is demonstrated by the facts of *Lovely & Orchard Services Ltd v Daejan Investments (Grove Hall) Ltd* (1977) 246 EG 651. An opening 'bid' in the tenant's application of August 1975 suggested a rent of £27,500 but this had been modified to a suggestion of a market rent of only £15,300 in a later affidavit of February 1977, by which date the new tenancy had not been granted or ordered. Presumably, if there is a rapid increase in rents, the balance of advantage in prematurely agreeing the rent would be reversed. So there are these good reasons for delaying settlement beyond the review date.

Whether for these reasons or mere pressure of business, if the rent review proceeds to a hearing it is most likely to be a hearing after the relevant review date, yet that earlier date is the one at which most review clauses will direct that the market rent is to be ascertained. The relevance of facts or evidence coming into existence after that date is the issue; it is necessary to consider both the extent to which such is admissible and (if so) the weight that should be given to it. It is worth stressing the interrelationship of the separate concepts of *relevance*, *admissibility* and *weight*. Post review date evidence can only be generally inadmissible if it is irrelevant to the issue; once admitted, its weight remains to be assessed.

(c)   The argument in favour of exclusion

(i)   Generally

The argument that the correct principle is one of non-admissibility for all post review date evidence is that the market at rent review date could have no knowledge of rents still to be settled, and for that reason evidence of those later settlements is not relevant to the issue. The same argument applies, it is suggested, to rents agreed at the review date 'subject to contract'. Judicial authority and support for a principle of non admissibility is found in three first instant decisions namely in *Industrial Properties (Barton Hill) Ltd v AEI Ltd* (Judge Fay QC sitting as Official

Referee), *Ponsford v HMS Aerosols Ltd* (3 February 1976, Whitford J) (both unreported but digested in Bernstein and Reynolds) and *Duvan Estates Ltd v Rossette Sunshine Savouries Ltd* (1981) 261 EG 364 (Robert Goff J).

Nevertheless, even a rule (if it existed) of strict exclusion of evidence of post-review transactions as matters of fact does not mean the expert witness need wholly ignore them. If he gives it as his professional opinion that, at the relevant date, rents were moving in such and such a direction or towards such and such a level, it may be quite impossible for him in all good conscience to be certain by the time of the hearing of the extent to which his opinion to that effect was merely corroborated by the later transaction and the extent to which the opinion was retrospectively formed with the hindsight of the later knowledge. The mental processes described by Megarry V-C in *English Exporters (London) Ltd v Eldonwall Ltd* [1973] Ch 415 in relation to hearsay evidence apply equally to the valuer's approach to post review date evidence. He says at 421C: 'it may be . . . possible for a valuer to fill a gap in his first hand knowledge of a transaction by . . . stating . .. that he made diligent enquiries of some person who took part in the transaction . . . but, despite receiving full answers to his enquiries, he discovered nothing which suggested to him that the transaction had any unusual features which would affect the value as a comparable'. The contrast is between opinion, buttressed by the existence of, as it were, retrospective vindication and factual evidence of post-review vintage.

The inadmissibility of evidence of post-review-date transactions was most strongly expressed in the rent review context in *Duvan Estates Ltd v Rossette Sunshine Savouries Ltd* where Robert Goff J accepted criticism of an arbitration award partly taking into account events and facts arising after the review date. He accepted the judgment of Whitford J cited above and held that there was no error of law since the reference to the post-review-date evidence (employed by both parties before the arbitrator) was not a reliance upon it but was rather saying, in effect, that it did not cause the arbitrator to depart from the conclusion he had already formed on the basis of relevant evidence. However, attention must be drawn to the fact that the respondent's counsel did not contest the principle of non admissibility, so the value of this third case in the series preventing the use of post-review date evidence is weak.

(ii)   Exclusion of evidence of post review date events

Though the argument in favour of general exclusion set out above was rejected in the *Segama* case (see below), there is judicial agreement that evidence of events and overall changes in the market occurring after the review date is not relevant and therefore inadmissible. Thus in the *Industrial Properties* case, Judge Fay was of the opinion that 'I must ask myself what a skilled valuer would have done at Christmas 1973 knowing all that had happened up to then but denied full knowledge of the catastrophes of 1974'. In the *Segama* case, which ruled in favour of admissibility of evidence of rents agreed after the review date, approval was expressed of this view that events or developments in the market must be left out of account. Thus in *Gaze v Holden* (1983) 266 EG 998 Judge Finlay agreed that subsequent prices could be looked at, but said that a valuer:

'. . . is not entitled to take into account events which happened subsequently and which resolve how these various possibilities and projects in fact turn out. To do so would be to introduce into the valuation a species of foreknowledge which would not be available to any willing buyer or willing seller entering into a contract as at the date when the property falls to be valued.' (at p 1004).

Whether the distinction between events and general developments on the one hand and evidence of rents agreed is a valid one may be open to doubt; what is certain is that if evidence of rents of comparable premises are relevant and admissible then the political and economic events both before and after the review date must then be relevant for assessing the weight of those comparables—as was accepted by Staughton J in the *Segama* case.

(d) The argument in favour of admissibility

The contrary view, in favour of the relevance and admissibility of, at least, evidence of rents of comparable premises finds judicial support in *Segama NV v Penny Le Roy Ltd* (1983) 269 EG 322 where the issue of post review date evidence in a rent review arbitration was squarely raised before Staughton J. The judge ruled that evidence of rents agreed after the review date was admissible and could be given in evidence before, and should be considered by, the arbitrator. He stated:

'If rent of comparable premises had been agreed on the day after the relevant date, I cannot see that such an agreement would be of no relevance whatever to what the market rent was at the relevant date itself. If the lapse of time before the agreement becomes greater then, as the arbitrator saw, the evidence will become progressively unreliable as evidence of rental values at the relevant date.' (at p 326).

Admissibility was upheld, but the issue of cogency is for the arbitrator to decide. Leave to appeal was refused. This is the only reported authority to the authors' knowledge as it relates to rent review, but it appears to represent the view on which practitioners rely. There is supporting authority from other fields on which Staughton J relied in the *Segama* case. The most persuasive of these is *Melwood Units Pty Ltd v Commissioner of Main Roads* [1979] AC 426, a Privy Council decision on valuation for compulsory purchase. The only available evidence of market value in that case was the price paid for adjoining land after the valuation date. Lord Russell stated at 436E:

'Now it is plain that in assessing values for the purpose of assessing compensation for resumption on compulsory acquisition a tribunal is not required to close its mind to transactions subsequent to the date of resumption. . . .'

No reasons were given, and the limitation of the statement to compulsory purchase should be noted but in the *Segama* case counsel's attempt to distinguish the *Melwood* case was rejected. The Lands Tribunal in the compulsory purchase case of *F W Woolworth & Co Ltd v Canterbury Corporation* (1953) 3 P & CR 367 had come to the same conclusion, subject to the caveat of adjustment to market conditions at the relevant date. *Silver v Holland House Estates Trustees* (1983) 266 EG 913, the decision of a Leasehold Valuation Tribunal under the Leasehold Reform Act 1967, and *Gaze v Holden*, above, a High Court decision arising out of a valuation under an option to purchase, each supported the admissibility of post-valuation date evidence or events though in *Gaze* counsel made a concession, the opposite to that made in the *Duvan Estates* case, that prices on subsequent sales could be looked at. Less persuasive in the rent review context is the *Bwllfa* principle, derived from *Bwllfa and Merthyr Dare Steam Collieries (1891) Ltd v The Pontypridd Waterworks Co* [1903] AC 426. In that case, the House of Lords held that the evidence of the value of coal after the date of a statutory compensation notice was admissible but in that context the valuer did have to assess a fact at a time in the future for the purposes of his valuation; so, as was recognised in the *Segama* case, the decision is not relevant to the determination of a market rent at a given date.

Nevertheless, the philosophy in all these decisions is the same and is most cogently expressed in a dictum of Uthwatt J in *In Re Bradberry* [1943] Ch 35 at 45

A principle is to be drawn from these authorities (viz *Bwllfa* and others) namely that where facts are available they are to be preferred to prophecies.

So also in *Gaze v Holden* (1982) 266 EG at 1004) Judge Finlay concluded:

'I have come to the conclusion that "valuation in the usual way" (on the exercise of the option) means taking into account the events which have happened as at the date when the property has to be valued . . . and taking into account not only the actualities at thàt date but the possibilities in relation to all the circumstances; and that the valuer has, as best he can, to form his own judgment as to how these possibilities and the various prospects that are inherent in the then existing situation affect the value of the property at that date . . .'

It is to be hoped that an appellate court will eventually resolve the issue of relevance and admissibility of post review date evidence in a rent review context though the likelihood of leave to appeal from an arbitrator's award on the point is limited (see the discussion at p 195 above). Nevertheless some more authoritative statement of principle one way or the other would be welcome particularly as Staughton J recognised that judges may take different views on the issue.

As has been pointed out in a comment on the *Segama* case at (1984) 269 EG 639, the practical consequences of allowing post review date evidence is that a landlord may try to delay a review in a rising market to fortify his claim by post review date comparables; or be inclined to initiate a review promptly in a sluggish or falling market. Such considerations tend to confirm the authors in their original stance in earlier editions of this book that post review evidence is better excluded.

The RICS Guidance Notes, which were published in September 1983, shortly before the *Segama* decision, took a similar stand (Note 3.7.6) but have been amended in the light of that case. It must be said that the constraints upon reliance on post valuation date rent comparables were apparently found irksome by many valuers and the relaxation which admissibility allows was welcomed with relief. Perhaps, in the end, there is only a marginal practical difference between, on the one hand, allowing such evidence to be admitted but insisting that weight is a matter for the arbitrator and, on the other, excluding it but allowing expert opinion which may be buttressed by retrospective reference to it.

9 Confidential and third party evidence

(a) The problem

There may be significant problems of confidentiality both in the use of rental evidence of comparable lettings and in obtaining vital details about those transactions, even where one party's expert may wish to undertake this sort of investigation and the other party's expert is willing to co-operate. An agent for principal X is not free to make use of information gained in that capacity in the interest of principal Y unless X freely consents. The agent's freedom to impart the information to a third party for the benefit of Z is, without X's consent, equally restricted. Yet it is just such a free exchange of information that is needed to allow the respective experts to operate to full effect, and it may well be that the normal courtesies between professionals would often permit it to be achieved in practice without strict observance of the more severe constraints.

(b) Confidential information is admissible

An arbitrator has power to refuse to admit hearsay evidence. Yet in respect of evidence obtained (or more accurately given) in breach of confidence he could not properly refuse to admit it on that ground alone—for the breach of confidence is not a matter for him (though there may be other grounds to object). Moreover, an opponent of a party whose witness gives evidence in these circumstances could not object to its admission, as the breach of the duty to the principal does not give rise to a power in him to object. So if the relationship of X and Y results in a confidential document only X and Y can waive the confidence. If Z comes by the document innocently, he can use it without consent subject always to the possibility of an injunction to restrain its use. This may explain the absence of authority and paucity of reported decisions on the point in the context of rent review disputes.

(c) Obtaining evidence from third parties

The fact that arbitrations and determinations are private may encourage disclosure of confidential information whether or not from third party sources. However, where a third party refuses to disclose documents or information there is nothing a party to a determination by an expert can do and there is little a party to an arbitration can do. This is because:

(i) An arbitrator's powers can only be exercised against the parties to a reference (s 12(1) of the 1950 Act).

(ii) A court order for inspection of a third party's property might be possible under s 12(6)(g) but the costs and complexity of such a procedure suggest it will be rarely worthwhile.

(iii) Though in an arbitration, a witness subpoena could be obtained (s 12(4)), an unwilling witness is unlikely to assist a case. Even if a witness is called in this way, he cannot be compelled by an arbitrator to answer so he may refuse to disclose information and may feel obliged so to refuse if the information is confidential.

(d) Practical restraints when deciding to disclose

There is an allied problem where a landlord wishes to cite as his 'comparables' the rents negotiated with tenants of other properties in the vicinity also owned by him. On the one hand, he may wish not to reveal to tenant A a rent agreed with a rival trader B, feeling a moral obligation towards the latter despite the absence of any legal duty of confidence. On the other hand, he may not wish to make the evidence available to the surveyor for one tenant where that would allow that surveyor then to seek, or even in effect to canvass, instructions from other tenants due to face reviews of their rents on the basis that such surveyor was 'first in the field' and had knowledge of the landlord's likely negotiating grounds not available to other surveyors. He may feel happier, as landlord, to negotiate with a number of different surveyors. It is hard to see how to solve this problem at least at the negotiation stage, for a workable formula to protect the use to be made of the disclosed information is not easy to devise. Similarly, a landlord may not wish to have the rents he has agreed, and revealed in negotiations with his tenants used as comparables in negotiations between other landlords and their tenants. It is hard to see how he could prevent his tenants, or their professional advisers, from so using them when disclosed in negotiations.

(e)   Use of information disclosed to an expert or arbitrator

Where such evidence is made available to an expert, it is submitted it can be furnished on the basis it is not communicated to the other party, but that could not be done in an arbitration. An arbitrator has power to order a party to disclose to the other all documents relating to the issue before the arbitrator (s 12). However documents so disclosed must not be put to an improper use—and proper use is limited to that in the course of the action or arbitration: *Church of Scientology v DHSS* [1979] 3 All ER 677. Further disclosure by the other party to others without consent is therefore improper and that restriction may well include other rent review arbitrations or determinations in which that other party is involved.

10   Evidence of 'comparables'

(a)   The basis of valuation by analogy

As has already been indicated, it is usual to adduce factual evidence of 'comparable' lettings to support and justify expert opinion evidence or even, in the circumstances most favourable to a landlord, to replace opinion altogether. Indeed, having regard to the possible difficulties of the phrase 'comparable lettings' (now used in the Agricultural Holdings Act 1986, discussed in Chapter 18, p 535) it may be wiser not to speak of comparable lettings but only of lettings of comparable property. Whilst a county court judge lamented in a renewal case that 'the ideal comparable property hardly ever exists' (*W Barratt & Co Ltd v Harrison* (1956) 167 EG 234), the use of comparables has been the practice under the 1954 Act since it came into force in October 1954. It was applied in rent review valuations not only by analogy to that litigation but by general principles derived from such sources as the need to establish market values in relation to compulsory purchase disputes, the practice in rating valuation, calculation of damages for breach of contracts for the sale of land and of goods or even to find the value of non-negotiable stamps issued in connection with a holiday pay scheme *(Building and Civil Engineering Holidays Scheme Management Ltd v Post Office* [1966] 1 QB 247). Forbes J in *GREA Real Property Investments Ltd v Williams* (1979) 250 EG 651 stated the matter in general terms at 653:

'It is a fundamental aspect of valuation that it proceeds by analogy. The valuer isolates those characteristics of the object to be valued which in his view affect value and then seeks another object of known or ascertainable value possessing some or all of those characteristics with which he may compare the object he is valuing. Where no directly comparable object exists the valuer must make allowances of one kind or another, interpolating or extrapolating from his given data. The less closely analogous the object chosen for comparison is, the greater the allowances which have to be made and the greater the opportunity for error.'

(b) 'Having regard to the open market rental values'

The authors' distaste for the use of the phrase 'having regard to' anywhere in a review clause (see p 278) is strengthened by the arguments it has engendered in the treatment of comparables. The phrase appeared in the 1979 and 1980 Model Forms but was sensibly dropped in the 1985 version.

The essence of valuation by analogy is that the expert may use such valuation evidence and method as appear appropriate to the case before him. The use of the phrase 'having regard to' does not therefore preclude the valuer from having regard to *other* matters not expressly set out. So a direction 'to have regard to rental values current at the relevant time' did not preclude the admission of rents agreed subsequent to the review date—*Segama v Penny Le Roy Ltd* (1983) 269 EG 322 (p 241, above); nor did it prevent a valuation by reference to profits where that was appropriate—*Ritz Hotel (London) Ltd v Ritz Casino Ltd* [1989] 2 EGLR 135.

(c) Assessing the weight of comparable evidence

Any letting can be a 'comparable' provided either that the transaction differs in no material aspect from that forming the basis of the assessment in question or that any material variation can be quantified with sufficient certainty to convince the tribunal. The Court of Appeal reversed the judgment below in the *O'May* case ([1981] Ch 216 reversing (1979) 249 EG 1065) because it found that the shift of the burden of rebuilding could not be accurately quantified and compensated for in a new rent, but it did not reject the concept of such 'compensation', and this view was vindicated in the House of Lords ([1983] 2 AC 726) where Lord Hailsham accepted that the reduction in rent by 50p per square foot was an adequate estimate of the compensation required—though it did not answer the question in that renewal case of where the risk was to lie.

There may be some truth in the notion that all lettings are potential comparables—it is just that some are much more comparable and cogent than others, cogency being the issue for the arbitrator to decide on the evidence. A useful illustration of the process of assessing the cogency of proffered comparables will be found in *UDS Tailoring Ltd v BL Holdings Ltd* (1982) 261 EG 49. Whatever evidence is adduced, it must be clear and relevant to the review at hand with any differences allowed for. In *Fine Fare Ltd v Kenmore Investments Ltd* [1989] 1 EGLR 143 it was never finally made clear to the arbitrator whether a vital comparable award was on a shell or fitted out basis, a difference which produced an alleged substantial discrepancy (which could not be corrected—see p 197).

Moreover, Staughton J in *Segama NV v Penny Le Roy Ltd* (1983) 269 EG 322 stressed that the greater the period of time between the fixing of the rent for the alleged comparable and the review date the less reliable the comparison would be. Staleness would go to cogency.

(d) Comparables for the unusual property

The more unusual the property, the period of the notional term for the rent review (see discussion of the constant rent problem at p 252, below) or the terms of the notional lease, the greater the problems of finding comparables. Thus in *Prudential Assurance Co Ltd v 99 Bishopsgate Ltd* (1984) 270 EG 950, Lloyd J observed that there were unlikely to be precise comparables for the building (a large city office block as a whole let with vacant possession—though the arbitrator had determined an alternative award on that construction). Similar sentiments were expressed in *National Westminster Bank Ltd v BSC Footwear Ltd* (1980) 42 P & CR 90 (see p 516, below).

In the early days of buildings of the 'high tech' type, it was claimed that the rent on review was improved by linking the rent on review to a stated percentage of the market rents of more conventional offices in the area, thus creating deemed comparables (see p 259, below).

These issues came markedly to a head in *My Kinda Town Ltd v Castlebrook Properties Ltd* [1986] 1 EGLR 121. The dispute turned on the issue of the correct comparables to be used in the rent review of a 'destination restaurant' to which customers would travel to enjoy, or perhaps just experience, the particular ambience or style of cuisine. The choice was between other specialist 'destination restaurants' in various Central London locations (some at a distance) or other more general restaurants in the immediate neighbourhood. The two factual findings by the arbitrators (interestingly, a Queen's Counsel and a chartered surveyor) were that the market consisted of those looking for premises suitable for the style of business already carried on at these premises. That market was spread over a particular area, so that the wider choice of specialist premises relied on by the landlord's valuer was appropriate and the tenant's attack on the award failed. The case demonstrates very clearly the need to select appropriate premises for comparison, and, in some cases, the degree of refinement in the choice that may be called for. By contrast, in the earlier case of *National Car Parks Ltd v Colebrook Estates Ltd* (1983) 266 EG 810 the judge somewhat brusquely dismissed the relevance of rents for other car parks put forward by the parties as comparable to the car park in question because of the variable elements involved.

(e) Making adjustments for variations in comparables

Now that the effect on rental values of many of the constituent elements of the lease has been recognised more widely it can no longer be sufficient to make the test of comparability by reference to such general criteria as location, size and rental details. If, say, restraints on alienation in one transaction differ from those in another, the relationship between them, and between each of them and the subject matter of the lease under review should be determined by reference to the effect in the market of the variations. There may be no evidence of such variation. In *Owen v Nightingale Page & Bennet* (1955) 165 EG 761, for example, a county court judge held that a use restriction was balanced out by the qualification that a change was permitted with consent, which should not be unreasonably withheld, and so the rent was not to be adjusted on that score. In *Janes (Gowns) Ltd v Harlow Development Corporation* (1980) 253 EG 799, a deputy High Court judge, having held that on the evidence of particular circumstances it was appropriate to include an upwards/ downwards review provision in the new lease, nevertheless held that the initial rent was not to be increased to reflect that potential advantage for the tenant (a conclusion queried in an editorial comment at (1980) 124 SJ 245). Where variations in terms do affect market values, however, their impact should be isolated. Sometimes this may not be easy. To what extent, for example, may a major national concern worried at its lack of presence in a particular locality be prepared to bid above the general market level to obtain the tenancy of vacant premises? Moreover, if a valuer acting for a tenant suspects that such a situation has arisen how can he show that to be so? The party negotiating for such a tenant is hardly likely to have disclosed his principal's attitude in this respect and the landlord's agent will be entitled to keep to himself his suspicions, as distinct from evidence, of the 'key-money' or premium element in his rent. Mr Justice Donaldson's 'list' of factors to be ignored in the ascertainment of the attributes of willing lessor and willing lessee in *FR Evans of Leeds Ltd v English Electric Co Ltd* (1977) 36 P & CR 185, is briefly discussed at p 393, is an indication of factors, potentially present in any new letting, to be detected and allowed for in an ideal exercise in comparability.

Even such basic elements as the respective floor areas of the subject premises and the comparables can cause difficulties because of different available methods of making the calculation. This is illustrated by the second limb of the decision in *National Westminster Bank plc v Arthur Young McClelland Moores & Co* (1985) 2 EGLR 13. A licence for alterations had contained a schedule of floor areas agreed to be used for rent reviews. After the areas were settled, a measurement code was introduced by the RICS. The arbitrator had used that code in his calculation of the fair market rent, and he was vindicated in so doing, despite his departure from the stated areas, because that was how a surveyor would proceed to advise a tenant. Moreover even if the arbitrator had adhered to the earlier measurements he would have needed to adjust rents derived from comparable properties measured by the later code.

As indicated in that case, some leases or ancillary documents include a statement of 'floor area', 'net floor area' or 'lettable area', frequently as a means of calculating a service charge recovery. If Lease A, for the property under review, and Lease B, for a comparable, each contain such a statement, it is tempting to accept that as giving a valid measure of one aspect of comparability. That is only so, however, if it can be shown that each figure was calculated on the same basis. It is not likely that the basis of computation will be stated in either lease. Considerable 'detective' work may then be necessary to arrive at a full picture. Opinions are divided over the utility of the practice in any event. Some who are unenthusiastic point to the problem such as we have just discussed or the risk that the figure given will be relied on when it has become inaccurate through later alterations or additions. Partly to cover this last point, it is safer to frame any statement by references to the situation at a given date—the date of the relevant measurement.

Where areas are stated but are shown to be factually inaccurate, there can be great difficulty in applying, for example, the zoning method of valuation (see below). Is the deficit or excess to be set against one element in the rent package or all; is it to be applied proportionately, whatever that may mean, or in some other way; is evidence on the source of the error to be admitted and so on? It is frankly impossible to give answers to such questions; the issues need to be addressed in the factual context in which they arise.

(f) Sources of comparables

(i) Open-market lettings

These appear to be the best materials for establishing comparables. However, they are most susceptible of distortion by specific factors that are not necessarily readily apparent but are factors to be eliminated in the hypothetical setting of the review formula. Particular difficulties occur when new lettings, or under-lettings, have involved a premium for there is no universally valid method of decapitalising such payments into a notional rent and the impact of taxation may add further distortions. The valuer must also be alert to detect the hidden premium where the tenant carries out work, or performs some other obligation, the cost of which would normally fall on the landlord. Rents achieved by tender may also be suspect, especially where they contain an element of 'over-bid' to secure a monopoly trading position. The point has been well made in a number of rating cases, for example *Thomas Cook Group Ltd v Price* (1980) 255 EG 547, but is equally valid in rent reviews. So also, as we have noted, in the *Segama* case, it was said that comparables from rents agreed between landlords and sitting tenants might have to be adjusted for a vacant possession valuation.

In *My Kinda Town Ltd v Castlebrook Properties Ltd* [1986] 1 EGLR 121 the review formula included the routine vacant possession assumption. It was mirrored by a similar assumption in the reviewed rents of some of the comparable leases and the fact of vacant possession in the initial rents of the others. Thus, on the face of it, like was being

compared with like. However, the extent to which difficulties in finding
vacant possession comparables may have been present in those other
reviews would have extended the inquiry to an intolerable degree. The
same problems could not exist with the evidence of comparable rents
achieved with vacant possession in fact.

(ii)   Rents agreed on statutory renewals

These are an obvious second source of comparables because of the
market rent basis for rent on renewal written into the Act. Pure
comparability can be affected by two factors—namely any specific
provision in the renewal lease not to be found in the lease giving rise
to the review and, in more general terms, the presumptions written into
the Act in effect to favour the status quo of the current tenancy, as
now amplified and explained in the *O'May* case, that may make the
renewal tenancy not truly comparable with the current lease on offer
in the market. Such differences produce a state of affairs that should
be reflected in the rent in the renewal lease and lead to possible adjustment
before it is used as a measure for the reviewed rent. The view has been
expressed by a surveyor that rentals determined by the court are much
less valuable than any others, includings rents agreed by the parties at
renewal, on the basis that a judge is not as good at analysing and weighing
the technical evidence of value (Holland, (1988) *Arbitration*, p 15). This
view must be of doubtful validity and it is not one likely to commend
itself to the judiciary.

(iii)   Rents agreed in other rent reviews

The third source of comparable transactions is other reviews but, once
more, care is needed to establish true comparability. The rent fixed under
a clause adopting a residue of the initial term basis may thus not be
an exact indicator of market rent under a 'notional term to equal initial
term' provision. It would need to be shown in this particular case, whether
the residue was restricted in a way that affected rental levels—for, whilst
that may happen, it is not always the case. Other factors may detract
from comparability (eg different disregards); the differing wording of
disregards may have to be allowed for but only if the completed review
to be cited as evidence of market rents can be shown to have been
one that would have been differently assessed had the disregard in the
lease coincided with those of the lease in dispute. The presence or absence
of an instruction to disregard a tenant's improvements is not relevant
if there are no such improvements. Considerable research may be needed
to ascertain this type of detail for a wholly accurate comparison to be
made; constraints of time and money may well mean that such a stringent
inquiry cannot be made.

Some support for this 'ranking' of evidence appears in the judgment
of *Wallshire v Aarons* [1989] 1 EGLR 147. The Deputy Judge explains,
at 149: 'The best evidence is the decision of the market, that is open

market lettings'. He goes on: 'Second best are rent reviews negotiated between valuers', but he warns that they 'can be unreliable because of the possibility of error piled upon error. They need an occasional window of reality provided by open market decisions'.

11 Zoning—an acceptable technique

In *Janes (Gowns) Ltd v Harlow Development Corporation* (1980) 253 EG 799 John Finlay QC, the Deputy Judge, discussed and approved the 'zoning' method of valuation followed by the expert witness in that case, a method having a long history of use in valuation, not least in rating cases, especially for valuing shops. In this method, a shop is divided into zones; Zone A, normally that nearest the entrance (and, hence, the street or other access) attracting the highest rent; Zone B, the area further into the premises (and so, it is postulated, not only less visible from outside but also likely to be 'penetrated' by a smaller percentage of potential customers) attracting a lower rent calculated as a fraction of the Zone A rent; and possibly Zone C, if there is one, comprising the 'farther recesses' of the shop and commanding the lowest rent of all, with a further reduced fraction of Zone A rent being applied. Further zones, suitably discounted, may be devised for interior ancillary accommodation and external ancillary accommodation respectively. Allied to the zoning process are such concepts as quantity discounts and allowances for poor layout or awkward shape and adjustments for restrictions on use may also be required. The Deputy Judge in the *Janes Gowns* case also approved an adjustment made by the landlord's valuer to reflect rising rents after the date at which the comparable rents had been settled, a trend of which evidence had been given. Added weight is given to the last point by the further ruling that the evidence or rising rents was to be disregarded in calculations on the interim rent, as at a date nearer the date of the comparables, when the trend was not established.

For rating decisions dealing with the zoning method and its application to large department stores see *Lewis's Ltd v Turner (V/O)* (1981) 260 EG 713 and *Lewis's Ltd v Grice (V/O)* (1982) 262 EG 775; and for a most helpful illustration of its use in a statutory renewal case, see *UDS Tailoring Ltd v BL Holdings Ltd* (1982) 261 EG 49. *Turone v Howard de Walden Estates Ltd* (1982) 262 EG 1138 and *Ratner (Jewellers) Ltd v Lemnoll Ltd* (1980) 255 EG 987 are further illustrations. In *Zermalt Holdings SA v Nu-Life Uphostery Repairs Ltd* [1985] 2 EGLR 14 both parties' valuers were agreed on an equated Zone A approach but the arbitrator rejected extrapolation of Zone A values from small premises to large. The award was set aside, not because the arbitrator's approach was wrong but because he not put his views to the parties for comment. An analysis of the zoning method in a rent review case appears in *Wallshire v Aarons* [1989] 1 EGLR 147. It is undeniable that it is now a universal technique, to the extent that rents expressed 'ITZA'—in terms of Zone A—is now part of the valuers jargon.

In *UDS Tailoring Ltd v BL Holdings Ltd* the judge referred to approaches to a market rent via turnover and by average rental per square foot instead of on a zoning basis. He did not find either of assistance but voiced no criticism of them as such. The former has already been discussed in relation to disregard of goodwill at p 232.

12 The 'constant rent' problem

(a) The theory outlined

Early in 1979 an article by Rose at (1979) 249 EG 531 ventilated what became known eventually as the 'constant rent' issue, the phrase being used later as a title for tables prepared by Rose and published in November 1979. The problem is easy to state: where a rent under a commercial lease is fixed (ie remains 'constant') for a period longer than the prevailing pattern of reviews (or, indeed, renewals), how can one render the equivalent to what the landlord's return over that period would be with reviews on a normal, or less abnormal basis? If a lay opinion may be ventured, the outcome would seem to be that, apart altogether from the mathematical niceties, there are two major obstacles to wide-spread adoption of this type of formula. First, the choice of the constituent elements of the formula—the Required Risk Rate, the Anticipated Growth Rate and so on—involve either such arbitrary choices (as for example in settling on what Risk Rate is in fact required) or such speculative assessments (as is obvious with an element labelled Anticipated Growth Rate) as virtually to ensure a departure from the actual performance of the market and of the economy in general. The second obstacle is that, whilst the *theory* of using mathematical formula to arrive at a constant rent (over, say 14 years, which produces over that span of time what might be obtained from an initial lower rent subject to periodical increases at 'normal' intervals) may be demonstrably sound, it is not possible in practice to obtain such a rent from a tenant. 'The traffic will not bear it', in short.

The whole episode is of value in emphasising the possible consequence of abnormal or atypical lease arrangements, but that is much less than the protagonists of the concept seem to have hoped for. The real test would come in a case where, for example, an arbitrator had to settle a rent on a 14–year review, where all the comparables were on a 5 or 7–year basis and there was overwhelming evidence of the current figures for returns on investment, risk rates, growth expectations and so on. If the tenant were to object to a rent based on constant rent calculations, claiming it was not a market rent, could the arbitrator properly award it? He cannot, as we have seen, deny that a market exists and he must fix some rent, but we find it hard to accept in the light of the continuing controversy that he could properly apply the constant rent solution on its purest form. The existence of the tables is no proof of a market view, although proof of their acceptance and use would be some evidence of professional opinion.

(b) Judicial response

The issue has arisen in three cases where 21–year leases contained options for renewal for a like term at a rent to be agreed or settled by arbitration—and where the framers of the option may well not have given thought to the rent review implications. The arbitrator had no power, it was ruled in *National Westminster Bank Ltd v BSC Footwear Ltd* (1980) 42 P & CR 90, to fix only a rent for the initial period of the new term with periodic reviews thereafter. That would be to introduce a new formula for the rent, not to fix it for the stated term and that is what the option required him to do. The alternative of a differential rent, following the lead given in *Fawke v Viscount Chelsea* [1980] QB 441, was also ruled out. The absence of evidence of market rents fixed for such long periods was acknowledged, but it was stated at 94 that 'Arbitrators are often faced with property which is of a peculiar nature and has, in practice, no market comparable, and yet they do not have the slightest difficulty in fulfilling the requirement that they shall fix the market rent then prevailing', a sentiment incidentally giving little encouragement to the adoption of constant rent tables. This decision was followed in *Bracknell Development Corporation v Greenlees Lennards Ltd* (1981) 260 EG 500, where the wording of the lease called for the arbitrator to fix a full and fair market rent. An additional argument that the effect of inflation was to cause frustration of the contract was also rejected. Similarly in *Lear v Blizzard* [1983] 3 A11 ER 662 the addition of a capital premium to compensate for the length of the new lease was also rejected, after consideration of arguments for it in an article at (1979) 76 *Law Society's Gazette* 332. *Lear v Blizzard* is significant because it is the first case which directly considered whether it was right to have a percentage uplift to take account of the fact that the new lease under the option would be for 21 years without a rent review. Tudor Evans J was of the view that to include a capitalised premium was really an attempt to include the effect of a rent review clause, which was a step prohibited by the *National Westminster Bank* case where Templeman J said 'What the landlords' predecessors in title gave away, these landlords cannot now take back'. The judge in *Lear v Blizzard* also considered that, even if a capital premium was permissible, an assessment of future rental inflation was entirely speculative and therefore inappropriate.

In *New Zealand*, the case of *Lear v Blizzard* was distinguished in *Feltex International Ltd v JBL Consolidated Ltd* [1988] 1 NZLR 668. Henry

J held that *Lear v Blizzard* only decided that a premium cannot be added in the form of discounted rent to take account of future inflation. What could be done, the judge held, was to take account of the length of the review period—the period for which the rent is to be payable. On that basis, he held that an arbitrator had been correct to have regard to the fact that he was fixing a rent for a five year period and that the rents for comparable properties all had three year review periods. An upwards adjustment in the rent of 10 per cent to take account of this fact was not an adjustment for inflation or an attempt to vary the terms of the lease. *Lear v Blizzard* and *National Westminster Bank Ltd v BSC Footwear* were expressly distinguished. It is submitted that the reasoning in *Feltex International Ltd v JBL Consolidated Ltd* is a strong one and accords with both valuation practice and legal principle and should be followed in England.

(c) 'Rule of thumb' percentages

In practice, it appears that valuers and arbitrators have not adopted any of the rigid mathematical formulae evolved in the constant rent debate but apply more or less 'rule of thumb' percentages to allow for review periods in excess of the norm (as in *Feltex International Ltd v JBL Consolidated Ltd* above), with a wary eye cocked on 'what the traffic will bear'. Some examples of this can be seen in reported cases:

> (i) *99 Bishopsgate Ltd v Prudential Assurance Co Ltd* [1985] 1 EGLR 72: there was an agreed 3 per cent uplift to allow for a 7-year review period against the normal 5-year period.
> (ii) *National Westminster Bank plc v Arthur Young McClelland Moores & Co* [1985] 1 EGLR 61: the allowance was 20.5 per cent on the finding that no review was to be assumed in the notional lease.
> (iii) *Electricity Supply Nominees Ltd v F M Insurance Co Ltd* [1986] 1 EGLR 143: the parties had agreed a 9 per cent uplift for a straight 25 year term instead of the same term with 5-yearly reviews.

The judgment in *Lear v Blizzard* casts some doubt on the correctness of such an approach in England, notwithstanding that the practice is widespread, by holding that to allow for inflation would be to provide, in effect, for a rent review. Yet the option in *Lear v Blizzard* provided a renewal 'at a rent to be agreed . . . or determined by a single arbitrator' and if the market practice could be shown to allow some uplift over the rent that would hold good over 5 or 7 years when the rent was to stand for 21, the authors find it far from easy to see why, wholly consistently with adherence to the *National Westminster v BSC* ruling, the arbitrator is not free to fix a rent consistent with that practice. *Lear v Blizzard* is only clear authority for the ruling that a landlord is not entitled to *compensation* for a long lease without rent review; it is still correct therefore, for an arbitrator, if he is satisfied on the material before him (including, within permissible limits, his own knowledge of the market) that a tenant would pay more for this lease than for one with a normal review pattern, to determine that higher amount as the appropriate rent, as held in New Zealand: *Feltex International Ltd v JBL Consolidated Ltd* [1988] 1 NZLR 668. What *Lear v Blizzard* clearly decides is that he may not now add further uplift to compensate the landlord for the effect of future inflation.

13 Valuation—the problem of disregards

(a) Valuing a disregard of improvements

Although the disregard of the rental effect of voluntary improvements was written into the Landlord and Tenant Act 1954, which greatly influenced the drafting of rent reviews, litigation on the valuation problems of the disregard, as distinct from other substantive issues, did not surface until 1979, and then in rent review cases. Two decisions of Forbes J discussed the valuation problems. The first—*GREA Real Property Investments Ltd v Williams* (1979) 250 EG 651—concerned the rare case of office premises let as a shell, the tenant having to build cloakrooms, lavatories and the like as well as to install office partitions and similar fitting-out items. The second—*Estates Projects Ltd v London Borough of Greenwich* (1979) 251 EG 851—arose from a more usual state of affairs where the tenant took on existing premises in need of rehabilitation to allow their use as offices with the alternative of shop use permitted for the ground floor. The judge disclaimed in the second case any intention that the court should act as a valuer. Rather more discouragingly, it may be thought, he added that the court could say that a valuation method was wrong but not necessarily what method was right. Both cases, it must be stressed, were 'appeals' by way of cases stated by arbitrators, so the judge's functions were relatively circumscribed. Discussion of a similar provision for disregarding the rental effect of improvements in agricultural rent arbitrations featured in *Tummon v Barclays Bank Trust Co Ltd* (1979) 39 P & CR 300 which is also discussed at p 445.

It should be stressed that the caution expressed by Forbes J is not a particular or personal reluctance confined to him alone. The same point was made by Sir John Pennycuick in the Court of Appeal in *Compton Group Ltd v Estates Gazette Ltd* (1978) 36 P & CR 148 at 159:

'All those questions .. concern .. the matter in which the surveyors ought to conduct their valuation: that is to say what particular circumstances and factors they should take into account in making their valuation, and what weight, or absence of weight, they should give to them ... the court is not concerned to give directions to the surveyors upon those points.'

The *GREA Real Property Investments* judgment stresses that in the valuation process the tribunal—arbitrator, expert or judge—must ascertain and give effect to the intention of the parties expressed in the lease set in 'the same factual matrix as that in which the parties were'. For that reason, the normal wording of the disregard provision requires that the rental effect of the improvements be disregarded, not that the existence of the improvements themselves be ignored. Further, as the normal formula refers to the effect on rent, a sharp distinction needs to be drawn between the *value* of the improvements and the *cost* of effecting (and also financing) them. Moreover, the valuation exercise has to be effected at the review date, so both the use of the historic cost, subject to an updating adjustment for inflation, and the estimation of cost at prices ruling at the review date may lead to error. Only if evidence showed that value and cost were synonymous should they be equated.

Forbes J stated in the first case (at 654) and reiterated in the second (at 853) that a rent freely agreed for other unimproved premises identical to those being valued but for the tenant's improvements is normally the best evidence of the rental value of the premises, disregarding the rental value of the improvements. He went on to recognise that 'when other things are not equal or . . . when no such comparable exists, then valuers may be driven to other shifts'. In the *Estates Project* case there was evidence of the rental values for comparable unimproved ground floor shop premises, a use permitted for that part of the property, and the judge ruled that such direct evidence should be followed in preference to a process of calculation of discounts from rental values of improved premises. For the upper floors of the property, where there was no proved comparable, a process of calculation was necessary. He remitted the arbitrator's award, because he had dealt with the upper floors by a process of devaluation from capital cost, which had not been shown to be a valid one. A comparable process had been rejected in the *GREA Real Property Investments* case for the same reason.

A method put forward in the *GREA Real Property Investments* case was to compare the rent actually agreed by the parties for the unimproved premises with rent for the premises in their improved site, derived from comparables, to arrive at a notional market rent for the premises as if unimproved, for which no comparable could be found. The judge expressed doubts on the validity of that approach at least in the absence of evidence that the effect, and possible variable effect, of inflation on the three elements of site value, the construction work and the improvement works would not vitiate the constant discount postulated. The landlord in the later case again urged that approach and the judge's doubts had clearly become less marked. The suggestion of arriving at such a discount and providing for its application on review by a provision in the rent review clauses in the lease was advanced by Aldridge in an article at (1980) 124 SJ 213. That may prove an acceptable practical compromise where a new lease is drafted or an existing lease can be modified; the problems must remain where the process is applied to a lease requiring disregard without reference to the ensuing valuation problems that took 25 years to reach the law reports.

Despite the wide-ranging, if ultimately inconclusive, judgments in this pair of 1979 cases, it is worth noting that neither dealt with what may be the most troublesome area of all. The work effected in the *GREA Real Property Investments* case was, in identifiable respects, work that the tenant would normally have expected the developer to carry out. The work in the *Estates Projects* case was work of modernisation and refurbishment without which the premises could not commercially (or, if the tenant's contentions were sound, legally) be put to their intended use. Improvements carried out during the term in the nature of addition to, or enhancement or embellishment of, premises that would continue, without them, to be quite commercially acceptable and even attractive in the open market will give rise to even more difficult valuation problems. They are clearly 'improvements' that can fall within the usual wording of the disregard, especially if the statutory formula has been followed. Further discussion of this matter will be found in the 1980 Blundell Memorial Lecture of Priday and Hoyes.

(b) Valuation of a 'fair allowance' formula

A bold and different approach to the problem was the distinctive feature of the ISVA Form A, reproduced in Part Seven. This required a fair allowance for any alteration or improvement voluntarily carried out during the term or in the 21 years preceding the rent review date. This is discussed at p 448, but mention is made of it here to emphasise the valuation difficulties of arriving at a fair allowance. Fair to whom? it may be asked. The likely dearth of comparable allowances is a difficulty, and the commentary (see (1984) 272 EG 57) that it caters for the situation of jointly financed works serves to stress that problem, as such financial co-operation is surely rare. It is suggested that these problems may account for the absence of welcome for this element of the form. 'Fair allowance was considered for inclusion in the 1985 Law Society/RICS Model Forms but rejected.

14   Valuing the incomparable

(a) The problem

The 1979 Blundell Memorial Lectures given by Bernstein and Hill dealt with this topic, the former dealing with cases where the use of the absence of comparables was the unusual term of the letting and the latter where the cause was the peculiarity of the property. Bernstein deals with unusually short notional terms, the premises let as a 'shell',

problems where trade fixtures are not removed at the end of one lease
where the review is under a continuation lease (possibly foreshadowing
his argument as counsel in *New Zealand Government Property Corporation
v H M & S Ltd* [1982] QB 1145), restrictive use clauses and planning
restrictions, the problems of subtenancies in the absence of a provision
to assume vacant possession of the whole, and the need to assume a
market for the premises. All of these issues have already been discussed,
and will not be repeated here. Hill's area of concern is, however, related
to the valuation aspects we are now discussing. His examples range from
the problems where there are few comparables—department stores and
hypermarkets are two examples—to the position when there are often
none—hotels, licensed premises and petrol-filling stations are his
examples. The authors could add to the latter list—coalyards, chemical
works, nursing homes, cattle markets, sports stadia and other facilities
and so on—the list is endless.

Trading potential, as Hill says, may often play a large part in negotiation
of rents and the disregard of goodwill becomes difficult. He cites *Corisand
Investments Ltd v Druce & Co* (1978) 248 EG 315 as an example of
the problem of valuing hotels and an excellent example it is. The solution
may have to be found in eschewing the open market rent basis of review
and using some other factor, whether index-linked or not (for which
see Chapters 20 and 21). In some cases, tests equivalent to the contractors'
test used in rating valuations of similar types of properties may be
admissible, and indeed a reversion to the old corn-rent concept by linking,
say, the rent of a coal yard to the price of coal might prove attractive
were it not for the risks of external interference with such price levels
by governmental legislation or exhortation. Ultimately in some cases
the matter will resolve itself into nothing more subtle or scientific than
the surveyor's feeling for 'what the market will pay'.

(b) Profit earning capacity

It has been judicially recognised that there are not two or three clear
cut methods of valuation—*Aik Hoe & Co Ltd v Superintendent of Lands
and Surveys* [1969] 1 AC 1 at 18. Consequently, if the standard practice
of using comparables proves difficult or impossible, then there is no
inherent reason why evidence of profits made from similar businesses
should not be used: *Cornwall Coast Country Club v Cardgrange Ltd* [1987]
1 EGLR 146; *Ritz Hotel (London) Ltd v Ritz Casino* [1989] 2 EGLR
135 where the profits valuation could be used in relation to casinos.
The problem of admissibility and discovery of such evidence is dealt
with in section 5 of this chapter, p 231 above. It is then a matter for
the arbitrator to assess the weight and cogency of such evidence properly
adduced.

(c) Linking or indexation to office rents

A technique first reported to have been used in 1983 lettings of 'high tech' buildings in a 'science park' development was to link the rents on review to those of offices of a designated type in a specific area, the revised rent to be a fixed percentage of the market rents of such other properties. It may be presumed that such percentage reflected the relative rents of the two classes of properties at the initial lettings of the (then) somewhat speculative and untried 'high tech' accommodation. However, even in 1983, it should have been appreciated that the general level of office rents could be affected by factors not relevant to the linked specialist properties. Moreover, subsequent events have revealed the difficulties with this approach. The 'high tech' properties have now shed their experimental flavour and established a definite market sector by the time for the first or later review. Now that a larger market of 'high tech' buildings exists it is less necessary to depart from the usual review basis but existing leases will have to be operated for some years. A discrepancy may then appear between this form of 'indexation' and the true market rent now established by sufficient comparables. This discrepancy may be exacerbated after the changes in the Use Classes Order with consequent ability to switch to and from 'high tech' use. Perhaps 'indexation' to office rents should only have figured as a (landlord's) option for review, as an alternative to open market rent.

The authors have met a similar index-linking, this time to a shops rents index, where the shop rent norm, as determined, was multiplied by a stated factor to produce a rent for a 'speciality' resturant.

(d) Creating a local index

Sometimes the benchmark is more closely allied to the subject premises. Such an approach, by means of a form of indexation, was adopted in *Standard Life Assurance Co v Oxoid Ltd* [1986] EGLR 123 which is more fully discussed at p 565; the dispute centred on the 'standard accommodation' norm. A similar measure was used in *Lansdown Estates Group Ltd v TNT Roadfreight (UK) Ltd* [1989] 2 EGLR 120 where the reviewed rent was to be 140 per cent of a standard warehouse building. The dispute was whether the actual yard, of 1.75 acres, was to be valued or the notional yard of 0.5 acres. The former was preferred on the facts because the actual yard fell within the wording of the formula as one of the 'facilities . . . in the remainder of the demised premises'. The decision emphasises the care needed in drafting this type of formula to cater for the unusual. In *Stylo Barrett Properties Ltd v Legal & General Assurance Society Ltd* [1989] 2 EGLR 116, discussed at p 569 but similarly relevant to valuation, 'proportion' was held to be capable of being a factor greater than one.

The moral that the draftsman must always consider the rent review provisions in the context of the specific lease and the particular property, and never in isolation, applies in greater force to the lease of the property which is, as here described, abnormal.

Chapter 8

Matters subsequent to the Review

Once the reviewed rent has been fixed, whether by agreement or by independent determination, a number of matters arise before the machinery of review can be concluded for the review period in question. In particular:

— From which date is the reviewed rent payable and at what date is the reviewed rent due for payment?
— In what circumstances can interest be claimed on the reviewed rent?
— What should be the form of memorandum to record the rent as agreed or determined?

1 Liability and time for payment of increased rent

(a) Liability from the review date

One of the very earliest appellate decisions on a modern rent review clause established the rule that there was no principle of law that would prevent the rent as reviewed being payable retrospectively to the review date: *C H Bailey Ltd v Memorial Enterprises Ltd* [1974] 1 WLR 728. It must be emphasised that it remains an issue of construction of the lease in question but every well drafted clause will clearly state the date from which the liability for the revised rent is to be calculated. Almost invariably this will be the review date. In a small minority of cases, leases of the 'notice' variety may state that, in the event of a late notice, the reviewed rent is only to take effect from the date of service of the trigger-notice and in such cases the express provision to that effect will prevail.

In the *United Scientific* decision, the House of Lords expressly approved the *C H Bailey* principle. It can faintly be argued that a contrary result should have been achieved by reference to the earlier decision of the House in *Tool Metal Manufacturing Co Ltd v Tungsten Electric Co Ltd* [1955] 1 WLR 761. It will be a brave litigant indeed who would challenge that aspect of the *United Scientific* decision; even if an argument can be sustained that the *C H Bailey* principle was decided per incuriam the *Tool Metal* case, it is probable that too many years have passed and too many leases drafted on the basis that retrospective liability is allowed for it to be overturned now.

(b)   Time when payment falls due

It is important to establish when the increased rent is payable, although a high rate of interest may provide an incentive to make payment in advance of the due date, of course. Each lease should make its own provision; the published precedents adopt various formats. The Model Forms in the 1979 version provided, in clause 3(5), for payment of the aggregate of increases on the first day for payment of rent after the revised rent had been ascertained, but the 1980 Revision made very different provision which was repeated in the 1985 Forms. Clause 4(C)(i) now requires payment 'forthwith upon the revised rent being ascertained', adding moreover, in clause 4(C)(ii), a definition of ascertainment which the 1979 version lacked and which avoids possible uncertainty. ('Forthwith' is not without problems of its own; it may only mean 'with all reasonable speed' though often intended to mean 'immediately'). Conveyancer Precedent 5–57 requires payment 14 days after ascertainment but does not define the latter concept; the EFP (4th ed) Forms all adopt the approach of payment on the rent day following determination and communication to the parties and *Kelly's Draftsman*, Form 14 specifies the rent day following the agreement or certifying of the revised rent.

The significance of the point was demonstrated by *South Tottenham Land Securities Ltd v R & A Millett (Shops) Ltd* [1984] 1 All ER 614. Rent with effect from 25 March 1980 payable in arrear was the subject of an arbitrator's award on 30 October of that year, of which the tenants were sent notice on 6 November. The lease was forfeited on 26 November for non-payment of the increases attributable to the June and September quarter days (the lease allowing for forfeiture if the rent was more than 21 days in arrear). The lessors' contention that the rent became due on the date the award was published was rejected. The lease contained no express provision to cover the late determination. The Court of Appeal, upholding the judge below, held that, in the absence of clear provision, the reddendum, providing for rent repayments on quarter days, prevailed and the increases had not been due until the December quarter day. The forfeiture was consequently premature and wrongful. An assessment of damages for premature forfeiture was ordered and the lessors' wrongful action meant that the rent for the period due in December 1980 was not recoverable; though the increased rent for the earlier quarters in September and June was still recoverable because the liability to pay had arisen before the forfeiture occurred (*Torminster Properties Ltd v Green* [1983] 1 WLR 676 applied). It was said, obiter, by O'Connor LJ (at 618) and Woolf J [1983] 268 EG 703 at 706 that an arbitral award of rent is published, and binding on the parties, when the arbitrator notifies the parties he has made his award whether or not they have notice of its contents; that being so, it was objectionable to have the rent falling due on the date of publication, for the tenant cannot be expected to pay an amount he does not or may not know, and this was a further reason for holding the rent fell due on the next quarter day. The *South Tottenham* case was applied in *Shield Properties & Investments Ltd v Anglo Overseas Transport Co Ltd (No 2)* [1986] 2 EGLR 112 so that reviewed rent was not payable and due until the first quarter day after an arbitrator's second, revised, award (nearly 2 years after the review date).

In any event, the advice of O'Connor LJ is to be heeded 'It is desirable that rent review clauses in leases should deal specifically with what is to happen where there is a delay in arriving at a new rent beyond the review date' (*South Tottenham* case [1984] 1 All ER at 618).

2   Provision for interest

Since a reviewed rent may be agreed or fixed a considerable time after the review date to which it relates, the landlord will be concerned to try and ensure interest is paid on the sum retrospectively due.

(a)   Not normally implied

Interest is not generally payable in default of an express provision. In *Trust House Forte Albany Hotels Ltd v Daejan Investments Ltd* [1980] 256 EG 915 Walton J held that an obligation to pay interest on a delayed review could not be implied on the 'business efficacy' principle, although it would have been commercially reasonable and not inconsistent with any other provision in the lease. The judge was of the opinion that, while the landlord may thus be disadvantaged, it was certainly not *necessary* to imply the term.

(b)   By virtue of an express provision in the lease

If there is express provision in the lease, either generally or specifically in the review clause, then interest will fall due in accordance with the express terms. The drafting considerations are considered in Chapter 4, p 81. If there is to be express provision for interest, then it is important to ensure that it applies to give interest from the review date. In *Shield Properties & Investments Ltd v Anglo Overseas Transport Co Ltd (No 2)* [1986] 2 EGLR 112, the lease only stated that interest was to be payable if the lessee 'shall make default in effecting payment to the lessor forthwith on demand of any monies becoming payable by the lessee'. The review date was 25 December 1982; an arbitrator made an award on 24 May 1983; before the next rent day, the tenants issued a notice of motion to set aside the award; on 3 April 1984, the award, though not set aside, was remitted to the arbitrator for further consideration (see [1985] 1 EGLR 7 and p 206, above) and on 20 November 1984 he made a substituted, and lower, award. The lessors claimed interest from the date of the original award but it was held that the tenants were not 'in default' under the lease. The original award had been annulled by the remission; under the revised award, the reviewed rent was not due until the next quarter day following the award (applying the *South Tottenham case*—see above); that had been paid by the due date so no interest was payable. If the clause had provided for interest as in the 1985 Model Forms, a substantial sum would have been payable as interest.

The deputy judge, Michael Wheeler QC, suggested that one remedy for the lessors, given that the lease did not make provision for interest, would have been for them to request that the tenants be put on terms as to interest when the motion to set aside the arbitrator's original award was issued.

In the absence of express provision, the circumstances where interest might be claimed are very limited.

(c) Arbitration Act 1950, ss 20 and 19A

An arbitrator has no general power to award interest: *President of India v La Pintada Cia Navegacion SA* [1985] AC 104. It appears that no argument has been raised on the possible application of ss 20 or 19A of the Arbitration Act 1950 in any rent review case the authors have been able to trace but the prevailing view is that they will normally not apply.

(i) Section 20
This provides:

'A sum directed to be paid by an award shall, unless the award otherwise directs, carry interest as from the date of the award and at the same rate as a judgment debt.'

The better view is that a rent is not 'directed to be paid' by any arbitral award which only determines a sum for which there is a pre-existing liability to pay from the lease itself. This is the view taken in the RICS Guidance Notes, Note 3.11.3 but the point awaits authoritative decision in the rent review context. *Knibb v National Coal Board* [1987] QB 906, a case decided by analogy to the powers of an arbitrator appointed by agreement between the parties, suggests that fixing a sum payable does not fall within the section; which would then be limited to sums awarded by way of damages or compensation. The section would have limited impact in any event since the power to award interest only covers the period from the date of the award, which will invariably be much later than the effective date of the retrospective increase. Further, if s 20 can be invoked, *Timber Shipping Co SA v London and Overseas Freighters Ltd* [1972] AC 1 restricts the arbitrator to either an award that no interest shall be paid or an award at judgment rate; no other rate can be awarded. *Rocco Giuseppe & Figli v Tradax Export SA* [1983] 2 Lloyd's Rep 434 held that the section only gives a right to interest at the rate prescribed at the date of the award and not at the rate as varied, by statutory instrument, from time to time.

(ii)   Section 19A

The Administration of Justice Act 1982 s 15(6) introduced a new s 19A into the 1950 Act permitting an award of interest:

> '(a) on any sum which is the subject of the reference but which is paid
>   before the award . . . ; and
> (b) On any sum which he awards . . .'

Once again, if the view is taken that a rent review arbitrator only determines a rent rather than awards a sum, then the section will not apply. The typical award in a rent review declares what the appropriate rent shall be and the payment obligation stems from the lease itself, not the award. It would be possible to frame the submission to arbitration to require an award of the sum payable; if that is not in the original lease, the tenant should not agree to it. If it is in the lease, one might also hope to find a provision for interest with full retrospective effect, in any event. If the section were to apply to rent review, then the award of interest can be 'at such a rate as (the arbitrator) thinks fit' but such award is limited to simple interest.

(d)   Determinations by an expert

An expert has no power to award interest unless the parties expressly give it to him. Conveyancer Precedent 5–57, for example, gives him a limited power to award interest for a lessee's delay.

(e)   Interest awarded under the Supreme Court Act 1981, s 35A

Section 35A of the Supreme Court Act 1981, inserted into that Act by the Administration of Justice Act 1982, s 15, and in force from 1 April 1983, gives the High Court discretion, in proceedings for the recovery of a debt or damages, to include in any sum for which judgment is given, simple interest at such rate as the Court thinks fit, subject to any maximum set by rules of court. This section (and there is similar provision for county courts under s 69A of the County Courts Act 1984) will permit a claim for interest wherever proceedings successfully allege reviewed rent is already due under covenants in the lease. It allows interest to be claimed even on sums paid before judgment, providing a writ had earlier been issued. Interest was awarded in a claim by a landlord against an original leesee for rent due from a defaulting assignee from

the date when each instalment of rent fell due, notwithstanding the fact
that the lease contained no provision for interest on arrears of rent (*Allied
London Investments Ltd v Hambro Life Assurance Ltd* [1985] 1 EGLR
45). The landlords therefore succeeded in obtaining interest from the
original lessee from the date each instalment of rent fell due. The court
held:

(1) The power under s 35A is a discretionary one to be exercised
    judicially.
(2) The fundamental principle is that interest is awarded because the
    plaintiff has been deprived of the use of the money due, not as
    a punishment.
(3) An original lessee has concurrent liability to pay rent as it fell due
    (by privity of contract).
(4) It is for the defendant to show cause why interest should not be
    awarded from the date of the loss. In the case, the defendants had
    been alerted by letter that a s 146 notice was being served and warned
    that they remained 'liable under your covenants'. This was sufficient
    to put them on notice that a claim might be made.

The procedure for such claims for interest is set out in a *Practice
Note* [1983] 1 WLR 377.

It was pointed out in the *Allied London Investments* case (at 950) that
the debtor tenant can avoid paying interest under s 35A by paying the
sum demanded before the writ is issued. In *President of India v La Pintada
Cia Navigacion SA* [1985] AC 104 an attempt in a charter-party arbitration
to obtain interest in such circumstances by persuading the House of
Lords to depart from its previous authority failed, and *London, Chatham
and Dover Rly Co v South Eastern Rly Co* [1893] AC 429 was upheld,
though with unanimous reluctance and regret and pleas for amending
legislation. There is a possibility of an EEC directive for interest on
debts but it is at too early a stage to judge if it will encompass rent
arrears.

(f) Interest on a s 27 Arbitration Act 1950 application

On a successful application for extension of time under s 27 of the
Arbitration Act 1950 relief may be granted on terms which may include
payment of interest even when the lease makes no express provision
(*Chartered Trust plc v Maylands Green Estate Co Ltd* [1984] 270 EG
845). Section 27 is more fully discussed at p 113, above.

3 Evidencing the varied rent

Whilst there is no statutory requirement that the revised rent arising
on a review be recorded in writing, the good sense of having a permanent

and undisputed record of the revised rent is evident. Some forms of drafting will render a written document at some stage essential. For example, where a landlord's notice must state a rent that takes effect in the absence of challenge or counter-notice by the tenant (see p 124, above) there must be at least one document. Similarly, an index-linked rent provision where the landlord must serve notice of the adjusted rent (discussed at p 571) is another instance where a document must come into existence.

(a) Arguments for and against agreements in writing

There are two schools of thought as to the desirability of requiring any agreement on rent to be effected by, or as a minimum recorded in, writing. On the one hand, the supporters of the requirement of writing emphasise the benefit of avoiding dispute or uncertainty and the value of bringing home to the parties, and particularly the tenant, the significance of the transaction that settles the obligation for increased rent for a period of some years. The opponents of the requirement point to the opportunities it provides for either party, repenting of a parol bargain in fact reached, to have second thoughts and decline to sign any document formally agreeing or recording the new rent. The arguments on both sides have already been fully explored over the years in relation to the wisdom of retaining s 40 of the Law of Property Act 1925, a debate now resolved by the Law of Property (Miscellaneous Provisions) Act 1989, s 2.

The Joint Working Party of the Law Society and the RICS do not require an agreement in writing in any version of the Model Forms. However, the authors of this book favour an agreement in writing (see Chapter 4, pp 59–64), especially as it avoids dispute not only on what was agreed but also over whether agreement had in fact been reached in what may have been informal or even casual conversations. Another argument is that it is a safeguard against the importunate agent for a landlord virtually bullying an unsophisticated and unrepresented tenant into a hasty and ill-considered oral agreement.

In most cases, a refusal to sign a document where one is required will not cause irreparable harm unless there is a time of the essence provision and the party with the right to invoke the 'fall-back' machinery of reference to a third party fails to do so in time, in reliance on the oral agreement arrived at. Whether in such a case the disadvantaged party could rely on either estoppel or his own part performance, akin to that formerly available to overcome the absence of writing under s 40, had not been put to the test in any reported decision. In principle, there is no reason why in appropriate circumstances one or the other principle should not be applied, though to establish either there would have to be clear proof of a concluded agreement. Apart from the minority of cases where time is of the essence, the remedy for a refusal to sign

an agreement, or a memorandum recording a concluded agreement, is
to proceed to the third-party reference. The refusal, if proved, could
have a bearing on the incidence of costs.

(b)   Evidence from written notices

Where notices have to be served as part of the review process, and
there is a requirement for the notice to be in writing, there will be written
evidence. The extent to which a mere mention of a notice, by probable
incorporation of s 196 of the Law of Property Act 1925, imparts the
requirement of writing has been discussed (in Chapter 5, at p 120). If
s 196 does apply, that will mean that notices must be written and these
will always be of evidential value. Where the notice has to state a rent,
and does so (see discussion of the issues at p 124) there will be a written
statement of the rent, but not where the notice is merely to initiate
some other procedure. The 'longstop' provision for a tenant's notice
in clause 3(6) of the Model Forms (clause 4(E) of the revised 1980 version)
should be borne in mind in this regard.

(c)   'Subject to contract' agreement will not bind

Agreement between the parties on a revised rent will often be by
exchange of letters between the parties or their advisers. In such a case,
a binding agreement can only be reached by 'open' letters. In *Henderson
Group plc v Superabbey Ltd* [1988] 2 EGLR 155 the landlord's proposals
for the new rent was contained in a letter headed 'Subject to contract'
and 'Without prejudice'. The tenant responded in an open letter that
the new rent was acceptable but resiled from that position before signing
a formal memorandum. It was held, applying well known propositions,
that the tenant's reply was governed by the 'subject to contract' condition
so there was no binding agreement on the new rent.

(d)   Arbitrator's award

The Arbitration Act 1950, like the 1934 Act but unlike the 1889 Act,
does not require the arbitrator's award to be in writing. Thus, any
obligation to put it in writing must be found in the submission to
arbitration, and then an award not in writing would be a nullity. If
the arbitrator were then to refuse to give a written award, he would
be guilty of misconduct. Signature of a written award does not appear
imperative. In practice, few arbitrators would refuse to give a written
award if asked, even where the submission is silent on the point, and
the authors have no doubt that the overwhelming majority of awards
are in writing and signed. The power of the courts under s 1(5) of the
Arbitration Act 1979 to require an arbitrator to give reasons, or more
detailed reasons where those given are insufficient for the appeal to
proceed, does not in terms impose an obligation to give them in writing;

again, in practice, it would be unlikely for such reasons to be given except in writing.

Mention should be made of the power in s 17 of the 1950 Act for the arbitrator to correct any clerical mistake 'or error arising from any accidental slip or omission' in his award. The second limb would cover, for example, arithmetical errors, but how much wider it may extend is not certain, for there is a marked dearth of decisions on the section. The powers are subject to any contrary intention expressed in the agreement, but such a provision would surely be rare.

(e) Expert's awards

There is no general obligation on the expert valuer to give a written decision but such an obligation can be imposed by the terms of the reference to him, whether in the original lease or as a matter of later agreement between the parties, and he would then be bound to comply with such a direction. In practice, the vast majority of awards will be in writing.

(f) Memorandum of reviewed rent

(i) Desirable as record of agreed or reviewed rent

Even where there is written evidence of the new rent, it may be in an inconvenient form. The parties' agreement may have been concluded in an exchange of letters, an award may be a lengthy document dealing with a lot of issues that one or other of the parties may not wish to have revealed to later assignees of the term or of the reversion, and so on. (Nevertheless, preservation with the title deeds of the award or determination and all documents relating thereto is desirable both to pass to later purchasers where appropriate and because of issue estoppel, as discussed at p 209.) Accordingly, the practice grew up amongst conveyancers providing for memoranda of the reviewed rent to be endorsed upon the lease and counterpart, recording the outcome of the review process, and signed by or on behalf of the parties. Early versions of the clause made it necessary for the tenant to return the lease to the landlord for his signature to a memorandum endorsed on it and for the counterpart likewise to go back to the tenant. This parting with original deeds is not altogether convenient, and may be particularly unwelcome to any third party holding the documents in connection with a security. Accordingly, it was found more convenient to provide for separate memoranda to be signed and exchanged, which are then placed with, or annexed to, the lease and counterpart respectively. This growing practice was reflected in the precedents first published in 1979, namely the first version of the Model Forms, and Conveyancer Precedent 5-57. The former added a suggested form of memorandum, which is reproduced in the Part Seven. There are also modern precedents in EFP

(5th ed) Forms 134 and 135 and memoranda will normally be signed and exchanged whether or not the lease makes express provision.

(ii)   Any guarantor should sign

Where there is a guarantor, whether in relation to the obligations of the initial tenant or of any later holder of the term, it is wise, for reasons discussed in Chapter 14, to provide that he also signs the memorandum. This should prevent his later claiming that he was not bound by the rent adjustment. It could be argued that the wording of subclause (1) of Conveyancer Precedent 5-57, referring to 'the parties', already suffices to achieve that result; the Model Forms refer in clause 3(3) (initial version) and 4(C) (revised version) to landlord and tenant and need to be adapted expressly to include the guarantor as a signatory. Express reference to the guarantor in Conveyancer Precedent 5-57 could defeat the possible argument that 'the parties' meant not the parties to the lease, which irrefutably include the guarantor, but the parties to the ascertainment of the new rent, of which the guarantor may not be one, so express reference would be safer.

(iii)   Absent or inadequate memoranda

Failure to endorse and sign a memorandum, or to sign a separate memorandum, does not have any substantive effect on the recoverability of the new rent previously ascertained, but could give rise to the very problems of proof and uncertainty that the provision is designed to avoid. If one party refused to sign, and the other was determined to insist on his rights, the court would seem to have ample power to order the defaulter to sign or to appoint someone to sign on his behalf.

What if the memorandum is erroneous? There might be a clerical slip in transcription, an arithmetical error in calculating a total rent from an ascertained rate per square foot, a measuring error in working out a floor area or a similar mistake. In *Equity & Law Life Assurance Society Ltd v Coltness Group* (1983) 267 EG 949 (fully discussed in Chapter 9 p 283, below) the mistake was as to the duration for which the reviewed rent was to be paid. Rectification would be available, as in the *Equity & Law* case, on proof of the mistake in recording the agreement (or, indeed, the award of the arbitrator or expert) subject to the usual qualification that third parties have not acquired rights which would make it inequitable to rectify against them. Other equitable defences (eg laches) would also apply.

4   Stamp duty aspects

Under the Stamp Act 1891, stamp duty is chargeable if an instrument falls within one of the various heads of charge listed in Sched 1 to the Act.

(a) Duty payable on the lease

The new lease attracts ad valorem stamp duty on the full rent by reference to the scale applicable to the length of the term created. As already discussed (p 49) the stamp duty on the lease with a rent review, or a rent subject to indexation, is assessed on the rent initially reserved on the basis that this sum is the minimum sum payable for the duration of the term. Only if the maximum rent payable later can be exactly calculated (eg as with a progressive rent) is there duty on the rent as reviewed, a result normally avoided (see below). This is because the standard rent review clause leaves the rent for subsequent review periods unascertained.

(b) Duty not normally payable at review

Some variations in a lease can only be achieved by a surrender of the residue of the existing term and the grant, or re-grant, of the amended lease. An extension of the original term can only be effected in this way—see dicta in *Re Savile Settled Estate* [1931] 2 Ch 210 at 217 and *Jenkin R Lewis Ltd v Kerman* [1971] Ch 477 at 496. A variation in rent, by contrast, does not normally involve such a transaction—*Gable Construction Co Ltd v IRC* [1968] 1 WLR 1246 and *Lewis v Kerman*— whether the variation comes from a new bargain or operation of review machinery (and see the discussion Chapter 2, p 17).

A variation does not attract under the heading 'Lease or Tack'— since it effects no demise. Moreover, liability under the heading 'Bond or Covenant' can be avoided.

(i) Memorandum which records change—no liability

Where the reddendum in a lease providing for rent reviews is drawn so as to reserve the rent as from time to time varied, then any consequent memorandum of the amount of rent as reviewed should be framed so that it merely records the ascertainment of the new level of rent. It should not itself purport to vary the rent under the original lease. In such cases there is no liability to duty under s 77(5) of the 1981 Act below. The recommended form of memorandum in the Model Forms meets these criteria; the reddenda in all the modern precedents reproduced in Part Seven meet the above-stated guide-lines too. The use of the wording in a memorandum of rent 'substituted' for the original rent is dangerous in relation to possible stamp duty and so is better avoided.

(ii) Liability if instrument effects the variation

Liability to duty under the the heading 'Bond or Covenant' was abolished in general by the Finance Act 1971, but s 64(1)(a) of that Act preserved it in so far as it related to documents varying rent payable under an instrument chargeable under the 'Lease or Tack' head. By s 77(5) of the Stamp Act 1891 it is further provided:

'An instrument whereby the rent reserved by any other instrument chargeable with duty and duly stamped as a lease or tack is increased is not to be charged with duty otherwise than as a lease or tack in consideration of the additional rent thereby made payable.'

Consequently, stamp duty will only be chargeable at rent review if the instrument itself varies the rent. This might occur if a review was agreed where the lease made no provision; or if a different rent review pattern was substituted. There must also be a risk that duty may have to be paid where a review is allowed to proceed by mutual agreement in a situation where, perhaps by missing a time-limit, one party has lost his right to review under the lease.

The effect of s 77(5), Goff J ruled in the *Gable Construction Co* case, was to limit the duty payable to the lease level but not directly to charge any duty on the variation deed. Normally the duty payable on the new lease would exceed that payable under the restriction imposed by s 77(5) and the duty payable under the Bond or Covenant head would exceed that on the restricted basis. The *Gable Construction* case was approved by the Court of Appeal in the *Lewis* case on the point of variation without surrender and re-grant, but the stamp duty issue was not relevant. It is interesting, nevertheless, to note that in the tenancy agreement in the later case the tenant agreed to pay 'the rent hereby recovered or any rent substituted therefore by agreement or by arbitration under s 12 of the Agricultural Holdings Act 1923'.

(iii) Memoranda under seal

Since a memorandum under seal or executed as a deed, even if not dutiable ad valorem, is chargeable to 50p stamp it is more convenient to have such memoranda signed by the parties and avoid any expession of intent that the document be a deed.

Chapter 9

Treatment of Inadequate or Erroneous Review Clauses

It is inherent in the nature of a rent review clause that any inadequacies, omissions or defects therein are only likely to be manifested on the occasion of the first review, usually some years after the lease has been executed—and the problems may be compounded by judicial rulings on particular issues in the meantime. Indeed, what may have seemed an entirely adequate clause may only have been shown to be less satisfactory by these decisions. In this chapter, we summarise how, and the extent to which, the courts try to ensure that inadequacies in review clauses do not frustrate the intent, presumed or otherwise, of the parties to the lease.

Inadequacies can be dealt with in a number of ways:

(1) A decree of rectification

This is the most radical and difficult remedy applicable when the deed contains a mistake. A deed may be rectified to accord with the actual intent of the parties in accordance with their agreement. The principles of rectification are considered in section 2 of this chapter, below.

(2) By implication of terms

A court is always slow to imply terms but will do so on the two grounds discussed in section 1 of this chapter, below:
  (a) The 'business efficacy' test: the implication is necessary to give business efficacy to the contract.
  (b) The 'officious bystander' test: the implication suggested is so obvious that the parties, if questioned on the point by an officious bystander, would have agreed that it was so obvious as to go without saying.

(3) By a process of construction

If neither of the above assist, then it will be a matter of the proper construction of the terms of the lease, a issue fully considered in Part Three. The principles and guide-lines referred to in Chapter 10 (p 297) may have the effect of securing a construction which accords with reality and the commercial purpose of the review clause.

(4)   An action for negligence

This will be the remedy of last resort when a party suffers loss from a defectively drafted or operated clause—see section 3 of this chapter, below.

1   Coping with inadequacies; implication of terms

We have already shown rent review clauses are treated as terms of a contract which fall to be considered within a continuing landlord and tenant relationship in which mutual rights and obligations have already arisen and are continuing. In striving to uphold the lease and the review clause, it has been easier for the courts, by necessary implication, to cope with omissions; for express words in a lease must be given some meaning if it is possible to do so and cannot just be ignored.

(a)   Review to 'rents to be agreed'

(i)   Implied term approach

It can be argued that a clause in a lease providing for review to a rent to be agreed by the parties ought to be of no effect since, in default of such agreement, the lease contains no formula or mechanism to resolve the dispute. For a court to step in, a process of implying words into a lease is required and this can be viewed as completing a bargain the parties failed to make for themselves. Such an approach has only found favour with one first instance judge. In *King v King* (1980) 255 EG 1205, which can no longer be considered good authority, the 'review' clause, having fixed a rent for the first 7 years of a 21–year term, merely prescribed 'such rent as may be agreed between the parties' for the remainder of the term. It was said that it was not proper to imply a standard of reasonableness enabling a reviewed rent to be fixed because it could not be certain that the standard of reasonableness is that which both parties would have intended to apply in the event of a disagreement. If the standard of reasonableness could not be applied if the reddendum had merely fixed such rent as may be agreed, a fortiori it could not do so where the revised rent is not to be agreed until some years later. However, the fixing of the rent for the first 7 years prevented the lease being void for uncertainty, and that sum was held to be the rent payable for the rest of the term. The contrary view has found favour with the Court of Appeal who have felt able in such cases to imply a term into the lease to give business efficacy to the contract. The first case in time is *Beer v Bowden* (1976) but only reported at (Note) [1981] 1 WLR 522. There a 'rent review clause' merely provided that from a particular date the rent was to be such figure as was agreed between the parties. There was no provision for what should happen in default of agreement (though it was clear that the rent originally reserved was to be paid only up to the review date) nor was there a reference to a formula or yardstick by which a rental figure could be ascertained. The only guidance was that it was to be not less than the rent for the first period and any improvements were to be ignored. The parties failed to agree yet the submission of the landlord that the lease was void, and the tenant's argument that the rent originally reserved continued, were both rejected. The Court of Appeal founded their judgments on the basis of an implied term to give business efficacy to the contract. They held that it was proper to imply that 'such rent as shall thereupon be agreed' should be read as 'such *fair* rent as shall thereupon be agreed'.

The reasons given for such implication were based on the principle of *The Moorcock* (1889) 14 PD 64. To allow the purported review clause to operate gave effect to the intention of the parties to reconsider and, almost inevitably, to increase the rent at the review date. The judgments stress the continuing estate in land (for which some rent should be paid) and the fact that any other construction of the lease would render the provision futile, for the tenant would never agree an increase. The liberal approach to the implication of terms is in accord with the guidance given by Lord Denning MR in a different context:

'In a commercial agreement, the further the parties have gone on with their contract, the more ready are the courts to imply any reasonable term so as to give effect to their intentions. When much has been done, the courts will do their best not to destroy the bargain (*F & G Sykes (Wessex) Lid v Fine Fare Ltd* [1967] 1 Lloyd's Rep 53 at 57).'

The *Sykes* case was cited with approval in *Thomas Bates & Son Ltd v Wyndham's (Lingerie) Ltd* [1981] 1 WLR 505 where as an alternative, subsidiary ground for decision it was said that the rent to be ascertained in default of agreement would be a fair rent between the parties, a conclusion in accord with the approach in *Beer v Bowden*. The principle established in *Beer v Bowden* was applied in option cases: *Trustees of National Deposit Friendly Society v Beatties of London Ltd* [1985] 2 EGLR 59; *Corson v Rhuddlan Borough Council* [1990] 1 EGLR 255. It has been followed in New Zealand: *Feltex International Ltd v JBL Consolidated Ltd* [1988] 1 NZLR 668 (the 'annual rental' to be reviewed was, by implication, to be the 'fair annual rental').

It may be open for one party to bring evidence to show that at the date the agreement was concluded he would not have found the suggested 'implied term' formula acceptable, and an observation to this effect was made at first instance in *Thomas Bates* (1979) 39 P & CR at 530, though in the light of the principles relating to construction of leases (discussed in Part Three below) this dictum may be doubted. If such evidence was accepted the court may be precluded from implying a term since the words to be implied could not be the presumed intent of the parties.

(ii)   Valuation basis of the term implied

A 'reasonable' rent may mean the same thing as a 'fair' rent, as the decisions in *Store Properties and General Investments Ltd v Darrington (Rustington)* (1978) 3 February (unreported) and *Thomas Bates* [1981] 1 WLR 505 at 519 assumed, but they may have a different meaning from an 'open market' rent (see *Ponsford v HMS Aerosols Ltd* [1979] AC 63, *Feltex International Ltd v JBL Consolidated Ltd* [1988] 1 NZLR 668 at p 671 and the discussion in Chapter 12, p 382).

The issue of the correct valuation basis arose in *Lear v Blizzard* [1983] 3 All ER 662 where, on exercise of an option to renew a 21 year lease for a similar term, renewal was at 'a rent to be agreed between the parties or in default of agreement at a rent to be determined by a single arbitrator'. The arbitrator posed four questions for the court, two of which are relevant to the present discussion. The first was whether what fell to be determined was an open market rent or a fair rent. The second was, if a fair rent was to be assessed, should it be what the particular landlord and tenant would agree reflecting the considerations each would have in mind in negotiating. It was held that a fair rent was proper, and it was to be determined subjectively, ie as indicated in the second question posed. The reasoning in *Thomas Bates v Wyndham* prevailed on the wording used in the option in the lease, the result in *Ponsford v HMS Aerosols Ltd* [1979] AC 63 of an objective approach being distinguished.

A consequence of the ruling in favour of a subjective approach was that the rental effect of certain improvements (initially unauthorised but retrospectively permitted with a rent increase) was to be ignored to the extent that the current tenant, in fact an assignee and successor in title of the party which did the work, might be found, on evidence to be given to the arbitrator, to have paid for them wholly or in part.

If evidence was tendered to show that there was a demonstrable difference between a fair rent and a market rent when applied to the particular demised premises, then it may be difficult for a court to decide which formula should be implied (*Lear v Blizzard*). In *Thomas Bates*, after the lease had been rectified (see section 2 of this chapter, below) it was conceded, with the approval of the court, that the agreement was one to arbitrate and not one to abide by a valuation and, in such circumstances, the rent should be a reasonable rent for the parties to have agreed under the lease, and not the market rent for the property. In the authors' respectful submission, it does not follow that one basis of valuation is necessarily more suited to an arbitral function, and another to that of valuation. In the *Lear* case, moreover, the emphasis was given to the initial provision for the parties to agree rather than to the nature of the later resolution of their failure to agree.

(iii)   Limited to one review

A lease providing for review of a rent during a term to a rent to be agreed but omitting to specify the basis or method of calculation in default of agreement will be valid if the court is able to imply a term into the lease. However, there are limits to what the court can do. If the lease provided for 'rents to be agreed' at a series of review dates specified in the lease, then it is probable that the *Beer v Bowden* principle would allow a review at each of those dates. On the other hand, in *Stedman v Midland Bank* [1990] 1 EGLR 146 a lease for a 71–year term reserved a rent of £800 rising by £10 per annum for the first 5 years and thereafter 'at a rent to be agreed or in default of agreement to be fixed by an arbitrator'. It was held that the proper construction of the lease was that the rent was to be fixed after 5 years for the whole of the remaining 66 years of the term. Since there had been an agreement to fix the rent at a date subsequent to the first 5 years, the landlord was not entitled to any further rent review. The contention that the lease provided for annual reviews was rejected. It is to be noted that there was no argument that there should be an implied term—the case was one of construction of the lease. However, it is thought that an attempt to argue that a term could be implied that there should not only be a fair rent but a fair or standard pattern of review periods would not succeed in the light of the decision in *National Westminster Bank Ltd v BSC Footwear Ltd* (1980) 42 P & CR 90 (discussed at p 516, below) and because it is not *necessary* to imply such a term. A bargain for a fixed rent for a period of 66 years may be unusual or a bad one for the landlord but it is a perfectly possible bargain. Indeed, a fixed rent in a long term, probably granted in return for a premium, is far more common than one fixed for, say, a 20 year term.

(b)   Absence of, or deficiencies in, the rent review formula

It will be clear from the foregoing that the total absence of a rent review formula will be met, where necessary, by the implication of review to a fair or reasonable rent. If wording is used which relates to agreement, or third party determination in default of agreement, the test will be a subjective one relating to the parties; otherwise it will be objective, but discounting the freak comparable. Such, at least, is the present state of the authorities.

Where the formula provided by the parties is imprecise, the test to be applied is whether someone genuinely seeking to discover its meaning is able to do so. The clause is to be approached with reasonable goodwill since the court seeks to avoid holding it void for uncertainty. In effect, the result is that the formula will be valid unless:

(1)   It is devoid of any meaning; or (more unlikely)

(2) There are a variety of meanings that can be fairly put on the provision and it is impossible to say which of them was intended.

This test was applied in *Brown v Gould* [1972] Ch 53, a decision of Megarry J, which deals with an option to renew in a lease. The principle that emerges is, however, equally applicable to the fluctuations of a rent during the currency of the lease. The option for the new lease in that case was for a term of 21 years 'at a rent to be fixed having regard to the market value of the premises at the time of exercising the option'. Any structural improvements done at the tenant's expense were to be taken into account. The formula, and with it the option, were upheld. It did not matter that the formula, if given to the parties' valuers, would produce figures which were not identical, for, it was said, 'valuation is like that'.

Thus, the courts accept some degree of uncertainty. One of the authors pointed out that the critical question not posed in *Brown v Gould* concerns the formula 'at a rent to be fixed having regard to the market value' (see Adams (1973) 68 *Law Society's Gazette*, 484, 529, also considering *Smith v Morgan* [1971] 1 WLR 803, a case displaying a similar lenient view on certainty when applied to a right of pre-emption). How can one say with certainty how much 'regard' (Adams at 531)? It is interesting to note that, within a year, the learned judge had occasion to consider the words 'having regard to' in the context of the Landlord and Tenant Act 1954, s 24A(3), where an interim rent is to be determined 'having regard to the rent payable under the terms of the tenancy' (*English Exporters (London) Ltd v Eldonwall Ltd* [1973] Ch 415). There he acknowledged that the term is 'almost of necessity bound to create difficulties' but they are difficulties the courts seem content to leave for valuers and arbitrators to resolve.

A more modern difficulty with any rent review formula is not likely to be its absence, but rather conflicting, confusing or inappropriate terms, often taken from standard precedents but unsuited to the lease in question. Construction of such clauses is dealt with in Part Three; but at this stage it should be noted that when ordinary construction principles still make a mockery of the review clause, then the court may adopt the same 'business efficacy' principle discussed in the previous section and imply a term into the lease, if—and only if—the rent review provision will not work without it. An example is *Law Land Co Ltd v Consumers' Association* (1980) 255 EG 617 (fully discussed at p 349, below); and a particularly striking illustration is *Jefferies v O'Neill* (1983) 46 P & CR 376. In that case, solicitors took a lease of first and second floor accommodation in premises adjacent to their own. The lease provided for a new access from the solicitors' existing offices, granted no other access to the upper floors and, indeed, the existing staircase was removed. The review clause was in usual form postulating hypothetical willing parties, an open market and providing for disregard of the solicitors' occupation—yet as the lease stood there could be no open market because only the solicitors could gain access. Neill J held that a disregard should be implied, namely of the existing first floor access and the absence of the staircase, since without such implication the whole rent review provision was of no practical effect.

Thus the courts may be able to rescue the parties to a lease from the consequences of their drafting errors, but any implied term must be necessary and in accordance with commercial realities. Thus, an attempt to imply a term into a lease and provide for an implied disregard of the possibility of amalgamation with adjoining premises failed in *Webber v Halifax Building Society* [1985] 1 EGLR 58. There the lease contemplated, in a provision for reinstatement, that the tenant building society would (as it did in fact) amalgamate the demised premises into its freehold office next door. A rather slipshod review clause failed to provide on review for an express disregard of this factor; so a valuer, considering the open market rent of the premises as a 'developer's shell', did not have to disregard the fact that the owners next door, and tenant in fact, might pay a special and higher rent for the premises. Unlike *Jefferies v O'Neill* (not cited in the *Webber* case), the review clause could operate as it stood and there was no room for implications on the 'business efficacy' principle.

Pleasurama Properties Ltd v Leisure Investments (West End) Ltd [1985] 1 EGLR 54 is a similar example. Nourse J rejected a claim that an obligation on a tenant to reinstate at the end of a term should be disregarded by necessary implication. There was no such necessity: indeed to do so would offend commercial common sense because such implication would require the landlords to suffer an increased burden— they had had no financial benefit from the alterations (construction of a dolphinarium) and the covenant to reinstate was their protection. This part of the decision was not challenged by the tenants in their, unsuccessful, appeal: [1986] 1 EGLR 145.

(c) Implication of the obvious—even if not necessary

If the suggested implied term is not strictly *necessary*, it may still be implied if it provides the obvious answer to an anomaly or difficulty raised by the express words. It must, however, be so obvious that the parties, if questioned on the point by the 'officious bystander' at the time of agreement, would have answered 'of course, that goes without saying'. An example of its application in a rent review clause is *Toyota (GB) Ltd v Legal & General Assurance (Pensions Management) Ltd* [1989] 2 EGLR 123 where the grant of a lease for 16 years followed by a reversionary lease of 34 years meant that a strict reading of the rent review clause for the review after 15 years postulated a notional term of only 1 year whereas the reality was that there was 35 to go. Words were implied so that reference to the residue of the term in the current lease included the additional term granted by the reversionary lease. This was considered to be obvious in the context of a 50 year total term with 5–year reviews.

(d) Absence of, or difficulties in, rent review machinery

If no machinery is stated for working out the formula, it was held in *Brown v Gould* that the court will if necessary determine the matter itself. The court is not precluded from resolving a dispute as to the rent payable under a lease if the parties disagree as to the application of a proper formula to the facts of the case. Where, however, there is machinery for determination, that machinery must be utilised. A number of authorities from the last century suggested that if the machinery breaks down the court will not step in (eg *Milnes v Gery* (1807) 33 ER 574), but as noted in Chapter 2 (p 13, above) these were overruled in *Sudbrook Trading Estates Ltd v Eggleton* [1983] AC 444. Where the machinery of rent review provided by the parties is a subsidiary or non-essential part of the contract, the court will substitute its own machinery to ascertain the agreed rent. It will not do so where the parties make it clear that the machinery they provide is fundamental and the sole method of reviewing the rent, either by making time of the essence— *Weller v Akehurst* [1981] 3 All ER 411, *Darlington Borough Council v Waring & Gillow* [1988] 2 EGLR 159—or by otherwise evidencing finality in the procedure they adopt—*Henry Smith's Charity Trustees v AWADA Trading and Promotion Services Ltd* (1983) 47 P & CR 607 and see generally Chapter 5, p 95 ff.

In *Wolverhampton & Dudley Breweries plc v Trusthouse Forte Catering Ltd* [1984] 272 EG 1072 there was a lacuna in the machinery the parties had provided for a review of the rent. The review clause was closely modelled on EFP (4th ed) Form 7:1 (set out in Part Seven, p 707) but subclause (3)(a) of the precedent was omitted and, though the words replacing that subclause provided for notice requiring a review of the rent, it did not require the notice to specify the reviewed rent. The reference in the lease to 'substitution of the said sum' (from subclause (3)(b) of the precedent) became meaningless and in default of agreement or a counter-notice by the tenant electing for arbitration (of which time was of the essence) there was no means of ascertaining the new rent. Harman J accepted the landlord's contention that the words 'specified in such notice or' should be read into the clause. He was satisfied that he could deduce from the lease that something must have been omitted *and* (more importantly) he was satisfied that the words suggested provided him with sufficient precision the nature of the omission. The tenant tried to argue for an alternative implication—allowing the lessor to be able to elect for arbitration—but that construction required altering the lease in four different places.

It is interesting to note that the judge made no reference to the principles of *The Moorcock*—the term was not implied to give business efficacy to the contract though it can be argued that the result can be justified on this basis. Rather the judge applied the principle from a wills case, *Re Whitrick decd* [1957] 1 WLR 884 at 887 and acted as a court of construction as discussed at p 288, below. As such, the *Wolverhampton and Dudley Breweries* case is a particularly striking illustration of how blunders can sometimes be corrected without the need for an action for rectification. There was no reference in the judgment to the existence of the precedent (Form 7:1), and the result, though in conformity with the form of the precedent, owed nothing to the precedent on which the rest of the review clause was based.

(e)   Effect will be given to what is provided

It can readily be appreciated that the decisions outlined strive to give effect to the presumed intent of the parties—to such a degree that it can be argued that inadequate drafting has sometimes been treated with undue tenderness. What the courts will not do is rewrite a contract which the parties have freely entered into, or ignore provisions in a lease altogether (eg *Kings Reach Investments Ltd v Reed Publishing Holdings Ltd* (1984) 21 June, CA, unreported, but see p 283, below). Effect must be given, if at all possible, to words, phrases and clauses in the context of the overall construction of the lease, a process further considered in Part Three.

Thus, if a construction can be given to the words the parties have used (which was not the case in *Jefferies v O'Neill*, above) then it will be adopted, even if deficiencies and unforeseen consequences remain. The court cannot and will not 'demolish and reconstruct' the parties' bargain—see *Freehold and Leasehold Shop Properties Ltd v Friends Provident Life Office* (1984) 271 EG 451.

(f)   Arbitrator or expert?

Where a review clause calls for independent assessment in default of agreement, it is necessary to know whether such referee is to act as an arbitrator or expert. If the clause fails to make it clear which status is conferred it will be necessary to decide this issue from the construction of the lease as a whole. This question is fully considered in Chapter 6, p 181.

2   Rectification

Rectification is an equitable remedy which will be available, in limited circumstances, where the lease does not embody the agreement reached by the parties; and it is a remedy which has been successfully obtained in a number of cases involving rent review clauses.

For a full discussion of the principles of the remedy, the reader is referred to the established texts on the matter, eg *Halsbury's Laws* (4th ed) Vol 32, paras 50–62; *Snell's Principles of Equity* Part VII, Chapter 4, p 610 ff. In the following discussion, the basic requirements to obtain the remedy, on the basis of either common or unilateral mistake, are set out with an illustration of their application to rent review. In either case, the burden of proof is on the party seeking the rectification; 'strong irrefragable evidence', ie something more than the highest degree of probability, is required, so exceptionally clear and convincing evidence is essential.

It was stressed in *Thomas Bates and Son Ltd v Wyndham's (Lingerie) Ltd* (see below) that it is not the standard of proof that is different in a rectification action from a normal civil action; but rather it is the evidential burden required to counteract the inherent probability that the written instrument truly represents the parties' intention which is unusual. To allege that a lease signed by the parties is erroneous is a serious allegation requiring a higher degree of evidential probability (cf *Hornal v Neuberger Products Ltd* [1975] 1 QB 247 at 258).

(a)   Common mistake

Mistake is central to the doctrine, and, normally, the mistake to be rectified must be one common to both (or, if a surety is involved, all) parties to the lease. To succeed on common mistake, it must be shown:

(1) That the parties entered into some agreement prior to the instrument (say, a lease) sought to be rectified; though this agreement need not amount to an enforceable contract (*Joscelyne v Nissen* [1970] 2 QB 86).

(2) That the difference between the prior agreement and the terms in the lease was due to a common mistake; in other words the original intent must continue with no decision by either party to alter the terms.

(3) That the mistake is one about the effect of the lease that it is sought to rectify—*London Regional Transport v Wimpey Group Services Ltd* [1986] EGLR 41.

(4) That the lease does not represent the true agreement of the parties at the time when it was executed; and

(5) That, if rectified as claimed, the lease will then carry out the agreement.

'Rectification ensures that the instrument contains the provisions which the parties actually intended it to contain, and not those which it would have contained had they been better informed' (Snell, p 613). The intent of the parties is the issue, so rectification is not available to correct a provision deliberately inserted into a lease which in fact means something different from what was meant. Clear evidence of a *mistake* is essential: *Lansdown Estates Group Ltd v TNT Roadfreight (UK) Ltd* [1989] 2 EGLR 120. So the remedy would not be available, for example, to correct a review clause where time was of the essence as a result of clauses or phraseology deliberately inserted even if the parties intended the general rule that time is not of the essence to apply but wrongly appreciated the import of the words they had used. *London Regional Transport v Wimpey* (above) is another example of this principle. A complex ground rent valuation formula, expressed algebraically, was agreed by surveyors. This was reduced to tortuous language by a solicitor and inserted into the agreement for a lease but the result, not appreciated by either party at the time, was to change the formula in favour of the tenant. Later, and pursuant to the agreement for a lease, the lease was executed and the parties agreed a new form of words for the rent review formula which they thought expressed both what the surveyors had agreed (which it did) and what was contained in the agreement for a lease (which it didn't). The tenants were unsuccessful in seeking rectification of the lease because there was no mistake in the lease. The mistake was contained in the agreement for a lease. On the contrary, if it had been necessary, it was the landlords who could have obtained the remedy to rectify the agreement for a lease.

The principles were applied in *Boots The Chemist Ltd v Street* (1983) 268 EG 817 where it was agreed that the lease should contain 5–yearly reviews in a 25–year term. The draft lease was modelled on a precedent of a 21–year term with reviews at 7 and 14 years and in the travelling draft references to 7 and 14 years had been replaced with 'every five years' except at one point in the lease. This error was carried over into the executed document; it was successfully rectified. In *Co-operative Insurance Co Ltd v Centremoor Ltd* (1983) 268 EG 1027 a lease, underlease and sub-underlease were granted contemporaneously as part of a development scheme. It was envisaged that rent increases at review should be passed on in proportions of 35 per cent to the underlessee and 65 per cent to the lessee. Owing to a common mistake over dates, the lessee only became entitled to his percentage 6 years and 9 months later. The Court of Appeal ordered rectification in favour of the lessee even though the mistake was in the sub-underlease, since such an order would give effect to the clear agreement between the parties. A claim on the basis of common mistake was upheld so as to rectify a memorandum on a lease recording the agreement for the reviewed rent at the first review date—*Equity & Law Life Assurance Society Ltd v Coltness Group Ltd* (1983) 267 EG 949. The memorandum recorded a rent agreed 'until the expiration of the within written lease'; this was a mistake not reflecting the bargain that was struck, namely that the rent should only continue at that figure until the next review date.

A decision of the Court of Appeal on rectification for common mistake is *Kings Reach Investments Ltd v Reed Publishing Holdings Ltd* (1984)

21 June, unreported, which arose from the sale and lease-back of an office development site. The plaintiff developers, later landlords, constructed the building for the defendant tenants, the former owners of the site. The plaintiffs would have preferred a building with a central core of lifts, with the lifts facing outwards, since it was apprehended a greater usable floor area would result, with a consequential increase in rental value. The defendants however insisted on inward facing lifts. The 99 year lease, as executed, provided for compensation for the plaintiffs during the first 7 years of the term by including within the net lettable floor space, as defined, the landings and lift lobbies resulting from the actual construction of inward facing lifts. However, the rent review clause, in a fairly standard form, which set the rent from the eighth year of the term, allowed for no such adjustment. The court unanimously upheld the judge below in his refusal to construe the lease and the review clause to accord with what the plaintiffs alleged it should mean, for on its proper construction, the meaning was clear. However, by a majority, the plaintiffs' claim for rectification succeeded. Eveleigh and Browne-Wilkinson LJJ held that there was evidence of an accord between the parties for a compensatory rent throughout the term and, though there was no common intention or agreement as to how the compensation should be assessed, such assessment was the mere machinery to work out their intent. The court, while ordering rectification, could include machinery (the appropriate 'rate per square foot') so as provide that the rent review was to assume construction with outward facing lifts. May LJ dissented, rejecting such a concept of implication which he saw as inappropriate to the remedy of rectification. Certainly the majority view may encourage more claims to rectify rent review clauses than have so far been the case. Moreover, it would follow that professional negligence insurers may more frequently deny responsibility if a claim for rectification could be argued to have been a reasonable step to have taken in mitigation of the loss.

(b)   Unilateral mistake

A mistake by one party will not normally give rise to a claim for rectification. There are two exceptions which may apply in rent review situations. The first is where the party who is not mistaken is fraudulent towards the other; perhaps unlikely in commercial leases with the parties bargaining at arm's length. The second exception, unilateral mistake, is a form of estoppel and is more important for rent reviews.

The conditions to be satisfied to establish a claim for rectification are established by the principles propounded in *A Roberts & Co Ltd v Leicestershire County Council* [1961] Ch 555, approved by the Court of Appeal in *Thomas Bates & Son Ltd v Wyndham's (Lingerie) Ltd* [1981] 1 WLR 505 and applied most recently in *Kemp v Neptune Concrete* [1988] 2 EGLR 87. The criteria to be established are:

(1) The party seeking relief was mistaken so that the deed as executed did not accord with that party's subjective intention and belief at the time of executing the deed.

(2) There was no mistake by the party against whom relief is sought; on the contrary, the other party intended or accepted the result achieved by the deed. The conditions for rectification for common mistake must otherwise be present.

(3) The party against whom relief is sought was aware of the mistake in his favour but stood by doing nothing to correct the error. However, the conduct of the defendant in standing by while knowing of the mistake must be such as either to amount to a degree of sharp practice, amount to unconscionable behaviour or, at least, make it inequitable that he should be allowed to object to rectification of the document. If these conditions are satisfied then the claim for rectification cannot be resisted by arguing the mistake is unilateral.

In *Thomas Bates & Son Ltd v Wyndham's (Lingerie) Ltd* (above) the review clause in the lease only provided for payment on review of 'such rents as shall have been agreed' but it was held that rectification (so as to provide for arbitration in default) was possible because:

(i) the landlord erroneously believed that the lease, executed in 1970, contained provision for arbitration in default of agreement, for the lease was executed after the exercise of an option to renew in an earlier lease which contained an arbitration provision;

(ii) the defendant tenants knew in 1970 of the omission of any reference to arbitration in the lease and they were taken to have recognised that this was the result of a mistake by the landlords' managing director (the necessity for actual knowledge by the defendant of the plaintiffs' mistaken belief was stressed in *Agip SpA v Navigazione Alta Italia SpA* [1984] 1 Lloyd's Rep 353 at 365);

(iii) the tenants had not drawn the mistake to the attention of the landlord; and

(iv) the mistake benefited the tenants.

It was not shown, nor, it was said, was it necessary, to prove the tenants were guilty of sharp practice: their conduct in failing to mention the error knowing that the lease did not embody the common intention sufficed. Eveleigh LJ (at 521) denied that it was even necessary for the mistake to benefit the tenant, averring that it was sufficient that the mistake was detrimental to the landlord.

These facts enabled the rectification principle to operate and an arbitration clause was inserted into the lease. Unlike the judge at first instance, however, the Court of Appeal held that, on rectification, the proper measure or criterion by which the arbitrator was to fix the rent was not the 'market rent' for the property, but a rent such as it would be reasonable for the particular landlords and the particular tenants to have agreed under the lease. The court recognised that a different result may well be reached to that fixed as an open market rent since an arbitrator could properly take into account all considerations that would affect the mind of either party in connection with the negotiation of such a rent (see p 386, above); the criterion is also different from a 'reasonable rent' or a 'reasonable rent for the premises': *Ponsford v HMS Aerosols Ltd* [1979] AC 63.

A similar failure to include a rent review clause occurred in *Central & Metropolitan Estates Ltd v Compusave Ltd* (1982) 266 EG 900. There was clear evidence of the agreement for a 20–year term with 5–yearly reviews but the landlord's solicitors, drafting the lease in the form of an earlier demise which contained no review, omitted to include any review provision at all. From the detailed evidence, the judge concluded the tenants were fully aware of the omission. Consequently, rectification was ordered, but on terms referred to below. As in the *Thomas Bates* case, the review was to be to a 'fair and reasonable' rent.

These two cases may be contrasted with two rent review cases where a claim for rectification of a lease on the ground of unilateral mistake failed. In *Taylor Barnard Ltd v Tozer* (1983) 269 EG 225 there was a clear agreement, but one subject to agreement and execution of the lease, that the lease should include a right of pre-emption in favour of the tenants. The lease as drafted by the landlord's solicitor contained no such right and the tenants' solicitor drafted an option to purchase the freehold for inclusion which was accepted by the landlord's solicitor and incorporated into the executed lease. It was held that the rectification claim meant the option to a right of pre-emption failed; the tenants could not be aware that a mistake had been made, nor was there any concealment on the tenants' part, but rather the submission of amendments for consideration in the usual way.

Kemp v Neptune Concrete (above) illustrates the difficulties in establishing a successful claim to rectify especially where the alleged unilateral mistake arises after a change in the terms agreed. The prior agreement was for a 'six year term with three year rent reviews' and the parties' solicitors drafted and considered a draft lease on this premise. After the tenant had been let into possession but before any lease had been executed the parties agreed to extend the term to 12 years. The draft was amended accordingly but no alteration was made to the review clause so that the lease only provided for one review at 3 years in the 12–year term. The claim to rectify failed on both the essential criteria for unilateral mistake. The landlord had made no mistake at the date of execution of the lease; his solicitor proffered a 12 year lease with a single review which was repeatedly reconsidered as the draft passed between solicitors. Nor had the tenant stood by unconscionably; he himself (it was held) genuinely believed that there was no error and though the tenant's solicitor 'must have been aware that the landlord's solicitor were under the impression that there was more than one review' the behaviour fell short of that required to justify equitable relief. The decision may seem harsh when compared to *Thomas Bates v Wyndham's* or *Central & Metropolitan Estates v Compusave* (above) but the key point is that there was no evidence of a prior agreement for a 12 year term with 3–year reviews. If there had been then the result may well have been different.

For the purpose of awareness of the mistake, the general principle is that knowledge of the solicitor agent is deemed knowledge of the client principal—*Bowstead on Agency*, art 102. Since solicitors have authority to receive all relevant information they have an obligation to communicate it to their clients (*Strover v Harrington* [1988] Ch 390 at 410). It would appear therefore that the knowledge of his solicitor can be imputed to the client if the former stands by unconscionably. It was so argued in *Kemp v Neptune Concrete* but Purchas LJ appeared unwilling to accept it though the decision that there had been no unconscionable behaviour in the case made it unnecessary for the point to be determined.

(c) Discretionary nature of remedy

Whether based on common or unilateral mistake, rectification is a discretionary remedy and is not available as of right. This has a number of important consequences. It is not available against an assignee of the lease or reversion who has given value and taken without notice of the claim for rectification. However in *Equity & Law Life v Coltness* (above) it was held that a lease could be rectified against assignees of the lease who were connected with the original tenants and who had not acquired the lease for value. In the *Taylor Barnard* case, it was said, obiter, that had the case for rectification been made out, it could have been ordered against the successors in title to the original tenant who became aware of the rectification claim after entering into a contract to purchase the lease but before completing the assignment. This conclusion, unnecessary for the decision in that case, is based on the old case of *Tourville v Naish* (1734) 24 ER 1077, and might well not be followed (cf *Smith v Jones* [1954] 1 WLR 1089). It must be borne in mind that, once rectification proceedings are launched, they become registrable as a pending action and, if not so registered, do not bind a purchaser without express notice—Land Charges Act 1972, s 5(7); for registered land s 59(6) of the Land Registration Act 1925 goes further in protecting even a purchaser with express notice.

Though rectification will not be ordered against a purchaser for value, the equity to have the lease rectified does pass to successors in title—Law of Property Act 1925, s 63(1); *Boots the Chemist v Street* (above).

As a discretionary remedy, rectification may not be given if there is undue delay or acquiescence once the mistake comes to light. Moreover, the party seeking rectification may have to submit to terms. Thus in *Central & Metropolitan Estates v Compusave* (above) rectification of the lease by ordering the inclusion of 5–yearly reviews was only granted on terms that the defendant tenant should have the opportunity of surrendering the term at the first review date by giving 3 months' written notice. It is also quite usual, after a successful claim for rectification, to make no order for costs since the need to rectify arises from the plaintiff's original mistake (*Boots v Street*; *Central & Metropolitan Estates v Compusave*).

Of course, only a court normally has the power to order rectification of a lease. However, 'there is no reason in principle why an arbitrator cannot make an order for the rectification of a contract, provided this is justified by law and by the arbitration agreement' per May LJ, *Ashville Investments Ltd v Elmer Contractors Ltd* (1987) 37 BLR 55 at 65. Nevertheless, an arbitrator appointed under a rent review clause in a usual form will not, unlike the arbitrator under the building contract in the *Ashville* case, have the necessary power under the terms of the lease and will therefore have no jurisdiction to rectify and must act on the terms of the lease before him unless or until a court otherwise orders or the parties agree otherwise. An arbitrator acting under a wider general arbitration clause (a rare occurrence in the rent review context) might be given powers sufficiently wide to rectify.

(d)   Rectification and construction of leases

In theory, rectification is clearly distinguishable from the process of construction of a lease; the latter aims to interpret the contract embodied in the lease, while rectification alters the contractual provisions so that they conform to the parties' common intent.

However, the two processes operate more closely in practice. In particular, a minor mistake in a written instrument may be corrected as a matter of construction in certain limited circumstances without the need for an action for rectification (Snell, p 611 and *Wilson v Wilson* (1854) 10 ER 811). However, the error must be an obvious mistake on the face of the instrument and it must be clear what correction ought to be made to cure the mistake. As such, this ability to correct is limited to obvious clerical blunders or grammatical mistakes. In *East v Pantiles (Plant Hire) Ltd* (1981) 263 EG 61, the Court of Appeal declined to rectify by construction a reference in a lease to payment of rent on '14 August' to read '1 August' even though other quarterly payments were due on the first day of November, February and May and notwithstanding that rent reviews fell due on 1 August every 7 years. The alleged 'mistake' was not clear and in the absence of a claim for rectification the executed lease could not be altered.

The process of construction of a lease can also result in 'radical surgery' to the wording of a lease if the words used are absurd—see *Pearl Assurance plc v Shaw* [1985] 1 EGLR 92 and p 299, below. However, when rectifying a lease the court alters the deed to accord with the parties' intention in the prior agreement; when dealing with absurdities as a court of construction the court will look to the purpose of a rent review clause and the presumed intention of the parties.

Yet even where a claim for rectification fails, and it is held there is no obvious mistake that can be altered by a process of construction, it may still be possible to construe the unamended wording of the lease to reach a satisfactory answer. Thus in *East v Pantiles* the Court of Appeal had to go on to consider how a rent review clause, which required a notice to be served (time being of the essence) 'at any time before the beginning of a clear period of two quarters' operated when one quarter's rent was due on 14 August and the review date was 1 August. It was held that 14 August was not indicative of when a quarter commenced; the quarter began on 1 August (though rent was due 14 days later) and the rent review notice was properly served. So, by a process of construction of the lease, the more bizarre consequences of an eccentric provision were avoided without the need for rectification. The process of construction is fully considered in Part Three.

3 Professional negligence

If a party to a lease suffers loss from an error which cannot be cured by agreement or by one of the methods discussed above, he may have a claim against the solicitor, surveyor or other adviser if he can establish negligence.

Claims of professional negligence in rent review valuations against a surveyor acting as an expert have been considered in Chapter 6, p 216, above. However, allegations of professional negligence may be made against any of the professionals acting in the review process and will often be the remedy of last resort for a party to a lease who considers it has suffered loss. In the following comments, we draw attention to matters of particular significance for rent review and for more detailed treatment the reader is referred to the standard texts, eg Dugdale and Stanton, *Professional Negligence*.

(a) A solicitor's duty of care

Solicitors may face assertions of negligence in drafting the lease or operating the review machinery. Their duty arises and is founded on contract (*Groom v Crocker* [1938] 2 All ER 394 and the view that there is a concurrent tortious duty (*Midland Bank Trust Co Ltd v Hett Stubbs & Kemp* [1979] Ch 384) has been questioned: *Lee v Thompson* [1989] 2 EGLR 151 at 153. Whatever its source, the duty is 'to use reasonable care and skill in giving such advice as the facts of the particular case demand': *Sykes v Midland Bank Executor and Trustee Co Ltd* [1971] 1 QB 113 per Salmon LJ. The standard required for perusal of a draft rent review clause is that of 'the reasonably careful and competent solicitor practising in this field': *County Personnel Ltd v Alan R Pulver & Co* [1987] 1 All ER 289 at 295 per Bingham LJ. This case provides a warning for all solicitors advising clients taking a lease with a review clause. The plaintiff company was the business medium of two ladies setting up an employment agency. Having agreed a 15 year lease of two rooms with 5–yearly reviews without the benefit of any valuation advice, they consulted the defendant solicitors. The review clause in the proposed underlease provided for the yearly rent agreed (£3,500, inclusive) and the reviewed rent for subsequent periods was to be 'an amount equivalent to the initial rent increased by the same percentages as the landlord's rent has been increased under the terms of the head lease'. The consequence of this unusual provision was only revealed in full at the first review; the head lease initially reserved a rent of £2,250 exclusive; the review to open market rent 5 years later resulted in an increase to £5,800. The rent in the underlease therefore rose proportionally to £9,022, whereas the open market value was £2,600.

The plaintiff company made three main allegations of negligence— failure to ascertain the initial rent under the head lease or warn of the risks of proceeding without such knowledge; failure to advise that a valuation opinion should be sought; and failure to advise on the operation of the review clause. The Court of Appeal, in holding the solicitors negligent, focused on the first and third allegations. They held that a competent solicitor would have taken account of two facts, namely, that the head underlessor was taking a head lease of the whole premises with a view to sub-letting part to the plaintiff company and that he did not wish to reveal the rent on the head lease. Though those matters might not have been sinister in themselves, in the light of the 'most unusual' rent review clause the defendant solicitors should have advised that, on existing information, it was impossible to say how the clause would operate in practice and that the risk of disadvantage could not be eliminated. This advice was not given and the defendants were liable in negligence. No clear ruling was given as to whether the plaintiff should have been told that valuation advice should have been sought. Bingham LJ was of the opinion that a solicitor is 'plainly unfitted' to advise in valuation. However, with respect, this is obvious and did not answer the issue. It is submitted that where it is common practice (as will be the case with many commercial leases) to seek valuation advice before entering into the lease then a solicitor with a client who does not have the benefit of that advice is under the limited duty to discuss with the client whether such a valuation is required.

The lessons from the *County Personnel* judgment would seem to be:

(1) A review clause which is not in 'a familiar standard form' requires more careful reflection.

(2) Anything in a review clause which might prove disadvantageous to the client must be drawn to its attention.

(3) A solicitor cannot ignore the financial implications of a rent review clause where they are inseparable from the legal consequences. As Binghan LJ remarked, 'the significance of the legal consequences lay in the financial implications' (at 296e)—a comment which is true of virtually every aspect of the modern rent review clause in both its machinery and the valuation framework.

(b) Negligence in operating the review machinery

Missing a time-limit or serving a defective notice will be obvious examples of possible negligence which can be raised against solicitor, surveyor or both. So in *Chartered Trust plc v Maylands Green Estatee Co Ltd* (1984) 270 EG 845 an action for professional negligence is referred to. The defence of the surveyors was that it was not within the scope of their instructions to give the necessary counter-notice and a second opportunity to give such a notice was missed because a solicitor and a surveyor each believed the other was undertaking the task. The risks with notices and the need for diary dates and care in operating this aspect of review machinery are too obvious to require further elucidation.

Other omissions to act properly in a client's interest at rent review can result in substantial liability for negligence. So in *Rajdev v Becketts* [1989] 2 EGLR 144 a surveyor acting for the tenant failed to submit representations to an independent expert making the determination in default of agreement within a time-limit specified in the lease. It was held the firm were negligent notwithstanding correspondence about whether the independent expert should withdraw on the grounds of a conflict of interest; they should have ensured representations were submitted on the client's behalf. By way of contrast, a surveyor was not negligent in agreeing to exclude corridors in a sub-lease arbitration before similar agreement had been reached in the related head lease arbitration for an error of judgment did not necessarily amount to negligence: *Thomas Miller & Co v Richard Saunders and Partners* [1989] 1 EGLR 267. Moreover, in respect of the negligence that had been established, the chain of causation had been broken by the decision of the arbitrator.

(c) Measure of damages

The basic measure of damages will be based on the principle of placing the plaintiff in the position that he would have been in but for the act of negligence—*Livingstone v Rawyards Coal Co* (1880) 5 App Cas 25 at 39. In property matters, the appropriate measure is often found by applying the diminution in value principle. The damages will then be the difference in value of the lease as it stands and what it should have been but for the negligence of the defendants. Thus in *Rajdev v Becketts* (above) the measure of damages was the difference in value of the lease with a rent determined by the expert and its value with an open market rent. The alternative (or additional) method of valuation advanced of valuing the loss to the plaintiff's business was rejected by the deputy judge. In *County Personnel Ltd v Alan R Pulver & Co* (above) however, the Court of Appeal said that damages will not invariably be assessed according to the diminution in value rule if its application was inappropriate. In that case, by reference to the overriding compensatory rule, the plaintiff was entitled to the cost of the enforced surrender of the lease. This was a certain figure and represented what the negligence had actually cost the plaintiff; a calculation of diminution in (negative) value would, in contrast, be speculative and unreal. The plaintiff was also entitled, if it could be proved, to any loss in value and goodwill of the business which the plaintiff would have established at these or other premises if it had been properly advised.

(d)   Problems relating to limitation periods

The error or problem arising as the result of the alleged negligence will often only come to light when the first, or even later review, is invoked. By that time, it may be too late to pursue the claim. It is in this regard that it may become significant whether the claim can be founded in tort as well as contract. In a contract claim, time will be running from the date of the breach of contract—so in the context of rent review, the grounds of the claim may be unearthed at a review date beyond the limitation period. Attempts to find a more favourable limitation period by using the tort of negligence have been unsuccessful.

In *Forster v Outred & Co* [1982] 1 WLR 86 the Court of Appeal held that damage accrued in tort and time began to run from the date when a defectively drafted mortgage was executed; the same court applied that principle to the defective sub-lease in *Costa v Georghiou* (1985) 1 Professional Negligence 201 (the facts are given at p 489, above) and to the failure to register a caution or charge, the time running from the date when the caution should have been registered: *Bell v Peter Browne & Co* (1990) NLJ 701. The Court of Appeal in *Forster*, moreover, found no concealment by fraud on the part of the solicitor who was unaware of his mistake, so the limitation period (6 years) was not to be extended. The availability of a remedy in negligence may, to a great extent, turn on the chance of whether the negligently drawn and defective lease provides for reviews at 5 or 7–year intervals.

The limitation period problem must now be considered in the light of the amendments made to the Limitation Act 1980 by the Latent Damage Act 1986 which came into force on 18 September 1986. If it can be shown that a negligently drawn review clause contains a latent defect, then a secondary period of limitation now applies, namely 3 years from the discovery of 'significant damage' attributable to that negligence. It is possible therefore that the operation of a review clause more than 6 years after the drafting and execution of the lease may reveal such a latent defect—but if it is shown that the plaintiff should have discovered the defect and the damage at an earlier date then that is the date from which the secondary period of limitation runs. The secondary limitation period is 3 years, and the detailed provisions are in s 14A of the Limitation Act 1980 (added by the later Act).

The 1986 Act also introduces an innovatory cut-off period or longstop provision (s 14B of the 1980 Act) whereby any action for negligence (other than for personal injuries) is barred 15 years from the act or omission alleged to constitute negligence.

The recent case of *Iron Trades Mutual Insurance Company Co Ltd v J K Buckenham* [1990] 1 All ER 808 supports the view that the operation of these provisions of the Latent Damage Act is confined to actions brought in tort. If this is correct, the period in contract runs from the date of breach irrespective of whether that breach could have been reasonably discovered. The possible difficult questions which might arise in a rent review under the Latent Damage Act will then be limited to an action in tort—if such an action is possible. Such issues are:

(1) In what circumstances would a lessor or lessee be expected to discover the negligent mistake?
(2) How is the mistake to be classified as latent?

For a detailed discussion of these points, the reader is referred to the specialist texts on the topic.

Part 3

The Construction and Interpretation of the Hypothetical Lease

Part Three examines what is the heart of any modern rent review clause. The parties have to agree, or the valuer or arbitrator has to assess, the rent for the notional letting postulated by the review clause. *Chapter 10* sets out both the general principles of construction and the guide-lines that are emerging which particularly relate to rent review. *Chapter 11* then examines the valuation and review implications of the actual property let and the terms of the actual lease which are incorporated into the notional letting. *Chapter 12* considers the hypothetical aspects of that valuation framework—the assumptions and disregards expressly or impliedly introduced into the open market valuation of the rent. At each stage, the drafting implications are considered. *Chapter 13* is concerned with the special aspects of ground rent reviews.

Part 3

The Construction and Interpretation of the Hypothetical Lease

Chapter 10

The Principles of Construction of Rent Review Clauses

There is no special quality about variable rent provisions that attracts or should attract particular rules of construction and interpretation. The ordinary rules applicable to the construction of deeds and contracts are applicable. However, the torrent of originating summons and motions seeking the proper construction of increasingly complex rent review clauses over the last decade or so has led to some 'guide-lines' or 'canons of construction' formulated within the context of rent review and particularly applicable to such clauses. These guide-lines appear to be a response to the onslaught of rent review cases, but they have still to be evaluated within the framework of the traditional principles.

It is not proposed to deal with these general principles at any length. At one time such detailed treatment in this new edition did appear to be warranted since there was little in print to assist the practitioner. The rules are stated and discussed in *Halsbury's Laws of England* (4th ed) Vol 12, in *Odgers' Construction of Deeds and Statutes* and in *Norton on Deeds* but the two latter specialist works are rather out of date. The gap in the literature now appears to have been filled to a considerable extent by Lewison, *Interpretation of Contracts* to which the reader is referred. In this chapter, therefore, we state those general principles succinctly and then deal with their particular applicability to rent review clauses. The detailed guide-lines that appear to be emerging which have especial reference to such clauses merit particular evaluation.

1 General principles of construction

Any attempt to precis the standard principles of construction runs the risk that brevity will impair clarity. The following nevertheless represents an attempt at a summary of those principles most pertinent to rent review clauses.

(a) The proper construction of a contract and therefore a rent review clause in a lease is a question of law but the ascertainment of the meaning of a particular word or phrase is a matter of fact.

This well established rule (the origins are discussed by Lewison, para 3.01) means that the construction process involves elements of fact and law, and the dividing line is not always easy to draw. In the context of rent review, the most significant consequences of the rule may be said to be:

(1) 'Rules' of construction are not rules of law and can be overridden by express provision by the parties to the contrary: *Equity and Law Life Assurance Society v Bodfield Ltd* [1987] 1 EGLR 124. Thus the presumption that time is not of the essence can always be expressly negatived by the parties (see Chapter 5, p 95).

(2) A decision by a court on the construction of one lease is a binding authority on the issue of law the case determines but it is easy to categorise the construction of the instant lease and its review clause therein as involving a different issue and, therefore, the interpretation of slightly different wording or of similar wording in a different context. The net result may be that a series of cases emerges that become difficult to reconcile and the advice to clients becomes uncertain. Further litigation is thereby encouraged (an example is the issue of deeming clauses—see p 99).

(3) Arguments on the construction of the lease and the contract embodied therein must not be based mainly on the consequences of one result or another of the construction issue before the court; the courts will at least traditionally resist being influenced by this factor. The most notorious consequence of this approach in the field of rent review is the *Arthur Young* saga (see p 333). The 'purposive approach' (below), by way of contrast, will look to the consequences of the arguments on construction to consider how they accord with the perceived commercial purpose.

The worst aspects of this rule of construction may be said to have been mitigated by the increasing use of the 'commercial purpose' approach to construction, discussed below, but they stand as a warning to those drafting and considering rent review clauses.

(b) The construction of a rent review clause, as with any contract, is a process of ascertaining the mutual intention of the parties from the meaning of the words they have used.

It is only legitimate to look to the words actually employed in the rent review clause.

'In other words, the question to be answered always is, "What is the meaning of what the parties have said?" not "What did the parties mean to say?". The latter question is one which the law does not permit to be asked . . . it being a presumption . . . that the parties intended to say what they have said.' (*Norton on Deeds*, p 50, approved in *Schuler AG v Wickman Machine Tool Sales Ltd* [1974] AC 235 (not a rent review case of course).)

This approach has the especial merit for any clause in a lease which is more likely than not to bind parties other than those who entered into the lease. At an assignment of the lease or reversion, the potential assignee will scrutinise the rent review clause but will have no means of inquiring whether the words used embody the desired original bargain. For this reason, if no other, it is and will remain the cardinal principle to be applied. It follows that the approach of the court to what the parties have actually said (rather than what may have been intended) is crucial.

(c)   Words used in the lease are to be used in their literal sense unless there is found a clear contrary intention or it would lead to some manifest absurdity.

This principle can be said to encapsulate the 'golden rule' that:

'In construing all written instruments, the grammatical and ordinary sense of the words is adhered to, unless that would lead to some absurdity . . .' (per Lord Wenseydale in *Grey v Pearson* (1857) 6 H L Cas 61 at 106).

The plain and ordinary meaning will be given to words and the court can look to dictionaries to elucidate that meaning (as in *Stylo Barratt Properties Ltd v Legal & General Assurance Society Ltd* [1989] 2 EGLR 116) but the scope of a word or phrase in a rent review clause will usually be decided as a matter of impression since the conveyance of meaning through ordinary language is 'intuitive' (*Norwich Union Life Assurance Society v British Railways Board* [1987] 2 EGLR 137 per Hoffman J).

The application of this principle can be demonstrated from many of the numerous rent review construction summons that have come before the courts. In some cases, the literal construction is firmly applied. An example is *Philpots (Woking) Ltd v Surrey Conveyancers Ltd* [1986] 1 EGLR 97 where a review clause provided that the reviewed rent was to be 'a sum equal to the aggregate of [£8,000—the initial rent reserved] plus the amount if any by which the fair rack rental value at the date of the review exceeds £8,000 or the yearly rent fixed at the previous date of review as the case may be'. Literally, the words meant that at second and subsequent reviews, assuming the fair rack rental value had increased, the reviewed rent would always fall short of that figure: only at the first review would the fair rack rent be the new reviewed rent. The landlord contended for a construction that meant the reviewed rent equalled the fair rack rental value and demonstrated by examples the curious and allegedly capricious results that might follow from the tenant's construction. The first instance deputy judge was duly persuaded but not the Court of Appeal, even though they agreed it was probable that the parties originally *desired* the result contended for by the landlords. That, however, was not enough—a court of construction took the interpretation from the words used and the tenant's construction gave full weight to all the words used. Even if the results were capricious they were not (it was held) absurd—and it is absurdity, said the court, which must be shown before the literal meaning is to be overthrown.

The *Philpots* case can be contrasted with *Pearl Assurance v Shaw* [1985] 1 EGLR 92 where the judge was satisfied the literal meaning was absurd. A clause directed that 'no account' was to be taken of 'any restriction on the user of the demised premises apart from such user as the landlord may from time to time permit'. Read as a whole, the provision was absurd since if all uses were to be left out of account, all possible uses could be taken into account. That conclusion enabled the judge to reject the literal reading and adopt a construction which resulted in the rent review taking account of the actual use—even though this meant radical surgery and the substitution of the words 'to the extent of' in place of 'apart from'. A strict approach can be seen in some of the machinery cases. In *Rahman v Kenshire* (1980) 259 EG 1074, for example, the relevant notice was to be given 'not less than nor more than twelve months before' the review date. The draft lease revealed that 'one' had been deleted between 'than' and 'nor' but no substitution made. In consequence the notice was to be given on one specific day and no other. Though the judge considered this unusual, eccentric and perhaps unique, it was clear in what it provided, it was not absurd and therefore fell to be applied as it stood.

(d)   Since the court adopts an objective approach in seeking the presumed intention of the parties, extrinsic evidence as to actual or subjective intent is rarely admitted as an aid to construction; but the court can take account of the 'matrix of fact' in which the transaction was concluded.

Evidence of the circumstances at the date of execution of the lease can be given for the purpose of elucidating and ascertaining the intention evidenced by the expressions used (*Shore v Wilson* (1842) 8 ER 450 per Erskine J). Consequently. the court can take judicial note of all the surrounding circumstances at the date of execution of the lease—the state and nature of the premises, the economic conditions then existing, the knowledge of the parties and the understanding of the law and cases reported at the time and the forms of rent review clause then current though the particular relevance of all or any of these factors will vary according to the issue before the court. In the words of Lord Wilberforce in *Reardon Smith Line Ltd v Yngvar Hansen-Tangen* [1976] 1 WLR 989 'No contracts are made in a vacuum' so regard must be had to the 'matrix of facts' in which they are set: *Prenn v Simmonds* [1971] 1 WLR 1381.

An illustration of the principle in the context of rent review is *Standard Life Assurance Co Ltd v Oxoid* [1987] 2 EGLR 140 (more fully discussed at p 565) where it was necessary for the court to rule on the meaning of 'standard accommodation' as defined. The context in which the lease was granted was taken to include the state of the financial and property markets and the existing industrial buildings in the locality and their then rental values at the time the lease was granted. Similarly, in *Hill Samuel Life Assurance Society v Preston Borough Council* (1989) 21 November, unreported, the construction of a ground rent review in a building lease was assisted by the fact that the terms of the lease as a whole indicated that the lessee for the time being would be holding the lease as an investment and would not be in personal occupation of the premises. 'It is part of the matrix of fact that it is legitimate and necessary to take into account' (per Scott J).

By way of contrast, though the state of the law is relevant to assist in understanding the background to the lease, an argument that the state of the law (as it was then thought to be) at the time of the execution of the lease could determine the construction of a lease was rejected by the Court of Appeal in the *Henry Smith's Charity Trustees v AWADA Trading and Promotion Services* (1983) 47 P & CR 607.

The types of extrinsic evidence relative to leases most frequently *excluded* by the established rules of construction are:

(i)   All evidence relating to the negotiations for the lease

This will include instructions for the lease, negotiations over its terms and the drafts submitted and amendments to them effected by the parties or their advisers. The rule against recourse to the negotiations was thoroughly dealt with in *Prenn v Simmonds* [1971] 1 WLR 1381, and *City and Westminster Properties (1934) Ltd v Mudd* [1959] Ch 129 is a good illustration of the rule of the exclusion from consideration of the drafts. There are a few limited exceptions. The two most relevant to rent review are:

(1)   In *Mudd's* case a valid collateral contract was found to exist in favour of the original tenant. Such a bargain, if truly collateral to, but consistent with, the primary instrument, is an exception to the rule (*Brikom Investments v Carr* [1979] QB 467).

(2)   An agreement for a lease or other antecedent contract concluded prior to the grant of a lease can be properly admitted. In *Ladbrooke Group plc v Bristol City Council* [1988] 1 EGLR 126 the draft agreed lease, annexed to a building agreement, was looked at to assist the construction of the rent review clause in the lease notwithstanding the fact that the terms of the lease departed from the draft in some respects.

Even in those cases where some extrinsic evidence is permissible to resolve ambiguity or uncertainty in the wording of the instrument, evidence of negotiations and drafts are still excluded.

*(ii)   Direct evidence of the subjective intention of the parties Schuler AG
v Wickman Machine Tool Sales Ltd* [1974] AC 235.

The reception of evidence within the factual matrix is probably limited
to objective facts; certainly 'the parties cannot themselves give evidence
of what their intention was' per Lord Wilberforce in the *Reardon-Smith*
case (above). It is a matter for debate whether this would admit reference
to the explanatory notes published by the Law Society-RICS Working
Party with each version of the Model Forms.

(iii)   Evidence of subsequent conduct of the parties

It was held in the *Schuler* case (above), that the normal rule is that
subsequent conduct cannot be looked at to interpret a written agreement.
However, if the subsequent conduct gives rise to an estoppel, then the
party so estopped may be prevented from relying on the true construction
of the lease (see Lewison, para 2.11).

**(e)   The document must be construed as a whole, and any part repugnant
to the clear primary meaning can, in the last resort, be ignored.**

Construction of the lease as a whole is so clearly illustrated by nearly
every construction case that it needs little further elucidation. In *Pearl
Assurance v Shaw*, (see above and at p 352) an absurd provision appeared
in a subparagraph in the lease. Vinelott J noted with approval that both
counsel accepted that the second limb of the subclause could not be
disregarded as a senseless addition to the first limb. 'Sub para (ii) must
be construed as a whole and if, taken as a whole, no intelligible sense
can be attributed to it, it must fall as a whole . . . ' [1985] 1 EGLR
92 at 93.

A user clause restricting use to the business of the actual tenant may
have to be modified when incorporated into the notional lease if, when
the lease and rent review clause are considered as a whole, it conflicts
with the overall intent to determine an open market rent. Thus, in *Law
Land Company Ltd v Consumers Association Ltd* (1980) 255 EG 617 the
intention of the parties as demonstrated in the terms of the rent review
clause was to enable a market rent to be determined. If the existing
user clause was to be incorporated into the hypothetical lease, as the
clause on its face appeared to indicate, then there would be only one
possible prospective hypothetical tenant. Since that result was inconsistent
with the idea of an open market, 'some modification has to be made
to the strict wording of the rent review clause if it is to work' (at 623).
The reference in the user clause to the actual tenant, the Consumers
Association, could be ignored and the name of the successful hypothetical
tenant in the market substituted. By way of contrast, where such a personal
permissive use was only one of three permitted uses there was no reason
to alter the literal wording; the hypothetical open market could exist
and be considered on the terms of the actual lease since there were

two further uses permitted within the lease: *James v British Crafts Centre* [1987] 1 EGLR 139.

There is the obvious need to construe the words of the rent review provisions by reference to any definition found elsewhere in the lease. The meaning of 'demised premises', for example, will frequently be found to be indicated with some particularity in the lease and we discuss its full significance at p 321 below. It must be remembered, however, that a reference to the demised premises will not automatically include a reference to part of the premises (see, for example, in relation to sub-letting: *Cook v Shoesmith* [1951] 1 KB 752); and so many leases contain a general provision to achieve that result. If it does not, then the reference, for example, in the Model Forms to the destruction of the demised premises will not apply to destruction of part of the property, but if it does then the extended meaning of the phrase must be borne in mind when construing the particular assumption required to be made. One of the possible dangers of the Model Forms, and of comparable rent review clause precedents, such as Conveyancer Precedent 5–57, is that such interrelation with the remainder of the lease may be inadvertently overlooked if the clause is simply grafted on to an existing precedent. The qualifications 'so far as the context permits' or 'unless the context otherwise requires' are, fortunately, only rarely used in private documents, unlike statutes where they are almost universal, and the difficulties associated with the phrases are largely avoided.

(f) The commercial purpose of the contract is a factor which may assist the court in the process of construction.

Lewison (para 1.06), while suggesting that this approach is not new, acknowledges that 'in the course of the last decade the court has increasingly sought to elucidate the commercial purpose of the contract under consideration'. Lord Diplock's words in *The Antaios* [1985] AC 191 have undoubtedly given impetus to this movement:

'. . . if a detailed semantic and syntactical analysis of words in a commercial contract is going to lead to a conclusion that flouts business common sense, it must be made to yield to business common sense' (at p 201).

Rent review cases have been in the vanguard of the trend to give increasing weight to this factor. Thus in *Pleasurama Properties Ltd v Leisure Investments (West End) Ltd* [1986] 1 EGLR 145 the court had to construe a Deed of Licence and the original lease to which it related. In accepting that the documents must be read together, Lloyd LJ stressed (at p 146) that

'. . . they must be read together so as to produce a sensible and business-like result.'

The exact relationship between the 'purposive' and 'literal' approaches is still being worked out. The currently predominant view would indicate that reference to the commercial purpose is not limited to the category of cases where the literal construction leads to an absurd result (*The Sounion* [1987] 1 Lloyd's Rep 230). As indicated in section 3 of this chapter, below, it is proper to have the commercial purpose of the clause in mind in all issues of construction (*Basingstoke and Deane BC v Host Group Ltd*) but for the commercial approach to be decisive, it may be that there has to be some doubt about what the words in dispute mean so that there is more than one possible interpretation (as in *MFI v BICC Properties* referred to below) and clear words certainly cannot be ignored just because they lead to an unreasonable or uncommercial result. Consequently, Lewison (para 1.07) suggests that the apparent commercial purpose is less likely to be helpful in a well-drawn clause than in a badly drafted one.

The use of the 'commercial purpose' as an aid to the construction and interpretation of rent review clauses is discussed in section 3 of this chapter, below.

(g)　Ambiguities may be resolved in a number of ways if a common intention cannot be ascribed to the parties by reference to detailed canons of construction; either against the lessor on the contra proferentem principle; or in favour of special conditions. If all else fails, between two contradictory expressions which cannot be reconciled by any of the above methods the earlier may be chosen in preference to the latter.

The modern trend in interpretation is against finding provisions void for uncertainty—particularly, it is submitted, where the parties are in a continuing relationship. *Brown v Gould, Beer v Bowden* and *Thomas Bates & Son Ltd v Wyndham's (Lingerie) Ltd* are discussed elsewhere (see Chapter 9, p 273 ff). Any one of a number of specific canons of construction (detailed in Lewison) may assist in any given case. The following may be of relevance in rent review.

(i)　Contra proferentem

This is a principle of construction clearly applicable to leases, and its justification (ie the superior bargaining power of the proponent of the relevant wording) is present in most if not all landlord and tenant negotiations. The phenomenon of the standard form of lease presented by landlord's solicitors to the tenant's solicitors on a 'take it or leave it' basis is very common, and it provides an obvious example where the rule should be applied if (and only if) an ambiguity is shown to exist. As long ago as *Willion v Berkley* (1562) 75 ER 339, however, it was held that the rule was not to be applied against the Crown and that any ambiguity should be resolved in its favour—without the ambiguity, of course, the principle does not come into play. The Crown in all its manifestations is sometimes said to be the tenant of more office space than any other single body, and it must equally rank high in the landlord league-table, so the point is not without practical effect. Whether this beneficent rule of construction in favour of the Crown would be applied where a government department was the lessor is not discussed in any recent lease case. An interesting parallel might be drawn from recent developments in the field of sovereign immunity where there is now a clear distinction between 'sovereign' activities and trading activities. On such a basis, the ancient principle might well not be applied in every circumstance for every manifestation of the Crown.

(ii) General and specific clauses

In standard form contracts, special conditions are accorded greater weight (Lewison, para 6.04.). Rent review clauses do not yet qualify as a standard form contract, but the approach may be applicable if one clause in a lease can be shown to be particular to that document and the conflicting provision from a standard precedent. A not dissimilar rule is that providing for typed or printed words prevailing over printed words (Lewison, para 8.10). In the era of the word processor and laser printers, the older idea could also be extended to provable adjustments from any model form, institutional precedent or standard letting condition.

(iii) Irreconcilability

It may be thought that incompatible phrases rarely occur in leases that are professionally prepared, but it must be recalled that the overwhelming majority of the clauses that have come before the courts, some of which have been roundly criticised by the judges, were professionally drawn. The authors have seen a provision requiring the new rent to reflect 'the general level of rents in the district and the rise [sic] in the value of the pound'. In such a case of irreconcilable incompatibility it may be necessary (at least in a case where the application of the 'commercial purpose' approach is not of assistance) to consider the principle of last resort which is to prefer the earlier provision to the later. This rule was stated in *Joyce v Barker Bros (Builders) Ltd* (1980) *The Times*, 26 February and said to be derived from *Slingsby's* case (1558) 77 ER 77 and repeated in other decisions. Like the *contra preferentem* rule, it will be applied with caution, especially after the statement in *Martin v Martin* (1987) 54 P & CR 238 that irreconcilable provisions must clearly be shown to be such and will be treated as if they appeared in two deeds or documents. The question is then posed whether the effect of the first could be reversed or altered by the second (in *Martin*, that could be done since the last two words in the phrase 'joint tenants in common' severed the joint tenancy created by the first). In the light of *Martin*, *Joyce v Barker Bros* may have been wrongly decided unless it can be distinguished on the basis that the purchaser had not executed the deed (see [1988] Conv 58). What has not yet been ventilated is whether a Schedule introduced by (say) clause 2 of a lease (a common drafting device for rent review) is treated as preceding something (say) in clause 4. It is hoped that it is to be so treated or the result will be even more capricious than the rule itself.

2 Application of the standard principles to rent review

It is suggested that rent review clauses have certain particular features which may create a few difficulties when the 'standard' principles of construction are applied or, at least, have characteristics which have encouraged the development of the 'commercial purpose' approach to construction and new guide-lines and canons of construction to be applied particularly to rent review.

(a) The 'time-scale' problem

Many commercial contracts which fall to be construed will have a limited application in time and will usually involve the original parties to those contracts. The parties to a dispute over the meaning of a rent review clause, by way of contrast, will often (if not usually) be assignees 'bound in' to a clause drafted and concluded by and between different parties some years before. The financial consequences of one construction rather than another being placed upon a rent review provision or some part of it can be very significant, so the parties have strong incentives to pursue their differences in interpretation to arbitration or litigation (either directly or by way of appeal from arbitration). Moreover, the volatile nature of the property world in recent years has heightened the extent to which the 'time gap' affects the construction issues. A party may wish, often with hindsight, to seek a particular interpretation in order to cater for the impact of particular events (or the consequences of certain circumstances) that were not fully allowed for, or possibly even contemplated, when the document was settled only a comparatively few number of years earlier. Developments and changes in drafting cannot be accommodated in existing clauses except by agreement which is unlikely to be forthcoming if one party considers the existing phraseology gives it an advantage, except as part of some wider readjustments of rights and duties.

(b) Review clauses as non standard form contracts

The construction of commercial agreements in standard forms is approached somewhat differently from other contracts. In such cases, the court particularly recognises the desirability of certainty, will pay closer attention to established construction of the standard clauses and the use of precedent is greater than with one-off contracts. Conveyancing agreements on standard printed forms will be construed to give effect to the underlying commercial purpose (see Lewison, paras 3.06–8).

Rent review clauses are not treated as standard form clauses—at least not yet. Each institutional lessor will have its standard draft and each commercial firm of solicitors its office precedent. These may bear close resemblance to existing precedents, but the drafting debt to such precedents will rarely (if ever) be explicit. The pace of developments in rent review has meant that in any event these standard drafts have been constantly updated and varied and individual lessees and draftsmen may respond in separate ways to new, or newly perceived, problems. A 'common denominator' approach may evolve over a few years but in the interim any number of different leases will have been put in place. These will last for many years and several reviews apiece. Rectification of any 'errors' will rarely be possible.

The consequence of treating rent review clauses as 'one-off' contracts is that certainty and precedent have not always been given the prominence that is probably warranted and a decision in any one case can be treated in isolation, its construction turning on the particular words of the lease. However, this can result in quite unjustifiable distinctions as witness the decisions in (say) *Drebbond v Horsham DC* when compared with *Touche Ross & Co v Secretary of State for the Environment* (see p 96) or in *Henry Smith's Charity Trustees v AWADA Trading and Promotion Services* when contrasted with *Mecca Leisure Ltd v Renown Investments* (see p 100).

The approach may be changing. In *Ipswich Borough Council v Fisons plc* [1990] 1 All ER 730 Lord Donaldson MR suggested that the sheer numbers of rent review clauses meant 'that there must be groups of clauses which bear so strong a family resemblance as not to be readily distinguishable from standard contract clauses'. The existence of the Model Forms and a limited number of published precedents give weight to this view. Moreover, once it is recognised that many of the constituent elements of the modern rent review clause appear in almost standard wording, the case for treating rent review clauses as standard form contracts (to which of course amendments can and will be made) increases. The trend is on-going—the publication in 1989 of the Rosscastle Letting Conditions (in Ross, *Drafting and Negotiating Commercial Leases*) is a deliberate attempt at standardisation which, if successful, will make it very much more difficult not to treat rent review clauses as standard form contracts. It must be recalled, however, that legislative innovation in this direction as embodied in the Leases Act 1845 was a signal failure.

(c) The pace of litigation

The recognition that a rent review clause in a lease cannot be treated as 'one-off' may have already arrived from the constant flood of litigation before the courts. The tide may have flowed from one issue to another but the flood of cases has been unrelenting. It is as these various points have surfaced that there has been a recognition that the issues in the cases are linked and similar treatment is required in the interests of certainty. This trend can be discerned, for example, in:

(1) The problem of whether time is of the essence which culminated in the *United Scientific* presumption.
(2) The litigation on the impact of delay in exercising the rent review machinery which was terminated by the rulings in *Amherst v James Walker Goldsmith and Silversmith (No 2)* [1983] Ch 305 (see p 158).
(3) The *Arthur Young* saga on the proper meaning of the assumption that the terms of the lease are to apply (other than those as to rent) which led to the guide-lines in the *British Gas* case fully discussed at p 333.

(d) New guide-lines to construction

The combination of these factors—the particular quality of a rent review clause applying over a period of time at periodic intervals, the growing recognition that a construction summons cannot, or at least, should not be determined in isolation as a one-off contract, and the sheer number of cases—has led to guide-lines or principles of construction which are of particular importance for rent review. These are developed in the next section.

3   Guide-lines particularly relating to rent review

In this section, we develop the general principles of interpretation, indicating how, particularly in cases in the last decade, certain emphases have emerged which may, in time, evolve into settled principles.

(a) 'Designed to be operated'

One overriding principle is that the courts seek to ensure that the rent review clause operates as it was designed to do. With regard to the *machinery* of review, this is amply demonstrated by the approach to time-limits, delay, inadequate clauses and other issues discussed in Part Two. However, it is also valid in relation to the *formula* which is the basis of the review.

The judgment of Donaldson J in *F R Evans (Leeds) Ltd v English Electric Co Ltd* [1977] 36 P & CR 185 contains in addition to his painstaking analysis of the constituent elements of the rent review provisions in that lease, a number of general statements of the proper approach to such provisions. Thus, he states at 193: 'I also agree that the possibility of the parties failing to reach agreement is to be disregarded; to borrow and adapt an immortal phrase: 'We are not interested in the possibilities of a failure to reach agreement. They do not exist''. In the same way, it is submitted, the absence of a market for a particular property, a state of affairs factually possible for a special type of property, must be ignored. Once the parties have postulated a given set of circumstances, it is up to the court to give effect to those hypotheses.

(b) Construction to accord with the commercial purpose

Reference to the 'commercial purpose' of a rent review clause now appears to have been elevated from a role as one, perhaps subservient, principle of construction to the dominant theme. The tension between the school of thought that gives precedence to a literal approach and that which emphasises the purposive seems to have been resolved, at least for the time being, in favour of the latter.

(i) Applicability

The use of the purposive approach to construction appears to apply both generally and particularly.

Generally, in all construction cases, it will be borne in mind constituting a constant guide in the whole process. In *Basingstoke and Deane v Host Group Ltd* [1988] 1 WLR 348 , the following guidance was given by Nicholls LJ (at p 353):

'The question raised on this appeal is one of construction of a rent review clause in a lease. In answering that question, it is axiomatic that what the court is seeking to identify and declare is the intention of the parties to the lease expressed in that clause. Thus, like all points of construction, the meaning of this rent review clause depends on the particular language used, interpreted having regard to the context provided by the whole document and the matrix of the material surrounding circumstances. We recognise, therefore, that the particular language used will always be of paramount importance. None the less it is proper and sensible, when construing a rent review clause, to have in mind what normally is the commercial purpose of the clause.'

Particularly, reference to the commercial purpose may be decisive if more than one possible meaning can be given to the words. In such a case, the court will prefer the meaning which accords with the commercial purpose. In *MFI Properties Ltd v BICC Group Pension Trust Ltd* [1986] 1 All ER 974 at 976d Hoffman J said 'if the language is capable of more than one meaning, I think the court is entitled to select the meaning which accords with the apparent commercial purpose of the clause rather than one which appears commercially irrational'. Similarly, in *R & A Millett (Shops) Ltd v BICC Group Pension Trust* [1985] 1 EGLR 103 (see p 341) the deputy judge preferred the construction which produced a 'sensible and business-like commercial result'. It may be that some uncertainty as to meaning must be demonstrated. Thus, in *British Home Stores v Ranbrook Properties Ltd* [1988] 1 EGLR 121 at 123 Warner J was of the (probably stricter) view that:

'. . . it is only where there is some uncertainty as to the meaning of a particular provision in a lease . . . that one can resolve the uncertainty by looking at its commercial purpose.'

(ii)   What is the commercial purpose?

The judicial perception of the commercial purpose of a rent review clause has been set out in Chapter 1, p 8. The modern emphasis recognises that such a clause is primarily designed 'to give relief to' ('load the scales in favour of'?) the landlord where, as is usual, the rent cannot be reduced on review (*Equity & Law Life Assurance Society v Bodfield* [1987] 1 EGLR 124); the overall aim is to combat both inflation and changes in property values; the particular purpose is to allow the landlord to obtain periodically the market value of the premises as if let on the same terms in the open market at the review dates (*British Gas Corporation v Universities Superannuation Scheme* [1986] 1 WLR 398). There is an increasing emphasis that the primary purpose is to 'allow the rent to be adjusted to reflect changes (usually only upward changes) in the monetary value of the building' per Hoffman J in *Tea Trade Properties Ltd v CIN Properties Ltd* [1990] 1 EGLR 155. This may reduce the emphasis and weight given to the idea of a rent review being a method of restoring the value of the bargain embodied in the lease—to both sides. So, as in the *Tea Trade* case, planning permission for supervening office use will certainly enhance the value of the premises but may effectively nullify the bargain if the tenant cannot and does not want to so use it and the original background to the lease was a building in an area not zoned for office use. At statutory renewal under the 1954 Act, it is right that the tenant seeking a new lease should always pay the market rent for the premises and for the continued use of the premises—for it is a renewal that is sought and if the area has moved 'up market' then the tenant cannot argue that he cannot afford it: *Giannoukakis v Saltfleet* [1988] 1 EGLR 73. It is less clear in a rent review if a rent review clause is perceived as of benefit for both sides (as in the *United Scientific* case) giving the tenant the security of a long term and the landlord a revised market rent for the property subject to the letting. As Bingham LJ said in *Toyota (GB) Ltd v Legal & General Assurance (Pensions Management)* [1989] 2 EGLR 123 'the object of rent review broadly is to ensure the tenant pays full price of what he is getting'; a landlord will seek to confine 'what he is getting' to the restored full value of the demised premises. However, the tenant will argue that he gets the property subject to a lease, for a term as yet incomplete and for the use and purpose of the tenant's business. Undoubtedly, the modern rent review clause is directed to the former and the judicial expressions of the general purpose reflect that fact; there is though then some tension with the trend and construction emphasis that the review should reflect 'the reality' and that a tenant should not pay for what he has not got. The further consequence may be that the tenant is 'worse off', in this aspect at least, at rent review than at a statutory renewal in that in the former there is no escape (except by a surrender or an assignment) from a rent review which the tenant cannot afford. This may be a factor in any trend by those tenants with sufficient bargaining power to seek shorter terms with options to renew or introduce options to determine after the conclusion of the rent review process.

The view in the *United Scientific* decision that rent review clauses are 'fair and reasonable' for each party (per Lord Salmon at 948D) is now somewhat less prominent; indeed the use of the purposive effect of construction is often a recognition that the literal effect of the words used produces a result that is exactly the opposite to one that is fair to each side. Many of the more prominent decisions, by insisting that a tenant should not pay for what he has not got (see section (c) of this chapter, below) and by preferring a construction which accords with the actual position between the parties, are in effect a recognition that the literal approach may lead to an unfair burden on one party (often the tenant) and do, in essence, look to the result of the construction process.

(iii)   The growth of the purposive approach
The insistence that a rent review clause in a lease is primarily a commercial document to be interpreted as such can be seen in the earliest cases. In *C H Bailey Ltd v Memorial Enterprises Ltd* [1974] 1 WLR 728 the recognition of this fact enabled the Court of Appeal to dispense with 'the highly technical points that stem from the intricacies of the ancient law of landlord and tenant'. In the *Law Land* case (see p 302, above), Brightman LJ stressed that the 'lease is a commercial document and we have to find a commercial solution to the problem posed'. The decision in *National Westminster Bank plc v Arthur Young McClelland Moores & Co* [1985] 1 EGLR 61, where Walton J chose to ignore any 'presumption' in favour of a a purposive approach and adopted the strict literalist position that every case 'must depend on the exact words of the lease', led to the assumption in that case that the notional lease was one without a rent review clause while the actual lease between the parties contained the review provision. This issue, fully discussed at p 333, was the basis from which the current emphasis on the commercial purpose of review came. It was one of those cases which occur from time to time which highlight or dramatise issues already raised in other cases and focus attention on it. Disquiet may result and consequently counter arguments are more strongly pressed in later cases and assist in the process of judicial reconsideration.

In *MFI Properties Ltd v BICC Group Pension Trust Ltd* [1986] 1 All ER 974 at 977g Hoffman J considered that the *Arthur Young* case 'gave less weight than I would have done to the commercial purpose of the clause there in question'; since the words in the clause before him, similar to that in the *Arthur Young* case, were capable of bearing the meaning in accordance with the context and the commercial purpose of a rent review clause, that was the construction to be preferred. The guide-lines proposed by the Vice Chancellor in the *British Gas* case, set out at p 334, consolidated the purposive approach to that particular problem once they received appellate approval in *Equity & Law Life Assurance Society v Bodfield* (above). *Basingstoke and Deane v Host Group Ltd*, previously referred to, may well become as significant a decision for the construction of rent review clauses as the *United Scientific* decision was for time-limits. Strictly, the decision is limited to deciding that in general the notional letting postulated by the rent review clause is to be a letting on the same terms (other than as to quantum of rent) as those still subsisting between the parties in the actual existing lease. The wider aspect is seen, however, in the principle which underlies the judgment— the intention of the parties is taken to be one 'that would accord with, and give effect to, the general intention underlying the incorporation by them of a rent review clause into their lease'.

The purposive approach is now expressed to be the starting point for a series of decisions on widely separated points of construction, for example in the *Toyota* case (above) and in *Trusthouse Forte Albany Hotels v Daejan Investments Ltd (No 2)* [1989] 2 EGLR 113.

(iv) Relationship to the literal approach

There are obvious limits to the purposive approach to construction. The guide-lines established apply only if and so far as the rent review clause does not provide 'either expressly or by necessary implication' to the contrary (per Nicholls LJ in *Basingstoke and Deane*); so if the words of a provision are clear, the court must give effect to them even if they have no discernible purpose (Lewison, para 1.07.).

The difficulty is in those cases which fall between the two extremes. If the literal reading results in an absurd result, the court has always been able to reject that consequence. If the words are clear, there is little or no room for the purposive approach. In the *British Gas* case the Vice Chancellor took a rather different approach to 'absurdity' than that taken in *Philpots (Woking) Ltd v Surrey Conveyancers Ltd* [1986] 1 EGLR 97 (above); namely that where words produce a result 'which is so manifestly contrary to commercial common sense' they should not be given literal effect ([1986] 1 WLR 398 at 403B). These words were uttered in the context of a rent exclusion provision requiring all provisions as to rent to be disregarded but the judge appeared to be attempting to formulate wider principles of construction. In the light of subsequent decisions, it is probable that absurdity does not have to be established if an alternative construction is available. It is sufficient to reject a literal construction if it is a result manifestly contrary to commercial common sense.

The more commercially unsound the result of a literal construction is perceived to be, the more likely it is that it will be rejected—and the burden may almost be on the person propounding the literal but uncommercial meaning to show that it is clear and unequivocal. In *Glofield Properties v Morley (No 2)* [1989] 2 EGLR 118, Nourse LJ was of the view that:

'. . . it is simply that it is contrary to the whole purpose of a rent review provision that the reviewed rent should be fixed by reference to values prevailing at a date significantly later than the start of the period for which it is payable.'

The question then became one of whether the judge

'. . . was correct in deciding that the parties have clearly and unequivocally expressed an intention in the sense for which the plaintiff contends. If they have not, it is open for the court to construe their language in such a way that as to produce the more sensible and realistic result' (at 119).

Fairly recent Court of Appeal decisions would also suggest that, to borrow the terminology of Lloyd LJ in *The Sounion*, not all the literalist goats have been persuaded to follow the purposive sheep. Decisions such as *Philpots* case, *Equity and Law v Bodfield* and *General Accident Fire and Life Assurance plc v Electronic Data Processing Co plc* [1987] 1 EGLR 112 (at first instance) reveal a different line. *Equity & Law Life Assurance Society v Bodfield* is particularly illuminating; notwithstanding the approval of the guide-lines in the *British Gas* case the actual decision by the Court of Appeal affirmed a construction which meant that the notional lease excluded the complex review provisions in the actual lease:

'Guide-lines . . . cannot entitle the court to construe and apply not the clause which the parties have entered into but the different clause which they might have, or probably would have, entered into if their lawyers had thought more deeply about how the intricate scheme they were setting up would work in practice' (per Dillon LJ at 126).

Moreover, it may not be possible to suggest that a particular member of the judiciary is to be classified as either a literalist goat or a purposive sheep. Nourse LJ for example, was a party to both the *Glofield v Morley* and *Philpots* decisions. All that can be fairly said is that a new canon of construction for rent review clauses may be emerging but is yet to be established.

(v) Limits and dangers

There are conceptual objections to the purposive approach now prevalent. The principal fear was expressed succinctly by Harman J in *General Accident v Electronic Data* (above) when he stated (at p 113G) that a judge could not approach a rent review clause

'. . . with some prior conception that its only purpose was to establish a true market rent of the premises from time to time upon the terms of the actual lease then in issue before the court. To so say would be to assert a power to shape all the clauses to a particular purpose whatever they may say.'

The problems with the purposive approach can be said to be:

(1) Since no evidence can be given as to actual intent, the court can never be sure as to the reason (if any) behind a particular assumption or provision. As Goulding J remarked:

'If I assume [the original landlord and tenant] had a common intention different from what the words express, I think I am merely guessing' (*Safeway Food Stores Ltd v Banderway Ltd* (1983) 267 EG 850).

(2) There must be a risk that the perceived commercial purpose is perceived wrongly so that the real intention of the parties, which may be judged by parties to commercial leases to accord with commercial practice anyway, is thereby frustrated. Perhaps some of the decisions on the notional term in the hypothetical lease and the date from which it is to run can be viewed in this way (see p 399). The danger is not so much that the overall purpose is misunderstood but its application in the words of the particular review clause chosen and drafted for a particular property and situation. As Lewison remarks (p 15, para 1.07), 'neither the advocates who argue points of construction nor the judges who determine them are commercial men.'

(3) Even if the purpose can be said to be ascertainable, the court may come very close to transgressing the cardinal principle and, in effect, re-writing the bargain. Some may consider this occurred in *Toyota (GB) Ltd v Legal & General Assurance (Pensions Management)* [1989] 2 EGLR 123 where the court was so concerned that the clear literal construction produced an uncommercial result that it was prepared to imply a term to avoid that result. It was not necessary to give business efficacy to the contract, as was recognised, but the authors also doubt if it could be truly justified on the alternative ground (put forward and accepted by the court) as being 'so obvious as to go without saying'. As long ago as 1676 Lord Nottingham observed: 'Chancery mends no man's bargain though it sometimes mends his assurance' (*Maynard v Moseley* (1676) 35 ER 1009 at 1011). In modern rent review the balance between not mending the bargain but sometimes effectively amending the terms of the lease is still being worked through.

(c)   Construction to accord with the reality

A further general principle which appears to have emerged is 'the presumption in favour of reality'—a description of Nolan J in *Lynnthorpe Enterprises Ltd v Sidney Smith (Chelsea) Ltd* [1990] 1 EGLR p 148 at 151. This approach to construction, which may (or may not) have developed from the emphasis on the commercial purpose of rent review, is better viewed as a separate if complementary principle. It was expressed in the *Lynnthorpe* case at p 151D to be:

'. . . the principle . . . that the construction of a rent review clause should be approached on the footing that, in the absence of clear words compelling a different conclusion, the terms of the hypothetical lease should not be held to be such as to cause the tenant to pay, by way of reviewed rent, either for more or for less than he actually enjoys under the actual lease.'

and by Hoffman J in *Norwich Union Life Assurance Society v Trustee Savings Banks Central Board* [1986] 1 EGLR 135 as

'. . . a presumption that the hypothesis on which the rent should be fixed at review should bear as close a resemblance to reality as possible.'

The principle is more specific than that relating more generally to the commercial purpose and is directed to the terms of the notional or hypothetical letting valued at rent review. The idea is that the tenant should not pay for what he has not got:

'The court should lean against a construction which requires a rent to be fixed on revision to be ascertained without regard for the use which, under the lease, the tenant is entitled to make of the demised premises, unless, of course, that intention is spelled out in reasonably clear terms. Otherwise the effect of the review might be to impose on a tenant an obligation to pay a rent appropriate to a very profitable use, but one very obnoxious to the landlord and one which he has been careful to forbid in the strongest possible terms—the effect, that is, of making the tenant pay for something which he not only has not got, but which he cannot require the landlord to give him' (per Vinelott J in *Pearl Assurance v Shaw* [1985] 1 EGLR 92 at 93).

The presumption applies, perhaps even more strongly, if there is a construction which gives the landlord a rental benefit which he could not even obtain in the open market. This consideration was at the root of the guide-lines in the *British Gas* case (see below and p 334) where it was held that the notional letting should normally contain provisions for rent review the same as those in the actual lease. The judge, Browne-Wilkinson V-C, referred to the purpose of rent review and stated that it would

'. . . be wayward to impute to the parties an intention that the landlord should get a rent which was additionally inflated by a factor which has no reference either to changes in the value of money or in the value of the property but is referable to a factor which has no existence as between the actual landlord and the actual tenant. Of course, the lease may be expressed in words so clear that there is no room for giving effect to the underlying purpose. Again, there may be special surrounding circumstances which indicate that the parties did intend to reach such an unusual bargain. But in the absence of such clear words or surrounding circumstances, in my judgment the lease should be construed so as to give effect to the basic purpose of the rent review clause and not so as to confer on the landlord a windfall benefit which he could never have obtained on the market if he were actually letting the premises at the review date' ([1986] 1 WLR at 401).

These passages received approval of the Court of Appeal in the *Basingstoke and Deane* case ([1988] 1 WLR 348 at 355). There, the landlord's construction, which was rejected, would have led to a rent inflated by a factor (the value of the site for the most profitable use) having no reference to the actual existing lease which contained user restrictions.

The reasons for this principle of construction is partly founded on the perceived commercial purpose as stressed in the *Basingstoke and Deane* case, though it must be remembered that the deputy judge came to the opposite conclusion in that case and considered the 'intention of commercial men' in reaching his conclusion. However, the prime justification is probably the judicial desire to achieve a construction which produces justice between the parties and does not offend business common sense. So in the Court of Appeal in *Basingstoke and Deane*, the landlord's arguments directed at the presumed intention of the parties were considered to be:

'. . . of little weight when put in the scales against the contrary argument based on the manifestly unfair result to which the landlord's case leads' (at p 357D).

Similarly, in *British Home Stores v Ranbrook Properties Ltd* [1988] 1 EGLR 121 at 123, the judge noted the counsel for the landlord

'. . . accepted that the construction for which he was pressing would be inequitable, because it would mean that the tenant would be paying for something that he was not getting, and that it was against the weight of the authorities.'

Stress on the 'common sense' aspect appears in *Pleasurama Properties Ltd v Leisure Investments (West End) Ltd* [1986] 1 EGLR 145. There consent was given by licence for the construction of a dolphinarium with a covenant to reinstate. The tenants then argued at review for a reduction to take account of the reinstatement obligation. This was rejected as offending against common sense; the parties could not have intended the tenant, for whose sole consent the licence was given, to reap an additional benefit by a reduction in rent at review.

The principle can be of equal assistance to a landlord. Thus where there was a ground rent review with an express disregard of the buildings constructed at the tenant's expense, it was held that the arbitrator had been right to take account of the full site value and the actual planning permission consequent on the existence and occupation of those buildings: *Railstore Ltd v Playdale Ltd* [1988] 2 EGLR 153. The planning permission was a factor which had actual existence between the parties and the tenant had the benefit of it. Just as the *Basingstoke and Deane* case shows the presumption that the landlord is not to get an uncovenanted bonus so too a tenant should pay rent on what he does in fact get:

there is a strong presumption against either the landlord or the tenant obtaining an advantage which is referable to a factor which has no existence as between the actual landlord and the actual tenant (per Knox J at 155).

(d) Detailed guide-lines

In addition to the general principles and presumptions, the courts have been prepared to formulate guide-lines for specific situations. Most of these have been set out in the cases already referred to and are more detailed applications of the 'commercial purpose' approach and the 'presumption of reality'.

These detailed principles are discussed more fully in chapters 11–13 below but for the sake of convenience they are briefly listed below together with a cross reference to fuller discussion.

(i) Rent review provisions normally included in the hypothetical lease

In the absence of clear words to the contrary, a rent review clause which requires the rent to be assessed on the basis of a notional lease containing the same provisions as the actual lease 'other than as to rent' or some similar formula is to be construed as excluding only the quantum of rent payable before the review date but including the provision for future rent reviews: *British Gas Corporation v Universities Superannuation Scheme Ltd* [1986] 1 WLR 398. The detailed guide-lines are discussed at p 334, below.

(ii) Notional lease on the same terms as actual lease

In the absence of a contrary indication, the parties to a rent review clause are to be taken as having intended that the notional letting assumed for the purposes of rent review is to be on the same terms (other than as to the amount of rent) as those subsisting in the actual existing lease: *Basingstoke and Deane Borough Council v Host Group Ltd* [1988] 1 WLR 348 (see p 330).

(iii) Notional term presumption

Unless the parties clearly indicate to the contrary, the length of the notional term in the hypothetical lease will be a period equal to the actual residue of the term in the actual lease: *Norwich Union Life Assurance Society v Trustee Savings Banks Central Board* [1986] 1 EGLR 135 (see p 398).

(iv) Review date as valuation date

Unless the parties clearly and unequivocally express an intention to the contrary, the reviewed rent will normally be fixed by reference to values prevailing at the review date, ie at the start of the period in respect of which the reviewed rent is payable: *Glofield Properties v Morley (No 2)* [1989] 2 EGLR 118 (see p 76).

(v) Improvements

Guidance on the approach to the disregard of improvements was given by Forbes J in *GREA Real Property Investments Ltd v Williams* (1979) 250 EG 651 (see p 256).

When considering all the guidance and approaches to construction set out in this chapter, the words of Lord Denning MR in *The Rio Sun* [1982] 1 WLR 158 in another context (see p 199) are apposite:

'. . . it must be remembered that they are only guide-lines. They are not barriers. You can step over guide-lines without causing any harm. You can move them, if need be, to suit the occasion.'

Chapter 11

The Valuation Framework: (1) Actualities

In both creating and interpreting the valuation framework for a rent review, the notional or hypothetical letting will be closely linked to the actual premises and the terms of the actual lease. The central assumption will be that the terms of the existing lease are to apply and thereby the valuer will be directed to the actual premises and the terms of the lease—but to be valued in the open market for a notional term at a particular date and, most significantly, assuming willing and prudent parties to the lease and not the actual parties. As Bingham LJ remarked in *James v British Crafts Centre* [1987] 1 EGLR 139 at 141M:

'The operation of any review clause involves the fusion of the actual and the hypothetical. The rent to be determined is that actually to be paid by the actual lessee . . . but the measure of that rent is to be determined by reference to what would be paid by the hypothetical willing lessee to a hypothetical willing lessor if the premises were available for letting on the open market, which of course they are not. Depending on the wording of the clauses in question, difficulties may arise . . . in determining where the actual ends and the hypothetical begins.'

In this chapter, it is the proper construction and valuation impact of the terms of the actual lease which are considered in turn. It is, though, because those actual terms are fused with the notional assumptions that they can assume a valuation significance at rent review which they did not necessarily have between the actual parties when the lease was entered into.

1 The property

The normal rent review clause will assume a notional or hypothetical letting; in doing so it will require, first of all, a property or premises to which that letting is to relate. In most cases, it will be the actual property which is the subject of the actual lease which will be incorporated into the notional letting. The premises will usually be the premises as defined in the lease subject to the express assumptions or disregards requiring the valuer to make notional adjustments to the property as they stand 'on the ground'. Departure from this principle will, of course, occur where the review formula prescribes indexation to a notional standard unit or (more generally) to rents per square foot of offices in a particular area.

(a) The property to be valued

As to the physical state of the property, the formula may well introduce assumptions as to the performance of covenants, the absence of improvements or even, as in the Model Forms, the non-destruction and absence of damage or depreciating activities, all of which are discussed in Chapter 12. Except to the extent that those assumptions otherwise provide, or where they are not included in a particular clause, the review process should take account of the physical state of the property and its location.

The valuation will, in the absence of express provision to the contrary, take the premises as they stand or stood on the review date: *Ponsford v HMS Aerosols Ltd* [1979] AC 63. The ramifications of this principle are as follows.

(i) The location of the property

There is no room for preserving the notional social standing and desirability of the area at the time of the demise (which applies for the assessment of repairing obligations on termination as in *Anstruther-Gough-Calthorpe v McOscar* [1924] 1 KB 716). By the same token, changes in the trading attractions of an area of such nature as to be reflected in market demand must be reflected in the assessment of new rent. There might be a case for seeking expressly to eliminate consideration of intense, but temporary, disturbances such as major roadworks in the area operative at a review date. (Consider the facts in *National Carriers Ltd v Panalpina (Northern) Ltd* [1981] AC 675.) These would suggest that the incoming tenant reduce his offered rent at least for a period equivalent to his estimate of the likely duration of the disruption, but drafting problems are not easy. A potential permanent dislocation of business by such activities, as exemplified in *Argyle Motors (Birkenhead) Ltd v Birkenhead Corporation* [1975] AC 99, should make the wise tenant of premises susceptible to such injurious affection wary of an upwards only review. The imminent opening of a new shopping centre likely adversely to affect the trading prospects of the premises involved in *Janes (Gowns) Ltd v Harlow Development Corporation* (1980) 253 EG 799 was expressly referred to by the deputy judge as justifying an upwards/downwards review in the new lease granted by him and the effect of the actual opening of such a competing development had to be assessed in *Ratners (Jewellers) Ltd v Lemnoll Ltd* (1980) 255 EG 987. A similar substantial depreciating effect could be caused by a new by-pass on a rent of a petrol sation, cafe, or other business which is heavily dependent upon trade from passing motorists (cf the facts of *Esso Petroleum v Mardon*

(1976) 2 BLR 82 which shows the impact on trade of having petrol pumps at a filling station facing the side street instead of the main road).

(ii)   The physical nature of the building

The presence of antiquated services, inconveniently large or small rooms, high ceilings, 'difficult' wall or floor surfaces, fluctuating floor levels, good or bad natural lighting and ventilation and all similar factors affecting the market for accommodation are all relevant, as are comparable limits or attributes in the immediate environs. The cost of combating and repairing the ravages of vandals is an obvious example, and such an element may or may not have entered into the respective calculations of the parties. Nevertheless, it and all other similar factors are relevant to the adjustment process and ideally may need to be evaluated in assessing the true weight of alleged 'comparables'. It would, of course, be possible to seek to eliminate one or more of them in settling the review formula, but the drafting problems are formidable and, save in the most favourable sellers' market, are likely to engender considerable tenant resistance. Moreover, as a general principle, the more artificial the 'package' of assumptions that have to be made about the property, the less the attractions of the reversion to potential purchasers. The grasping landlord may find that the gap between actual and notional worlds leads only to tenant insolvency and empty premises.

(iii)   Improvements and subsequent buildings

Any building works to the property will become part of the land and therefore part of the 'demised premises' under basic principles. For this reason the express treatment of the disregard of improvements is vital if the tenant is not to pay rent on capital projects he has financed— see the *Ponsford* decision and the full discussion at p 386. Similarly, ground rent reviews can cause difficulty if it is not made clear that the valuer is to value the bare site instead of the land with the buildings constructed by the tenant: see *Ipswich Town Football Club v Ipswich Borough Council* and Chapter 13 p 464, below.

(iv)   Surrender of part

It follows that if part of the property has been surrendered at the review date, the valuation would be of the remainder.

(v)   Constructing notional premises to be valued

It is open to the parties to construct notionally, for the purposes of review only, premises entirely different to the actual property. This technique is valuable if the premises are unusual or where there are likely to be no suitable comparables. Very often this artifical creation is a 'standard' or index to which the rent is then related and this concept is explored and discussed in Chapter 20, p 564. It should be noted that it may then become much more difficult to bring in any of the actual provisions that operate since the terms of the lease may not fit well with the notional premises so constructed. Conseqently, prior agreement on the original rental value per square foot for the premises with an agreed formula to relate this to the hypothetically constructed notional premises will ensure the actual property is at least brought into account through the indexation process. The parties might even be prepared to trust the referee only to apply the lease terms to the notional property 'so far as reasonably applicable'.

(b)   The 'demised premises' as defined

There can be few formal commercial leases that do not contain a more or less detailed specification of what is leased, compendiously defined as 'the demised premises' or by some similar label, and such definition will normally be carried over into the rent review clauses. The definition therefore becomes the starting point for the proper ascertainment of the extent of the property to be valued. The description will normally be sufficiently precise and may even contain a statement of the floor area. Unless this is expressly stated as the agreed area for the purposes of review, it will not be conclusive. Some modern leases now provide that the then current edition of the RICS/ISVA *Code of Measuring Practice* shall apply to calculations of area and this will ensure that the market practice at the date of review is adopted.

In informal residential leases or tenancy agreements the description may be more exiguous and this may create extra problems but even detailed leases for longer terms can give rise to disputes. In *Graystone Property Investments Ltd v Margulies* (1983) 47 P & CR 472 the issue was whether voids between the false ceilings were included in the demise or not; it was held they were and so could be incorporated into proposed alterations of a flat, subject to permission which could not be unreasonably withheld. More surprisingly, it was held that, where a lease was silent on the issue of the exact horizontal boundary, the 'normal expectation' was that the upper limit of one flat was the underneath of the floors of that above. The authors confess to some doubts whether that would have been the normal expectation of many conveyancers. Neverthless, an analagous result was reached in *Hatfield v Moss* [1988] 2 EGLR 58 when it was held that the demise of a flat in the roof of a large building included adjoining roof space which was on the same horizontal level. At a review, the prospect of utilising any such space would be a factor to be taken into account.

Where a tenant occupies land adjoining the demised premises not included in the lease but nevertheless occupies it in connection with the demised premises, then the land so occupied is an adjunct to and an addition to the land of which he is truly a tenant: *Smirk v Lyndale Developments* [1975] Ch 317. It follows that such additional land can form part of the demised premises at review. Thus in *Kensington Pension Developments Ltd v Royal Garden Hotel (Oddenino's) Ltd* [1990] 27 EG

79 a hotel had been partially constructed on land not included in the lease but to which the landlord hoped to get title and grant a lease to the tenant. In fact, though the landlord had obtained a leasehold title to this extra land it was for a term substantially less than the 150–year term of the hotel lease and no title had been granted to the tenant. At the first review after 25 years, it was held that since the tenant had actually occupied the additional land as part of the hotel and in connection with the demised premises, it formed part of the demised premises as defined for the purposes of the review. The potential difficulty of valuing an hotel shorn of one corner was thereby avoided.

(c) Relevance of plans

It may prove necessary to establish exactly how far the definition extends in order that the process of valuation and adjudication can proceed on a proper footing. The extent to which reference can be made to plans and drawings incorporated in the lease is limited. Where the plan is for the purpose of identification only, it is only permissible to look at the plan if the parcels clause is not clear—so measurements on such a plan cannot be used. Even where the parcels are not explicit, if the plan is inaccurate or unhelpful, little weight may be given to it as it is only one factor to be considered: *Hatfield v Moss* (above). If the premises are 'more particularly delineated' or 'as shown' on the plan (much less usual for a commercial lease) then the plan and any details it provides can be referred to—but only to the extent the plan is not inconsistent with the lease. In *Trusthouse Forte Albany Hotels Ltd v Daejan Investments Ltd (No 2)* [1989] 2 EGLR 113, there was the need to value specific areas of the hotel 'as shown edged red on the plans annexed hereto'. The two relevant areas were each divided into two by extra red lines but the Court of Appeal were satisfied that the extra red lines were inconsistent with the words of the lease requiring the two areas to be let as a whole and they were treated as a manifest clerical error. In *Kensington Pension Developments Ltd v Royal Garden Hotel (Oddenino's) Ltd* [1990] 27 EG 79 the lease demised 'a piece of land . . . together with the new building erected thereon . . . more particularly delineated on the plan'. The premises constructed (as both parties knew) went outside the land so delineated onto a portion of land to which the landlord hoped to get leasehold title. Harman J held that the edging on the plan prevailed so that as a matter of strict construction the 'demised premises' excluded a portion of the hotel building constructed and the plan prevailed over the landlord's attempts to argue that the parcels clause showed an intent to grant a lease of the whole hotel building (though it was further held that the additional land could be treated as part of the demised premises, see above).

(d) Easements expressly granted

Practices vary amongst draftsmen whether, for example, express easements and exceptions and reservations are comprehended in the defining phrase or not. For the purposes of rent reviews, the particular technique may matter little provided that the formula allows for the ascertainment of a rent at the revised figure on the basis of the terms of the lease, since thereby all the express provisions of those parts of the lease dealing with easements, exceptions and reservations (where those attributes are not within the definition of 'the premises') have to be brought into account. More difficult may be rights and restrictions granted or imposed by implication or rights and restrictions that can only be established by interpretation of the lease itself. For example, in *Re Webb's Lease* [1951] Ch 808 it was held that the demise of a flat extended to the exterior surfaces of the walls thereby securing to the lessee and not the lessor the benefit of advertising displays thereof (although the landlord had maintained advertisements there for nearly 11 years). In *Sturge v Hackett* [1962] 1 WLR 1257 it was held that an exterior decorative cornice was included in a demise of a flat, and in *Re No 1 Albemarle Street* [1959] Ch 531 the valuable rights to exhibit illuminated advertisements fronting Albemarle Street and Piccadilly were held to be rights that should be included as part of the new tenancy to which the tenant was entitled on a statutory renewal as no sufficient reason was adduced to exclude them from the renewal. The offending advertising signs in *Kelsen v Imperial Tobacco (of Great Britain and Ireland) Ltd* [1957] 2 QB 334 provide a further illustration of advertising positions that might be included by implication in a demise. The point is particularly important where potential rights of this nature have not been exploited but take on a new significance owing to a relaxation of planning constraints or the growth of a new demand for product advertising, directional signs or display space that could be shown to have a demonstrable influence on market rent at the relevant review date. (The restrictive provisions of the lease, as well as the planning restraints, may be the overriding factor, as well as an established pattern of landlord consents, a matter further discussed under 'Use clauses' at p 342 ff, below.) Similar considerations might apply to, say, unused but available open storage space or even trading forecourts in the case of those retail trades (ironmongery and flower shops, for example) that often utilise such areas.

(e) Implied easements and rights

The impact of the Law of Property Act 1925, s 62, may also fall to be considered as attaching to the property valuable rights not apparent on the face of the lease, rights that prior to the granting of the lease may have been enjoyed by licence or other concession. By virtue of s 62 all privileges, easements, rights and advantages enjoyed with the land demised at the date of the lease will pass for the benefit of the tenant. For example, it cannot be denied that, had the new tenancy in *Wright v Macadam* [1949] 2 KB 744 contained provision for a variable rent, the right to use of the coal-shed would have been a factor in finding the market rent. Many leases contain provisions designed to oust the effect of s 62, of course; a prudent landlord may have sought to determine all precarious rights in fact enjoyed in relation to premises before letting or re-letting them so as to avoid their carrying over and ripening into full easements under the new lease. Both factors should be considered. Where, as is not infrequent, premises are occupied under an agreement for lease prior to the making of the formal lease, whilst the agreement for the lease will not activate s 62 *(Borman v Griffith* [1930] 1 Ch 493), rights in fact exercised during the period of occupation under the agreement may ripen into rights attached to the property on the grant of the lease (see *Goldberg v Edwards* [1950] Ch 247). At review, the lawyer to each party should thus check what exact assumptions have been made by the valuer acting for his client as to the existence, and continued availability, of such ancillary rights and benefits as fall within s 62 (or for that matter the rule in *Wheeldon v Burrows* [1879] 12 ChD 31). At a later stage he should check the assumptions on these aspects made by the other party's valuer. In drafting new leases, the existence of s 62 encourages careful delimitation of the express rights granted combined with a provision excluding operation of the section.

(f) Rights enjoyed under licence

In the not unusual state of affairs where certain valuable rights— for example parking for staff, visitors and customers—are enjoyed not under the lease but under either a parallel licence or under the authority of a sideletter that are coterminous with the lease, it is necessary to consider how, if at all, these valuable rights will be taken into account at review. The existence of such rights may have a marked effect on market rentals and it is the authors' view that, whilst the device of the separate licence will mean that ancillary rights are not part of the property to be valued, their existence, and the ascertainable prospects of their continued existence are elements properly to be considered in establishing market rental if that is the relevant standard of comparison (cf *Kensington Pension Developments Ltd v Royal Garden Hotel (Oddenino's) Ltd* [1990] 27 EG 79, discussed above). Even if such rights are personal to the existing tenant, the prospects of such terms being available for the notional willing tenant may be taken into account. Thus, the existence, situation and nature of public facilities for car parking would be a factor in assessing market rents in many cases, whereas in some residential lettings with variable rents the proximity of public (or private) parking areas could be a negative factor (see *Redspring Ltd v Francis* [1973] 1 WLR 134): a fortiori, therefore, the benefit of private parking. The same applies to other benefits enjoyed under separate but linked arrangements. Benefits in fact enjoyed under terms permitting their termination or withdrawal during the pendency of the lease will have little or no effect on market values, although much must depend on all the facts.

At the drafting stage, if such ancillary rights may have an impact on the valuation, it will be wise to provide expressly that they are to be either taken into account or disregarded, as the case may be.

(g) Fixtures

In the absence of express assumptions, the valuation will proceed on the basis of the demised premises ignoring both the tenant's chattels and fittings and the tenant's fixtures which he is entitled to remove. Where, however, those items are of considerable value, their assumed *presence* or *absence* in the hypothetical letting at rent review can be significant and the lessor may wish to argue that items originally chattels and introduced by the tenant have become first fixtures and secondly landlord's fixtures and so part of the demised premises for the purposes of review. Such issues raise the complex interrelation of the law relating to fixtures and the express provisions of the lease and review clause.

(i) The problem analysed

In analysing whether items originally chattels have become part of the demised premises for the purposes of rent review, it is suggested that the following questions need to be addressed:

(1) Have the chattels concerned become fixtures within the well known principles? If not, they will be ignored at review.
(2) If they are fixtures, do they qualify as *landlord's fixtures* or *tenant's fixtures*? If the former, they have become part of the demised premises, but if the latter they remain removable by the tenant while occupation continues (and, indeed, for a short extra period to allow removal). While the right to remove exists, they will not be part of the demised premises.
(3) Given the status of the fixtures, do they fall to be taken into account or disregarded at review? The decision as to whether they are landlord's fixtures or tenant's fixtures may not be conclusive but must be an issue to be decided in the light of the valuation framework and particularly the provisions relating to vacant possession and the treatment of improvements.

(ii) What is a fixture?

For a detailed treatment of the considerable case law, reference may be made to the standard texts (eg Hill and Redman (18th ed) Vol 1 para 2416ff, Megarry and Wade, *The Law of Real Property* pp 730–8). In summary, there are two traditional tests, namely:

(1) The degree of annexation; and

(2) The purpose of annexation.

The primary test is the degree of annexation (*Holland v Hodgson* (1872) LR 7 CP 328) and a substantial degree of annexation will put the onus on the party contending the item remains a chattel. Traditionally, the purpose of the annexation was a subsidiary test so that if the purpose of the annexation was to enjoy the item as a chattel, it never became a fixture (*Leigh v Taylor* [1902] AC 157) but the more recent cases suggest that considerations of purpose and intent are now of first importance (*Hamp v Bygrave* (1983) 266 EG 720). However, the intention of the person who annexed the item is only material in so far as it can be presumed from the degree and purpose of the annexation (*Hobson v Gorringe* [1897] 1 Ch 182; *College v H C Curlett Construction Co* [1932] NZLR 1060). It is now possible to argue that the one test is now the object and purpose of annexation and the degree of annexation is one significant piece of evidence to that end but it is doubtful whether the authorities yet go that far.

What is undoubted is that it is a question of fact in each case; the factors taken into account in other cases and the actual decisions are no more than a guide. Some of the most relevant for commercial leases and rent review situations are:

(1) Items brought in to equip the land for use will be more readily inferred to be chattels, even if the degree of attachment is small or non-existent. An example would be an airconditioning unit standing by its own weight on the roof of a building (*Belgrave Nominees Pty Ltd v Barlin-Scott Airconditioning Pty Ltd* [1984] VR 947 (Australia)—a fixture even before the unit was connected to the electricity supply). It is on this basis that the decision at first instance in *Young v Dalgety plc* [1987] 1 EGLR 116 can be justified. Mervyn Davies J held that fitted carpets ranked as fixtures and, though the Court of Appeal ([1987] 1 EGLR 116 at 119E) did not find it necessary to decide if he was right, a similar result has been reached in Canada in the case of wall-to-wall carpeting in an hotel (*La Salle Recreations Ltd v Canadian Camdex Investments Ltd* (1969) 4 DLR (3d) 549).

(2) If it is apparent that the items were brought in for temporary use, they remain chattels. Thus the same items may remain chattels in one set of circumstances but be clearly fixtures in another, as with theatre or cinema seats—compare *Lyon & Co v London City and Midland Bank* [1903] 2 KB 135 (temporary and therefore chattels) with the *New Zealand Government* case below and *Vaudeville Electric Theatre v Muriset* [1923] 2 Ch 74 (permanent seating).

(3) To rank as a chattel, the article must be capable of removal without irreparable damage: *Spyer v Phillipson* [1931] 2 Ch 183; but light fittings which cause damage to plaster on removal may be still be

chattels or, if tenant's fixtures (see below), still be removable: *Young v Dalgety plc* [1987] 1 EGLR 116.

(iii)   Tenant's fixtures

Before an item, which is admittedly a fixture under the general principles outlined, falls to be considered as part of the premises at rent review it must be shown that either it was not a tenant's fixture or, if it was, the tenant has lost the right to remove it.

'Tenant's fixtures' is a term given to a series of exceptions to the general rule that fixtures become conclusively part of the land. The exceptions were developed in the landlord/tenant relationship to mitigate the harshness to the tenant of the uncompensated benefit the lessor would otherwise receive. Tenant's fixtures include ornamental or domestic items and (by statute) agricultural fixtures but the most significant for rent review purposes are items which are affixed for the purposes of the tenant's trade or business. Unless the lease otherwise provides, these are removable by the tenant while the term continues or while he remains in possession. 'Landlord's fixtures' is then the phase used to describe fixtures attached to the land by a tenant but which are not tenant's fixtures. The better view is that tenant's fixtures, since they are fixtures, become the property of the landlord until they are lawfully removed by the tenant, though it can be argued (Gray, *Elements of Land Law*, p 24) that the rules relating to tenant's fixtures are really instances of the court's applying more exacting standards in the landlord/tenant relationship so that the items never lose their character as chattels. Whatever, the proper view, tenant's fixtures will usually fall to be disregarded at rent review. As Fox LJ remarked in *Young v Dalgety plc* at 119E:

'Were these items tenant's fixtures or landlord's fixtures? If they were landlord's fixtures, then they must be left for the landlords and it would therefore be proper to bring them into account in relation to a rent review. However, the position is otherwise and it is not in dispute if they were tenant's fixtures.'

The right to remove tenant's fixtures is not lost by a surrender and re-grant so the right to remove items installed during the term of the first lease is preserved during the new lease: *New Zealand Government Property Corporation v HM & S Ltd* [1982] QB 1145. Dunn LJ stated the rule to be that:

'. . . a tenant has the right to remove tenant's fixtures so long as he is in possession as tenant, whether by holding over, . . . or upon extension of a lease of business premises under Part II of the Landlord and Tenant Act 1954.'

Consequently in that case the new rent was assessed on the basis that the tenants had not lost the right to remove substantial fittings installed in a leading theatre over a period of over 70 years; notwithstanding the length of time involved they were not part of the demised premises for the purposes of rent review.

(iv)   The impact of express provisions in the lease

It is not sufficient to conclude that tenant's fixtures will always be excluded from consideration at a review, since the terms of the lease may have an impact.

(1) A lease may negate the right of the tenant to remove fixtures; such a covenant would ensure that they fell to be taken into account at review.

(2) The fixtures may have been installed by the tenant under an obligation or covenant but they may still rank as tenant's fixtures and be removable: *Young v Dalgety plc*. Only if there is a clear indication that the items so installed are to become landlord's fixtures will the general position be altered.

(3) Most reviews will proceed on the usual 'vacant possession' assumption (either expressly or by implication) and this will bring in the hypothesis that the outgoing tenant has removed all he was entitled to remove. However, it does not necessarily follow that the absence of the assumption of vacant possession will bring tenant's fixtures into account. So where there is a review of a head lease on the basis of actual sub-lettings there is no reason why the head lessee's fixtures (eg carpets and lighting in the common parts) should be taken into account. By analogy with the *New Zealand Government* case, the actual tenant *could* have removed them the day before the review date and reinstalled them thereafter—and since that is the case, it seems inappropriate to bring them into account. The issue may turn on whether tenant's fixtures which are removable form part of the demised premises until removal; the authors prefer the view that they are not.

(4) There will be the related or separate issue of whether fixtures (whether or not they are classified as tenant's or landlord's) or 'non fixtures' (ie fittings) may rank as improvements, the treatment of which will depend on the wording of the relevant provisions. If the installation of a chattel ranks as an improvement falling to be disregarded it will not matter for the purposes of rent review whether it is a fixture or not but will turn on the exact wording of that disregard.

There is a dictum in the *New Zealand Government* case (per Lord Denning MR at 1160C) that 'improvements', at least under s 34 of the Landlord and Tenant Act 1954, apply only to 'landlord's fixtures'. If this a correct view applicable to all improvements then classification as a chattel or tenant's fixture may be significant to a tenant where improvements do not fall to be disregarded. The disregard of improvements is covered in Chapter 12, p 427, below.

(5) In modern review clauses, an assumption that the premises are fit and available for immediate occupation and use may well negate the adverse valuation consequences for the landlord that it is assumed the tenant has removed all he is entitled to remove.

2   Assumption that the terms of the lease apply

The assumption that the terms of the actual lease are to be the basis of the hypothetical letting is often expressly stated in the rent review provision and, in those cases where it is not (as with many earlier clauses), the proper construction of the clause will usually lead to the same result.

(a)   Fixed terms applying in a notional future market

The actual terms of the lease apply between the parties for the time being to the lease and will continue to do so after the review. Yet in the open market, the standard terms in new leases fluctuate and consequently some of the actual terms may prove to be obsolete, outdated or financially disadvantageous in that market at review.

The position at review must be contrasted with that at a statutory renewal under the 1954 Act. There, under s 35, the new lease shall be upon such terms 'as may be agreed . . . or as, in default of . . . agreement, may be determined by the court; and in determining those terms the court shall have regard to the terms of the current tenancy and to all relevant circumstances'. It is clear that, despite the presumption in favour of the status quo, variations can be imposed by the court in the absence of agreement between the parties by the order for a new lease. The matter was discussed in *O'May v City of London Real Property* [1983] 2 AC 726 (and see p 514) where the decision to change the burden of repairing obligations from landlord to the tenant was reversed on appeal. The case demonstrates changes in market attitudes and requirements and illustrates how the court, granting an order for renewal of a lease, may respond to them. The lease with a rent review provision has equally to be considered in the context of a fluctuating market, but the lease terms cannot be changed (in the absence of mutual agreement or, very rarely, waiver). The requirement of ascertaining a market rent for the property on the terms of an outmoded lease, which is what the lease will have become in the event of substantial shifts in the market, thus involves adjusting the rent from the level prevailing for 'comparables' on modern terms to reflect the departure, in the provisions of the actual lease, from what has become the market norm. The facts agreed between the valuers in *O'May* prove the point. The revised rent on renewal on the basis of the former service charge, providing the landlord only with partial recoupment of its probable total outlay, would have been £10.50 per square foot. On the basis of a revised service charge, providing full recoupment, it was lower, at £10 per square foot, and the judge's order for a new lease was on the latter basis. (The reversal of the order on appeal does not vitiate use of the figures as an illustration.) However, with identical facts on valuation, the rent review process would have proceeded in reverse order:

(*i*) Open market rent on 'modern' service charge basis is £10 per square foot; (*ii*) in instant case, either (*a*) the open market rent on the basis of the outmoded service charge is shown to be £10.50 or (*b*) there being no available evidence of rents being now fixed to allow for only partial recoupment, the known market rent of £10 per square foot has to be adjusted by virtue of the benefit enjoyed by the tenant; and (*iii*) this gives a figure of £10.50. It will be seen, therefore, that in this case the rigidity of the rent criteria produces a rent higher than prevailing market rents because the fixed terms of the lease favour the tenant. Indeed, it was held in the *O'May* decision that the variation could not be compensated for by a rent reduction to reflect the uncertain burdens of the total maintenance (or even reconstruction) of the building. If the burdens have thus generally moved to landlords, one would expect them to respond by seeking rents reflecting the increased liability, and so the current market rents on the changed basis will be higher than what is appropriate for the lease into which the parties are locked. In other circumstances (eg the *Norwich Union v British Railways Board* decision discussed at p 373, below) a lease may impose obligations on the actual tenant that tenants as a whole never have accepted or will no longer readily shoulder so the open market rent on the onerous terms will then be lower. However, the lesson that may be drawn from the *Plinth Property* decision (see p 345 below) is that the prospect that the landlord might vary the terms of the lease, in return for a premium of rent-adjustment or both, is normally too speculative to be allowed as a factor in the determination of a market rent.

(b) Implied if not express

It is now established that the notional letting at any rent review will be on the terms of the actual lease unless the parties otherwise provide: *Basingstoke and Deane Borough Council v Host Group Ltd* [1988] 1 WLR 348 where Nicholls LJ giving the judgment of the court said:

'Of course, rent review clauses may, and often do, require a valuer to make his decision on a basis which departs in one or more respects from the subsisting terms of the actual existing lease. But if and in so far as a rent review clause does not so require, either expressly or by necessary implication, it seems to us that in general, and subject to a special context indicating otherwise in a particular case, the parties are to be taken as having intended that the notional letting postulated by their rent review clause is to be a letting on the same terms (other than as to the quantum of rent) as those subsisting between the parties in the actual existing lease.'

The ruling is in line with (and quoted with approval) dicta in *Ponsford v HMS Aerosols* [1979] AC 63 where both Viscount Dilhorne and Lord Fraser (at 76G and 83) referred to valuations of premises 'on the terms of the lease'. It is justifiable on the basis that as the review relates to the rent to be paid for these premises under this lease, it must be on the terms of the lease except in so far as contrary provision is made. This is akin to the *rebus sic stantibus* doctrine regularly resorted to in rating valuation, and accords with the rule for contractual interpretation within the 'factual matrix' (as enunciated in *Reardon Smith Line Ltd v Yngvar Hansen-Tangen* [1976] 1 WLR 989 and see Chapter 10, p 300). The *Basingstoke and Deane* case is therefore a rejection of the counter-argument which would have given less weight to the actual existing terms. Such views emphasised the review to a *market* rent and linked that to the underlying rationale of rent review. It was said that to reproduce the rent bargain that the parties negotiating afresh at arm's length in the market place might well have produced necessitates a reference to the then going terms in that market. Decisions such as *Law Land Co Ltd v Consumers' Association Ltd* (1980) 255 EG 617 discussed below at p 349, and *Avon County Council v Alliance Property Co Ltd* (1981) 258 EG 1181, discussed at p 407, might once have been viewed as giving some support to this approach.

The rule now established in the *Basingstoke and Deane* case was the preferred approach of the authors in earlier editions of this book and probably that also of the majority of those professionally involved. The landlord, it may be argued, is already getting the benefit of a measure of hindsight in re-negotiating the rent, an advantage for which admittedly he has bargained, so why should he also obtain the benefit of re-thinking and rewriting the other terms, normally in his favour, when he had not the foresight to bargain for that opportunity? Consequently if the lessor wishes to have a review which is on a basis which departs from the actual terms in any particular then such departure should be explicitly stated.

In two decisions prior to the *Basingstoke and Deane* case the court felt it equally appropriate to imply that the valuer should assume that the terms of the original lease, other than as to rent, were to apply and these now stand as examples of how the implication applies:

(1) *Sterling Land Office Developments Ltd v Lloyds Bank plc* (1984) 271 EG 894 concerned a 1960 lease of bank premises for 42 years with a 21 year review; the review clause described by the judge as in the very simplest of terms, merely provided for the reviewed rent to be 'an amount equal to the market rental for the demised premises with vacant possession'. In such a case, Harman J held that the most natural assumption was to assume that the terms of the lease were to apply; in the context of existing premises the only alternatives were to assume that 'usual covenants' applied or allow the valuer to assess them. Neither alternative was attractive when compared to the actual terms under which the parties operated—which accorded with reality.

(2) *Scottish & Newcastle Breweries plc v Sir Richard Sutton's Settled Estates* [1985] 2 EGLR 130 involved the interpretation of an early

review clause (1962) in an underlease for 42 years with one review after 21 years taken by the plaintiff brewers of part of a development. Here the *landlords* successfully argued for the implication of the assumption that the terms of the lease applied, expecting on this basis for a higher rent (21 years without review); if the arbitrator could have assessed his own terms and conditions, he would be expected to assume a more modern review pattern with a consequential lower rent.

In the light of the *Basingstoke and Deane* ruling, it is submitted two earlier cases came to the wrong conclusion:

(1) In *General Accident Fire and Life Assurance Corporation plc v Electronic Data Processing Co plc* [1987] 1 EGLR 112 there was no express assumption that the terms of the actual lease applied; rather there were eight express assumptions most if not all of which are common in review clauses and were not inconsistent with an implied assumption that the actual terms applied. Harman J refused to apply his own decision in *Sterling Land* (above) since it would duplicate some of the express assumptions and adopted the strict (and now less favoured) approach to construction exemplified in *Philpots (Woking) Ltd v Surrey Conveyancers Ltd* (see Chapter 10, p 299). The better view is that this decision is unsound.

(2) The decision by the arbitrator in *Lucas Industries plc v Welsh Development Agency* [1986] 3 WLR 80 can no longer be justified. The lease was silent as to the terms of the notional lease and the problem for the arbitrator was whether it was to be assumed to be in Type A, the standard form of the defendant landlord at the date of the lease (and, indeed the form of the lease itself) or Type B, the standard lease at the date of review. The latter relaxed tight use and alienation restrictions in the former. Each variation could affect the rent on review significantly. The arbitrator found that the notional lease should be taken in Form B. On appeal, the Vice-Chancellor, despite a reference to the arbitrator's 'carefully reasoned award', was left with 'a real doubt whether [he] was right'. The authors understand the matter was resolved by agreement but the correct approach now would be to take the terms of the actual lease. If an institutional lessor wishes a review to be conducted on the basis of its then standard draft, then it must so provide in the lease. Any such provision must be carefully drafted. What if the landlord has a choice of standard forms at the date of review, each differing from the other and also from the current 'outmoded' lease? How is the choice of the most appropriate new form for the hypothetical lease to be settled? A tenant could be substantially disadvantaged and not just because the review will be 'moved away from the reality'. Could a tenant inquire into the reasons for any change in such

standard terms? Can the tenant insist on evidence that the draft so offered is acceptable in the current market? For all such reasons tenants will rightly resist any attempt to allow an institutional lessor expressly to substitute at review its current standard draft as the basis of valuation.

(c) Exclusion of terms relating to rent—the 'Arthur Young' saga

There is, of course, one term of the actual lease which cannot be assumed to apply and must be disregarded—the amount or quantum of the rent originally reserved and the amount of current rent actually payable. This is axiomatic and implicit in a review to open market rent. It is for this reason that the ISVA Forms of rent review clause (set out in full in Part Seven at p 669) do not bother expressly to state that the amount or quantum of rent is to be disregarded. However, it is not surprising that draftsmen seek to make the point explicit. In earlier review clauses, this was often done by stating an assumption 'that the terms of this lease *(other than as to rent)* are to apply' to the notional valuation. The exact wording varied but the problem in a host of reported cases was the same—did the valuer or arbitrator, in addition to disregarding the quantum of the rent, also have to disregard the fact that the actual lease contained a rent review clause? If that was the result, the rent payable in the market for a long term lease without review (described by Hoffman J as an 'animal not so much fabulous as extinct' in the *MFI v BICC* case, below) would be one fixed without reference to comparables (which do not exist) resulting in a more or less arbitary upwards adjustment to the rent which the premises would command on a letting with a normal review clause. In a series of cases, of which the *Arthur Young* case is the most notorious, lessors sought to argue that the rent review clause in the lease had that effect. Where they were successful, the lessee would usually end up paying a rent inflated by the assumption that there was no review clause but applied to a lease where there was such a clause—by the very same clause that was assumed not to exist! The *British Gas* case has now formulated guidelines which will often ensure this unjust result does not occur but clear words can still leave a lessor with this unmerited benefit.

(i) The Arthur Young case

A dozen or more, largely first instance, decisions have occurred in the last few years where the court has had to construe a rent review clause to decide if the postulated hypothetical lease *either*

> EXCLUDED the provisions for rent review (argued by landlords seeking a higher rent as a result); or
>
> INCLUDED those provisions—as was the case in reality (tenants urged the justice of the result).

The most notorious of these was *National Westminster Bank plc v Arthur Young McClelland Moores & Co* [1985] 1 EGLR 61 a decision of Walton J (26 November 1984), a decision which spawned much subsequent litigation. The rent review was to be 'Subject to the provisions of this . . . lease other than the rent hereby reserved'. The judge, applying a very literal approach to construction and rejecting the view that there was a presumption in favour of a commercial result, decided that the review clause was excluded from the hypothetical lease. As a consequence, there was a rent uplift as determined by the arbitrator of 20.5 per cent. Unfortunately, an attempt to appeal in the *Arthur Young* case failed (see [1985] 2 EGLR 13, as the case began as a motion under the Arbitration Acts and not an originating summons and no leave or certificate was given under s 1(7) of the 1979 Act) but subsequent cases (summarised in section (iii) below) revealed a different judicial approach to the construction of similar clauses. This process culminated in the *British Gas* guide-lines. Subsequent litigation (see p 209) between the same parties to the *Arthur Young* decision at the next review have led the Court of Appeal to categorise the decision by Walton J as 'plainly wrong' (*Arnold v National Westminster Bank plc* [1990] 1 All ER 529).

(ii)   The 'British Gas' guide-lines

The 'principles of construction' and 'correct approach' enunciated by the Vice Chancellor in the *British Gas* case will now be applied as the starting point for any construction of a similar provision in any lease. These are:

(a) words in a rent exclusion provision which require *all* provisions as to rent to be disregarded produce a result so manifestly contrary to commercial common sense that they cannot be given literal effect;

(b) other clear words which require the rent review provision (as opposed to all provisions as to rent) to be disregarded (as those in *Pugh v Smith's Industries Ltd*) must be given effect to, however wayward the result; and

(c) subject to (b), in the absence of special circumstances, it is proper to give effect to the underlying commercial purpose of a rent review clause and to construe the words so as to give effect to that purpose by requiring future rent reviews to be taken into account in fixing the open market rental under the hypothetical letting.

These guide-lines were welcomed and approved by the Court of Appeal in *Equity & Law Life Assurance Society v Bodfield* [1987] 1 EGLR 124 and in *Basingstoke and Deane v Host Group Ltd*. It was stressed in the former case that they are not mechanistic rules to be applied rigidly but only guide-lines to assist in construction of the particular review clause in question.

'Guide-lines such as the Vice-Chancellor's cannot entitle the court to construe and apply not the clause which the parties have entered into but the different clause which they might have, or probably would have, entered into if their lawyers had thought rather more deeply about how the intricate scheme they were setting up would work in practice'. (at 125G).

Consequently, the *British Gas* case guide-lines do not ensure that on every review the hypothetical lease will contain the rent review provisions in the actual lease. The question will be one of construction of the actual words in the light of those guide-lines.

(iii)   Summary of the decided cases

Before attempting a synthesis of the present state of the law, it is worth listing and summarising, each of the decisions, noting the words of the review clause concerned with a brief précis of the thread of reasoning involved and the result reached.

Two decisions decided shortly before the *British Gas* case are in accord with the decision in that case. They were quoted with approval and the reasoning in each was adopted by the Vice-Chancellor. They have been influential in establishing the broad commercial purpose to construction:

(1) *Datastream International Ltd v Oakeep Ltd* [1986] 1 WLR 404, Warner J. 'Subject to the provisions of this lease (other than the amount of rent hereby reserved).' Referring with approval to *Lister Locks Ltd v TEI Pension Trust Ltd* (below) and *Pearl Assurance plc v Shaw* (1984) 274 EG 490 the judge preferred the construction which produced a reasonable and fair result and did not require the lessee to pay for a benefit it was not enjoying, namely a lease with no review clause in it. The reasoning of the *Arthur Young* case was not followed; the review provisions were to be included in the calculation process.

(2) *MFI Properties Ltd v BICC Group Pension Trust Ltd* [1986] 1 All ER 974, Hoffman J. 'Having regard to the terms of this lease (other than those relating to rent.' Placing emphasis on the commercial background to a rent review clause, the judge rejected the literal interpretation of the words which would give the valuer an extraordinary set of assumptions, since the long lease of commercial premises without rent reviews was an 'animal not so much fabulous as extinct'. Inclusion of the review provisions into the hypothetical lease was preferred as in accordance with the context and commercial purpose.

(3) *British Gas Corporation v Universities Superannuation Scheme Ltd* [1986] 1 WLR 398 Browne Wilkinson V-C. 'By means of a lease containing the same provisions (other than as to the yearly rent).'

In construing the lease, the judge gave effect to the underlying purpose of the rent review clause and held the rent review provisions were to be included in valuing the lease. The judge formulated principles of construction (set out above).

Subsequent cases have applied the *British Gas* guide-lines:

(4) *Electricity Supply Nominees v FM Insurance Co Ltd* [1986] 1 EGLR 143. 'Upon the terms of this lease other than as to rent.' A deputy judge again preferred adoption of the construction which is consistent with the commercial purpose of rent review clauses with the result that the review provisions were again included.

(5) *Amax International Ltd v Custodian Holdings Ltd* [1986] 2 EGLR 111. Hoffman J applied the general principles of construction from the *MFI* and *British Gas* decisions. The words were again 'other than as to rent', this time in the same clause as the reservation of the original rent. The attempts of counsel for the landlord to found sufficient 'contra indications' to the prima facie approach to construction propounded in the *British Gas* case conspicuously failed.

(6) *British Home Stores plc v Ranbrook Properties Ltd* [1988] 1 EGLR 121, Warner J. 'Upon the terms and conditions (save as to rent) herein contained.' It was held that the words were at the very least ambiguous and therefore did not fall within guide-line (b); applying guide-line (c) and giving effect to the commercial purpose it was right that the review provisions were to be taken into account for otherwise the tenant would be paying for something it did not get.

In some decisions, both before and after the *British Gas* case, the words of the clause have been clear and the hypothetical lease has excluded the review provisions (and thus can not be categorised as falling within guide-line (b)):

(7) *French Kier Property Investments Ltd v Marconi Co Ltd* (unreported, but noted at [1982] 132 NLJ 993–4) where the assumption was the inclusion in the notional lease of the covenants and conditions in the lease 'other than the amount of rent and the provisions of the present clause for reviewing the rent'. It was held that the valuer must find a rent appropriate to a term equal to the unexpired residue of the term without review notwithstanding the fact there would be later reviews periodically. The express reference to the review clause means that the result would still be the same today. Applying the *British Gas* approach, guide-line (a) would not assist since the words directed a clear disregard of the whole review clause within guide-line (b).

(8) *Pugh v Smiths Industries Ltd* (1982) 264 EG 823. 'But excluding therefrom the provisions of this clause.' Once again, these very clear

words could not be disregarded and were given effect though it was recognised that this one-sided assumption produced an unfair result. The tenant's attempt to argue that the clear words should be disregarded on the basis of absurdity or repugnancy failed as did a late claim for rectification. The *British Gas* case itself recognised that this case was rightly decided within guide-line (b).

(9) *Safeway Food Stores v Banderway* (1983) 267 EG 850. 'On the same terms and conditions as are in these presents contained (save for this proviso).' The proviso referred to was that providing for the rent review and it was accepted that the literal meaning excluded all the review clause. The judge said that there was nothing absurd or insensible so the literal meaning must prevail. In the light of the *British Gas* guide-lines it is possible that an opposite conclusion would now be reached but on balance it would appear to be a correct application of guide-line (b).

(10) *Securicor Ltd v PosTel Properties Ltd* [1985] 1 EGLR 102. ' . . . there being disregarded this clause.' Since this, poorly drafted, clause clearly directed disregard of the whole review clause, the review provisions were excluded from the notional lease to be valued.

(11) *General Accident Fire and Life Assurance Corporation plc v Electronic Data Processing Co plc* [1987] 1 EGLR 112. This case differed from the others summarised above in that there was no express assumption that the terms of the lease applied. Eight matters were to be assumed but provisions for rent review were not one of them. Harman J refused to imply any further terms and so the valuation was to assume that there were no review provisions. It is submitted that, after the *Basingstoke and Deane* case, this decision is wrong; the assumption that the terms of the lease are to apply should have brought in the review clause and a similar matter would now be decided differently.

(12) *Equity and Law Life Assurance Society plc v Bodfield Ltd* [1987] 1 EGLR 124. Court of Appeal. 'Upon the terms of this lease other than as to duration and rent.' The lease contained, in the body of the review clause, a provision whereby the tenant only paid 85 per cent of the net rental value ascertained on review. The purpose of the 15 per cent discount was not revealed. It was held that the terms of the lease as to rent would include a reference to the rental discount since the review was to the 'net rental value' defined as the best rent which the premises might fetch and not 85 per cent of the best rent. Since this part of the review clause was 'a term as to rent' then the rest of the review provisions were also such terms and the hypothetical lease therefore contained no review clause. The presence of the 'gearing' provision or discount within the review clause itself led to the exclusion of the whole clause. It is submitted that a more robust application of the *British Gas* guide-lines could have led the court in this instance to the opposite result; the review obligation

could have been incorporated but the concession to 85 per cent of the net rental value excluded by necessary implication as in the *Guys 'N' Dolls* decision (below). The rejection of this argument by Peter Gibson J, however, received appellate approval.

Finally reference may be made to *Telegraph Properties (Securities) Ltd v Courtaulds Ltd* (1981) 257 EG 1153 which concerned a second lease drafted to incorporate and be on the same terms as an earlier lease between the same parties except as to (inter alia) 'the rent reserved'. Notwithstanding the fact that the review clause in the first lease was not specifically excluded from the second lease (as was the case with some provisions), it was held that the 'rent reserved' included a reference to the rent review provisions which were therefore not carried over into the second lease. This case was overruled on the issue of delay (see p 159) and the construction issue might well be decided differently today.

(iv)   The current state of the law

In the light of these cases, it is possible to make the following propositions:

(1) It is quite possible for the parties to agree upon a rent review clause where the valuer is to assume a long lease at rack rent without reviews. In the absence of a claim for rectification (see Chapter 9), the court cannot rewrite the bargain where the words are clear: *Pugh v Smiths Industries*; *Securicor v PosTel*.

(2) Where such an assumption appears, a valuer has to postulate a lease which has no counterpart in the real world (except, perhaps, in options to renew at market rent in long leases granted many years ago without review). An uplift in rent of anything between 10 per cent and 20 per cent results, either by agreement (eg *Electricity Supply Nominees* case) or by 'some more or less arbitrary readjustment' (per Hoffman J) by the valuer or arbitrator.

(3) If the lease is silent on this issue, the passing rent will be impliedly disregarded as this has to be done to arrive at a hypothetical lease into which the new rent can be inserted (see opinion to this effect in the *Datastream* and *Electricity Supply* cases). In such a case, the review provisions would be left intact.

(4) Where the words 'other than as to rent' (or similar phraseology) occur, leaving an ambiguity as to whether this refers to all (or some) provisions relating to rent or only to the quantum of rent initially reserved, then provided that ambiguity can be established or provided that the court is convinced that there are two possible constructions to the provisions, then guide-line (c) of the *British Gas* guide-lines will be applied—*British Home Stores v Ranbrook*.

(5) Fresh leases should avoid the problem exemplified by these cases and ensure the lease only excludes the quantum of passing rent from the hypothetical lease and expressly includes the provisions for review

(as with all versions of the Model Forms—the ISVA clauses chose to rely on the implicit assumption arising from silence). Vigilance is still essential when advising on the assignment of a lease. It appears that tenants locked into *Pugh v Smiths Industries* types of lease have sought redress against their professional advisers for alleged negligence, either in relation to the actual grant or in respect of advice allegedly not given on assignment.

(d) Impact of other terms incorporated

The issue of whether the rent review provisions in the actual lease are incorporated into the hypothetical lease, vividly demonstrated by the *Arthur Young* saga, culminating in the *British Gas* guide-lines, is only the most prominent aspect of the wider principle, namely, that the lease should construct a valuation framework which excludes from consideration those terms (and only those terms) of the actual lease which are not relevant to the determination of the open market rent for the property in issue. There are occasions when certain provisions in the actual lease will be brought into account by the usual express assumption 'that the terms of the lease apply' and may distort the valuation process as much as the exclusion of the rent review provisions. Consequently, it behoves a draftsman incorporating an assumption that the other terms of the lease are to apply to check carefully each of these and expressly to exclude any which are inappropriate, or, alternatively, to clarify exactly how they are to apply at review. Particular problems can arise from:

   (i) Rent discounts or premiums applied to the initial rent or payable as extra rent and still payable after a rent review; do these fall to be taken into account?

   (ii) Non-standard review formulae designed to ensure the rent as reviewed is higher than that which would otherwise be determined; would the hypothetical willing lessee pay less as a result?

   (iii) Options or special rights, privileges or provisions which fall to be operated at a particular point in time during the term. The valuation impact of thse may depend on whether they are assumed at the review date to operate at the actual date or a notional date.

   (iv) The impact of use, alienation and other standard clauses is discussed in separate sections below.

(i) Rent discounts or premiums

Where there is an obligation to pay an extra rent, the courts will lean towards a construction which disregards the existence of that obligation, if necessary implying a term to that effect. Similarly, it follows that the benefit of a rent concession will usually fall to be ignored, particularly if there is a clear reason established for such concession. The explanation is that unless such extra payments or concessions in the actual lease fall to be disregarded in the review process, a review to open market rent will be difficult if not impossible to determine. The willing lessee, if obliged to pay an extra rent, will reduce the basic rent he is willing to pay; or increase it to get the benefit of a rental concession. Thus in *Lister Locks Ltd v TEI Pension Trust Ltd* (1982) 264 EG 827 there was a reservation of both a basic rent and an 'extra rent', the latter being a fixed sum based on the cost of expenditure to meet the original tenant's special needs. The review was to be to 'the fair rack rental market value' for a notional lease 'subject to similar covenants (other than the amount of the rent)' as in the actual lease. After the review, the extra rent was to be increased in the same proportion as the basic rent. It was held that, though the literal words of the lease required the obligation to pay the extra rent to be taken into account (since the disregard was only of the *amount* of the rent reserved), a term was to be implied to give business efficacy to the contract to exclude the extra rent provision from the calculation of fair rack rental value. Otherwise, the landlord would have been compensated twice—once in the reviewed rent and once in the continuing (and increased) extra rent. Similarly, in *Guys 'N' Dolls Ltd v Sade Brothers Catering Ltd* (1983) 269 EG 129, the review was to be 'in all respects on the terms and conditions of this lease'; there was no qualification at all; '(other than as to rent)' was not added. For the second and third periods of the lease, the annual rent (under the lease) was to be £7,500 above the sum determined as the fair rack market value as agreed or settled on third party reference. It was held, first, that the excess £7,500 would have to be disregarded on the first review and, secondly, (reversing the judgment below on this point) that on the first review the future obligation to pay that excess over the rack rent ascertained at the second review, should also be disregarded. These rulings rejected the literal construction of the words which would have required the excess to be taken into account; to do otherwise would result in an 'Alice in Wonderland construction' whereby the obligation to pay the £7,500 would merely be subtracted at review. The result was achieved, again, by implication of terms on the ground of necessity and to give business efficacy to the contract. The Court of Appeal, approving the *Lister Locks* decision, impliedly restricted the strict literal meaning to give effect to the commercial object of the parties.

Not every rent concession or extra rent provision will fall to be disregarded. In the *Lister Locks* decision, emphasis was laid on the factual matrix and the surrounding circumstances which showed how the extra rent represented a rentalised cost of special requirements built in for the original tenants; and in the *Guys 'N' Dolls* case, Robert Goff J was of the view that the result might have been different if the extra rent payable had not been a constant sum. In such a case, the valuer at the first review could take account of the fact the extra rent would be different at the next review. Nevertheless, the strength of the desire not to hinder the calculation of open market rent by taking account of rent concessions or extra rents is shown by *Equity & Law Life Assurance Society v Bodfield* (above) where the court was clear that the provisions for calculating 85 per cent of the net rental value were excluded—even if this meant that the review clause itself was also excluded.

(ii)   Unusual rental formulae

It may not be possible to disregard impliedly some forms of 'extra' rent. Both the *Lister Locks* decision and the *Guys 'N' Dolls* case concerned fixed or proportionately related rent premiums. In other leases of which the authors are aware, attempts have been made to 'build in' express comparables (in the belief that these comparables will produce a higher rent at review) or postulate a notional property in a nearby location where it is believed higher rents per square foot are likely to be obtained and if the rent obtainable for such notional property is higher than that for the actual premises then it is substituted. These provisions will be an integral part of the review clause and, as in *Equity & Law Life Assurance Society v Bodfield*, the review clause will be incorporated into the notional letting as a whole or not at all. The willing lessee in such circumstances will, it is submitted, take account of the impact of such rental formula. Indeed if a poorly drafted review clause in the actual market can affect the value of the reversion and the assignability of a lease (as it does) then it should also be a factor taken into account by the willing lessee to the hypothetical lease.

(iii)   Options and fixed rights and obligations

An option or other right or obligation available to a party at a particular point in time during the term will usually be incorporated into the notional lease but adjusted to fall at the actual date on which the option, right or obligation arises. This will accord with the reality between the parties to the lease. In *R & A Millett (Shops) Ltd v Legal & General Assurance Society Ltd* [1985] 1 EGLR 103 a 35 year lease with 6 yearly reviews contained an option for the landlord to terminate the lease for certain specified purposes (eg to demolish or reconstruct). This option could be given 'after the expiration of the first 12 years of the term hereby granted' by giving the tenant 6 months' written notice. This term was assumed to apply to the hypothetical lease falling to be reviewed at the second review date. The landlord argued that the notional lease should contain the clause verbatim so that for the purposes of rent review the 12 year period commenced again. This approach was rejected; not only would it be a curious provision at the final review date but also it did not accord with the actual state between the parties—for the tenant now held under a lease where 6 months' notice to determine could be given at any time. The deputy judge was of the opinion that where some provisions in the original lease cannot, or cannot sensibly, be read literally into the notional lease (he referred to redecoration covenants as an example) then 'minor adjustments' must be made. In deciding in favour of the tenants construction, he relied upon the object of review clauses to produce a sensible and businesslike commercial result.

If it is desired to exclude such options or other rights, an express disregard will be required—and will be resisted by the party who considers a disadvantage will follow. Similarly, an express provision or clear words will be needed to incorporate the option in the notional lease at a date other than that on which it actually falls.

(e) The precedents

Of the forms reproduced in the Part Seven, all versions of the Model Forms, EFP (5th ed) Form 22 (clause 1.3.6) and Conveyancer Precedent 5–57 introduce the assumption of a letting on the terms of the lease other than that as to the rent reserved but including the review provisions. The three obsolete EFP (4th ed) forms (Form 8:1, Additional Form 76 and Form 7:1) which are still the basis of many review clauses in current leases use the form 'on the same terms and conditions other than *the amount* of the rent . . . as are herein contained'. The italicised words will limit the disregard to fixed amounts (usually only the sum originally reserved) and not include amounts ascertained by means of the rent review formula: *Datastream International Ltd v Oakeep Ltd* [1986] 1 WLR 404. In clauses adopting this wording, the review provisions for the future will be taken into account on each review. *Kelly's Draftsman*, Form 14, surprisingly for a 1979 precedent, does not contain the standard assumption. Now, following the *Basingstoke and Deane* case, it will be implied in such clauses that the valuation is to be on the terms of the actual lease except as to the quantum of rent.

3   Use clauses

A use clause, a common if not invariable provision in all types of commercial lease, may have a significant impact upon the calculation of the revised rent at review and draftsmen should be aware of their implications. Where a lease provides that the premises are confined to use of a particular trade, or even the particular trade of the tenant, this will result in the calculation of the rent being based on that use. The common assumption that the terms of the lease (other than as to the quantum of rent) are to apply have often led to these particular problems in relation to clauses in the lease restrictive of the use of the premises, not only in rent review cases but also in the partly analogous situation of an application for a new tenancy under the 1954 Act where the use clause is (or is most likely to be) carried over into the new tenancy. The construction placed on the lease in such circumstances has significant valuation consequences. The valuation is made in the light of a restricted use, carried over from the actual lease, in the notional letting on review (unless that limitation is expressed not to be taken into account in the rent review valuation or some alternaive or wider use is postulated) or (in cases decided under the 1954 Act) as carried over into the new statutory tenancy.

(a) Use clauses under the 1954 Act

The cases decided under the 1954 Act give some assistance to the problem and, although the situation is not directly comparable in view of the discretion of the court to alter the terms in the new tenancy, they have been influential in later rent review decisions. Thus in *Aldwych Club v Copthall Property Co Ltd* (1962) 185 EG 219, the covenant in the existing lease read not to use the premises 'other than as a club without the previous consent in writing of the lessors which consent shall not be unreasonably refused'. The tenant sought to maintain the same restricted use in the new lease and argued for the rent under the renewal to be for club use and put forward £2,500 p a on that basis. The landlord, who had applied for and obtained planning permission for use as offices, argued successfully that the use clause in the lease should be modified to club or office use and consequently obtained a rent of £5,200 reflecting club or office use. By obtaining permission the landlords prevented any argument that the probable difficulties of obtaining planning permission would depress the market rent. In other circumstances, the poor prospects of obtaining the necessary permission from local authorities of other statutory bodies would be a significant factor to be taken into account.

In another case under the 1954 Act, *Charles Clements (London) Ltd v Rank City Wall Ltd* (1978) 246 EG 739, the relevant clause restricted the use to that of a retail cutler, or any other purpose with previous consent. The landlords were arguing for a relaxation in the new lease by the addition of the qualification 'such consent not to be unreasonably withheld', and stressed the benefit to the tenant of the improved assignability this would bring to the lease. The tenants objected that they did not wish to have to pay the new rent that would follow from the modification, and it was held that the new lease should mirror the old and contain the restricted clause only. The landlord was contending in the proceedings for a rent of £15,000 and the tenants for £9,000; it was stated in argument that the relaxation of the restriction would affect the rent by a figure of £1,750.

Both these decisions were referred to with approval in the *O'May* case (see p 329, above); so that on the one hand the courts will reject an attempt by the landlord, as a means of raising the rent, to force on the tenant a relaxation of the covenant limiting uses which would be of no value to the tenant (see Lord Hailsham's précis of the *Charles Clements* case in *O'May* at 741B), but they will ensure the market rent is paid; so in the *Aldwych Club* case (unlike the *Charles Clements* case) the landlord could not have reasonably refused consent to a change of use to offices, and they were consequently successful in altering the wording of the use clause and obtaining the (higher) rent for office use.

(b)   Use clauses at rent review

The rulings in these statutory renewal decisions are mirrored in the problems at rent review. If the actual lease contains an absolute prohibition, or a qualified limitation (ie 'without consent'), these clauses will also appear in the hypothetical letting. The pool of willing lessees can only include those who are able to comply with those known limitations. Since there is no statutory provision incorporating a proviso that consent is not to be unreasonably withheld, a clause postulating consent will be treated as virtually equivalent to an absolute limitation. On the other hand, an express fully qualified covenant ('except with the consent of the landlord, such consent not to be unreasonably withheld') will open up the pool of willing lessees for all those uses for which consent cannot be unreasonably withheld.

(i)   Exact wording vital

The exact wording of the restriction, and its relation to assignability (and any restriction thereon), are central to construction of the lease and the valuation consequences of that construction. On a rent review, unlike statutory renewal, there is no prospect, short of agreement by both parties, of changing the framework laid down in the lease. There is no room, as in the actual market, for any bargaining to alter or remove the use restriction. The hypothetical lessee, however 'willing', is one whose bid will be made in the light of the known restriction.

(ii)   'Positive' and 'negative' clauses

The type of use clause may be positive or negative, usually the latter (eg 'not to use the premises other than for . . . '). A positive covenant 'to use for (particular use) only' penalises non-use as well as a use contrary to the permitted one (*Creery v Summersell* [1949] Ch 751). The type of covenant requiring the tenant to keep the shop open during normal business hours is a positive one. Though it seems that it cannot be enforced by injunction (*F W Woolworth plc v Charlwood Alliance Properties plc* [1987] 1 EGLR 53), breach may give rise to substantial damages: *Costain Property Developments Ltd v Finlay & Co Ltd* [1989] 1 EGLR 237; *Transworld Land Co Ltd v J Sainsbury plc* [1990] EGCS 49 (where the damages included a substantial sum for the adverse effect on other rent reviews of closure of an 'anchor' tenant). If, as a result of the implications of the *Costain* decision, such covenants are perceived as a potential burden and unacceptable in the market, then their presence at a review may have a some depressing effect on the rent. The risk, which cannot be discounted, that an appellate court would allow injunctions, may add to the perception by tenants that such clauses are no longer to be accepted without question.

The more significant issue, however, is whether the covenant (whether positive or negative) is qualified by the words 'without consent, such consent not to be unreasonably withheld', as in the *Aldwych* case. Here, the valuation consequences are less severe, for the valuer can assume the most profitable use for which consent would reasonably be forthcoming. On the other hand, an absolute limitation of use, without qualification, can have a very marked impact at review.

(c)   Absolute limitations on use

A restriction on use, which does not admit of the possibility of consent to a change, allows a lessor to refuse any request for a change—however reasonable that request might be. A willing lessee will make his rental bid in the light of that restriction if it is carried over, as is normally the case, into the hypothetical letting.

(i)   The Plinth Property decision

An absolute limitation on the use to which the demised premises may be put in the actual lease will bind the notional willing tenant and no account can be taken of the possibility that it might be waived: *Plinth Property Investments Ltd v Mott, Hay & Anderson* (1978) 38 P & CR 361. The lease there restricted use to 'offices . . . in connection with the lessee's business of consulting civil engineers'. The arbitrator found that the rent was to be £89,200 p a if the requirement in the rent review clause to have 'regard to . . . the provision of this (under) lease other than the rents hereby reserved' precluded consideration of a possible consent to change of use or under-letting of the whole or part (which was also forbidden), or £130,455 if it did not.

The court dealt with two questions of law submitted from the arbitrator, holding first, on the construction of the lease, that the premises could only be used for the business of consulting engineers throughout the term and any assignee would be bound by that restriction; and secondly that the arbitrator could not take account of the possibility that the use clause might be waived or modified by the lessor. Unlike the earlier two cases under the Landlord and Tenant Act 1954, no questions of relaxing the covenant (and reflecting that change in the level of rent) arose; the arbitrator had to interpret the lease as it stood. Slynn J at 368–9 based his judgment at first instance, upholding the lower rent, on the proposition that:

'. . . the right course is to look . . . at the wording of the lease (at 368–9);
I do not consider that (the arbitrator) was required to consider whether it would be more or less likely that consent would be given for a change of user, or for what purpose the change of user might take place . . .'

In the Court of Appeal, which upheld the judge below, Lord Denning laid stress on the second element:

'[The arbitrator] could not possibly assess the rent on the basis that the landlord would always relax or waive a clause of this kind wholly gratuitously. A landlord would never do that unless he were paid a considerable sum—and how is one to work that sum out? It is all hypothetical. It is so intangible it cannot be done' (at 372).

That approach leaves open the prospect of taking account of possible relaxations in restrictions where evidence is available to remove the element of hypothesis. Brandon LJ's brief judgment takes a stronger line, which would not support such a broader view. He said (at 373):

'The arbitrator is not to say to himself "Those who have rights may not enforce them and those who have obligations may not be required to perform them". He is to assume that the rights will be enforced and that the obligations will be performed. He is to look to the legal position of the parties and nothing else.'

The final sentence is particularly uncompromising. The third member of the Court of Appeal, Shaw LJ, favoured the Denning view.

There has been some criticism of the decision—for example, by Bernstein in his Blundell Memorial Lecture of 1979 (at p 11) and by Hill in the same lecture (at pp 28-9)—and the criticism is not unnaturally repeated in Bernstein and Reynolds at para 5-5. The approach of Lord Denning is questioned because the reasoning is based on matters of fact on which no finding had been made in the actual case and on which findings might vary—so that in some instances it may be possible to find evidence that lessors do willingly relax use restrictions without payment (and ironically, after the *Plinth Property* decision, they have every incentive to do so!). The approach of Lord Brandon is clearly a proposition of law but it is argued that if the real world is one where absolute restrictions may be waived then arbitrators should be able to assess that prospect. There is force in these submissions but the contrary view is to return to the actual arrangements between the current parties to the lease. They are bound by its terms and these can only be altered by mutual consent. The object of the review is to ascertain the open market rent subject to those terms which will continue to bind the parties after the review. The *Plinth Property* decision does therefore accord with the trend to ensure that the tenant 'pays for what he gets' and to assume, unless the contrary is expressed, that the terms of the hypothetical letting are the same as those under the actual lease.

Whatever the merits of the *Plinth Property* ruling, a further concern is the wide disparity between the two levels of rent established by the arbitrator's award which is regarded with some scepticism. In particular, the critics ask: 'Was the initial agreed rent affected by the 'tight' restriction on use?' If not, they say, the differential on review is hard to justify (see also p 257). At least, any attempt to cite the decision as establishing a given numerical discount will be most unlikely to be persuasive.

(ii) Limitations to the Plinth Property principle

The decision in the *Plinth Property* case has been distinguished in two first instance decisions and the judges have declined to follow its reasoning in cases where they might well have done so.

In the *Forte & Co Ltd v General Accident Life Assurance Ltd* [1986] 2 EGLR 115 Peter Gibson J treated the *Plinth Property* case as one turning on the wording of the particular lease—which permitted only one form of use. In the case before him, the complex use clause resulted in a wide variety of uses, prohibiting some but permitting others. In superior leases of the property, however, more tightly drawn use clauses applied, and the judge held that an arbitrator or valuer *could* take account of the fact that the superior lessors might authorise other forms of use and relax those restrictions. It was a matter for the arbitrator. He might say that the possibility of the superior lessors acting arbitrarily (as they were entitled to do) meant that the specified forms of use were the only permitted ones for valuation assessment. Equally he could say that a hypothetical lessee would pay more for a lease which did contemplate the possibility of a change of use, if evidence was forthcoming that that was a real factor. With respect, it seems difficult to reconcile this reasoning with the Court of Appeal ruling.

In *Rushmoor Borough Council v Goacher* [1985] 2 EGLR 140, Mervyn Davies J decided that the *Plinth Property* decision had no relevance where the landlord, successfully, claimed that an arbitrator could take account of development potential. The lease directed the valuation 'to have regard to all the circumstances then existing including any (planning) permission'. Any development potential was an existing circumstance if shown by professional evidence to exist; the fact that the lease also directed attention to the existing use and extant planning permissions was no ground for preventing the arbitrator from taking proved development potential into his calculations. (Development potential is further discussed at p 377, below).

(d) Use confined to the particular business of the tenant

The first principle of law in the *Plinth Property* case—namely that the restricted use applied throughout the term and was therefore a term also of the hypothetical letting—will apply to those clauses where assignees are bound by the same restriction, such as 'the business of consulting engineers'. Thus in *SI Pension Trustees Ltd v Ministerio De Marina de la Republica Peruana* [1988] 1 EGLR 119 the use clause read: 'not to use the demised premises otherwise than as offices in connection with the lessees' business as mortgage and finance consultants'. It was held that the willing lessee would be one using the premises for a mortgage and finance consultancy and an assignee would be equally restricted.

Attempts to urge a construction which treated the reference to the business as surplusage failed; nor could the *Law Land* decision, below, be called in aid to write in a blank space for the hypothetical lessee's business.

The *Plinth Property* principle may not apply if the clause only refers to 'the business of the lessee' as such a wording could bring in the business of any assignee of the term. It will be a question of construction in each case as to whether the reference to the lessee's business is only descriptive or permissive (in which case it will not bind either an assignee or be a factor in the hypothetical letting) or mandatory (when it will so bind). Thus in *J T Sydenham & Co Ltd v Enichem Elastomers Ltd* [1989] 1 EGLR 257 the relevant clause read:

'Not to carry on upon the premises any trade or business of an obnoxious or offensive character but to use the demised premises for the ordinary purposes of the tenant's business that is for the manufacture and export of synthetic rubber and latices . . .'

The nature of the clause enabled a construction which read the reference to the tenant's business as a permissive one—which was fortunate for the lessor since there were only six companies in the United Kingdom in the synthetic rubber business who could have formed the pool of willing lessees had the restriction been carried over into the hypothetical lease.

(e)   Use confined to a particular tenant—'personal use' clauses

There is a particular problem with 'personal use' clauses which confine the use to the original and named tenant. This may be illustrated by the unreported case of *London Scottish Properties Ltd v Council for Professions Supplementary to Medicine* (8 November 1977) and the difficulty of relating such clauses to rent review shown by *Law Land Co Ltd v Consumers' Association Ltd* (1980) 255 EG 617. Both cases were decisions of the Court of Appeal and dealt with use clauses confining use to the particular tenant.

(i)   Construction of a 'personal use' clause

In the *London Scottish* case, use was confined to 'offices in connection with the lessees' business for the purpose of the Council for Professions Supplementary to Medicine'. The originating summons sought determination of the true construction of the use clause for the purposes of rent review, the lessors contending that the words 'for the purpose (etc)' were descriptive only. This was rejected, notwithstanding the fact that use only in connection with the purposes of the Council meant that the lease was rendered virtually unassignable. It should be stressed that this decision related to the meaning of the use clause in the actual lease and not to the proper construction of the rent review clause— for the Court of Appeal was not asked to rule whether the clause was incorporated into the hypothetical letting.

(ii)   The Law Land decision

The *London Scottish* decision was distinguished, as relating only to the construction of the use clause and not to the rent review clause, in the *Law Land* case where the Consumers' Association had agreed not, without prior consent of the landlord, to use the premises otherwise than as offices for the Association and its associated organisations. While reaching a similar conclusion to that in *London Scottish* on the terms of the actual lease (namely that there was to be use only by the Consumers' Association etc) nevertheless the review clause postulated an open market, vacant possession and willing lessor and lessee, in accordance with the provisions of the lease; in other words, it created a hypothetical situation. To write in a restriction of use to the actual tenant, it was held, would make nonsense of the review clause, for there would be only one hypothetical lessee. To avoid that result, it was held that the surveyor was to assume that the open market notional lessee would be entitled to a lease in the form of the existing lease, save that his name would be substituted in the use clause. Assuming, say, a multi-national corporation (and its associated companies) as a potential tenant in place of the non-profit making actual tenant had obvious valuation effect.

It seems clear that in the *Law Land* case, the court was determined to avoid the absurd result of a valuer being directed to set an open market rent, yet having to assume that the premises could only be let to one specified tenant, and whatever view one might have on the logic of the argument, the result is closer to what one can presume was intended by the parties. This early landmark decision accords with the now dominant approach that the commercial purpose of rent review means that the court should seek to ensure that the review clause is made to operate but it is not to move 'away from reality' more than is required for that purpose.

The *Law Land* decision certainly does not mean that the restriction on use had no valuation implications at review. The hypothetical lessee would be taking a lease which might be difficult, if not impossible, to assign (because the tight use restriction still operated) and that factor may well lead to a depressing effect on the market rent. Nevertheless, it is a little ironic that the result may be that an actual restriction to a particular tenant can or may have a smaller impact on valuation than one (as in *Plinth Property*) with a restriction to a trade or profession with a limited number of operators. Just such a result occurred in *SI Pension Trustees Ltd v Ministerio De Marina de la Republica Peruana* (above) where the *Law Land* decision was distinguished as relating to a named individual; it was not posssible to write in a blank for the words 'mortgage and finance consultancy'.

Finally, it is significant that there was no attempt in the *Law Land* case to argue that the possibility that the landlord might consent to a change of use should be taken into account—notwithstanding the fact that the restriction on use in the lease postulated that consent might be forthcoming.

(iii)   Limits to the applicability of the Law Land ruling

Use clauses which restrict use in some way to the particular original tenant will only be amended in the hypothetical letting if and so far as it is necessary to ensure an open market calculation: *James v British Craft Centre* [1987] 1 EGLR 139 where the decision in *Law Land* was distinguished. The relevant use clause prohibited use except for:

> (i)   high class business, commercial or professional offices; or
>
> (ii) in respect of such part of the premises 'occupied and used by the lessee (here meaning the British Crafts Centre)' for storage sale and display of craftsmen's work and as an office and studio for the trade of designers, advertising and press agents.

The Court of Appeal, upholding Scott J, rejected the landlord's submission that the court should prefer a construction which did not cut down the number of potential lessees for the hypothetical lease. The hypothetical lease should contain the tenants' covenants from the original lease; otherwise an assignee of the term (not the British Crafts Centre) would be obliged to pay for an assumed permitted use (storage, etc) which was not actually permitted. The tenants' construction which treated subclause (ii) as a personal privilege to the British Crafts Centre, and not a general right of storage and sale of craftsmen's work was therefore preferred. The reference to British Crafts Centre was to remain in the hypothetical lease.

The *Law Land* case was distinguished and treated as a case where 'some change had to be made' and where removing the actual tenant's name from the use clause was necessary to enable sense to be made of the requirement of an open market rent. As May LJ remarked of the *Law Land* decision:

'. . . in that case one has to do a certain amount of injury to the literal wording of the lease in order to enable just that open market to be looked at as and when the review dates came up.'

In the *James* case there would be a substantial market for 'high class business, commercial or professional offices' so an open market rent could be assessed notwithstanding the *additional* limited permitted use in favour of the British Crafts Centre in the hypothetical letting. 'The hypothetical open market can well exist and can be easily considered on the terms of the instant lease as they stand'. Once again therefore the courts ensure that the actual terms are incorporated in the hypothetical letting except in so far as is necessary to achieve an open market valuation:

'Effect must be given as closely as possible to what the parties have agreed;

otherwise there would be a disparity between the effect of the actual lease under which the rent after all is to be paid and the effect of the hypothetical lease which is to provide a measure of that rent' (per Bingham LJ at 142D).

The *James* case can be contrasted with *Sterling Land Office Developments Ltd v Lloyds Bank plc* (1984) 271 EG 894 where the *Law Land* decision was applied where the use clause was limited 'not . . . for any purpose other than a branch of Lloyds Bank Ltd' and Harman J found the analogy between the case before him and *Law Land* compelling. In this lease, some change did have to be made. Consequently for the purposes of the determination of the market rent, the use clause read 'not to be used for any purposes other than the premises of the hypothetical willing lessee'.

Reference may also be made to the unusual use clause in *C & A Pension Trustees Ltd v British Vita Investments Ltd* (1974) 272 EG 63 where the tenant could not use the property for any purpose other than a trade or business authorised in writing by the lessor. A consent was given by deed in a detailed way for the foam, textile and fibre business of the tenant. An attempt by the lessors, 9 days before the review date, unilaterally to authorise the tenants to use the premises for any business within three stated classes of the Use Classes Order and so widen the use assumption at review failed. An authorisation under the lease presupposed a request by the tenant. The clause made no reference to whether the authorisation of the lessor could be unreasonably withheld but the decision can be justified if the view was that it could. The decision was criticised by Hoffman J in *Tea Trade Properties Ltd v CIN Properties Ltd* [1990], 1 EGLR 155 who was of the view that:

'The question at rent review is not the use to which the actual tenant might wish to put the premises, but the purpose for which the hypothetical tenant in the open market might wish to use it.'

The authors repectfully agree; but with the proviso that the actual tenant must also be able legally to use it for the same (more profitable) purposes should he so wish. It is to this latter issue that the *Plinth Properties* decision is concerned.

(f) Use clauses with the addition of the words 'without consent'

This form of use clause, which featured in the *Charles Clements* case (above), differs from an absolute use restriction, in that it postulates consent might be forthcoming; yet it does not state in terms that consent cannot be unreasonably withheld. Moreover, though s 19(3) of the Landlord and Tenant Act 1927 imports a term into such use clauses that no premium, fine or sum of money in the nature of a fine shall be payable for the lessor's licence or consent to change of use, there is nothing comparable to s 19(2) of the Act to import a term that consent shall not be withheld unreasonably, though s 19(3) does import a term that no fine or premium is to be required for consent where change involves no structural alteration. Here the landlord has an arbitrary right to refuse consent but, if it is granted, cannot demand more than costs and a sum for diminution of value, where appropriate.

It had been argued on the basis of a dictum in *Bocardo SA v S & M Hotels Ltd* [1980] 1 WLR 17, that s 19(2) merely makes statutory what would have been an implied term of the contract; so that, if the words 'without consent' appear in a use clause, it can be implied that consent cannot be unreasonably withheld. The argument was a logically attractive one that, if there is no such implied term, the words 'without consent' add nothing to, and subtract nothing from, the effect of the clause without those words. However, the point has been rejected: *Guardian Assurance Co Ltd v Gants Hill Holdings Ltd* (1983) 267 EG 678. Mervyn Davies J declined to follow the *Bocardo* dictum and held that no such term could be implied.

This decision was contrary to the prior tendency in practice to apply the *Bocardo* dictum; but until the point is raised in a higher court (as it might well be) the *Guardian Assurance* decision shows that use clauses which do not expressly provide for consent not to be unreasonably withheld will have to be treated as absolute limitations (subject only to s 19(3)) from which the valuation consequences of the *Plinth Property* decision may flow.

The approach of *Guardian Assurance Co Ltd v Gants Hill Holdings Ltd* was followed in *Pearl Assurance plc v Shaw* [1985] 1 EGLR 92 where Vinelott J also declined to apply the dictum in the *Bocardo* case in another context. The lease in question provided that 'the tenant should not make any application for planning permission without the prior written consent of the landlord'. The judge noted that while, on their face, the words requiring consent added little to the bald prohibition of the making of planning applications, nevertheless the clause as a whole would have read oddly without them, prohibiting both a change of use without planning consent and a covenant not to apply for such consent. The judge also felt that in the context of a professionally drawn lease, the omission of the words 'such consent not to be unreasonably withheld' must be taken to be deliberate.

(g) 'Fully qualified' use clauses

A use clause which permits other uses 'with consent of the lessor, such consent not to be unreasonably withheld', (a 'fully qualified' use clause) enables the valuer or arbitrator to value the demised premises for the actual use or for any other more profitable use for which the lessor could not reasonably refuse consent. The review to open market rent, prima facie, means that the valuer must consider every potential tenant for any purpose for which the premises could be physically and legally used. This principle was established in the statutory renewal case of *Aldwych Club v Copthall Property Co Ltd* (1962) 185 EG 219, noted above, and has been confirmed for rent review by *Tea Trade Properties Ltd v CIN Properties Ltd* [1990] 1 EGLR 155, Hoffman J. There the fully qualified use clause provided for use as commercial premises with ancillary offices. A change in planning policy meant that the area had beeen re-zoned for general office use and the lessors had obtained planning permission for such use. At review, the tenants sought a declaration of an assumed use of commercial premises with ancillary offices but the judge rejected this and granted the lessors a declaration that it be assumed that the premises can be used entirely as offices. There was no physical objection to such use, and attempts to show a legal objection from the terms of the lease were unsuccessful. The proviso to the landlord's consent governed the whole clause; a request by the hypothetical tenant for use as offices could not be unreasonably refused. A clause prohibiting development was also construed as not preventing use as offices.

A tenant should consider carefully when taking the grant or assignment of a lease with a fully qualified covenant when the proposed actual use may carry a lower rental value than an alternative use for which consent could not, or may not in the future, be unreasonably withheld. For example, a lease of licensed premises in a new shopping arcade limits use to that of a public house but the use clause is fully qualified so that consent for change to retail use could not be unreasonably refused. At the date of the lease, the local planning authority insist on at least one licensed premises in the development so the original rent reflects that appropriate for licensed use. By the review date, the view of the planning authority has changed so that retail use would be accepted. The review will, prima facie and subject to the terms of the lease, be at the more profitable rent for retail use. It then becomes important to consider two further factors:

(i) Any assumption that the premises are fully fitted out (see p 418) can work injustice. It is one thing to assume the premises are fitted for the actual use; quite another for an assumed use which would require fitting out in the real world.

(ii) The tenant can be further disadvantaged by sub-letting. Thus on the facts in the *Tea Trade* case, or in the example postulated, the tenant could always seek to assign for the more profitable office or retail use if the reviewed rent was more than the business could bear. If, however, there has been a sub-letting (say) for the actual use as a public house without the possibility of change of use to retail premises the tenant under the head lease may find the reviewed rent reflects the more profitable retail use while recovery of rent under the sub-lease is on the basis of licensed use.

(h) General approach to construction of the use clause

If the nature of the use restriction can have such a significant impact at review, it is not surprising that litigation as to the meaning of the use clause often occurs in the context of rent review.

(i)   The commercial purpose emphasised

The recent trend of emphasising the underlying commercial purpose of rent review clauses as an aid to construction of leases (see p 309) can be seen in both the result and the judicial comments by Vinelott J in *Pearl Assurance plc v Shaw* [1985] 1 EGLR 92. The judge had to construe a provision 'to take no account of . . . any restriction on use of the demised premises apart from such use of the demised premises as the landlord may from time to time permit'. This was an 'absurd provision' as the judge noted since if all restrictions are left out of account, all possible uses, permitted or not, can be taken into account. Counsel for the landlord attempted to give some meaning to the words by relating them to later clauses in the lease, but this involved some artificiality. The tenant boldly argued that the words 'to the extent of' should be substituted for the words 'apart from'—a substitution of words of precisely the opposite meaning. In accepting the tenant's submission, the judge held:

(1) He should have regard to the purpose of a rent review clause, namely to bring the rent up to date, or to that the parties might have been expected to agree in the light of conditions prevailing at the time of the review. On that basis, he considered a court should lean against a construction which requires the rent to be fixed without regard to the use which, under the lease, the tenant is entitled to make of the demised premises—unless such an intent is clearly spelt out. The judge considered that to hold otherwise would be to make the tenant pay for something he not only has not got but which he cannot require the landlord to give him.

(2) The words 'may from time to time permit' pointed to permission subsequent to the lease and *not* given by the lease, which did not accord with the landlord's construction.

(ii)   Use clause by reference to use classes

The use to which the premises may be put in the notional letting may be defined by reference to the Use Classes Order. This may be the result of either the clause in the actual lease containing such a reference and being incorporated into the notional letting or the review clause itself postulating the use assumed at review.

There has been a tendency, particularly since the *Plinth Properties* decision, not only to avoid narrow use clauses but, on the contrary, to make a consent to a change of the permitted use fully qualified and to define, in the use clause in the lease, the range of permitted uses to which consent to a change of use will not be unreasonably withheld.

This ensures that, at review, the lessor secures the rental value of the most profitable of this range of uses to which the premises could be put at review. Reference to a particular class of the Use Classes Order has the advantage, for this purpose, of securing the rental value of all those uses for which planning permission need not be obtained. A tenant must always appreciate that the consequence may be that the reviewed rent will be based on a use that the tenant does not actually adopt, does not wish (perhaps) to adopt, but could legally do under the terms of the lease.

There is no presumption that any reference to a statute or statutory instrument in a lease is a reference to the law for the time being in force. Where there is a reference to the Use Classes Order, it will be a matter of proper construction of the terms of the lease whether the reference is to the existing order when the issue arises or the one in force when the lease is executed: *Brewers' Company v Viewplan plc* [1989] 2 EGLR 133. In that case, the reference in the lease was to the 1972 order; there was no reference to any future statutory modification (as there was with references to primary planning legislation). The landlord's attempt to secure a ruling in favour of a more profitable reference to class B1 in the 1987 order failed. A specific reference in a lease to the possibility of statutory modification of the Use Classes Order is probably required to take advantage of any changes in use classes.

A usual wording in leases is that references to either a named statute or statutes generally are taken as references to any statute re-enacting or modifying the statute and any orders or regulations made thereunder. So far as re-enactment is concerned, the provision is probably redundant having regard to s 17 of the Interpretation Act 1978. In the context of any Use Classes Order, however, the issue arises as to whether 're-enactment or modification' only relates to statutes or also covers regulations. Thus the Use Classes Order 1988 was made under the same statute as the order it replaced. It may be sheer chance whether future orders are made under the same or a new or amending statute. The usual wording could have an arbitrary effect so that orders under later statutes were not included. It may be better to recast the phrase to refer to 'orders and regulations made under the [specified] statute or any statute, order or regulation re-enacting or modifying such earlier statute order or regulation'.

The position where the reference is to the Use Classes Order, without any version indicated by year and with no 'widening' definition, is uncertain. The decision in *Brett v Brett Essex Golf Club Ltd* [1986] 1 EGLR 154 (see p 446) may lend support for the view that reference is intended to the version in force when the lease is made—especially if (as in that case) the particular class referred to can only make sense in that version. On the other hand, the trend towards 'reality' may point to the opposite result. (The possibility that any new order would resolve the private law issue by providing that references in existing documents will be to the new order is remote).

It may be appropriate to define the use in the notional lease expressly by reference to the appropriate class in the dated Use Classes Order where the actual use is an unusual or unique one. However, if the actual use is one which does not fall into any of the classes, problems may result. Thus, in *Wolff v London Borough of Enfield* [1987] 1 EGLR 119 the lease provided that the reviewed rent was to be the best annual rent for a letting as a whole with vacant possession 'for use for any purpose within Class III of the Town and Country Planning (Use Classes) Order 1972 or any other class within which falls the use or uses of the demised premises permitted by the planning authority from time to time'. The premises were former light industrial works and Class III was the class appropriate for light industrial buildings. The premises were used as a non-teaching service unit for the Middlesex Polytechnic. The planning permission for such use was personal to the Polytechnic as a non-teaching Service Unit and the actual uses to which the property was put included offices, printing and storage. The Court of Appeal held that the planning permission authorised a composite use which did not fall within any of the class or classes of the Use Classes Order. Consequently, the rent was to be reviewed upon the basis of a value of the premises as a whole for light industrial use—their actual use had to be ignored.

(iii)   Prohibited uses and actual uses

Where a use clause is in the form of a series of prohibitions, followed by provisos modifying those prohibitions, it has been held that the use is not thereby confined to the actual use to which the premises are put for review purposes: *Forte & Co Ltd v General Accident Life Assurance Co Ltd* (1986) 279 EG 1227. The lease in question was of premises used as the Cafe Royal and the provisos expressly envisaged use as a high class licensed cafe restaurant. The tenant's argument that the effect of these provisos were to limit the permitted use to the actual use failed. For example, the only prohibition on office use was the rather quaint one preventing use as a railway or carrier's parcels office. It followed, said the judge, that all other office use was allowed and this should be a factor, if relevant, in the assessment of the reviewed rent.

(iv)   'High class uses'

References to 'high class' categories of particular uses are not, as the authors must confess to having once suspected, surplusage or window dressing. At the lowest, four cases can now be cited in which judges have sought to give effect to the epithet, namely, *Rossi v Hestdrive Ltd* (1984) 274 EG 928, *Patoner Ltd v Lowe* [1985] 2 EGLR 154 and *Patoner Ltd v Alexandrakis* (1984) 272 EG 330. The first of these cases concerned consent to assignment; the latter two were both actions for possession which successfully alleged that subtenancies breached a covenant requiring high class furnished accommodation. In *Ropemaker Properties Ltd v Noonhaven Ltd* [1989] 2 EGLR 50, the phrase was 'not to use . . . other than as a high-class restaurant/night club to include music, dancing and cabaret and gambling'—a somewhat ironical description as the basis of forfeiture was the incidence of sexual immorality based on the premises and the activities of its hostesses.

(j)   Use clauses and assignability

An absolute use restriction may have a substantial effect on the assignability of a lease (*Sykes v Midland Bank Executor and Trustee Co Ltd* [1971] 1 QB 113); so a draftsman of a lease, or the valuer at review, must consider the interrelationship of the use clause to any clause prohibiting or limiting the right to assign the lease. If there is a wide use clause, or none at all, coupled with a right to assign with consent, the lessee is quite free to assign a suitable person; the presence of the common clause prohibiting assignment unless the tenant first offers to surrender and the landlord does not accept (a device which received the Court of Appeal's approval in the *Bocardo* case) will limit the likelihood of the tenant obtaining a premium on assignment, and with the problems raised by the decision in *Allnatt London Properties Ltd v Newton* (1982) 265 EG 601 there may well be adverse valuation consequences on review (we discuss the issues further at p 368, below).

The impact of restrictions on alienation are fully discussed below (p 365). The point to stress is that it is the combination of a tight use clause coupled with an absolute or restricted prohibition on assignment which can lead to valuation difficulty, often reducing the open market rent as in the *Plinth Property* decision. Even in cases like *London Scottish Properties* and the *Law Land* decisions the combination of an apparent right to assign to third parties with consent, coupled with a use clause restricting use to the particular tenant, created incongruity in the leases and raises the complex questions of construction and valuation previously discussed, showing that even freedom to alienate will be a hollow right if there is a very limited permitted use.

The lease in *James v British Crafts Centre* [1987] 1 EGLR 139 contained an absolute prohibition on alienation of part or sub-letting or sharing possession of the whole as well as use restrictions. A proviso to such alienation restriction did allow the lessee to share occupation with a holding or subsidiary company 'but only while the lessee is the British Crafts Centre'. It was held by Scott J that in the hypothetical lease to be valued at review the reference to the name of the lessee should be left blank. The judge viewed the alienation clause proviso of giving a privilege to the first person who happened to be the lessee and not a personal privilege to the British Crafts Centre. As noted more fully at p 367 below, there was no appeal on this conclusion but the Court of Appeal doubted its correctness when upholding the judge on the interpretation of the use clause.

The exact combination of the use and alienation clauses will depend on the construction of the particular lease and it behoves the draftsman to consider them together and their operation at review. Alienation covenants will normally be 'fully qualified' (ie it will be expressly, or by virtue of s 19 of the 1927 Act impliedly, subject to a proviso that consent will not be withheld) in relation to assignment of the whole but may be more restricted in relation to alienation of part or sharing possession. User clauses will either be expressly fully qualified, or contain little by way of restriction or contain a variety of restrictions which may be more or less severe. Nevertheless, four broad categories of lease will be found:

(i)   Those with a fully qualified or relatively unrestricted use clause and a fully qualified alienation clause

There should be little or no valuation difficulties at review for the lessor. The tenant needs to be aware that the open market rent for such a lease may reflect a rent for a use other than that for which it is actually used (see, eg, the *Tea Trade* decision, above).

(ii)   Those with a restricted or limited use clause, not fully qualified, but no abnormal restrictions on alienation

Such leases may result in an adverse valuation impact at review for the lessor. The exact consequence will depend on the construction and effect of the use clause as discussed above.

(iii)   Those with a fully qualified or relatively unrestricted use clause but a more limited right to alienate

This will be an unusual combination. The valuation effect will depend solely on the extent to which the restrictions on alienation would be unacceptable to the willing lessee. An absolute or very restricted right to alienate may make the lease practically unassignable but available on that basis to the willing lessee for any use for which consent could not be unreasonably withheld.

(iv)   Those with both a tight or absolute use clause and with absolute restrictions on alienation

Such leases will have the greatest impact on review if the result is to present the notional willing lessee with a lease which is effectively unassignable and only on offer to a limited pool of lessees.

(k)   The valuation consequences

The cases discussed illustrate the necessity to construe the review clauses in the context of the lease as a whole and show again how the hypotheses on which a review is to be conducted can lead to a result, in relation to rent, removed from the reality of the tenant's true position. A central factor will be the actual wording of the restrictive use clause itself. At one end of the spectrum, a clause restricting use to 'offices' may be of no valuation consequence since it is commonly occurring and may be the purpose for which the premises are designed. By way of contrast the *Plinth Property* case shows that an absolute prohibition can have a significant effect on the rent (it being stated that the open market rent without restriction would be £130,455; but with the use limited to consulting engineers, only £89,200—a reduction of some 30 per cent).

Between the extremes of absolute prohibition on the one hand, and a very general limitation (or none at all) on the other, many varied examples of use clauses will occur. No doubt, in conducting the valuation exercise, the impact of the particular restriction on the market will be a matter of professional valuation judgment. There will be additional problems where the use restrictions are cast in the form of the 'trading monopoly' style, listing what may be sold in one property and preventing such sales in other adjoining properties. Discussion of the topic in detail is beyond the scope of this work but the decisions to be studied include *Lewis & Co (Westminster) Ltd v Property Trust Ltd* [1940] Ch 345, *Bier v Danser* (1951) 157 EG 552, *Labone v Litherland Urban District Council* [1956] 1 WLR 522, *Rother v Colchester Corporation* [1969] 1 WLR 720, *Calabar (Woolwich) Ltd v Tesco Stores Ltd* (1977) 245 EG 479 and *St Marylebone Property Co Ltd v Tesco Stores Ltd* [1988] 2 EGLR 40. There are many others. The previous comments show the danger of trying to generalise the valuation consequences. Nevertheless, the presence of use clauses at review or renewal may lead to a discount in the rent obtained of between 10–30 per cent. A few examples can be given:

(1) In *Duvan Estates Ltd v Rossette Sunshine Savouries Ltd* (1981) 261 EG 364, an arbitrator made a 10 per cent reduction (from £7,500) on review in the light of an absolute prohibition (not to use the premises for any purpose other than making meat pies and pasties). The court held he had applied the correct principle of law and the amount of reduction was one purely for his own judgment.

(2) By way of contrast, there is the renewal case of *UDS Tailoring Ltd v BL Holdings Ltd* (1981) 261 EG 49. There the reduction was also 10 per cent (from £23,761), though the use clause was very different. Though the use was restricted to bespoke and ready-to-wear tailors and outfitters, the lessor could not unreasonably refuse a change of use to one not in conflict with another retail trade or business in the particular block. Taking the two cases side by side, it may be thought that a greater reduction was appropriate in the former case or perhaps it is merely confirmation that the art of valuation is not a science.

(l) Use clauses—the drafting response

From the *lessor's* point of view, a decision must be made as to the extent of control required by the use clause and the valuation impact of such control on the willing lessee in an open market at review. If the degree of control desired will or might depress the rent, then a choice must be made between control and income. The only alternative is to attempt to divorce the actual control in the lease from a wider assumed use at review. This will naturally be resisted by tenants; moreover, in the absence of clear words separating the actual terms from the notional letting, the courts may prefer a construction which accords with the reality (see Chapter 10, p 314). From the *tenant's* point of view, the main concern will be, first, to ensure that at review the interrelation of the use, assignment and review clause does not result in the tenant paying for what he does not get and, secondly, to seek to limit the problem exemplified by the *Tea Trade* case where the tenant pays at review for a use it does not want. The consequence may well be that the traditional roles are reversed; the tenant may seek a more restricted use clause than the lessor.

There are a number of possible approaches:

(1) To 'delete' the use clause, or put in a clause consistent with the market's perception of what is an acceptable level of use control, so that any valuation consequence is minimised. For the lessor this is probably the best course of action unless there is a good reason for restricting the use of the premises more tightly than the market at review would accept. An example of a use clause which ought to have little or no effect on review or renewal is one restricting the use to office or retail use or the purposes relevant to the premises within a particular class or classes of the Town and Country Planning (Use Classes) Order.

(2) To provide in the lease for the lessor to have power to waive the use requirement. As an express term, a valuer would be both entitled and bound to have regard to it on review within the ratio of the *Plinth Properties* decision, and a court, on renewal, would be in a similar position under s 35 of the 1954 Act. There are disadvantages, however. Thus, a lessor with a sound rationale for the use restriction in the first place may not wish to waive it, yet may wish to avoid permanent financial disadvantage; and if the use restriction has not been waived, there may be some discount on the rent at review. If that is the case, this form of clause merely defers the choice beteen control or income to the review date.

(3) To maintain the use restriction, but provide in the rent review for a wider assumed use. This might be done by either requiring the valuer or arbitrator to disregard that restriction in settling the open market rent but few lessees will accept such a wide disparity between the actual and the notional. A more acceptable compromise is to provide for review on the basis of any use falling within a particular class of use within the Town and Country Planning (Use Classes)

Order—the class chosen to be the one into which the actual use allowed falls. Such a clause must be carefully drafted to aviod the possible pitfalls illustrated by *Wolff v London Borough of Enfield* (above); and it must be made clear that the hypothetical lease is to contain the wider use clause—it is not enough merely to 'have regard to' rental values for similar property within the same use class: *SI Pension Trustees Ltd v Ministerio De Marina de la Republica Peruana* [1988] 1 EGLR 119.

An example of a lease separating the actual use from the assumed use occurred in *Trust House Forte Albany Hotels Ltd v Daejan Investments Ltd* (1980) 256 EG 915, where the premises were in fact used as part of the Strand Palace Hotel but the review clause required the assumption that those areas were actually let or available for letting for shopping and retail purposes. As a matter of construction it was held that valuation should proceed on the basis that there was no legal obstacle to such uses, but it did not have to be assumed that the relevant areas had been physically adapted for such use. In *Bovis Group Pension Fund Ltd v GC Flooring and Furnishing Ltd* (1984) 269 EG 1252, the valuer was directed to set a rent reasonably expected for office purposes. There was in fact no planning permission for such use of the premises as a whole, nor did it accord with the actual use. Following the *Trust House Forte* case, the judge at first instance, (1983) 266 EG 1005, held that the valuer was to presuppose the office use without illegality, or, in other words, with the necessary planning permission; and, by a majority, the Court of Appeal upheld his reasoning (see also the discussion of these cases at p 363–5 and 425 ff, below).

The solution which divorces the hypothetical world of rent reviews further from reality, is superficially attractive to the lessor, obtaining as he does the best of both worlds—a tight use clause, but a rent as if there was no restriction. The lessee clearly suffers, particularly if there are also restrictions on assignment—though he may find even a right to assign illusory if the rent is above that which the market can stand. Moreover, the lessor may be left with a problem on renewal under the 1954 Act. There, the court under s 34 is settling the open market rent for a lease containing a restrictive use clause, notwithstanding the assumptions on review. Consequently, a discount on the rent remains likely at that stage.

Whilst landlords cannot necessarily be blamed for exploiting their superior bargaining power to obtain the 'best of both worlds' the authors would repeat the warning that too marked a divergence between the actual state of affairs (in which the tenant has to trade to be able to pay his rent and meet all his other obligations under the lease) and the assumed and notional state of affairs (by reference to which the rent is to be revised) may ultimately prove counter-productive. There can come a point where the tenant can no longer sustain the burden and may be forced into insolvency, whereupon disclaimer of the lease may become a risk. Tenants should be alert to avoid the unfortunate effect of this combination of provisions and similar leonine bargains. (The impact of use clauses is more fully discussed by one of the authors (see Clarke (1983) 4/1 RRLR 31) and by N J Harker at (1984) 4/2 RRLR 132.

4   Statutory restrictions on use

The assumed use in the notional lease may be complicated by statutory restrictions on use. The planning legislation embodied in the Town and Country Planning Acts will affect all business premises; particular trades, occupations or professions may be subject to more particular, and often detailed, legislation. The Gaming Acts have raised difficult construction issues in rent reviews of casinos, the Licensing Acts may have a similar impact in leases of public houses and there are plenty of other situations, eg legislation such as that controlling sex shops, horse riding establishments or relating to hazardous fuels or occupations—to mention but a few.

(a)   Planning restrictions on use

A use which would be permitted by the lease will often be unlawful without planning permission. Most leases will contain a prohibition against use which contravenes planning control. Moreover, most leases contain an assumption that all the tenant's covenants have been performed. On this basis, any use which contravened either the use restriction or this more general obligation to observe statutory provisions, would have to be ignored and its effect on rent should be eliminated. However, if the use in breach of planning law was not caught by the wording of any other provision of the lease, the situation is less clear. Whilst an implied obligation against illegal use arises without express wording, it must be remembered that a material change of use, or other development without planning permission or in breach of conditions does not become illegal until an enforcement notice has been served and possibly a following appeal has taken effect. So the problem may have to be faced in several different circumstances. It is submitted the position is as follows:

(1)   Normally, the possibility of any future use of the premises in breach of planning control must be excluded from consideration: *Compton Group Ltd v Estates Gazette Ltd* (1978) 36 P & CR 148. However, a valuer can have regard to the possibility of obtaining planning permission for a use currently unauthorised if this would be a factor in the rent a willing lessee would offer: *Rushmoor Borough Council v Goacher* [1985] 2 EGLR 140.

(2)   Particularly having regard to the *rebus sic stantibus* principle of

valuation, where the actual use is unauthorised but is not a use which is not actually forbidden by the lease, then it must be taken into account to the extent that there is a market demand for it, bearing in mind that the tenant currently so using the property is one component element of the market. Prima facie there might need to be reflected in the assessment that measure of discount which the market would require as an allowance for the prospect of intervention by the local planning authority or other public body. The *Plinth Properties* decision militates against this valuation approach but *Pivot Properties Ltd* v *Secretary of State for the Environment* (1979) 39 P & CR 386 provides warrant for it, especially as it relates to the market's assessment of the prospect of the intervention by an independent body and not of relaxation by the landlord with a direct financial interest. Thus in *Sixth Centre Ltd v Guildville Ltd* [1989] 1 EGLR 260 a building was actually used as offices, the relevant lease restricted use to showrooms or offices but there was no planning permission—indeed consent to a change of use had been refused. Yet no enforcement proceedings had been taken. It was held that the valuation should proceed on the basis of the authorised use (as a warehouse) but *hope value* of obtaining change of use could be taken into account and regard could be had to the lack of enforcement proceedings. The case for reflecting the market assessment of the contingency is a matter for the valuer. Which party will be so arguing depends of course on whose interests will be best served by its acceptance. The position at rent review can be contrasted with that in the statutory renewal setting. In *Turner & Bell v Searles (Stanford-le-Hope) Ltd* (1977) 33 P & CR 208 the use of premises for a coach operator's business had been the occasion of successful enforcement proceedings under the planning legislation, although not implemented, it seemed, because of the operator's activities on behalf of the local education authority. Renewal of the lease for the illegal use was refused.

(3) Where the rent review clause postulates a use as the basis of valuation, then it may be assumed that planning permission exists for that purpose: *Bovis Group Pension Trust Ltd v GC Flooring & Furnishing Ltd* (1984) 269 EG 1252 (the reviewed rent was to be that which 'might reasonably be expected to be let for office purposes'—the case is further discussed in Chapter 12, p 425). A similar result was reached in *Sixth Centre Ltd v Guildville Ltd* (above). A second lease to a different tenant in the same building directed that the premises be valued for use as offices. That direction meant that (unlike the first lease discussed above) an assumption of lawful use was required.

(b)   *Other statutory restrictions on use*

The complexities which may result from statutory restrictions on use, other than those relating to planning, when applied to valuation of a hypothetical lease on review are illustrated in the case of *Daejan Investments Ltd v Cornwall Coast Country Club* [1985] 1 EGLR 77. The premises were used as a casino and although the use clause permitted a wide range of uses the case was argued on the basis that the most profitable use was as a casino. The landlord contended that the hypothetical letting for review purposes should be on the footing that the lessee can use the premises lawfully for the purpose of a casino from the rent review date, with the implication of an assumption that the lessee must have the necessary certificate of consent from the Gaming Board and a gaming licence. On the construction of the lease, the judge (Peter Gibson J) rejected any such implication, which one would have expected to have been explicit. The *Bovis Group* case was distinguished as a situation where the parties introduced an artificial assumption explicitly (namely office use) to which deemed planning permission was to be attached as an attribute of the premises. In the *Daejan* case, however, a gaming licence was precarious, and attached to a person. The lease was let with use as a casino as one of the permitted uses, not for use as a casino (*Hill v Harris* [1965] 2 QB 601 applied). It is interesting to speculate whether the issue would have been affected if the assumption that personal 'planning or other consent', now to be found in the ISVA Model Form (set out in Part Seven p 669), had been present in the *Daejan* case.

The *Daejan* case may be contrasted with the decision of *Exclusive Properties Ltd v Cribgate Ltd* [1986] 2 EGLR 123 where the permitted use was limited to a film and photographic studio with necessary ancillary offices. The lease contained provisions for installing the essential fire precautions without which the (hazardous) permitted use would not be lawful. These works were executed by the landlord and there was provision for the cost of the works to be paid for by the tenant as additional rent over the first 10 years of the term of the lease. On the first review, the lease provided for an express assumption that the works actually done should be ignored and that the premises should remain unimproved. This meant that the review clause operated on one of two bizarre hypotheses; either

(1) that the tenant was unable throughout the review period to use the premises except in their unimproved condition and would have the gravest difficulty in complying with the use covenant because of the lack of fire precautions; or
(2) that the tenant could lawfully carry out the intended business without the fire precaution works.

Knox J preferred the latter construction on the basis that there was a clear intention in the lease that the premises should be used; and used as a film and photographic studio. The *Daejan v Cornwall Coast* case was not discussed but the judge did find assistance from the *Bovis Group* and *Trust House Forte v Daejan* cases: 'availability denotes legal propriety but does not necessarily connote the execution of necessary building works'.

5   Alienation covenants

(a)   The valuation impact

The measure of restriction imposed on assignment, under-letting, parting with possession, or sharing or parting with occupation bears directly and forcefully upon the rent to be expected in arm's length negotiations. Evidence for judicial acceptance of this largely self-evident proposition can be found in *Cardshops Ltd v Davies* [1971] 1 WLR 591, where the court refused on a statutory renewal to substitute an absolute prohibition for a qualified covenant as in the existing lease. A prohibition on assignment prevents the tenant from realising the value of his goodwill, of his stock in trade and of the residual value of any shop-fitting or other tenant's works. He may be bound for the residue of the term to pay the rent for, and other outgoings on, property for which he has no further use. The market of willing lessees at a review ready to accept a lease with absolute prohibitions against alienation will be much smaller than for leases containing more marketable fully qualified provisions and the rent they would be prepared to pay in consequence will be much lower, especially with a residue of any length.

(i)   The nature of the restriction

There is, of course, a 'spectrum' of possible clauses relating to alienation stretching, on the one hand, from an absolute prohibition on both assignment and under-letting of whole or part to a lease granting (or allowing) complete freedom to the tenant. Neither of these extremes is likely to be encountered in a modern commercial lease of any length but the possible variations between the two extremes are of many types. From the rent review standpoint, the theoretical ideal is for the alienation clause to conform to the 'band' of clauses acceptable and appropriate in the market for the nature of the property and letting in question. If that is done, then, providing there is no significant change in the market practice in relation to the format of alienation clauses, there will no adverse valuation impact at review. If the lessor seeks to impose restrictions greater than those normally acceptable to the market, then the price for such control may well be paid at review in the form of a discount to the tenant. At the other end of the spectrum, a clause more generous than that normally occurring in the market may just possibly enable the claim for a (small) rent uplift on the basis that a willing lessee will pay more—but few if any lessors will relinquish the degree of control given by the generally acceptable qualified clause in return for an uncertain and limited benefit at review.

The 'band' of acceptable clauses is founded on the standard 'fully qualified' covenant, namely, against assignment of the whole without consent of the landlord, such consent not to be unreasonably withheld (if the covenant is one against alienation 'without consent' then the effect of s 19(1) of the Landlord and Tenant Act 1927 is to imply the proviso that consent is not to be unreasonably withheld and so convert the 'qualified' covenant into a 'fully qualified' one). Whether or not there are then absolute or fully qualified provisions relating to assignment of part, or sub-letting of part or the whole will depend on the nature of the property in question (see below). The provisions of the Landlord and Tenant Act 1988 have adjusted the balance of advantage where assignment is requested in favour of the tenant by imposing statutory duties on those whose consent is required and by providing a remedy in damages in the case of a dilatory landlord who fails to fulfil the duties so imposed to deal expeditiously with a request to assign. However, the 1988 Act is unlikely to have an impact on the rent review process except in so far as a willing tenant in the market should now be more ready to accept the constraints of a fully qualified covenant.

The possible combination of alienation provisions, and their impact on rent review are well illustrated by *Five Ways Properties Ltd v Secretary of State for the Environment* [1990] 31 EG 50. A covenant against alienation (except to another government department) was followed by a proviso allowing assignment or sub-letting of the whole premises with consent. However, a further proviso required the assignee or sub lessee to give a direct covenant with the (head) landlord against any further disposition by that assignee or under lessee. Arguments that one or other of the trio of provisions was repugnant to one of the other failed. The arbitrator held that the combination of provisions permitted one alienation only and this was upheld on appeal: the rent would reflect that somewhat uneasy situation.

Incidentally, the freedom of disposition to another emanation of the Crown is not infrequently sought by the Property Services Agency. It differs only slightly from the usual freedom in relation to subsidiary and associate companies in its possible width. Moreover, in so far as it both widens the range of potential occupiers and avoids any problems over the dissolution or disappearance of a particular occupier it may even assist a landlord at review—governments have a habit of still being in the market when others have withdrawn.

(ii) Interrelationship with use clauses

The clauses in the lease relating to alienation have to be viewed in the light of the provisions relating to use. If the use clause is tightly drawn (and is not fully qualified), it may be difficult or even impossible to find a potential actual assignee in the market who could observe the terms of the use clause. If that is the case, then however generous the alienation clause, the willing tenant at review taking the hypothetical lease with these terms as to both use and alienation would treat the lease as one where assignment was impossible for all practical purposes. The net result in terms of valuation at review is as if the lease contained an absolute prohibition against assignment—namely, a lease with no prospect of building up a premium value, the likelihood of being bound by the covenants for the whole term and (in the case where extrication from the lease is required) the financial burden of a surrender with a reverse premium. Such factors will have a substantial adverse impact on the rent proffered by a willing lessee.

At issue in *International Drilling Fluids Ltd v Louisville Investments (Uxbridge) Ltd* (1986) 277 EG 62 was refusal of consent for assignment to an assignee proposing the provision of 'serviced office accommodation' in small suites, fully furnished, with services of a receptionist, telephonist and typist plus word processing, telex, photocopying and telephone services. The use clause specified 'offices'; the proposed arrangements would break no provision of the lease. On the evidence the judge found that the proposals would not affect the result obtainable at review, and doubted the professional opinion expressed that the value of the reversion would be seriously diminished. It was held refusal of consent was unreasonable. However, circumstances are readily imaginable where only slight changes in these facts where the use clause covers a rather 'unorthodox' style of the permitted activity could have significant valuation consequences on review. The market rent might be more or less than the rent for a main-stream permitted use.

The full interrelationship of use and alienation clauses and the cases relating thereto have been considered in the section on use (p 357, above).

(iii)   Relaxation in favour of named lessee

Where there is a fairly tightly drawn alienation clause combined with a express relaxation to the (named) original tenant, it will be a question of construction as to whether the relaxation is a benefit which would be enjoyed by the notional willing tenant in the market under the terms of the hypothetical lease. In *James v British Craft Centre* [1986] 1 EGLR 117 there was an absolute prohibition against assigning, sub-letting or sharing possession of part; a proviso allowed the lessee to share occupation with a holding or subsidiary company of the lessee 'but only while the lessee is the British Crafts Centre'. Scott J had to decide if this was a personal privilege restricted to the British Crafts Centre (and so not available to the hypothetical willing lessee) or a personal privilege available to the first original hypothetical lessee whoever that might be. The issue is similar to that arising in respect of personal privileges relating to use (see p 348). The decision of Scott J was that the concession was available to the hypothetical original tenant in the market and the hypothetical lease would contain a blank for insertion of the name. In the Court of Appeal ([1987] 1 EGLR 139) this result was doubted by two Lords Justices and May LJ stated (at 141H) that he would have reached the opposite conclusion but the appeal related to the point of construction on the use clause (see p 350) and no appeal was made on the alienation clause. Thus, as with all personal concessions in leases, whether relating to use, alienation or otherwise, it is advisable for express provision to be made as to their treatment at a review either by an assumption that they are to be available to the notional lessee or by way of disregard. It must be remembered that a notional disregard at review still leaves the restriction or privilege untouched in its direct application.

(b) The 'offer to surrender' device

There may be an impact for rent review from the common form clause which requires a tenant to offer to surrender the term prior to seeking consent to assign. This 'offer to surrender' device was upheld in *Adler v Upper Grosvenor Street Investments Ltd* [1957] 1 WLR 227, criticised in *Greene v Church Commissioners for England* [1974] Ch 467 but vindicated in *Bocardo SA v S & M Hotels Ltd* [1980] 1 WLR 17. However, the practical efficacy (as opposed to the legal validity) of the 'offer to surrender' obligation in business lettings (not in point in the *Bocardo* case) is open to grave doubt in the light of s 38 of the Landlord and Tenant Act 1954, as first interpreted in *Joseph v Joseph* [1967] Ch 78 and confirmed in *Allnatt London Properties Ltd v Newton* (1983) 45 P & CR 94. There the Court of Appeal upheld the decision of Megarry V-C at first instance that the agreement for surrender created by the landlord's acceptance of the tenant's (mandatory) offer to surrender could not be enforced against the tenant. However, the offer having been accepted, the tenant's right to assign with consent did not arise and the tenant was left with a lease he could not assign. The uncertainty, and possible stalemate, resulting from the juxtaposition of the *Bocardo* and *Allnatt* decisions may perpetuate the depreciatory effect on rent of such clauses, which contain the potential for the landlord to turn a conditionally qualified bar on assignment into effectively an absolute one by insisting on the offer of surrender being made and then accepting it. However, the landlord does not gain the benefit of surrender, if that is what he wants, if the tenant, though thwarted in his desire to leave the premises, prefers to 'stick it out' rather than surrender. Variants of the traditional clause, designed to take advantage of the power in s 38 for the court to approve agreements to surrender, have been devised in the wake of the *Allnatt* decision. It may take litigation to establish the validity of such clauses and the prospect of needing to go to court is a depreciatory factor that an intending tenant may allow for by offering a reduced rent.

(c)   *Restrictions on underlettings*

(i) Absolute restrictions on under-lettings, particularly on under-letting part of the demised premises, have a greater or lesser effect on rental values according to the nature of the property and changes in the market— witness the growth of demand for 'working suites' or so-called 'flatted factories' in otherwise unfashionably large mills and warehouses suitably adapted for such break-up operations. Many such small units are not sub-let but occupied under licence and it is a matter of construction whether the alienation covenants restrict such transactions. If they do, and it is quite usual for that to be the case, the restrictions will affect rent levels for properties having a potential for such treatment. Finally, the myth (for it may have been nothing more) of the attraction of the single tenant of undoubted standing for the major development (associated, however wrongly, in the public mind with the early history of Centre Point) underlines the possible impact on the rent review of the exact form of the alienation covenant.

(ii) Qualified restrictions on sub-lettings may not always nullify the valuation impact, particularly in relation to sub-letting of part. For if it is reasonable for the lessor to withhold consent to a division of the holding a tenant may find he is unable to achieve a profitable under-letting of part. Consequently, at review, the rental value attached to possible future fragmentation may be lost if the willing lessee could not be sure consent would be forthcoming.

A combination sometimes found is a prohibition on sub-letting with a relaxation that consent will not be unreasonably withheld for subtenancies of parts contracted out of the protection of Part II of the Landlord and Tenant Act. In the early years of the head lease, the possible length of sub-leases will be unlikely to deter potential subtenants or cause them to offer reduced rents; accordingly the head lease rent may be little affected at review by this form of alienation provision. However, as the lease runs on, the restriction on the permissible length of contracted-out sub-leases may produce a falling off in the supply of willing subtenants and a reduction in the rent offered for the sub-leases: at that stage some tempering of the head rent, for a lease now different from the usual lease, may be expected. Indeed, on general grounds, this restricted form of alienation provision introduces an adverse element to the notional lease of which the tenant's valuer will make such use as he can. None of the alienation provisions in the reported cases have been in this form; its relationship with the assumption of a notional term on renewal equal to the full term running from review date may create further complications.

(d)   *Impact of conditions imposed on alienation*

The issue of how far the presence of a condition imposed on alienation in the actual lease and carried over into the notional lease affects the market rent at review is, once again, a matter of valuation in the circumstances of each case.

(i) The requirement of a direct covenant from an assignee to pay rent and observe covenants creates an obligation that lasts for the residue of the lease (*J Lyons & Co Ltd v Knowles* [1943] KB 366), though possibly not beyond into statutory extensions (*Junction Estates Ltd v Cope* (1974) 27 P & CR 482) (see the discussion at p 480). It should accordingly be resisted by the sophisticated or well-advised assignee for the reason that it outlasts his ownership of the leasehold interest. Where the obligation is already contained in the lease, however, there has not yet been any reported decision that it is unreasonable (there are, indeed, dicta to the contrary in *Balfour v Kensington Gardens Mansions Ltd* (1932) 49 TLR 29) and there appears to be no market resistance to it known to the authors. Its presence could be a slight bargaining factor. These issues are further discussed in Chapter 14, p 479.

(ii) The requirement of any under-letting to be at full market rent is a provision frequently encountered. Thus the Rosscastle letting conditions, clause 3.7:6.1, contain a covenant to ensure that any underlease:

'. . . is granted without a premium at a rent approved by the landlord (such approval not to be unreasonably withheld) and no lower than the open market rent.'

Bernstein and Reynolds (para 5–38) rightly point out that since the open market rent is a matter of valuation opinion, there is plenty of scope for dispute, consequent delay and loss of the potential assignee. However, it is only if such clauses are perceived in the market to be troublesome, and leading to a willing lessee reducing his rental bid thereby, that an adverse effect at review should occur.

The reasoning behind such clauses stems partly from *Town Investments Ltd's Under Lease* [1954] Ch 301 pointing out risks if the head lease is disclaimed in insolvency; the same hazard applied if a large portion of the sub-rent is paid in advance but that is rarely forbidden.

(e) Prospect of modification to be ignored

Unilateral offers to modify tight restrictions on alienation, or a market assessment of the likelihood of such concessions being forthcoming, are to be ignored. A subsidiary element to the prospect of consent to a change of use being obtained in *Plinth Properties Investments Ltd v Mott, Hay and Anderson* (1978) P & CR 361 was the prospect of modification of another prohibition on any under-letting to allow under-letting of whole or part. What was said about the former equally applies to the latter, so the discussion at p 345 above is relevant. Thus the present approach must be to ignore the prospect of relaxation. Moreover, it must be recalled that, whilst acknowledgement of the continuance of the tenancy with knowledge of a prohibited sub-letting, assignment or sharing (see *Metropolitan Properties Co Ltd v Cordery* (1979) 251 EG 567) may be a waiver of the right to forfeit for breach, the remedy in damages would remain (if loss could be proved, as for example by the creation of a protected residential tenancy). The covenant itself, as distinct from the specific breach, could only be waived by very compelling evidence of abandonment.

6   Repair obligations

(a)   The theoretical and practical background

Just as with any other onerous term of the lease, an onerous repairing obligation in the actual lease may, when incorporated into the hypothetical lease, cause a reduction in the assessment of the market rent to reflect the obligation perceived to be more onerous than the market will bear: *Norwich Union Life Assurance Society v British Railways Board* (discussed in section (*b*) below). Similarly, a much less onerous covenant than that now accepted in the market (eg the lessor bears external repairs and there is no service charge recoupment) may or will cause an uplift if the pool of willing tenants in the market perceive this as a benefit for which they will pay some additional rent: cf *O'May v City of London Real Property Ltd* [1983] 2 AC 726.

At one time market conditions dictated that various types of obsolete industrial buildings were let in their rather scruffy condition on the basis of limited repair obligations on the tenant—'to keep the premises in no better conditions than they are now in', 'wind and water tight' or the like. The apparent attractions of this trade-off technique soon palled; tenants often found that, despite the absence of obligation, practical considerations (including pressure from employees or their unions) produced the need to effect minimal but often expensive repairs—to roofs, main walls, wiring, floors, and so on—or to carry out 'improvements' to adapt the premises to modern industrial or commercial use or comply with health and safety requirements. Combined with growth of conservation, the pattern changed to the modernisation and adaption of the premises on full rents and FRI (Full Repairing and Insurance) terms. Some of the former style of leases will still continue; on review the tenant's experience of the need and cost of some measure of maintenance and repair will be prayed in aid to balance any suggestion that the willing tenant would pay a higher rent to obtain a lower level of repair and maintenance obligation. So the steam has gone out of the issue in respect of a whole sector of the market. Individual lettings on such a basis may still be found. The initial tenant may enjoy a lower repair obligation and be content to carry out his business operations in a run-down setting. This sort of tenant may often operate in a 'bad neighbour' activity which would have inevitable adverse effect on the premises if they had been put in good order so their unkempt condition is quite tolerable. Nevertheless, other potential tenants would want, or need, to put the premises into a better condition than they are in and would pay little heed to the absence of usual repair obligations. No question of extra rent in recognition of the below average repair covenant would arise. In these circumstances, accordingly, the rental effect of the relaxation of normal repair burdens may be minimal or absent at review.

The introduction of the nature of the repair covenant into the rent review equation must be set against the background of changes in the nature and obligations imposed on tenants as to repair, reconstruction and service charge recovery. Older leases falling for review may contain provisions which no longer reflect the market norm. Thus, the obligations imposed on tenants in relation to responsibility for the structure of the demised premises, both directly and indirectly (through service charges covering work to be carried out by landlords), increased markedly in he lessors' markets of the 1960s and early 1970s. The scope of even traditionally framed covenants was widely thought to have been extended by *Ravenseft Properties Ltd v Davstone (Holdings) Ltd* [1980] QB 12 (which largely contradicted the views on 'inherent defects' canvassed in the Blundell Memorial Lecture of 1976 by Plume and Dunnett), and may have shifted the boundary between repair and replacement. (The possible difficulties of what falls within the scope of 'repair' are discussed in the context of the meaning of improvements in Chapter 12 at p 428, below). The relevant clause in the lease in the *Ravenseft* case, and in many others, covered 'rebuilding', 'replacement' and the like, although the judge expressly did not found his judgment on those words. Such clauses sometimes continued by stating that such obligations should apply notwithstanding the presence of initial or inherent defects in the design or construction of buildings, the unsuitability of the ground or other similar 'hidden' factors. For a time, such widened obligations were more or less passively accepted by tenants, or, more probably, their advisers, as representing the usual provisions in a newly granted lease (including, it seems obvious, renewals of protected business leases under the Landlord and Tenant Act 1954, where departure from the previous lease to a 'modern' form was not challenged). The publicity afforded to the *Ravenseft* decision and one or two spectacular building failures (or the need for expensive remedial measures to prevent such calamities) seemingly produced an awareness of the potential liability and increased tenant resistance. The House of Lords' decision in *O'May v City of London Real Property Ltd* [1983] 2 AC 726 laid stress on the potential burden if a tenant is fully liable for the building's very existence. In any particular case, therefore, it can properly be argued, and may be susceptible to proof by evidence, that the presence of a repairing obligation in an unduly onerous form should be reflected in a lower rent than where a less extreme set of liabilities was imposed.

(b) The Norwich Union v British Railways case

The decision of Hoffman J in *Norwich Union Life Assurance Society v British Railways Board* [1987] 2 EGLR 137 decides that where the terms of a repairing obligation, as interpreted, place upon the tenant a more onerous obligation than the market will bear, then it is right and proper that the rent as determined at review should be discounted to reflect that burden. The decision of the arbitrator to reduce the market rent by 27.5 per cent was upheld though it must be stressed that the appeal approved the construction and effect of the covenant not the level of discount which was a matter for the arbitrator.

The context of this decision should be noted whenever the valuation impact of a repairing obligation is raised:

(i) The terms of the repairing clause were 'to keep the demised premises in good and substantial repair and condition and when necessary to rebuild, reconstruct or replace the same and in such condition yield up the same at the expiration or sooner determination of the said lease'. This was construed to be a covenant both to repair and then to renew when necessary; it related to the whole and not to a part of the whole.

(ii) The length of the term was 150 years. In the context of such a long term it could be assumed that the tenant may well have accepted the obligation to reconstruct—so that there was no commercial reason to question the straightforward construction of the clause notwithstanding the fact that it was not usual. Moreover, it was not inconceivable that, whatever the present standard of the building, in a lease of 150 years duration replacement might well become necessary.

(iii) The current state of repair of the premises does not appear to have been a factor in the decision but in other circumstances the age of the demised premises and the imminence of the need to replace or reconstruct could enter into the equation.

(iv) The covenant was a more onerous obligation than repairing obligations in leases of comparable properties.

The lease in the *Norwich Union* case was for a period of 150 years so the need for complete rebuilding over that period was a real possibility; in the *O'May* case the lease was only for 5 years and being renewed for a further 5 years. Most business leases fall between the two extremes but we have not found a reported decision where a 'discount' related to the rebuilding obligation has been a factor in such a lease.

When renewal or onerous repairing clauses are evaluated within the hypothetical lease, the aptness and level of discount will be a matter for the arbitrator or valuer in the light of the valuation evidence and the impact of the obligation within the notional term and in relation to the particular property. Most tenants will argue strongly for some allowance.

(c) Impact on assignability

The impact of onerous repairing or rebuilding covenants on
assignability must be taken into account. On the one hand, a landlord
faced with a request for consent to assign might properly consider not
only the ability of the proffered assignee to pay rent and other outgoings
but also the ability of such an assignee to fund the rebuilding operation
should that become necessary. The assignability of a lease is an element
of its attractiveness in the market and any restraint on assignability beyond
what is usual will depress the rent. On the other hand, the presence
or even the risk of the presence of serious inherent defects that a tenant
would have to make good would affect both the pool of willing tenants
and the rent they would offer (or, once more, the future ease of assignment
of a lease, which would also operate upon the mind of the hypothetical
initial tenant). In *Civil Aviation Authority v Langford and Camden Borough
Council* (1978) 247 EG 957 the presence of certain design weaknesses
and the use of High Alumina Cement were held, upholding the decision
of the Lands Tribunal, to render the premises virtually unlettable, and
rateable values, based on a notional letting of £950,000 gross, £791,638
net, were reduced to a nominal £1 (the issues were discussed by Bowhill
(1982) 79 *Law Society's Gazette* 556).

(d) Repairing obligations and the notional term

The effect of traditional repair covenants in relation to premises nearing
the end of their useful life is further considered in the discussion of
the notional length of the assumed term for the review in Chapter 12
at p 396. The effect of 'concessionary' repair covenants in relation to
ascertainment of the market level of rents should be allowed for,
preferably in the drafting of the lease or by being recorded in some
contemporaneous memorandum referred to in it. This avoids, on the
one hand, the risk that the fact of the covenant being concessionary
will become the subject matter of a later dispute and, on the other,
doubts whether or not the link is to be perpetuated at later reviews.
Equally, where a concessionary rent reflects an unduly onerous repair
obligation, both the facts and the parties' intention as to future treatment
of the interrelation should be placed on record.

(e) Statutory repairing obligations

Statutory obligations under such enactments as the Offices, Shops
and Railway Premises Act 1963, the Fire Precautions Act 1971, and
the Health and Safety at Work Act 1974 are not usually borne in mind
when assessing repair obligations and are often provided for in a covenant
in general terms. Nevertheless, compliance with requirements so imposed
can be both costly and disruptive, and they are matters to be borne
in mind in assessing market rent levels. Some of the relevant provisions

(eg s 73 of the Offices, Shops and Railway Premises Act 1963 and s 28(3) of the Fire Precautions Act 1971) allow apportionment and recovery of part of the cost incurred from the landlord. The prospects of such recovery may be a material factor adding yet a further complication to the process of valuation. Indeed, the provisions just cited permit the county court to modify the lease in respect of the rent payable. Will the county court judge take off what, say, the arbitrator has recently added?

(f) The actual state of repair and common assumptions

The hypothetical letting will normally involve a notional letting of the actual property let with the repair obligations from the actual lease incorporated into the notional lease. The basic premise that would then follow is that the valuation proceeds to value the property as it exists and in its actual state of repair at the review date.

Such a premise can easily work injustice if the property is in disrepair. Consequently, most review clauses will contain assumptions as to the state of repair and so require the valuer, so far as directed, to disregard the actual state of the demised premises. These common assumptions are:

(1) that the tenant (and sometimes also the lessor) has fully performed his covenants; and/or
(2) that all covenants as to repair have been fully performed; and/or
(3) that the demised premises are fit for immediate occupation and use; and/ or
(4) that, in the case of the demised premises being destroyed or damaged, they have been fully restored. These assumptions and their impact are discussed in Chapter 12.

(g) 'No person can take advantage of their own wrong'

In the absence of any of these express assumptions to be applied at rent review, the general principle that no person can take advantage of their own wrong will apply to the landlord/tenant relationship as embodied in the commercial lease. Thus a lessee who is in default of tenant's repairing obligations imposed by the lease cannot benefit from the default and argue that the rent should be reduced in consequence of the dilapidated state of repair: *Harmsworth Pension Funds Trustees Ltd v Charringtons Industrial Holdings Ltd* [1985] 1 EGLR 97, applying *Family Management v Gray* ((1980) 253 EG 369, a dilapidations case) and *Hibernian Property Co Ltd v Liverpool Corporation* ([1973] 1 WLR 751, compulsory purchase). In the *Harmsworth Pension Funds* case, defects in a modern industrial building appeared after the commencement of the term and the tenant was engaged in proceedings against the developer. By holding that, in so far as the tenant was in breach of its repairing covenants, the diminishing effect on rent should be disregarded it became unnecessary to determine the extent to which the tenant was in fact in breach of its obligations. Warner J said that the view, adopted by Bernstein and Reynolds para 4–53, that valuation in a dilapidated state is not unfair (since the lessor can recover the shortfall by way of damages) was unsatisfactory and the authors respectfully agree with the learned judge. There can be no guarantee, even in the real world, that the lessor would recover by way of loss of value to the perhaps distant reversion a sum fully equivalent to the immediate diminution in rent; to then transfer this idea to the notional letting is inappropriate.

By way of contrast, a lessor who is in breach of any landlord's repairing obligations cannot, in the absence of an express assumption, rely on an implied assumption that his covenants have been performed. The premises fall to be valued in their actual state though, at review, a differential rent is not possible: *Clarke v Findon Developments Ltd* (1984) 270 EG 426 distinguishing, (on the issue of differential rent) *Fawke v Viscount Chelsea* [1980] QB 441 (where it was held that in determining an interim rent under s 24 of the Landlord and Tenant Act 1954, it was proper to have regard to the actual condition of the premises at the date when the interim rent was assessed). The different approach to landlord's repairing covenants is justified since it again accords with the principle that no person should profit from their own wrong. The lessor has failed to repair, the rent receivable is thereby diminished. It should be noted, however, that this position is often negated by the express assumption that all covenants have been performed (see p 413). Express power for a referee to determine a differential rent at review to reflect disrepair under a lessor's repairing obligation is possible in theory but unthinkable in practice!

7 Covenants against alterations and improvements

Where the demised premises have the potential for alteration, improvement and development by a hypothetical willing lessee, then that prospect of enhanced value can, prima facie, be taken into account at rent review. As with other areas, there is little room for the argument that the actual tenant does not wish to take up these opportunities if the hypothetical letting will permit them to the pool of willing tenants. However, in many cases, the incorporation of the express terms of the lease will limit the scope for an uplift in rent on this basis because of covenants restraining such activities.

(a) Absolute prohibition in the lease

A covenant against alterations and improvements which is unqualified will largely negate any development potential; the decision in the *Plinth Properties* case prevents speculation about the likelihood of consent being forthcoming. It is true that a tenant may have a statutory right to carry out 'improvements' within Part I of the Landlord and Tenant Act 1927 but the complex procedure of that Act is little used and has been recommended for abolition (Law Comm 178, 1989). This suggests that a notional willing lessee taking a lease with an absolute prohibition will give little weight, if any, to development potential.

(b) Fully qualified prohibitions

A prohibition of alterations without consent, subject to a proviso that consent is not to be unreasonably withheld (if not express, the proviso will be implied by the Landlord and Tenant Act 1927, s 19(2)), will permit development potential. It is then a matter for valuation evidence as to the extent to which, if at all, the letting value is enhanced. Given the capital cost, possible difficulties with planning permission and the practical fact that compensation is rarely sought or granted at the end of the term under the statutory provisions, enhancement of the rental letting value by the prospect of development potential is likely to be the exception rather than the rule. Moreover, restrictions on use or alienation which are incorporated into the notional letting may negate the impact of development value to the willing lessee. An illustration of the way the use clause interrelates with development potential is *Tea Trade Properties Ltd v CIN Properties Ltd* [1990]. There, as a consequence of re-zoning, the tenant's commercial premises had the potential for full office use (instead of the existing restricted and partial office use); planning permission for such change had already been granted to the landlord. Neither the use covenant (see p 353) nor the detailed covenant not to contravene the Planning Acts made the change to total office use legally impossible under the terms of the lease. The prospects of alterations and improvements for such potential use was therefore to be taken into account. The argument by the tenant that the necessary works would have been so expensive so as to make the building in practice unattractive to a potential office tenant was a question for the valuer and was not a matter for a declaration by the court.

8   Insurance and other covenants

(a) Insurance

Increasingly in commercial leases, landlords insure and recoup the insurance premiums from tenants, often in the form of additional rent. Even in older leases where tenants insure, landlords either expressly establish the level of cover or could indirectly do so by seeking a ruling whether the tenant had indeed insured for 'full value', 'full insurable value', 'full re-building value' (or 'cost'), 'full reinstatement value' (or 'cost') and so on, whatever phrase the original draftsman had used. The ingenuity of draftsmen in responding to their clients' perceptions of advisable estate management in relation to insurance produces increasingly complex and potentially burdensome obligations. Although there is no immediate evidence that opposition to the more onerous of these provisions has yet developed, there is no reason to suggest it might not—whereupon the presence of a particularly 'fierce' insurance (or repayment of premium) provision must be given effect to in the review process. Moreover, where the effect of a particular obligation can be shown to be significant, its presence or absence in an alleged 'comparable' should be ascertained and some appropriate adjustment or allowance made where necessary in assessing the full relevance of the 'comparable'.

(b)   Other covenants

Covenants to keep open for trading during certain hours, not to open save during certain hours, not to hold sales by auction, or even to comply with any regulations subsequently made by a lessor, may all prove in particular circumstances to have an adverse effect on market rentals. The first of these is discussed at p 344.

9   Alterations to the lease by later deed or licence

Where there has been a modification to the terms of the lease by later deed or licence, it may be important to determine whether the notional lease at review incorporates the terms of the original lease or the lease as modified by the subsequent deed or licence.

Ideally, the question should be addressed and answered by the later deed itself. A permanent modification of the terms, binding on assignees, will affect the valuation exercise at review. Sometimes, the substantive variation will merit an express modification of the basis of valuation in the review clause. The same result will rarely be desired in the case of a personal licence to the existing tenant; if, however, it is to be given effect to at review, in reference to the particular tenant, it should be made clear whether the effect will be eliminated on assignment or not. In some instances, particularly where the alteration is solely for the benefit of the tenant and of no value at review, the lessor may wish or be prepared to disregard it in the review valuation; if it is not so disregarded, the lessee may wish to ensure that his ability to assign is not restricted because of the higher rent which may be determined at review reflecting a concession his successor will not enjoy if it is a factor in the review.

Where no express thought or provision has been made for the rent review consequences at the time of the variation, the question of whether the amended terms are incorporated into the hypothetical letting will depend on two factors:

(a) the terms of the review clause in the original lease; and
(b) whether the subsequent deed or licence did actually purport to vary the terms of the original lease.

(a) The terms of the original lease

If the lease refers to the review being on the terms of this lease 'or as subsequently varied' (or words to that effect), there will be no obstacle to incorporating the later deed—provided it does vary the terms. Even where there is no such reference, if the subsequent deed does purport to vary, the courts may well construe the review to be on the basis of the varied terms: *Pleasurama Properties Ltd v Leisure Investments (West End) Ltd* [1986] 1 EGLR 145. In that case, the review was to be on the basis of the terms and conditions 'herein contained' and Lloyd LJ was of the view that:

'In the case of a deed of variation the effect of which was to widen the permitted user, then I could well understand the courts holding that the words 'herein contained' should be read as referring to the covenants as varied.'

If this (obiter) view is correct, then the vital issue is the terms of the later deed and whether it does in fact vary the lease. However, in *SI Pension Trustees Ltd v Ministerio De Marina de la Republica Peruana* [1988] 1 EGLR 119 one of the reasons for the decision of Mervyn Davies J in refusing to incorporate the variations to the use clause in a licence to assign was the fact that the review clause referred to 'the provisions of the lease, not the provisions as they may be varied from time to time'. The Court of Appeal decision in *Pleasurama* was not referred to and may not have been cited. Both the *Pleasurama* decision and the *SI Pension Trustees* case were cited to Judge Hayman in *Apus Properties Ltd v Douglas Farrow & Co Ltd* [1989] 2 EGLR 265 where his view on the construction of a review clause 'on the same terms as the present demise' was that it spoke at the date of the lease and so did not incorporate a subsequent variation of the use clause. The judgment stressed both the fact that the lease did not refer to the terms 'as varied from time to time' and the omission to deal with the issue of amendment to the review basis of valuation in the subsequent deed. However, it is now clear that there is no general proposition that a provision in a rent review clause requiring it to be assumed that the hypothetical lease contains covenants similar to those in the actual lease is to be construed as requiring any subsequent variation to be ignored: *Lynnthorpe Enterprises Ltd v Sidney Smith (Chelsea) Ltd* [1990] 1 EGLR 148; and the case has been upheld on appeal: [1990] EGCS 60. There Warner J referred to the 'presumption in favour of reality' which he considered:

'requires the terms of the hypothetical lease to reflect any variations (other than perhaps variations personal to the particular tenant) in the terms of the actual lease.'

The authors consider this is the correct approach (but with the deletion of the word 'perhaps'). It has the merit of being consonant with the treatment of review on the liability of the original lessee. So in *Centrovincial Estates plc v Bulk Storage Ltd* (1983) 46 P & CR 393 at 396 Harman J indicates:

'. . . the assignee is the owner of the whole estate and can deal with it so as to alter it or its terms. The estate as so altered then binds the original tenant, because the assignee has been put into the shoes of the original tenant and can do all such acts as the original tenant could have done.'

He applied *Baynton v Morgan* (1888) 22 QBD 74 and held the tenant liable for rent increased by agreement as allowed for in the lease. The decision was followed in *Selous Street Properties Ltd v Oronel Fabrics Ltd* (1984) 270 EG 643 (the cases are discussed at p 486–7). If variations have this retrospective effect, then why should they not equally, or even more compellingly, have prospective effect?

Nevertheless, the better course, particularly in the light of the *SI Pension Trustees* and *Apus Properties* decisions, is to ensure that, especially where the review clause only refers to the terms of the lease, that the subsequent deed which varies the terms of the lease also corrects or confirms the basis of the subsequent rent review valuation(s)—if this is desired. Failure to address the issue may be grounds for a claim in professional negligence.

(b) The terms of the subsequent deed

It will be a question of construction as to whether the subsequent deed or licence actually purports to vary the original lease. Where the deed is stated to be a licence, it will be somewhat more difficult to argue that it varies the lease: *Pleasurama Properties v Leisure Investments* (above). Similarly, a deed which is expressed to be personal to the assignee or tenant or other persons who are parties to the deed is unlikely to vary the lease: *SI Pension Trustees Ltd v Ministerio De Marina de la Republica Peruana* (above). By way of contrast, in *Lynnthorpe Enterprises Ltd v Sidney Smith (Chelsea) Ltd* (1990) (above) the subsequent 'Deed of Variation' stated that the underlease 'is hereby varied as follows'. There was a difficult issue of construction as to the extent of the variation but an attempt to argue that this was a personal variation failed.

The effect of expressing the later deed to be 'supplemental' to the first, though often done, is more problematical. The Law of Property Act 1925, s 58, merely states that this has effect as if the original deed were recited in full in the later deed and is largely directed to other issues. It is by no means certain that it has any greater effect than avoiding repetition, by way of recital, of the earlier deed. Despite that, the use of the device might increase the chances of it being given effect as an intention to vary the original lease.

10   Conclusions and drafting considerations

There are common threads and themes which are common to the whole area of the relationship of the *actual* provisions governing the relationship of the parties for the time being to the lease and the terms incorporated into the *hypothetical* letting.

The overriding lesson is that a benefit, provision or covenant in the lease which gives a benefit to one party which is unusual, considered unduly onerous or generally unacceptable in the open market will or may rebound on the party so benefited at review by a rent discount or uplift, as the case may be. In the case of use, alienation and alteration covenants the lessor must normally chose between income and control. If he opts in any of these areas for a degree of control greater than the market at review considers is justified, then the income obtainable at review may well be reduced. The beneficial consequence, in general terms, is that new leases are normally couched in terms which accord with the 'broad band' of acceptability in the market. Clauses relating to use, alienation and so on are, in consequence, possibly less restrictive currently than was once the case. Rumblings of tenant discontent with 'oppressive' standard institutional leases nevertheless continue.

The temptation, particularly in a lessor's market, is to divorce the actual from the hypothetical; to impose some strict or tight provision relating to use or alienation but to provide a disregard of these matters at review. The courts have shown their distaste for such provisions and a willingness to construe clauses so that they accord with what the tenant actually gets. Any departure form the actual at review, which may be justified in certain instances, needs to be spelled out in unequivocal words that make the position at review clear.

Chapter 12

The Valuation Framework: (2) Constructing and Interpreting the Hypothetical Letting

The modern rent review clause constructs a notional framework for the valuer to assess the rent to be paid:

- Notional parties, willing and ready to grant and take the lease.
- A notional lease, based on and usually incorporating the terms of the actual lease but often for a different term and commencing on a different date.
- Notional property, where the actual premises demised may be subject to certain assumptions and disregards requiring actuality to be modified with hypotheses, thus creating a property which only exists for the purposes of the rent review valuation.

Each rent review clause should, and normally will, state a 'criterion of value' usually directed to obtaining the open market rent of the notional letting. In the older review clauses, where the description of the notional lease was brief or non-existent, these criteria were of some significance as the only directions to a valuer in the lease; in a modern review clause, it will be the meaning and valuation impact of the notional lease which will be decisive.

1 Criteria of value

The exact label of value specified in the lease is not critical provided a full definition and elaboration follows with all the assumptions and disregards appropriate to that property. However it must not be assumed that the differences between one formulation and another are of no consequence.

(a) Market rents

The most usual practice is for a clause to provide that the new rent shall be 'the market rental value of the property' and then proceed to define that term for the purpose of the lease. However, it is remarkable that many different variants of even this basic theme are in common use. In addition to the 'market rental value' numerous variations on the theme have been adopted, such as 'open market rental value', 'market rent', 'yearly rent', 'full yearly market rental', 'commercial yearly rent', 'current market rental value', 'full rack rental value', 'current rack rent' and 'current letting value'. The received wisdom is that the exact phrase used does not matter—it is the detailed definition which follows which is crucial, and in most cases this will be true.

This view has judicial support in *Royal Exchange Assurance v Bryant Samuel Properties (Coventry) Ltd* [1985] 1 EGLR 84 where Peter Gibson J was of the opinion that in the phrase 'full current market rack rental value', 'market' did not add anything of great significance to 'rack' nor 'rack' to 'market'; and the addition of the word 'full' added nothing to the already cumbersome phrase. The phrase as a whole had the 'ordinary meaning' of what the hypothetical tenant was willing to pay the hypothetical landlord for the premises. Similarly, in *Sterling Land Office Developments Ltd v Lloyds Bank plc* (1984) 271 EG 894 Harman J rejected an argument that an 'open market' rent had a different meaning to a 'market' rent. At most, 'open' merely makes express what the review process implies—that the premises are available to all.

In some instances, a note of caution must be entered.

(i)   Yearly rent

The use of the term 'yearly rent', or any of its derivatives, is not uncommon; indeed the Model Forms, in all versions, adopt this term which on its face would appear to mean the same thing as a market rent. However, the authors must confess to slight unease on the use of the criterion 'yearly rent' in case it may be thought to import the notion of a 'yearly letting', an arrangement virtually unheard of in the commercial and industrial field in today's circumstances and a source of some difficulty when employed in s 24A(3) of the Landlord and Tenant Act 1954 as one of the criteria for settling the size of an interim rent award. For example, in *English Exporters London Ltd v Eldonwall Ltd* [1973] Ch 415 it was said that 'the process of applying section 34 to a hypothetical yearly tenancy is one that, at least under present conditions, may often have an air of unreality about it which would puzzle the most expert of valuers', per Megarry J at p 430. Some illuminating figures can be found in *Ratners (Jewellers) Ltd v Lemnoll Ltd* (1980) 255 EG 987 where Dillon J deducted 15 per cent for the difference between the rent payable for a term of years and that payable under a yearly tenancy. Moreover, on such a yearly tenancy there would be little point in providing for rent review machinery. No doubt the phrase 'yearly rent' is meant to refer to '£x pa' but it is not completely certain that this is achieved. As far as the authors are aware, no argument on the precise meaning of 'yearly rent' has been raised in any reported rent review decision; on the contrary, there are decisions (eg *99 Bishopsgate*

Ltd v Prudential Assurance Co Ltd (1984) 270 EG 950) which appear to assume the phrase refers to the annual market rent.

(ii) 'Having regard to'

In the first revised version, (1980), the Model Forms, while still maintaining the criterion of 'yearly rent', then proceeded (after the usual assumptions and elaboration of the criteria) to state that the yearly rent was to be fixed 'having regard to open market rental values current at the review date'. Far from removing the doubts, this approach raised the issue of how much regard the arbitrator is to have, and the spectre that the open market rental values might not be decisive in a special case. The authors' distaste for the phrase 'having regard to' is reinforced by the decisions in the *99 Bishopsgate* case (above), which reveals the valuation uncertainty it can cause and in *Stroud v Weir* [1987] 1 EGLR 190 where it was provided that 'regard shall be had' to three items including the Index of Retail Prices. The judge in the latter case was of the opinion that the rent was not required to go up by the increase in the index; it was just a factor to be taken into account. The reference to 'having regard to' has wisely been dropped from the 1985 Model Forms Revision but the authors would still prefer the Model Forms to direct determination of an open market rent specifically rather than a yearly rent.

(iii) Rack rents

It is also perhaps advisable to avoid the phrase 'rack rent' and similar variations such as 'current rack rent' or 'full rack rental value'. In *Compton Group Ltd v Estates Gazette Ltd* (1977) 36 P & CR 148, Sir John Pennycuick pointed out that 'rack rent' may mean either: (a) the rent which represents the full annual value of the holding or (b) the maximum rent permitted by law. Though his Lordship indicated that the former is the primary meaning of the word in legal language, there is a risk in a time of rent 'freeze' or other statutory limit on rents imposed in the future (see Chapter 19) that the latter meaning could apply. A similar risk existed where part of the premises were residential and subject to a registered rent: *Newman v Dorrington Developments Ltd* [1975] 1 WLR 1642. In our view, therefore, the more traditional 'market rent' is to be preferred (see also the discussion in *Langham House Developments Ltd v Brompton Securities Ltd* (1980) 256 EG 719 at 720).

(iv) Fair market rents

In a few review clauses, the concept of a 'fair' or 'reasonable' rent has been combined with that of a market rent to produce a criterion of a 'fair market rent'. In one arbitration of which the authors are aware, it was argued that it had a meaning different from a market rent; namely, that a market rent was to be determined in the usual way in the light of the provisions of the lease but, as a final step, the arbitrator had to consider if the result was objectively fair as between the parties and make any adjustment necessary to reflect that assessment. This may or may not be a sound argument (see the discussion of the *Ponsford* case below) but there is no good reason for the draftsman ever to allow it to be raised. An attempt to draw a distinction between market rents on the one hand and fair rents on the other failed in *99 Bishopsgate Ltd v Prudential Assurance Ltd* [1985] 1 EGLR 72. Counsel urged that where the arbitrator was to *have regard to* current open market lettings with vacant possession and was then to fix a *fair* yearly rent, the arbitrator need not assume the premises concerned are themselves to be let with vacant possession. In the construction of the clause in that case, the court held that 'fair' did not mean 'fair' between these particular parties but what the hypothetical tenant would fairly be expected to pay taking the premises from a hypothetical landlord.

It would seem, therefore, that when the parties presuppose an elaborate hypothetical framework, it is inappropriate for an arbitrator or valuer to use the direction to impose a 'fair rent' to exercise a degree of judgment if such exercise will involve acting in contrary manner to the hypothetical framework postulated—even if he is only directed to 'have regard to' those considerations.

(v) Full market rent

In *Royal Exchange Assurance v Bryant Samuel Properties (Coventry) Ltd* [1985] 1 EGLR 84 an attempt by counsel for the landlord to give the meaning of 'undiscounted' to the word 'full' failed; the judge preferred to give the phrase 'full current market rack rental value' its ordinary meaning of the rent a hypothetical tenant taking the demised premises under a single lease would pay. In *Dennis & Robinson v Kiossos Establishment* [1987] 1 EGLR 133 Dillon LJ was discussing a 'full market rent' and said that 'though it is assumed that there is a market, there is no assumption required as to how lively that market is' though it does not appear that the impact of 'full' had been argued.

The possibility of argument on the effect of 'full' should not be wholly discounted. In a time when the market is depressed, slack or sluggish, 'full' might be considered to allow the valuer to seek some adjustment (however slight) in the comparability of market rents in a depressed market on the basis that they are market rents but not full market rents. The argument might be stronger where there is a rent review in a development or complex where recent lettings have been subject to discounts perhaps unrelated to the wider market but the result of a temporary policy or financial needs of the actual lessor. If a willing lessor was not subject to those factors, then there is room to argue that the lettings with such discounts are lettings in the market but not 'full market rents'. The strongest point in favour of such an approach is that it does give meaning to the word 'full' and that would accord with accepted canons of construction (see p 299). It is perhaps more likely to be rejected on the basis that even a complex development creates its own market and if that market is depressed (for whatever reason) the reviewed rent should reflect that fact.

(vi)   Percentage of market rent

Particular care with drafting is required whenever a review to market rent is contained in a lease which provides for rent to be, for example, a specified percentage of such market rent, or, on the other hand, contains provision for extra rent over and above the market value, perhaps to cover some specified expenditure. Some such difficulties are illustrated by the *Lister Locks* and *Guys 'N' Dolls* cases at p 340; the *Royal Exchange Assurance v Bryant Samuel* case (above) provides another example. The rent there was to be '75% of the full current market rack rental value' where the demised premises was 130,000 square feet of land on which there were to be 32 warehouse units. The purpose of the discount was unexplained. The landlord's contention that the market rent was to be an aggregation of the market value of the individual units failed (if that is what the parties intended they should have said so). The words had their ordinary meaning, and if that meant that a tenant, who was likely to be an investor, got a double discount (ie the costs of and potential profit needed to be derivable from the intermediate lessor from the sublettings being reflected in a single open market rent for the whole, and then a 25 per cent deduction), then that was the result of the ordinary meaning of the words used.

(b)   'Reasonable rents' or 'fair rents'

Less commonly, a rent is to be assessed as 'the reasonable rent for the demised premises' or 'a reasonable rent'. A similar term which may be used is a 'fair rent'. In the context of commercial leases, 'fair rent' and 'reasonable rent' may mean the same thing—indeed, they were treated as interchangeable terms in *Store Properties and General Investments Ltd v Darrington (Rustington) Ltd* (1978) 3 February, unreported (QBD) where it was said that 'a rent could not be fair unless it were reasonable and could not be reasonable unless it were fair' (see also *Feltex International Ltd v JBL Consolidated Ltd* [1988] 1 NZLR 668 at 671). Nevertheless, it can be argued that the terms express a different meaning to that of open market rent. Thus, according to Sir Raymond Evershed MR in *John Kay Ltd v Kay* [1952] 1 QB 258 (a case that ruled on the interpretation of 'reasonable rent' in the Leasehold Property (Temporary Provisions) Act 1951), a reasonable rent acquires the application of a subjective test of what the judge thinks right and fair; whereas, for an open market rent, an objective test is to be applied of what the evidence shows is the market value. This straightforward approach was distinguished in *Ponsford v HMS Aerosols Ltd* [1979] AC 63 by a bare majority of their Lordships who held that 'a reasonable rent' in the lease in that case had a different meaning to a rent that was 'in all the circumstances reasonable', the phrase which occurred in the *Kay* case. A rent that took account of *all* the circumstances could take the particular circumstances of a tenant into consideration, including the fact that the tenant had paid for improvements to the demised premises whereas a 'reasonable rent' is a rent that is (objectively) reasonable for the premises and not a rent that would be reasonable for the (particular) tenant to pay. The demised premises included the improvements effected by the tenant when a damaged part was repaired from insurance proceeds and thus the reviewed rent had to take account of the improved premises. Consequently, the fact that the improvements in that case had been paid for by the tenant was to be ignored. It was acknowledged that this led to an 'unreasonable' result as between this particular tenant and this particular landlord since the tenant was to pay rent on items he had paid for (at 84B-C, 86F), but it was still a reasonable rent for the premises since a surveyor is to take the premises as he finds them.

On this basis, a 'reasonable rent', or 'a reasonable rent for the demised premises', would appear to produce an identical result to an assessment on the basis of an open market rent. This was indeed the view of Lord Keith, one of the majority in *Ponsford*, who opined that the meaning was 'a rent at which the demised premises might reasonably be expected to be let' and could envisage no circumstances in which a different result would be reached on an assessment based on a market rent. Viscount Dilhorne and Lord Fraser, who with Lord Keith formed the majority in the case, adopted the reasoning of Megarry J in *Cuff v Stone (J & F) Property Co Ltd* (Note) [1979] AC 87; while a reasonable rent was only to be read in a valuation sense it still meant a rent that was right and fair for those premises, and therefore it might be different from an open market rent since an exceptional or freak rent need not be taken into account. It allows 'the surveyor to reject a rent which though obtainable in the open market by reason of special circumstances appears to him to exceed a rent which is right and fair' (per Megarry J at 90H). Since the dissenting Lords in *Ponsford* were of the opinion that a 'reasonable rent' did allow a tenant's personal circumstances to be considered, and was therefore quite different to a market rent, no majority view as to the meaning of reasonable rent emerges. Some further assistance can be obtained from *Lear v Blizzard* [1983] 3 All ER 662. In that case, an option to renew was to be 'at a rent agreed between the parties'. In distinguishing the *Ponsford* case, Tudor Evans J held that the emphasis in the option on 'agreement between the parties' meant that the rent to be assessed by an arbitrator was not the objective market rent or a reasonable rent for the premises but a subjective assessment of what the parties would have agreed (despite the fact that they hadn't!). The view of Tudor Evans J has been followed and applied in New Zealand: *Feltex International Ltd v JBL Consolidated Ltd* [1988] 1 NZLR 668.

The issue of a 'fair and reasonable market rent' fell squarely for decision in *ARC Ltd v Schofield* [1990] NPC 3, another option case. Millet J held that 'fair and reasonable' might have a subjective or an objective meaning depending on the context. Allied to 'market rent', as in the instant lease, it was to have an objective meaning, not as introducing a qualification as to what, subjectively, the particular parties might have agreed. If upheld on appeal, this may be helpful in the future; at least it counters Lord Wilberforce's concession in *Ponsford v HMS Aerosols Ltd* [1979] AC 79 that he found the phrase so obscure as to be incomprehensible, a remark to which the NPC commentator drew attention.

It is submitted that the position now is:

(1) A review clause that requires a surveyor to assess a 'reasonable rent' or 'a reasonable rent for the demised premises' will probably produce a figure identical to a valuation on an open market basis. It need not be reasonable for the tenant but only reasonable for the premises. However, the surveyor can ignore a rent that, though obtainable, is not right and fair for those premises or he may reject a 'comparable' rent obtained for similar premises as exceptional by reason of special circumstances (per Viscount Dilhorne and Lord Fraser, Lord Keith contra).

(2) A review clause providing for assessment of a rent that is 'in all the circumstances reasonable' (*Kay*) 'which is reasonable for the tenant to pay' (per Lord Fraser in *Ponsford* at 83F) or 'reasonable for the parties to agree' (*Lear v Blizzard*) shifts the emphasis and requires the surveyor to take account of circumstances affecting a particular tenant and possibly a particular landlord. This may produce a figure markedly lower than the open market rent if the market rent is inflated (for example) by circumstances of shortage (per Lord Evershed in *Kay*). In a case of local over-supply, it could exceed a 'depressed' market rent. The value of improvements paid for by a tenant, as those made in *Ponsford*, may then be disregarded. Indeed, such a result was held possible in *Lear v Blizzard* where the option to renew at a rent to be agreed was held to require a rent which the parties would reasonably have agreed, discounting the effect of improvements to the extent the tenant had paid for them. The case is more fully discussed at p 276.

(3) There is little authority as to the meaning of a review clause whose criterion of value is 'a fair rent', probably because the phrase has quite properly been avoided by reason of its use in Rent Act legislation. However in *Compton Group Ltd v Estates Gazette Ltd* (1977) 36 P & CR 148 (considered more fully at p 548, below) the Court of Appeal discussed the meaning of 'fair rack rent', in the course of which it was said that 'fair' suggests the upshot of free negotiation rather than an amount imposed by statute (per Sir John Pennycuick at 155). On the basis of *Ponsford* it may well be that a 'fair rent for the demised premises' would be distinguished from a 'fair rent for the tenant to pay' in the way outlined above, though

the danger exists that the particular approach applied to Rent Act valuations would be adopted. In some judgments, 'fair' and 'reasonable' are used interchangeably or in tandem, although not used at all in the provision under consideration.

If the authors may be permitted a little speculation on one possible meaning of 'fair rent' or 'fair market rent' it is that its effect may be to eliminate from consideration of the market and from evidence tendered of comparables any transaction which is in some demonstrable way out of line with normal behaviour in the market in question. The 'special lessee'—eg the multiple prepared to pay above the going rate to secure representation in a particular location— is not always to be ignored in assessing a market, for there may be several such tenants in competition, but there would at least be an argument to ignore or discount the rent bid or agreed by such an abnormal tenant as a comparable where 'fair' is the chosen epithet, especially if linked to a market rent. The example chosen is not the only instance that might occur. This approach is supported by a passage in the judgment of Tudor Evans J in *Lear v Blizzard* [1983] 3 All ER 662 at 671, where the word fair was implied and construed to exclude a 'freak offer' from an exceptional tenant. *Kelly's Draftsman*, Form 14 (printed in Part Seven) incorporates a reference to 'fair market rent'.

(4) The addition of 'market' to the 'fair and reasonable' attribute is likely to rob the latter phrase of most of its force: (*ARC Ltd v Schofield* [1990] NPC 3).

In conclusion, none of the criteria of value based on a reasonable or fair rent commend themselves—particularly the use of 'a fair rent', which should be shunned. If a 'reasonableness' test is adopted care should be taken in choosing the words to make it clear whether reference is to a 'reasonable rent for the premises' or a 'reasonable rent for the tenant to pay'. The only advantages of such criteria would be a situation where the parties to the lease of a unique or unusual type of premises wish to avoid extreme fluctuations that might occur to the market value of such premises.

(c) 'Best rent'

A standard phrase that is often found in draft rent review clauses emanating from landlords and their solicitors is that of 'best rent', whereby the rent payable on review is to be the best rent obtainable for the demised premises, a concept that has gave rise to tenants' complaints at the time they first appeared (see (1979) 76 *Law Society's Gazette* 647). There are, of course, the usual variations on the theme such as 'best market rent' or 'highest rent'. In most instances the resultant rent produced will be identical to that produced by the more usual 'market rent' basis. In a minority of cases, however, the formula may result in a higher rent. This could occur where there are 'comparables' (ie recently obtained rents for comparable premises) and one of these comparables is particularly high (for example, for premises to let to a large company to whom the rent is no object and who were prepared to pay a seemingly excessive sum to secure the premises they desired). That one high figure may well be the guide and criterion by which the 'best rent' will be measured and the surveyor will have to ignore other comparables at more moderate figures.

'Best rent' formulas may tend to 'drive up' rental values over a particular area and, therefore, are desired only by landlords. For example, 'best rent' criteria in leases from a common lessor encourage the landlord, on review, to select the most vulnerable tenant first and use the rent agreed or settled on that review as the standard for comparable reviews. An even less desirable situation would arise if one tenant was associated with or beholden to the landlord thus enabling an unreal 'best rent' to be fixed, though in such circumstances the sum so produced might be liable to be set aside (see *Finchbourne Ltd v Rodrigues* [1976] 3 All ER 581).

In the review clause in *Daejan Investments Ltd v Cornwall Coast Country Club* (1984) 50 P & CR 157 the rack rental value was defined as the 'highest rent at which at the rent review date the premises ought reasonably be expected to be let in the open market'. It was the opinion of the judge that a letting in the open market is the highest rent obtainable; the word highest adding no more than emphasis. On this basis, it can now be strongly argued that a 'best' rent is likewise no different from an open market rent but, on the other hand, there remains the real possibility that the points made above could apply. There are many instances where a number of cases (or even a particularly convincing single decision) appear to have settled a particular line of construction but later causes have nullified, qualified or even reversed the initial trend, which explains the rather tentative nature of these comments.

The prudent tenant will still seek to avoid 'best rents' in new leases, but if faced with one on review, should argue for a meaning identical to that of the usual market rent. This will be particularly true where the term 'best rent' or 'best yearly rent' is used in the context of defining the open market rent.

(d) 'Economic rent'

In modern use, 'economic' is often used as synonymous with 'market' or 'arrived at by the forces of supply and demand' in contrast to a price or charge that is subsidised, concessionary or otherwise shielded from what are regarded as the laws of economics. It is in frequent use in this way in consideration of public monetary policies. Although it has not been traced in any reported case, it is submitted that it would be equated with market rent in a rent review context, and not accepted in its other sense of cheap or restricted.

(e) 'Return on freehold value'

One of the Forms published in 1984 by the Incorporated Society of Valuers and Auctioneers incorporated a concept of return on freehold value, put forward as best suited to residential property or commercial premises leased for a premium or on a building lease. As can be seen from the Form, printed in the Part Seven, it provides for the ascertainment of a freehold value, on certain assumptions, and the calculation of the revised rent as a percentage of that notional price. Clearly more complicated variations are possible, eg a variable percentage linked to market returns or some other index, assumptions of a cleared site, alternative uses, and so on. Virtually any method by which an initial rent might be calculated by a developer or other owner could be adapted and adopted. Potential problems can be envisaged, especially if fiscal or other factors distort freehold values without, at least in the short term or to the same extent, having similar effect on market rentals. If the percentage is fixed it may vary above or below the market range of yields at the time of each review. If it is variable, the problems of ascertainment may be acute if the market is in a state of uncertainty at the review dates. On the other hand, this formula may provide a sure basis for unusual properties, discussed at p 257

'Return on freehold' differs, of course, from valuing the rent on an assumed 'bare site'. 'Site value' was the basis adopted in the lease in *Basingstoke & Deane Borough Council v Host Group Ltd* [1988] 1 WLR 348 and it is a valuation basis frequently found, for example, in New Zealand (see *Duncan v Mackie* [1939] GLR 503). Ground rent reviews are fully considered in Chapter 13, below.

(f) Position where no criterion of value is stated

It is possible to have a valid rent review clause without a standard by which the rent can be ascertained. A clause of this nature was accepted without question or comment from either counsel or judge in *Kenilworth Industrial Sites Ltd v E C Little & Co Ltd* [1975] 1 WLR 143 and upheld in two cases (*Store Properties & General Investments v Darrington (Rustington) Ltd* (1978) 3 February, unreported (QBD) and *Thomas Bates & Son Ltd v Wyndham's (Lingerie) Ltd* [1981] 1 WLR 505 (see the discussion in Chapter 9, p 274 ff). Though it is valid a valuer or arbitrator is left with the thankless task of setting a new rent without guide-lines, and thus such a clause is a source of potential conflict.

(g) Early basic valuation directions based on s 34

Though the detailed wording will vary, the standard review clause

will have a basic definition which directs the valuer or arbitrator to
fix an open market rent or, in the words of s 34(1) of the Landlord
and Tenant Act 1954 (the section which defines the rent payable under
a new tenancy granted under the Act) a rent:

'at which, having regard to the terms of the tenancy (other than those relating
to rent), the holding might reasonably be expected to be let in the open market
by a willing lessor.'

The formula from s 34 was the basis of many early forms of review
clause. It is no longer suitable as it stands—in particular the cryptic
disregard 'other than those relating to rent' requires reformation to ensure
clarity (see p 333) and an express reference to a willing lessee is also
appropriate.

Adopting a basic framework in early rent review clauses similar to
that in s 34 meant that the valuation under a rent review was on similar
criteria to the valuation, in the absence of agreement, on a tenant's
application for a new tenancy under the 1954 Act. This arguably meant
that the 'field of comparables' was widened or, at least, tended to eliminate
differences in valuation on review and on statutory renewal although
it is now too late to point to empirical evidence to support this view.
Thus, on this basis, in a 15–year term with reviews every 5 years for
a new notional 15–year term the rent that is reviewed every 5 years
will be determined in a similar manner to that determined on an
application under the 1954 Act at the end of 15 years; moreover, the
new tenancy under the Act may well include provision for varying the
rent (see s 34(3)) and these periodic reviews will also adopt the same
criteria. Now that the rent review criteria incorporated in many lettings
are far more complex and there are usually plenty of comparables from
other rent reviews and open market lettings the need for a formula based
on the statutory formula has been weakened.

The wording of such a clause based on s 34 is nonetheless clear enough
to be the basis of a valuation that fairly balances the parties' interests
and flexible enough to allow for the provision for specific matters while
the basic wording remains unchanged. The valuation has to pay regard
to the terms of the tenancy and it was usual to add to the definition
those matters expressly stated to be disregarded in s 34.

One early addition to the substance of the s 34 wording, now made
by the Model Forms, was the provision that the tenant is 'willing', so
that the rent reflects that which would be expected in the open market
'by a willing lessor to a willing lessee'. In the context of s 34, there
might be an argument that the additional words are not required because
the tenant must be 'willing' since he is applying for a new tenancy but,
in view of a tenant's right to withdraw from a new tenancy ordered
by the court (see s 36(2)), this argument is difficult to sustain. The same
does not apply to the lessor, who has no choice but to renew, so the
need to specify a willing lessor is obvious. Another possible argument

is that the use of market rent implies a sufficiency of willing tenants, although that does not meet the hypothesis of eager or over-willing tenants. In fact, on renewal, there will be degrees of enthusiasm ranging from the tenant who is half-hearted and constrained by circumstances to the one who wants a renewal very much. At a review, a lessee who has seen market forces or local conditions change against him may be most unwilling. Thus, there is a counter-argument that, even on renewal, a different result may occur from the exclusion of the requirement that the lessee be willing, for what is sought is the market rent and a rent in a market of only willing lessors may be a different rent to one in a market of willing lessors *and* willing lessees. For example, one could envisage a state of affairs in a particular area where all potential lessees suffered those very attributes that Donaldson J in the *Evans* case (discussed below) said must be disregarded in construing the hypothetical willing lessee. The additional words ensure that the particular qualities and situations of both landlord and tenant are ignored in the assessment of the new rent. The problems of the assumptions for rent review when s 34 is carried verbatim into the review formula is discussed at p 446.

2 Notional parties

(a) Meaning of 'willing parties'

The usual express assumption of a willing lessor and a willing lessee provides the first and central notional aspect of the hypothetical letting.

The importance of the words may be illustrated by the case of *F R Evans (Leeds) Ltd v English Electric Co Ltd* (1977) 36 P & CR 185. The wording of the review clause was: 'The yearly market rental . . . shall mean the rent at which the demised premises are worth to be let with vacant possession on the open market as a whole between a willing lessor and a willing lessee'. Regard was to be had to the terms and conditions of the lease and there were various matters to be disregarded. Donaldson J, whose detailed reasoning and judgment were upheld and apparently fully approved on appeal ((1978) 245 EG 662) acknowledged that there was no authority giving guidance upon how a rent review clause was to be operated. (The principles in relation to a willing vendor and a willing purchaser in a compulsory purchase statute had been laid down by the Privy Council in *Vyricherla Narayana Gajapatiraju v Revenue Divisional Officer Vizagapatam* [1939] AC 302 in terms remarkably consonant with the judge's analysis of willing lessor and willing lessee.) He examined the instructions in this wording and distilled three valuable guide-lines:

(1) the new rent is to be that which the premises are worth for letting on the open market with vacant possession on the review date (the tenants are deemed to have moved out of the premises);

(2) the premises are being offered in their actual condition, subject to any direction in the lease to the contrary such as to maintenance and repair; and

(3) there is a rent upon which a willing lessor and a willing lessee could and would agree.

In his Lordship's view, the 'willing lessor' and 'willing lessee' were both abstractions—hypothetical persons, one actually desiring to lease premises, the other to obtain premises to satisfy the needs that these premises would fulfil. The consequence is that the willing lessee (or the lessor as the case may be) is not identified with the actual lessee (or lessor). Therefore, either party's reluctance or, for example, cash flow crisis is irrelevant; so is the fact of occupation by the tenant prior to the review date.

The notion of the 'willing lessee' is closely analagous to that of the 'prudent lessee' laid down in New Zealand as long ago as 1912 in *Drapery & General Importing Company of New Zealand Ltd v Mayor of Wellington* (1912) 31 NZLR 598 in the context of ground rents. This is further discussed in Chapter 13 p 466 below, but it is worth noting that in applying this test in *Wellington City Council v National Bank of New Zealand* [1970] NZLR 660 North P stated that the test meant that a valuer or umpire was only obliged to consider what factors would be taken into account by a prudent lessee; 'in short he was only concerned with matters which will affect the mind and ultimately the judgment of a prudent lessee in making his offer to the landlord'. So too in *Feltex International Ltd v JBL Consolidated Ltd* [1988] 1 NZLR 668 Henry J observed:

'. . . the inquiry is to what a prudent lessee would pay for these premises, having regard to the term and conditions of the lease. This must represent the amount which he can reasonably expect to pay for the rights and obligations which are undertaken in the lease.'

(b) 'Willing parties'- an implicit notion

In the case where reference to a willing lessee (or less commonly, to willing parties at all) has been omitted, whether by accident or design, it can be implied or assumed from the nature of the open market valuation postulated by the usual review clause that there is to be an assumption of a willing lessor and a willing lessee: *Dennis & Robinson Ltd v Kiossos Establishment* [1987] 1 EGLR 133. There the Court of Appeal approved the dictum of Templeman LJ (as he then was) in *Law Land Co Ltd v Consumers' Association Ltd* (1980) 255 EG 617 where, in discussing a clause which expressly defined the market rent he said:

'That clause envisages the existence of an open market, an offer with vacant possession, a willing lessor and, by implication, a willing lessee.'

A similar view was taken by Peter Gibson J in *Daejan Investments Ltd v Cornwall Coast Country Club* (1984) 50 P & CR 157 at 162 where, in a clause expressly providing for a willing lessor, he said: 'the hypothetical lessee . . . must, I think, be taken to be a willing lessee'.

In the *Dennis & Robinson* case the rent review clause was unusual for one so relatively recent (1982) in that, while the reviewed rent was to be that 'at which the property might reasonably be let in the open market . . . for a term of 25 years with vacant possession and otherwise on the same terms and conditions as this lease (including the provisions for rent review at the intervals herein specified)' it did not provide for the commonly occurring hypothesis that the letting was to be by a 'willing lessor' to a 'willing lessee'.

The landlords sought a declaration that the valuer was to determine a rent which would be expected to be agreed between a willing lessee and a willing lessor. Though protected to some extent by a minimum rent provision, they argued that reference to the 'full yearly market rent' and 'the rent reasonably expected in the open market' postulated a willing lessor and a willing lessee. The tenant asked for a declaration that a valuer could not make any such assumption but must, in valuing the open market rent, determine if 'anyone would wish to take a lease on the terms offered'. The tenant supported his argument by reference to the clause prohibiting assignment without a prior offer of surrender to the lessor; such surrender offer was to be at 'its fair market value as between willing buyer and willing seller'—the view being that if the concept was express in that clause, its absence from the rent review clause was crucial, and so it should not be implied.

The deputy judge took the view that the presence of the phrases 'willing lessor' and 'willing lessee' added little or nothing to the requirement of an open market rent but was unwilling to assume that there would be a letting in the market. He considered that there might be no willing lessees in the market, that was a matter for the valuer and he declined to make either of the rival declarations sought. The Court of Appeal reversed his decision but also chose to make no declaration.

Referring to the review clause in that case, Dillon LJ said:

'These phrases assume that there is a market in which agreement will be reached for a hypothetical letting of the premises to a hypothetical tenant. That necessarily imports a hypothetical landlord who is willing to let the premises and a hypothetical tenant who is willing to take the premises on the terms prescribed by the rent review clause.'

Fox LJ (at p 134H) formulated the following assumptions in relation to the phrase 'rent at which the property might reasonably be expected to be let in the open market':

(1) There will be a letting of the property . . . in my opinion this must be so. The language . . . expressly contemplates a letting in the open market.
(2) There is a market in which that letting is agreed.
(3) The landlord is willing to let the premises. Equally, the supposed tenant is willing to take the premises. The notion of a letting in the open market

between an unwilling lessor and an unwilling lessee (or between a willing lessor and a unwilling lessee) makes no sense.

The tenant's argument that the result produced artificiality was rejected; the assumptions were implicit and the result of the bargain reached.

The Court of Appeal decision restored the meaning of open market rent and the implicit nature of willing notional parties in that market to that reflected in the *F R Evans* judgment. However, just as Donaldson J in that case accepted that there might be a paucity of willing parties, so too the *Dennis & Robinson* decision leaves no doubt that there may be degrees of enthusiasm between willing lessees and there is no assumption as to how lively the market is. As Fox LJ remarked:

'. . . the clause requires the assumption of a willing lessee. But the willing lessee is not going to pay more than the market requires him to pay.'

The case has exorcised the spectre of a market totally bereft of participants—nothing more.

3   Notional period of letting

The notional lease to be valued at a rent review will normally incorporate the terms of the actual lease—and the valuation consequences and the construction aspects of such incorporation are fully discussed in the previous chapter. Apart from the necessary disregard of the amount or quantum of the rent, the other terms need not be altered. The parties *may* move the lease to be valued away from the reality by express assumptions or disregards as to, for example, the use of the premises (see below) and it is important to ensure that the notional lease includes the actual provisions for rent review (see Chapter 11, p 333, above). The most important notional aspect of the hypothetical lease is, however, the notional period of letting which is to be assumed at each review date.

(a)   The notional period of letting—the alternatives

There are at least five possible alternative approaches which can be adopted:

(1) The 'review period approach'—ie a term equal to the number of years between each review date.

(2) The 'residue approach'—ie a term equal to the actual 'remainder of the term' at each relevant review date, so that the period of notional letting decreases at each subsequent review date.

(3) The 'original term approach'—ie a term equal in length to the original term.

(4) An express compromise—the lease may expressly specify a fixed or varying term to be assumed (different from the first three possibilities).

A particularly common compromise between the residue and original term approaches is to have a notional term equal either to the unexpired residue, or, say, 10 years, whichever is the greater. In longer terms, then the compromise may well be the residue or a period of 20 years, whichever is the greater (as in *Basingstoke and Deane Borough Council v Host Group Ltd* [1988] 1 WLR 348).

(5) A 'best notional term at valuation' approach. This is found in some modern leases so, for example, the notional term might be:

'. . . for such a term (but not exceeding the length of the [original] Term) as would at the relevant review date then command the best rent with vacant possession.'

This approach leaves the expert or arbitrator to determine the term and then determine the rent; yet the length of the term and the amount of rent as reviewed may be interdependent—which is to be fixed first? Such a provision may also move the rent review valuation further away from the reality between the parties.

The choice in the precedents, and the preferred practice, has changed over the years. The 'review period approach' was never common and as the periods of review dropped from long periods of say 14 years to the now usual 5 years or less pattern it became particularly inappropriate. It would produce a rent related to a period rarely found in the market and lower than rent being negotiated in the market for longer terms. It was once usual for the 'residue approach' to be chosen rather than the original term approach but the latter is now increasingly common. Lack of judicial sympathy with the use of the 'original term' means that the issue must be put beyond doubt by express words in the lease if what is truly intended is a review equal in length to the full term. Where the lease is silent, or there is lack of clarity, then the 'residue approach' will most often be implied (see below).

The length of a notional term can have significant impact on the reviewed rent. Thus, specifying in a 25–year term that it shall be assumed that there are 25 years to run on the review after 20 years may cause the revised rent to be greater than with a 5–year term residue assumption. Occasionally, however, it could have the opposite effect. The argument in favour of the short period stems from the fact that the tenant would often have preferred a much shorter term in the first place—perhaps with an option to renew; the longer term hypothesis is one that normally benefits the institutional landlord seeking to obtain a long guaranteed income return. The 'residue approach' then seeks to balance these conflicting demands. The 'original term approach' can be theoretically justified by more that just the supposed benefit to the landlord. For a review is substituting a rent within a 25–year term (to return to our example) with a revised rent and it is a rent that is supposedly applicable to that length of time. It is seeking to nullify the effect of inflation and restore the bargain made by the parties in the first place—and the bargain was for a term of 25–years. As the Background Notes to the revised Model Forms point out, the assumption of a term equivalent to the original term does not normally prejudice the tenant's interest and it avoids a false temporary reduced rent and a consequent temporary reduction in investment value at the last or later reviews. However, at the drafting stage, it must be borne in mind that the valuation implications of the alternative approaches will vary according to the nature of the property and the state of the relevant segment of the market. In some situations, a notional shorter term may command rents equal to, and even in excess of, longer terms—perhaps because the property is in need of repairs in the medium term future which a shorter period would avoid or if there is a glut of longer terms available in the market where many of the willing tenants would only be seeking the shorter period.

(b) Where no notional term is specified

If a review clause is silent as to the period of time on which the rent falls to be calculated then it will be necessary for an arbitrator, expert or judge to decide which approach is most appropriate. Indeed, the parties' valuers will have to make the same decision. In the absence of any clear provision in the lease or any express and admissible evidence as to the parties' intention the 'residue' approach will normally be the assumption implied and applied since that is the actual term of years remaining between the actual parties and, after all, what is being settled is the rent for the specific lease. Consequently, the correct approach is for the valuer, expert or arbitrator to assume a lease for the residue of the term.

This, it must be said, is a trend that has become much firmer in the last few years as part of a general trend to favour the actual state of affairs when no express contrary indication is given (see Chapter 10, p 314). In *MFI Properties Ltd v BICC Group Pension Trust Ltd* [1986] 1 EGLR 115 Hoffman J described the assumption of the actual residue as a 'prima facie assumption', justified by the purpose of rent review clauses. In *Norwich Union Life Assurance Society v Trustee Savings Banks Central Board* [1986] 1 EGLR 136 an arbitrator had decided that he should assume the 'residue approach' when construing a clause otherwise silent on the issue. In declining to grant leave to appeal the same judge, Hoffman J, was of the opinion the arbitrator was right since there is 'a presumption that the hypothesis upon which the rent should be fixed at review should bear as close a resemblance to reality as possible'; the landlord 'would be having it both ways if he was entitled not only to adjustment for changes in the market and changes in inflation but also to the assumption that what was being granted on the rent review date was a brand new lease rather than what was in fact the case, a lease which by then was 12 years expired'. He justified his opinion by reference to *Ponsford v HMS Aerosols Ltd* [1979] AC 63 at 76H (Viscount Dilhorne) and *Pearl Assurance plc v Shaw* [1985] 1 EGLR 92 at 93 (Vinelott J) though it should be noted that the comments in those two cases were where the relevant lease in question expressly provided for the rent to be assessed for a period equal to the unexpired residue. The criticism of 'having it both ways' is not entirely convincing either. To assume a new letting and a new term equal to the original term granted may give a double benefit; it is not however, the process of both relying on and simultaneously denying one concept which is the usual meaning of the phrase 'having it both ways'. Nevertheless, in the light of the *Basingstoke and Deane* case and the decisions noted in the next section, the presumption of a valuation of the actual residue in the notional lease is currently a very strong one.

Where there is a reference to an 'open market rent' and the market practice is to provide for and calculate reviews by reference to a term of the same length as the original term running from the review date, it is still just arguable that the implication of the shorter period should be displaced and the 'original term approach' implied but the recent decisions suggest it is an argument unlikely to engender judicial sympathy. It would need compelling evidence of the provisions in comparable leases to establish the original term as the market norm. That evidence is now less likely to be found than, say, 10 or 15 years ago when it was the dominant approach. The publication of the ISVA Forms in late 1984 marked the change in sentiment and the 1985 revision of the RICS/ Law Society Model Forms also made the switch. Both adopt the 'compromise formula'—ie a notional term which is either actual residue or a set period of medium length whichever is the greater.

(c) The 'original term approach'—the need for clarity

Where the notional period chosen is the original term, or the unexpired residue of the term, it is essential (except with the second choice at the final review) to establish if the notional lease for that term includes the rent review mechanism so as to see if it should be taken account of in the actual review in hand—an issue fully discussed in the previous chapter at p 333. The lease litigated in *Pugh v Smiths Industries Ltd* (1982) 264 EG 823 provided for review by reference to a notional lease for a term equal to the unexpired residue of the term, originally 25 years, on the basis that the lessee would observe covenants as in the lease but excluding the review provisions. The landlord succeeded in his contention that on the first review he would obtain a rent appropriate for a 20–year term without reviews, notwithstanding that he would in reality obtain further reviews every 5 years, on a 15 and 10–year like basis for the first two of them. The wording of the exclusion allowed no latitude in the matter, as the whole clause part of which created the reviews was excised from the notional lease.

The second issue that must be made clear if the notional period is to be equal to that of the original term is the date from which the notional period is to run. Modern precedents state 'that such term begins on the relevant review date' (EFP (5th ed) Form 22); older precedents merely state that the rent is that 'obtainable on the relevant review date . . . for a term equivalent to the original length of the said term' (Conveyancer Precedent 5–57). A series of recent decisions have come to indicate that a lease of the latter type may be construed to be a term calculated from the date of the actual lease and not the relevant review date. Where this occurs, the practical result is a notional term equivalent to the residue of the lease (except for the notional impact of a notional statutory renewal of the term—see below). The impetus for such construction appears to be the prevailing desire to make the notional term accord as far as possible with reality, but it may be less welcome in this respect than in other manifestations of the new sentiment.

In *R & A Millett (Shops) Ltd v Legal & General Assurance Society Ltd* [1985] 1 EGLR 103 the review clause expressly provided for the notional term to be the unexpired residue of the lease. The lease also contained an option to determine to apply after the expiration of the first 12 years 'of the term hereby granted'. For the purposes of the hypothetical lease to be valued at review, this was construed to mean a term beginning when the actual lease began, so the option was not to be carried forward into the notional lease at every renewal. In *Dennis & Robinson Ltd v Kiossos Establishment* at first instance, (1986) 280 EG 200, where the clause required a reviewed rent 'for a term of 25 years . . . on the same terms and conditions as this lease (including the provisions for rent review at the intervals herein specified)', notwithstanding the fact that the point was not argued, the deputy judge (Michael Wheeler QC) opined that 'term of 25 years' meant 25 years from the date of the commencement of the lease—so that the hypothetical lease was on the basis of a term equal to the residue of the existing underlease. He supported his view by reference to the 'intervals herein specified' taking this to mean the *actual* dates of review rather than the 5 year time span. In the Court of Appeal, this part of the judge's order was set aside not on the merits of the argument but on the basis that the parties were not in dispute on the point. The landlord's counsel conceded that the deputy judge should not have ruled upon it.

A direction that the notional term was to be 'for a term equivalent to the said term' was construed to mean a term for the unexpired residue of a term dated from the date of the lease: *Lynnthorpe Enterprises Ltd v Sidney Smith (Chelsea) Ltd* [1990] 1 EGLR 148; upheld on appeal [1990] EGCS 60. Since the 'said term' was defined as 'a term of 15 years from the date hereof' there was some justification for the conclusion but it is still unlikely to be what the draftsman intended. It is less easy to justify the result in *Ritz Hotel v Ritz Casino* [1989] 2 EGLR 135 where the valuation direction was for 'a term equivalent to the term hereby granted'; the view of Vinelott J was that the natural construction of these words was a term of 21 years (the original term length) from the date of the lease. This view, though now in the ascendant, is, with respect, questionable for if that is what the draftsman had intended surely a direct reference to the unexpired residue would have been expected. The result in these cases can be criticised on a number of grounds:

(1) Although the *Lynnthorpe* case (at first instance) does not refer to the earlier *Ritz Hotel* decision, both purport to apply the *Basingstoke and Deane* 'presumption in favour of reality' and the *Norwich Union v TSB* presumption in favour of a term equal to the residue of the actual lease. However, the authors find these arguments unconvincing since the result does not reflect the reality—which is an occupying tenant with a residue of a term which has existed since it was granted not a fresh term in the market for a term commencing many years before its date of execution. Moreover, the *Norwich Union v TSB* presumption was made in the context of a lease which was silent on the notional term point (Warner J in the *Lynnthorpe* case partly recognised this and stressed the reality presumption).

(2) A new lease for a term commencing many years before the review date is not something for which there is in the real world a market since it is a creature which does not exist. (A common start date for all terms in a development with an increasing measure of back-dating as the later leases are granted is a different matter.) It is one thing for the parties to create notional improbabilities; it is less defensible when they are created unnecessarily by a process of construction. Nevertheless, Warner J preferred this answer to a term of years equal to the unexpired residue (which was the only other alternative if the 'full' original term approach was to be rejected) since the prospects of being granted a long term at renewal under the Landlord and Tenant Act 1954 (see section (*e*) below) was greater with a term retrospectively dating from the actual date of the lease.

(3) Both judgments proceed on the assumption made by Hoffman J in *Norwich Union v TSB*, namely that the original term (running forward from the renewal date) approach produces a manifestly unjust result. However, not only is there a strong theoretical justification (see above) but also the residue approach can be equally unfair to a lessee at the end of a lengthy term when the lease contains provisions appropriate to that longer term. The point is that the valuation consequences are not clear cut or necessarily one sided and it is submitted that the intentions of the parties in the lease as derived from the literal meaning of the words they used should be allowed to operate, for better or worse, in this instance. Unfairness to the tenant because of the terms of a standard lease imposed by the landlord with the predominant bargaining power has been a feature of the English landlord and tenant scene for many years.

No general power to redress the imbalance exists (see *Maynard v Moseley* and Chapter 10, p 314) nor do the judges seem to have hankered for it. Hence its emergence in this one setting is a departure from the usual 'hands off' attitude.

An appeal against the *Ritz Hotel* decision was dismissed by consent following a settlement between the parties. It is thought that more litigation on the issue is likely and perhaps, as in other areas of particular concern, appellate guide-lines may eventually follow but the cases do indicate the strength of the current judicial preference for the 'residue' approach, and the contrast with the earlier views on the meaning of 'equivalent', 'equal' and synonymous phrases.

(d) The 'residue approach'—the need for clarity

The meaning of what is meant by an express direction that the notional term is to be equal to the residue of the actual term is less likely to cause problems than a direction that it is to be equivalent to the original term—though the fact that a particular lease was contracted out of the 1954 Act would mean that there would be no statutory continuation of the term and no prospect of statutory renewal (see below).

Where, however, there is a reversionary lease granted contemporaneously with the existing lease and taking effect as the existing lease expires, a construction may follow that in *Toyota (GB) Ltd v Legal and General Assurance (Pensions Management) Ltd* [1989] 2 EGLR 123. There it was held that a direction to value a lease 'equivalent in length to the residue unexpired at the review date' should not be read literally. To do so in that case would have meant that a review after 15 years would be on the basis of a notional term of one year (since the existing lease was for a 16 year term) when the reality was that there was 35 years to run (34 of them under the reversionary lease). Not only would that review have produced a yearly rent (see the problems of this discussed at p 383) for the last year of the first lease but the rent for the first 4 years of the reversionary lease would also be determined on that basis. This literal reading of the lease was, however, said to produce an absurd, irrational and capricious result enabling the Court of Appeal to imply an assumption so that 'the term hereby granted' in the first lease included the term granted by the supplemental lease. The intention of the parties was to ensure the tenant paid the market value and the implication was one on which the parties would have agreed without question had the point been raised. The authors are less confident of the inevitability of that finding than was the Court of Appeal. The obvious reason for the use of two leases was the saving for the tenant in stamp duty. Doubtless if the attention of the landlord's advisers had been focused on the possible consequence of the split this accommodation of the tenant's wishes to save stamp duty might have been refused. With its attention centred on the stamp duty saving (it is not easy to postulate another explanation for the two lease approach), the tenant may equally have overlooked the possible bonus of the literal meaning of the first lease standing alone. Because of the artificiality of the conveyancing device, the outcome is not unjustifiable in itself, but the assumption of 'what the parties would have agreed' is rather shaky. Moreover, there are certainly other cases where the parties have had to accept a strictly literal interpretation of the wording used despite its harsh or capricious impact on the interests of one party—see, for example, the *Pugh v Smith Industries* line of cases. (For a discussion of implication of terms, see p 273.)

(e) Prospect of statutory renewal

Where the notional period of letting is short, or shorter than the ideal term in the market for the premises in question, then the prospects of statutory renewal of the notional term can be taken into account: *Pivot Properties Ltd v Secretary of State for the Environment* (1979) 253 EG 373. The acute problems that a short notional period for letting can raise, as well as the financial consequences that may result from any notional period, are vividly illustrated by the decision. A 42–year lease of 'very large' premises provided for periodic reviews. Though the period between reviews varied (from $3\frac{1}{2}$ to 7 years), most of the periods between reviews were of $5\frac{1}{2}$ years and there was a direction that the review was to be to 'the best rent at which the demised premises might reasonably be expected to be let in the open market as a whole for a term not exceeding five years and one half of another year'. Phillips J pointed out an odd feature of this phraseology: the inclusion of the words 'not exceeding' were peculiar, for the exact length of the notional period ('one of the principal features by which the rent is to be fixed') was thereby left to the parties to agree or the third party to determine. In fact, the parties agreed on $5\frac{1}{2}$ years, but difficulties might have arisen had they not done so. The first lesson to be derived from the case is, therefore, to ensure that the exact notional period is specified. The judgment also contained the observation that the notional letting period of $5\frac{1}{2}$ years in a lease of 42 years was unreal as it did not accurately reflect the situation, except at the end of the term—an observation critical of the review-period approach and in accord with the later trend towards preference for the 'residue approach' and its accord with the reality of the parties position.

The issue in the *Pivot Properties* case was whether, assuming the notional letting period of $5\frac{1}{2}$ years, account could be taken of the possibility of continuation or renewal under the Landlord and Tenant Act 1954, Part II. It was held that account could and should be taken for, although the parties ('willing') and the term ($5\frac{1}{2}$ years) were hypothetical, the figure has to be determined according to the facts as they are and in such a situation the well-known provisions of the 1954

Act would be borne in mind. Unlike *Plinth Properties Investments Ltd v Mott, Hay and Anderson* (1978) 249 EG 1167 (where the possibility of a relaxation of a user covenant was held to be too intangible to be assessed) there was a definite possibility to be taken into account that could not be disregarded merely because of attendant uncertainties. As a result, in the *Pivot Properties* case the rent was assessed at £2,925,000 pa instead of £2,100,000, and it was estimated that, by taking renewal under the 1954 Act into account more than £14 million additional rent would be payable over the 42-year term. The first instance decision was upheld by the Court of Appeal (*Secretary of State for the Environment v Pivot Properties Ltd* (1980) 41 P & CR 248), that court stressing that the valuation approach approved by the judge was not one of assessing rent for a period longer than that specified in the rent review period but rent for a term of the length specified yet reflecting the market's assessment of the potentiality or prospect of statutory renewal. Speculation on that prospect may not have been too difficult in the circumstances of that case—an extremely large office development, a government department as tenant and a property company landlord—but could be far more difficult in other conditions. What if the landlord is a trading company, or the parent or subsidiary of a trading company in a group, where instead of the actual reversion in, say, 15 years' time one must assume a reversion of a third of the period and prophesy a likely course of action under the 1954 Act? Will the prospects of resistance to a renewal on grounds of reconstruction, demolition or construction (s 30(1)(f) of the 1954 Act) or 'own' occupation (s 30 (1)(g)) have to be assessed, as they might have to be in the market, or is that too speculative and so disallowed? It is rather remarkable that the issue has not been litigated where the specific circumstances have differed from those in the *Pivot* decision.

Yet, as a consequence of the *Pivot Properties* decision, the possibility of statutory continuation or renewal will have to be taken into account in assessing the rent payable on review unless the lease expressly provides otherwise. It is a factor that will be of particular significance where, as in the *Pivot Properties* case, the notional letting period is for the period of review only. It will be less important where, as in the Model Forms, the rent is to be calculated by reference to the length of the original term, for as the notional letting period is increased, so the impact of possible renewal is reduced.

The issue has arisen in a slightly different form. It is not unusual to prohibit sub-letting or restrict it to subtenancies contracted out of 1954 Act protection. Whether that will reduce the willing lessee's bid in the market for the whole property may then depend on the potential length of such permitted sub-letting. The longer the period a subtenant could obtain, the lower the impact of possible non-renewal on the rent he will pay (or so it can be argued) and consequently the lower depressive effect on the head-rent of the mandatory contracting out.

(f)   Drafting considerations

In normal circumstances, the landlord will benefit from the designation or implication of a notional term equal to the full original term running from the renewal date. Indeed, the choice of that notional term stemmed from the attraction of valuing the rent at each review on the length of term which was proving most popular in the market for new lettings (at a time, moreover, when the relative volatility of market sentiment and practice was less readily acknowledged than it now is). The actual residue formula produced at the last review, or even the last two reviews, a notional term shorter than that for which there is market demand and the rent would then be discounted accordingly. However, in one particular set of circumstances, the valuation process could reverse the preference, and that is where the property is reaching the point of dilapidation where substantial repair and refurbishment is needed. A tenant would argue that any tenant taking a 25 or 20 year term on a full repairing basis would reduce his bid to reflect that foreseeable and possibly heavy expenditure. Such a case for reducing the rent might not hold good if what was being valued was, say, only a 5–year term unless which the tenant could see himself 'in and out' before crisis-point arrived. This is the rare exception to prove the rule and indeed may no longer be attuned to current views on valuation.

There has been a change in market sentiment over the way a rent payable for a short term is to be treated, at least for certain types of property and for certain classes of tenant. The typical property for this treatment would be prime office, shop or hightech premises: the typical tenant would be a sophisticated body with a strong covenant to give it bargaining power. Foreign banks and similar institutions fitted this specification and their dislike for terms over 5 or 10 years gave impetus to the change of attitude. A greater desire for flexibility and willingness to move are two factors in the shift of opinion; continuing liability of the original lessee and, possibly, later assignees (discussed at pp 486–488) is doubtless another. In such cases the former discount between rent levels for 'normal' and for 'short' terms disappeared or was even reversed.

This movement in specific areas of the property market prompted change in the precedents. The ISVA Forms of 1984 and the 1985 Revision of the Model Forms—both 'institutional' products—adopted variants of the mid-way approach adumbrated above as a 'compromise'. The former postulated a notional term of the longer of the actual residue or the number of years being a multiple of the review periods closest to 10; the latter followed a similar pattern. The ISVA Note claims that this choice of notional term holds a fair balance on 'the last review', but it may affect more than one review if the cycle is less than 5 years. The clear aim is to eliminate at one extreme a notional term longer than the tenant has and commanding a premium rent, and at the other

extreme too truncated a notional term resulting in a depressed rent.
The Joint Working Party argues the case for the new 'minimum notional
residue' at greater length in its Note 6. EFP (5th ed) Form 22, para
1.3.7, leaves the choice open between the three alternatives—the original
term, the residue or the 'compromise formula'. The published precedents
may reflect the influence of 'institutional' views; the risk is that a lawyer
acting in respect of a more modest property will too unthinkingly adopt
the institutional approach.

Of the older precedents included in Part Seven, Conveyancer Precedent
5–57 adopts the same approach as the earlier Model Forms, namely
the original term approach. EFP (4th ed) Form 8:1, and the amended
version of it, Additional Form 76, specified the period to the next review
(review period approach), but the other EFP (4th ed) forms stipulate
the unexpired residue. The former produced the perceived disadvantage
of the short term at each review not merely those at the end of the
term. The form from *Kelly's Draftsman*, surprisingly, states no notional
term. However, after the *Norwich Union v TSB* decision (above), the
unexpired residue is, by implication, to be taken as the notional term
on the 'reflecting reality' principle.

4 Notional property

The hypothetical letting valuation will be on the basis of the demised
premises (see Chapter 11, p 318) but modified by the stated assumptions
and the valuation framework stated in the review clause. Assumptions
about the presumed state of the actual premises produce a notional
property more or less like the actual property depending upon the extent
and nature of those assumptions. These may relate to the physical state
of the premises or they may relate to its occupation or use but what
is central to any open market valuation is that the actual tenant is not
in occupation. This raises the issues of the desirable assumptions, express
or perhaps implied, of whether the premises are to be assumed to be
available with vacant possession, whether they are to be treated as only
let as a whole or available for subdivision, and how actual or potential
sub-lettings are to be treated. The detailed assumptions and disregards
relating to improvements, fitting out, destroyed or damaged premises
and so on are considered in sections 5 and 6 of this chapter, below.

(a) Vacant possession

The requirement of ascertaining the rental value on an assumption
of a letting with vacant possession is found in the most modern precedents
and in the Model Forms. A number of issues arise:

> (i) If the assumption of vacant possession is not expressed, when
> will it be implied?

(ii) What is the meaning of this phrase and what are the valuation consequences?

(iii) How does 'vacant possession' relate to other valuation assumptions?

(i)   Implication of a vacant possession valuation

The basis of most rent review clauses is that of a review to open market rent; this will normally involve an implied assumption that the premises are let with vacant possession: *Scottish & Newcastle Breweries plc v Richard Suttons SE* and *Forte & Co Ltd v General Accident Life Assurance Ltd* discussed below. However, the issue is essentially one of construction and the courts, while stating this prima facie starting point, have in a number of cases found that in the lease before them the review is not one which is to be valued on that basis. Important factors in these decisions have been whether there were sub-lettings at the date of the lease or whether such sub-lettings (of all or part) were contemplated.

The fact of an existing subtenancy, as with all other circumstances, will be taken into account in the process of construction but the cases suggest that the fact of such subtenancy means that the courts will be less ready to imply an assumption of vacant possession. No such assumption is to be found in the Landlord and Tenant Act 1954 and it was held in *Oscroft v Benabo* [1967] 1 WLR 1087 that the effect of a statutory subtenancy on open market rental had to be allowed for.

The cases on the issue are set out to assist in assessment of review clauses which are silent on the question of vacant possession.

(1) The criterion of 'rack rental market value' was employed in the rent review provisions of the lease considered in *Avon County Council v Alliance Property Co Ltd* (1981) 258 EG 1181, and the lease also listed various sub-leases and licences to occupy parts of the building in force when the lease was granted. Vacant possession of the whole was to be assumed, it was held, in the particular circumstances of which the rental formula was one of the most compelling. Obviously, listing sub-leases and licences does provide the tenant with an argument for modifying the effect of the vacant possession assumption although it failed in that case. The emergence of the 'preference for reality' approach to construing rent review provisions, and the subsequent decisions, reinforces the possibility of this argument now succeeding.

(2) *Scottish & Newcastle Breweries plc v Richard Suttons SE* [1985] 2 EGLR 130 concerned a single review after 21 years in a 42 year term entered into in 1962. Judge Paul Baker QC was of the opinion that an assumption of vacant possession was the normal one to make, and is likely to be the intention unless expressly provided to the contrary. In the lease before him, however, the parties at the time the lease was granted contemplated extensive sub-letting;

the original rent was calculated by reference to rents receivable from sub-letting and the formula adopted then found its place in the review provision. The most significant factor, it was held, was that the sub-lettings, if continuing beyond the single review date, were themselves subject to review, so the tenant would be in receipt of full rack rents of the part sub-let, and for the purposes of the single review, the lease to be valued would be with vacant possession of the part occupied by the tenant and full rents of the remainder. For these reasons, the judge considered an assumption of vacant possession was inappropriate.

(3) In *Forte & Co Ltd v General Accident Life Assurance Ltd* [1986] 2 EGLR 115 Peter Gibson J similarly considered that ascertainment of the open market rental of premises would ordinarily involve an assumption of vacant possession. On the lease before him, however, of the premises substantially used as the Cafe Royal, one shop unit was subject to an underlease of 54 years from 1949, which was an existing demise when the lease to Forte was granted in 1967 for 35 years, and the judge considered entirely different considerations applied in such circumstances. The judge declined to follow the *Avon CC* case (above); though he saw differences between the scheduled leases in the *Avon CC* case and the 1949 underlease, he was aware that there was sufficient similarity between the facts of the two cases to consider whether, in the interests of certainty, he should follow the reasoning in the *Avon CC* case. By choosing to depart from the *Avon CC* decision, and suggesting that it might be inconsistent with dicta in *Oscroft v Benabo* (above), the way has been left open for further litigation on the issue.

(4) In *SI Pension Trustees Ltd v Ministerio de Marina de la Republica Peruana* [1988] 1 EGLR 119 Mervyn Davies J had no difficulty in assuming a vacant possession basis for offices where the review clause directed regard to be had to comparable property on a vacant possession basis even though the clause was silent as to whether the hypothetical letting was to be on that basis as well.

(ii) Meaning and effect

The presence of a vacant possession basis of valuation will mean that the actual tenant's occupation has to be disregarded; this was treated as virtually axiomatic by Lloyd J in *99 Bishopsgate Ltd v Prudential Assurance Co Ltd* (1984) 270 EG 950. Moreover, it also seems to require, when expressly provided as a basis of the review, that any existing subtenancy must be ignored. The latter may be particularly significant where part of the property is sub-let to a residential occupier though this aspect reduces in importance now that new lettings will normally produce assured tenancies at market rents.

In *The Law Land Co Ltd v Consumers' Association Ltd* (1980) 255 EG 617 the presence of 'vacant possession' as an assumption assisted the Court of Appeal to reach the conclusion that an open market rent had to be determined on review without giving full effect to a clause restricting the use to the Association and its associated organisations. That is a far-reaching consequence, although whether the phrase would have had that result on its own did not arise for discussion in that case. Similarly in the *99 Bishopsgate* case, the vacant possession provision helped to lead the judge to the conclusion that the rent for a 30 floor city office block was to be assessed on a notional letting of the building as a whole and not on a floor-by-floor basis and a substantially lower rent followed as a result.

As with many of the usual assumptions, there are circumstances where the wording inserted to assist the landlord may be found to be to the tenant's advantage. Thus, where the tenant has managed to effect a particularly lucrative sub-letting, he can insist that it be disregarded as a *direct* factor in the vacant possession valuation (though it may be considered indirectly as evidence of the potential value to be reflected in the open market value). At its highest, the ascertainment of the value could reflect the possible effect on the market of the general prospects of securing such a sub-letting as the tenant has in fact achieved.

Other aspects of the assumption are less obvious. So far as vacant possession relates not to the absence of legal or equitable estates or interests but to physical circumstances as in *Cumberland Consolidated Holdings Ltd v Ireland* [1946] KB 264 and *Norwich Union Life Insurance Society Ltd v Preston* [1957] 1 WLR 813—or even legal constraints— see *Topfell Ltd v Galley Properties Ltd* [1979] 1 WLR 446—the assumption can affect the issues in several ways. The assumption that the premises are bereft of fixtures and fittings, which it would take a certain period to acquire and install, may depress the offer of a hypothetical bidder in the open market and so should reduce the rent. (The topic of fixtures and fittings is fully discussed in Chapter 11, p 325).

The statement of opinion in the preceding paragraph was vindicated in full measure by the Court of Appeal decision in *New Zealand Government Property Corporation v HM & S Ltd* [1982] QB 1145, overturning the former law that a tenant taking on a renewal lease without removing tenant's and trade fixtures or making a special bargain over them would forfeit his former right of removing them at termination of his lease. Mr Bernstein (one of the counsel in the case) had foreshadowed that result in his 1979 Blundell Memorial Lecture. The full impact of this on review can be quite startling, because such a review must periodically reflect the fact that on taking a new lease on a vacant possession basis the hypothetical tenant in the market would often expect and be granted a period of rent-free or reduced rent occupation for fitting out or adaptation, even of 'second hand' accommodation. Such a concession might also be looked for to reflect delay in installing telephones, telex, data transmission and similar services. To have to repeat the possible concession every 5 years, or other review period, will be an unwelcome shock to some landlords, where a vacant possession assumption was intended for other purposes. This suggested effect of the vacant possession assumption appears to have been common ground in *99 Bishopsgate Ltd v Prudential Assurance Co Ltd* (1984) 270 EG 950 where the competing contentions advanced by counsel (Mr Bernstein appearing for the landlord appellants) differed on whether the valuation reflecting a notional rent-free period was to be effected on a floor-by-floor basis or an assumed letting of the whole. The judge clearly accepted the point in the course of ruling in favour of the whole building approach. *99 Bishopsgate Ltd v Prudential Assurance Co Ltd* was upheld on appeal [1985] 1 EGLR 72. The Court of Appeal accepted that a direction to have regard to current rental values for property let with vacant possession meant that the tenant's occupation was to be disregarded. Moreover, the court rejected the landlord's main argument on the appeal, namely that since the arbitrator was to fix a *fair* yearly rental and was only to *have regard to* values with vacant possession, the arbitrator could adjust the guide-line to eliminate the substantial discount which resulted from a vacant possession criterion applied to a large office building. On review, therefore, the rent fixed properly reflected the discount applicable to a substantial rent free period which would be offered on an open market letting with vacant possession. The worse aspects of this result of the vacant possession basis are often mitigated by the presence of an assumption that the premises are fully fitted out (see p 418).

Circumstances where vacant possession might not enhance the value because of the risks of vandalism are discussed on p 456, below. Whether the requirement of vacant possession being assumed postulates a need to envisage a tenant who had to start a business from scratch is not considered in any reported rent review case known to the authors. In *Naylor v Uttoxeter Urban District Council* (1974) 231 EG 619 it was stated that the rental value for premises suitable for only one type of business (then a cattle-market) should upon a statutory renewal be assessed on the basis of the business in question being freshly started up; as the 1954 Act does not embrace the condition of vacant possession the effect of that decision on the assumption of vacant possession on a review may be slight. Nevertheless, if allowance has to be made for starting up, it should reduce the level of rent.

An argument that a review provision requiring valuation with vacant possession would preclude the reception of evidence of rents agreed with sitting tenants of comparable properties was rejected in *Segama NV v Penny Le Roy Ltd* (1983) 269 EG 322 at 332, the judge ruling that such evidence could be admitted but might fall to be adjusted. That aspect is further discussed at p 238.

The vacant possession assumption may have relevance in the transitional phase of the 1990 re-rating (see Chapter 15, p 501).

(iii) Relationship to other assumptions

It might be thought that the vacant possession assumption duplicates the disregard of occupation by the tenant or his subtenant that is found in many rent review provisions. However, whilst there is a large overlap, occupation by, say, a licensee for a substantial period would not be caught by reference to subtenants but would be ignored on a valuation on a vacant possession basis.

The assumption that the premises are fit for immediate occupation and use (found, for example, in the Model Forms and further discussed below, p 418) counters the depreciatory consequence of the assumption of vacant possession, but such deemed fitness is not provided for in every clause requiring valuation on a vacant possession basis. Where it is, the authors suggest that, being the more specific, the fitness for immediate use assumption would prevail over the vacant possession assumption, or rather over that aspect of it which might lead to a discount for fitting out, even though, once more, the result must be fortuitous in as far as the reasons for incorporating the fitness assumption may have been different. Less attractively, a similar result can be argued for where the order of wording of the Model Forms is strictly followed by virtue of the residual rule of construction that given irreconcilable inconsistency earlier provisions prevail over later (noted and discussed at p 304) although the relative order of the clauses may be a matter of chance.

(b) Assumptions as to letting 'as a whole'

The facts of *F R Evans (Liverpool) Ltd v English Electric Corporation Ltd* [1977] 36 P & CR 185 provide a striking example of the difference that the incorporation of this phrase can make. The 60–acre Walton Works involved in that case provided a good example of premises that might well have lent themselves to subdivision and exploitation to better advantage by the creation of separate units. Donaldson J referred (at 188) to the arbitrator's findings on this point:

'(a) in adapting the property for letting or sub-letting in parts the landlords or their single tenant would need to demolish parts in order to provide accessways and loading facilities (b) any letting or sub-letting in parts would entail considerable delays in finding tenants for all the various parts (c) any single tenant intending to adapt the property for sub-letting in parts would require a lease for a term of much longer than 18 years [the unexpired residue in that case] and would expect a rent-free period and a reduced rent during the early years of the term).'

It follows from this that, whilst the presence of the phrase meant that the prospect of a developer interested in such an operation being in the market so as to affect the rental was not to be ignored, it was unlikely his assumed presence would have taken the rent above the level of that to be paid by a single lessee who was to occupy the whole.

The same position could apply to office buildings susceptible of division into small suites, possibly with the provision of central services in excess of basic lighting, cleaning and maintenance of common areas and the provision of central heating. This is particularly so in the light of the valuation evidence in *International Drilling Fluids v Louisville Investments (Uxbridge) Ltd* [1986] Ch 513.

The discussion of the *99 Bishopsgate* case at p 409 above shows how a vacant possession assumption resulted in a valuation of the rent in relation to the whole building, not as an aggregation of the floor-by-floor rents. It is submitted that had 'as a whole' been used (perhaps unlikely in a 1975 lease) the point would have been virtually beyond dispute. The lower rent awarded by the arbitrator of £6,065,000 for the whole building contrasted with his award of £6,700,000 for the aggregate of floors figure, although even that was being challenged by the landlords, who were seeking £7,451,000. The arbitrator had allowed a 10 per cent discount for size; it must be the case that the bidders in the market for a massive building is more restricted than the number and choice of tenants willing to take parts of it and given the risks of voids and rent defaults, and the burden of management, a lower rent is the obvious result of a single rent for the entire property. (See also the facts in the *Pivot Properties* case (1980) 256 EG 1176.) The Court of Appeal in the *99 Bishopsgate* case, upholding as they did the judge below and the lower rent awarded of £6,065,000, did not have to deal with the issue of the 10 per cent discount for size in the arbitrator's alternative award.

The phrase 'let as a whole' is a useful provision in all cases except those where the prospect of sub-letting is a factor in the original bargain. It was not usual in the published precedents prior to the *Evans* decision but it now appears in at least some of them—namely Conveyancer Precedent 5–57 and all versions of the Model Forms but not EFP (5th ed) Form 22 or the ISVA Forms; its presence or absence is a factor to be considered in the valuation process. Where the lease is silent it is a matter of evidence to establish to what extent the potentiality of subdivision would be a market consideration in the light of the planning and like legislation and the terms of the lease (but ignoring, once again, a market assessment of the mere commercial prospects of relaxation if the principle of the *Plinth Property* decision discussed at p 345 holds good). Equally, if the rent review clause were to provide expressly for an assumption of subdivision, or for the possibility of subdivision to be taken into account, it would be incumbent on the parties, or the referee if the decision falls to a third party in default of agreement, to seek to give effect to such provision even though it might not reflect an actual market state of affairs at the relevant time. Once the parties have provided for the hypothetical state of affairs, the assessment process cannot be carried through in defiance of the instructions given. However, if there was evidence of a lack of demand for subdivision, the uplift provided for by the assumption will be small, nominal or nil.

(c) Without a premium

Additional points of clarification relating to the letting of the notional property can be made. First, that the property is let 'without a fine or a premium' (eg Model Forms, clause 3(A)(i)(a)), so that it is then clear that the valuation will be on the basis that no fine or premium is being taken. This might well be covered in the usual phrase 'might reasonably be expected to be let in the open market', but the Model Forms prefer to make the point explicit. Indeed, since one can envisage an open market in which premiums become usual practice (perhaps for fiscal or accounting reasons) there is merit in such express exclusion.

It is possible to argue that if the absence of a premium is expressly stipulated comparables involving the de-capitalisation of rents associated with payment of a premium should be wholly disregarded. At one time, following an adjustment in the statutory formula for agricultural rents it was suggested that tendering should be conducted by means of acceptance of a rent made known by the letting agent and by those tendering bidding a premium to secure the tenancy. It is not clear how widespread this practice was or how long it lasted.

5 Assumptions

(a) Assumptions that all covenants have been performed

(i) Effect on repairing covenants

This assumption can be framed in a number of different ways with varying effects on the review. The most general formula—namely, that all the covenants in the lease have been performed to the relevant date—normally works to the landlord's advantage; or, to put it another way, it prevents the tenant from taking advantage of his own wrong. He cannot obtain a rental valuation of the premises that reflects their defective state, if disrepair has been brought about by breach of his own obligations. There can be no quarrel with its fairness in that respect. However, the general assumption may be unfair to the tenant where the landlord also has obligations under the lease, say, to repair the structure or common parts or to provide or maintain services that have been broken. It was held in *Fawke v Viscount Chelsea* [1980] QB 441 that such a state of affairs could be allowed for in renewals under the Landlord and Tenant Act 1954 (where, of course, no such assumption is stated) by setting both the interim rent and the rent under the new lease at a certain level till the defects were remedied and then at a higher level when the work had been done. The Court of Appeal in *National Westminster Bank Ltd v BSC Footwear Ltd* (1980) 42 P & CR 90 stressed the statutory basis of that earlier decision and the *BSC* case was followed in *Clarke v Findon Developments Ltd* (1984) 270 EG 426, rejecting the *Fawke v Chelsea* solution. In the *Clarke* case, the landlords had repair obligations as to the exterior, alleged to have been broken. The parties agreed, ultimately, that the arbitrator in settling the rent should not only reflect the existence of any breach by the landlords but also should take into account the prospects of the landlords remedying them or the tenants recovering compensation 'equivalent to the cost of remedying the same' (sic). The judge held, however, that a differential rent varying with the state of repair could not be fixed on a review, largely because of the agreement on the first issue. However, where there is split repair liability but the assumption is in the general form of all 'covenants performed', the parties have committed themselves, in advance and irrespective of the true facts, to a valuation on the basis of full compliance on both sides. Even the 'half-way house' of the *Fawke* case is denied them.

In *Harmsworth Pension Funds Trustees Ltd v Charringtons Industrial Holdings Ltd* [1985] 1 EGLR 97 Warner J held that any diminishing effect on the market rent occasioned by any failure of the tenant to repair the demised premises in breach of its full repairing covenants were to be disregarded for the purposes of rent review. The lease contained no express disregard to that effect, but directed a review 'on the basis that the tenant would be obliged to perform and observe the covenants and conditions on the part of the tenant herein covenanted to be performed and observed by the tenant'. The judge relied upon the decision in *Family Management v Gray* (1979) 253 EG 369, a dilapidations case, for the proposition that subtenants could not rely, in diminution of the rents that they were to pay under their new statutory leases, on the want of repair of the premises attributable to their own breaches of covenant. He distinguished *Fawke v Chelsea* (above) as relating only to a *landlord's* failure to repair; and in so far as the judges' statements in the *Fawke* case related to a tenant's breach of an obligation to repair they were obiter and uttered without the benefit of argument.

The *Harmsworth* case would suggest that valuation in the dilapidated state is inappropriate wherever the hypothetical lease assumes the terms of the current lease are to apply—since that assumption thereby incorporates the tenant's covenant to repair and a further assumption that it has been performed. The *Harmsworth* judgment stresses the maxim that no man can take advantage of his own wrong. On that basis, the *Fawke v Chelsea* principle—that a landlord's failure to fulfil his obligations to repair can be taken into account—should continue to apply, unless, of course, an 'all covenants performed' formulation excludes that approach.

The tenant can, of course, take action to try to force his landlord to meet his repairing obligations by seeking an injunction (see *Jeune v Queens Cross Properties Ltd* [1974] Ch 97 and *Francis v Cowliffe Ltd* (1976) 33 P & CR 368) or damages. The issue of the correct measure for damages is somewhat unsettled. *Hewitt v Rowlands* (1924) 131 LT 757 established that the normal rule is the difference in the value of the premises in their actual state and in the state they should have been in. The 'cost of remedying' measure has so far been applied only in respect of self-help remedies (under *Lee-Parker v Izzett* [1971] 1 WLR 1688; *Asco Developments Ltd v Gordon* (1978) 248 EG 683 by way of deduction or in cases relating to failure to repair common parts (*Marenco v Jacramel Co Ltd* (1964) 119 EG 433) and, most strikingly, in *Loria v Hammer* [1989] 2 EGLR 249 (failure to do repairs said to have a cost of £150 leading to ultimate award of nearly £17,000). In comparable fields the two measures have been treated as closely linked, the cost of repair being treated as a good starting point for the loss of value assessment. Moreover, the traditional formulation has now also to be reconsidered in the light of *Calabar Properties Ltd v Stitcher* [1984] 1 WLR 287 which goes some way to support the 'cost of repair' measure of damages and may well herald a general move in that direction. The difficulties of the 'agreed formula' in *Clarke v Findon* of compensation equivalent to the cost of remedying are still not wholly resolved.

The wording of various statutory provisions emphasise the possible difficulties of ascertaining the scope of 'repair'. Thus, s 18 of the Landlord and Tenant Act 1927 restricts the measure of damages for breach of a repair covenant 'expressed or implied . . . general or specific', yet even that extended meaning does not cover a covenant to spend a stated annual sum in maintenance *(Moss' Empires Ltd v Olympia (Liverpool) Ltd* [1939] AC 544) or to pay a fixed sum in lieu of dilapidations (*Boyer v Warbey* [1953] 1 QB 234). The Leasehold Property (Repairs) Act 1938, in contrast, simply refers to covenants to repair. There is also the perennial problem of the borderline between repair and improvements (see p 428). The more extensive the work done by a tenant the more likely it is to improve the property and the more anxious the tenant will be to have it excluded. An assumption of performance of covenants of repair will not have that effect and so the effect of those (probably unauthorised) improvements will depend upon other elements in the review formula.

A particularly harsh consequence of the distinction manifested itself in *McDougall v Easington Borough Council* [1989] 1 EGLR 93.

The conclusion, that the limitation of the relevant assumption to performance of covenants of repair thus creates problems that would be better avoided, will be reached by many landlords. Similarly, tenants may be wise to avoid the possible misunderstandings to which it could give rise. Resolution of the possible doubts can involve time, expense and the risk of souring the landlord-tenant relationship. Some more general formula may be preferred, although similar problems can also arise with other wording.

(ii) Effect on improvements or use covenants

The effect of ignoring improvements has been a problem in a number of reported cases, which are discussed at p 427 ff, below, and the consequences of having to discount the sort of breaches now under discussion may also be a difficult valuation exercise—but it is the hypothesis postulated by this assumption in the lease. In many cases of unauthorised works, an aggrieved landlord may have waived his right to forfeit on account of the breach—perhaps only because the inspection of the premises, in readiness for the rent review, will have given him notice. At least, whether or not he has in fact waived the breach he may be held to have done so. If the breach is continuing, as with a continuing change of use, his remedy of forfeiture will remain open to him, and the tenant would be likely to get relief only on relinquishing the irregular use, but the carrying out of works is not a continuing breach. Where the breach has enhanced the value of the reversion and forfeiture is not available, the landlord will be denied immediate benefit from it by the assumption and moreover, he might not have a sustainable or worthwhile claim in damages (especially if the unauthorised work increased the value of the reversion) and his chances of obtaining an injunction to remove the unauthorised improvement may be uncertain. As we have stated above the tenant nevertheless runs these risks.

In one set of circumstances, however, a provision that all covenants have been performed might assist a tenant. Where a tenant has carried out work, or altered a use, without seeking prior approval from the landlord as required by the lease and this has in fact improved the rental value, he could ask that the beneficial effect of his breach be ignored in the review, albeit at the risk of drawing attention to what has been done and inviting a demand for re-instatement. The agreed assumption is that he has not done that which was forbidden. The Model Forms limit the disregard of improvements, for example, to those 'carried out with consent [*sic* consent of anyone, not just the landlord] where required', so manifesting an intention to penalise that errant tenant by taking account of unauthorised improvements that increase the rental value. However, it is submitted that this wording does not necessarily or always override the force of the assumed performance of covenants assumption where both provisions are present in the same lease. The initial (1979) version of the Model Forms used the formula 'written consent of [the] immediate landlord (where required)', but that does not affect the present argument.

The presence of this assumption was, however, held not to assist a tenant who had omitted to obtain written consent to improvements as the lease required in the *Hamish Cathie Travel* case discussed at p 416, below. It could not be assumed improvements had been carried out with consent so as to allow the improvements to be disregarded at review, when they had not.

(iii)   Effect a matter of construction

If the assumption is not in the general form quoted above, its effect depends on the true construction of the words used. For example, the obsolete EFP (4th ed) Forms 8:1 and Additional Form 76 provided for the assumption that the tenant has complied with all his 'obligations as to repair and decoration'. On the one hand, the unfairness to the tenant where a landlord has broken his covenant to repair but is assumed not to have done so under a general formula would be avoided as there would be no implied assumption that the landlord had complied. On the other hand, there may be some doubt about the meaning of the formula where the repair covenant proper is limited in some way (by exclusion, say, of fair wear and tear or a proviso that the tenant need not put the premises in a better state of repair than they were on a given date). Matters not falling within its scope may be re-introduced in part by a different covenant—say, to observe statutory obligations. Is the latter type of clause a *repair* obligation in any event? It is not cast in terms of 'repair' , yet part of its effect is to require some types of repair to be done.

(iv)   Effect on other covenants

Problems could arise from the specification of this assumption on other types of covenants, say on use or against alteration or alienation so far as it concerns sub-letting or parting with possession. Difficulties of interpretation of the exact wording of those covenants in the particular lease might arise and could be compounded by the problems of the valuation effect of any breach that has to be disregarded. The treatment of breaches of positive and of negative covenants may differ. Admittedly, such wording is rare in practice, but might arise where particular stress on these aspects in the lease has led to this form of assumption being included.

(v)   The choice in the precedents

The various published precedents adopt different and conflicting approaches to the problem of whether the assumption is to be that *all* covenants have been performed or *all the tenant's* covenants have been met at the review date. Thus, it will be observed that while the initial (1979) version of the Model Forms used the 'all covenants performed' formula, so covering landlord's covenants, the revised version in 1980 referred only to 'covenants on the part of the tenant' and the current 1985 version reads:

'That the covenants herein contained on the part of *the landlord and* the tenant have been fully performed and observed.'

The Background Notes to the 1980 Forms did not go into the reasons for the change, nor did they warn landlords who undertake obligations in the lease that they are less well protected than they were, however unfairly, under the initial version. Background Note 8 to the 1985 Forms remedied this omission and now refers to the fact that the assumption of the landlord's covenants being fulfilled on review being included as an option. This note (see p 668 in Part Seven) recognises injustices can occur either way so considers that it is a matter for negotiation in all the circumstances of the particular case. Conveyancer Precedent 5–57 uses an 'all covenants and conditions' formula and the obsolete EFP (4th ed) Forms in the Part Seven assume compliance with all tenant's covenants as to repair and decoration. The form from *Kelly's Draftsman* contains no assumption on the point while Form 22 in EFP (5th ed), clause 1.3.3, adopts the compromise wording of the 1985 Model Forms. The ISVA Forms follow the 1980 Model Forms formula.

If the phrase used is observance of 'all the tenant's *obligations* under this lease', this would bring in any statutory or implied obligations binding on the tenant. This may be potentially wider than a reference just to performance of his covenants, since one never finds a covenant to observe implied obligations—that would be almost self-contradictory.

(b)   Assumption that premises are fit for immediate use and occupation, or fully fitted out

This particular assumption is to be found in the Model Forms ('that the premises are fit and available for immediate occupation') and is increasingly to be found in one form of words or another in institutional leases. The wording, for example, in EFP (5th ed) Form 22 para 1.3.5 is much more explicit and is as follows:

'that the premises are ready for and fitted out and equipped for immediate occupation and use for the purpose or purposes required by the willing tenant . . . and that all the services required for such occupation and use are connected to the premises.'

This is mirrored by a further express assumption introduced into the 1985 Model Forms:

'(iv) that no reduction is to be made to take account of any rental concession which on a new letting with vacant possession might be granted to the incoming tenant for a period within which its fitting out works would take place.'

It is clear that a potential tenant in the open market would lower his bid or otherwise negotiate for some concessions over rent where he could not immediately move in and use the premises as intended. Landlords sometimes offer a rent-free period to allow time for fitting out, or, in a more extreme form, to tempt tenants into unoccupied premises that are proving to be hard to let. Thus the assumption rules out what would be a market factor producing a low rent, if only for a short period or a discount on the rent as reviewed to reflect this factor.

To the extent that the vacant possession assumption necessitates a valuation of the premises as cleared of all tenant and trade fixtures, and third party apparatus, and so imports a notional rent-free or reduced rent period, an issue fully discussed at p 410, above, it is contradicted by these assumptions, which are thus of much greater significance since the *New Zealand Government Property Corporation* case. There could be little doubt, it is submitted, that this *express* provision would override that *implied* construction.

To a considerable extent the assumption that all covenants have been performed will cover much of the same ground, but some situations not caught by the assumption of performance will be covered by this assumption. It seems clear that 'fitness' is a general concept covering not only the physical state of the property but such matters as the provision or connection of services (as made explicit in EFP (5th ed) Form 22) and facilities or the obtaining of statutory or other permissions. It also extends to non-physical constraints on use or occupation, as may be seen from the analogous decision in *Topfell v Galley Properties Ltd* [1979] 1 WLR 446 where a restriction on the number of permitted occupants of a house created breach of a vacant provision term for the property where those in one part satisfied the number allowed to reside although the rest of the property was empty. It might thus relate to premises occupied or used in breach of an unfulfilled condition in a planning permission, s 52 agreement or fire certificate prohibiting occupation or use until the condition is met.

Delay arising from the time needed to cater for such factors could cause an incoming tenant to seek a reduction in rent or a rent-free period so, once more, this assumption favours the landlord. Thus the absence of this assumption in *Tea Trade Properties Ltd v CIN Properties Ltd* [1990] 1 EGLR 155 meant that, though the fully qualified use clause meant that the commercial premises were available for office use by the willing lessee, the cost of conversion was a factor. Hoffman J remarked:

Such [office] use would no doubt have required alterations and improvements . . . The tenant says that they would have been so time consuming and expensive so as to make the building in practice unattractive to a potential office tenant. If that is right, the theoretical potential of office use may add little to its existing use value, but that is a question for the valuer . . .

The sheer logistical problem of fitting out and moving into a large office complex means that the fitness assumption may be very significant, especially if the assumed term of the lease to be valued is short or shorter than the market would bear for the notional fitting out. There were instances reported in the 'trade press' some years ago where the long delay to obtain telephone services caused the ending of negotiations to take assignments or sub-leases of Central London offices. The *Estates Times* of 11 February 1983 reported a case where an appeal from a Local Valuation Tribunal, based on a long delay in obtaining telephones for empty offices, was compromised on the basis of a reduction to one-third of the former rateable value and the Lands Tribunal made a consent order accordingly. Again, it seems likely that this assumption would require such a factual state of affairs to be ignored should such circumstances return.

It is easy to assume that fitness for occupation involves fitness for occupation for the use(s) permitted or required by the lease. Much will, however, depend on the wording of the lease and there must be a chance of litigation on this point, although in the context of recent moves towards a more robust style of construction (see Chapter 10) it seems unlikely that implication would be denied. Perhaps the matter will be more arguable in those difficult cases where the lease contains a restriction on use or is actually used for a less valuable use but requires or permits review on the basis of a wider or even 'open' use assumption. In one lease of which the authors are aware, the premises were used as a public house but consent for a change to retail use was permitted by the lease and consent to such a change could not be unreasonably withheld. The valuer was required to value 'the public house' and there was an assumption that the premises were 'fit for immediate occupation and use'. In the circumstances of that case, it could be argued that the premises were only deemed fit for occupation and use as a public house and a willing lessee paying for a higher retail use rental would reduce the rent bid because of the need to bear the costs of conversion—as indeed he would in the real world if the public house came on the market for retail use. Modern precedents (eg EFP (5th ed) Form 22) may prevent such an argument by providing that the 'premises are ready for and fitted out and equipped for immediate occupation and use *for the purpose or purposes required by the willing tenant*'. The ISVA Forms require the assumption that the premises are 'fully fitted out and equipped so as to be ready for immediate occupation and use' and, since the forms import 'the terms of this lease' as a basis for the review, less room for doubt on the issue exists.

Tenants should consider the form of wording in EFP (5th ed) Form 22 or the Model Forms assumption (iv)—especially where the use clause permits a wider use which would necessitate fitting out in the real world in any event. It is one thing to require an assumption that the premises are fitted out for the actual use, or for a use consistent with the state of the premises at the date of the lease, since the 'fitted out' basis merely negates the effect of the *New Zealand Property* case and ensures that the tenant cannot claim for notional fitting out discount at review when the premises are actually fitted out. The wider words of Form 22 potentially allow the lessor a notional benefit that he could not get in the real world, namely a rent for a new use for premises which are not actually fit and ready for that use. The reason the Joint Committee gave (Background Note 9 reproduced on p 668) for including the new assumption (iv) was that a rent free period for fitting out was a 'one-off' concession made by the landlord to the tenant in respect of the full term of the lease and it was not therefore a benefit which should be granted to the tenant at each subsequent reviews. There is some force is this argument but a tenant may not appreciate it if he ends up paying a rent for the premises not only on the basis they are used for a some more profitable use but on the basis they are fitted out for that use.

(c) Assumption that there are no depreciating works

(i) The nature of the assumption

The original (1979) version of the Model Forms required an assumption that 'no work has been carried out by the tenant or its predecessors in title during the said term which has diminished the rental value of the demised premises'; the revised (1980) version merely added 'its subtenants' after 'the tenant' and refers to 'their' predecessors. Both versions contain a possible ambiguity on whether 'during the said term' qualifies when the work was carried out or the particular other parties involved—moving the phrase to after 'carried out' would make this clear. The current 1985 version reads:

'(iii) That no work has been carried out to the demised premises which has diminished the rental value . . .'

The provision is not found in the earlier published forms the authors have traced, but it does appear in other modern precedents such as EFP (5th ed) Form 22, clause 1.3.1. The effect of such an assumption is obvious enough—one tenant's embellishments may well be another tenant's eyesore, or worse, and the rectification or removal of such works a factor with adverse effect on the market rental. Something of this concept is to be found in s 19(2) of the Landlord and Tenant Act 1927, under which a tenant may be required to reinstate the premises where improvements do not 'add to the letting value of the holding'. In many circumstances such depreciatory works will have constituted breaches of covenants and so be covered by the general clause already discussed but there can be circumstances where this independent assumption may have independent effect.

The ISVA Forms do not include the assumption, so any depreciatory effects must be allowed for in assessing the rent, unless they are ignored under some other assumption, such as due performance of covenants. Perhaps the stated predilection of the sponsors for the *rebus sic stantibus* principle explains the omission.

(ii) When and by whom the works are done

The wording of the earlier Model Forms did not expressly cover such works carried out under any period prior to the start of the term proper, a point that is picked up and covered in the wording of the disregard of tenants' improvements. This is not the correct interpretation if the ambiguity in the 1979 and 1980 Forms noted above requires reference to 'the tenant or predecessors in title during the said term'. A person who is currently the tenant or happens to have been a predecessor in

respect of the current term might have done work before the term and
the reasoning in the case of *Hambros Bank Executor and Trustee Co
Ltd v Superdrug Stores Ltd* [1985] 1 EGLR 99 would then apply. The
pre-current term work would then have to be disregarded because of
the identity of the person who did it though done before the current
term.

The 1985 Model Forms use different wording (set out above), which
does not confine depreciating work to that done by the tenant and specifies
neither by whom the disadvantageous work was done nor when. They
just refer to a factual state of affairs. No reasons for the amendments
are given in the Background Notes issued by the sponsors, but one can
envisage circumstances where the revised wording could unfairly penalise
the tenant. For example, the works might have been carried out by
the landlord or by an earlier tenant under an unrelated lease. The words
could even cover the situation where works intended to enhance the
property turn out, in fact, to have the opposite effect, perhaps some
years later, and are then to be ignored. Could a lessor claim to disregard
work done many years which existed at the commencement of the term?
EFP (5th ed) Form 22 maintains the references to tenant, predecessor
and the term and provides:

'that no work has been carried out on the premises by the tenant [its] subtenants
or their predecessors in title during the term which has diminished the rental
value of the premises [other than work carried out in compliance with clause
. . .]'

The concluding words allow express reference to obligatory works done
under the terms of the lease.

(iii) Works other than to the demised premises

Where the depreciatory works are not to the demised premises, there
is no such assumption. If property associated with the demised premises,
but not let as part of them, has been dealt with in a way depreciatory
of the value of what is let, that consequence must be reflected in the
assessment of market rent. This may be unfair to the landlord if, say,
the tenant has caused disfigurement of a car-park, amenity or entrance,
in a way outside the landlord's control or remedy, and may be unfair
to either party if, say, other occupiers have done so. The impact of
the more or less immediate environs of the actual holding, to use the
statutory concept, has been largely, and curiously, ignored by draftsmen
of rent review formulae.

(d) Assumption on destroyed or damaged premises

(i) The form and effect of the assumption

Given the notional world of rent review, it is no surprise to find in
the Model Forms and in other modern precedents such as EFP (5th
ed) Form 22 the assumption of the rebuilding or restoration of the

premises if they have been destroyed or damaged. The impact of destruction or damage may be thought self-evident, but evidence of its valuation consequences is vividly illustrated in the context of rateable values by the decision in *Plessy & Co Ltd v Eagle Pension Funds Ltd* [1989] EGCS 149. Where the lease also provides for the assumption of performance of all the lessee's covenants, the provision may be otiose where the other provisions include obligations for repair and rebuilding— 'to keep in repair' of necessity importing 'first to put in repair' (*Proudfoot v Hart* [1890] 25 QBD 42). However, where rebuilding is linked to damage or destruction by an insured risk and the property had been affected by an uninsured, or even uninsurable, risk the present provision would extend beyond the 'performance of covenants' assumption. It could well be thought to prove unfair to the non-defaulting tenant. Moreover, a reasonable time for reinstatement is allowed: *Fasimani v Gates* (1984) 271 EG 887; so if a rent review date fell in the permitted interval between the damage and the date to start the work, the tenant would not be in breach of covenant. So this specific assumption there assists the landlord. Another problem will arise where any relevant statutory authority for re-building has been refused (see *Sturcke v S W Edwards Ltd* (1971) 23 P & CR 185—tenant liable under lease for failure to repair where permission refused, but liability under further covenants in licence held subject to implied 'subject to permission' condition). This might even terminate the lease by way of frustration; if it does not, the basis of valuation in the absence of this assumption will be problematical.

Similarly, a tenant should be wary of the provision where rebuilding is, in whole or part, a landlord's obligation. Where the landlord is in default of his rebuilding or repairing obligation, the tenant might well recoup as compensation for the breach that portion of his new rent attributable to the notional state of affairs now being considered because it is assumed that the landlord has repaired or rebuilt. The tenant would claim a sum either as part of his damages for the landlord's breach or by way of equitable set-off (*Melville v Grapelodge Developments Ltd* (1978) 39 P & CR 179). However, the mere fact that the rebuilding or restoration was not complete, or perhaps not even started, would not inevitably show the landlord to be in breach of his obligations although *Vural v Security Archives Ltd* (unreported except at (1989) *Estates Times*, 29 September) has clarified the implied obligations of the landlord.

The ISVA Forms include the assumption that destruction or damage has been made good and expressly provides for that to be so 'even if compliance with the Tenant's obligations herein did not so require'; that qualification is implicit in the wording used in the Model Forms which is unchanged in the 1985 Revision. There may be some discernible difference, in particular circumstances, between merely 'made good' (the ISVA phrase) and 'fully restored' (the Model Forms wording). Moreover 'herein' in the ISVA formulation might be a slight trap if there were relevant covenants only in a licence or other collateral instrument. The trap may be illustrated by the unsuccessful arguments for the tenant in *Pleasurama Properties Ltd v Leisure Investments (West End) Ltd* [1986] 1 EGLR 54.

(ii) The meaning of 'destroyed'

The exact meaning of the premises being 'destroyed' may need to be ascertained, for it is not entirely free from doubt whether the word in this context connotes some element of calamity or lack of intention or whether it could also comprehend deliberate demolition. Take the example where a local authority, having acquired by negotiation or compulsory procedures the freehold and sub-leasehold interests in a property, demolishes it before coming to terms with the mesne lessor on compensation for its interest (the facts, in part, of *Re King, Robinson v Gray* [1963] Ch 459). Could the authority be allowed to argue that the physical disappearance of the building should be ignored in a relevant review of the headlease rent, so increasing the rent payable and hence reducing the compensation payable for that lease-hold interest? That result seems inequitable, but by no means impossible. Equally, where demolition of, say, a worn-out superfluous out-building or extension has been allowed, care should be taken by the tenant so acting to ensure it is not notionally re-erected overnight for the purposes of a rent review (or a number of rent reviews, to put it at its worst) if, despite its dilapidation or obsolescence, the notional restoration increases the rent. In some circumstances, of course, selective demolition may enhance the rental value of a property by improving appearance, access, pedestrian or vehicular circulation or the ease of handling materials. There the assumption that the former less satisfactory state of affairs still exists, ie that the 'destroyed' element has been 'fully restored', will result in a lower rent on review so a landlord should bear the point in mind where his licence for demolition has been needed or he funds the work at the tenant's request.

Where the assumption is to be applied, the necessity for either party to be able to establish the position prior to the destruction or damage will apply as it does in respect of any disregard of improvements, as discussed below.

(iii) An alternative solution

A better solution for these difficulties might be to postpone the effective review date till the work has been done, the loss of rent element in the insurance being so framed as to provide the landlord with the additional return he would have received had those operations in fact been complete on the contractual review date and an increase then payable.

Where a review date is so postponed, care must be taken to provide for the consequences, both as to whether the next review is postponed and also as to the notional term of the lease to be assessed in the delayed review. These issues are further discussed below in relation to similar provisions in 'rent freeze' clauses (at p 545). It must also be made clear whether the review date remains the original date, with notional back-dating of the reinstatement and restoration or is a later date related to the work. If the latter is chosen the ascertainment of the date should be stated expressly to avoid complications (see *Glofield v Morley (No 2)* and also p 76).

(e) Assumption on availability for different use

(i) Effect of this assumption

The bargain between the parties to a lease may result in the inclusion of an assumption that premises in fact used for one purpose are to be deemed susceptible (to use a neutral term for the present) of use for another. Indeed, from the discussion of the *Aldwych Club* and *Tea Trade* cases at p 353, it can be seen that such an assumption can be involved where there is a fully qualified use clause which permits other uses for which consent cannot be unreasonably withheld. However, in *Trust House Forte Albany Hotels Ltd v Daejan Investments Ltd* (1980) 256 EG 915 the assumption was expressly stated. The rent review clause required that certain parts of the demised premises, in fact used as part of the Strand Palace Hotel, should be assumed to be 'actually let for or available for letting for shopping and retail purposes'. The judge held that the valuation should proceed on the basis that there was no legal obstacle to such uses, so that no breach of covenant, planning or similar legislation or the like would result, but that it did not have to proceed on the supposition that the relevant areas had been physically adapted for the lettings postulated. This narrow construction meant the assessment of rental potential of the designated areas would have to reflect both the time needed to adapt them and the cost of adaptation. At the next review date, this same lease threw up further complex issues of construction, again largely centring on the assumption of availability for letting for shopping and retail purposes: *Trust House Forte Albany Hotels Ltd v Daejan Investments Ltd (No 2)* [1989] 1 EGLR 133. A similar result was reached in *Bovis Group Pension Fund v GC Flooring and Furnishing Ltd* (1984) 269 EG 1252 where an assumption of a notional letting for office purposes was to be made in respect of shop premises. It was held in the Court of Appeal, by a majority, that the existence of planning permission for such change of use should be assumed. How widespread this judicial approach may become is unclear, although it is undoubtedly consistent with the *contra preferentem* principle of construction (see p 304) and, if applied at all widely, could limit the worst consequences of the notional wide use formula discussed at p 360.

The impact of *Wolff v Enfield London Borough* [1985] 1 EGLR 75 has been discussed at p 356 above; and for a decision distinguishing the *Bovis* case, see *Daejan Investments Ltd v Cornwall Coast Country*

Club discussed at p 364. The decision in *Rushmoor Borough Council v Goacher* [1985] 2 EGLR 140 (and see p 347) shows development potential of land can be taken into account in appropriate circumstances, and where the construction of the lease allows, even in the absence of an existing planning permission. Since such assumptions will be made in the market it is hard to criticise such decisions. In *Basingstoke and Deane Borough Council v Host Group Ltd* [1988] 1 WLR 348 the valuer was directed to assume a bare site only. The property was in fact developed and used as a public house and in the absence of any express provision, the 'presumption of reality' meant that the site was to be valued on the basis of the potential exploitation for the actual use.

(ii)   Essentially a matter of valuation

It has been made clear, however, that it is not for the court to give guidance to a valuer and direct him exactly what considerations he must take into account beyond those enjoined in the lease expressly or by implication. So in *Forte & Co Ltd v General Accident Life Assurance Corporation* [1986] 2 EGLR 115 the judge held the use clause allowed user other than that carried on at the review date (see p 408, above). The landlord's subsequent attempt to seek a declaration that, in so far as he took into account the possibility of different uses, the valuer should also take account of the degree of likelihood of planning permission being obtained and the cost of any necessary works of conversion and adaptation failed as the judge refused to make such a declaration, applying *Compton Group Ltd v Estates Gazette Ltd* (1977) 36 P & CR 149 at 159.

(iii)   Assumption of availability of existing planning consent

The two forms published by the Incorporated Society of Valuers and Auctioneers in 1984 each require an assumption that the benefit of 'any planning or other consent' is available for the notional willing tenant. This is justified, in the Society's Notes, because it 'prevents premises which are actually being used by the tenant for a use for which he has a personal planning consent having to be valued as if that use were not an established use by reason of the 'disregard' of the effect on rent of the occupation of the actual tenant'. However, once the rent has been reviewed on that hypothetical basis, it will continue at that level to the next review even if the tenant with the benefit of the permission vacates. Assignment by that tenant, at a rent probably higher than that payable without the benefit, may be rendered more difficult as a consequence. At the next review, the personal permission has lapsed and so would no longer be 'current'.

The virtue for a landlord of the ISVA approach is that it excludes the argument that an open market valuation should ignore a permission which is not generally available, but the unreality of the assumption harms the tenant. Perhaps the relaxation in planning policies so that restricted permissions are readily 'depersonalised' is some justification for it, although the Society does not advance that justification.

A possible solution to the problem of the personal planning consent would be a differential rent whereby the reviewed rent would reduce if the personal planning consent lapsed, but this solution is faced with the obstacle of the decision in *Clarke v Findon* discussed at p 414. Of course, such a differential rent could be expressly provided for.

Similar considerations would apply to 'local user' planning conditions or even agricultural occupant restrictions affecting all or part of the demised premises, although the former are now out of fashion and the latter increasingly susceptible of modification and the market takes that into account.

6   Disregards of improvements

The aim of this common disregard is to ensure that any increase in rental value of the demised premises attributable to the existence at the relevant review date of any improvement to the demised premises will be disregarded when calculating the new rent. The desirable conditions, commonly expressed, will be that:

(i)   any consent required has been obtained (for improvements will often require the written consent of the reversioner(s));

(ii)   the tenant was not obliged to carry out the improvement in pursuance of an obligation to the landlord or the predecessors in title (an important proviso, for though it is right that a tenant should not be assessed to any rent on capital improvements he has financed, it is equally just that works that are the result of obligations the tenant freely entered into should be taken into account); and

(iii) the improvements were carried out by the *tenant, its subtenants or their respective predecessors in title* (emphasis added) during the term of the lease or during any period of occupation prior thereto that arose out of an agreement to grant such a term. Where the relevant improvement was carried out before the occupation permitted under any prior agreement to grant the term, the improvement may still be disregarded provided it was carried out by any present tenant or subtenant and provided that, since the improvement, the landlord or its predecessors in title has not had vacant possession of the relevant part of the demised premises.

The aim is to ensure that a landlord is unable to claim an increased rent for improvements done at the tenant's (or another's) expense. The italicised words in the preceding paragraph represent an amendment to the first draft of the Model Forms where reference was made to 'the tenant or its predecessors in title or subtenant'. On this wording it is possible that improvements undertaken by a sub-undertenant could not be disregarded, and this would create a lacuna. The reference to 'subtenants' in the revised formula may be wide enough to meet the problem but any doubt would be resolved if the phrase 'by the tenant, its subtenants, their predecessors in title or persons deriving title mediately or immediately under them' were adopted. Where appropriate, the disregard of clause 3(B)(iii) may be limited to improvements completed in the 21 years preceding the review date and the (optional) concluding words of the paragraph in the 1980 Model Forms so provided.

Lear v Blizzard [1983] 3 All ER 662 shows the effect that an absence of this disregard might have. In that option case (discussed at p 276, above) the arbitrator had to determine the rent which was stated to be 'a rent to be agreed'. Though holding that this involved a subjective assessment, it did not follow that improvements were to be automatically disregarded because in that case they had been paid for by a tenant's predecessor in title. Consequently, it was for the tenant to show, as a matter of evidence, that in the process of assignment he paid wholly or contributed partly towards the cost of improvements in the premium he had paid.

(a) Improvements—meaning and scope

There is a vast amount of material to assist in the often difficult issue of whether particular work falls to be included as an 'improvement'.

(i) Authority from repair covenant disputes

The dividing line between repairs and improvements has never been an easy one to draw. It has arisen, and will continue to arise, in a number of contexts beside that of rent reviews and statutory renewals, the source of its introduction in the formative years of rent review. The distinction has been put in the following terms:

'. . . if the work which is done is the provision of something new for the benefit of the occupier, that is, properly speaking, an improvement but if it is only the replacement of something already there, which has become dilapidated or worn out, then albeit that it is a replacement by its modern equivalent, it comes within the category of repairs and not improvements' (per Denning LJ in *Morcom v Campbell-Johnson* [1956] 1 QB 106 at 115).

The distinction runs through a whole series of well-known cases in which the point being litigated was, of course, the scope of a repairing clause rather than the distinction between repairs and improvements as such. In *Lister v Lane and Nesham* [1893] 2 QB 212 remedying the defect (a bulging wall caused by the rotting of timber foundations in muddy subsoil) would have required work going beyond repair; in *Wright v Lawson* (1903) 19 TLR 510 making good a dangerous bay window would have involved building pillars or columns that would have been beyond the scope of the repair covenant (in fact, the tenant had replaced the demolished bay by a window flush with the front wall of the house); insertion of a damp-proof course was held to be beyond the scope of repair in *Pembery v Lamdin* [1940] 2 All ER 434; *Sotheby v Grundy* [1947] 2 All ER 761 followed the *Lister* case on comparable facts (though there the original defective foundations were illegal—a nice point in the context of an 'observance of covenants' assumption discussed at p 413, above); *Collins v Flynn* [1963] 2 All ER 1068 was to like effect too; and finally, in *Brew Bros v Snax (Ross) Ltd* [1970] 1 QB 612, repair of defective drains, the demolition of a flank wall, the building of new foundations and the rebuilding of the wall were all held to be outside a repair covenant. On the other side of the line, in *Lurcott v Wakely and Wheeler* [1911] 1 KB 95 the rebuilding of a dangerous front wall although in modern materials and to standards required by current bye-laws, was held to be within a repair covenant; and in *Ravenseft Properties Ltd v Davstone (Holdings) Ltd* [1980] QB 12, a similar ruling applied to replacing the concrete cladding of a block of flats, inserting expansion joints and a sufficiency of 'ties' to rectify their earlier omission. Emphasis was placed on two factors; namely, a need to judge each dispute on its particular facts and the relevance of cost of the remedial work proportionately to the value or cost (the two are not differentiated) of the premises. For a view that the former ground was a departure, and an unwelcome departure, from the principle of distinguishing repair and renewal in the earlier cases, see Smith [1979] Conv 429.

In *Smedley v Chumley & Hawke Ltd* (1981) 44 P & CR 50 case, a landlord's covenant for structural repairs was held to require him to bear both the cost of rectifying an unstable foundation 'raft' and the tenant's losses while the newly built premises were unusable. In contrast, a lessor was not liable for ineffective damp courses under a covenant to repair in *Yanover v Romford Finance & Development Co Ltd* (1983) 29 March, unreported, but noted in (1983) 4 CSW 70. However, in *Elmcroft Developments Ltd v Tankersley-Sawyer* (1984) 270 EG 140, a landlord was held responsible under a covenant to repair the exterior and (inter alia) main walls, for remedying extensive damp due to a defective damp course in a late Victorian block. The case illustrates once more how much the issue is one of fact and degree. In *Halliard Property Co Ltd v Nicholas Clarke Investments Ltd* (1984) 269 EG 1257 forfeiture for breach of a repair covenant was denied as rebuilding an inherently defective rear extension was held, on the facts, to fall beyond the dividing line of repair and total replacement, viewing, somewhat surprisingly, the extension independently of the whole building of which it was part.

Further cases illustrate the borderline between repair and improvement. In *Mullaney v Maybourne Garage (Croydon) Management Co Ltd* [1986] 1 EGLR 70 wooden windows, a constant source of problems, were replaced by modern maintenance-free metal ones; a lessee of a flat who objected to having the cost of the work apportioned to a service charge only covering repair succeeded in her contention. By way of contrast, in *Sutton (Hastoe) Housing Association v Williams* [1988] 1 EGLR 56, on wording only distinguishable with difficulty and on similar facts, the opposite result was reached. In *Quick v Taff-Ely Borough Council* [1985] 3 WLR 981 a local authority landlord was held not liable on the implied statutory repair covenants for failing to cure substantial problems caused by damp. Repair would not have remedied the cause of the damp which was due to basic design defects, and so was an item the remedying of which would be an improvement. The opposite result, yet again, occurred in *Stent v Monmouth District Council* [1987] 1 EGLR 59 founded on different arguments and closely related facts. In *McDougall v Easington District Council* [1989] 1 EGLR 93 the landlord council, before starting extensive works, agreed to pay the tenants £50 for damage to decorations. That sum proved quite inadequate when the works were complete. The tenants sued for compensation on the basis that the works were repair (see *Bradley v Chorley Council* (1985) 83 LGR 623 and *McGreal v Wake* (1984) 13 HLR 109) but the claim failed as the works constituted improvements.

Similar issues to those in the *Mullaney* and *Sutton (Hastoe)* cases have arisen in commercial service charge cases. In both *Holding and Management Ltd v Property Holding and Investment Trust plc* [1990] 1 EGLR 65 and *Plough Investment Property Ltd v Manchester City Council* [1989] 1 EGLR 244 landlord's proposals for remedial works were held to go beyond repair so that, in the first case, professional fees for pursuing the proposals and, in the second, the cost of preparatory surveys fell outside the ambit of contributions recoverable as service charge payments.

(ii) Repair cases not always helpful

However, whilst these cases may provide a guide-line to what constitutes an 'improvement', the issue may have to be approached differently in a rent review context (as against a breach of repair covenant dispute). 'Renewal' is used more often than 'improvement' in the reported cases on repairing obligations, and most are concerned with the replacement of defective elements of buildings. In the review context, perfectly sound parts of the building may have been swept away to allow different and more convenient structures to take their place. The amended premises may have a more convenient layout, eliminate unwelcome changes in floor levels or ceiling heights, allow cheaper or quicker cleaning or decorating, enhance a modern 'image' or appearance or have some other such advantage to offer. Consequently, an improvement may well have resulted without any necessity that the former state of affairs constituted a state of disrepair. Accordingly, the repair cases will not assist greatly in deciding whether or not there is an improvement to be reflected in the new rent as the work will not have remedied disrepair.

(iii)   Guidance from statutory concepts

In some ways, therefore, the concept of improvements embodied in ss 1–3 and s 19 of the Landlord and Tenant Act 1927 ought to be a better guide to the meaning to be given to the word in the 1954 Act and in the rent review clause originally framed by reference to the statutory model. Surprising though it may seem, there is no statutory definition. Guidance on the meaning of the word can be found in *Woolworth & Co v Lambert* [1937] Ch 17 and *Lambert v Woolworth & Co (No 2)* [1938] Ch 883 where the decision eventually turned on the issue of whether the correct test for what was an improvement was whether what was proposed to be done on the demised premises, combined with what was to be done on adjoining property, benefited the tenant or whether it had to be decided by seeing if it benefited the landlord. The majority favoured the former test and the paradox of this in a rent review provision is obvious. An instruction to disregard improvements effected by the tenant is normally thought to be intended to benefit the tenant, but in a case like that litigated in these cases to ignore the effect of improvements would benefit the landlord if something, which happened to be of advantage to the particular tenant and so an improvement on the *Lambert* test but not a benefit to the reversion, has to be eliminated and this has an effect on the open market rental value adverse to the tenant. It would have such an adverse effect if the majority of tenants would pay more for the premises without the improvement.

The last-cited cases arose under s 19(2) of the 1927 Act under which covenants against improvements without consent become subject to a proviso that such consent shall not be unreasonably withheld. The statutory regime that allows a tenant (putting it broadly) to claim compensation for improvements that are shown to have enhanced the letting value of the premises on termination of the lease is to be found in ss 1–3 of the 1927 Act. The meaning of the term in decisions under s 19(2) was said to be of doubtful assistance in relation to issues under s 3(1) by Morton J in *National Electric Theatres Ltd v Hudgell* [1939] Ch 553 at 567. To the extent that the two sets of provisions are thus not to be treated as *in pari materia* for the purposes of the 1927 Act itself, the influence of either upon the meaning of the words in the disregards specified in s 34 of the 1954 Act (and, therefore, indirectly, in rent reviews based upon the later Act) is much reduced. However, one thing can be said; namely, that if a tenant had successfully invoked the 1927 Act compensation procedure, or at least the first stage of it in s 3, the existence of an improvement could not be denied in a later rent review. In practice, the procedure seems very rarely to be resorted to; it is thought to be cumbersome and slow, and the prospect of future compensation (when the impact of what has been done may well be diminished by the overall state of the building) may be judged or be thought so remote or speculative as not to justify present effort. Indeed, if the residue is of any length, forecasting a future increase in letting value is itself speculative.

The Leasehold Reform Act 1967 (as amended in 1974 and by statutory instrument SI 1990 No 434) allows a tenant to seek an adjustment in rateable value (so as to bring his property within the enfranchisement limits) by reference to his 'improvements made by the execution of works amounting to structural alteration, extension or addition' (s 1(4A) as introduced by s 118(3) of the Housing Act 1974). In *Pearlman v Keepers and Governors of Harrow School* [1979] QB 56 the word 'improvement' was not separately discussed but Lord Denning MR, speaking of the whole phrase, said at 66F: '[the words] are simple English words'. The decision turned on whether the installation of a modern central heating system was a 'structural alteration' and it was held to be so. The doubts cast on the decision in *Pearlman* in subsequent cases (eg *Re Racal Communications Ltd* [1981] AC 374) are doubts of jurisdiction and do not question the interpretation of the statutory formula.

The 1954 Act follows the 1927 Act in eschewing any definition, an omission not remedied when the 1969 amendments to the treatment of improvements were enacted. In the only major reported case on the point, which led to some of those amendments (namely *Re 'Wonderland' Cleethorpes, East Coast Amusement Co Ltd v British Transport Commission* [1965] AC 58), no question arose on the meaning of improvements.

(iv) Guidance from taxation cases

The distinction between repair and improvement is also important in taxation matters in that, for example, expenditure on repairs may be deductible from current income whilst making good of an accumulation of past failures to repair may be treated as capital expenditure and so disallowed as a deduction. The test of what constitutes a repair enunciated in *Lurcott's* case has been referred to in some of the taxation cases, but no direct statement of what constitutes an improvement can be found. Nevertheless, the cases would lend some support to an argument that at some stage the making good of accumulated past neglect to repair might constitute an improvement that could become relevant to the disregard of improvements where up-grading or refurbishment could well have taken place during the life of a lease and may cover disrepair pre-dating the lease. If it was effected at the outset, there would be the additional obstacle that a covenant to keep in repair may involve an obligation first to put into repair (*Proudfoot v Hart* [1890] 25 QBD 42), bringing into conflict the taxation concept that, at some stage, 'catching-up' becomes improvement.

Interest on loans for the improvement of 'an only or main residence' attracted tax relief (Finance Act 1972, Sched 9, para 1(b)) until the Finance Act 1988; expenditure for 'enhancing the value' of an asset may enter into the computation of any capital gain (Capital Gains Tax Act 1979, s 32); and the various bases for development land tax all permitted expenditure on relevant improvements to be taken into account and there is a definition in Sched 3 to s 44 of the Finance Act 1988. It is not thought particular decisions under those provisions provide any general guide to the meaning of 'improvement' but, in any specific case, Revenue rulings on the issues should at least strengthen an argument that particular work constituted an improvement within the disregard provision. There was a spate of litigation on a comparable issue in relation to VAT, which has tailed off with the removal of the distinction in the 1984 Budget, save for listed building improvements.

(v) Works which become part of the demised premises

Works which are, or become, part of the demised premises will not be improvements. Modifications to a wall and drains in the landlord's building in the course of construction by the prospective tenant and at the tenant's expense was not an improvement, but part of the original building: *Scottish & Newcastle Breweries plc v Sir Richard Suttons Settled Estates* [1985] 2 EGLR 130 at 137. Similarly, what was once an improvement may cease to be one on the grant of a new lease. In *Brett v Brett Essex Golf Club Ltd* [1986] 1 EGLR 154 the Court of Appeal, reversing the judge below, held that the erection of a golf clubhouse and the creation of a golf course in 1973–75 could not be 'improvements' within the context of a 1978 lease, for under that lease they formed part of the demised premises. The works may well have constituted improvements under an earlier lease but the incorporation of s 34 in its original wording (see below) meant that the principle of *Re 'Wonderland' Cleethorpes* (below) applied and the substantial works done by the tenant during the earlier lease could not be disregarded as improvements. A similar result was reached and the *Brett* case applied in *Panther Shop Investments Ltd v Keith Pople Ltd* [1987] 1 EGLR 131.

Another area of difficulty is that of distinguishing between improvements and other tenant's installations which rank as fixtures, especially trade fixtures or mere chattels (a topic considered in detail in Chapter 11, p 325; and see *Young v Dalgety plc* [1987] 1 EGLR 116). A tenant who, at the end of a lease, would be anxious to be able to claim the right to remove certain types of equipment or elaborate fittings, might face a dilemma on an early rent review in a moderately lengthy term whether or not to advance the same arguments. As a matter of valuation, disregard of the rental effect of the items regarded as improvements would have one effect, but their notional absence as trade fixtures under a vacant possession assumption could have a different effect. Their significance in relation to notional permitted use could have a valuation effect—if the conduct of the alternative business would necessitate some such installation that produces a different result from the case where it is marginal, optional or frankly excessive. Vacant possession may be countered, in this respect, by assumptions of fitness for (immediate) use or express disallowance of fitting out concessions, as discussed at p 418. An obligation to effect improvements may negative the disregard, as we have seen, but if installations not becoming part of the premises can be discounted in one of the other ways just discussed then the fact they fell within a contractual obligation to provide them may be irrelevant. The carpets, light fittings and flooring in the *Dalgety* case fell quite squarely on the tenant's fixtures side of this line but other installations may be more difficult to categorise. Will pre-fabricated, modular false ceilings and partitioning be regarded as still demountable or will the purpose and degree of installation test attach them to the freehold, so as to qualify as improvements?

Technological advances and changes in attitudes to the desirable working, shopping or living environment over the life of a lease may present new problems at successive reviews. The remarks in *Ratners (Jewellers) Ltd v Lemnoll Ltd* (1980) 255 EG 987, concentrated on the absence of rental effect of extensive and expensive shop-fitting rather than this landlord's fixtures/tenant's fixtures/chattels distinction. The differentiation process to effect this categorisation suffers both from a dearth of modern examples and the overlap between disputes as between landlords and tenants, mortgagor and mortgagee, possibly mortgagee and finance house with goods on hire-purchase or conditional sale, vendor and purchaser or life tenant and remainderman.

The existence of an express requirement to disregard improvements does not settle the question, when improvements have been done, of whether regard should be had to an obligation to eliminate such improvements and reinstate the premises to their former condition at the end of the term, a future expense that can be argued to affect the mind of the willing lessee: *Pleasurama Properties Ltd v Leisure Investments (West End) Ltd* [1986] 1 EGLR 145 (CA). The court declined to construe a licence to alter premises as equivalent to a deed of variation to a lease. A covenant by the tenant in the licence to reinstate was not, therefore, to be read as one of the tenants' covenants contained in the lease and was not, therefore, to be taken into account at review. the possible confict was thus side-stepped in that case but will arise if the licence is by way of variation of the lease (see p 378 for a discussion of subsequent variation of the lease).

(vi)   The problem of records
These varying lines of authority show that difficulty may be met in deciding what is an improvement as a matter of law. An equally difficult practical problem may have to be faced in ascertaining at or about a review date the facts of what a tenant has done, and what the state of the premises would be had the changes not been made. Not all tenants and not all landlords keep detailed records of the physical state of property from time to time sufficient to demonstrate the 'before' and 'after' state of affairs (see, for example, *Kensington Pension Developments Ltd v Royal Garden Hotel (Oddenino's) Ltd* [1990] 27 EG 79 where the form of the

review clause necessitated reference to the nature of the contributions to the building development 25 years previously). Moreover, the tenant negotiating the review may not have been the tenant who carried out the work and may have failed to take over the records of the earlier tenant. The same position may exist on the landlord's side. Quotations and invoices, even if preserved, may not elucidate the problem, working plans may have been lost or destroyed (although in some circumstances a local authority may hold copies), or work may have been done without plans. The cumulative effect of a series of small adjustments may have been to bring about what the tenant retrospectively puts forward as an improvement.

The potential problem in divining the 'before' and 'after' state of affairs was illustrated by *Young v Dalgety plc* [1987] 1 EGLR 116. The improvements carried out by the lessees and directed to be disregarded at review, could not be identified, still less described, because the drawings had been lost and the building had since been extensively refurbished. That difficulty necessitated the parties to the lease asking the court by originating summons to identify what, if any, assumptions were to be made as to the work which was likely to have been done.

(vii) Drafting to cope with the definition problem

Accordingly, it is suggested that future drafting techniques may seek to eliminate some of the difficulties noted. First, it is felt that one of the existing definitions would provide a useful reference for the particular lease, it could be incorporated in the clause. The authors do not find any of them sufficiently clear or helpful to nominate it as a candidate for consideration. A draftsman could always devise his own definition in the light of all the factors stated above. Secondly, to prevent arguments about what has been done, it could be provided that the only improvements to be disregarded are those notified (possibly within a stated period from start or from completion) and claimed as such by the tenant. Of course, the result may be achieved indirectly because of the existence of covenants requiring prior consent, following the submission of plans and specifications, to the carrying out of the more or the less usual (but very worthwhile) provision that the value of a tenant's improvements will only be added to the insurance cover following notification of what has been done. Provisions such as these may be valuable, particularly because challenges to the claim that an improvement has been effected can be promptly made and settled rather than forming merely part of the later negotiation or other resolution of a rent review. The settlement can cover the two aspects of establishing both what has been done and whether it ranks as an improvement within the criteria of the particular lease.

The original 1979 version of the Model Forms required that improvements must be 'shown to be such by the tenant', but that has been dropped in the revised versions. The phrase in question made it clear where the onus of proof lay, and one effect of its omission would be to throw the parties back on the basic rule of evidence that the onus would be upon the party seeking to assert that the disregard of alleged improvements should or should not be applied. The revised versions also bring the Model Forms back into line with s 34 in this regard, but whether the Joint Working Party's second thoughts are an improvement on the first is a matter of conjecture. The Background Notes do not give any hint of the thinking behind the change.

(b) Improvements—by whom carried out

Section 34(1)(c) of the Landlord and Tenant Act 1954, providing for the disregard of improvements, applies to improvements carried out by 'a person who at the time it was carried out was the tenant'. It is usual to render this, in rent review provisions allegedly or apparently based on the statute, as a reference to 'the tenant or his predecessors in title'. A further protection is to add 'or any subtenant'; and this will be found, for example, in the Model Forms. Indeed, most of the 'standard' clauses limit the description of those who have carried out works, in addition to the tenant, to its 'subtenants' or 'undertenants' (and their respective predecessors in title). The words occur in the 1985 Model Forms, the ISVA Form A, and EFP (5th ed) Form 22. Only Conveyancer Form 5–57 uses the wider phrase 'person lawfully deriving title under the Lessee'. However, the word 'subtenant' or 'undertenant' may be capable of bearing the wider meaning so that it comprehends all sub-underleases, at least where the title derivation is by means of a lease. Some support can be found in the conveyancing decision of *Becker v Partridge* [1966] 2 QB 155 that 'sub-lease' was probably a sufficient description of a sub-underlease. The point is not without substance, given the layers of leases frequently found between the freeholder and the ultimate occupier and where such a hierarchy has been built up over the years the phrasing in each of the leases is not always consistent.

EFP (5th ed) Form 22 goes somewhat further than 'person lawfully deriving title under the lessee' in providing that the disregard extend to improvements carried out:

'by the tenant [its] subtenants or their respective predecessors in title [or by any lawful occupiers] during the term . . .'

The phrase *or by any lawful occupiers* is optional; it is not discussed in the footnotes but its potential width is obvious. It would cover, for example, licensees. In some settings, such as 'in-store franchisees' or similar concession arrangements, such occupiers may be in lawful possession for considerable periods and may well invest in works which could rank as improvements and affect the rental value. This is not to argue against the extension to the form of words in this precedent but rather to show circumstances where it might take effect.

The original version of the Model Forms excluded from the disregard improvements 'to the extent [they] shall have been carried out without any liability on the part of the immediate landlord to reimburse the cost thereof'. It is obviously right that if the landlord has to bear the cost he should not have to forgo the benefit of that expenditure on revision of the rent, but the words are not without difficulty. Do they cover the liability to pay the statutory compensation under the 1927 Act where the reasonable cost of the work, as if carried out at the time for assessment of compensation, is a possible measure of the compensation? It is doubtful that the words cover such a potential and contingent liability especially as it only matures on the expiry of the term; in any event the words have been dropped in the revised versions.

Works done by the landlord's contractors were 'carried out by the tenant' since the tenants requested the work and paid for it—*Scottish & Newcastle Breweries* case [1985] 2 EGLR at 137B, but they may not rank as an improvement—see (*a*) above. Similarly, work done prior to the grant of a lease was held to be an improvement to be disregarded in the *Hambros Bank v Superdrug* case (see below) since it was done by 'the Tenant' which was construed to mean the party named in the lease. Compare however the result in the *Brett* and *Euston Centre* cases (discussed at pp 441-3).

In *Daejan Investments Ltd v Cornwall Coast Country Club* (1984) 50 P & CR 157 a deed of licence acknowledged that certain improvement works had been executed to the landlord's satisfaction. This was held by Peter Gibson J to estop the landlords from later asserting that the works were carried out by someone other than 'the tenant' for the purpose of disregard of improvements.

(c) Absence of obligation

(i) Nature and source of 'obligation'

Section 34(2) of the Landlord and Tenant Act 1954, defining what improvements fall within s 34(1)(c), continues 'otherwise than in pursuance of an obligation to his immediate landlord', and that too is reproduced in most of the published or litigated clauses providing for this disregard. Section 2(1) of the 1927 Act referred only to 'an obligation . . . in pursuance of a contract entered into . . . for valuable consideration'. The 'trap' this created was sprung in *Owen Owen Estate Ltd v Livett* [1956] Ch 1 where a tenant was denied compensation because the improvement was an obligation he had entered into as landlord vis-à-vis a subtenant. Where 'open' wording akin to that has been used, the reasoning of that case would apply and the disregard would not be effective if the tenant was under an obligation to anyone, possibly even only under some statutory duty. There is no reason for limiting 'obligation' to those arising in contract.

In a county court case, *Appleton v Abrahamson* (1956) 167 EG 633, the judge went so far as to hold that 'obligation' did not necessarily mean a legally enforceable obligation, and might include a moral obligation. As the lease stated that it was granted 'in consideration of the expense which the tenant had [incurred] and would incur' in renovating the premises, it might have been possible to find an implied obligation that would justify not disregarding the improvements on renewal. Despite the rather unsatisfactory reasoning of the case, it does raise the issue of what nature of obligation suffices, on which we have not traced any other reported decision.

Once more, all the covenants in a lease must be considered, not just the obvious case of a covenant to do work. A covenant to observe statutory requirements, for example, could involve an obligation on the tenant to effect improvements in view of the width of those requirements, as discussed at p 374, above, and it would not be impossible that a covenant not to vitiate insurances would, in extreme cases, have a like effect. A covenant, now sometimes found, to carry out work required by the insurers would more obviously be caught. Moreover, the obligation might be found not in the lease itself but in the agreement for lease preceding it—a point expressly covered in the drafting of the Model Forms. The Model Forms refer simply to 'an obligation to the Landlord'—so covering all the three limbs just discussed (direct covenant; indirect covenant and collateral covenant); and the revised version adds 'or its predecessors in title', which ties up a possible loose end and should be contrasted with the wording in the first version. Other wording may not pick up all the possible sources of an obligation.

A licence allowing improvements or alterations may also be the source of an obligation. Such a licence often imposes an obligation to reinstate at the end of the term as in *Pleasurama Properties Ltd v Leisure Investments (West End) Ltd.* Such an obligation could restrict the increase in rental value created by the improvement, especially if the review is to be a short notional term, a matter further discussed below. The licence to carry out improvements that was granted in *Godbold v Martin the Newsagents Ltd* (1983) 268 EG 1202 imposed conditions on the tenants if they chose to carry out the works, but imposed no obligation to do the work. Accordingly, the improvements were not carried out in pursuance of an obligation to the landlord and their effect on rent was to be disregarded. Probably the majority of licences giving consent to improvements are of such a type, leaving the tenant free to decide whether or not to effect the work, but the point is one for both parties to bear in mind in considering the form of any licence. (This can also affect statutory compensation—see the discussion in the notes to Conveyancer Precedent 5–72.)

(ii)   Necessity for consent

It is also a condition of disregard of improvements in the Model Forms that any necessary consent has been obtained, although the wording has changed from 'the written consent [of the] immediate landlord (where required)' in the 1979 version to mere 'consent where required' in the 1980 and 1985 Model Forms. There are at least two possible consequences of the changed wording, one being that the second version may provide for the circumstances where consent is required of someone else besides the immediate landlord—a superior landlord, for example—and the other the prospect that 'consent' might comprehend acquiescence, which 'written consent' would not. Consent might also extend to permissions to be obtained from public authorities, too. There is in all versions a possible conflict with the assumption that the tenant has complied with all his covenants, a point already discussed above in relation to that assumption. The absence of consent where necessary, or the carrying out of improvements in defiance of a covenant not to effect them without consent, may have a substantial effect on the rent at review, for it can be argued that a tenant bidding in the market would pay nothing extra for the benefit of improvements which the landlord could insist on being removed, with the attendant cost of removal and making good the disruption attendant on that work and the return to the unimproved condition of the premises. That proposition was accepted in *Selous Street Properties Ltd v Oronel Fabrics Ltd* (1984) 270 EG 643 at 743. In that case, retrospective consent had been given and the judge found that the works in question had not significantly affected the reviewed rent because of their relative insignificance as compared to the premises as a whole. So, if the Model Forms wording is adopted, the tenant will argue 'If the work was unauthorised, it should be disregarded at review on general principles; if it was authorised, the same result flows from the wording of the disregard'.

Care is required to ensure that if written consent is required, that it is obtained and the precise terms of the disregard are met. In *Hamish Cathie Travel England Ltd v Insight International Tours Ltd* [1986] 1 EGLR 244 the lease provided for no account to be taken of improvements to which the landlord had given written consent. No written consent was ever given to the improvements undertaken, despite a history of complex negotiations. The landlords successfully claimed that, on review, the improvements were not to be disregarded. Notwithstanding the *Hamish Cathie* case, the absence of *written* consent, for example where the circumstances demonstrate such a degree of acquiescence that removal would not be ordered, might still lead in other cases to the disregard being applied. This would be possible if the court followed decisions in other areas of law where the absence of writing has been brushed aside if a binding non-written consent has been found. Moreover a landlord may not wish to argue against himself, as it were, that he has acquiesced; he will have to balance the effect on rent levels of taking account of the improvement not approved in writing against the loss of his right to insist on removal. He may give a consent (so, as in the *Selous Street* case, facilitating an assignment) against an agreed rent adjustment. There remains a possibility that if the disregard refers to consent yet there is in fact no need for consent or no prohibition on making improvements, admittedly an unlikely and probably inadvertent combination the absence of written, albeit unnecessary, consent will negate the disregard.

(iii)   Improvements in pursuance of statutory obligations

An improvement which is required by statute may still be done 'in pursuance of an obligation to the immediate landlord'. Thus in *Forte & Co Ltd v General Accident Life Assurance Ltd* [1986] 2 EGLR 115 the tenant covenanted to execute 'all works as under or by virtue of any Act or Acts of Parliament'. It was held that this meant that substantial works done by the tenant pursuant to statutory requirements were carried out in pursuance of an obligation to the immediate landlord. It mattered not that they were carried out under a statutory obligation as well; their rental effect was thus not to be disregarded.

The risk that a covenant to observe statutory duties would result in an improvement not being voluntary, and so not to be disregarded, has been addressed by the Joint Working Party in the 1985 Revision of the Model Forms. The wording will be found in clause 3(B)(iii) of each of the variants:

'except obligations requiring compliance with statutes or directions of Local Authorities or other bodies exercising powers under statute or Royal Charter.'

There may be some dangers in the reference to 'directions' where a local authority (or cognate body) is also a lessor; the word is not necessarily to be restricted to directions *dehors* the lease but could include requirements that the lessor makes in that capacity (the converse of the situation produced by normal provisions in such leases that its actions as lessor do not bind it as local authority).

(iv)   Possible problems for a tenant

Where new shop-fronts are to be fitted, indeed are necessarily to be fitted, into 'shell' shopping units, some landlords omit imposing any positive obligation on the tenant to install the same (whilst still retaining full control by requiring consent to the details of any shop-front in fact installed). The device seeks to eliminate tax liability arising through the works being treated as a deemed premium under s 34(2) of the Income and Corporation Taxes Act 1988, where the lease is a 'short lease' of less than 50 years. The lessor relies on the practical neccessity for the tenant to carry out the work. The benefit of thus avoiding tax can still be obtained, but to avoid a continuing adverse effect on any rent review the landlord who agrees to the disregard of improvements voluntarily effected should be required by the lease to exclude from the disregard the initial shop-fitting works, and indeed later replacement shop-fitting works as well. The latter point is of general importance as a matter to be considered. In some trades and locations it may be virtually routine for an incoming tenant to replace the existing shop-front, and less frequently to remodel interior fittings and fixtures; indeed, without any change of tenant it may be usual to alter the appearance or 'image' of shops in an intensely fashionable sector several times during a 14 or 21–year lease. Accordingly, the existence of a particular combination of windows, doors, shelving racks and other display units, decor or lay-out may have no demonstrable effect on the hypothetical market, especially in the case of mass-volume units in 'prime' shopping pitches, and it will matter little whether or not the review includes a provision to disregard such improvements or their effect on rent. Thus, in *Ratners (Jewellers) Ltd v Lemnoll Ltd* (1980) 255 EG 987 the judge, in fixing an interim rent under the 1954 Act, accepted the valuer's evidence that a particular shop-front would not affect the market rent, despite evidence that an incoming tenant might spend £30,000 on his own shop-fitting. However, when the premises are not of that specialised type but one or more changes of shop-fitting may or may not take place during the term, to the extent that such work is an improvement it will be fair that it should be disregarded and the lease should provide accordingly. In practice, the usual formulation of the disregard, which eliminates only the impact on rent of the improvement, may often achieve this effect. This is discussed in (*e*) below.

(d) Improvements—when carried out

Whether or not 'improvements', executed prior to the grant of a lease, fall to be disregarded will depend very much on the exact terms of the lease; if s 34 of the Landlord and Tenant Act 1954 is incorporated then it will be crucial whether the lease incorporates s 34 as originally enacted or as subsequently amended in 1969. The problems when the s 34 disregard is incorporated by reference into the lease is discussed in section (*f*) below.

(i) Clauses with the 's 34' wording

Where the disregard is in the form of s 34 in its original wording, either expressly or by incorporation, the improvement must have been carried out 'by the tenant or a predecessor in title of his'. *Brett v Brett Essex Golf Club* [1986] 1 EGLR 154 makes it clear that, in such circumstances, the principle of *Re 'Wonderland' Cleethorpes* applies so that only improvements carried out by the tenant and effected during the term of the current tenancy fall to be disregarded. The *Brett* case was applied in *Panther Shop Investments Ltd v Keith Pople Ltd* [1987] 1 EGLR 131. The works in question had been undertaken during the currency of a previous lease between the same parties. They were part of the demised premises as far as the current lease was concerned and the terms of an express disregard modelled on s 34 did not extend to those earlier works. The *Hambros Bank* case (see p 437) was distinguished.

The 1969 amendments to s 34 of the 1954 Act, consequent upon *Re*

'Wonderland' Cleethorpes, extended the disregard to improvements carried out not only during the current tenancy but also those in the 21 years preceding the application for a new tenancy where there had been a continuity of 'protected' business tenancies thereafter and no tenant under any such tenancy had quit on termination. Where the disregard is in the form of s 34, as amended, or expressly in one of the Model Form variants, the problem which arose in the *Brett* case will not apply (but working out the s 34 formula may present the problems discussed at p 446).

(ii)   The approach in the precedents

The first version of the Model Forms, amongst other precedents, followed the model of s 34 as amended, but avoided the time-limit difficulty with that section (see p 447) by stipulating a period 21 years before the commencement of the relevant review period (although the wording is not particularly elegant). The revised 1980 version achieved much the same result, although there is clearly a difference between the provision that no previous tenant has quit during the relevant period and the amended provision that the landlord has not had vacant possession of the relevant part of the premises. In the 1980 version, the 21–year period was made an optional element of the Model Forms in recognition of the possibility that such a limit will not always be appropriate. The current 1985 Model Forms retain the 1980 wording but have now eliminated completely the 21–year time-limit, except where there is a break in continuity. This means that if the tenant's improvements retain value after 21 years they still fall to be disregarded. The disregard of improvements in EFP (5th ed) Form 22 is almost exactly the same as that in the 1985 Model Forms and this form of words, without any time-limit, now appears to have evolved into the standard form of wording in many modern clauses. Conveyancer Precedent 5–57 contains no time-limit.

The ISVA form for review to open market rent uses a different 'fair allowance' approach, which is discussed at p 448, below. As part of that contentious fair allowance provision, it uses 21 years immediately before the relevant review date as the alternative to confining the allowance to improvements during the term.

(iii)   Diminishing impact on valuation

As Forbes J pointed out in *GREA Real Property Investments Ltd v Williams* (1979) 250 EG 651, the older the improvement, the less effect on rental values it may well have and there may come a stage where even what was an improvement when it was made has itself become outmoded and in need of replacement. The more fashionable or 'trendy' the work was, the more likely it is to fall out of fashion, or there may be higher standards of safety that come to be applied—for example, on ceiling tiles, PVC filling in furniture 'built in' or in the use of asbestos.

A continuing obligation to treat the premises as they were at the date of the lease can thus introduce an element of unreality that will become increasingly intense with the passage of time. Added to the problems of proof of what the unimproved state of the premises was, this makes the case for some time-limit a strong one, notwithstanding its elimination from the Model Forms. Moreover, since the exclusion of tenant's voluntary improvements is designed to be fair to the tenant, it is not unfair to remove that protection when the tenant has himself recouped the full benefit of the work and long since written off the capital cost in his accounts.

(iv) Meaning of 'predecessors'

Disregard of improvements under s 70(3)(b) of the Rent Act 1977 fell to be considered in *Henry Smith's Charity Trustees v Hemmings* (1983) 265 EG 383. The Court of Appeal held that the statutory formula 'any predecessor in title of the tenant . . . under the regulated tenancy' meant only a predecessor in relation to the current lease, so improvements carried out by the person holding over under an earlier lease, as part of the consideration for a new lease, were not to be disregarded. It made no difference, moreover, that, when the second lease was granted it created a term 'starting' at the expiry of the earlier lease and so encompassing the period when the work was done. Where the amended s 34 is incorporated, predecessors under earlier leases are included, provided the other conditions are met; where the phrase 'predecessors in title' stands alone, it remains to be seen whether the *Re Wonderland, Cleethorpes/Hemmings* construction would be followed or not.

(v) Work done prior to grant of a lease

Care must be taken by a tenant in carrying out voluntary improvements in anticipation of a lease where the disregard relates only to those effected during the term or by the tenant. In *Euston Centre Properties Ltd v H & J Wilson Ltd* (1981) 262 EG 1079, work was carried out by the party which became the lessee under the terms of an agreement, which the judge found to have been a licence to occupy and an agreement for a lease conditional on completion of some works by the landlord and of the works the intended tenants chose to carry out. When those works were done they were not 'carried out by a person who at the time it was carried out was the tenant', which was the wording used in the lease (probably a standard form of words to mirror the 1969 amendments to s 34). Accordingly, the rental effect of the works was not to be disregarded, enabling the landlord, as the judge remarked, to 'reap where it has not sown'. The wording would have shut out work carried out by a predecessor under an earlier term; but it also shut out the very party who had incurred the expenditure as being only the putative tenant at the time. The Model Forms extend to improvements 'during any period of occupation prior [to the term] arising out of an agreement to grant such term' and Conveyancer Precedent 5–57 was amended, by a similar addition, following the *Euston Centre* decision. The old EFP (4th ed) Forms incorporate s 34 by reference, with attendant difficulties discussed at (*f*) below, as does the *Kelly's Draftsman*, Form 14.

Work done by a person who later becomes the tenant may fall to be disregarded if there is no requirement that the work be done during the term: *Hambros Bank Executor and Trustee Company Ltd v Superdrug Stores Ltd* [1985] 1 EGLR 99. The defendant tenants were allowed into possession during the last months of a former lease, but in advance of the grant of the lease to them, to carry out shop-fitting works. These included installing a new staircase to the upper parts at the rear of the property to replace that at the front, so adding a considerable Zone A frontage. The landlord urged, citing the *Euston Centre Properties* case, that these works were not to be disregarded at review. Scott J avoided an 'unconscionable' result because the lease directed disregard of 'any effect on rent of any improvement carried out by the tenant' and *not* as in the *Euston Centre* case 'any improvement carried out by a person who at the time it was carried out was the tenant'. Since the work was done by the actual person defined by the lease as 'the Tenant' it mattered not that the work was in advance of the grant of the lease.

(e) Nature of the disregard

It is important to note that the statutory provision introduced into s 34 of the 1954 Act by the Law of Property Act 1969 does not require the existence of the improvement to be ignored but only its effect on rent, a point on which its lead has been followed by many other forms, including the Model Forms and EFP (5th ed) Form 22 which require disregard of 'any increase in *rental value*'. However, some clauses will almost certainly be found in leases that require the very existence of the improvements to be disregarded. Although we know of no reported decision on the point, we submit that the proper construction of such a clause requires the valuation to proceed on the further hypothesis that any part of the building actually removed for or destroyed in the course of the improvements be notionally re-instated. The ruling of Morton J in *National Electric Theatres Ltd v Hudgell* [1939] Ch 553, noted at p 431, above, that demolition constituted an improvement, reinforces this view. Indeed, where the provision requires disregard of the effect on rent of improvement, a similar notional re-creation of the unimproved state of affairs is also implied. In both cases, what is to be assumed is not necessarily restoration of the status quo, for some other provision—namely, that of assumed compliance with repair obligations—may require the valuation to relate to the former physical facts, save that any actual disrepair that existed when the improvement was effected be treated as made good (and so maintained) sufficiently to have complied with the repairing obligation. The county court judge in *Tummon v Barclays Bank Trust Co Ltd* (1979) 39 P & CR 300, deciding a special case stated by an arbitrator under s 8 of the Agricultural Holdings Act 1948, had to consider the meaning of the statutory words requiring the arbitrator not to take into account 'any increase in rental value . . . due to improvement', where the tenant had laid out roads and built toilet blocks and other facilities so as to comply with the conditions of a planning provision to use some 9 acres of a 300 acre farm as a caravan site. He held that the potential in the site for the new, profitable and, incidentally, non-agricultural use and the realisation of the latent value must be dealt with separately. The tenant's efforts, expenditure and work had secured the latter and that was the element to be disregarded, but the rental value inherent in the site to allow that improvement was not to be denied to the landlord who should be rewarded for the situation and general suitability for the use brought to fruition by the development. The release was 'due to' the improvements but the pre-existing factors, including the planning permission or the prospect of securing it, were not. It is submitted that a comparable analysis would be appropriate on the wording of many of the disregard formulae, whether the wording is of a rent effect 'due to' the improvement, some more neutral phrase such as 'attributable to' (the Model Forms usage) or merely a reference to 'the effect of' improvements (as in Conveyancer Precedent 5–57).

The statutory formula of disregarding *effect* on rent covers not only the most common situation where the improvement enhances rental value, where the disregard will reduce the rent assessed, but also the infrequent circumstance where the improvement depresses market rental, no matter how convenient it may have been to the actual tenant. The tenant may thus pay a rent above what the hypothetical incoming tenant would pay in the market. Such a construction would apply to any clause following the statutory wording in this regard: see Conveyancer Precedent 5–57, for example. It is a perfectly defensible result.

The Model Forms, in contrast, in both original and revised versions seek only the disregard of 'any increase in rental value *attributable*' to the improvements there detailed. On that wording, the tenant is not penalised by this disregard for improvements reducing value. His joy may be short lived, however, for the 'absence of depreciatory works' assumption, discussed at p 421, will serve in most instances to eliminate this negative aspect of the works carried out. The official 'Notes' to each version give no hint at the reasoning behind this particular departure from the statutory norm, which as we have just seen is largely negated by the countervailing assumption. That may not be true of those leases following the Model Form only in adverting to 'increase in rental value' but omitting the 'no depreciatory work' element.

The valuation aspects of the disregard of improvements are examined in Chapter 7, p 255.

(f)   Incorporation of s 34 by reference—which s 34?

The advice to avoid the incorporation of s 34 by reference has been strengthened by one point arising for decision in *Brett v Brett Essex Golf Club* [1986] 1 EGLR 154; the issue arose whether a direction in a 1978 lease to 'disregard (if applicable) those matters set out in paragraphs (a)(b) and (c) of s 34 of the Landlord and Tenant Act 1954' was a reference to the section as originally enacted in 1954 or to the section as amended and substituted by the Law of Property Act 1959.

In *Euston Centre Properties Ltd v H & J Wilson* (1981) 262 EG 1079, Cantley J assumed that such a reference in a 1975 lease was to the amended version. In the *Brett* case, the Court of Appeal agreed it was the more natural and reasonable assumption in the majority of cases but denied that there was any presumption to that effect. On the lease before them, it was decided (per Slade LJ) that the following factors pointed to a reference to the unamended 1954 wording.

(1)   The reference was to 'paragraphs (a) (b) and (c) of s 34'—an accurate reference to the 1954 wording whereas the amended section is s 34(1).
(2)   The unamended paragraphs (a)–(c) can more readily be incorporated into a rent review clause (they avoid the reference to s 34(2)).
(3)   The difficulties inherent in the amended section would indicate that a draftsman intending to refer to it would have been expected to specify in greater detail the manner in which the provisions were to apply in the review clause.
(4)   Elsewhere in the lease, references to statutes (eg s 196 of the Law of Property Act; the Arbitration Act 1950) either explicitly referred to the amending version or to any statutory modification then in force.

Although primarily an issue of construction of each lease, the views expressed in the *Brett* case are likely to be decisive in similar cases. It is submitted therefore:

(1)   References to s 34 in a lease entered into before the 1969 Act came into force will be to the original unamended wording.
(2)   References to s 34 in leases entered into after that date will be a matter of construction of the lease. An incorporation of the unamended version is likely particularly where (like old EFP (4th ed) Forms 7:1 and 8:1) the reference, as in the *Brett* case, is to 'paragraphs (a)(b) and (c) of s 34'. If the reference is just to 's 34' the issue is more finely balanced and may depend on whether references in the lease to other amended statutes make express reference to the amendment or not. The argument for the statute as amended will stress that, after the 1969 Act came into force, the 'the Landlord and Tenant Act 1954' means the amended version.

(3) Express reference to 's 34 (as amended)' as in *Kelly's Draftsman*, Form 14 and EFP (4th ed) Additional Form 76 will be sufficient to incorporate the new wording. A similar result is likely to follow where the lease incorporates 's 34(1)'. If the 1954 Act is further amended in relation to the disregards, there may be a difficult question as to whether future amendments are referred to.

(g) Possible traps from incorporation of s 34 by reference

(i) In relation to time-limits

Particularly in early leases, disregards have been incorporated in leases by direct reference to s 34(1) of the 1954 Act. Priday, in his 1980 Blundell Memorial Lecture at p 80, drew attention to a possible danger of this in relation to improvements. His example is of a renewed lease for 10 years with a rent review at 5 years of premises formerly held on a 21 year lease where improvements were carried out in the third year of that earlier term. The substantial effect of those improvements had to be ignored when the rent for the new lease was settled. Will they still be ignored at the review when they are 23 years old? Priday argues they may not. The construction difficulty is that s 34(2) defines relevant improvements as those 'completed not more than 21 years before the application for the new tenancy was made' and the process of review is clearly not such an application. Only if it is treated as such, by analogy, will the problem postulated in the lecture arise, and the authors are inclined to doubt the validity of such a construction. Priday's advice to the tenant's adviser was to 'make sure that the rent review clause is so worded that his client obtains the benefit of the improvements throughout the new tenancy'; the authors doubt if there can be any such general guide-line. In many ways, the device of incorporation is better avoided—consider also the problems of introducing the concept of 'the holding' where there have been sub-lettings yet rent for the whole of the demised premises is to be reviewed. Indeed, the problems involved in the introduction of the statutory concepts do not end there. What of voluntary improvements in the immediate vicinity of the premises which undoubtedly enhance the premises but which affect only its environs and not any part of what was demised? It may be said that a tenant may be foolish to incur such expenditure, but it will often be commercially opportune to tidy up a scruffy entrance, service area or car park area. If the wording of the disregard applies only to improvements 'to the demised premises' then 'outside' improvements, eg surfacing a previously unmade parking area over which the tenant had only easements, would not have to be disregarded. Each of the precedents reproduced in Part Seven which expressly provides for improvements to be disregarded refers to improvements to the demised premises. and it is virtually standard usage. Those precedents which incorporate s 34 of the 1954 Act incorporate its wording including para (c) of subs (1) which only specifies 'any effect on rent of an improvement to which this paragraph applies' and the application of that para (c) by subs (2) does not state that it applies only to improvements to the holding (or indeed to the demised premises). The reference to 'the holding or any part of it *affected* by the improvement' supports, or is, at least, not inconsistent with, a construction that improvements off the premises but demonstrably enhancing them are within the statutory disregard; that it must have been carried out by a person who was the tenant is, it is submitted, neutral on this issue. Perhaps this should be put in the scales in favour of incorporation of the statutory formula, which is generally better avoided.

The 21–year period in the amended s 34 must precede the date of the application for the new lease, a date to some extent within the tenant's control. Straightforward incorporation of the statutory formula, quite frequent in early rent review clauses, created the problem of translating that period to rent review where no application had to be made. That difficulty provides the strangest argument against mere incorporation by reference; today only the most unsophisticated lessor will use it. The issue of whether the nearest equivalent should be the start of the term (either the actual date of the lease or the date from which the team was calculated), the relevant review date on successive reviews or some other date appears never to have been raised in a reported case. Whilst the rental effect of improvements effected (say) 21 years before the start of a lease when on the fifteenth year review they are 36 years old might be slight, that result could follow if, on general principles, the provision was construed, *contra proferentem*, against the landlord. indeed, to revert to Priday's example, improvements disregarded after 18 years might be taken into account after 23.

(ii) 'Carried out'

It may be difficult to ascertain the correct meaning of 'carried out'. In *Dennis & Robinson Ltd v Kiossos Establishment* [1987] 1 EGLR 133 s 34 was incorporated with the qualifying proviso that 'improvements' was only to cover works carried out on or after 31 July 1982, the lease being dated 20 October 1982 and the term running from 31 December 1981. In such circumstances, 'carried out' might be troublesome if the work was started before the reference date and finished after. Subject to that, the case illustates one way which was adopted to deal with the statutory wording.

(h) Treatment of improvements in the ISVA Forms

(i) The 'fair allowance' concept

The particular treatment of tenants improvements was a major and innovatory feature of the ISVA Form A on its publication in December 1984. The provision required the making of a fair allowance to the tenant for voluntary improvements. The improvements might be those made during the term or those during a rolling period of 21 years before the relevant review date. By clause 1.4(I) the term 'tenant' includes a permitted undertenant, an issue discussed at p 436. The Society's explanatory notes explain that the fair allowance method 'avoids the difficulties which arise in respect of the disregard of the effect on rent of tenant's improvements— eg, the problems of fitting out time or of works paid for partly by the landlord and partly by the tenant'. The earlier discussion shows what those difficulties are or can be; the problem for the draftsman in deciding whether to follow this lead is whether those difficulties are avoided only to be replaced by others. For example:

(1) Whilst disregarding the effect of improvements on rent requires the contending valuers to determine what that effect is, the solution of that valuation problem may be easier than quantifying a fair allowance. That calculation may be based on one or more valuation techniques and the valuers may legitimately differ on which is the most appropriate.

(2) The major element leading to uncertainty is the central concept of an allowance that is 'fair'. Is that judged as fair to the tenant, fair to the landlord or fair to both? Is the test objective or subjective? The former seems the more likely and we refer to the discussion of the meaning of 'fair' as a qualification of market rent, discussed at p 384. Where the work has been done by an undertenant the exact arrangements between that undertenant the exact arrangements between that under-tenant and the mesne landlord may have a substantial effect on what can be considered fair for the latter as against the head landlord. A referee might well be urged to make some allowance in those circumstances; it cannot be forecast that he will do so.

(3) This emphasises the main worry of the ISVA concept, namely the room for uncertainty it gives. The disregard approach builds on the substantial experience over a period of years gained first from its incorporation in the 1954 Act, then from rent review provisions modelled on the renewal provisions and finally from express clauses based on the familiar wording. The fair allowance approach has no such history and was not a usual provision in leases prior to the promulgation of the ISVA forms. The form sought to lead rather than to follow the market; it did not even link the question of an allowance to the rental effect of what had been done.

Professional opinion gave little welcome to the new approach. The Background Notes to the 1985 Model Forms of the Law Society/RICS Working Party tersely state that it 'was considered but rejected' and it appears to have won few friends and gained little following or use.

(ii)   The alleged benefits assessed

The authors commented, in their 1986 Supplement to the Second Edition, that the justification advanced in the Notes and expanded by Finch, one of the draftsmen, that it catered for the situation where the work had been jointly financed 'rather disguises the fact that such shared expenditure is uncommon'. Moreover, we then thought that shared funding would 'normally be the subject of prior negotiations in which the rent consequences would be discussed'. Finch's comments, in an article at (1984) 272 EG 57, were followed by comments by Freedman and Fogel at pp 496 and 618 and his response at p 1274 of the same volume. The first laid stress on the common sense of the solution, making the valuers' own expertise an important part of the review clause. The commentary by Freedman and Fogel advanced many of the criticisms here made, and the response may be thought a little on the defensive. The suggested amendment to cater for 'negative improvements' has not seen the light of day. In fact, a far more convincing case for the fair allowance solution can be made out and the landlord's contribution reason served largely to weaken the case for it. The *rebus sic stantibus* justification (in Finch's final article) foreshadowed the emphasis on reality which came later to inform or to be claimed to inform, a series of decisions. A number of situations thrown up in the preceding discussion of the more usual disregard could be resolved by the fair allowance device if only the parties would accept the chances of a possibly arbitrary decision that could result. That risk—the risk of an unwelcome opinion arrived at, however conscientiously, by an unknown third party at some distance ahead must be what has tempered or even stifled, any support for what the ISVA produced with such enthusiasm.

The second problem allegedly addressed by the fair allowance, namely 'fitting out time' is solved in a different way by, say, the Model Forms by disregarding any rent-free or reduced rent period. At least, that is the solution if that is the problem being tackled—and the ISVA Form itself contains an assumption that 'the premises are fully fitted out and equipped and ready for immediate occupation and use'. If it is meeting some other aspect of fitting out—disruption of the tenant's business or enjoyment of the property while the work is done, the cost of funding any borrowing to pay for the work or of supervising it or so on—then it is hard to see why those temporary disadvantages should be rejected in a subsequent rent adjustment. The authors have never met a rent concession allowed to a sitting tenant who chooses to call in the builders, nor would we expect many landlords to respond sympathetically to such a request.

(iii)   Some consequential difficulties

Some other points fall to be made on the ISVA Form. It covers alterations as well as improvements, which differs from the Model Forms, and most 'private' forms which only cover the second. This may mean that not only must repair be differentiated from improvement itself (no easy task as has been demonstrated—see p 428) but it must also be distinguished from alteration. The expense and trouble of deciding both what constitutes an alteration and then what amounts to a fair allowance for the alteration could well prove quite disproportionate to the resultant rent adjustment. The alteration or improvement only ranks for an allowance where made 'otherwise than pursuant to any obligation of the tenant'; the potential trap of this formulation has already been discussed, at p 437. Limitation of the qualification to consent of the landlord, and further exclusion of obligations merely to observe statutory requirements should commend themselves to the well-advised tenants prepared to adopt the ISVA formulation.

The Society's notes state, obviously enough, that the option of work in the 21 years preceding a review date should only be used for a renewal lease to a former tenant or undertenant—a new lease to an undertenant is not strictly a renewal—and then discusses work during the currency of an agreement for lease or otherwise preceding the lease. The note counsels specific agreement on the treatment of such work and appropriate provisions in the lease. Ironically enough, this seems to be equally sound advice to cater for the infrequent event of shared expenditure on alterations or improvements! Finally, the provision appears in clause 1.4 H 'for the avoidance of doubt no value shall be attributed to the equipment and other property of the tenant in the demised premises'. Unfortunately a provision designed to avoid doubt creates some doubt of its own by its wording, for it may be arguable whether 'equipment and other property' relates only to fittings and chattels or includes tenants' and trade fixtures as well. That issue has arisen in other contexts—see p 325—but not in relation to this wording in any reported decision. Indeed we have traced no reported decision on any review clause readily recognisable as derived from the ISVA model.

(iv) Isva Form B

Form B, which is based on a return or yield on capital value, does not provide for any effect of alteration or improvement. The note suggests it could be reflected in the percentage; but, with all respect, it would not be sufficient to make a once-and-for-all adjustment long before the work was done. If the fair allowance route is to be followed, machinery for adjusting the percentage when the nature and extent of the relevant works become known is required, thereby introducing a further and arguably regrettable element of uncertainty. A further complication would be to allow for the tapering-off of the percentage adjustment as the rental effect of the improvement diminishes, a feature already discussed in the earlier treatment of the conventional disregard.

7   Other disregards

(a)   Exclusion of goodwill

(i)   Rationale

Section 34(1)(b) of the Landlord and Tenant Act 1954 excludes the effect on rent of goodwill attributed to the carrying on of the business of the tenant or his predecessor in that business. The presence of a disregard of goodwill is almost universal in early rent review clauses (often via the s 34 wording) and in current precedents (eg, EFP (5th ed) Form 22, clause 1.4.2; Model Forms, clause 3(B)(ii)).

In the context of the 1954 Act a disregard of goodwill was, and remains, wholly understandable, building as it did on the compensation for goodwill provisions of the 1927 Act. The case for including it in rent reviews is rather less compelling compared to, say, the case for disregarding the effect of improvements. A tenant may decline to carry out work that will only result in his being saddled with an increased rent—the unhappy outcome of *Ponsford v HMS Aerosols Ltd* [1979] AC 63, for example; it is an incentive to him to do work without that penalty that its effect is excluded, and the landlord in any event may obtain the benefit of the work in due course. The attraction of goodwill, however, is a less conscious operation in that it will accrue and adhere to the property incidentally through the efforts of the tenant largely directed to improving the profitability of his business, which happens to be in the premises. Of an improvement it can properly be said 'you can't take it with you', but the same is not always or even often true of goodwill. If, however, the goodwill of the business does adhere to the premises it could be argued that such a consequence is no less a piece of good fortune to the landlord than a general rise in property values in a neighbourhood or an upturn in the economic climate from which he should and does benefit at review. Nevertheless, the disregard is commonly provided for.

(ii)   Meaning

No definition of goodwill was provided in the statutory schemes of 1927 or 1954. There are definitions to be found in the cases, ranging from Lord Eldon's words in *Cruttwell v Lye* (1810) 17 Ves 335 at 346 ('the probability that the old customers will resort to the old place') through the House of Lords' statements in *Trego v Hunt* [1896] AC 7 and *IRC v Muller & Co's Margarine Ltd* [1901] AC 217 and a more 'modern' statement in the textbook by Merlin on *The Landlord and Tenant Act 1927* (2nd ed, 1931) employing a complex 'cat', 'dog' and 'rat' classification based upon the differing habits of customers who might or might not be attracted back. Maugham LJ, scornful of the analogy in any event, sough to add the rabbit category to this menagerie (*Whiteman Smith Motor Co Ltd v Chaplin* [1934] 2 KB 35 at 50). In the *Muller's*

Margarine case, Lord Macnaghten at 223 said of goodwill that 'It is a thing very easy to describe, very difficult to define', a counsel of mild despair echoed in other cases and not unlike the statement of the Master of the Rolls noted at p 432 that 'improvement' is a 'simple English word'. What the cases show is that it may be or become attached to the premises or it may be derived from the occupier; it is the latter alone that review provisions following the statutory model seek to exclude. In a particular case is the goodwill 'the benefit and advantage of the good name, reputation and connection of a business' (per Lord Macnaghten in the *Muller's Margarine* case at 223–4)? Is it something deriving from 'the one attribute common to all [sic] cases of goodwill . . . locality' (again, Lord Macnaghten a few lines later in his speech)? The last statement is surely too sweeping. Thus, goodwill attached to the premises has been held to be included by implication in a mortgage of them (*Re Kitchin, ex parte Punnett* [1880] 16 ChD 226) but goodwill personal to the occupier has been held not to be included (*Cooper v Metropolitan Board of Works* [1883] 25 Ch 472). Thus, it may not be easy to identify the existence of goodwill, where it has to be isolated, and to establish its character to see if its effect on rent is to be discounted. If an enterprising tenant takes on improving premises in an unlikely area—doubtless at an initial rent reflecting those drawbacks—and establishes a thriving business before a review date so that, indeed, to quote Ralph Waldo Emerson, 'the world will make a beaten path to his door', it may be a matter of great dispute how much of the consequential improvement in market rent is due to the inherent but dormant value of the property and how much due to the entrepreneurial flair of the tenant creating goodwill for purposes of the valuation exercise (compare the discussion of *Tummon v Barclays Bank Trust Co Ltd* at p 445, above). It must largely be in the specialist trades—the starred, rosetted or otherwise outstanding restaurant, the pioneering craft business in the long-neglected 'historic' warehouse or the enterprise capitalising on some (forgotten) dramatic, literary or scientific association—that the issue will arise and falls to be settled.

The situation under the 1927 Act was exhaustively discussed in *Whiteman Smith Motor Co Ltd v Chaplin* [1934] 2 KB 35 and the difference between the effect of situation and the impact of the tenant was rehearsed. In *W J Barton Ltd v Long Acre Securities Ltd* (1982) 263 EG 877, the Court of Appeal held that the tenants' trading records were protected from disclosure for the purpose of ascertainment of the market rent on renewal, for the success (or otherwise) of the business carried on was generally irrelevant in 'the ordinary case of shop premises'. The case of *Harewood Hotels Ltd v Harris* [1958] 1 WLR 108 was distinguished, as being one of the few cases where the open market rent may depend on an assessment of the profitability of a business for which the premises are peculiarly adapted (there an hotel, but other examples would be a theatre, a race-course or other sports facility or perhaps petrol filling station). It is submitted that these renewal cases are directly relevant to review cases adopting the statutory formula. The issue arose in a rent review case in *ARC Ltd v Schofield* [1990] NPC 3. Having held that 'fair and reasonable market rent' imported an objective test, Millett J ruled that trading accounts were thus inadmissible (although the arbitrator had ordered discovery of them) he added that he doubted whether they would have been admissible even if the test was subjective. (For a full discussion of admissibility of trading accounts, see Chapter 7, p 231.)

(b) Exclusion of effect of tenant's occupation

(i) Wording

Once more, the model for the inclusion of a disregard of the effect on rent of the occupation of the tenant is s 34(1)(a) of the 1954 Act. The statute refers to occupation of the tenant 'or his predecessors in title'; s 25 of the 1927 Act contained a definition of that phrase that was interpreted in the cases to mean strictly a former holder of the tenant's interest and not a subtenant (*Williams v Portman* [1951] 2 KB 948) nor the person who sold his business but surrendered his lease so the purchaser could take up a new one (*Passmore v Whitbread & Co Ltd* [1953] 2 QB 226). To what extent the 1927 Act decisions govern the meaning of the words in the 1954 Act, particularly in the absence of any definition in the later Act, is not certain and so their relevance in interpreting the words used in a lease is unsettled.

The original Model Forms ran the disregard of goodwill and occupation together, differentiating between the predecessor in title to the business in regard to the former and predecessor in title simpliciter in regard to the latter. The 1980 version separated them and specified occupation of subtenants, which the original version did not, so that if *Williams v Portman* does apply to the unembellished phrase it cannot to the later version. The 1985 Model Forms (EFP (5th ed) Form 22 is identical) has a disregard which reads:

'(i) any effect on rent of the fact that the tenant its subtenants or their respective predecessors in title have been in occupation of the demised premises.'

(ii) Effect

Disregard of occupation can have a positive or negative effect. The effect of disregarding the occupation of the tenant was said in *Harewood Hotels Ltd v Harris* to eliminate not only increases but also sitting tenant concessions—Lord Evershed MR expressly approving a passage in Woodfall to that effect. In some respects its effect may overlap with the goodwill provision, and so be likely to assist the tenant to argue for a lower rent, but not in all cases. However, whilst 'negative' goodwill is not necessarily covered by the goodwill disregard, it is submitted that the adverse effect of occupation may be a valuation factor. Consider, say, premises now occupied by a respectable tenant but which until recently has been the haunt of criminals, prostitutes, drug addicts, hooligans or other undesirables. It cannot be doubted, first, that in most cases the sordid associations would depress the market rent (and few landlords, it is surmised, would overtly argue that they welcome the additional rent they could demand for such unsavoury use of their property) and, secondly, that the present disregard would apply to counteract that bad effect. There may just be an argument that it would be the use and not the occupation as such of the former tenant that has given the premises a bad name, but we do not see that the distinction could be sustained. Taking similar facts but considering the case where the undesirable activities have been carried out by a subtenant, the effect of not applying the disregard to the subtenant's occupation becomes obvious. There may be no basis for the tenant to restrain the detailed conduct of his subtenant's business and no provable breach of the head lease terms. Indeed, the mesne landlord may be astute not to find a ground of complaint if he can argue on the review that he is to reap the benefit of the unwelcome activity as something that depresses the head lease market rent. Extending the disregard to the subtenant's occupation prevents that approach.

A contrary argument relative to the use made by the occupying tenant may occasionally be prayed in aid by the tenant. Given a lease with a reasonably wide use covenant, a particular tenant may institute a specific trade or activity which undoubtedly adds to letting value, at least if it were to be offered to another tenant in that line of business. However, if such tenants are few and far between, and unlikely to be attracted to the premises in question, their presence in, and effect on, the market level of rent could be shown to be slight or non-existent. The rent must then reflect demand from the generality of tenants for the use permitted by the lease, and so discount the particular use of the tenant in fact occupying.

Another matter of dispute may be whether the stress is on the fact that the tenant has been in occupation or on the fact that the premises have been occupied by anyone at all. The main thrust of the provision is undoubtedly to deny the landlord the benefit of the contribution to the market attractiveness of the premises properly attributable to the personal standing of the tenant—the phenomenon of the 'key' tenants in the marketing of accommodation in new shopping centres comes to mind—but it is submitted that it is not the only possible meaning. Many 'twilight' areas are so prone to vandalism, and worse, that an incoming tenant may pay more (possibly only a little more, admittedly, but still more) by way of rent to take over premises that have not been left empty and possibly attracting the depredations of the lead-strippers, the aerosol-sprayers and the like. In some respects, the effect of having to disregard occupation may, in these specific circumstances, equate with the assumption of vacant possession, discussed at p 406, above. In a rating case before the Lands Tribunal, *Hardy v Board* (1983) Lands Tribunal, 28 January, unreported, the rateable value of a flat was reduced because of the extraordinary risk of vandalism (apparently because the property backed on to Highgate Cemetery!). We do not overlook the significance that the wording of s 34(1)(a), and of lease provisions modelled on it, is that the tenant or a predecessor 'has been' and not 'is' in occupation but little seems to turn on it, especially as it may well properly be interpreted as meaning 'has up to immediately before the relevant time been' in occupation. Moreover, in *Family Management v Gray* (1979) 253 EG 369, where the issue was the measure of damages for disrepair on expiry of a long lease, damages were reduced in respect of certain shops comprised in that lease where the subtenants had negotiated new leases with the freeholders at rents not below the open market level, notwithstanding elements of disrepair. The court seems to have accepted that those subtenants might have paid a little more because their own default should not have led to a lower rent. It is suggested, in a note at [1980] Conv 244, that the only statutory basis for this is the disregard of the tenant's occupation in s 34(1)(a) of the 1954 Act. Alternatively, it may be seen as just a particular example of applying the maxim that a party should not profit from his own wrong. If the suggestion is right, this is another possible meaning to be ascribed to this particular disregard in a review clause, although the assumption of performance of the tenant's obligations will often cover the point more directly.

The notes to the two forms published by the Incorporated Society of Valuers and Auctioneers suggest that the disregard would require excluding any weight being attributed to the existence of a planning or other consent personal to the tenant. The validity of that construction has not yet been litigated to the writers' knowledge, but they do rather doubt if it would be upheld. Consideration of whether the notional willing tenant would be able to persuade the planning or other authority to renew a personal permission in his favour may be precluded by the principle in the *Plinth Property v Mott Hay & Anderson* case, discussed at p 345; but might be allowed if the approach of *Rushmoor Borough Council v Goacher* prevailed (see p 347). We have already remarked on the relaxed approach to 'depersonalising' such permissions.

(c) Other disregards

Although most leases will probably limit themselves to the statutory disregards in s 34(1) and most omit that in s 34(1) (d) (licensed premises) because of its specialised nature, it is quite open to the parties to agree upon and include any other disregard they feel appropriate or desirable. In *Langham House Developments Ltd v Brompton Securities Ltd* (1980) 256 EG 719, for example, there was added to the s 34 disregards a disregard of 'any statutory restrictions on the amounts of rentals'. The

Vice-Chancellor was at pains to stress, first, that the wording required the valuer to ignore certain matters but not to make any particular positive assumption—such as whether or not the flats which formed part of the property were let on regulated tenancies. The surveyor, in contrast, should take cognisance of the fact that lettings had been on non-regulated tenancies and should consider whether or not such a state of affairs would continue. He was instructed by the phrase in question to ignore all restrictions on rentals at all levels of sub-letting, not merely as between the landlord and the immediate tenant. Emphasis was laid on the use of 'rental' rather than 'rent'. In the context of the letting, the disregard was wholly understandable, but it must be said that not all 'non-standard' disregard clauses would meet the tests of aptness or accuracy. The same warnings must be sounded, to landlords no less than tenants, of the dangers of unreal and highly notional disregards as have been voiced above in respect of constituent elements in review formulae or assumptions to be made. They produce, or can produce, acute or even extreme difficulties in valuation, and, as a consequence, have an adverse effect on both the value of the reversion and the attractiveness of the term. The lesson to be drawn, as ever, must be for restraint in seeking to construct over-elaborate structures. Agricultural rents have to be settled in the light of disregards embodied in the 1986 Act which are discussed in Chapter 18, below.

(d) Other disregards—can they be implied?

If the parties fail to expressly provide for disregards, it is unlikely that they will be implied. To do so, the usual strict tests for the implication of terms will have to be met. Such terms are not implied unless they are *necessary* in the sense of required to allow the bargain the parties have made to operate—'to give business efficacy to the contract': (see *The Moorcock* and the discussion in Chapter 9, p 273).

Without that necessity, the court is likely to reject an argument to imply a disregard, and attempts in the context of rent review have been largely unsuccessful Thus in *Webber v Halifax Building Society* [1985] 1 EGLR 58 (more fully discussed at p 76) the possibility of amalgamation with adjoining premises was not to be impliedly disregarded.

Implication of a disregard may be made in two instances. First, it may be implicit from the wording of the rest of the review clause: *Pleasurama Properties Ltd v Leisure Investments (West End) Ltd* [1985] 1 EGLR 54 (more fully discussed at p 434) where, had it been necessary, the court was prepared to say that a disregard of improvements extended to a disregard of an obligation to re-instate. Second, it will be done to make commercial sense of the rent review: *Jefferies v O'Neill* (1983) 46 P & CR 376. In that case, without the disregard of the fact that the actual access was through the tenant's adjoining freehold premises, a review to an open market rent was impossible as the actual tenant would be the only possible lessee.

(e) The choice in the precedents

The Model forms (in all versions), EFP (5th ed) Form 22 and Conveyancer Precedent 5:57 include disregards of tenant's occupation, goodwill and tenant's voluntary improvements, in differing formulations which have been discussed above under each of those headings. The obselete EFP (4th ed) Form 8:1, Additional Form 76 and Form 7:1 and *Kelly's Draftsman*, Form 14 all incorporate para (a), (b) and (c) of s 34(1), by reference, although the first three, pre-dating the 1969 amendments, describe them as paragraphs of s 34, and only *Kelly's Draftsman* refers to s 34(1).

8   Conclusion

The various notional elements of the valuation framework of rent review clauses have of necessity been examined separately but the interrelationship of one element with another, with the actual lease and property (see Chapter 11) and indeed with the remainder of the lease, has been stressed throughout. This is the major lesson to be drawn from the on-going spate of litigation and also gives proper emphasis to the need for the drafting to be a co-operative effort between surveyor and lawyer. The latter's drafting ought to reflect the former's valuation skill and experience. Sadly some of the reported cases show the absence of such joint consideration or, at least, the absence of such consideration in sufficient depth or detail.

Chapter 13

Ground Rent Reviews and Rents in Building and 'Shared Development' Leases

'The term 'ground rent' is well understood and has a definite meaning: it is the sum paid by an owner or builder of houses for the use of land to build on': *Barlett v Salmon* (1855) 43 ER 1142 at 1145 per Lord Cranworth. This early definition encapsulates a key feature of all ground rents—the landlord supplies the land but retains the freehold rather than selling to the builder or developer and the latter adds the building. The rent then represents the continuing value of the land contributed to the total development. On this basis, there can be a fairly standard rent review of ground rent lettings differing only (but vitally) from the normal pattern in that there is either an assumption of a bare site or a disregard, not just of improvements, but of all the buildings on the land so that the valuer is directed to value only the site. However, in many major developments, the land provider or land assembler may wish to partake in the future value of the site *as developed* and not only the value of the notional bare undeveloped site. Moreover, there is an considerable element of unreality about the valuation of land that is not in fact undeveloped which has created problems for valuation in ground rent reviews. The extent to which the site's potential is to be disregarded—ignoring what in many other contexts is identified as hope value—is just one problem. Consequently, there are other approaches that can be adopted as an alternative to the straightforward ground rent, including forms of turnover and equity rents or the use of some type of indexation, and we draw together all these possibilities in this chapter, with cross reference to other sections of the book where appropriate.

1 Methods of ground rent review

This section might be better entitled (if it were not too cumbersome) 'methods of periodically readjusting the appropriate monetary return on the value of land contributed to a development of it by others'. All the alternatives really mirror some of the basic forms of variable rent already discussed in Chapter 3 but adapted for the specific purpose of

459

the building lease or shared development. They can be summarised as follows:

(a)   Normal ground rent reviews

In a normal review of ground rent, the valuer will seek the rental value of the site notionally undeveloped and without the actual buildings. Such reviews often raise particular problems of valuation and are fully discussed in section 2 of this chapter, below. If such a normal review is not suitable, either because of those difficulties or for any other reason, then one of the following alternatives are available.

(b)   Rent reviews linked to the capital value of the freehold

This is a variant of the normal ground rent review and seeks to meet the particular problem, which may often exist, of the lack of comparable evidence of similar lettings with ground rents. Instead of directing a rental valuation, the valuer is first to place a capital freehold value on the assumed site at the review date—for which it should be easier to locate comparable valuation evidence. The rent as reviewed then bears the same proportion to the reviewed capital value at review as the original ground rent bore to the freehold capital value (usually agreed and stated in the lease) of the site at the date of the lease. This fixed element in the calculation is what distinguishes this approach from the first category. Ground rent reviews to a capital value are discussed in section 3 of this chapter, below.

(c)   Geared rent reviews

A geared rent review is particularly appropriate where the head lease reserves a ground rent, the tenant develops the land and then sub-lets the whole at an open market rent with normal reviews. The rent reviews in that head lease can then be geared and linked to those in the sub-lease and timed to occur at or about the same time. The sub-lease rent review is determined and the head lessee then pays by way of ground rent a percentage of the reviewed rent, the amount of the percentage being determined and agreed in the lease. Geared rent reviews are discussed in section 4 of this chapter, below.

(d)   Indexation

Indexation will not normally have a significant role to play in ground rent reviews—at least not in the strict and usual form of linking the rent to an external index. Certainly, a ground rent can be linked and periodically reviewed by reference to the Index of Retail Prices but the effect will only be to preserve the value of the sum so reserved and so combat inflation but it will bear no necessary or functional relation to the future value of either the property as developed or the bare site.

More loosely, however, fixed percentages of market rents received or receivable, or of total value of the development, will be found but such rents are better understood as 'equity rents' where the rent represents a fixed proportion of the income of the head lessee or a return from the combined investment of the landlord's land and the tenant's development.

The device of indexation to a notional rent review of a defined standard property (discussed at p 564) could be adapted for a ground rent if desired and the issue of indexation generally is fully explored in Chapter 20.

(e) Turnover rents

In this case the rental value of the land is recovered as a proportion of the 'gross turnover' achieved by the occupying tenant's business. The rationale is that the potential profitability of the occupying business activities flows from the location and inherent attraction of the site. A turnover rent will be suitable for ground rents of developments of retail units but probably only where the rents in the retail sub-leases are also formulated by reference to turnover. Such variable rents are fully covered in Chapter 21, p 584.

(f) Equity rents

In an equity rent, the rent is calculated as a defined proportion of the income received by the tenant from occupying subtenants at full market rents. The rent can either be tied to the actual receipts (with specific provision for voids) or linked to the market rents which should be receivable (whether or not they are actually received). This topic is also discussed in Chapter 21.

2 Normal ground rent reviews

A normal ground rent review will contain most of the features of a usual rent review clause but with the additional assumption (for example):

'that the demised premises are a bare site only clear of all buildings . . .' (the wording of the clause considered in *Basingstoke and Deane Borough Council v Host Group Ltd* [1988] 1 WLR 348).

An analogous definition can be found in the formula for determining a new rent of an extended tenancy granted under the Leasehold Reform Act 1967, s 15(2)(a):

'the rent shall be a ground rent in the sense that it shall represent the letting value of the site (without including anything for the value of the buildings on the site) for the uses for which the house and premises have been put since the commencement of the existing tenancy.'

A precedent for a rent review for premises which are assumed to be a vacant site without buildings has been published as EFP (5th ed) Form 120.

(a) Difficulties facing normal ground rent reviews

There are two principal problems: there may be insufficient evidence of comparable lettings to allow the rent review to operate satisfactorily when the time for review comes round and, even if there are such lettings, the valuation process may be subject to considerations which have a much greater impact on the quantum of reviewed rent than in a full open market rent review.

(i) Comparable lettings

The parties will usually agree, the lessee would be expected to insist and the courts will assume, in the absence of provision to the contrary, that the site is to be valued for the use to which it was actually put and is being used and as available for letting on the terms of the actual lease. This 'accords with reality' (see Chapter 10, p 314 and the *Basingstoke and Deane* case). This immediately raises the issue of whether there will be sufficient evidence of comparable lettings on the review date. No doubt a vacant site available for any lawful use or on terms of what would be agreed in the market at the review date *may* not normally pose this problem but as soon as the actual use and the terms of the actual lease are brought into consideration the situation may change. A site for a public house may not, on its face, pose too many valuation problems since there will be a need for a number of licensed premises in any area. However, if no other public house is let on a ground rent and all other vacant sites for such a purpose are sold freehold or only in the developed state and let at full market rents, then even there there may be no suitable comparable evidence. Thus in *Tesco Holdings v Jackson* [1990] 1 EGLR 153 the ground rent review was that of a site for a supermarket and, because of the difficulty of the absence of any direct comparables when the review fell to be determined, the valuers had no option but to proffer alternative methods of valuation which led to a dispute whether the valuer had adopted the correct method. Where the danger of future lack of comparables is perceived at the drafting stage, then an alternative stratagem may well be appropriate. Thus in *Wallace v McMullen & Sons Ltd* [1988] 2 EGLR 143 the requirement was to reappraise periodically the site value of agricultural land leased for the purpose of being laid out as a golf course. Suitable comparable lettings were inherently unlikely so the chosen alternative was an increase of the initial ground rent by reference to the increase in capital value of agricultural land in the vicinity. Valuing agricultural land with hope value for use as a golf course may now be easier since there is likely to be more comparables.

(ii) Particular valuation issues

Even if a market of comparable lettings on ground rents exists, the very nature of a ground rent will give rise to valuation problems which, though found in normal rent reviews, are exaggerated in the circumstances of valuing a notional bare site. This point can be illustrated by reference to the body of New Zealand case law on ground rents which goes back to the start of the century. It appears to have been common practice for local authorities and other land owners to release land for development by way of long term building leases reserving a ground rent. Even at this early date, such ground rents in long term leases were subject to review—an interesting contrast to the absence of such devices in England and Wales where a high proportion of urban housing was based on ground rent leases. That system grew up over several decades but the concept never developed variable rents or reviews. There *was* a market in New Zealand of comparable lettings but difficult issues arose (which are often mirrored by problems in the more modern English rent review context):

(1) To what extent was the subsequent development and improvement of the land to be taken into account in assessing the ground rent? -according to *New Plymouth Borough Council v Bonner* [1929] NZLR 217 they fell to be ignored.

(2) Could a ground rent let as a site for an hotel be valued for a more profitable site use? A negative answer was given in *Duncan v Mackie* [1939] GLR 503.

(3) In the last review after 40 years in a 50–year term, what was the proper valuation basis given that all buildings would pass to the landlords without compensation at the end of the term and the assumption was a bare site? The holding that the valuer was to assume a term of 10 years on the terms of the lease without compensation for improvements at the end of the term, probably meant that the lessor was condemned to receiving a tiny fraction of the rental value of the site without that qualification and a small fraction of the value of the site value on the assumption that the existing buildings had in fact been constructed—*Re Lund's Lease* [1926] NZLR 541.

(4) Was the valuer to assume the terms of the existing lease applied? Indeed they did, even if that meant that the rental bore 'little relation to the value of the land'—see *Ziman v Auckland Grammar School Board* [1929] GLR 208; though if the lease was on favourable terms this would weigh with the prudent lessee and may induce him to pay a higher rental as in *Blenheim Borough Council v Gibson* [1939] GLR 121.

In other words, the familiar valuation issues, assumptions and disregards have to be approached afresh within the context of a notional site value. Where the draftsman has not catered for them, elements may have to be implied. English draftsmen would do well to consider the New Zealand experience.

(b) Judicial approach to the construction of ground rent reviews

In addition to the principles of construction, both specific and relating to rent reviews in particular, discussed in Chapter 10, the following guidelines can be identified specifically in relation to ground rent reviews:

(i) The general rule is that the subject matter of any review is the demised premises as they stand

In the absence of a clear direction that the valuer or arbitrator is to value only the bare site, the rent to be valued is the land with the buildings then erected, even if they were paid for at the expense of the tenant: *Goh Eng Wah v Yap Phooi Yin* (1985) [1988] 2 EGLR 148 (Privy Council); *Ravenseft Properties Ltd v Park* [1988] 2 EGLR 164. In the former case, on appeal from Malaysia, the rent originally reserved for 21 years was only $700 per month and the tenants had paid for and erected a cinema which they covenanted to insure for $320,000. The lessor's counsel acknowledged that the rent originally reserved was 'low' although the relationship of the figures did nothing to resolve the uncertainty as to what the parties intended. The lease was silent as to the basis of valuation of the reviewed rent and there was no disregard of improvements or assumption of a bare site—so the general rule applied. This result accords with the facts and the reality (there were buildings) and is in line with the result in, say, *Ponsford v HMS Aerosols Ltd* [1979] AC 63 (see p 386) which held that improvements formed part of the demised premises so a reasonable rent for the demised premises included the improvements for which the tenant had paid. Whether or not it was what the parties intended is uncertain. The general rule was also applied in *Ravenseft Properties Ltd v Park* where the defendant had contributed land towards a joint development to which the plaintiffs, the owners of adjoining land, had constructed a supermarket so it was partly on their own and partly on the tenanted land. As in *Goh's* case, the intention *may* have been that the reviewed rent was to attributable only to the site but there was no express direction to that effect and there was insufficient evidence from the lease to displace the normal presumption—even though that meant that the survyor had to value half a supermarket building. The judges's view that it was not a problem likely to defeat a surveyor who would be used to problems of hypothetical valuations is not to easy to support.

The prima facie rule will not only be displaced by a clear direction to value a bare site or suitable assumptions and disregards but also by sufficient evidence from the lease as a whole and the context in which it was executed to indicate to the contrary: *Ipswich Town Football Club Co Ltd v Ipswich Borough Council* [1988] 2 EGLR 146. The football club had had a series of leases of the land since 1888 and had over the years erected all the stands and buildings on the site, with one minor exception; the background to the existing 1969 lease for a fresh term of 99 years was the imminent implementation of expensive 'ground improvements' by the club. The rent review clause in the lease, however, referred to the 'current market value of the demised premises' and the council sought a full market rent to include the rental value of all the buildings. The rest of the lease carefully referred to the land demised as the 'sports ground' and distinguished it from the buildings erected thereon. The judge was therefore enabled, by reference to that careful drafting and the background factual matrix against which the lease was entered into, to construe the reference in the review clause to 'the demised premises' as a drafting slip (and it may well have been the careless incorporation of a rent review precedent). The rental value was to be determined on the hypothesis that the land was free of buildings.

(ii) In the absence of a contrary indication, a review of a ground rent will be a notional letting on the same terms (other than as to the amount of rent) as those subsisting in the actual existing lease

This is merely a detailed application of the general rule enunciated in *Basingstoke and Deane BC v Host Group Ltd* [1988] 1 WLR 348. This case concerned a ground rent and applied what was said to be a principle of rent reviews relating to land and buildings to the ground rent of a public house. The court rejected the argument that the principle should be modified in the case of a ground rent where the actual lease is of land and buildings and the notional lease is of a bare site. The Court of Appeal was of the view that a valuer was to disregard the buildings but was not to be taken, in the absence of express provision, to disregard the terms of the lease and (specifically) the use restriction it contained. The fact that some of the covenants thereby incorporated in the notional lease, though unexceptional in a lease of buildings, would be inappropriate to a simple lease of a bare site was not sufficient to reject the basic presumption. On the contrary:

'those covenants will or may have some materiality in assessing the up-to-date rental value of the premises demised by this lease (which includes buildings) even though no rental value is being attributed to the buildings themselves. They will or may have materiality in assessing that value because they impose obligations on the tenant' (per Nicholls LJ at 356H).

It was said in the *Basingstoke and Deane* case that counsel's researches had not brought to light any previous case in which the subject matter of the review clause was a ground rent. This may be correct in relation to English cases but as mentioned above there are many reported examples in New Zealand. Though decided in ignorance of those cases, the principle in the *Basingstoke and Deane* case bears a close resemblance to the ruling as to the proper basis of valuation of a ground rent set out by the Court of Appeal of New Zealand in *Drapery and General Importing*

Company of New Zealand Ltd v Mayor of Wellington [1912] 31 NZLR 598 and applied in the cases referred to in the previous section:

'the true basis on which the valuers must proceed is that there are no buildings and improvements on the land. They must ascertain what a prudent lessee would give for the ground rent of the land for the term, and on the conditions as to renewal and other terms mentioned in the lease. They must put out of consideration the fact—if it be a fact—that there are buildings and improvements on the land' (per Stout CJ at 605).

Reservations can be entered about the widespread adoption of the 'reality' principle (see Chapter 10, p 314) but in this context its impact is correct and acceptable.

(iii) An assumption of a bare site or a disregard of improvements or of buildings on the site, or of any effect of improvements, will only extend to the disregard of the existence of the buildings; planning permission or any other benefit extrinsic to the land itself will be taken into account

If, as the *Basingstoke and Deane* and *Drapery and General* cases decide, the terms of the actual lease are to be incorporated into the notional letting at the ground rent review, then the existence of those buildings is disregarded only for the purpose of the ground rent valuation. As Nicholls LJ remarked (at 3578):

'Where the subject of the lease is land and buildings and the subject matter of the valuation is the up-to-date rental value of the leased property but excluding the buildings, it is not surprising if the notional lease thus predicated is a somewhat odd looking creature.'

The disregard of the buildings will thus be taken no further than is rendered imperative for the purposes of the valuation exercise. An express disregard of any effect of improvements will only extend to the disregard in value attributable to the existence of the buildings so constructed. It will not extend to require a disregard of the actual planning permission situation consequent upon the existence and occupation of those buildings: *Railstore Ltd v Playdale Ltd* [1988] 2 EGLR 153. Thus, in that case the tenants unsuccessfully argued for a valuation of a piece of vacant land; the reality was the site benefited from an existing planning permission which was a factor in the relationship of landlord and tenant and the fact that it was granted subsequent to the lease was not relevant. The tenant had the benefit of it and it was a factor in the review; only the existence of the buildings themselves fell to be disregarded. Even if there is no actual planning permission in existence, the *prospect* of obtaining such permission will be a factor weighing with the willing lessee: *Wolff v London Bororgh of Enfield* [1987] 1 EGLR 119 (and the discussion in relation to normal review clauses at p 356).

This approach again coincides with earlier experience in New Zealand. In *Cox v Public Trustee* [1919] NZLR 95 Hosking J said:

'Land in a natural state may receive an increase in value from two factors—

one intrinsic, consisting of what has been done on or to the land itself and may be comprised under the term "improvements"; the other consisting of extrinsic circumstances, such as public roads and railways, public systems of drainage, public services brought within reach or other causes to which the tenant does not contribute.'

Such 'extrinsic' factors will fall to be taken into account in a ground rent review to the benefit of one or other of the parties. Thus in *Railstore v Playdale* the rental value to the lessor was increased by the planning permission but on another area of land included in the demise in that case and earmarked as a site for a building a 'nil' value had been given as there was no hope of development until a new road access was made. No doubt if, by the next review, such access had been constructed, or the view of the planning authority had changed, then a value could be given to that vacant site.

There is possible conflict between such external factors which may be perceived to increase the rental value of the site and the terms of lease. For example, a planning permission may be obtained, where there is a lease of an office block subject to a ground rent, for demolition of the existing building and the erection of a more modern structure. Since this will usually not conflict with the user clause in the actual lease the landlord may well argue successfully for a ground rent which reflects the availability of the site (which is assumed to be free of buildings) for the more attractive development—unless there is some other term in the lease which clearly conflicts with this. If the original lease was only granted after the existing buildings were constructed then there may well be some provision or reference to the type, nature or construction of the buildings which the lease of the notional site presupposes which will prevent the site being treated as available for the more modern development.

Even if no such conflict with the actual terms of the lease exists, the *Basingstoke and Deane* case does leave open a possible wider issue. To what extent should the valuer reflect the reality and value the site for the actual buildings so constructed, particularly if (as will be commonly the case) the actual buildings were jointly envisaged by the parties and approved by the then landlord? The problem will be acute when the premises were constructed some decades ago and are not up to modern standards of construction and amenity. The market rental of a site for a pub, office, or factory unit newly constructed to meet current demands may be higher, even on the terms of the existing lease than the rental for the site of the pub, office, or factory unit which actually exists. Conflicting approaches to this issue can be taken. The straightforward argument will stress that the review is on the assumption of a bare site so the valuer can assume the most valuable development within the terms of the lease. A contrary contention might be based on the 'presumption of reality', namely that between these parties there are actual buildings for which the ground rent is payable and the tenant is unable to have the advantage from the notional better development (for any one of a number of reasons—perhaps it would be prevented by the terms of subsisting sub-leases or even because the premises have been designated as a listed building!). Though the matter is not beyond dispute, the better view must be the former and can be tested by reversing the process. If a time should come when the historic nature of the actual buildings reverses the relative values, surely one has to sweep away the extra value of those buildings to arrive at the bare site for review. Nevertheless, the whole area of inherent value is difficult.

(iv)   If there are no comparable lettings at review, an alternative method of valuation will have to be used to determine the rental value

The absence of any comparables will not mean that the review is lost or aborted. Some other valuation method must be found to find the rental value as defined. In *Tesco Holdings Ltd v Jackson* [1990] 1 EGLR 153, the landlord's expert successfully argued before the arbitrator for a calculation based on the capital value of freehold sites; the tenant's valuer unavailingly put forward open market rental values to which he had applied a gearing ratio. This does not mean that the approach upheld in this case would be right or appropriate in every situation; the court stressed that the acceptance or rejection of such evidence is a matter of fact and not law and therefore a matter entirely within the competence of the arbitrator. In some circumstances, a 'profits valuation' based on the trade or turnover may be a possibility: *Cornwall Coast Country Club v Cardgrange Ltd* [1987] 1 EGLR 146 and see the discussion in Chapter 7, p 232. However, in a lease of an assumed bare site it might seem strange to then value the ground rent by reference to trade or turnover after development takes place—even if the ground rent review is on the basis of the terms of the actual lease and the use is limited to that trade. In an early New Zealand decision, *Duncan v Mackie* (above), the value of the trade from the actual premises was rejected as a basis for valuation of the ground rent of an hotel but the arbitrators were to consider 'generally any factors touching the possibilities of a hotel trade in that locality' which may admit evidence more generally of profits to be expected from the trade or use in question (compare the *Harewood Hotels* decision discussed in Chapter 7 at p 232).

(c)   Drafting ground rent reviews

The aim when drafting a rent review of a ground rent should be to eliminate or at least to mitigate all the problems discussed and produce a valuation framework which will enable a rental to be determined which will balance the conflicting interests of the landlord and the tenant. However, the legal drafting cannot hope to cater for two inherent difficulties. First, unless the letting occurs in a market where leases with ground rents are commonly found and will still be found at the date of future reviews, there will be the likelihood, if not a probability, that at the review date evidence of directly comparable lettings cannot be obtained. Agreement on the reviewed rent then becomes more difficult and alternative valuation methods may be the only answer (*Tesco Holdings Ltd v Jackson*). Secondly, the valuation will be of the letting value of an assumed bare site which will presuppose a letting on a building lease with the notional tenant commencing development. If the review date happens to fall in a time of economic recession and high interest rates then the ground rent for the subsequent period may be depressed by what may turn out to be a only cyclical downturn in the market. This is a possible feature of all rent reviews of course but may affect ground rent reviews proportionally to a greater extent. On the other hand, valuers may discount this factor to some degree because of the longer time scale of ground rent reviews compared with those of rack-rent and the rapidity of change in the economic climate.

The most basic choice that needs to be addressed is whether the ground rent is to be for one on the terms of the actual lease (ie for the site as developed but with a disregard of the actual buildings constructed) or for the the bare site assumed to be available for development generally on the best terms and for the best use at the review date. The tenant will seek the former since, on the latter assumption, the ground rent after review may bear no relation to either the terms of the lease (which bind him) nor the realities of the site as developed. On the other hand, the field of possible comparable lettings may be substantially wider if one assumes the best terms and use available. A ground rent review which sought to evade the *Basingstoke and Deane* implied assumption that the terms of the lease apply might well adopt the very wording of the declaration unsuccessfully sought in that case:

'That the valuer shall assess the up-to-date rental value on the basis that the demised premises are available for letting on the terms and conditions of a hypothetical lease containing such terms and conditions as the valuer regards as reasonable for a bare site for development current at the relevant date.'

The tenant must appreciate that such a valuation basis seeks to substitute a notional best development and notional best terms basis while he will still have the actual buildings on the existing terms. The effect could be mitigated by a clear delimitation of the use and purpose of the development postulated by the hypothetical lease so that it accords with that in the actual lease. It may also be mitigated, in the absence of such detail, by the market's distaste for a valuation on a notional basis too obviously divorced from reality.

Whether or not there is an assumption that the terms of the lease apply, the following points need careful attention:

(1) Though the cost of development will be borne by the willing tenant in the hypothetical lease as well as in the actual lease, it is wise specifically to state that it is to be assumed that no claim can be

made for reduced ground rent or a rent-free period by any willing lessee. Such would commonly occur at the commencement of a lease with a ground rent but must be disregarded at review (cf the *New Zealand Government* case discussed at p 327).

(2) The notional term is vital. Ground rents invariably occur in long leases and the cost of the development can be amortised over such a long period. In a normal rent review, as has been seen, there is a presumption that the notional term in the hypothetical lease at each review date is a period of years equal to the residue of the term. If this is not expressly countered, then the ground rent will be substantially reduced, perhaps even to a nil value, if any development for a relatively short notional term would not be viable. The lease should explicitly assume that the term of the hypothetical lease is a term of years equivalent to the full length of the original term and calculated to commence at the review date—or, at least, that should be the starting point for negotiations.

(3) It will be worth considering whether certain assumptions should be stated which may be of special relevance to a ground rent review. A disregard of any premium may be appropriate and express assumptions as to the planning position and allied statutory controls may commend themselves. Of particular relevance in a long term might be an assumption as to the physical state of the site, which in an increasingly environmental conscious world may become unsuited, less suited or contaminated for the actual use postulated in the lease—so that the actual lessee with existing use rights can continue but a willing lessee with a bare site to develop would be prevented from such activity. In the same vein, an assumption as to the continued enjoyment of the proper access and other services would not be out of place.

3 Ground rents to freehold capital value

The particular problem with even a well drafted ground rent review clause is that there may be no suitable comparables at the date of the review. There may be comparable sites or developed properties but if they are not, respectively, available to let or already let on ground rents there may be no comparable lettings. A review linked by a formula to the capital value of the land will usually avoid these problems. Nevertheless, the valuation may still be one of a bare site for development and in such a case it will still be subject to the vagaries of the market in development sites and thus subject to the economic pressures from the economy such as interest rates, recession and the costs of building. The alternative, as with the ISVA Form B, is to base the rental on a formula linked to the freehold value of the site as developed.

(a) General drafting considerations

In a review clause of this type, the valuer is directed to ascertain the capital value of the land (either the site, or the site as developed) on an open market freehold vacant possession basis. It cannot be the valuation of the freehold reversion since that value is largely dependent on the rent reserved by the lease the revalorisation of which is the purpose of the exercise. It is often necessary for the parties to agree the capital value at the date of the lease and the reviewed rent will then be the same proportion of the reviewed capital value as the initial ground rent bore to the agreed capital value at the date of the lease. Alternatively, it may be possible to devise a formula for the reviewed rent to represent the ruling rate of rent on capital value—ie the commercial yield current at the date of review, although the room for dispute on the ruling rate may be considerable. Whatever the basis, it is advisable to express any formula algebraically: *London Regional Transport v Wimpey Group Services Ltd* [1986] 2 EGLR 41.

Since the valuation will not reflect the terms of the lease, any easements rights or obligations which the parties wish to figure in settling the capital value assessment must be clearly stated. In *Wallace v McMullen & Sons Ltd* [1988] 2 EGLR 143 farming land was let for a term of 99 years for the purpose of the construction of a golf course at the expense of the tenants. At each 7–year rent review, the valuer was directed to value the freehold value of an 'equivalent and comparable area' of agricultural land 'with similar rights and obligations attaching thereto' and with planning permission for a golf course. If such valuation showed an increase over a stated capital value per acre then the ground rent was to rise by the same percentage as the increase in the value per acre. It was held that this did not import any of the tenant's covenants and obligations so (in particular) it did not require the notional willing tenant to construct a golf course. This result was reached after a detailed analysis of what 'rights and obligations' meant under the terms of this particular lease.

The use of the land must be addressed and the tenant will be concerned to ensure that the capital value assessed is to be one on the basis of the actual use or, at least, on the basis of only the possible uses at the date of the lease. To revert to the facts of *Wallace v McMullen* (above), the capital value was to be of agricultural land with planning permission for the actual use. If the lease had directed a valuation of the actual site without restriction and changes in planning policy by the review date meant that planning permission for residential or commercial development would be forthcoming, or had been given, then the capital value of the demised land would be very much greater and the reviewed ground rent would reflect that fact and that potential use and not the actual use.

(b)   The ISVA Form B

The second of the two rent review clauses promulgated by the Incorporated Society of Valuers and Auctioneers in 1984, Form B, is a form for return on freehold value and is set out in Part Seven (p 673). The freehold value is that of the demised premises and not the site for development. It is not, therefore, designed to be limited to ground rent reviews but is likely to be adopted, at least when used for commercial premises, primarily for such purposes. The rental value is defined as a percentage of the price that the demised premises might be sold in the open market by a willing vendor freehold and with vacant possession. The notes to the form give a simple example of how the chosen percentage, in the case of a ground rent review, must reflect the agreed return based on the site value in the development. Express assumptions are directed primarily to the use and physical state of the property so that the property is assumed to be fully fitted out for use for the purposes permitted by the lease and that the benefit of any planning consent current at the review date is available to the purchaser. It is assumed that any destruction or damage to the premises have been made good at the relevant review date and that all the tenant's covenants have been complied with.

If this form is taken as the basis of a review clause, the draftsman should consider (inter alia):

(i)   Adding the assumption 'to a willing purchaser';
(ii) Deleting reference to any of the tenant's covenants which would be irrelevant to a notional sale freehold with vacant possession;
(iii) Considering carefully the use clause in the lease as any undue restriction will be carried over into the assumption of use at the notional sale of the freehold;
(iv) Incorporating expressly any easements, rights or privileges which would be granted to the purchaser of the freehold (see *Wallace v McMullen & Sons Ltd* above)

(c)   The problem of the ratio or percentage

Even if the capital value is to be for the use of the land for the actual use, the parties must appreciate that the ratio between any ground rent letting value and the capital freehold value may alter substantially; if expressed as a percentage of the capital value as in ISVA Form B, the percentage so expressed may in the future become either more or less than the market will bear. If this moves against the tenant, the ground rent payable after the review may be higher than the market norm and so substantially reduce the value of the leasehold interest. This has been a particular problem in residential ground rent reviews. Following the Leasehold Reform Act 1967, many freehold estates in London apparently adopted a policy of leases with ground rents subject to review. The original ground rents so reserved were, it seems, fixed at a level high enough to ensure that the rent did not initially qualify as a 'low rent' within the Act. This meant that the ground rents might be fixed at a higher figure than might otherwise have been the case. Such ground rents were then subject to review (often at 21 year intervals) and many appear to have adopted a capital value formula. At the date of the leases, apparently, the proportion of the ground rent reserved to the capital value of the land as a site for residential building was 1 to 35. With the dramatic increase in land values, the site value of such houses may in some cases have become as much as 70–80 per cent of the freehold value of the whole property instead of the 'usual rule of thumb' at about 25 per cent. More recent ground rent review formulas are apparently at levels of about 1 to 60 and no doubt reflect the later much lower proportion of ground rent reserved when compared with the then capital value. In such cases, the tenants of properties with an adverse percentage ratio would have benefited from having a normal ground rent review to the current level of ground rents reserved.

A possible compromise which would avoid the worse aspects of both normal ground rent reviews and reviews to capital value is to provide for a capital value review but temper the increase to the current ground rent letting value for comparable properties. This method would ensure for the tenant that the reviewed ground rent does not increase beyond the market rate but satisfy the lessor that, in the event of a change in the market so that no comparable lettings exist, an alternative method of valuation is to hand.

4 Geared ground rents

A 'geared' ground rent is a form which refects both features of the normal ground rent and of the fully developed 'equity' rent linked to rents received or receivable by the tenant considered in Chapter 21. It recognises that a review to capital value or a normal ground rent review with an assumption to ignore the terms of the lease may divorce the valuation exercise from the actual position between the parties. More positively, it reflects what may be the intention when the original lessor contributed his land to the development, namely, that both parties were to share rateably in the future value of the development. This is particularly the case when a good site and a sensitive building produce an attractive development which enhances the value of both.

The geared ground rent review will aim to produce for the head lessor an agreed proportion of the rental value from time to time of the site and buildings. This has attractions for both parties. The landlord receives a share in the value of the site as developed which avoids the problems with a normal ground rent review; the tenant is assured that the ground rent will only reflect the value of the site as it has been developed and is used and not for some notional better development or use. The essential features of such a geared ground rent review are:

(1) The ground rent reviews in the head lease are timed to occur at the same time and at the same frequency as in the open market rent reviews in the sub-lease.
(2) The ground rent is reviewed to a specified fraction of the sub-lease review; once again, an algebraic formula is to be preferred: *London Regional Transport v Wimpey Group Services Ltd* (above).
(3) Normally, the review in the head lease need only involve a mathematical calculation of the sum agreed on the sub-lease review. However, the head lessor may well insist on involvement in the sub-lease review process or at least ensure his consent is required to any agreement at such review to protect the rental return.
(4) There should be provision for the contingency of the sub-lease review not taking place. The sub-lease review could conceivably be lost or compromised or the sub-lease itself surrendered (cf *R & A Millett (Shops) v Leon Allan International Fashions Ltd* [1989] 1 EGLR 138). The easiest way of ensuring protection is to provide for a fallback rent review of the land and buildings between the head lessor and sub-lessee to open market rent but with only the agreed percentage being paid after such determination.

Geared rent reviews in this form become less suitable once the premises contained in the head lease are subdivided (as will often be the case). The value of a letting as a whole may be different, often less, than a letting in parts (consider the issues in the *99 Bishopsgate* case discussed at p 412). To value the open market letting as a whole when it is in fact sub-let creates a unreal assumption but if the lessor seeks a proportion of the letting value of the parts then the tenant will wish to take account of management costs and so forth. Additionally, it may become difficult to ensure that the review dates always coincide and this is essential for a just operation of a geared rent review. If they are at different dates then either the landlord is not obtaining his full share or the tenant is not able to recoup from his own subtenants until the next sub-lease review.

An example of an ineptly drafted geared ground rent is *Hill Samuel Life Assurance Ltd v Preston Borough Council* (1989) 21 November (unreported) where the rent was to be reviewed to the same proportion of 'the market rack rental value' at the date of review as the original ground rent (£28,000) bore to the 'initial market rental value' of the building at completion. The initial market rental value was defined as 'the exclusive rent for the premises ascertained on the footing that the tenants by which the same is payable are liable to bear the cost of' certain stated items. This was held to refer to the sum of the rents payable by a letting of the individual parts; a figure had been agreed by a letter subsequent to the lease to be £172,000. The market rental value at review, however, was defined quite differently as the rent at which the premises might reasonably be expected to be let in the open market. No guidance was given as to whether vacant possession was to be assumed or whether it was to be taken to be let as a whole or in parts. As a matter of construction, the letting was held to be taken to be with vacant possession and as a whole. However, the judge stressed that the fact that it was an investment rent. This meant that the calculation for the letting as a whole with vacant possession would be the occupancy rents for the units that would be let and these would then form a basic guide that an investment lessee would pay for the premises as a whole.

For these reasons, in large scale developments, geared rents are redrafted so that they become true 'equity' rents. The freeholder or head lessor receives by way of ground rent an agreed proportion of of the income actually received or receivable by the subtenant. Such forms of equity rents are dealt with in Chapter 21. Reference may also be usefully made to EFP (5th ed) Form 141, a form of rent schedule providing for head lease rents to be determined by reference to the underlease rents.

Part 4

Special Situations and the Impact of Statute

In this Part, rent review clauses are examined in the context of parties other than the lessor and lessee for the time being and the impact of various statutory provisions in the law of England and Wales are fully covered. *Chapter 14* looks at the review in the light of the potential liability of the original lessee who has assigned, the guarantor or surety of the lessee and the inter-relationship of sub-lease and head lease rent reviews. *Chapter 15* considers the impact of value added tax on the review and assesses the contingencies that can be built into the clause at the drafting stage. It also deals with the impact on rent review of the 1990 rates revaluation, the introduction of a Uniform Business Rate and the phasing relief. *Chapter 16* examines rent review in leases granted under the provisions of the Landlord and Tenant Act 1954, Part II. *Chapters 17 and 18* respectively assess the use of rent review clauses in the statutory regimes applicable to residential tenancies and agricultural holdings. *Chapter 19* briefly advises on the incorporation of clauses to meet the contingency of statutory restrictions on rent increases (a 'rent freeze') during the currency of the lease.

Chapter 14

Guarantors, Original Lessees and the Problems of Sub-Leases

A guarantor or surety of a lease and the original lessee (who has assigned the term) have a not dissimilar interest in the outcome of a rent review. Both may find that they are called upon to pay a reviewed rent yet neither may have been involved in agreeing that figure. This chapter deals with the continuing liability of such parties and the drafting issues. A not unrelated problem is that of the parties to a sub-lease. A subtenant may find his own rent review is directly or indirectly related to the review contained in the head lease. Such a tenant may need to bargain for involvement in the head lease review or he, too, may find that he has to pay a reviewed rent under his sub-lease, the amount of which has been fixed without reference to him. A mesne lessor will have to consider two related reviews, perhaps interlinked but often determined at the same review date, and will wish to ensure that the margin between the rent paid on the head lease and that received in the sub-lease is not eroded. The issues raised in drafting rent reviews in sub-leases have been raised in Chapter 4, p 85, but the interrelationship of the head lease rent review and the sub-lease rent review is discussed in this chapter.

1 Guarantors

A landlord will wish to ensure that the contract of guarantee will bind the surety to pay the rent as reviewed; the surety may be seeking to bargain for a say in the review process.

(a) Basic principles

(i) Surety covenants 'run with the land'
After a series of cases which revealed some judicial disagreement on the topic, it has now been held that a surety or guarantee covenant 'touches and concerns' the land and is, therefore, enforceable by an assignee of the reversion against the guarantor (*Kumar v Dunning* [1989] QB 193; approved and applied in *P & A Swift Investments v Combined Stores plc* [1989] AC 643). It is now clear, therefore, that a guarantor will be liable on his surety covenant to both the original landlord and

any subsequent assignee of the reversion. Similarly, a covenant by a surety of a tenant to accept a lease in the event of the tenant's insolvency is a covenant that runs with the land and is enforceable by an assignee of the reversion: *Coronation Street Industrial Properties Ltd v Ingall Industries plc* [1989] 1 WLR 304.

(ii) Liability for rent as reviewed

Since a rent review clause is contemplated and provided for in the contract embodied in the lease, it is submitted (and is widely accepted) that the guarantor will be liable, not only for the rent as originally reserved, but also for subsequent increases agreed or settled on review: see *Torminster v Green*, discussed below. The only possible risk to a landlord is that the guarantor may be released from his guarantee if what takes place in the course of a review is found to be a variation of the contractual obligations of the tenant. Where the terms of the surety covenant are so drafted so as to make the guarantor liable as a principal debtor, then there can be no question of release.

The general conclusion that a guarantor is liable for rent as reviewed receives some support from two decisions. In the first, the guarantor was liable for mesne profits arising after termination of the lease on the principle that a guarantor normally guarantees not only rent payments under the lease but also observance of the covenants. In *Associated Dairies Ltd v Pierce* (1982) 265 EG 127 a lease was forfeited for non-payment of rent and an application for relief subsequently failed, the (former) tenant having remained in possession in the meantime. Mesne profits, assessed, as is common, at the rent formerly payable, were awarded against the tenant, and sought to be recovered from the guarantor. His obligation as surety for rent ended when the lease terminated, and it had never been reinstated. However, the tenant, having failed to yield up on termination in accordance with the standard form covenant to that effect, thereby effected a breach of covenant for which the guarantor was liable; the mesne profits, whilst technically an award of damages in tort for trespass, provided the measure of damages for the breach of covenant. Similarly, when the tenant asserts a right to possess after termination by forfeiture and fails to deliver up in accordance with its covenant, the guarantors remain liable for mesne profits: *Capital and City Holdings Ltd v Dean Warburg Ltd* [1989] 1 EGLR 90.

The position on rent review may be contrasted with new rents agreed or settled on statutory renewal. In *Junction Estates v Cope* (1974) 27 P & CR 482 where the lease was extended by virtue of the Landlord and Tenant Act 1954, it was held that the guarantee on its particular, but entirely usual, wording only covered rent falling due during the contractual term of the lease. The decision was followed in *A Plesser & Co Ltd v Davis* (1983) 267 EG 1039 where a distinction was drawn between the contractual term and statutory continuation as concepts.

By analogy, a review during the contractual term will not normally discharge the guarantee.

(iii)   Release of a guarantor

In *National Westminster Bank plc v Riley* [1986] FLR 213, BCLC 268 it was held that a non-repudiatory breach of the contract as between the primary parties will not without more discharge a surety. Consequently, it is most unlikely that the principle of release by any variation from the strict contractual position (as shown by the earlier case of *Holme v Brunskill* (1878) 3 QBD 495) could now avail a guarantor to enable him to escape his obligations for a reviewed rent. He would have to argue that the parties to a lease had departed from a principal term of the lease in a manner which could be described as 'not insubstantial'. This situation is unlikely to occur except when the parties to a lease negotiate an express variation of its terms.

An express variation of the terms can release a guarantor, unless he consented to the variation: *Apus Properties Ltd v Douglas Farrow & Co Ltd* [1989] 2 EGLR 265. In that case, it was argued that a use restriction had been varied by a deed and licence to sub-let. If that argument had been successful (see p 379), then it was said, obiter, that the guarantor of the original tenant would have been released but not the guarantor of the defaulting assignee who on the facts had clearly consented to the variation. On this point, the position of a guarantor may be better than that of an original tenant who is not necessarily discharged by a subsequent variation of the lease (see p 486, below).

A surrender of a lease will release the tenant, and his guarantor, after the date of the surrender but such surrender does not destroy liability under a rent review clause which has already accrued. Thus, in *Torminster Properties Ltd v Green* [1983] 1 WLR 676 guarantors were held liable for reviewed rent due from a company in liquidation for the period between the review date and the surrender by the liquidator, even though the increase was settled by an arbitration commenced after the winding-up and concluded after the surrender. This, it was said, was because the obligation to pay arose on the review date and the right was not destroyed by the surrender. Similarly, the forfeiture of the lease for non-payment will not destroy the guarantor's accrued liability but liability will terminate once the forfeiture occurs. Where rent is payable in advance, guarantors are liable for the whole quarter notwithstanding forfeiture during the ensuing quarter—*Capital and City Holdings Ltd v Dean Warburg Ltd*, above, it was not then necessary to determine the exact date of the forfeiture.

There is scope for argument in particular circumstances which, if successful, could displace the general proposition that a guarantor is liable for rent as reviewed. First, it could be said that where there is no agreement between the parties on the revised rent and there is a reference to arbitration which is then followed by agreement between the parties, which in effect compromises the dispute referred to the arbitrator for decision, the guarantor is released because of a departure from the terms of the bargain which he had guaranteed—see *Bowmaker v Moore, Shireff and Trelfs* (1819) 146 ER 954. However, that case may now be of doubtful authority in the light of the new formulation in *National Westminster Bank plc v Riley* (above). The same argument can be raised where the reference is to an expert valuer and the exercise of his judgment is pre-empted by an agreement reached after the reference is made. In the view of the authors, such an argument would fail since it is the almost invariable feature of a review clause to envisage agreement between the parties on the new rent. It should not matter that the agreement is only reached after reference to an expert or arbitrator. Even where time is of the essence, and landlord and tenant agree on a rent review out of time, it might be hard for a disgruntled guarantor to convince the court that there was such a variation of the terms of the lease as to show he was released.

Secondly, recourse could be had to the doctrine that a guarantor may be released if, even without variation in the fullest sense, the creditor 'gives time' to the debtor in a binding manner; only in the limited (and inherently unlikely) case of the tenant allowing a review notwithstanding that the landlord has missed a strict time-limit could the guarantor's argument that he has been released succeed.

There may be a slight risk for landlords that they may accidentally bring about a release for the guarantor by some quite amicable dealing with a tenant which is not actually envisaged by the lease but results in an increased rent (eg compromise of a dispute about rent review notices). It may only be a partial release so that, for example, the initial rent would still be covered by the guarantee but not the excess of the increased rent, but that is a far from happy state of affairs. The landlord could protect himself by express provision in the lease or, when he is too late to do so, by involving the guarantor in the review process or settlement of the dispute.

(b)   Drafting and operating a review clause with a guarantor

When drafting, the words of the guarantee of the rent could be expanded so as to refer to the rent 'hereby reserved or as subsequently increased'. It may be safer not to say 'as subsequently increased under the provisions contained in Clause—hereof' in case that is construed to involve strict compliance with all the terms of the relevant clause, with the possible adverse consequences of departure from them in any material degree just discussed. Perhaps 'as subsequently increased under the provisions contained in Clause—hereof or otherwise agreed or settled between the landlord and the tenant' would be acceptable to all three parties, and the guarantor could hardly then claim to be released by some departure from the exact review machinery.

Most leases with a guarantor as party will contain a more or less standard clause whereby the giving of time or other indulgence to the tenant does not release the guarantor—indeed, it is a standard provision in many other forms of guarantee as well. This general wording seems wide enough to cover most, if not all, types of landlord-tenant relaxation of strict performance of review clauses, although there appears to be no reported decision on the point. In *Selous Street Properties Ltd v Oronel Fabrics Ltd* (1984) 270 EG 643 and 743, a guarantor was not released when a landlord retrospectively consented to the retention of building work carried out in breach of covenant, imposing an obligation to reinstate at the end of the term. That was held to fall within the 'giving of time' wording in the standard proviso. *Burnes v Trade Credits Ltd* [1981] 1 WLR 805 did, however, establish that the 'standard' clause in a mortgage did not prevent the release of a guarantor where the interest rate was increased and the repayment period was extended, so there may well be some extreme measures of landlord-tenant adjustment which will release the guarantor notwithstanding the usual clause. Rent review is an obvious area for such far-reaching amendments to be arrived at.

Where a guarantor is introduced at a later stage in the life of a lease, as, for example, on an assignment, the guarantee should include, at least, the standard wording if not wording specifically to deal with reviews which are late or otherwise effected in a way different from that laid down. Similarly, of course, the obligations of the guarantor should be extended, if this is desired, to last beyond the contractual term to any statutory extension, so dealing with the *Junction Estates v Cope* problem.

The alternative approach is to take steps to involve the guarantor in the review process. A cautious landlord could serve copies of all relevant notices or correspondence on the guarantor, in the manner exemplified by, say, the Consumer Credit Act 1974. The guarantor should be informed of any reference to an arbitrator or expert and of the latter's award. Indeed, the arbitrator may need to consider how far he must involve a guarantor in the whole arbitral process or run the risk of misconducting it. There is a strong case to require the guarantor's signature to any memorandum of the new rent, an issue earlier discussed in Chapter 8. In the case of *Cressy v Jacobs* (1977) 14 October (unreported) a guarantor was held to be a 'party' to the lease and, as such, since the lease provided for the revised rent to be agreed by 'the parties', with independent determination in default, it was held that an agreement which excluded the guarantor was unenforceable against him.

It is interesting to note too, that in *Langham House Developments Ltd v Brompton Securities Ltd* (1980) 256 EG 719 the guarantor of the lease was made second defendant to the originating summons.

(c) Protection for a guarantor

(i) By express provision

So far we have considered the law and drafting aspects from the landlord's point of view. However, it also behoves the guarantor to seek to protect his own position. First, he might bargain to include in the lease a provision allowing for his release providing a suitable substitute surety is provided (an example is Conveyancer Precedent 5-74A), perhaps with particular emphasis on assignment. Secondly, he could bargain for service of copies of relevant rent review notices on him or to otherwise be made a party to any agreement on the revised rent, for a right to be party to any reference to a third party and so on. In *Cressey v Jacobs* (above) the need to involve the guarantor was probably not intended where the review provisions referred to 'an agreement between the parties'. It is a matter to be considered whether these rights should only last while the party whose obligations he has guaranteed is a tenant. Where the guarantor has guaranteed the original lessee's performance of his covenants or where, as is common, the guarantor of an assignee undertakes and is required to undertake responsibility for the residue of the term and not merely the assignee's holding of it, the case for the protective rights to last for the residue of the term is a strong one. Whilst, in many instances, there is often a close link between the guarantor and the original principal debtor—the former being a director of a private limited company, a parent of the tenant or a substantial member of a group of companies of which the tenant is a less substantial member and so on—that link will not normally continue after an assignment. Where there is a community of interest the guarantor may not wish to take a stand on the relevant principles relating to the effect of variations or the giving of time—although the attitude of the court to the risks of a 'parent' company abandoning its subsidiary in *Re Greater London Properties Ltd's Lease* [1959] 1 WLR 503 may no longer represent commercial reality.

Once the link between current tenant and guarantor is broken, the incentive to call in aid the established doctrines for the guarantor to claim release by inconsistent dealings between creditor and principal debtor is much stronger. In the *Junction Estates* case, in fact, there had been such an assignment; moreover, the initial guarantors also took an indemnity from persons connected with the assignee. This probable break in community of interest enhances the arguments for the wisdom, from the guarantor's viewpoint, of building in the protection of service of notices, his consent for any agreement on the reviewed rent, and the like. Even if it is not in the lease, he should seek similar protection by his bargain with the tenant, and, more particularly, he should obtain covenants from any assignee to keep him informed of the progress of future rent reviews and for his consent to the new rent or compromise of independent determination. The alternative for the guarantor is not to take any such precautions at all and hope either that the reviewed rent is to his satisfaction or, by a stroke of luck perhaps, that there may be such a course of dealing between landlord and future holder of the residue of the term as to release him.

There are other precautions the guarantor can take as against the tenant. For example, he can insist on the tenant allowing him to conduct the rent review negotiations; Aldridge, in an article at (1980) 77 *Law Society's Gazette* 787, suggests a power of attorney irrevocably appointing the guarantor the agent of the tenant for these purposes. It would probably be necessary to link this with an undertaking by the tenant to take no part in the review himself. Moreover, it is unlikely that the initial guarantor could effectively be appointed, as it were, the standing agent of the tenant for the time being, but a covenant binding assignees to appoint the guarantor on request might overcome that difficulty. Even in the absence of any precautions it is no great extension of the holding in *Standard Chartered Bank Ltd v Walker* [1982] 1 WLR 1410 that a mortgagee exercising his power of sale owes a duty of case towards the guarantor of the mortgagor, to find that a lessor invoking a rent review owes some implied duty of care to the guarantor of the lessee, or of a predecessor in title of the current lessee, and such an extension, at least in extreme circumstances, is a possibility for the future. If such a step were to be taken, it would provide a measure of protection for the guarantor.

(ii) Reimbursement

In the *Selous Street Properties* case (above), it was held that both the assignee in possession and his guarantor had an implied obligation to indemnify the guarantor of the original lessee, as well as the latter personally. Similarly, in *Becton Dickinson UK Ltd v Zwebner* [1989] QB 208 it was held that the assignee and its guarantor had 'ultimate' responsibility for the rent due. Liability was independent of contract so that an original tenant who had paid the arrears of a defaulting assignee could recover from that assignee's guarantor, even though the guarantor was not a party to the assignment and had, indeed, expressly refused to be a party and to covenant with the original tenant. On this basis, the guarantor of a tenant who has assigned may seek reimbusement from a later guarantor in the chain.

Notwithstanding the *Becton Dickinson v Zwebner* decision, a guarantor should still try to procure, on an assignment by his principal debtor, that the indemnity covenants of the assignee, and his guarantor if any, are expressly extended to cover him—the statutory covenant only extends to the conveying parties. There remain doubts whether the reimbursemnt or subrogation principle survives the liquidation of the party whose obligations were guaranteed. In *Becton Dickinson v Zwebner* the current tenant whose obligations the defendant had guaranteed was in liquidation but no argument was addressed on the issue. In *Bradley v Eagle Star Insurance* [1989] AC 957 the House of Lords held, in a different context, that insurance subrogation rights did not survive a liquidation. Consequently, a direct covenant giving a contractual remedy remains the safer option.

2 Original lessees

(a) Liability for rent as reviewed

Whilst it is sometimes said that the original lessee, by virtue of his lease-long liability, is in the position of a quasi-surety, his position is not assimilated to that of a guarantor in the strict sense. The covenant by an original tenant is not a contract of guarantee (*Baynton v Morgan* (1888) 22 QBD 74), but rather the primary liability of the original tenant. He can, for example, be called upon to pay a rent or meet other obligations without prior demand on the current tenant and he is not released by disclaimer of the lease by the trustee-in-bankruptcy of the tenant, although the latter's guarantor is (*Warnford Investments Ltd v Duckworth* [1970] Ch 127). Accordingly, he will not be able to claim the benefit of the rules protecting the true guarantor. This proposition is further and firmly demonstrated by *Allied London Investments Ltd v Hambro Life Assurance Ltd* (1983) 269 EG 41 where it was held that the release by the lessor of the surety of the assignee did not also release the original lessee from his continuing direct primary liability.

An original lessee can be liable for the full amount of reviewed rent agreed between a lessor and an assignee. In *Centrovincial Estates plc v Bulk Storage Ltd* (1983) 268 EG 59 the defendants as original lessees denied liability for increased rent agreed on review in accordance with the terms of the lease between the plaintiff and the current lessee which the latter had failed to pay. The defence failed, the judge applying *Baynton v Morgan* and following *Haslemere Estates Ltd v British Olivetti Ltd* (1 June 1977, unreported). In this latter case, it was said that since an original tenant puts the assignee 'in his shoes' for all purposes, the assignee for the time being is the proper person to reach agreement as to the amount of the reviewed rent. The continuing liability of the original lessee was further demonstrated in *Selous Street Property Ltd v Oronel Fabrics Ltd* (1984) 270 EG 643 and 743, where the rent, it was claimed, might have been affected by works carried out by a later tenant increasing the value of the demised premises. Judgment was given against the original lessee. The inability of the original lessee to perform covenants, eg to yield up possession at termination or to repair, is no defence to a claim in damages for breaches by a later assignee: *Thames Manufacturing Co Ltd v Perrots (Nichol & Peyton) Ltd* (1984) 271 EG 284.

There remains the question of whether the original lessee would be bound by a rent agreed on review in a manner not envisaged by the lease, for example, agreed notwithstanding the failure to observe strict time-limits. Just as a guarantor could argue that he is released (above), so also the original lessee could say that he is only liable to the extent of the obligations he entered into. In the *Centrovincial Estates* case, Harman J indicated at one point in his judgment that only an agreement by a specified date would be effective (if time was of the essence) but later he was of the opinion that an assignee of an estate can alter its terms and 'the estate so altered binds the original tenant'. It is submitted that the better view is that the original tenant should not be liable for a rent agreed otherwise than as envisaged by the terms of the lease, although minor departures from the procedure might well be overlooked.

On the issue whether an original lessee ought to be liable for rent due under a statutory continuation of a business tenancy, it remains to be seen whether or not the principle established in *Junction Estates Ltd v Cope* (1974) 27 P & CR 482 (and applied in *A Plesser Co Ltd v Davis* (1983) 267 EG 1039, see above) would be applied to a claim against an original lessee, or a subsequent assignee who had given a direct covenant to the lessor, for rent unpaid or some other obligation unperformed in relation to a period during the statutory extension of the terms after expiry of the contractual term. On the one hand the relationship of the original, or later, lessee to the term is much closer than that of the guarantor. On the other hand, the cited cases point strongly in the opposite direction and French J in the *Plesser* case stressed the distinction between the contractual term and the statutory extension.

The argument in the *Plesser* case that the guarantor should not be taken to have undertaken an obligation of indefinite duration applies a fortiori to the original lessee of a pre-Act lease, and the case to exempt him from post-expiry liability is even stronger than for a post-1954 lease; though that proposition is weakened a little by consideration of *West Layton Ltd v Ford* [1979] QB 593. The original lessee, if liable, could claim indemnity from his assignee, that assignee from his assignee and so on, and on the issue of whether or not such liability to indemnify may only extend to the end of the contractual term it is worth noting that the statutory implied covenants in respect of unregistered land apply 'at all times, from the date of the conveyance', but that no final date is stated. For registered land the transferee's covenants are expressed to last 'during the residue of the term' (Law of Property Act 1925, s 77(1)(c) and Sched 2, Part IX; Land Registration Act 1925, s 24(1)(b)).

The assignee in possession and his guarantor have an implied liability as those ultimately reponsible to indemnify the original lessee, and his guarantor, as decided in the *Selous Street Properties* and *Becton Dickinson* cases. The implications of the various rulings in that case (and kindred decisions) are discussed by Reynolds and Fogel in their 1984 Blundell Memorial Lecture, an edited version of which appears at (1984) *Law Society's Gazette* 2214.

(b) Protecting the original lessee's position

An original lessee (or even a subsequent lessee liable on indemnity covenants) can consider three possible measures to protect his position:

(1) When entering into the lease, he could seek to limit his liability so that it terminates on assignment. Notwithstanding that this limitation would accord with the Law Commission recommendations (Law Comm No 174, 1988), such a limitation is unlikely to be acceptable to a lessor unless and until those plans to limit the liability of the original lessor are enacted. An attempt to argue, in the *Centrovincial* case, that the particular terms of the lease excluded the general principle of liability, was rejected.

(2) On assignment, the tenant could take a covenant from the assignee to provide for involvement in the later review processes. This might give the original lessee some say in rents later agreed, but at some cost in time and effort to all concerned. Moreover, breach of the covenant by the assignee might only come to light when the original tenant was faced with a claim by the landlord at which point the covenant from the assignee could well have little value. Moreover, further assignments would complicate the position and make such covenants of little direct value.

(3) Rather than trying to get involved in later review processes, an original lessee, or a later assignee with a direct obligation for the rest of the term, may protect himself from future unforeseeable liability from rent reviews as part of the general financial protection. Assessing the financial standing of the proposed assignee is always crucial. Though direct covenants in licences to assign are very common and express indemnities virtually universal the assigning original tenant does not always seek the same protection. If a landlord will not accept an assignee without a guarantor then neither should the tenant. Indeed, a surety covenant from a suitable guarantor of the assignee is always a wise precaution for an original tenant.

(4) The only real protection, as Harman J observed in the *Centrovincial* case, is for the original lessee to sub-let on identical terms to the original lease save for a nominal reversion. This would preserve the lessee's full rights of involvement. The price for such protection is the cost of remaining fully committed as an intermediate landlord in premises in which the original lessee has otherwise no interest. The rent review provisions in the sub-lease must be properly linked to the head lease rent reviews as discussed below, and the cost and disruption of those two reviews on a regular cycle is another factor to be weighed in the balance when deciding whether or not to follow the sub-lease route. Few parties to a lease will be willing to shoulder these burdens for the (relatively) small protection received.

3 Sub-leases

In this section, the difficulties in operating linked head lease and sub-lease rent reviews are considered. The drafting considerations are set out in Chapter 4, p 85. Errors in drafting can be costly and some of the dangers are shown by *Costa v Georghiou* (1984) 1 Professional Negligence 201. In a sub-underlease, which mirrored rent review provisions both in the sub-lease and head lease, a solicitor omitted to ensure that the relevant figures were inserted into the blank spaces providing for the second review. The sub-underlessor lost his review, but was subject to one himself. No claim for rectification was made; nor was it sought to allege that the review clause might still operate though each of these remedies may be available in appropriate circumstances. Instead a claim for negligence was launched, which failed, though negligence was admitted, because the claim was held to be statute debarred since the cause of action occurred more than 6 years before action. The cause arose at the execution of the lease—yet it was not likely to be discovered until the second review, 9 years later.

(a) Defective sub-lease review clauses

The courts have been prepared to go to some lengths to 'rescue' or 'salvage' inept or defective drafting in sub-lease rent reviews. In *Lorien Textiles (UK) Ltd v SI Pension Trustees Ltd* (1981) 259 EG 771 the amount of rent originally reserved in a sub-underlease was identical to the sum so reserved in the underlease. The review clause in the sub-underlease provided that if the rent under it had not been fixed by a certain day it was to be 'as shall be fixed in accordance with the covenants and conditions' in the underlease. The underlease had, however, been surrendered at the date of the review but the argument that that rendered the rent review in the sub-underlease inoperative was rejected. It was decided that the superior lease was available for reference and the sub-lease referred to only the review formula in the head lease and not the actual revised rent which by reason of the surrender would never fall to be ascertained.

Where the process of cross-reference between head lease and sub-lease breaks down, the missing machinery may now be supplied by the court through application of the principles in the *Sudbrook Trading Esate Ltd v Eggleton* [1983] 1 AC 444, discussed at p 13. Thus in the *Lorien Textiles* case, had the wording been construed as referring to the revised head-rent and not merely the method of revision, this approach might have been resorted to, so saving the day. Just such a result, though without reference to the *Lorien Textiles* decision, was reached by the majority of the Court of Appeal in *R & A Millett (Shops) Ltd v Leon Allen International Fashions Ltd* [1989] 1 EGLR 138. The rent reserved by an underlease was to be 'seventy eight eighty fifth parts of the rent payable by the lessors . . . as fixed in the manner provided by the said superior lease'. The superior lease referred to was later surrendered, though there was a lease back subject to the underlease. The majority view was that the underlease could be construed as an arrangement to pay a fair market rent calculated on the market rent for the the whole property and then reduced to 75/85ths of that sum. The machinery for ascertainment (namely the superior lease rent review mechanism) having failed, then the court could substitute its own machinery—*Sudbrook Trading* case (above). Balcombe LJ dissented on the basis that this would mean that a sub-lease rent review could proceed even if a head lease rent review had not been activated; but, with respect, this would not be the case since the specified machinery would not have failed.

There is some force in the argument that a sub-lease rent review should be construed, in cases of doubt or ambiguity, to occur on the same dates as those in a related head lease even when the sub-lease commences subsequently to the head lease: *Finger Lickin' Chicken v Ganton House Investments Ltd* [1989] EGCS 99. However, in that case the construction was clear; the review dates were fixed by reference to the first 7 years of 'the said term', the next 7 years of 'the said term' and then to the remainder of the term. It was held that 'the said term' had to relate to the term of the sub-lease and not to that in the head lease so the review dates were later in the sub-lease and the rent review notices were given in time.

(b) Practical issues—negotiating tandem reviews

Where the settlement of the rents in the head lease and the sub-lease(s) is, in default of agreement, by arbitration, there may be circumstances where it would be convenient, and less costly, to seek to combine the arbitrations. Unfortunately, the absence of powers of consolidation or other provision for multi-partite arbitration is one glaring weakness of the English law of arbitration, a matter of increasing concern in the field of commercial arbitration which may lead to eventual reform to mirror amendments in other common law jurisdictions offering commercial arbitration facilities. It may be possible, by agreement, to achieve some measure of linkage between the parties but not, it would seem, full integration.

Consequently, professional advisers to a mesne lessor dealing with both a head lease and sub-lease arbitration need to ensure that agreement on one does not compromise the other. In *Thomas Miller & Co v Richard Saunders & Partners* [1989] 1 EGLR 267 an agreement to exclude the rental value of corridors in the sub-lease arbitration left the mesne lessor unable to cover the cost when the corridors were included for the purposes of calculation of the rent in the head lease arbitration. The outcome was a claim in professional negligence against the mesne lessor's surveyors.

Similarly, whether the relative timing of head lease and sub-lease rent reviews is that order of precedence or the reverse, the adviser should be careful not to depart from that order save for good reason, ideally agreed with the client after full consideration of the tactical issues.

Chapter 15

The Impact of Taxation—
Value Added Tax and the
Uniform Business Rate

1 Value Added Tax

The issue of VAT on rent did not call for treatment in any earlier edition of this work. Rent might be an exempt supply or zero rated but while the difference might be vital to the landlord, as affecting the ability to recover VAT it had paid or was to pay, the tenant was not affected. The miscellaneous types of property transactions attracting standard rated tax rarely required or lent themselves to variable rents and the rarity of instances where such a rent was present justified the absence of treatment of the topic.

(a) The 1989 Finance Act changes

The Finance Act 1989 changed the situation radically and the long term results have yet to emerge and even forecasts of what they may be remain speculative. The Act flowed from the judgment of the European Court on 21 June 1988 which obliged the United Kingdom drastically to overhaul its VAT system to bring it into line with general European regimes. The prior pattern of exempt and zero-rated supply was replaced by one of a retention of zero-rating only for the sale and leasing (for more than 21 years) of dwellings and buildings designed and used for certain specified residential or charitable purposes, where the vendor, lessor or assignor constructed the building, and otherwise standard rating or exempt supply. Special rules applied for a limited period in various transitional circumstances. Extended treatment of all the issues are outside the scope of this book, but the rent review aspects require, first, a brief exposition of the general aspects.

(b) General aspects

(i) Zero-rating

Zero-rated transactions are unlikely to attract variable rents in most cases. Where they do, the issues described below in respect of the impact of VAT on review, especially in regard to the impact of the tenant's VAT status on market rent and the problems associated with the use of comparables, will arise and the relevant considerations must be applied.

(ii) Exempt supply

Exempt status for rent is basically attractive for a tenant who does not have to find an extra 15 per cent on each rent payment, even where, as (in the usual case) such VAT paid can be reclaimed later by way of set-off. Whether it is attractive for a landlord depends on the extent to which it has incurred VAT on supplies of goods and services to it in providing the premises, whether newly built, adapted or re-furbished or in the later supply of services to the finished building. In cases where such payments have been made, VAT paid to it, as an addition to rent, can be set against the payments and so improve the net financial position of the landlord or, at least, restore a balance between VAT paid and received. Accordingly the legislation allows the landlord to opt for taxation of the rent or, more strictly, to elect to disapply the exemption. The rent will then attract standard rate tax. In some cases, the small landlord may have paid so little VAT that he sees no point in waiving the exemption. He may hope thereby to increase the potential pool of tenants to his properties.

(iii) Standard rating

Standard rate tax is also payable, much as it was before April 1989, on various miscellaneous categories or property transactions—which may involve variable rents though most are likely to be on a short-term basis and so offer little scope for elaborate review mechanisms. The transactions in the list include the grant by lease, licence or other contract of rights in respect of shooting and fishing, hotel and boarding accommodation, holiday accommodation, caravan pitches, parking, storage of aircraft or storage and mooring of boats and ships, timber, accommodation at sporting, theatrical or other entertainment events or sporting and recreational facilities. Other categories of standard rated supplies, namely freehold sale of new or part completed buildings other then dwellings or the special categories or of land with civil engineering works or surrenders are irrelevant for present purposes.

(iv) The tenant exempt from VAT

However, there is a major exception to this pattern. A significant group of tenants for particular types of buildings provide tax-exempt supplies and will thus be unable to recover, by set off, tax payable on rent. The major group of potential tenants so treated is those providing financial services, normally attracting tenants of good standing and who may enjoy substantial bargaining power. Other groups are those supplying medical or educational services. Moreover, there is a substantial body of such tenants with a range of activities on the totality of which they can be treated as partially exempt.

(c) The impact of the new rules

The consequences of the new regime have been widely debated since the 1989 Budget. Advice and opinion have flooded the property press, the conference circuit and brochure and circulars distribution networks. Unlike the not dissimilar impact of commercial property rates revaluation and the Uniform Business Rate (discussed at p 501), the impact will not be relatively short-term, for many leases will continue, and rent review elements will operate, for many years, though prepared under the pre-1989 regime, and before the European Court decision (which did prompt some anticipatory redrafting). Rents and rent review will be susceptible to re-appraisal under the new rules. Accordingly it is necessary first to consider what may be termed for convenience pre-1989 leases, by which we mean leases, whenever drafted, which do not reflect the changes effected by the Finance Act 1989.

(i) On pre-1989 leases

The pre-1989 lease may well be silent on the issue of VAT. In that case, the basic general rule is that the specified sum is VAT inclusive. That rule lacks impact if the rent remains exempt, but comes into play if a landlord elects to waive exemption. The Finance Act 1989 altered s 42 of the Value Added Tax Act 1983 so as to provide that such an election entitles the landlord to charge VAT on the stated rent, unless the lease otherwise provides. A pre-1989 lease will hardly provide to the contrary in direct wording, but some forms of general wording might be thought to have that effect. An example given in a brief note in the *Law Society's Gazette* of 12 July 1989 ((1989) 27 *Law Society's Gazette* 12), where the tenant agrees to pay 'all existing and future taxes, duties, charges, assessments, impositions and outgoings whatsoever . . . *other than taxes payable by the landlord in respect of rents payable under the lease*' is wrong (apart altogether from the present authors' doubts if the particular form of words is common) because s 42 was also amended to require the contrary provision to refer expressly to VAT or s 42. Few pre-1989 leases will do that. Even so, if such a contrary provision is incorporated in a lease the possible adverse effects of election must be allowed for, both in the initial decision to elect or not and, more importantly, in rent review both of the offered rent and in any use made of such a review as a comparable in the review of other rents. A new landlord is not bound by his predecessor's election, and there may well be grounds to eliminate the actual landlord, who has ill-advisedly elected, from the notional cadre of willing landlords who figure as dramatis personae in the review scenario, who may be taken not to have so elected.

(ii)   Tenant's covenant to pay VAT

A general provision to pay all VAT frequently appears in pre-1989 leases and will put matters beyond doubt unless cast in very restricted terms. All new leases should sensibly contain a widely drawn tenant's covenant to pay VAT coupled with a landlord's obligation to provide VAT invoices, although there is a statutory obligation to do so anyway.

(iii)   Landlord's covenant not to elect

So what else should appear in post-1989 leases? A tenant whose trading activities are wholly or partially exempt will wish to pay rent which is also exempt, and will try to bargain for that result, seeking confirmation that the proposed landlord has not elected to waive exemption status and will not do so before or after granting the lease in question. An assignee with similar VAT status may try to establish the like situation in relation to the landlord, although from a much weaker bargaining position. Whether the landlord will concede the obligation depends on the circumstances. A building designed as a banking hall, say, or one incorporating the large open dealing floors so much in vogue before and after 'Big Bang' virtually dictates non-election as the best landlord's policy. So, even more strongly, would purpose-built medical or educational accommodation. Unless the covenant not to elect is given, the negotiable rent will reflect the inability of the initial tenant to recover any VAT added by later election. The effect upon tenants in the market of the actuality or potentiality of election, if the landlord has not deprived itself of the option, will be strenuously argued at review and will thus also affect the market value of the reversion. With the purpose-built building, accordingly, non-election provides a state of affairs that may be sought to be made permanent.

Whether such an obligation entered into by the original lessor binds successors has been raised in various commentaries to date (eg by Fogel and Plumbe in their article at [1989] 16 EG 76). The right to elect is personal to the landlord and the present authors regard the promise not to elect as one which does not 'touch and concern' the reversion, and thus is not binding on a successor. Fogel and Plumbe rather incline to the opposite view; Ross, in his 1990 Blundell Memorial Lecture takes the present authors' view. The 'safest approach', advocated by Fogel and Plumbe, is to bind the landlord to require a new covenant on assignment from the new landlord in favour of the tenant and his successors. We agree—indeed we would expand the provision to make it clear that the landlord would only assign (or sub-let) to a new landlord who has already covenanted both not to elect for waiver, and to accept a similar restraint on disposition by himself. The restriction can be noted on the Land Register if the reversion is registered, but if unregistered can not unfortunately be registered as a D(ii) Land Charge as it is a landlord-tenant restriction. An assignee would take with notice of it, but that is irrelevant if the assignee is not bound. The major sanction against such an assignee who elects for tax will be the adverse effect on review, but in the interim the tenant's remedy will be against the previous landlord for breach of the covenant. The irrecoverable VAT to be paid by the tenant will be the basis for assessing damages.

(iv)   Mixed premises—the 'hiving-off' solution

The position may be much less clear-cut then in the above discussion. For example, the banking hall element may only be part of the building, but election must be on a building by building basis. 'Buildings' linked internally or by covered walkways 'part of a parade precinct or complex' are, moreover, treated as one. The attitude at the time of writing appears to be to give a wide meaning to the 'complex' concept and to apply it, for example, to a business park. The use of sub-leases may alleviate this problem, as each landlord's election only relates to those parts of a building in which he has an interest thus achieving a remedy by 'hiving-off' those parts in respect of which no election is to be made. The intermediate landlord should not be in the same VAT group as the head landlord; the rent the former pays will attract standard VAT by reason of the latter's election relative to the whole building but the sub lease will provide for VAT-free rent. The figures must reflect that to ensure that the benefit of attracting VAT-exempt tenants for the 'financial services' elements is not unduly diminished by the different treatment of head-rent and sub-rent for the portion hived-off.

(v)   Premises with tax-exempt potential

However, greater problems arise when financial services or other exempt use is only one of a number a potential uses of a building or part of a building or complex. Many offices, most shop units (in the light of building society/finance-providers' use) and even some types of storage and warehousing buildings will have that potential. Should the landlord agree to forego election if his first tenant seeks that concession? It is a relaxation that can be given by the normal side-letter, applicable only to that tenant and terminable on assignment, if the building is a single building and the lease is of the whole of the building or the 'hiving-off' route is followed. Whether such a limited concession will satisfy the initial exempt tenant depends on an assessment of who will be likely assignees in the future, and whether they will seek a similar election and whether a lasting concession will be given depends largely on the relative strengths in the bargaining relationship. If the premises to be demised are only part of a building, in the extended statutory meaning, the circumstances in which a promise of non-election will be given to the 'abnormal' tenant will be rare indeed. The landlord and tenant will instead have to negotiate a rent reflecting the 15 per cent (less for the partially exempt) which is irrecoverable by the tenant from Customs and Excise (though obviously still a tax-deductible expense for a trading tenant) but which the landlord will have to account for, if only by way of set-off against the payments of VAT it has to make on its own expenditures.

Alternative approaches to collateral warranties are possible. For example, a landlord who has already elected to waive exemption for a whole building could agree with an interested but exempt tenant of part to forgo that portion of the total of rent plus VAT payable under the lease as drawn needed to reduce the tenant's outlay to the rent net of VAT. The concession could be limited to that tenant or extend to any 'tax-alike' assignee. The concession could be framed to continue beyond any review. Indeed, once an election has been made, this may be the only way to accommodate this 'abnormal' tenant. One advantage of this method is to eliminate distortion of the reviewed rent, and enhance its utility as a comparable perhaps for the remainder of a complex or other nearby buildings owned by the landlord. It spares the review valuers the task of adjusting the atypical rent.

Some commentators have suggested that an initial tenant not exempt from the tax who foresees the possibility of future assignment to exempt traders might also seek a landlord's non-election undertaking. A tenant, not itself wholly or partially exempt, occupying 'custom built' financial services accommodation might just conceivably make that choice, but only, we submit, in the very remote circumstances where assignment to such a special assignee is a real and relatively immediate prospect and the likely benefits of such a sale outweigh the self-inflicted wound of payment of irrecoverable VAT on other supplies without VAT on the rent to off-set it in the interim. This combination of variables strikes the authors as almost fanciful, we doubt if it will occur often in practice.

(vi) Summary

Summarising all these considerations produces the following conclusions:

(1) Premises designed wholly for categories of use wholly exempt on current VAT rules are likely to be leased on the basis of non-election before or after the letting.

(2) Desirable tenants of non-specific property with VAT exempt status may hope to bargain to persuade landlords not to waive exemption, especially on a whole building transaction but sometimes via the hiving-off route using the intermediate sub-lease.

(3) It remains to be seen, writing in mid-1990, whether tenants will have to pay a modest increase in rent to obtain the concession at (2).

(4) Many landlords will want the right to elect and VAT-exempt tenants will have to shoulder the VAT burden, if they want the relevant premises, as they already do for all other vatable supplies; and

(5) The new VAT regime introduces new elements into the rent review field.

We now turn to those rent review aspects.

(d) Drafting rent review provisions

The effect of these new rules must be allowed for in the drafting of rent review clauses in new leases. If there is a covenant not to tax, ie not to waive exemption, how should it be treated for rent review purposes?

(i) General considerations

A tenant which has used its bargaining strength to obtain the concession will retain that advantage on review under a normal 'terms of the present lease (except as to the quantum of rent)' basis. The landlord must decide if that result satisfies his financial and investment strategies and whether it will affect the marketability or value of his reversion. Rent review to market rent should reflect the optimum market; unless the potential market overwhelmingly consists of tenants in the exempt categories the carrying-over of the freedom from VAT introduces artificiality. The landlord obtains a rent return which has no bearing on his own net VAT bill; the exempt tenant may find assignees prepared to pay some premium to obtain premises at a VAT-free rent.

Suggestions have been made that the non-exempt tenants will not mind paying VAT on rent, for that will be an input to be deducted from the output of VAT charged by them on goods and services supplied to their customers. That may not truly reflect the psychology of many traders and it ignores the whole element of cash flow and the interplay of when VAT on rent is paid out, when VAT on supplies is received from customers and when remittances to Customs and Excise must be made. The tenant not paying VAT on rent will have to pay larger sums to the Customs and Excise to reflect the VAT he has charged his customers than if he had paid VAT on his rent but he will not have had to find or fund that latter payment in the first place. So whether the non-exempt tenant will pay a bonus to obtain a VAT-free lease may not be as routine a question as some have assumed. If the non-exempt assignee is shown to be largely indifferent to the freedom from VAT on rent, so that it becomes a nil or marginal factor in his decision to take the premises, some of the present predictions will not be fulfilled. Continued freedom from VAT would then not add much potential for profit to the tenant's ownership of the lease, and should not then be reflected in any increase in the rent on review.

Against this, the presence in the market of a body of exempt potential assignees may produce a rent at a level above that obtainable from non-exempt assignees; if, indeed, the evidence of what the market actually produces at the valuation date for review demonstrates such an enhanced rent then the landlord will want to review on the basis of non-election. So the policy issues may be finely balanced, and future trends could increase uncertainty. For example, the shop-front building society office, 'see-through' banks or 'lobby service' provisions of automatic machines and money shops are all features of High Street premises virtually unheard of 20 or 25 years ago when many existing leases were settled and who can tell what the next decade or two will bring? The rise and fall of what is perceived as the desirable tenant, or the most desirable tenant, provides a second of the variable factors in the property market which rent reviews have not proved capable of legislating for in every respect; provisions, as suggested by Fogel and Plumbe, that willing lessees in the market are all engaged in non-exempt activities are thus another possible artificiality which may or may not turn out to the advantage or disadvantage of either landlord or tenant in the unknowable future. They go on to illustrate the possible valuation arguments to which that assumption can give rise, by which a tenant tries to turn an unreal assumption to his own benefit. The phrase they use for the tenant with exempt activities is 'disadvantaged'; the meaning is clear but the value-judgment is perhaps more questionable for, whilst it is a disadvantage to have to pay out VAT on supplies received, is it truly an advantage to have to charge it on supplies made? Johnson and Ross, in their Blundell Memorial Lecture, use 'VAT adverse' as the label (omit the 'd' and it is even more apt!).

(ii) Assumption in the formula

If the landlord's assessment is that rents without the landlord's right to elect will settle down above the level of rents actually or potentially liable to VAT, an assumption of no election and no right to elect (or rather a covenant not to elect) can be written into the review formula. The clause drafted by Fogel which appears as part of Conveyancer Precedent 5–105, which is printed in Part Seven, follows much of this pattern. It also provides for a tenant to require the landlord to make an election to waive the exemption (which, as drafted, does not seek to bind a later successor) and extends to part disposals. The gain will be to obtain the benefit at review of the expected uplift in starting rents that exempt tenants will be offering over rents from non-exempt tenants. That result will be achieved if those expectations are realised and continue to be realised at future review dates. A contrary result may be produced if resistance arises among non-exempt tenants to rents assessed on a basis different from that on which they will have to pay, especially if any expected differentials melt away. Artificiality of itself may engender tenant resistance as has been mentioned elsewhere in this book: it has already produced a judicial reaction in favour of 'reality' and can well effect valuation sentiment which then comes to be reflected in the awards of arbitrators and experts. The awards reinforce the market sentiment, so professional opinions become firmer which is reflected in further settlements and awards and so the process continues.

Drafting attempts to eliminate such reaction to artificiality lead to only further artificiality and the process feeds upon itself unless kept in check. So, for example, a freedom for the landlord to choose at each review, (i) for valuation either on the basis of election not having been made or having been made, (ii) of a future election to waive being possible or not being possible, or (iii) for the class of willing tenants to be taken to be exempt, non-exempt or a mixture can be provided as a matter of bargain and drafting. This range of possibilities on which the landlord can fasten is no wider or narrower than other menus from which landlords in the past have been able to pick and choose. The policy decision remains as to whether such a one-sided set of provisions does not ultimately render the lease less attractive to good tenants and the reversion less valuable to investors in the market.

(iii) Vat aspects of comparables

The landlord who opts for a formula based on the factual situation must not expect all others to do the same. He may decide that the prospects of a financial services tenant being attracted to his corner shop, office or warehouse are so slender that he will omit provisions designed to cater for that chance. Yet when the first review comes around, there can be no certainty that the original landlords who settled the forms of lease for comparable properties were equally circumspect. Equally, the fact that the lease of the comparable property is silent on the ability of the lessor to elect leaves open questions of whether the actual landlord (who may not be the original lessor) has chosen to waive the exemption or bound himself, by side letter or other collateral promise, not to do so and, if he has, whether only to the current tenant or generally. Such facts may or may not be ascertainable when needed. So the rent review formula should sensibly guide the valuers, and any third party referee, involved in the revaluation of the rent in their treatment of such comparables. Some of these adjustments will flow naturally from the like-for-like comparison inherent in valuation by reference to comparable lettings. Fogel, in his Notes to the relevant part of Conveyancer Precedent 5–105, points to the danger that the referee may even regard express direction so to act as 'impertinent'. Like him, the authors regard that risk as one worth running, for fear of the possible ill-effects if 'approximation' or 'calibration' is not carried out. His clause requires the third party to assume a different rental than that shown for the other property, as being the reasonable rent the actual tenant would have paid if not unable to recover any VAT payable on the rent; indeed it requires the referee to assume a higher rental on the hypothetical basis. As suggested above, time will tell if the valuation reasoning behind the required assumption is sound. He rejects an alternative approach of disqualifying as comparables any property the rent of which is reduced by VAT factors, a decision we support.

Ross, in the specimen clauses which accompany his 1990 Blundell Memorial Lecture, provides for an assumption of a warranty against pre-lease election and a covenant against post-lease election.

Other provisions are possible in particular circumstances. For example, where an initial tenant has obtained, because it is engaged in VAT-exempt activities, a covenant not to elect but, in return, has paid some increase in the rent it would otherwise have offered, it would be possible to identify that increment and provide for its treatment on review. This would deal with the problem identified by Johnson in his section of the 1990 Blundell Memorial Lecture (given jointly with Ross) of not being able retrospectively to isolate the exact effect on the initial rent of the exempt status of the initial tenant. The present authors hesitate, in these early days, to say this should be done; it could be done. We agree wholeheartedly with Johnson and Ross that each transaction should be dealt with on a specific consideration of the best VAT solution applicable to it. In that regard, it will be interesting to see whether Johnson's forecast of likely valuation approaches are vindicated or not.

(iv) Tenant responses

A tenant in a strong negotiating position may equally wish to have review valuation on a basis eliminating or varying valuation factors related to VAT. It may argue for opposite provisions to those discussed above from the landlord's viewpoint. It may seek a collateral undertaking to review, or rather to only recover rent following review, on a basis different from that provided for in the lease. The need to recover VAT paid on rent may require one entity to become the tenant but with power to allow occupation by a subsidiary or associated company which could not do so, when the commercial objective has always been occupation by the second company.

2 The Uniform Business Rate

April 1990 saw the abolition of domestic rates and new valuations of all other property (based on 1988 figures) combined with a centrally fixed Uniform Business Rate (UBR). The combined effect of the second and third elements produced rates bills which in many areas are substantially in excess of the amounts previously payable under the application of rate poundages determined locally to the rateable values in existence before April. Measures of interim relief for tenants remaining in possession apply for a 5 year period. The impact of these provisions, assuming the relevant provisions of the Local Government Act 1988 (as adjusted by the Local Government and Housing Act 1989) remain untouched, will need to be taken into account in rent reviews to market rent for some years.

(a)   Valuation impact of UBR on open market rents

For some years, professional opinion amongst valuers has stressed the concept of total occupation cost, represented by the combination of rent, rates and service charges, the first liable to increase (perhaps substantially) at intervals of several years and the second or third increasing annually. Indexation or turnover related rents make all three liable to annual increases or perhaps even more frequent adjustment. The substantial increase in the rates element, which happens to coincide with a period of recession or at least slow growth in economic activity, can be predicted to produce restraint generally on rents obtainable in the market. If the predictions prove true, and it must be stressed that evidence of actual events always outweighs the most confident opinion of likely trends, the comparable rents at review based on achieved market rents should produce rents at review lower than there would have been without the heavier burden of rates produced by the combination of revaluation and the UBR. Evidence of lower rents, or, pending the emergence of such evidence, the expectation of lower rents, will influence negotiated settlements of rents at review or on renewal; such negotiated rents will be used as comparables in yet further rent settlements or awards and so the process continues until the sharply increased level of rates payments fades from the scene and rent levels settle down against what will then become the background of UBR on the 1990 valuations (until the next upheaval).

(b)   Considerations at a rent review

One can safely predict that a rent review formula countering either limb of the 1990 package will be a rarity of the highest degree. A new lease negotiated when the shape of the pending 1990 adjustments was known might just cater for the constituent elements of the package but such a result is unlikely to have been reached. Now that the 1990 pattern is known, and might provide a model for future adjustments, albeit at unknown times, one may find counter provisions written into leases but a time of slack demand, which has coincided with UBR, is hardly the time for landlords to experiment with novel assumptions adverse to tenants. They are rather more frequently offering tenant inducements and incentives. Two aspects need to be considered.

(i) Comparable rents

First comparable rents need to be scrutinised, so far as that can be done, to establish the extent to which the prospect or actuality of UBR played any part in the negotiating process. Evidence that a prospective tenant, or the valuer for such a party, relied on it as a factor in support of a particular bid or offer of rent would obviously be admissible to establish the 'authority' of a market rent then negotiated. Absence of such evidence, or just silence on it, will allow a valuation argument that a negotiated rent must be discounted to form a proper comparator now UBR has arrived. The negotiating valuers, or the referee, must give that argument such weight as professional opinion and market sentiment suggested it deserves. That represents common practice for any feature of a market-based process.

In some cases, more complicated arguments can be foreseen. For example, it might be argued, for a landlord, that the rateable value of a comparable property is too high and would be reduced on appeal (whether or not an appeal has in fact been lodged). But for that, it would be urged, the rent would be more so the rent fixed for that property should be increased to arrive at a proper comparison. Either party may seek to argue that the property to be used as a comparable bears the same rateable value as the review property which demonstrates that the valuation officer considers them of equal value. That equation can be upset if one value was the original sum on revaluation and the other fixed on appeal or if one figure reflected a substantial reduction for tenant's improvements not applicable to the other. If nothing like that can be shown, then the coincidence for the two values may have some evidential weight which an arbitrator or valuer must consider. Such arguments may become very tenuous and the tactical advantage may not justify the expense of inquiries to find all relevant facts, such as the rating returns made by the 1988 occupier. Nevertheless, the prospects of such disputes cannot be ruled out completely.

(ii) The position of the 'sitting tenant'

Assuming, however, that UBR does produce some provable reduction in rent levels, at least in its immediate wake, the special bargaining position of the 'sitting tenant' calls for special treatment. The tenant in occupation on 31 March 1990 can claim phasing relief, so that for up to 5 years he pays only his previous rates bill adjusted for inflation based on the Retail Prices Index and a 20 per cent increase (or 15 per cent for premises with lower rateable values in the new lists). A minimum (new) rateable value of £500 is also requisite for any relief to be attracted. He will argue that the market rent is that obtainable in the market, probably from willing lessees (see this discussion at p 393). He may be one of the bidders making up the tenant element of the market. Dicta in the cases go either way on this. If Donaldson J's analysis of the attributes

of the willing tenant (see p 394) hold good this personal relief to the
actual occupier is a good example of a factor to be ignored.

Similar concessions apply to a tenant in occupation on 31 March 1990
who retains ownership when the whole premises later become unoccupied.
A tenant who owns premises on 31 March on which date they were
totally unoccupied but who had occupied all or some on some occasion
between 1 April 1988 and 31 March 1990 can also obtain phasing relief
if he retains ownership up to the date of claiming relief. In these cases,
the presence of subtenants, licensees or other occupiers may be relevant
to the issue of the whole premises being empty and should be looked
into when the availability of relief becomes relevant. Both the occupying
tenant and the tenant within these other categories must make a claim
for relief.

(c)   Relevance of common rent review assumptions

Two usual assumptions reinforce the view that the occupying tenant
can require his privileged position to be disregarded. First comes the
usual disregard of the fact that the actual tenant is in occupation. The
rationale of the disregard is discussed at p 454; obviously, elimination
of phasing relief under UBR has not been a factor in the inclusion of
that disregard. That it is a consequence seems undeniable. The tenant
who goes out of occupation after 31 March 1990 does not forfeit phasing
relief so long as he retains ownership and the premises are wholly
unoccupied. Can the landlord argue that, although the tenant's
occupation is to be disregarded, his ownership is not? The tenant will
counter that by arguing that review to an open market rent assumes
property available to whoever offers a market rent so his ownership
is also to be disregarded. Fogel, in his article at [1990] 06 EG 26 appears
to accept that argument; it commends itself strongly to the authors as
likely to succeed.

The second string to the tenant's bow consists of the vacant possession
assumption. Unlike the disregard just discussed, it may well be implied
if not expressed (see p 407). Vacant possession must involve cessation
of the tenant's occupation, and the strength of the concept, going beyond
physical presence, enhances the prospect that it requires continued
ownership also to be treated as ended. It is not axiomatic that that
will be the construction but the tenant's prospects of so successfully
arguing are good. It is not, however, sufficient just to point out, as
Fogel does, that vacant possession means the tenant has moved out,
as that does not resolve the cessation of ownership point. However,
in *F R Evans (Leeds) Ltd v English Electric Ltd* (1977) 245 EG 657
Donaldson J went so far as to say of the vacant possession assumption
that:

'It is implicit in this instruction that the tenants are deemed to have moved out *or to have never occupied the premises*' (emphasis added).

It is not clear if this two-limbed analysis proceeded from substantial argument on the point. However, if the dictum is accepted, it means that the impact of a vacant possession assumption will be to disregard the privileged position of the actual tenant. Ownership of the premises only earns phasing relief if the owner has previously occupied part (at least) of the property.

Whilst recognising the limited opportunity to introduce amendments to counter the tenant's 'bonus', Fogel states they are not introducing artificialities, but correcting the anomaly of the rates' respite to the sitting tenant. Such anomalies potentially exist whenever the willing tenant appears on the review stage—the authors are not convinced that the landlord should be entitled to benefit by sharing in the legislative tenderness extended to perceived victims of UBR by obtaining an increased rent from him. Moreover, if the landlord does obtain an increased rent to reflect the beneficial effect of reduction of the rates element of the sitting tenant's total occupation cost, that good fortune ought not to continue for any part of a review period following assignment. The reviewed rent should drop to a lower level on assignment, so as to avoid a penalty or disadvantage on the tenant's ability to assign, and preventing the landlord carrying forward his bonus not only to the next review but even perhaps beyond it through the medium of a minimum rent proviso. The relevant drafting is not easy, as the reduction in rent in favour of an assignee to eliminate the protected status of the assignor who had pre-April 1990 occupation must encompass several variables. One is the annually reducing amount of the transitional relief, using a formula partly based on the fluctuations of the Retail Prices Index. Another may be to isolate the mathematical measure of the adjustment made for the tenant's privileged treatment. The authors suggest, as in other areas, that whilst it can be done it may not often be done in practice, especially over the short period of the transition. These variables, of course, also need to be borne in mind when appraising comparables allegedly affected by the impact of phasing relief.

Where part of the demised property ranks as domestic premises within the definition in s 66 of the Local Government Act 1988, abolition of domestic rates and the substitution of community charge may affect the market rent at review. Market rents of residential accommodation may demonstrate the adverse impact of the charge as compared with rates. If so, market rents of premises with residential elements should reflect that development. Inclusive rents present a number of special issues, discussed by one of the authors in an article at [1989] 40 EG 22. Where, as is possible, the change-over gives the mesne landlord an unexpected increase in net income that should be taken into account on any review of the rent under that landlord's own lease before the temporary bonus effect has lapsed, although again it may be short-lived and hard to isolate in the valuation process.

Chapter 16

Rent Reviews on Statutory Renewals and under Options to Renew

In earlier chapters (see pp 391, 441), reference has been made to the rental formula contained in s 34 of the Landlord and Tenant Act 1954 (which is concerned with the rent payable under a new tenancy granted by order of the court) and to s 34(3), which allows the new tenancy as determined by court order to include provision for varying the rent. The detailed procedure for renewal under the Act is beyond the scope of this work and readers are referred to the standard texts. The purpose of this short chapter is to summarise those aspects relating to the inclusion, and terms, of rent reviews (and other variable rents) when an order for the grant of a new tenancy is made under the Act; to contrast the position under that Act with that where a tenant exercises an option to renew contained in the original lease.

1 The statutory principle

The 1954 Act, as originally enacted, did not specifically provide for the incorporation of rent review clauses, though it was argued that they could be included provided that the rent at which 'the holding might reasonably be expected to be let in the open market' (s 34(1)) was one that would be subject to review. Alternatively, there may have been power to include a rent review clause under s 35 of the 1954 Act, the general jurisdiction to determine the terms of the tenancy. Provision for a review of rent half-way through a term of nearly 14 years granted under the 1954 Act was included in *Re No 88 High Road Kilburn, Meakers Ltd v DAW Consolidated Properties Ltd* [1959] 1 WLR 179 by Wynn Parry J although the judge made no reference to the jurisdictional basis of his decision. Doubts as to the courts powers persisted however, and sub-s (3) was inserted into s 34 by the Law of Property Act 1969, s 2, following the recommendation of the Law Commission (Law Comm No 17, 1969). The subsection reads:

'Where the rent is determined by the court, the court may, if it thinks fit, further determine that the terms of the tenancy shall include such provision for varying the rent as may be specified in the determination.'

The 1969 Act also inserted s 24A into the 1954 Act, whereby a landlord may apply to the court for what is commonly called an 'interim rent' (though the term does not appear in the section)—namely, a rent that it would be reasonable for the tenant to pay while the original tenancy continues under the Act but before the application for a new tenancy is adjudicated upon. There will be occasions where either party might seek to make such a rent subject to variation.

2 Scope of s 24A

The legislative purpose of s 24A has been judicially expressed as one primarily to prevent a tenant spinning out the procedural steps under the Act so as to prolong unfairly the continuation of the old rent. However, by directing regard should be had to the old rent, the tenant was to be cushioned against the shock of an immediate increase to the full market rent directly the lease was determined: *Charles Follett Ltd v Cabtell Investments Ltd* [1987] 2 EGLR 88 per Nourse LJ.

It will be unusual for there to be a need for a variable rent to be sought as an 'interim' rent under s 24A. There is certainly no express provision permitting this similar to that in s 34(3) and though s 34(1) and (2) apply to the determination of the interim rent (s 24A(3)), s 34(3) does not. Since a rent determined under s 24A is to be a rent payable as if it were a tenancy from year to year and will be of a limited duration (and often only determined retrospectively at the time of the main hearing for the grant of a new tenancy as in *Conway v Arthur* [1988] 2 EGLR 113) a rent review appears inappropriate.

In *Fawke v Chelsea* [1980] QB 441, however, the court held, though with some hesitation, that a differential interim rent could be ordered to reflect the state of disrepair. It was stressed that since an interim rent can only be applicable for a short time such a rent will usually be a fixed one. Only where the evidence is strong will the court be justified in departing from the usual practice. In that case, the disrepair was serious, with extensive damage by dry rot, and a differential rent might have been justified; so the Court of Appeal remitted the case for further hearing. They stressed that the rent had to be in accordance with s 24A(1); namely, a rent reasonable for the tenant to pay on the basis of a tenancy from year to year for the whole of the property comprised in a tenancy. It is possible that this formula will admit forms of variable rent other than a differential rent to reflect the state of disrepair. Thus, where a tenant applies for a new tenancy under the Act and his current lease provides for (say) an index-linked or turnover rent, then an 'interim' rent under s 24A might also be index-linked or based on turnover since it might well be reasonable for the tenant to continue to pay rent on similar terms to his existing tenancy.

In the more usual case of the lease containing a standard rent review clause, it will be difficult to persuade a judge to depart from ordering a fixed 'interim' rent under s 24A. In *Charles Follett Ltd v Cabtell Investments Ltd* [1986] 2 EGLR 76 the first instance deputy judge calculated the appropriate interim rent at £40,000 pa, but then declined to make a determination, accepting instead an undertaking by the tenant to pay £25,000 before a particular date and £40,000 thereafter. The Court of Appeal ([1987] 2 EGLR 88) held that this was an improper exercise of the judge's discretion under the section and 'as between the alternatives' of the original rent (£13,500) or the interim rent (£40,000) for the whole period, chose the latter. It does not appear that *Fawke* case was cited, nor was it argued that the court had power to, or should, determine a differential interim rent (as opposed to accepting undertakings) but the tenor of the appellate judgment is not encouraging to the concept.

3 Scope of s 34

In the large majority of renewals, the landlord and the tenant will be able to reach agreement upon the terms of the new tenancy. In such cases, the parties are free to incorporate the form of rent review they prefer—or indeed any other variable rent.

A more modern form of rent review clause can be substituted by agreement if the existing wording is considered defective. The amount of rent only falls to be determined by the court in default of such agreement and s 34(3) is only expressed to apply where the rent is so determined. On such determination, s 34(3) allows a rent review clause to be included in the lease, thereby enabling the court to fix a term of years up to the maximum allowed by the Act (14 years) while enabling the landlord to obtain a rent which is fairer than a fixed rent would be. Of course, s 34(3) is discretionary and the court does not have to include a rent review clause, but in practice such inclusion has become a widespread if not an almost invariable feature of statutory renewal.

(a) Can any form of variable rent be included?

In *Fawke v Viscount Chelsea* [1980] QB 441 at 452B, Goff LJ was of the opinion (obiter) that 'section 34(3) authorises nothing more than the inclusion of a rent review clause'. The dictum occurs in the context of the power of the court to order a differential rent where the demised premises are out of repair as a result of the landlord's failure to observe a repairing covenant, and the judge was of the opinion that s 34(3) did not authorise the latter. In the same case, Stephenson LJ also equated 'variable rent' in s 34(3) with 'a provision . . . varying the rent by a rent review clause' (at 522), but also in the context of contrasting this variation with a differential rent allowing a lower figure until repairs are affected. Consequently, it is submitted that the case is not an authority to prevent the inclusion of forms of variable rent other than a rent review clause in a new tenancy granted by court order where there are good grounds for so doing. Indeed, in *Naylor v Uttoxeter Urban District Council* (1974) 231 EG 619 the rent determined by the court under s 34 in a new tenancy of a cattle market was a percentage one; namely, 20 per cent of the gross commission earned by the tenant auctioneers.

However, even if a restricted interpretation of s 34(3) is adopted—so that it only authorises the incorporation of a rent review clause, and nothing more—there is now authority (paradoxically from *Fawke v Chelsea*) to the effect that s 34(1) may authorise a rent increasing at fixed amounts at specified times if supported by evidence that this would be the manner in which 'the holding might reasonably be expected to be let in the open market' (s 34(1)). Thus, if the market rent was a rent that varied during the period according to the state of repair of the premises, the court would have power to determine (and, indeed, per Brandon LJ at 521E, would be obliged to determine) a differential rent accordingly. The same argument applies in other situations. Thus, in a shopping centre where all the units are let on retail percentage leases, incorporating a turnover rent, evidence might well be adduced that the market rent for any one unit in the centre would be one incorporating a turnover rent.

Thus, it is the authors' view that the court has power to include any form of variable rent on statutory renewal under s 34(3); but if, contrary to our view, s 34(3) is limited to rent review clauses, there is power under s 34(1), providing suitable evidence is forthcoming that such a rent is the open market rent for the holding.

(b) When should a review clause be included on renewal?

Assuming a rent review clause is the most likely form of variable rent, a review clause will be appropriate whenever a rent subject to review is the rent at which the holding is likely to be let in the open market. Given the near universality of rent review in business leases, the effective burden of proof is likely to be on any tenant who suggests that a review clause is inappropriate. Consequently, a review clause is only likely to be omitted when the duration of the term of the new lease is less than the current market pattern for frequency of review.

Where a reduced term of years is granted under the Act, the rent review clause is still likely to follow the market patterns (*Edwards & Sons Ltd v Central London Commercial Estates Ltd* (1984) 271 EG 697—7 year lease, review after 5 years).

(c) What should be the terms of the rent review clause?

Given the wide variety of review clauses available, dispute is more likely to centre on the details of the clause and the frequency of review. Where the current tenancy contained a review clause, it is usual for the existing clause to be carried over into the new lease. Indeed unless the clause is clearly inadequate, the burden of persuading the court to change the details (eg) of the machinery or assumptions is a heavy one and would have to be justified on the principles laid down in *O'May v City of London Real Property Co Ltd* [1983] (discussed in the next section, p 514, and also more generally at p 329). On the other hand the correction of drafting defects is likely to be approved. In *Charles Follett Ltd v Cabtell Investment Co Ltd* [1986] 2 EGLR 76, the deputy judge declined to alter a well drafted review clause 'in a form which has stood the test of time' merely to remove the strict time-limits which it contained and this aspect of the judgment was not challenged on appeal. In the absence of evidence justifying a change, or agreement to alter the form of the clause, the existing review clause will be carried over into the new lease on the basis that it represents terms originally agreed. Where there is no review clause in the existing lease, the determination of the exact review terms is a more open issue. It is submitted that evidence of the terms of review clauses in current open market lettings, with reference to the statutory guide-lines (eg the express disregards in s 34 of the 1954 Act) would be important factors in such a determination.

(d)   What should be the frequency of reviews?

Where there is no review clause under the existing lease, the issue will be settled by reference to market practice. Where there is an existing review clause and an outmoded review pattern then, notwithstanding the provisions of s 35 (below) and the direction to have regard to the existing tenancy, the market frequency of reviews will be substituted. Thus in the *Charles Follett* case, a 5 year review pattern was substituted for the original 7 year pattern without dissension for, as the judge noted, the valuation evidence was on the basis of 5 year reviews.

Disputes will only be likely on the issue of what is the market practice. In *WH Smith & Son Limited v Bath City Council* (6 November 1984, unreported, Bath County Court) the landlord council successfully argued for a 4 yearly review pattern, bringing evidence to show that the local market showed higher than average rental growth and that, as landlords in the city, they had carried out a successful local estate mangement policy of insisting on 4 yearly reviews and there was no shortage of demand for units. These arguments prevailed over the evidence of the tenant retailer who could demonstrate that the vast majority of its 300 outlets were on a market pattern of 5 year reviews. A 4–year periodicity, it was said, was fair and reasonable, and the outcome would be the same whether the matter fell to be determined under s 34 or s 35 of the Act.

(e)   Can an 'upwards only' review be included?

It was pointed out in Chapter 1 that, on two occasions, it has been held that a review clause included in a new tenancy under the 1954

Act should provide for the rent to be adjusted either up or down—
a so called 'upwards or downwards' review (*Stylo Shoes Ltd v Manchester
Royal Exchange Ltd* (1967) 204 EG 803 and *Janes (Gowns) Ltd v Harlow
Development Corporation* (1979) 253 EG 799). In the *Stylo Shoes* decision
Cross J observed 'what is sauce for the goose is sauce for the gander'.
However, the authors respectfully suggest that his Lordship's enthusiasm
for a well-known metaphor may have led him to too sweeping a
generalisation and provision for a downwards review will not be
automatically included in every renewal for two reasons. Primarily, if
the current lease contains an upwards only review clause, then the court
is directed under s 35 of the Act (see below) to have regard to the terms
of the existing tenancy; indeed following the *O'May* case (discussed below)
the prima facie result would be to carry over the existing provision so
a strong case will have to be made to change that clause. Even if the
court agrees to depart from an existing upwards only review, or where
there is no restriction in the current lease, it is submitted that an upwards/
downwards review clause will only be appropriate if the 'market rent'
is one that includes the possibility of a downwards review. If the evidence
is that upwards only reviews are the norm, then this should be the right
result on renewal. Support for this approach is found in the *Janes (Gowns)*
case itself where, though an upwards or downwards review clause was
included on the tenant's application, the judge reached that conclusion
on the evidence he had heard about the development of a new shopping
centre nearby that might cause the rental value of the demised premises
to fall (at 803). A tenant on the open market would, therefore, be in
a position to bargain for a downwards review that was part of the open
market rent. Similarly, if evidence was given that the practice in a
particular market was for landlords to insist successfully on 'upwards
only' reviews, that could properly result in an 'upwards only' review
in the new statutory tenancy.

This view of the authors, expressed in earlier editions, was vindicated
by the decision of the judge (which was not challenged on appeal) in
the *Charles Follett* case (above). The upwards only review clause in the
original tenancy was carried over into the new tenancy since there was
no evidence to justify a change. Consequently, it is now clear that the
two earlier cases do not mean that upwards only reviews cannot be
properly included under the Act.

4   Variation of the terms of the tenancy

Section 35 of the 1954 Act provides:

'The terms of a tenancy granted by order of the court under this Part of this
Act (other than terms as to the duration thereof and as to the rent payable
thereunder) shall be such as may be agreed between the landlord and the tenant
or as, in default of agreement, may be determined by the court: and in determining

those terms the court shall have regard to the terms of the current tenancy and to all relevant circumstances.'

In the context of variable rents, two matters call for detailed comment.

(a) 'The rent payable thereunder'

When determining the terms of the new tenancy, the court is to 'have regard to the terms of the current tenancy', but the section does not apply to 'the rent payable thereunder'. It is not clear whether this means the court is only to disregard the *amount* of the rent originally reserved or whether it further requires the court to disregard the *manner* in which it is reserved. It will be remembered that when drafting a rent review clause it is advisable to direct that the valuer or arbitrator acts on the assumption of a letting 'subject to the terms of this lease (other than the amount of the rent hereby reserved but including the provisions for review of that rent)' (Model Forms, proviso (A)(i)(b)). This clarification makes it clear that only the *amount* of rent originally reserved is to be disregarded. Statutory clarification, in another context, appeared in the Counter-Inflation (Business Rents)(Transition) Order 1974 No 1030 (see Chapter 19, p 545), perhaps an indication that provision (as in s 35) 'other than . . . to the rent payable' is equivocal as to whether the review provisions are themselves part of the provision as to rent. In the context of s 35, where there is no such clarification, the matter might assume importance in circumstances where (say) the original lease provided for an index-linked rent. On statutory renewal it is clearly open, within s 35, for the parties to agree to change the rent to one subject to rent review. If, however, the parties cannot agree and one party requests the court to maintain the index-linked basis, and the other seeks a change, it would be important for the court to decide whether or not the terms of s 35 required them to 'have regard to' the original index-linking. In our submission, the court should and would be so required. Certainly the words of the section—namely, 'other than terms . . . as to the rent payable thereunder'—are wide enough to comprehend the method of varying the rent and enable the court to disregard the original position. However, the method of varying the rent may well have a substantial effect on the amount of rent payable thereunder—indeed, a landlord seeking change from an index-linked rent to a rent review pattern may do so primarily because he believes an increased income may result. Consequently, the method of varying a rent will be an important term of the tenancy and have as much effect (if not more) on the amount of the rent as (say) the incidence of repairing obligations.

If the court does 'have regard to' the method of varying the rent under s 35, this does not prevent a change on renewal provided the party seeking the change can show a valid reason therefor, which is the position for a departure from any of the other terms of the current tenancy (*Cardshops Ltd v Davies* [1971] 1 WLR 591). In the cases, the judges have tended to avoid the issue, and in the *WH Smith v Bath* decision, the judge did not find it necessary to decide if the issue of frequency of rent reviews fell under s 34 or s 35. In the light of the decision in *British Gas Corporation v Universities Superannuation Scheme Ltd* [1986] 1 WLR 398 (see p 334, above) the better view must be that 'the rent payable' in s 35 only refers to the quantum of rent; so that a court will have to 'have regard to' the form of a review clause under s 35. This accords with the first instance decision in the *Charles Follett* case (not challenged on appeal) where the judge declined to remove a time of the essence provision from the existing review clause, though once again it appears that the judge considered he was applying an unfettered discretion under s 34 rather than his more circumscribed powers under s 35.

In *O'May v City of London Real Property Co Ltd* [1983] 2 AC 726 it was held that an alteration in the burden of repairing liability for the demised premises, and a consequent alteration in the payment of the service rent, fell to be considered under s 35. As Brightman LJ said in the Court of Appeal 'the substantial issue is not the amount or calculation of the rent but the incidence of certain financial burdens which have the effect of controlling the rent' ([1981] Ch 216 at 227D). In the authors' view, a party seeking a change in the method of varying a rent will be in an exactly similar position and will be subject to s 35. The court will 'have regard to' the form of variable rent that has the effect of controlling the amount of rent payable. Thus, in a disputed renewal, the court should first determine the manner in which a rent will vary (form of review) under s 35 and then approach its task under s 34 of determining the quantum of rent (*O'May* case, at 740). In practice, it seems the process is often subsumed into a single issue.

(b) Departing from the existing rent review terms

If the above view is correct the second question arises: namely, what circumstances enable the court to depart from the terms of the existing tenancy under s 35—and change the original terms relating to the manner of rent review or form of variable rent? The tests propounded by Goulding J in the *O'May* case at first instance (1979) 249 EG 1065 and applied by the Court of Appeal (which nevertheless reached the opposite conclusion) have been discussed earlier (see Chapter 10, p 329). The House of Lords confirmed the approach and the decision. Lord Hailsham at 740G was of the view that while s 35 does not in any way bind the parties to the terms of the current tenancy in any permanent form, he did believe that the court should begin by considering the terms of the current tenancy, with the burden of persuading the court to impose a change resting on the party proposing the change. Imposing this evidential burden is also clear when the judge purports to act under s 34 (as in the *Charles Follett* case). Thus, a change in the form of variable rent, or manner of rent review, will be subject to this approach and the overriding test that the change must be fair and reasonable.

5 The use of 'eleventh hour' reviews to avoid the disadvantages of statutory renewals

The prolongation of the contractual term by s 24 of the 1954 Act provides an incentive for tenants to drag out the renewal process to gain the benefit of the old rent; in the absence of agreement the former term is extended by s 64, until 3 months after the application for a new lease has been finally disposed of. Where there is no appeal, that point is reached on the expiry of the time allowed for appealing. Section 24A was expressly designed to counter this tactic, but it only does so partially because the interim rent is invariably set somewhere between the old rent and the new market rent under s 34. An 'eleventh hour' review seeks to protect a landlord from this disadvantage. The rent is revised with effect from a date, say, 1 month before expiry of the contractual term, so the extended term will be at an updated market rent, which in practice will only be fixed after the end of the term. Indeed, the negotiations of such a revised rent may well be combined with attempts to settle the rent for the renewal lease. No application for an interim rent need be made and would usually be pointless in any event. It would be well within the scope of s 34(3) to include such a provision in a new lease, whether or not it was in the old lease. As yet, it is unlikely that many leases containing such a provision have come up for renewal, as the device is of fairly recent origin. The authors believe, however, it is an increasingly common provision in modern leases but tenant resistance to the device indicates that it is not standard practice. It would also protect a landlord against the unfortunate state of affairs illustrated by *Nevill Long & Co (Boards) Ltd v Firmenich & Co* (1984) 47 P & CR 59 whereby, on a division of the reversion, all the landlords must act together and if a part—any part, however small, it would seem— of the revision comes into the hands of an 'ally' of the tenant the lease can never be terminated and a new rent fixed. To avoid the consequences of a continuing lease which cannot be ended (the *Long v Firmenich* dilemma), a wise precaution in situations where the reversion may be divided is to provide at the drafting stage for reviews at the agreed intervals however long the lease continues. Alternatively, the answer is to negotiate to avoid the situation when the sale of part of the reversion is made; for a precedent providing for different approaches to be negotiated on a sale of part of the reversion see Conveyancer Precedent 16–68.

The drafting of 'eleventh hour' rent reviews and the problems relating thereto are discussed in Chapter 4, p 78.

6 Rent reviews in options to renew

The exercise of an option to renew contained in a lease is analogous to the exercise of the statutory right to a new tenancy under the 1954 Act. Indeed, where such an option to renew exists, it is an alternative course of action for a tenant who will opt for one way or the other to obtain a fresh term, no doubt making his choice in the light of the perceived advantages and disadvantages, some of which we discuss below.

(a) Options in leases with an existing review clause

Options to renew are fully dealt with in Barnsley, *Land Options*, Chapter 8, and differ principally from the position on statutory renewal in that, once validly exercised, the tenant has an absolute right to a fresh term, the terms of which are governed entirely by the terms of the renewal covenant. The standard precedents provide that those terms will be at a rent to be determined but otherwise will be the same as the stipulations in the existing lease, except for the clause renewal.

Thus, as regards rent review clauses (or any other form of provision for variable rent for that matter) in the old lease, the fresh lease will contain review clauses on identical terms both as to the machinery and as to the frequency of review. It will not be possible to vary these provisions (except by agreement between the parties), as the court has power to do on an application under the 1954 Act, save in the unlikely event that the wording of the option allows such a variation.

(b) Options in leases with no existing review clause

Where the existing lease contains no provision for varying the rent but provides for the new rent, on exercise of the option, to be fixed by an arbitrator, it is not open on such arbitration to introduce rent review machinery into the fresh term where none existed before. In *National Westminster Bank Ltd v BSC Footwear Ltd* (1980) 42 P & CR 90 there was a ruling on an option to renew in a lease for a 21–year term for a further 21 years at the 'then prevailing market rent'. It was held by the Court of Appeal that the arbitrator had no power to introduce a periodic review provision into his determination of the new rent. The lease empowered him to determine the amount of the prevailing market rent, not to impose a new formula. Nor could the arbitrator introduce a differential rent; *Fawke v Chelsea* (see p 508) being distinguished as a decision limited to the statutory power on renewal (a view since repeated in *Clarke v Findon Developments Ltd* (1983) 270 EG 426). The absence of evidence of market rents fixed for such long periods was acknowledged, but it was suggested (in a dictum quoted fully at p 253, above) that arbitrators, when faced with no market comparables, do not have the slightest difficulty in fulfilling the requirement that they shall fix the market rent then prevailing. Some may think Templeman LJ's conclusion rather optimistic. The result is, however, consistent with the interpretation of 'rack rent' in a review clause where the view of Sir John Pennycuick was that a rack rent 'must be a rent which will continue to be payable throughout the whole of the term' (*Compton Group Ltd v Estates Gazette Ltd* (1977) 36 P & CR 148 at 154.)

It was stressed in the *National Westminster* case that the lease had to be construed in accordance with the intention of the parties at the time the lease was made (1957); and the fact that the result proved disadvantageous to the lessors in 1978 could not affect that process of construction. This Court of Appeal decision was followed in *Bracknell Development Corporation v Greenlees Lennards Ltd* (1981) 260 EG 500, where the wording of the lease called for the arbitrator to fix 'a full and fair market rent'. The lessor argued (unavailingly) that 'a full and fair market rent' in an option to renew for a term of 21 years could not be either full, or fair to the lessor, if fixed for 21 years without review; but it was held (with evidence being given) that it would be possible to determine a rent fixed for the whole term. A further argument that the lease was frustrated because the fixed rent was necessarily unfair was rejected for not dissimilar reasons.

Similar unwillingness to rescue the parties, or, more significantly the landlord, from the consequences of what time and inflation has rendered a poor bargain was expressed in *Lear v Blizzard* [1983] 3 All ER 662. The judge refused to sanction either a premium as such or a decapitalised premium as extra rent. The principle in *National Westminster v BSC Footwear* was also applied in *Stedman v Midland Bank* [1990] 1 EGLR 146 (see p 277).

(c)   Choosing between exercising the option or statutory rights

A tenant whose current lease contains no rent review, or (perhaps more likely) a rent review pattern favourable to the tenant (eg only every 7, 10 or 14 years) may well conclude that exercise of any option to renew such a term will be more favourable—certainly as regards rent review—than relying on the statutory rights under the 1954 Act. Any option to renew is also likely to be preferred for other reasons, particularly the guaranteed length of term afforded, and as a particularly effective means of blocking any opposition by the landlord on one of the prescribed grounds in s 30 of the 1954 Act.

Reliance on the statutory provisions may be preferable when, perhaps, the tenant considers that he has a case to alter the rent review mechanism or wishes to employ the assumptions contained in s 34 of the Act in setting the new rent which may be more advantageous. Additionally, application for a new tenancy under s 26 may hold the rent at a lower level for a longer period of time (whether or not the landlord applies for an interim rent, but particularly if he neglects to do so). Reasons unrelated to the rent may play a part; thus the tenant may not desire a further long term but, knowing the lessor will oppose any statutory renewal under s 30, the tenant may nevertheless apply for a new tenancy of short duration hoping at least to obtain compensation under s 37 if he gets no new lease, and 'carrying forward' that right if he gets a short renewal. In some circumstances, the tenant may have to fall back on his rights under the 1954 Act, for an option requires strict compliance with the terms and conditions on which it is granted, eg as to performance of any repairing covenants (*West Country Cleaners (Falmouth) Ltd v Saly* [1966] 1 WLR 1485; but compare *Bassett v Whiteley* (1982) 45 P & CR 87) whereas in dealing with an application under the statute, the court has a measure of discretion when considering opposition to such a tenancy under s 30(1)(a)–(c) and the tenant's conduct has to be very much more culpable (eg *persistent* delay in paying rent or *substantial* breaches of his obligations).

It is not thought likely, where a tenant deliberately chooses to rely on the statutory provisions rather than exercise an option to renew, that any argument could be raised that he *should* have chosen to exercise the option instead, for an option is only a privilege which the tenant can choose to ignore, and when the original term expires the tenancy will continue under s 24 of the 1954 Act. A tenant seeking to exercise an option after 27 September 1989 will need to do so in the light of the possible effects of s 2 of the Law of Property (Miscellaneous Provisions) Act 1989 (see [1990] Conv 9.

For the more difficult considerations of the interrelationship of the 1954 Act with options to determine, see the discussion in Chapter 3, p 32, above.

Chapter 17

Residential Tenancies

Though rent review clauses have always been a contractual possibility in residential leases, the statutory framework of the Rent Acts gave little room for their operation. The legislation now contained in the Housing Act 1988 offers wider scope for all types of variable rent.

1 The statutory framework

(a) Rent Act control—entered into before 15 January 1989

Tenancies of a dwelling house entered into before 15 January 1989 will be subject to the 'twin pillars' of the security of tenure and rent control provisions of the Rent Acts unless they came within one of the exceptions to that Act. In a protected tenancy, however, there was no prohibition on the parties agreeing to any form of rent review clause in their tenancy agreement. Indeed, standard forms available from stationers included review clauses—for example, clause 44 of the National Letting Provisions (Residential) 1981 (Oyez Conveyancing Form 26). It is not clear to what extent such clauses operated according to their terms but they were certainly precarious in law. By application for and registration of a fair rent, a tenant could, at any time, render any contractual review nugatory. Any contractual increase consequent upon any review would be irrecoverable to the extent that it was higher than the rent so registered. Thus, though rent reviews have been refined and honed over a 30-year period into an essential feature of every commercial lease, the rent review in a residential lease was a 'Cinderella' and has, until 1989, only been of real significance in specialist situations outside Rent Act control, such as the luxury flat (see eg *Davstone (Holdings) Ltd v Al Rifai* [1976] 32 P & CR 18). Now that the cause of this blight—rent control—is consigned to history (at least for new tenancies) it is no longer appropriate to consider to what extent rent reviews were possible under the old regime. Readers who encounter a rent review problem in a residential tenancy entered into before 15 January 1989 are referred to the full discussion of the issues in the second edition of this book at pp 39–51.

(b)   Under the Housing Act 1988

The abandonment of the idea of rent control has given a new freedom periodically to increase rent by contract in residential leases entered into on or after 15 January 1989. A landlord has choices in most situations: there is a statutory system to increase the rent in assured periodic tenancies; he can choose his own rent review clause and the type and form of such clause; or he could opt for short term shorthold lettings with the opportunity to agree an increased rent for a fresh term.

The Housing Act 1988 creates a completly new statutory framework. It is beyond the scope of this book to do more than sketch the outline of this system. The Act creates two main forms of private sector residential tenancies. The assured tenancy retains a degree of security of tenure; the assured shorthold is a fixed term tenancy (exceeding 6 months) where, providing the requisite notice is given before the tenancy is entered into, possession may be recovered at the end of the term. For both forms of tenancy, the Rent Act principle of rent control is abandoned. Rent assessment committees will have a very limited role of curbing excessive rents in shorthold tenancies and determining market rents under fixed term assured tenancies if the statutory procedure for rent increase is adopted.

For the purpose of considering rent reviews, the new forms of private residential tenancies can be divided into four categories:

(i)   Fixed term assured tenancies

Traditionally, residential tenancies have been for periodic terms or for an initial, fairly short, fixed term and thereafter from (say) month to month. Where, however, a fixed term assured tenancy is agreed it will be essential for the landlord to address the question of rent review during that fixed term. This is because the statutory method of increase (s 13) only applies to assured periodic tenancies, though this will include the statutory periodic tenancy which arises when the fixed term assured tenancy expires (s 5(2)). On the other hand, a fixed term assured tenancy may prove attractive in some circumstances (at least to landlords) since the initial rent agreed and any rent review process or rents reached or agreed thereunder cannot be challenged later by a tenant. The reference of excessive rents under s 22 to a rent assessment committee only applies to assured shorthold tenancies.

(ii)   Periodic assured tenancies

Contractually agreed rent review clauses can also be inserted into periodic tenancies if desired. The issue is not so important in the sense that if there is no such clause the landlord can take advantage of the statutory mechanism for increase contained in s 13. However, any provision in such a tenancy 'under which the rent for a particular period of the tenancy will or may be greater than the rent for an earlier period' (s 13(1)(b)) will preclude any statutory increase. The landlord's choice at the outset therefore is either the inclusion of an express rent review in the agreement or reliance on the statutory scheme. A landlord cannot use both.

As with fixed term assured tenancies, there is no way a tenant can challenge a rent initially agreed as being too excessive; a rent review mechanism and rents agreed thereunder are similarly immune.

(iii) Statutory periodic assured tenancies

A statutory periodic tenancy arises under s 5(2) of the Act whenever a fixed term assured tenancy comes to an end (otherwise than by court order or surrender or other action by the tenant). The points to stress as far as rent reviews are concerned are:

(1) Section 5(3)(e) provides that the terms of the statutory tenancy are to be the same as those of the fixed term assured tenancy which has come to an end, so that any rent review clause will be carried over into the statutory periodic tenancy.

(2) Section 6 of the Act provides for either party to give notice, during the first year of the statutory tenancy, of proposed changes in the terms of the statutory periodic tenancy. If a counter-notice is served by the other party to the lease, the new terms are determined by a rent assessment committee as those reasonably expected to be found in an assured periodic tenancy of the dwelling house concerned (s 6(4)). There is scope therefore for a tenant to propose the deletion or amendment of any rent revision clause in the fixed term tenancy or for the landlord to propose that one be inserted, though it might be hard to convince a rent assessment committee to put one in where there was none before.

(3) Under s 6, the rent assessment committee has power to adjust the amount of rent when they determine new terms (s 6(5)). The adjustment can be made whether or not the parties have requested it. Though the parties in their notice can also propose such an adjustment, such rental changes under this section appear to be limited to adjustments to take account of the proposed new terms.

(4) The statutory method of rent increase under s 13 also applies to statutory periodic tenancies and a literal reading of s 13(1) would suggest that it also applies even if the statutory periodic tenancy contains a rent review clause carried over from the fixed term assured tenancy since s 13(1)(a) applies the section to all statutory periodic tenancies. In contrast, s 13(1)(b) applies it to any other periodic tenancy except one under which rent for a particular period will or may be greater that the rent for an earlier period.

(iv) Assured shorthold tenancies

The assured shorthold tenancy looks superficially attractive to landlords—as it was no doubt designed to do. At the moderate cost of a minimum fixed term of 6 months and notice to the tenant in advance, the landlord is not only free of the restrictions of security of tenure (the benefit of the old protected shorthold) but also need have no fears of artificial rent control now that fair rents are a thing of the past. There is the restriction that the landlord must not include any power to determine the tenancy during the first 6 months (s 20(1)(b)) but this does not include a power of re-entry or forfeiture for breach of any term or condition of the tenancy (s 45(4)).

Rent reviews will be an important consideration in the longer fixed terms; though, for the more common shorter terms of up to a year, landlords may choose to leave rent increases for negotiation in succeeding shorthold tenancies and by virtue of s 20(4) there will be no need for a fresh notice under s 20(1). They will know that they can give 2 months' notice to determine the original term if the tenant declines to agree any increase. In such circumstances, there is the additional freedom of knowing that that when the original assured shorthold comes to an end, a new tenancy of the same or substantially the same premises under which the landlord and tenant are the same at such ending will be an assured shorthold even if the basic conditions of s 20(1) are not met. In other words, it can be of any length, no notice need be given and it can contain a power for the landlord to determine (ie a break clause) in the first 6 months.

For assured shortholds only, the tenant has the right under s 22 to apply to a rent assessment committee for the determination of the rent which, in the committee's opinion, the landlord might be expected to obtain in the open market. The idea (as reflected in the marginal note to the section) is to curb excessive rents. It is submitted that it will do no such thing and that landlords have little to fear from this section because:

(1) It is wholly inapplicable to assured tenancies where one might have expected it to have had greater impact. Given the prospect of indefinite periodic terms buttressed with some security of tenure, tenants would have had some incentive to challenge their landlord. No such encouragement exists in the precarious shorthold.

(2) It does not even apply to second or subsequent shorthold agreements of the same premises between the same parties as entered into the initial agreement (s 22(2)(b)). Only one application under the section can be made during the first shorthold term so the timing of the application will be vital.

(3) Few tenants are likely to make application in the context of a short fixed term shorthold since they will fear, with possible good reason, that any success before the rent assessment committee will be a pyrrhic victory when they are given due notice at the end of the term.

(4) Even where a tenant is both in a position to apply and does choose

to refer a rent under s 22, the rent assessment committee cannot make a determination unless they consider–

'(a) that there is a sufficient number of similar dwelling houses in the locality let on assured tenancies (whether shorthold or not); and

(b) that the rent payable under the assured shorthold tenancy is significantly higher than the landlord might reasonably be expected to obtain under the tenancy, having regard to the level of rents payable under the tenancies referred to in paragraph (a) above (s 22(3))'.

In practical terms, a reference under s 22 is going to be the exception rather than the rule; a successful reference is going to be difficult to achieve given the need to establish both a local market of assured tenancies and that the rent agreed is *significantly* higher than the market rent.

2 Appropriate forms of residential rent review

Practitioners accustomed to the complex forms of commercial rent review will have to adjust to more simple forms for the residential tenancy. The rental return over a given period from the lease of even a substantial house will be much lower than that from most commercial premises; the parties may be less sophisticated and will often wish to operate the rent review without the expense of professional assistance; and disputes on esoteric points of law or valuation will rarely, if ever, assist the client. These factors would suggest that the most appropriate forms of rent review will combine the virtues of simplicity, cheapness (for both parties) and certainty. An impartial observer might wish to add that the review process should be fair to both parties but sadly one expects that, if the experience of commercial rent reviews are any guide, achieving a 'fair result' will not be a high priority.

On this basis, the following forms of rent review merit consideration:

(a) Unilateral notice by the landlord

The lease could simply provide that from a given date, and perhaps on each annual anniversary thereafter, the rent will be such sum as that specified in a notice given by the landlord to the tenant. Until such notice was given the rent originally agreed would continue to be paid. A precedent embodying this idea has been published as Conveyancer Precedent 5–103, reproduced in Part Seven, p 725, below.

The validity of varying a rent by a notice in this way was upheld by the Court of Appeal in *Greater London Council v Connolly* [1970] 2 QB 100 where both the timing and the amount of an increase in rent of a council tenancy depended on the whim of the landlord council. Despite the doubts of Glidewell LJ in *Dresden Estates v Collinson* [1987]

1 EGLR 45 at 47 that a 'tenancy agreement itself cannot give a landlord power to alter a rent unilaterally', the *Connolly* decision and the views of the Privy Council in *A-G for Alberta v Huggard Assets Ltd* [1953] AC 420 at 440 would seem to be a sound basis for this form of residential rent review (see Chapter 3, p 29 for fuller consideration).

Time need not be of the essence for such a notice though it might be sensible, as well as fairer to the tenant, if the notice did not have retrospective effect. Though the case of *C H Bailey Ltd v Memorial Enterprises Ltd* [1974] 1 WLR 728 is clear authority allowing retrospective increases, the courts might well shrink from allowing a landlord to make a retrospective increase by unilateral notice of the *Connolly* type.

Though few tenants will be happy to have rent increases in this way, in a situation of housing shortage they may have little choice but to accept. Their advisers should at least ensure that they have the right to break any fixed term assured tenancy on the receipt of such notice; in a periodic assured tenancy they could always choose to leave by giving any requisite notice to quit (assuming that they can find an alternative home); in an assured shorthold (which is the first such term between the parties) there is a remedy under s 22 if the tenant feels that the rent specified in a notice is excessive.

Though landlords may consider that unilateral notice gives them a means of rent increase which is simple, cheap and easy to operate and certain in its result, a note of caution should be entered. Since it is potentially so harsh on a tenant (eg if the rent in the landlord's notice was set at an inordinately high figure) it is possible that the views of Glidewell LJ, quoted above, may find some support and the *Connolly* principle might be restricted in future decisions.

The final, somewhat worrying, scenario is that this form of rent increase could be used by unscrupulous landlords as a means to winkle tenants out and bypass the usual grounds for possession for an assured tenancy. A notice increasing the rent to an impossibly high figure could be given; the tenant would obviously refuse or be unable to pay; he might well vacate and if he did not, the landlord could, some 3 months or so later, take proceedings for possession under the Act (see s 5(1) and ss 7 and 8) using ground 8 of Sched 2 (more than 3 months' arrears of rent), a ground on which the court must order possession if the ground is made out.

(b) By notice and counter-notice

The form of rent review that commences by one party (usually the landlord) serving a 'trigger-notice' is well established in commercial lettings, though currently out of favour for new leases. The landlord serves a notice stating the revised rent; this takes effect unless the tenant serves a counter-notice in due time with his own proposals as to the rent. In the absence of an agreement, the revised rent is fixed by an independent valuer.

A form of rent review for an assured tenancy along these lines has been published as Conveyancer Precedent 5–100 (reproduced at p 724, below), with the variation that the valuer adopts the 'flip flop' process of valuation. The valuer will have before him the figures put forward by both the landlord and the tenant in their notices and any later written representations in support of their respective figures. He will then set the revised rent as the figure which in his opinion is the nearer to the market rent. The idea is both to reduce the cost of decision making and to put each party under pressure to put forward a realistic figure in their notices.

The aim of such a form is laudable, but arguably the advantage of the balance it gives between the parties is outweighed by other considerations:

(1) The procedure is not simple, requiring proper service of a notice, specifying a figure and demanding an appropriate response from the tenant. The case law on commercial rent review notices is vast and the mistakes in the process, often made by professionals in the field, show how easy it is to get it wrong (see Chapter 5, p 119 ff, above). If commercial rent review draftsmen have largely abandoned the formula, one can reasonably doubt the wisdom of adopting the idea in the residential context.

(2) The procedure will not be inexpensive if a valuer is involved—it is inevitable that a valuer's fee will seem large in relation to the rent reserved for a moderately sized residential property especially if the process is an annual one. Burdening the tenant with payment of all or even half of the fee might be resented. Conveyancer Precedent 5–100 provides for each party to pay one half of the valuer's fee; there is provision for the valuer to decide that one party should pay the whole fee if the valuer decides that that party has acted unreasonably.

(3) The form provides that all time-limits must be strictly observed which gives certainty but at the expense of classic time-traps—for both parties.

Different variations of 'notice' rent review could be drafted to eliminate or minimise these disadvantages. Thus the 'time-trap' for the landlord could be eliminated by allowing him to serve a notice at any time after a certain date, but the time-limit on the tenant's response would have to remain in the interests of certainty. However, for reasons outlined below, the statutory system of revision under s 13, which is a not dissimilar process but with attendant advantages, is to be preferred for those periodic tenancies to which that section applies.

(c) *By agreement, valuation in default*

The simple yet classic form of rent review will have much to commend it, namely by providing for agreement on a new rent between the parties to take effect at the specified rent review date, with independent valuation in default of such agreement. Problems of time-limits, forms of notice and other peripheral issues will be avoided. The landlord can approach his tenant by formal or informal means and in many such cases an amicable or acceptable new rent will be agreed. It need then only be endorsed on the tenancy agreement—and then only as evidence of what has been agreed. In the event of failure to agree, then independent valuation can resolve the issue.

Such rent reviews offer a much more informal basis for agreement which is particularly appropriate to the residential tenancy; and the only disadvantage is the expense of a valuer in default of agreement—but that fact may be an incentive to reach agreement, especially if the cost is to be shared. A precedent of this type has been published as Conveyancer Precedent 5-104, see Part Seven, p 726.

Clause 44 of the National Letting Conditions is basically of the type envisaged, save that an element of formality is introduced by requiring a written notice to set the review in motion and specifically envisaging that either party can make time of the essence (for service of such notice or reference to the arbitrator) by later notice. Since either party has power to initiate the relevant steps in the review process, it is submitted that introducing such potentially complex issues into a residential rent review is counter productive (compare *Factory Holdings Group v Leboff International* [1987] 1 EGLR 135). Moreover, the form requires the independent determination to be by an arbitrator and it is submitted that the additional formality and extra expense of an arbitration will rarely be justified in a residential tenancy.

(d) *By indexation*

Superficially, an index-linked rent for a residential tenancy might appear to be attractive. It offers a simple mathematical calculation ensuring that the rental return steadily rises in line with the inflation rate as measured by the Retail Prices Index ('RPI'). One obvious potential disadvantage is the same as that for commercial rent reviews—namely that the RPI measured increase may be lower than the national or local rise in residential rental levels. There are practical problems too. If the increase is to take effect too frequently (eg every month or quarter) there will be the regular time-consuming chore of making the calculation, communicating it to the tenant, and collecting the revised sum. Regular payments through bank standing orders would be difficult if not impossible. For the relatively moderate extra return, it is thought that such regular revalorisations will be not worthwhile. On the other hand, if the index-linked adjustment only takes place every year, the attractions of one of the other forms of rent revision may outweigh the mathematical simplicity of indexation. One suspects that most landlords will distrust the RPI and prefer a greater say in the amount of rent as reviewed.

An index-linked rent clause for an assured tenancy has been published as Conveyancer Precedent 5–99, see p 723, below. It provides for revision on 'every anniversary of this tenancy' and in the interests of brevity does not provide for the abandonment of the RPI.

Indexation may be worthy of consideration in longer term fixed term assured or shorthold tenancies. In such cases, it could be combined with an overriding rent review. This would ensure that, if the index got out of line with residential rental levels, the rent review would restore parity and a new base level for future indexed rises. For discussion of index-linked rents generally, see Chapter 20.

(e) A progressive rent

The simplest way to vary a rent is to avoid rent review and revert to the idea of a progressive rent providing, say, for a 10 per cent increase, compound, on each anniversary of the term. Each of the methods discussed above has one or more drawbacks—uncertainty for the tenant, cost, relative complexity, delay and so on—and however long they may last in fact, the potentially short life of many residential tenancies compared with the average commercial lease emphasises the disadvantages. No pattern has emerged as the dominant mode.

There is some evidence that a progressive rent with annual predetermined increases has proved attractive to companies operating under the Business Expansion Scheme. They will let properties on assured tenancies for a period of 4 years or so with a progressive rent. The crudity of the method, which led to its abandonment for commercial lettings, is set against its administrative simplicity and rough and ready answer to inflation. Tenants who cannot meet the increase, it appears, are readily replaced by others if they leave; if they refuse to pay, the remedies discussed above (p 524) apply. The guarantee of a regularly increasing return over a moderately long period with tax incentives has proved sufficient to outweigh the the lack of sophistication and disadvantages of progressive rents noted in Chapter 3, p 324.

3 Statutory rent review under s 13

As has already been noted, the increases of rent allowed by s 13 of the Housing Act 1988 only apply to statutory periodic tenancies and other periodic tenancies which contain no contractual provision 'for the time being binding on the tenant, under which the rent for a particular period of the tenancy will or may be greater that the rent for an earlier period'. This would appear to cover not only the various forms of rent review already discussed, but also any express differential rent, eg £100 for the first month and £250 thereafter. Landlords should beware of offering initial rent discounts, for whatever reason; otherwise they may be denied the benefit of s 13. Section 13 will, however, encompass most assured tenancies, which are likely to be periodic or for a short fixed term and thereafter from month to month.

The statutory system may come, over a period to commend it in preference to the contractual forms outlined above. Advocates of its use point to various benefits and opponents to some of the drawbacks:

(1) The rent revision will be by a landlord's notice. Though this must be on a prescribed form, there are *advantages* in using a form obtainable from stationers since it should be less likely that errors and omissions will occur. The *drawback* is that experience over the years with statutory forms under the Landlord and Tenant Act 1954, reveals mistakes will still be made and technical arguments about validity and form will be raised.

(2) Regular increases of rent under the section will be possible. There is a minimum gap between rent increases of 1 year—the proposed new rent can only take effect after the first anniversary of the date on which the first period of the tenancy began or (if the rent has previously been increased in this way) after the first anniversary of the date on which the the previous increase took effect (s 13(2)(b)and(c)). Otherwise such notice can be served at any time—there are no 'time-traps'—except for the dilatory tenant who does not refer the matter to the rent assessment committee. Since the prescribed forms will contain a statement of the tenant's right to refer and a warning of the consequences of his failure so to do, the objection to time-traps is of much less weight.

(3) The proposed new rent will take effect automatically, in the absence of a reference by the tenant to the rent assessment committee, at the beginning of a new period of the tenancy specified in the notice (s 13(4)). However, this date must occur after the expiry of the 'minimum period' after the date of the service of the notice. This minimum period is a period equal to the period of the tenancy but it will never be less than 1 month and will be 6 months in the case of a yearly tenancy (s 13(3)). For the usual weekly or monthly tenancy therefore, 1 month's notice is all that is required. Since the notice will have to specify a date at the beginning of a new period, a landlord will only need to wait between 1 and 2 months for his increase—unless the tenant refers the notice to the rent assessment committee under s 14. A notice under s 13 served, say, on 23 January, in the case of a monthly tenancy commencing on the first of a month, could propose a new rent to take effect from the 1 March. The *disadvantage* of the procedure is the requirement of the nomination of a specific date. This introduces an element of technicality similar

to that relating to the common law rules for notices to quit a periodic tenancy.

(4) If the tenant is dissatisfied with the new rent proposed, then at any time before the beginning of the new period specified in the notice the tenant may in the prescribed form refer the notice to a rent assessment committee (s 13(4)(a)). The rent assessment committee will then determine a new rent—that at which the dwelling house concerned might reasonably be expected to be let in the open market by a willing landlord. The detailed valuation directions given to the committee by that section are designed to ensure the rent will reflect true market conditions and some reflect basic concepts which are a standard feature of commercial rent review clauses. Thus there is a disregard of relevant improvements carried out by the tenant (s 14(2)(b) and (3)); the landlord benefits from the disregard of any effect on the rent of the sitting tenant and of any reduction in value which would have been attributable to a failure by the tenant to comply with any terms of the tenancy (s 14(2)(a) and (c)). There is therefore no theoretical reason for landlords to avoid this process. The rent so determined will take effect from the beginning of the new period specified in the landlord's notice—unless it appears to the rent assessment committee that this would cause undue hardship to the tenant (s 14(7)). Only if the rent assessment committee is generous in its interpretation of 'undue hardship' might landlords regularly find that their rent increase under the section is delayed. This optimism, based on an analysis of the section, has to meet the pragmatic *disadvantage* that the new rules will be applied by rent assessment committees which have had a long involvement with settling fair rents under the Rent Acts and who will retain a concurrent involvement in fixing fair rents for existing protected tenancies for some time to come. The consequent fear is expressed that there will be a legacy of a tendency to set allegedly market rents at too low a level. The evidence of comparables, the critics say, will inevitably be patchy and arguably unreliable and the committees will be persuaded to be cautious or in the minds of fiercer critics, restrictive. None of these misgivings may be justified and the authors reject the criticisms implicit in them since they may do injustice to the integrity and professionalism of panel members.

(5) The parties are free to agree a rent change at any time notwithstanding the fact that the statutory procedure has commenced. If the rent assessment committee is already in the process of determination under s 14, then the parties can give written notice that they no longer require such a determination (see ss 13(5) and 14(8)). Section 13(4)(b) also ensures that later agreement between the parties overrides the rent proposed in a s 13 notice. Though such an agreement need not be in writing, it will be wise to have documentary evidence to ensure that one party does not resile from the agreement reached

and then seek to rely on the rent stated in the notice. The *disadvantage*, sceptics would argue, is that if agreement between the parties becomes at all usual then the statutory scheme is either unnecessary or will produce distorted results in the small number of cases where it is operated.

This statutory system, when theoretically analysed, meets most of the principles for a residential rent review suggested at the start of this section. It is straightforward in its operation, certain in its result and should prove to be relatively inexpensive. The giving of notices in a statutory form, the avoidance of privately funded valuation and the lack of any time-traps into which the landlord may fall, suggests that this is a better choice than a contractual notice and counter-notice rent review. There is the added advantage of a degree of balance between the interests of both parties and the issue of rent review need not be addressed in the tenancy agreement. Certainly, a landlord granting an assured periodic tenancy need only adopt his own contractual review if he has clear reasons for so doing. Nevertheless, there is a wariness about involvement in a system still associated with the restraints of the fair rent rules and a reluctance to accept that the Housing Act has brought in fundamental change. There may be a risk of a self fulfilling prophecy in this hostility. If only a few cases go to the committees then atypical results may corroborate doubts. Only experience will prove if optimism is justified.

4   Drafting summary

(*a*) *For an assured periodic tenancy, or one for a short fixed term and thereafter for a periodic term*, there may be some good reasons for relying on the statutory system of rent increase under s 13. The parties to such an agreement can alternatively opt for a contractual review form if they so wish (or if the landlord so insists) and any such form and the rents agreed thereunder will be immune from challenge under the new Act.

(*b*) *For a longer fixed term assured tenancy*, consideration of a contractual rent review will be essential as the statutory scheme is inapplicable until the term expires and the statutory periodic assured tenancy arises. It is suggested that the best solution is to provide for a rent review by agreement with independent valuation in default and thus avoid the problems of notices, counter-notices and time-traps. The issue of cost and delay must be accepted as necessary elements and if these are considered too high a price for achieving periodic review then the cruder but simple reservation of a progressive rent is an option.

(*c*) *For an assured shorthold*, much will depend on the length of the term. For the periods of up to a year (which will probably be the norm) there is much to be said for leaving rent increases to be agreed informally as each fixed term expires. For longer terms, the rent can only be increased during the fixed term by rent review in the agreement. Once again, there is a wide choice of forms of review and the benefits and disadvantages of each are set out above. All rents in assured shortholds, whether fixed in advance or later by a review, can be challenged by the tenant if he considers them 'excessive'. However, there is only one opportunity for this and timing will be vital.

5 Residential tenancies outside the Housing Act 1988

Certain tenancies of residential premises cannot be assured tenancies—see Sched 1 to the Housing Act. Many such categories (eg tenancies of houses with high rateable values, those at a low rent, licensed premises etc) mirror exceptions to the Rent Acts which received some discussion in previous editions since reviews could only be relied on in tenancies outside the Rent Acts.

Now that rent reviews are viable in assured tenancies, it is no longer necessary to explore the boundaries of these exceptions. Even where a tenancy, initially at a low rent (Sched 1, para 3), becomes an assured tenancy by virtue of an increase in rent, the new regime will continue to allow the contractual rent review to operate without hindrance.

Chapter 18

Agricultural Holdings

The vast majority of tenancies of agricultural holdings are subject to the control of the agricultural holdings legislation (the Agricultural Holdings Act 1986 (the '1986 Act')), and thereby the rents of such tenancies are subject to a measure of control. It does not necessarily follow that most agricultural land farmed by persons other than freeholders is covered by the legislation. It is not just that certain tenancies may be beyond the scope of all or part of the statutory provisions, it is rather that owners of agricultural land intending to hand over farming operations have sought to evade the legislation completely. Tenancies may be avoided and some agricultural land falling vacant has been made the subject of partnership agreements (a would-be landlord being a sleeping partner) or other devices—for example, interposing a 'tame' head tenant, often a company controlled by the owner of the land (see Conveyancer Precedent 10–19). For detailed consideration of the agricultural holdings legislation reference should be made to Scammell and Densham's *Law of Agricultural Holdings* or Muir Watt's *Agricultural Holdings*. The discussion that follows is confined to consideration of how far a variable rent may be provided in a tenancy of agricultural land.

1 Definition of agricultural holdings

(a) The statutory definition

An agricultural holding is defined by the 1986 Act as meaning the aggregate of land (whether agricultural or not) comprised in a contract of tenancy which is an agricultural tenancy (s 1(1)); and a contract of tenancy, means an agreement to let or a letting for a term of years or from year to year (s 1(5)). A contract of tenancy for an agricultural tenancy is defined (s 1(2)) as any contract of tenancy relating to land where the whole of the land comprised in the contract is let for use as agricultural land, having regard to the terms of the tenancy, the actual or contemplated use of the land at the time of the contract or subsequently, and any other relevant circumstances. An exception is made for a letting to an employee of the landlord while his employment continues (s 1(1)). 'Agriculture' is not exhaustively defined by the 1986 Act but by s 96(1) it includes horticulture, fruit growing, seed growing, dairy farming and livestock breeding and keeping, the use of land as grazing land, meadow land, osier land, market gardens and nursery grounds and the use of lands for woodlands where that use is ancillary to the farming of land for other agricultural purposes.

(b) Exceptions

A tenancy must be in substance a tenancy of agricultural land to be within the scope of the Act and must meet the requirements of s 1(2) outlined above. Where the dominant purpose is non-agricultural the Act will not apply and under a not dissimilar definition in the Rent (Agriculture) Act 1976, s 1, it was held that the employment of a gamekeeper to rear pheasants for sport was not an employment in agriculture (*Earl of Normanton v Giles* [1980] 1 All ER 106). However, the definition is otherwise a broad one and little is allowed to escape the net of the Act; if a letting is an agricultural holding at the outset, the court will be reluctant to find that it has subsequently moved into the 1954 code by a gradual change of emphasis in the mode of use: *Short v Greeves* [1988] 1 EGLR 1. By s 2 lettings for a period of less than a year and, importantly, licences to occupy agricultural land (which would qualify as agricultural holdings if they had been yearly tenancies) are to take effect as if they were agreements from year to year, and are, therefore covered by the Act. By s 2(3) grazing and mowing agreements are excluded from the Act; and ministerial approval prior to an agreement otherwise covered by s 2 will prevent such agreement becoming an agricultural holding.

By virtue of s 4 and s 5 of the 1986 Act, there are exceptions to s 3 (which provides generally for security of tenure and continuation of tenancies). These apply where the tenant dies (s 4) or where the parties, prior to the grant of a tenancy for a term of not less than 2 and not more than 5 years, agree that s 3 shall not apply and obtain ministerial approval to such agreement. The other important type of agricultural tenancy excluded appears to be one for a term greater than a year but less than 2 years (*Gladstone v Bower* [1960] 2 QB 384) as a consequence of a lacuna in the statutory framework (See Scammell and Densham, pp 25–7), although this exception is strictly construed. Thus in *Keen v Holland* [1984] 1 WLR 251 a tenancy agreement granting a tenancy for a period of 13 months, but signed a few days before the term was due to expire, was a tenancy for less than a year since a grant of land cannot take effect retrospectively. Apart from these exceptions, any consideration of inclusion of a form of variable rent in a tenancy of an agricultural holding must take account of the impact of the control of rent contained in s 12 and Sched 2 of the 1986 Act.

2 Control of agricultural rents (s 12 and Sched 2)

(a) Statutory arbitration

The object of s 12 is to enable rents to be adjusted at reasonable intervals to take account of changed circumstances. Either party by notice in writing served on the other may demand a reference to arbitration to determine the rent properly payable at the date of reference (and not at the next termination date at which the reviewed rent takes effect—see Sched 11, paras 1(3) and 31 for the date at which the arbitrator is taken to have been appointed). The arbitrator then has power to increase or reduce the rent payable or direct that it continue unchanged. The new figure is payable from the 'next termination date' (s 12(2)) after the date of reference upon which the tenancy could have been determined by notice to quit.

(b) Fixed term tenancies

The scheme of s 12, providing as it does for reference to arbitration payable from the next termination date, ie the next day following the date of demand on which the tenancy could have been determined by notice to quit, has the effect of excluding fixed term tenancies from its scope, since a notice to quit is inapplicable in such circumstances and therefore there is nothing upon which the machinery of s 12 can operate (*Edell v Dulieu* [1924] AC 38). This is so notwithstanding the inclusion of such tenancies within the security of tenure provisions of the Act by s 3. In only two circumstances may the arbitration provisions of s 12 be invoked in fixed term tenancies:

(1) In all cases, at the expiration of the term, by virtue of s 3 (which provides that a fixed term tenancy is to continue as a tenancy from year to year, terminable by at least 1 year's notice at the expiry or anniversary of the term). Such notice is deemed to be a notice to quit (s 3(2)) enabling the machinery of s 12 to operate.

(2) In those fixed term tenancies that contain a 'break-clause' providing for an option to determine the tenancy before the expiration of the term by a notice to quit there is a day on which the tenancy can be determined and thus s 12 is applicable (*Edell v Dulieu*); the tenancy might have been determined at that date and it is not necessary that this in fact happened: *Wallingford Estates v Tench* [1954] EGD 22. If such 'break-clause' gave only one party the option to determine, a difficult question of construction would arise as to whether the other party was able to invoke arbitration under s 12. The better view would seem to be that he could.

Consequently, in all other fixed term tenancies except the two instances outlined above, the parties are free to stipulate for their own rent review provisions untrammelled by the provisions of s 12. An example is *Million Pigs Ltd v Parry and Another (No 2)* (1983) 268 EG 809 (fixed term lease of 21 years in 1972 with a rent review clause effective every 3 years). (See further p 541, below.)

(c) The statutory procedure

The salient features of the arbitration procedure are as follows:

(1) The scheme was designed and largely operates as a code of variable rent for tenancies of agricultural holdings. It is an essential element of a code that bestows a substantial measure of security of tenure upon agricultural tenants.

(2) The initiation of the procedure rests solely with the two parties to the tenancy and if they choose not to apply, or fail to take the proper action, the existing rent and contractual provisions as to the rent payable will continue.

(3) The section is designed to ensure that increases of rent under the section cannot occur more frequently than once every 3 years. In particular:

    (i) no reference to arbitration can be demanded under s 12 in any circumstances where a resulting increase or reduction of rent would take effect from a date earlier than 3 years from the commencement of the tenancy (Sched 2, para 4(1)(a)); so during this period the contractual arrangements as to rent will be fully effective;

    (ii) no reference to arbitration can be demanded so as to cause a resulting increase or reduction within 3 years of 'the date as from which there took effect a previous increase or reduction of rent (whether made under this section or otherwise (Sched 2, para 4(1)(b))'. The latter provision has especial import when considering the effectiveness of the inclusion of the parties' own variable rent provision in the lease (considered on p 544, below).

(4) The statutory formula for determination of the rent in force until 1984 appeared to ensure that the rent of the agricultural holding was periodically set at the open market value that the landlord would have been able to obtain had the security of tenure provisions of the Act not prevented him from obtaining possession. However, the new rental formula adopted in 1984 now omits direct reference to the 'open market', though the rent is still to be that at which the holding might reasonably be expected to be let by a prudent and willing landlord to a a prudent and willing tenant taking into account all relevant factors. These phrases point the arbitrator back towards a market letting, though the authors wonder what, if anything, 'prudent' adds to 'willing' bearing in mind the interpretation of willing

parties by Donaldson J in *F R Evans (Leeds) Ltd v English Electric Co Ltd* (1977) 36 P & CR 185. The important disregard of scarcity value introduced in 1984 (now Sched 2, para 1(3)(a) of the 1986 Act) provides a qualification to the market objective, by providing that the arbitrator shall disregard 'any element of the rents in question which is due to an appreciable scarcity of comparable holdings available for letting on such terms compared with the number of persons seeking to become tenants of such holdings on such terms'. The disregard of scarcity in the formula may now be less significant than formerly given changes in the market. Section 13 of the 1986 Act gives the right to a landlord to increase rent where improvements have been carried out by him in the circumstances set out in s 13(2) of the Act—particularly, for example, at the request of or in agreement with the tenant.

The new rental formula was the result of a desire to remove scarcity value from the rent formula and thereby ensure that arbitrally determined rents were not unduly inflated by the level of rents obtained for first lettings in a market hit by a dearth of land available for fresh lettings. The requirement of *appreciable* scarcity and the presence of all the other elements in the rent formula suggests that the valuation impact will not be as great as the similar provision in the old Rent Act legislation; but this disregard, together with the disregard of 'marriage value', does explain the removal of the direct reference to open market rent.

It appears that both the operation and interpretation of the formula has caused difficulty and met with dissatisfaction (see Law Com 162 (Cm 145), para 4(64)). To take one example, the rent is to take account of 'all relevant factors'; but the factors include 'the current level of comparable *lettings*' (our emphasis). This is, no doubt, meant to refer to comparable property, but the wording used invites problems. Could an institutional landlord with a standard lease argue that all its other lettings were suitable comparables regardless of location or rental value? Could a tenant, faced with rents for undeniably comparable properties, seek to show how the tenancy agreements in question differed sufficiently so as not to be a comparable? We doubt if either argument would be allowed but the exact meaning of a comparable letting is an open issue. For a detailed consideration of the rent formula, reference may be made to the standard texts previously referred to at p 532 above.

(5) The procedure of fixing the rent is that of independent arbitration. This allows expert evidence and submissions by the parties in the usual way. The appointment of the arbitrators is now by the President of the Royal Institution of Chartered Surveyors rather that the minister, thereby giving the statutory procedure a further link to contractual rent reviews. (For further details of the procedure, reference may be made to Muir Watt, pp 43–66).

3   Effectiveness of the statutory code

It appears that the provisions of s 12 are allowed to take effect on a wide scale, although in the overwhelming majority of cases the amount of the new rent payable is agreed by negotiation without necessity for arbitration. No doubt the original provision that the properly payable rent shall be that at which the holding might reasonably be expected to be let in the open market has contributed to the general satisfaction (among lessors, at least) with the mechanism, for the rent fixed by an arbitrator will not be dissimilar to what he would arrive at if appointed under a rent review clause containing similar provision. Assuming that rents determined by arbitration do not depart too far from those available at first letting, then the well tried procedure is likely to continue to enjoy general confidence of the parties. The tenant has the benefit not only of security of tenure but also of (usually) at least a year's notice of a possible rent increase since demand for reference to arbitration must be to determine the rent payable from 'the next termination date' on which the tenancy could be determined by notice to quit (s 12(4)). A full year's notice to quit is the relevant period expiring on the renewal date for the tenancy (s 25). This will normally result in a period of any time between 1 and 2 years before a revised rent can operate as the result of a demand for arbitration. In practice, a demand for arbitration must be made during the second year of any review period to ensure the earliest possible increase at the end of the third year. (The only possible exception is where a shorter period of notice to quit can be given under s 25(2), the most important of which for the purpose of s 12 would appear to be a notice by a tenant to a subtenant (s 25(2)(c)).) It is not clear if a prior agreement allowing for a short period of notice for possession for a non-agricultural purpose (s 25(2)(b)) thereby allows a similar short period of notice for s 12 but it has now been decided that if a notice is given for a period shorter than 12 months, the parties are then free to agree that it is to take effect as a valid notice—*Elsden v Pick* [1980] 1 WLR 898. The normal 12–month period allows time for negotiation in an attempt to agree a figure, though either an arbitrator must have been appointed by agreement between the parties or an application must have been made to the President of the RICS for the appointment of an arbitrator. This is the result of s 12(2) and on the latter point effectively overrules *Sclater v Horton* [1954] 2 QB 1 and *Master & Fellows of University College, Oxford v Durdy* [1982] Ch 413. Nevertheless, the reasoning in those cases, where it was held that an arbitrator had to have accepted his appointment for the reference to be effective, could still apply to the appointment by agreement limb under s 12(3)(a). Provisions as to arbitration, which are contained in

Sched 11 to the 1986 Act, state that the award shall be made within 56 days of appointment.

In practice, rent changes by agreement are the most common method of adjustments in agricultural rents; but it is the provisions of s 12, and the prospect of arbitration in default, that provide the incentive for a new rent to be proposed and agreed. Only an intractable difference of opinion will normally necessitate a full arbitration procedure under the Act. A suggested deed to provide for an increase in rent agreed instead of proceeding to an arbitration is provided in EFP (5th ed), Vol 2, Form 36. Such an increase will by Sched 2, para 4(1)(b) be an increase in rent made otherwise than under the section preventing a further reference taking effect within the 3–year period.

It is likely that for the majority of agricultural holdings within the Act's code the use of the statutory system to vary rents will be perfectly adequate.

4 'Contracting out' of the statutory code

This section considers whether it is possible to 'contract out' of the statutory code and thereby enable substitution of a form of variable rent desired by the parties. The new rent formula of s 12, since 1984, and the removal of scarcity value, may provide an incentive for agricultural lessors to substitute their own rent review if this can be done.

(a) Direct contracting out

For some time it was not clear whether it was possible for both parties to an agricultural tenancy to provide in the tenancy agreement that the provisions of the Agricultural Holdings Acts were not to apply and thereby 'contract out'. If this were possible, it could only be done with respect to some of the Acts' provisions, for some sections expressly state that 'this section shall have effect notwithstanding any agreement to the contrary' or by some similar words (see eg s 5(1), s 24 and s 78(1) of the 1986 Act repeating similar wording from the Agricultural Holdings Act 1948). It was argued that since other sections were silent (as is s 12) then it must be possible to contract out of those provisions. This argument came up for consideration in the House of Lords in *Johnson v Moreton* [1980] AC 37 on the interpretation of the similar provisions in the 1948 Act. The case concerned a lease of an agricultural holding for 10 years from 1 January 1967 that provided, inter alia, that the tenant would not serve a counter-notice (after the landlord's notice to quit) under s 24 of the 1948 Act. The tenant did serve such counter-notice in response to a notice to quit and thereby claimed the benefit of the security of tenure provisions of the Act whereas the landlord sought to uphold the validity of the clause in the lease and possession for a breach of that covenant. In holding that the clause in the lease was unenforceable and the attempt to contract out had failed, their Lordships advanced three reasons:

(1) The argument from silence carried no weight, for two other sections of the 1948 Act expressly permitted contracting out (s 12, s 30(2)) thus cancelling the idea that by the silence of the section contracting out was implicitly allowed (at 49G, 57G, 65E and 73A).

(2) The language of s 24 (now s 26 of the 1986 Act) is mandatory and therefore expressly makes any agreement to the contrary unenforceable. Reference was made to the words 'notice to quit *shall not* have effect' (at 51B and 58F) and this requirement could not be overridden by any principle of freedom and sanctity of contract nor by maxims allowing the renunciation of a term introduced entirely in favour of (in this case) the tenant, for here the public had an interest in the nation's farms and therefore this was not a waiver of an entirely private right (at 59A and 67H).

(3) The policy and objective of the 1948 Act, when looked at as a whole (involving as it did an element of protection of the nation's food supplies), made it clear that the Act was intended to benefit all tenant farmers and was applicable to all tenancies whether created before or after the Act came into force. The wording of the section, with its mandatory words, was consistent with this overall policy, thereby indicating that contracting out was not allowed. To have decided otherwise would have tended to defeat the object of the statutory provision and, moreover, create anomalies and 'curious quirks' in application of the Act as a whole (at 52G, 61D, 73B).

These reasons of their Lordships were directed to one particular section (s 24; now s 26 of the 1986 Act) but have been set out in full as, it is submitted, they apply with equal force to s 12 and Sched 2, which contain the provisions for variation of rent:

(1) Section 12 is equally silent as to contracting out and thus the rejection of the idea that silence allows contracting out in *Johnson v Moreton* is directly relevant.

(2) The section contains the equally mandatory words 'the landlord or tenant may . . . *demand* a reference to arbitration . . . and on a reference . . . the arbitrator *shall* determine the rent properly payable' (our emphasis).

(3) In a period of steadily increasing land and rental values it might be argued that s 12 arbitration is of as much benefit to the landlord as s 24 (now s 26) (giving security of tenure) is to the tenant and may be waived as a benefit by that party. Just as the argument failed in *Johnson v Moreton* with respect to the benefit to the tenant so, it is submitted, would it fail in relation to s 12.

Thus, it is suggested that any provisions that *directly* purported to exclude either party from making a demand for arbitration under s 12 may be unenforceable in the same way as the security of tenure provisions were held virtually inviolate in *Johnson v Moreton*.

(b) Indirect contracting out

In a fixed term tenancy, since the use of s 12 is not possible during the term, the parties indirectly contract out of s 12 for the duration of the term whether they wish to or not, and they must make their own arrangements for review of the rent; though a statutory review under s 12 can be obtained at the expiry of the term. For a long time, agricultural leases for fixed terms were only occasionally found; but after the 1984 changes to the statutory rent review formula, there appears to be a shift in opinion in favour of fixed term agricultural tenancies. In such fixed terms, provision for a contractual review can be and should be made. A number of forms of variable rent may be considered appropriate in such cases:

(1) A progressive rent may be stipulated that gives figures that rise each year by an amount fixed in the lease.

(2) Agricultural leases are particularly suited to a type of royalty rent (an adaptation of the old corn rents) by the taking of rent in kind whereby the basic rent can be supplemented by an additional rent calculated as a certain percentage of the tenant's revenue from the net yield of a crop per acre of the 'revenue from dairy produce . . . expressed in terms of gallons of milk', a phrase found in a lease considered in *Bolesworth Estate Co Ltd v Cook* (1966) 116 NLJ 1318. In this way the rent will increase (or decrease) according to the productivity of the farm, which may be a formula that finds favour with both parties since a landlord will get increased rent as prices paid for agricultural produce rise and the tenant will have some compensation in the eventuality of a poor year or bad harvest. However, such extraneous factors as, say, milk quotas may distort revenue which would then distort the rent.

(3) The rent could be indexed for the term of the lease to the more usual indices or perhaps to the Ministry of Agriculture's 'Table of Newly Determined Average Rents', thus enabling the rent payable to keep in line with the annual increases. Such a clause would have to be carefully drafted since the tables, which have shown increases of 40–50 per cent in some years, reflect change over a minimum of 3 years since a previous change and thereby would indicate a lower annual rate.

(4) There is no objection to a rent review clause in an agricultural lease for a term of years; indeed, the lease in *Johnson v Moreton*, a 10–year term,

contained provision for review after 7 years. Another example is *Million Pigs Ltd v Parry*, previously referred to on p 535.

It may be that, in some instances, a landlord may wish to stipulate for a fixed term rather than a yearly tenancy to enable a contractual rent review to be adopted. Thus, a rent review clause might offer the prospect of a better financial return than arbitration under s 12. For example, there would be no elimination of scarcity value so a review might lead to a higher figure. To take another example, a different procedure could be adopted that is more advantageous to the landlord, such as providing that he should suggest a new rent in his notice initiating review and that such a figure is to be applied unless the tenant objects and sets the review mechanism in motion. Whatever the form of variable rent contracted for, at the end of the fixed term, reference to arbitration under s 12 will become possible by virtue of the statutory continuance of the tenancy as a tenancy from year to year.

Tenancies within s 5(2), ie for a term of not less than 2 and not more than 5 years, excluded from the security of tenure provisions of s 3 by prior agreement, will be fixed term tenancies and a rent review or other variable rent can be included.

Finally, one possibility must be considered—namely, whether the inclusion of rent review clause might effectively exclude the provision of s 12 even in tenancies from year to year. This arises because of the words in Sched 2, para 4(1), which prevent a reference to arbitration within 3 years of the date from which 'there took effect a previous increase or reduction of rent (whether made under that section or otherwise)'. Therefore, on the face of it, a rent review clause that provided for a review to *take effect* every 3 years (or, preferably, every 2 years 364 days or any lesser period) would mean there was never a period of 3 years after which an arbitration could be commenced. It would be necessary to draft the review clause to ensure that the review of the rent always 'took effect' within the 3–year period, perhaps by imposing strict time-limits. If such a provision was successful in evading s 12 it could be attractive for landlords because they could then adopt whichever of the rent review clauses or methods appear to be most appropriate.

However, doubts must be expressed as to whether s 12 is effectively ousted by this device. In the *Bolesworth Estate* case a county court judge held that it failed. In that case, the rent was of the royalty type and varied annually but the judge decided that such changes, calculated by reference to a formula, did not prevent a reference under s 12. The short report might indicate that the case was decided on the narrow ground that the rent was fixed by the agreement and it was only a change in the datum figures by which the rent was calculated rather than an 'increase of rent' for Sched 2, para 4(1). If this is so, it would be open to argue that a review clause (unlike a royalty rent) was an increase under the agreement. However, the judge also felt that the tenant's contention that the agreement had in effect meant the parties had contracted out of s 12 was 'contrary to the general intention of the Act which was clearly that the parties should, upon failure to agree, be entitled to resort to arbitration'.

A single county court decision in a royalty case is by no means conclusive. Though a strong case can be made by arguing that a rent, reviewed according to the original tenancy agreement, is an increase or decrease of rent, it is submitted that a court would hesitate before allowing the free operation of a rent review clause that would result in reference to arbitration under s 12 being forever excluded. If however s 12 was excluded the way would be clear for a widespread use of review clauses in yearly tenancies in preference to s 12 arbitration.

5 Using a variable rent in conjunction with s 12

Even in tenancies from year to year that are subject to s 12 inclusion of an appropriate form of variable rent is worthy of consideration.

(a) First 3 years

The provision of Sched 2, para 4(1)(a), which prevents a reference to arbitration taking effect in the first 3 years of the tenancy, allows continued operation of contractual rent provisions in that period. A progressive or royalty rent might be most appropriate over such a relatively short period of time. To include a review clause (eg on an annual basis) would be a relatively expensive operation and, whatever the period between reviews, it will only be worthwhile if it is effective after the initial 3–year period. As has been suggested, it may be possible to ensure that reference under s 12 is precluded.

(b) In subsequent years

Such variable rents will remain effective after the initial 3–year period until one party demands a reference to arbitration. So, if both parties are happy with the arrangements made there will be no problem. Even if one party does demand a reference it will be usual to agree the new rent, and the parties will be free to agree a rent that will vary in the manner they previously agreed or in any other way. If, however, they fail to agree then the question arises as to whether the arbitrator has power, when finding the rent properly payable, to award a form of variable rent.

(c) Variable rent in an arbitrator's award

In Sched 2, para 1(1) the arbitrator is directed, when fixing a rent properly payable, to 'take into account all relevant factors, including (in every case) the terms of the tenancy (including those relating to rent)'.

This means an arbitrator can have regard to the fact that the contractual tenancy includes a variable rent directly as a basis for a similar provision in the award he makes. Moreover, there is nothing expressly to prohibit an award including new provision for variation. Further, the arbitrator will be able to take account of the submissions of the parties, either or both of whom may request the inclusion of the variable rent they think suitable. The heart of the matter will be whether the arbitrator decides that the rent which is properly payable is one including provision for variation. We suggest this may well be the case when land rentals are increasing steadily and inflation is at a high rate. A prudent and willing landlord may insist on some protection—even for a 3-year period—and a prudent and willing tenant may be happy to pay, especially if the variation is of the royalty kind and linked to the money value of milk or crops produced, for he will know that the rent will only increase as a percentage of his gross income. A variable rent may be the open market rent, and the fact that the original tenancy agreement included one may be evidence of the fact. It would appear anomalous if an arbitrator did not have this power when a similar power was first taken in the case of business tenancies (*Re No 88 High Road Kilburn* [1959] 1 WLR 279) (on almost identical wording to that of Sched 2, para 1(1) and later confirmed by statute in the Landlord and Tenant Act 1954, s 34(1), as amended). It is submitted that this power is available and thereby the case for the inclusion of a variable rent in the original agreement is immensely strengthened especially after the 1984 amendments now embodied in the 1986 Act; for the more usual it is to include provision for variation in an agreement, the more likely the arbitrator will conclude that this is a part of the open market rent that is properly payable. Judicial approval of this approach was indicated in *Fawke v Viscount Chelsea* [1980] QB 441 at 453 on construction of similar words in the Landlord and Tenant Act 1954, s 34(1), where it was stated that variation of the determined rent may result if supported by evidence that this would be the manner in which the holding might be let in the open market by a willing landlord to a willing tenant.

6 Agricultural partnerships

As mentioned, partnership arrangements are sometimes used to avoid the agricultural holdings legislation. Obviously, if there is no 'tenancy' there can be no question of a variable 'rent'. Instead of rent the would-be landlord usually receives the first £x of the profit. (See Conveyancer Precedent 10–19, clause 7.) This clause could be amended to allow for an increased share to keep abreast of inflation (eg by indexation or as a first percentage of profits). It might be more difficult to 'review' the sum, for any clause providing for an increase to an 'open market rent' might be a strong basis for showing that the whole 'partnership' was a sham and in reality was a tenancy. Indexation to one of the agricultural rent indices should avoid that risk, and have achieved a measure of wide acceptance not accorded to other rent indices.

Chapter 19

Rent Reviews and a Rent 'Freeze'

In 1972, statutory controls on rents of business, agricultural and residential premises was introduced in the United Kingdom. The control—the 'freeze' as it became known—ended in 1975 and has not been repeated to date though a not dissimilar period of rent freeze was in force in New Zealand from 1982–84. Any such rent freeze in the future will have a similar effect on the operation of rent review clauses, and other methods of varying rents and in such circumstances the cases reported in the aftermath of these freezes will proably be of relevance. The earlier experience with control has resulted in the introduction of provisions in leases to cover the contingency of rent freeze, none of which have been put to the test in reported litigation to the authors' knowledge.

In this chapter, we briefly summarise the case law and consider the lessons from past experience for the drafting and consideration of proposed clauses to deal with any rent freeze.

1 The form of past statutory control

A brief summary of the past forms of temporary rent control will enable a better understanding of the drafting issues.

(a) United Kingdom

The statutory control of rents in the United Kingdom was derived from two statutes: the Counter-Inflation (Temporary Provisions) Act 1972 and the Counter-Inflation Act 1973 (which superseded the former). Each merely gave power for the making of control orders by statutory instrument and a series of such orders was the means of detailed control. The initial orders under the 1972 Act—the Counter-Inflation (Agricultural Rents) Order 1973 (SI No 1489), the Counter-Inflation (Business Rents) Order 1972 (SI No 1850), and the Counter-Inflation (Rents) (England and Wales) Order 1972 (SI No 1851)—just imposed a standstill. No rent was payable at a rate exceeding that payable on 5 November 1972, which was the day preceding that on which the legislation was announced. This was later termed the 'standard rent' and was extended to the rent last paid in the preceding year where no tenancy subsisted on 5 November 1972. Increases for improvements were still permitted, and a rent payable on the given date included one where the amount was fixed later. The standstill extended to rents on the re-letting of premises already let on the 'base' date, but no control was imposed on rents under new lettings.

The orders made under the 1973 Act in relation to business rents continued the approach of the 1972 Orders but added requirements (such as control of rents under 'superior tenancies', rules for apportioning or aggregating rents where premises were let consisting of part of larger premises or of a number of smaller premises, where in both cases there was a standard rent for those other premises) and permitted 'proper' adjustments to reflect changes in lease terms on renewal or change of use. The second 1973 Order for agricultural rents, however, went beyond the pattern set by the 1972 and the first 1973 Order by permitting one-half of any increase in rent payable over that of 5 November 1972 (either through agreement or the arbitration process) to be recovered. A similar relaxation was achieved in the Counter-Inflation (Business Rents) (Transition) Order 1974 (SI No 1294), which permitted rent to be recovered up to open-market levels at 5 November 1972 (if higher than the actual rent then payable). The order contained a formula, closely modelled on the provisions of Part II of the Landlord and Tenant Act 1954, by which the open market rent was to be established (art 5). The assessment was to reflect the unexpired length of the term on a transition date, determined according to a table to the order by reference to the date on which the restriction on rent first operated in fact to restrict recovery, and disregards equivalent to those in s 34 were to apply. Such market rents were to be agreed or, in default, settled in court. Incidentally, it is worth noting that the draftsman indicated that the rent should reflect all the other terms of the lease 'other than as to the rent payable . . . but including any provisions for varying the rent periodically'. This indicates an official opinion that a provision for review on all the terms of the lease other than as to rent may be equivocal as to whether the review provisions are themselves part of the provision as to rent—an issue which later led to the *Arthur Young* saga and the guide-lines in the *British Gas* decision (see p 333).

It cannot be stated with certainty how common the implementation of these provisions proved to be. The Counter-Inflation (Business Rents) Transition Order 1974 was made in July to come into force on 1 November, but the decontrol orders of 1 February 1975 ended control, upon service of 6 weeks' notice, on the later of 19 March 1975 or expiry of notice. For superior tenancies, decontrol was universal on 19 March. So, after something just under $2\frac{1}{2}$ years the rent freeze ended.

(b) New Zealand

The New Zealand legislation was contained in the Rent Freeze Regulations 1982 and 1983. Like the United Kingdom legislation, 'the rent payable' in respect of any letting was frozen at a particular day and the rent during the freeze was in force was not to exceed the rent so payable at that date. Under both the 1982 and the 1983 Regulations any contractual rent reviews could take place or be completed but where its effect was to increase the rent, the increase was not to take effect until the date of decontrol.

2 The effect of the controls

(a) Statutory impact on rent review

This simplified outline of two past periods of rent freeze indicate that during their currency landlords were denied the benefits of provisions for review or other revisions of rent. Increased rents on negotiated or court-ordered renewals could also not be recovered, and indeed the various United Kingdom orders expressly provided for a right to recover over-paid rent by deduction from future payments (as well as in other more usual ways). What the statutory wording did not do was to prohibit the operation of review procedures, as distinct from implementation by recovery of the adjusted rent.

This conclusion can readily be drawn from various parts of the different orders, especially art 9 of the Agricultural Rents Order of 1972. This reads:

'Nothing in this order shall render unlawful any agreement or determination increasing a rent to which this order applied, but, subject to the provisions of this order, no increase of any such rent provided for or determined by agreement or arbitration shall have effect in respect of the standstill period.'

Whilst periodic review of farm rents by agreement or arbitration is a statutory feature of the system for agricultural holdings, this provision illustrates a clear intention in general not to interfere with the establishment of a new rent level, but to prevent recovery of the increase.

The New Zealand legislation was more specific:

'Where, at any time during [the relevant period], the rent payable in respect of any property falls due for review under any Act or in accordance with the terms of any lease or agreement, that review may take place or be completed, as the case may require, but, where its effect would be to increase the rent payable, the increase shall not take effect . . .'

Consequently, a review could proceed but the increase was delayed.

(b) Judicial interpretation

The approach adopted by the English courts to this legislation was 'broad and business-like' so that the standard rent payable was not necessarily the technical legal rent. Thus the Court of Appeal in *Secretary of State for Social Services v Rossetti Lodge Investment Co Ltd* (1975) 235 EG 501 determined as the standard rent a sum provisionally agreed before 5 November 1972 even though embodied in a lease executed after that date. A point that weighed heavily with the court was the fact that the tenant was in occupation under a statutory continuation of the old tenancy and (but for the agreement) a new tenancy would have been ordered by the court before the control came into effect. In New Zealand, by way of contrast, a new rent agreed under a right to renew the lease but where the new lease was not to take effect until after the freeze came into force could not be recovered: *Westminster Flats Ltd v E N & E M Law Ltd* (1983) New Zealand Conveyancing Bulletin 89. Judicial determination to interpret the legislation so that it 'cut across contractual relationships as fairly as possible' (per Scarman LJ in the *Rossetti Lodge* case) was also demonstrated in other decisions (see eg *London Transport Executive v Gray Brothers (East Finchley) Ltd* (1981) 259 EG 629 and the cases there cited).

A brief summary of the propositions established in the cases litigated under these former rent freezes may assist in interpreting any future legislation and in drafting.

(i) The machinery of rent review can normally proceed even if the legislation is silent as to the issue: Compton Group Ltd v Estates Gazette Ltd (1978) 36 P & CR 148

The rent was to be reviewed there to the 'fair rack rent . . . payable'. The judge in the court below (Goulding J), finding that the 1973 Business Rents Order was in force at the relevant review date, held that its effect was to render the 'fair rack rent' unascertainable, so the rent continued for the review period at its former level. The Court of Appeal overruled him and decided that the review should proceed, the statutory control not preventing such a procedure. In the context of the lease, 'fair rack rent . . . payable' referred to the full annual value of the holding and not the rent originally reserved and the current maximum recoverable under the rent freeze.

(ii) The 'rent payable' for the purposes of the freeze means the rent is legally recoverable at the relevant date

The primary meaning of the words 'rent payable' is the rent required by the terms of the lease to be paid and the primary meaning of the words 'rack rent' is a rent which represent approximately the full annual value of the premises—Stephenson LJ in the *Compton Group* decision at 162 relying on *Re C R Sawyer and Withall* [1919] 2 Ch 333. It was this meaning to which the Court of Appeal gave effect. Although distinguished in the *Compton Group* case, the case of *Newman v Dorrington Developments Ltd* [1975] 1 WLR 1642 was there cited to support the statement that 'a legislative limit on rents, which exists at the time a lease providing for a revaluation of the rent is executed, may give such words ['payable rent'] in the lease that meaning [of 'recoverable rent']' (per Stephenson LJ at 162). Similarly, *Rawlance v Croydon Corporation* [1952] 2 QB 803, a Housing Act case, showed that 'a rack-rent may in a statutory context mean the full rent which the landlord is permitted by the law to receive', but it, too, was distinguished in the *Compton Group* case.

Subsequent to the *Compton Group* decision, 'letting value', for the purposes of application of the Leasehold Reform Act 1967, was held in *Manson v Duke of Westminster* [1981] QB 323, to include a decapitalised premium as well as the maximum rent recoverable under the Rent Acts. Doubts were cast on *Gidlow-Jackson v Middlegate Properties Ltd* [1974] QB 361 in which it was held that letting value means rent lawfully recoverable. Presumably, the reasoning in the *Compton Group* case should also have been applied to the determination of market rents under art 5 of the Counter-Inflation (Business Rents) (Transition) Order 1974 during its short existence. We see no distinction between 'market rent' in a general sense and 'rack rent'.

(iii) Provided that there was liability for the rent at the relevant date, it will not matter that the amount payable has yet to be determined

This was stated in the 1972 Order ('the rate at which rent was payable whether or not determined as to the amount') and in the *Rossetti Lodge* case (above) this assisted in the conclusion reached in that case. In New Zealand, it was held that where a rent review date fell due before the rent freeze came into force, the 'rent payable' was the rent contractually payable even if not yet ascertained even if the review had not been commenced at the relevant date: *Transport (Nelson) v Johnson* [1984] 2 NZLR 355; *Peter Fortzer v Ryan* (1983, New Zealand).

(iv) Where there is an indexed linked or turnover rent, 'rent payable' will be the rent so payable in respect of the period which included the relevant date

It will again not matter that the actual figure cannot be ascertained until the gross sales are known: *MLC Assurance Co Ltd v Takapuna Hardware Supplies Ltd* (1983) New Zealand Conveyancing Bulletin 90. However, there will always be potential problems with subsequent periods; it is likely that it will be held that the legislation overrides the formula in the lease so that the maximum recoverable during the freeze is the sum payable at the relevant date: *Fletcher Trust and Investment Co Ltd v Guthrie's Pharmacy Ltd* [1984] 2 NZLR 419.

(v)   A review occurring during a freeze may result in a lower rent since the existence of the freeze will be a valuation factor: Compton Group Ltd v Estates Gazette (1978) 36 P & CR 148

The review would reflect the existence at the relevant date of the 'freeze' (and, indeed, in that case, the knowledge of its pending relaxation). It will be apparent from what has been said at p 240, above that the fact that the control ended in March 1975 would have to be ignored (even though the review would be much later) and the parties would have to indulge in the theoretical exercise of trying to establish what the market at the review date thought of the prospects of eventual repeal. In the same way, rents determined after the relevant date, but fixed in relation to a review date before the freeze was announced, would have to be fixed as if no control had been imposed. However, in so far as the market was responding to the prospect of control, that factor had to be retrospectively allowed for. The political nature of the imposition, relaxation and removal of this type of control makes market sentiment very speculative. The judgments in the *Compton Group* decision stress that the imposition of rent control overtook, as it were, the provisions for review and was not in prospect when the lease was drafted, agreed and made.

3   The drafting responses to a rent freeze

(a)   In early leases

Various solutions to cope with a rent freeze were evolved by the drafters of leases during and after 1972-75. It must be remembered that the Court of Appeal's decision in *Compton Group Ltd v Estates Gazette Ltd* (1978) 36 P & CR 148 on the effect of the imposition of control was not given until May 1977, and even the judgment at first instance was dated 13 April 1976; so it was necessary long before then for individual draftsmen to form a view of what the statutory constraints might do to the particular variant of rent review adopted in any new lease. Some may have favoured the view that was taken in the High Court; some the one that emerged from the Court of Appeal; and yet others may have reached different conclusions. The particular drafting response was likely to follow from the assessment so made of the effect of the Act. Furthermore, the drafting was being done at a time of the emergence in the cases of the distinction between 'machinery' and 'option' types of review clause and before the emergence of the presumption that time was not of the essence, which continued until the *United Scientific* decision. Accordingly, allowance must be made for these factors in assessing the efficacy of any clause drafted in the 1972-75 period, or afterwards for that matter. To date, moreover, there has been no occasion to litigate any of these clauses, and it is most unlikely that a clause in a lease of the last month of 1972 or the first few months of 1973 would have fallen to be operated before March 1975; so none of the clauses have been put to the test.

(b) In new leases

The first decision is to decide whether to include any such provision at all—ie 'Is it wise to include 'anti-freeze' provisions in new leases to guard against the risks of future control?' This is a question that receives different answers from the published precedents, and from leases in general use. The political climate in both countries which have experimented with rent freeze have since been philosophically opposed to any similar ventures for the future so the need for such clauses can be questioned; and the draftsman will, in any event, inevitably have to face the difficulty of attempting to deal with potential legislation of unknown scope. However, governments and governmental philosophies can change—sometimes very quickly indeed—and the inclusion of provisions to cover any future rent freeze, at least in longer leases, is still frequent. Even if no control is in force or in prospect when a new lease is granted past experience makes future control a possibility the parties should bear in mind. The Joint Working Party of the Law Society and the Royal Institution of Chartered Surveyors, however, included no such provision in any version of the Model Forms. The omission is not commented on in the Background Notes, but it is understood that the reason for the decision was that it was felt the possible variations in future statutory intervention made it difficult to devise and recommend any one comprehensive formula to cater for the contingency. The discussion above shows the validity of these arguments, but the authors do believe that, nevertheless, the attempt should be made, at least in the longer terms.

(c) Drafting considerations

(i) Postponing the ascertainment of the review

Though past rent freezes have not prevented the review machinery operating, an early response which is now standard practice is to provide that if at the relevant date statutory control of rents prevent the operation of a rent review provision the landlord is free to operate it when the control is lifted or appropriately modified—and by reference to an interim review date (see (ii) below). In early clauses, with the emphasis on time-limits then common, this aspect of postponement and the substitution of a new timetable would be covered in some detail. These early clauses did not always distinguish fully between statutory prohibition on invoking the review process and prohibition on recovering the adjusted rent, and the consequence of postponing the review in different circumstances must be considered.

The reason to postpone is because if the review goes ahead without postponement the rent will be fixed, under the usual type of formula, in a market depressed by the existence of the known restriction of unknown future duration on what landlords can recover and thus on what tenants will pay. New lettings, as has been shown, were not subjected to this bout of rent control in 1972–75, but the alternative of taking an assignment of existing premises at 'frozen' rents would be present in the mind of the hypothetical willing tenant. Unless there was compelling evidence that tenants in the market were offering 'two-tier' rents (ie one rent until controls were lifted and then a higher rent), it would hardly be open for a referee to fix such a rent and rents reviewed during a freeze will almost certainly be depressed by the statutory controls. The rent so determined in the unusual context of the freeze will hold good throughout the whole review period, even if the restrictions are lifted at an early point during that period. From this point of view, therefore, postponement of the review is likely to benefit the landlord even where the legislative controls only deny recovery of increased rent not its assessment, unless the landlord faces a downward plunge in rents after decontrol, a most unlikely event.

A simplified approach commonly found and embodied in EFP (5th ed) Form 22, Second Schedule, para 5 (see p 676), is to allow the landlord to proceed with any review that has been prevented by the service of a notice once the restrictions on recovery of any rent increase has been removed or modified.

(ii) Postponement of the relevant review date

From the landlord's point of view, he will wish to ensure that the relevant review date under a postponed review is also postponed to the end of the freeze so that the rent can be valued in a market free of control. Consequently, modern precedents allowing notice of review at the end of the freeze provide for the landlord to specify the review date (Rosscastle Letting Conditions, Form 1, clause 7.5) or state the the review date is the date of the expiry of the notice (EFP (5th ed) Form 22). The latter is preferable since it both covers the eventuality of failure to state a date and prevents the landlord choosing a date beyond the expiry of the notice.

(iii) Fitting in the postponed review

The draftsman should check that the postponed review fits with the rest of the review clause. In particular:

- Consider the 'notional term' of the lease to be valued at the postponed review. Different results will flow from the particular wording used and its interaction with other parts of the rent review clause.
- Ensure that the date and timing of any subsequent reviews are not affected (see EFP (5th ed) Form 22, para 5.2.1.). For, if the postponement triggers off a like postponement of all later reviews, the result may be to deprive the landlord over the residue of the term of some of the increased rents he expected under the review

provisions in the lease. Conequently, the rent determined under the postponed review will only run for the period from decontrol to the next regular review date.

(iv)   Timing the postponed review

The timing issues are whether to allow the landlord to give a notice at any time after the end of the freeze and, secondly, whether the initiation of that postponed review should coincide with the date at which the reviewed rent is to be assessed (see (ii) above). These are interrelated issues and the tenant will be concerned to ensure that the landlord cannot either delay the review beyond the end of the freeze to a more favourable time or specify a review date that is most favourable to him. From the tenant's aspect, the better position will be to make time of the essence for the instigation of the postponed review by notice (Form 22 contains such an optional provision) and to ensure that the date for valuation of the reviewed rent is the date that that notice expires. The landlord will prefer to avoid any such strict time-limit which runs the risk of losing the review and opens the door to possibility of a dispute about the date from which time runs (is 'the date of the restriction being removed'—Form 22—the date relaxation is permitted or the date of any required notice to the tenant under the decontrol provisions?). If the landlord successfully insists on having no time-limit the tenant may wish to bargain for the protection of initiating the postponed review himself.

(v)   Express disregard of the freeze

Normally, this will not be required if the review is to be postponed to the removal of restrictions. However there is an argument for such a disregard if the review is not to be postponed and will therefore take place at the normal time and, if there is a rent freeze, in the abnormal context of an operative restriction on rents recoverable, lasting for an uncertain time. A disregard of the freeze could be difficult to operate in fact where no open market could be shown to exist and even new lettings could be affected by the availability in the market of premises with frozen rents. A bolder approach found in some leases requires the effect of any control, or any statutory restriction relating to rent, to be ignored in the review (see eg *Beaconscross Ltd v Norris* (1989) (unreported) 'there being disregarded . . . all restrictions whatsoever relating to rent . . . contained in any statute..'). This may give rise to problems as already discussed when all the market comparables are affected by the rent freeze restrictions.

(vi)   Statutory control on the process of review

If control were to be imposed in future on invoking the review process itself, it is to be hoped that the legislation would provide for the consequences of the prohibition, at least where the lease contained no express provision. If that were not done, then it is suggested that the more relaxed attitude to time-limits deriving from the House of Lords decision in the *United Scientific* case might provide a solution by implying a postponement. Nevertheless, express provision for postponement may avoid these potential problems and further attempts to cope with this unlikely event are not recommended.

(vii) Later recovery of sums frozen?

One possible approach to the imposition of control is to provide that any 'excess' rent rendered irrecoverable by the 'freeze' would be, as it were, held in suspense and become payable as a matter of contractual obligation on the ending of the control. The authors have no knowledge as to whether this device was widespread at the time of the last freeze but art 8 of the Decontrol Order of 1975 effectively countered it by providing that any agreement made before the order came into operation was ineffective to permit subsequent recovery of any 'frozen' element. It is safe to assume that a similar precautionary provision would form part of any future package of statutory control, so we do not recommend this approach.

(d) Available precedents

The drafting in EFP (5th ed) Form 22 has already been referred to and this precedent is reproduced in Part Seven, p 676 below. The Rosscastle Letting Conditions (in Ross, *Drafting and Negotiating Commercial Leases* Form 1, para 7.5) is a similar but simplified version of the same approach save that there is no optional 'time of the essence' provision relating to the giving of the notice initiating the delayed review and the rent review date is that specified in the landlord's notice rather than the date of the termination of the notice. Both these modifications potentially favour the landlord.

An earlier example of a rent freeze provision is in Conveyancer Precedent 5–57 reproduced at p 684. This precedent does not postpone the operation of the rent review which will operate in the normal way, albeit subject to the valuation problems alluded to above. This does involve settling a 'depressed' rent (ie one affected by the legislative prohibitions, even though it may be known at the later date that they have ended). The precedent deals separately with restraints on recovery of rent (clause (j) providing that the lessee shall pay rent at the highest level recoverable under the restrictions) and any restrictions (if any) on carrying out reviews. The effect of the second provision in that Form (clause (k)) would then allow a postponed review with the usual notices initiating review under that form once the restrictions are lifted.

4   Operating a review in a time of rent freeze

If control relates only to rent recoverable, then in the absence of any postponement provision in the lease, the review machinery can, and normally should, be operated normally. Delay in operating it carries the problems and possible risks associated with delay discussed in Chapter 5. Moreover, a delay serves little point, if the post-review-date *events* are generally inadmissible in evidence or argument (see a fuller discussion of admissibility of such evidence in Chapter 7, p 238).

The precedents referred to and many clauses in leases will allow recovery of rent at the highest level recoverable under the statutory controls. If however, the statute requires some action on the part of the landlord, the lease is unlikly to override that specific statutory requirement: *London Transport Executive v Gray Bothers Ltd* (1981) 259 EG 629.

5 Index-linked and turnover rents and 'freeze' legislation

Various techniques of index-linking are discussed in Chapter 20. 'Freeze' legislation restricting recovery of increased rent would not prevent the operation of 'automatic' indexation, although the sum payable will be held during the operation of the statutory restrictions. However, the impact of the statutory controls on, say, the Retail Prices Index, would affect the performance of the Index as against what it might otherwise have registered. Such legislation would be unlikely to prevent the service of notice to claim an index-linked adjustment where that approach has been adopted. It is unlikely that control directed to the very exercise of the review process would be so worded as of itself to interfere with the operation of the second type of indexation, and it would be irrelevant to try to prevent the first, as a matter of mere calculation. If the drastic step of direct control of review were to be taken, however, it is possible that adjustment on an index-linked footing activated by notice would be expressly dealt with too (especially as forms of index-linking are common in other areas). Precautionary clauses could be added to cover this contingency, but they would not be easy to draft and we have not found any example in practice. Indeed, as has already been pointed out, the prospect of direct governmental interference with prices, rents and other incomes is one of the factors against indexation as a medium of rent adjustment and inflation proofing.

The New Zealand decisions of *Fletcher Trust and Investment Co Ltd v Guthrie's Pharmacy Ltd* [1984] 2 NZLR 418 and *MLC Assuirance Co Ltd v Takapuna Hareware Supplies Ltd* (noted at p 544, above) reveal that the impact of a rent freeze on both index linked and turnover rents can be particularly difficult to apply and even be harsh on one or other party. This will be so, for example, when a freeze is imposed on a turnover rent in a cyclical industry at a low point in sales. The gross rent recoverable under the legislation may be limited to that 'payable' during the period the freeze was imposed notwithstanding the fact that sales in later periods are very much higher and would normally be reflected in a higher rent.

Part 5

Variable Rents other than Rent Review Clauses

This last part of the text covers those forms of variable rent other than the review clause. *Chapter 20* deals with indexation of rents, particularly to the Retail Prices Index but also including the form of rent review clause which combines rent review with indexation to a notional standard property as defined. *Chapter 21* examines two distinct but related concepts, namely the turnover rent (or 'percentage lease') where the rent varies in line with the turnover of the lessee's retail business and the equity rent where the rent in a head lease varies in line with the rents received or receivable by the lessee from sub-lettings.

Chapter 20

Indexation of Rents

The concept of indexing a rent reserved in a lease is, at first blush, theoretically attractive to the party seeking protection against the effect of inflation during the currency of a lease. After all, such provision allows the parties to provide for the rent to rise automatically on a scale commensurate with the index figures, and thus the intrinsic value of the rent reserved is maintained. A pattern similar to a rent review can be set up with the rent being adjusted in line with the index every 3 or 5 years but, if desired, this may be done more frequently and even each time a payment of rent falls due; whereas a rent review is only feasible at periodic intervals (which will rarely be more frequent than every 3 years). The problems of giving notices, negotiating a new rent, and the expense of arbitration or valuation are avoided.

Yet, though indexation has been sanctioned and precedents published, indexation of commercial rents is exceptional in the United Kingdom. One reason for this involves the inability of most index-linked rents to react to fluctuations in property values that are not associated with inflation; another is the difficulty of financial planning when the amount of rent due in the immediate future is always, to some degree, uncertain. Indexation may, however, be appropriate in some instances and there may be room for its use in conjunction with reviews. Certainly, indexation of rents is an accepted feature of commercial life in other jurisdictions, so, although a growth of index-linked rents at the expense of the familiar review clause is unlikely at present, it is not an impossible prospect, especially if circumstances should change. Indeed, there are periodic suggestions that it is time to reconsider appropriate indexation on the basis that the machinery of revaluation or arbitration is comparatively more expensive (eg [1979] Conv 236-9); such calls are presently still falling on deaf ears.

The form of indexation that is increasingly common is rarely recognised as such and is certainly not simpler or cheaper than the usual rent review. This involves the creation of a local property index, for example 'standard warehouse accommodation' on an industrial estate, and indexation of the particular rent to that standard. This is a combination of rent review and indexation requiring determination of the rent of the standard accommodation and indexing the sum so agreed or determined.

1   The principle of indexation

The idea of indexation is relatively simple. The monetary obligation to pay rent is made to vary in line with increases (or, possibly, also decreases) in an index chosen by the parties to the lease. The index selected by the parties will be one that measures (for example) the level of domestic price inflation. Thus, by increasing the rent in line with the index, the lessor achieves some protection against a fall in the value of money. The central feature of an indexation provision is, therefore, the index selected by the parties. It needs to be reliable, readily available and identified with certainty in the lease so that the calculation of the additional amount payable can be made at the appropriate time. A properly drafted clause will set out the method of computation, make provision for both changes in the index (and the method of its presentation) and any cessation of publication.

As detailed in Chapter 2, indexation of rents (and, indeed, monetary obligations in other forms of contract) has been known since at least the 1930s both in this country (*Griffiths and Diggens Ltd v Great Universal Stores Ltd* [1953] CPL 657 concerned a 1932 lease) and in Australia (see (1931) 4 ALJ 315). Precedents were in print soon after the last war (1948) 12 Conv (NS) 322; and they also find a place in current publications (EFP (5th ed) Vol 22, Forms 137 and 138; EFP (4th ed) Vol 11, p 302, Precedent 2:13; and Conveyancer Precedents 5–11 and 5–11A; some of these are reproduced in Part Seven).

Indexation of a rent, provided (as always) it is properly drafted, is quite acceptable in law and certainly satisfies the now diluted requirement that a rent be certain. Challenges to index-linked obligations failed in both *Stanwell Hotel Co Ltd v Leslie* (1952) 26 ALJ 35 (Australia) and in the *Griffiths and Diggens* case, and the principle was applied without question in *Blumenthal v Gallery Five Ltd* (1971) 220 EG 31. In the *Stanwell Park* case, where the challenge was to the principle of indexation, it was said that there is nothing to prevent parties to a contract adopting a fixed figure as the primary monetary expression of liability and then varying the liability by providing that more or less money must actually be paid as the index varies—since the index only measures the actual liability contracted for.

2   Choosing an index

Though index number calculations began as early as 1707 by the then Bishop of Ely, it is only in the last 100 years or so that official, comprehensive and reliable indices have been published on a regular basis (see Crowe, p 97). Though in theory the parties to a lease could elect to index the rent payable to any one of the large number of index numbers regularly published in this country or abroad, in practice there is little choice because the index must be suitable for the task in hand (namely, reducing as far as possible the distortion produced by inflation on the bargain made by the parties and embodied in the lease). In his book on index numbers, Crowe points out that an index is only as good as the components on which it is based and postulates that these should satisfy certain conditions (p 16). They should be relevant to the primary purpose of showing either the general rate of domestic inflation or, perhaps more specifically, the average increase in rental values. They need to be representative and reliable so that the parties can be assured that they enable the index to achieve the purpose for which it is designed. Finally, the component parts of the index need to be comparable, able to cope with the inevitable changes that occur over a period of time and remain up to date. In particular, such considerations mean that the choice of an index is limited.

(a) Retail Prices Index

The index most frequently chosen, and adopted in the published precedents, is the Retail Prices Index (RPI). It is published monthly by the Department of Employment and seeks to record changes in the level of prices most people pay for the goods and services they buy. It includes a broadly based and representative selection of about 600 prices of food, clothing, fuel, household goods, housing costs, transport and services divided into 80 sections of expenditure. These are given a relative importance according to a formula aimed at reflecting the average patterns of spending of most households in the country. The RPI is, thus, a consumer price index of the type often used as an indicator of the rate of inflation. Indeed, the Department of Employment recognises that the most important present function of the RPI is to act as a general measure of domestic price inflation. A concise but comprehensive guide to the RPI can be found in an article in (1987) *Employment Gazette* 393.

The RPI, as a well-established index that has been carefully compiled to ensure it is reliable and representative, offers substantial advantages to the parties to a lease who are seeking to index rent over a period of time:

(i) It is published regularly and the figures are readily available

The prices are collected on a Tuesday in the middle of the relevant month. The RPI is published on the Friday $4\frac{1}{2}$ weeks later (ie the middle of the following month) in a press release and appears in full in the *Employment Gazette* at the beginning of the next month. *British Business* also publishes the monthly RPI figures. For example, the RPI figures for 14 February 1989 were published on 23 March 1989 and appeared in the April edition of the *Employment Gazette*.

(ii)   It is likely to continue indefinitely

As an official index, cessation of publication of the RPI is improbable. Fundamental changes in its structure are unlikely to be implemented since it has assumed a significant function as the nation's barometer of inflation. Indeed, there was significant opposition to suggestions that there be major alterations in 1979. Certain recognised changes have been made to the RPI and will be made no doubt in the future, such as the alteration of the base date. Such alterations can be predicted and a draftsman can and should provide for such contingencies.

(iii)   It is flexible

The presentation and publication of the RPI allows it to be used for annual, quarterly or even monthly adjustments in the rent paid—though movements in rents as often as every month would be exceptional and complicated to operate.

The main disadvantage of the RPI is that it is a consumer price index and as such a lessor can only hope to achieve the preservation of the purchasing power of the rent reserved. It does not ensure that he will continue to receive the open market rent, for variations here depend upon factors additional to that of inflation. Commercial rents are notable by their absence from the components of the RPI—understandably so, since the average consumer is not immediately concerned with them— but it does mean that movements in the property market have no direct impact on the RPI figures. Moreover, users of the RPI should be aware that it may be affected by matters other than purely economic ones. Thus, consumer prices can be subsidised or artificially restrained for political reasons or be modified substantially by fiscal measures. Thus, the RPI for April 1980 showed an 8.5 point rise, 2.75 points of which were the result of tax changes in the 1980 Budget.

Other indices, similar to the RPI, that might be used are, eg the Taxes and Prices Index, introduced with some flourish in August 1970 but now largely ignored, and the Producer Price Indices (first published in August 1983, replacing the Wholesale Prices Index), all of which are regularly compiled and published by the Central Statistical Office on a monthly basis and appear in *British Business*, a weekly publication of the Department of Trade and Industry. The Taxes and Prices Index, which consistently shows rates of increase below that of the RPI, is hardly likely to appeal to landlords; though the former Wholesale Prices Index has, to the authors' knowledge, been used in some commercial leases subject to an overriding rent review (see p 578, below) it is not thought that the current Producer Price Indices are widely adopted.

(b)   A property rent index

In theory, an index reflecting movements in the market rent of commercial properties ought to be more suitable than the RPI for indexation of rents since it should produce a result more in line with current market rental values at any given time. Unfortunately, no such index can be recommended for this purpose. Most of the property indices that are compiled are privately produced and based on the records of the larger firms of valuers (perhaps the best known are the Investors Chronicle/Hillier Parker Rent Index first published in October 1977, see (1978) 245 EG 209 and (1978) 247 EG 449 and the Jones Lang Wootton Property Index constructed around a typical institutional portfolio of 142 properties (see (1983) 266 EG 954). Any that are independent of the principal agents are relatively limited in scope (eg the RICS/Institute of Actuaries City Rents Index); which was discontinued in 1986 only to be revived in 1988 [1988] 06 EG 58).

A comprehensive property index commanding wide acceptance does not appear to exist at the present time, and the difficulties that such an index might encounter may be illustrated by reference to the initial problems faced by the privately produced indices (see (1977) 244 EG 358; (1978) 264 EG 455). Criticisms were directed at both the choice of base year (1965, the base year for the Investors Chronicle Index, might be thought to be a time when the market was in a slump) and at the selectiveness of their approach (the one basing itself on standard properties and the other on prime commercial properties). They must be used with care; and, it must be remembered, they are certainly not designed to be used to index the rent in a lease but rather as a service provided by the leading agents to their clients. These property indices have been useful in general terms (eg by illustrating that commercial rents in late 1981 failed to keep pace with inflation (see (1981) 260 EG 863) with an even slower growth rate a year later (see (1982) 264 EG 762); by comparison, Central London office rents doubled in 1987, a growth which vastly outstripped inflation in the same period—(1987) 284 EG 1154).

These pioneering indices may one day lead to a more comprehensive index, and hopes have been expressed that this could be achieved. Immense difficulties would have to be overcome. In truth, such an index would have to be a series of indices, distinguishing between shops, offices and industrial property, prime sites and secondary locations and between different areas of the country. As a neat illustration of our point, a table was published in February 1983, quoting apparently comparable rents for a series of locations within 100 miles of, but not including, London. The quoted rents per square foot varied from £15 per square foot in Slough to £4.50 in Maidstone. More recently, 1987 rises were measured at 45.4 per cent in the central City but 87.3 per cent in Holborn/Marylebone area. Any comprehensive index would certainly need a focal point, probably on 'official' and recognisably impartial source, in order to command wide acceptance. The Royal Institution of Chartered Surveyors has been suggested as a suitable body to have the co-ordinating role but such a step would involve considerable (perhaps prohibitive) cost and demand a close degree of co-ordination to produce the necessary evidence ((1978) 247 EG 618). A possible mode for such a property index is shown by the Agricultural Rent Indices, which achieve a degree of accuracy and relevance, though the impact of the Agricultural Holdings legislation means the scope for indexation of agricultural rents is very limited.

In 1984, it was announced (271 EG 330) that four large firms of surveyors planned to produce a new 'Super-Index' of property performance. This is now published annually as *The Property Index* and is compiled as at 31 March in each year. With a sample size whose capital value was £4.1bn in 1988, the aim was to provide 'a reliable measure of performance', with sub indices for different property types. The scheme has the RICS blessing (but not participation at present) with an independent body to collect and process data and thus satisfy confidentiality. It is not designed to be used as a property rent index and, even if so used, the method of compilation of the index would only allow annual changes to the rent in any lease which was linked to the index.

(c) Creating a local property index—rent review by reference to hypothetical premises

In the absence of a suitable existing property index, there remains the possibility of constructing and creating a very 'local index' within the terms and framework of the lease. This device will be useful where the land or premises are unusual or otherwise out of the ordinary so that a standard review clause is inappropriate because of the lack of comparable lettings. Examples are unimproved land to be used as a golf course (*Wallace v McMullen* [1988] 2 EGLR 143), an industrial building whose features are not standard (*Standard Life Assurance Co v Oxoid Ltd* [1987] 2 EGLR 140) or a hypermarket with terms of letting not normally found in the market (*Tesco Holdings Ltd v Jackson* [1990] EGLR 153 where there was a normal review clause for which comparables could not be found resulting in a valuation dispute). The essence of the procedure is that a standard property is defined in the lease and this notional property is subject to a normal rent review valuation; subsequently, a pre-determined algebraic formula is applied to fix the rent of the subject premises. This formula may alternatively relate to a rental value per square foot of letting area by first determining the market rent per square foot of the 'yardstick' premises. In this way, there is a standard rent review but the indexation copes with the perceived difficulty of the lack of exact comparables. A precedent has been published as EFP (5th ed) Form 122, but this form is, of necessity, only an outline for guidance on which the details of the particular case will have to be grafted.

A good illustration is *Standard Life Assurance Co v Oxoid Ltd* [1987] 2 EGLR 140 where the draftsman of the lease attempted this form of indexation, which created, in effect, a local property index solely for the purposes of the lease in question. This was apparently done because of the unusual nature of the premises which were ten times the size of the other units on the industrial estate and (particularly) contained over twice the proportion of office space. The parties were able to agree at the time of the lease that 65p per square foot was the 'standard' rent for single storey industrial accommodation in the locality; and the 'lease rent' reserved was at the rate of 95p per square foot. So, the review clause provided for the lease rent to be increased by the same proportion—in other words, having ascertained the rent for standard accommodation, as defined, the rent was increased by multiplying by 95 and dividing by 65. In effect, the lease combined standard rent review and indexation to determine the rent—first the review to an open market rent of 'standard accommodation'; then a mathematical indexation with that rent ascertained as the denominator.

The dispute arose on the definition adopted of standard accommodation, but there is no reason why this form of indexation should not be used provided there is a very clear definition of the 'standard accommodation' to be valued. The drafting points to bear in mind are:

(1) The Court of Appeal decision in the *Standard Life* case shows that the premises which are to provide the 'standard accommodation' or index to which the rent is tied must be defined with great particularity so that a surveyor is in no doubt as what is to be valued. It is likely that disputes will follow if this is not done. In *Lansdown Estates Group Ltd v TNT Roadfreight (UK) Ltd* [1989] 2 EGLR 120 the rent was to be 140 per cent of the 'Standard Warehouse Rent'. Once again, this form of review was because the defendant tenant wanted a warehouse built to its own specifications and with a larger than average yard area. The definition of the 'standard warehouse' failed to clarify the extent of the yard area—was it the standard area or the actual area? On the construction issue, the judge concluded that a standard unit of accommodation would have the (actual) larger area of yard so that the rent for the premises required a higher base rent for that element and the formula then left the tenants paying 140 per cent of that sum. The tenant's claim to rectify the lease on that issue (arguing, in effect, that they were paying for the larger yard twice over) was rejected.

(2) A decision must be made as to whether the terms of the lease are to apply to the notional standard accommodation—just as in reviews to a freehold capital valuation (*Wallace v McMullen*) or with ground

rent reviews (*Basingstoke and Deane BC v Host Group Ltd* [1988] 1 WLR 348)—for some of the terms may be inappropriate and it may be questionable whether the *Basingstoke and Deane* assumption (that it is to be implied that the notional letting is on the terms of the actual lease) will be appropriate. The *Lansdown Estates* case might suggest that this form of rent review is one to which it will not be assumed that the terms of the lease or the actual state of affairs applies for the parties have chosen to value a notional property quite distinct from the actual premises.

(3) The appropriate index linking must be established in the lease and the parties must be satisfied that the differential will stand the test of time. Changes in market demand may result in one or other of the parties repenting of the bargain he has made.

(d) Rate of exchange for sterling

The London stock-market is provided with a rate of exchange for the pound sterling at the close of business for each trading day and thus produces an index of the value of sterling against other currencies. In *Multiservice Bookbinding Ltd v Marden* [1979] Ch 84, a clause indexing the repayment of capital sums and interest due under a mortgage to the rate of exchange between the Swiss franc and the pound sterling was upheld and an argument that such an approach was void on the grounds of public policy was rejected. This decision would seem to confirm that a rent may be made to vary in a similar manner. Until the *Marden* case, it could have been argued that indexing rents to currency values might be struck down on the authority of *Treseder-Griffin v Co-operative Insurance Society Ltd* [1956] 2 QB 127, where the lessees were required to pay the yearly rent of £1,900 by equal quarterly payments 'either in gold sterling or Bank of England notes to the equivalent value in gold sterling'. The lawfulness of a 'gold clause' in a domestic transaction was doubted in no uncertain terms by Denning LJ (as he then was). However, the decision was strictly on the basis of the construction of the clause; and in that lease the reference to a fixed sum of £1,900 (when even at the date of the lease the selling price of £1,900 worth of gold sovereigns was over £3,300) and to 'equal quarterly payments' led the majority to construe the reddendum of the lease as fixing a rent of £1,900— the clause merely indicating alternative modes of paying that sum. There is, moreover, nothing in the judgments of Morris LJ or Harman J to prevent the price of gold, or a rate of exchange, being used as a standard of value—indeed, Harman J was of the view that even the clause in *Treseder-Griffin* could be construed this way. Significantly, Lord Denning MR, while discussing inflation in the later case of *Staffordshire Area Health Authority v South Staffordshire Waterworks Co* [1978] 1 WLR 1387, referred to 20 years' experience of continuing rampant inflation and considered that the views he expressed in *Treseder-Griffin* may have to be revised (at 1397, 1398). Since, therefore, as Browne-Wilkinson J pointed out in the *Marden* case (at 104), there is no difference between revalorisation by reference to the price of gold or indexing to the value of the Swiss franc and indexation to any other yardstick, indexation of rent to price of gold or foreign currency is as valid as any other index-linked obligation.

Whether or not parties to a lease would be wise to agree to rent to be indexed in this way in view of the uncertainties of currency movements is more debatable, for currency values are not only subject to fluctuating economic pressures but can also be altered for political reasons. Indeed, although the Swiss franc index used in *Marden* is often thought of as demonstrating a highly attractive indicator, the movement in the rate of exchange, from 12 Swiss francs to the £ in 1966 (September) to just over 4 francs to the £ in 1976 (October) was less than the increase in the RPI over the same period from 117.1 to 366.6. Experience in 1983 has further demonstrated the lack of congruence between relative values of particular currencies and other economic indicators, which may be said to be the strongest reason to be distrustful of such an index for rent purposes (for an example of the use of indexed currency escalation clause in a charter-party, see *Agip SpA v Navigazione Alta Italia SpA* [1984] Lloyd's Rep 353).

(e) The capital value of the property

Indexation of mortgage loans to the underlying capital value of the property offered as security has become quite popular (see Conveyancer Precedent 7–22 and the decision in *Nationwide Building Society v Registrar of Friendly Societies* [1983] 1 WLR 1226) and could theoretically be used for indexing rents, permitting a constant return reflecting that proportion of capital value which the base rent bore to the then value. However, the problems of re-valuation of the capital value may be substantial, especially where the value in some way reflects rental potential, and perhaps costly. The draftsman must be alert to ensure that the capital valuation basis and assumptions (if any) are clear. Unlike a standard rent review, it will not be appropriate to assume the existence of the lease or any obligations which arise thereunder but any assumptions as to the state of the land or property and as to planning or development should be stated. Failure may result in a dispute as to the capital valuation basis from which the indexation is derived. An example of the problems is the lease litigated in *Wallace v McMullen* [1988] 2 EGLR 143 which provided for 7-year reviews of rent in a 99–year term. The land had been demised in its agricultural state with the object that the land should be laid out for use as a golf course. The assumed capital value of the land at the date of the lease, with permission for the development, was stated in the lease and the reviewed ground rent was to be the same percentage increase over the rent originally reserved as the percentage increase in the capital value of an equivalent and comparable area of land at the date of the review. No doubt a standard rent review clause was considered inappropriate because of the difficulty if not impossibility of finding suitable comparable lettings. The dispute arose because the valuer was to assume that the notional land to be valued had 'similar rights and obligations' as the actual land. It was held that this only brought in the rights and easements granted by the lease and not all the covenants applicable as between a landlord and a tenant. For the use of capital value as a valuation method in ground rent reviews see Chapter 13, p 470.

(f) Residential rent indices

Residential rents could be linked to one of the house price indices— eg that of the Nationwide Anglia Building Society introduced in 1989; but rental values in a particular area will bear little relation to fluctuating capital values which may fall while rental values remain buoyant.

3 Drafting index-linked rents

When the parties to a lease agree to index link the obligation to pay rent, the draftsman as always must choose provisions and language most suited to the property and transaction in question. In so doing, the precedents in EFP (5th ed) Forms 137 and 138 or Conveyancer Precedents 5–11 and 5–11A may offer some guidance and some of these precedents are reproduced in Part Seven. Amendments have been made or suggested to these published forms and may be desirable. Clause 2.2 of Form 138 provides for reference to the RPI in verbal language; following the advice of Hoffman J in *London Regional Transport v Wimpey Group Ltd* [1986] 2 EGLR 41 a revised clause is suggested (in (1988) 39 *Law Society's Gazette* 40) which links the rent to the index by an algebraic formula. Conveyancer Precedent 5–11 **has** been improved since first publication and Conveyancer Precedent 5–11A is a variant of Conveyancer Precedent 5–11; references made below to Conveyancer Precedent 5–11 will be appropriate for Conveyancer Precedent 5–11A also unless otherwise stated.

(a) Basic rent

The starting point will always be the sum that the parties agree for the rental period prior to first revalorisation. This basic rent, which will be reserved in the usual way and stated as the rent for the initial period will form the point of reference for the indexation of the rent for the future periods (see Conveyancer Precedent 5–11, clause 1; Form 137, clause 4(1)).

(b) Variable rent

The variation in the rent alongside the index may be achieved in one of two ways. It may either be reserved as an additional rent (the approach of Form 137) or the basic rent may be multiplied by a variable factor calculated according to movements in the index (as in Conveyancer Precedent 5–11 and *Kelly's Draftsman*, Form 14, also reproduced in Part Seven). The former method can ensure that a fall in the relevant index (at the present time unlikely with the RPI but quite possible for a rent linked to the value of a foreign currency against sterling) will not reduce the rent below the rent first reserved, whereas use of the variable factor approach requires express provision if it is desired to prevent a fall in rent below the original figure. However, neither procedure would operate to prevent a fall in rent for a third or subsequent period after an earlier rise in the index to a figure greater than that first reserved but lower than that payable for the immediately preceding period though it is equally likely that express provision will be made. Thus, both clause 4 of Conveyancer Precedent 5–11 and clause 4 of the Second Schedule of Form 137 provide that, on revalorisation, the rent, if not greater than that previously payable, shall be deemed to be the same as the amount payable for the immediately preceding rental period. A fall in the rent cannot occur if such provision is included. It is, however, important to provide whether the future calculations revert to the actual index figures or proceed thenceforth as if the rent so substituted, to prevent a fall in rent, had in fact reflected a different figure for the index from that published.

It has been held that a 'proportion' is not confined to a meaning of a portion or a part but may mean a comparative relation or ratio. Consequently, a percentage or fraction in excess of one can be a 'proportion' within the terms of the lease: *Stylo Barrett Properties Ltd v Legal & General Assurance Society Ltd* [1989] 2 EGLR 116.

(c) Periods between revalorisation

The intervals between revalorisation may be as short (or long) as is desired. Where the rent is to be varied in line with the index only every 3 or 5 years, indexation of a rent becomes a substitute, and perhaps a poor substitute, for a rent review. More frequent adjustments are more effective in securing to the landlord the value of the rent originally reserved, but at the cost of attendant uncertainty as to the exact amount of rent payable for the immediate future. Thus, Form 137 provides for quarterly adjustments (and the lessor has to give notice of the additional rent due each quarter); Form 138 is designed for annual change. Different approaches in drafting may be appropriate according to the length of the period both as regards the relevant index figures to insert in the lease and as to suitable provisions catering for the cessation of publication of the index. An example of an 'indexed rent review'—that is reviewing the rent every 7 years by reference to the RPI—can be seen in the lease considered in *Costa v Georghiou* (1984) 2 May, unreported, CA (but see report in (1985) 1 *Professional Negligence* 201). The clause originated from a 1964 head lease and would be unusual today.

(d) Reference to the index

Most indices adopt a fixed-base or chain-base system whereby a date is chosen and the published index numbers reflect changes from that date. The RPI base date is at present 13 January 1987 (when the RPI figure was taken as 100; it was previously 15 January 1974 and 17 January 1962). It is not necessary to refer specifically to this base date in the lease, though if it is done the correct date should be checked as a change in the present base may have occurred.

The reference that must be inserted is the index figure, relevant to the date of commencement of the lease, that the parties choose to correspond with the basic rent. If the RPI is used, this could be either the figure for the month in which the lease is executed, or the average monthly figure for, say, the 3 months or the 12 months immediately preceding the date of the lease. The choice may depend on the period between revalorisation. Where this is at intervals of a year or more an average monthly figure for the preceding calendar year or relevant 12–month period may be more appropriate. It will have the advantage that the seasonal trends or monthly movements unrepresentative of the underlying trends are largely eliminated. Conveyancer Precedent 5–11 adopts this approach. However, at times when inflation is running at annual rates of 15 per cent or 20 per cent or more such averaging of figures may have the effect of reducing the rent payable from that which would have prevailed had the latest figures been taken. Form 137 prefers the alternative mode by providing that the base figure to be inserted into the lease shall be that for the month preceding the execution of the lease. This form is particularly suitable where each payment of rent (due quarterly) rises in line with the index, since the very regularity of rises will reduce the impact of any seasonal or unusual variation in the index. It is less reliable in Form 138, which provides for annual adjustments but the increase is only linked to the preceding monthly figure. Conveyancer Precedent 5–11A also adopts this approach, referring to 'the Index of Retail Prices last published' prior to the start of the relevant year (adjustments to be made annually). *Kelly's Draftsman*, Form 14 refers to the index figures on the first day of specified months. Given the timing of collection of data and of publishing of the RPI, as explained at p 561 there is little point in giving a day of the month, and, whilst quite accurate, a reference to a middle Tuesday would probably prove quite mystifying to the average landlord, tenant or adviser.

It is advisable to ensure that the index figure or figures on which the revalorisation depends will be available and published by the time payment of the revised rent falls due. Though it may not be essential for this to be done, since it is now clear (contrary to old belief) that the full amount of rent due need not be known with certainty at the date when it becomes payable (*United Scientific* [1978] AC 904, 935, 947, 964), practical difficulties will thereby be avoided. The lessor will not have to wait beyond the due date for payment of the rent nor will the lessee be in the position of not knowing the rent due for the current period. In particular, conflict with express provisions in the lease that presuppose prior publication of the index or payment on the due date will be avoided. Particular care is required for references to the RPI and it is by no means certain that Conveyancer Precedent 5–11 ensures that the index figures are available by the due date. The more recent Forms 137 and 138 are better in this respect since the original base figure is to be from the month preceding the grant of the lease; and each quarterly revalorisation is based on a similar preceding figure, but this does not guarantee availability.

Thus, the additional rent under Form 137 is calculated by reference to 'the Increase as at the month preceding that quarter day' (clause 4.3.). Increase is defined as 'the amount (if any) by which the Index for the month preceding each quarter day exceeds the Base Figure'. As has been noted, the figures published in the middle of 1 month relate to the RPI for the middle of the previous month. Consequently, where rent is due on 1 quarter day (say 25 March), the figures for the 'preceding month' (February) will only be available on or about 18 March in a press release and in the April *Employment Gazette* at the beginning of the next month. So if the landlord is to calculate the additional rent before the quarter day the latest figures available to him will be those for January published in mid February, and it is to these figures that the clause as it now stands would appear to refer. This is supported by reference to clause 3 of the Second Schedule of Form 137 which provides for written notice to the tenant of the additional rent due before the quarter day; and, though since the *United Scientific* decision giving such notice in time will not be of the essence, reference to the later figures published just before the quarter day would make notice in due time improbable. Nevertheless, it is thought that disputes could arise on the present wording of Form 137 since the relevant month's figures are not clearly identified. Consequently, it is suggested that clause 2.11 be amended to read 'by which the index *recorded and published during* the month preceding' thus pinpointing (for a March quarter day) the January RPI published in February. If it is desired to use the February figures published in March, reference might be 'to the increase *for and relating to* the month preceding'. Since this will only give about a week from publication of the figures to the relevant quarter day, clause 3 of the Second Schedule will also require amendment to allow a longer time for notice of the additional rent to be given.

Conveyancer Precedent 5–11, until it was amended, made reference to 'the figure representing the average monthly Index of Retail Prices for the calendar year (or other period of a year to which the Index may refer) immediately preceding the year of commencement of that rental period' (clause (D)). However, where payments are due in advance the figures may not be available on the date due (eg for a rental period beginning on 1 January, the figures will not be available until 16 January at the earliest). The parties, as before, will not suffer any drastic consequences but only the inconvenience of a delay in ascertaining the sum due, and this may be avoided if the draftsman ensures reference is to figures normally published prior to the day the rent becomes payable. Clause 1(i) of Form 5–11 (reproduced in Part Seven) achieves this purpose by reference to the 'average figure . . . of the twelve Indices last published prior to the Adjustment Date'.

Reference to the RPI will also require either a verbal or algebraic formula. Conveyancer Precedents 5–11 and 511A have always used algebraic notation (see 5.11A, clause 2(b)). Algebraic notation is to be preferred in the opinion of Hoffman J in *London Regional Transport v Wimpey Group Ltd* [1986] 2 EGLR 41:

'Rent formulae can often be expressed more simply and unambiguously in algebraic form.'

Consequently, the verbal reference in Form 138:

'Such revised rent for any review period shall be the amount which bears the same proportion to the initial rent as the increase bears to the same figure . . .'

can be amended to:

'The revised rent for any review period shall be determined by multiplying the initial rent by the index [for and relating to] [published during] the month preceding the review date at the beginning of the review period and then dividing the result by the base figure.'

(clause 4 of the form is then deleted).

The original wording is not 'wrong' as has been suggested ((1988) 39 *Law Society's Gazette* 40) since in the context of indexation to the RPI it appears unambiguous and clear but the algebraic formula is probably better.

In *Costa v Georghiou* (1984, above), a 1969 lease which provided for index-linked reviews of rent was not in the form adopted by any of the precedents discussed. Instead, the rent was to be increased by £20 12s 10d for each point by which the RPI rose above the figure at which it stood at the date of execution of the sub-underlease. Such a method of indexation will give quite different rents at review (perhaps markedly so) than the more usual fixed base system.

(e)   Providing for changes or errors in the RPI

The most probable change in the RPI, as in any index of prices, is a change in the reference base. Thus the base was fixed as 100 at 15 January 1974 and reached 396.4 before a further new reference base was fixed of 13 January 1987 = 100. In earlier years, a new reference base was adopted when the RPI approached 200 to reduce possible confusion, but the present approach is to use one reference base for as long a period as possible (see *Department of Employment Gazette*, February 1978, p 150); and the latest change was only made after 13 years and as the index approached 400. So a draftsman should always provide for a change in the base date as is done in clause 1 of the Second Schedule to Form 137 and clause (2) of Conveyancer Precedent 5–11. The former relies on the relatively simple approach of arithmetically converting the new index figure into the figure it would have shown had the reference base remained unchanged; the latter connects the calculation directly to the new RPI by substituting the new figures and relating them not to the initial basic rent but to the rent being paid immediately before the commencing date of the new reference base.

If a lease fails to make provision for a change if the base date it has been held in Australia that the indexation clause continued to operate after a change in the reference base as this was only a change in the way the index was expressed and an arithmetical reference to the earlier index could be made. Consequently, a clause in the lease to operate 'in the event of any suspension or discontinuance of the Index' did not come into operation. A change in the reference base was not a suspension or discontinuance: *Tanner v Stocks and Realty (Premises) Pty Ltd* [1972] 2 NSWLR 722.

Attempts have been made to meet other contingencies. In *Blumenthal v Gallery Five Ltd* (1971) 220 EG 31 the parties provided for the rent to be adjusted in line with the RPI after 7 years of a 14–year term, but the rent was to be fixed by valuation if any of four conditions existed. One of these was 'if such index was to take into account other matters besides retail prices'. It was held that the indexation provision was not displaced by the fact that some of the component parts of the RPI were the cost of services, for this was the basis of the RPI when the lease was executed. Probably. the parties were concerned to ensure that a fundamental alteration in the RPI could be met with an alternative method of fixing the rent. If this is a matter of concern, then more careful wording should be adopted such as 'if the said index should no longer substantially concern itself with the extent to which retail prices for goods and services have changed from month to month'.

In *Cumshaw v Bowen* [1987] 1 EGLR 30, a service charge in a 1960 lease was indexed to the RPI; but an alternative method of calculation was to be used 'if the Index shall cease to be published . . . or for any reason is no longer available to the public'. The lessor argued, unavailingly, that the alternative method should operate; neither the changes in commodities and services and the relative weightings given to such items nor the changes in the RPI base in 1962 and 1974 was sufficient. The RPI had been *revised* (and, indeed, the commodities and weightings are revised annually); but it was still the same index and the changes were minor. Even though the parties had not made provision for the alteration in the mathematical base, a simple calculation was possible and the lease could be construed to accord with the parties intention. The decision accords with the *Tanner* and *Blumenthal* decisions though neither are referred to in the judgment.

The revelation in December 1987 that, as a result of a computer error, the RPI had been understated by up to 0.1 per cent for a period of 21 months suggests that provision to cope with such events might be made in the lease. Since the published figures were not retrospectively adjusted on this occasion, a landlord would probably not be able to claim a compensating increase in rent to cover such an error without such express provision.

(f) Providing for delay in publication

Since compilation of the RPI depends upon the labours of field researchers, statistical experts and printers, it is quite possible for delays to occur in publication. A few years ago, disputes in the printing industry caused delays in the appearance of the *Department of Employment Gazette.* Moreover, as mentioned above, there may also be difficulties in calculating the additional rent by the date it is payable. It will be prudent, therefore, to provide in the case of delay for interest to be paid once the rent is determined and for the pre-existing rent to be paid in the meantime. Conveyancer Precedent 5–11 has a clause (5(ii)) on these lines but it only operates if the indexation provisions lapse. It might be appropriate to widen the scope to cover any delay. A lending rate should be chosen usually one based on the base rate of the landlord's bank, or that of a bank notified by the landlord or agreed in advance by the parties, or one of the statutory rates.

(g) Providing for cessation of publication

However unlikely it may seem, a well-drawn indexation clause must make provision for the eventuality of the index being suspended, discontinued or otherwise ceasing publication owing to an event making it impossible or impracticable to implement the indexation provisions. It must provide an alternative method of calculating the rent. A number of possibilities present themselves:

(i) A review clause

This is the approach of Conveyancer Precedent 5–11, which provides for reference to arbitration. Such a clause is advantageous since it can also embrace the determination of 'bona fide disputes' as to the amount of rent payable and the 'construction and effect of this clause' as well as cessation of publication. The clause will be otherwise similar to a standard review clause and will operate only in those circumstances set out. It is the most appropriate method when indexation only occurs every few years. It does, however, raise the issue of whether rent review would have been more appropriate in the first place. It also raises the certainty that when rents determined by review are substantially out of line with the rises in the index one party or the other will attempt to bring the default clause into operation (as in *Blumenthal v Gallery Five Ltd*).

(ii) A substitute index

In theory, a substitute index would most closely accord with the original bargain. For an Australian audience, Lang suggested that if the chosen index ceased publication: 'there shall be substituted for the said Index an index which in the opinion of an expert appointed in default of agreement between the parties by the President for the time being of . . . most closely reflects changes in the cost of living [or other appropriate criterion]' (Precedent 4, p 72). This would be suitable for use with the RPI, save that the reference to 'cost of living' should be a reference to 'retail prices and services' (the RPI is not a cost of living index although it is popularly referred to as such).

(iii) Reference to arbitrator

Form 137 adopts an approach containing elements of both the previous methods. Once again, an arbitrator assumes responsibility for determining the rent, with the advantages previously outlined; but he does not review to determine the open market rent but rather 'to determine on such dates as he shall deem apposite what would have been the increase in the said index had it continued . . . '. On the face of it, this would appear to impose a nigh impossible task, and it may be preferable expressly to allow such an arbitrator to make reference to an index that most closely accords with that originally chosen as in (*ii*) above. This will allow one reference to arbitration to be sufficient for more than one revalorisation. Certainly a clause on the lines of (*ii*) or (*iii*) will be more appropriate where indexation is at frequent intervals. Perhaps an expert rather than an arbitrator would make a more appropriate category of referee, and the President or other senior officer of the Institute of Actuaries a more appropriate appointor than his RICS confrère.

(h) Drafting and perusing drafts generally

It is particularly important for the details of the reservation of an index-linked rent to be precise. Indexation is primarily an arithmetical exercise and provided the method of calculation is clearly set out the revision of the rent is simple and automatic. What must be avoided is wording such as 'shall be revised so as to take into account the rise in the cost of living and the level of rental values in the area'. The authors have seen a lease drafted in such terms. It at one time appeared possible that such a clause, in the absence of an arbitration clause, would be ineffective to review the rent and the basic rent would continue (as in *King v King* (1980) 255 EG 1205) or the lease might even be void for uncertainty but *Beer v Bowden* [1981] 1 WLR 522 and *Thomas Bates & Son Ltd v Wyndham's (Lingerie) Ltd* [1981] 1 WLR 505 render this result unlikely, though those cases, and others also discussed in Chapter 9, do show that the exact outcome might be difficult to predict. The phrase 'taking into account' is certainly inappropriate for the arithmetical calculation required for indexation. The result of only requiring the RPI to be taken into account means that it merely becomes a factor in the valuation process. Thus, in *Ex parte Yuco Pty Ltd* [1978] Qd R 235 (Queensland) an option to renew was to be at a rent agreed upon between the parties 'taking into account any increase in the basic wage for adult males in Queensland . . . '. It was held that no arithmetical calculation was to be made; but in default of agreement the arbitration clause was to apply and, though the valuer could take such wage increases into account, all the other usual factors impinging on the valuation process would also be at large. Similarly, in *Stroud v Weir Associates* [1987] 1 EGLR 190 the arbitrator of an annual pitch fee of a caravan site was 'to have regard to' three items one of which was the RPI which, it was held, was the only factor allowing scope for an increase. It was held that the rent was not *required* to go up by the relevant increase in the RPI; it is a factor to be taken into account. However, the judge had not been wrong to increase the rent by the full amount of the RPI when there was a relatively low rate of inflation in the relevant year. One recalls the misgivings expressed by Megarry J in *English Exporters (London) Ltd v Eldonwall Ltd* [1973] Ch 415 at 426D over a comparable phrase; '. . . the term 'have regard' is almost of necessity bound to create difficulties. How much regard is to be had, and what weight is to be attached to the regard when it has been had?'

It is also wise to work through the formula and apply it and test it to ensure it works fairly for the client. Index linked rents based on the precedents already referred to should give no difficulty. In the '*Blue Dolphin*' leases, however (see (1988) 34 *Law Society's Gazette* 10), the revised rent was allegedly determined and increased in line with and according to the RPI but the original rent was added back in to the sum so determined so that the tenant was left paying a sum far in excess of what straight indexation would have produced—and a number of solicitors were left facing negligence claims.

4 Delay

As with rent reviews, there may be a failure to revalorise the rent in line with the index at the time envisaged by the lease through forgetfulness or default by either or both of the parties. The consequences of such a delay are unlikely to be calamitous but the detailed position may depend on the manner in which the indexation clause is drafted or even on the length of the time that has elapsed since the due date.

A well-drafted index-linked clause should ensure that problems are eliminated or at least kept to a minimum. This will be achieved provided the indexed rent is reserved without any conditions or provisos making (for example) the revalorisation an option to be exercised by one of the parties or consequent upon a notice. In other words, the rent should be self-adjusting requiring only the mathematical calculations to be made by either party. Thus Conveyancer Precedent 5–11 provides for the basic rent to be multiplied by a variable factor set out in the Schedule. Consequently, any increases in the rent as a result of increases in the index are merely fluctuations in the liability envisaged and contracted for by the parties. Arrears of such rent may be recovered by the usual remedies. It is submitted that this may be prevented only if a tenant can found an equitable estoppel by showing reliance on the landlord's representation that he intended not to take the increase of rent to which he was entitled (see discussion in Chapter 5). It would not seem to be possible for the tenant to claim the revalorisation is lost by an unreasonable period of delay by the landlord (even if such a claim is theoretically sound—which is now unlikely, see p 147)—there has been no default by him but rather an omission to recalculate the rent due under the lease, a calculation the tenant is as able to make as their landlord.

Where a rent is to be adjusted at the 'option of a landlord' or express notice of the amount of the increase must be given by him, different considerations may arise where the landlord fails to give the requisite notice or delays for a period before seeking the increase in the rent. Form 137, by incorporating in clause 3 of the Second Schedule provision for the written notice of the increase to be given, is a clause of this type—for the additional rent is only to be paid 'provided that' these steps are taken. However, the principles of the *United Scientific* case ([1978] AC 904) will apply, so that the time for calculation of the sum due and notice thereof will not be of the essence. So default by the landlord will not normally deprive him of an increased rent but the tenant will face the same practical difficulties when there is such a delay as he does on rent review (fully discussed in Chapter 5, above). The difficulties will become serious if the delay is substantial, and the tenant faces a claim for a large retrospective increase in the rent. In Australia, in *Re Ipswich Road Properties Pty Ltd's Lease* (Queensland) [1974] Qd R 215 it was held that, in a case where the rent was to be adjusted by indexation at the option of the landlord, the option had to be exercised within a reasonable time of the publication of the index and where this was not done the rent could only be increased in respect of rent due after the giving of the requisite notice. However convenient such a result may seem, it cannot be a guide to the determination of a similar issue in England in view of the *United Scientific* decision where it was held that an obligation to review a rent (and, by analogy, to index a rent) is an inseverable part of the whole consideration of the landlord's grant of the lease. This will mean that delays in giving requisite notices will neither prevent the increase (at a later date) in line with the index nor the retrospective recovery to the due date. Unlike 'self-adjusting' clauses, however, a claim on the basis of prolonged or unreasonable delay might be founded by the tenant so that the right to revalorisation may have been lost because the landlord has been guilty of an unreasonable delay in taking the necessary steps provided for in the lease, especially if a further calculation date has passed. However, the seeming rejection of all such defences based on delay in *Amherst v James Walker Goldsmith and Silversmith Ltd (No 2)* [1983] Ch 305 (see p 158) suggests that even in such cases a late adjustment to the rent can be made.

5   Use of indexation in conjunction with rent review

There would seem to be no objections to parties to a lease contracting and providing for a rent to be both indexed and subject to periodic review, or indeed to index other forms of variable rent (in *Re Ipswich Road Properties Pty Ltd's Lease* (Queensland) [1974] Qd R 215 a progressive rent was subject to optional indexation). Some instances of combining reviews with indexation have come to light (see, for example, (1976) 237 EG 356 for a particularly interesting example from the Netherlands); but, so far as the authors are aware, these are not the subject of reported decisions.

In Australia, the case of *Hely v Sterling* [1982] VR 246 involved litigation of a rent review clause postulating agreement with arbitration in default, but with a proviso that the amount payable in each relevant review period should not be less than the amount payable in the previous period and 'shall correspond with an increase made by the Consumer Price Index'. It was held that the proviso operated as a covenant to pay rent and imported an obligation to pay not less than the minimum, that minimum being adjusted in accordance with the stated index, unless and until the lessor chose to seek arbitration.

(a)   An indexed rent with overriding rent review

This is the possibility that has attractive features for lessors since it offers a form of rent offering protection both against falls in the value of money in the short term and against movements in the property market independent of inflation in the longer term. It is a form of variation which has been used regularly by one major property company in recent years. A typical example might be a lease for 21 years of commercial premises at a rent fixed for the first year and annually indexed thereafter to the RPI. To give a measure of certainty—and a measure of protection to the tenant—it is possible to limit any increases otherwise payable by the annual indexation so that rent shall (notwithstanding the indexation calculation) not exceed (say) 110 per cent of the rent payable in the previous year (ie no more than 10 per cent pa). At the end of the fifth year, there would be a review to the open market rent and this rent, once agreed or determined, would both be the rent payable for the sixth year and provide a new base rent for indexation during the four subsequent years to the next review. The annual indexation of the rent ensures that the lessor's income from the property does not fall in real terms when compared with the rate of inflation while the rent review enables account to be taken periodically of the movements in property values that affect the particular property in question. It is accordingly a particularly efficient form of inflation-proofing. It is not, however, without its problems— quite apart from the fact that tenants may resist a rent that offers no advantages to them. Thus, it suffers from the uncertainties of forward planning and vagaries of inflation movements common to all rents indexed to the RPI. If there is a fall in the rates of inflation, indexation with overriding rent review is less attractive. Certainly, one property company with a policy of indexation with quinquennial reviews offered tenants a change to a more conventional 3–year rent review pattern and apparently less than half took up the option (see (1983) 267 EG 1093).

A particular problem can arise on review where the open market value of the premises proves to be lower than the index-linked rent paid in the previous year. Take an example of a rent originally reserved at £1,000. Let us assume that, by virtue of the index-linked rises, it is £1,500 for the fifth year of the term and at the end of that year the open market rent of the premises is agreed or determined at £1,750. No problem occurs since the rent for the sixth year will be the figure of £1,750 and this figure will be the base rent for indexing the annual rent for the next four years. The position is very different if at the end of that fifth year the open market rent is (say) £1,250, the tenant having paid £1,500 the previous year. In such circumstances, there are three very different solutions:

(i)   The rent payable will fall to that payable on the open market
Namely, in our example, £1,250. This figure will be the new base rent for subsequent annual indexations. This solution will be preferred by tenants since it is most advantageous to them. It is also the 'fairest' solution and should not be rejected because a rent review clause does not permit a downwards review, for it is not a directly comparable position. Thus, in our example of a rent originally reserved at £1,000, if a straight rent review every 5 years had been agreed rather than indexation with overriding review, the rent determined on review would still have been £1,250, the open market rent, and more than the sum originally reserved. By means of the indexation, the landlord has already achieved a financial advantage. Nevertheless, lessors will dislike the

prospect of a reduction in the return from their investment and if their bargaining power permits may seek one of the two following solutions to meet the situation where the rent as reviewed is lower than that previously payable.

(ii) The rent payable subsequent to the review will be the amount for the last rent period prior to the review, but the (lower) open market rent will form the new base to which future rises in the index are linked

In our example, therefore, £1,500 would continue to be paid in the sixth year but the annual indexation calculation will be applied to the figure of £1,250. Only when the index causes the 'notional rent' to rise from £1,250 to over £1,500 will an increased actual rent be paid. This ensures that the lessor never suffers an actual reduction in the amount of rent he receives but prevents the rent payable by indexation from moving too far out of line with the property value.

(iii) The open market rent, because it is lower than that obtained by application of the indexation formula, is ignored and the indexation provisions apply as before

In other words, the overriding rent review only applies if it results in a higher rent; otherwise it is disregarded. This solution gives the lessor the best of both worlds. He is protected from the vagaries of indexation but the tenant is not. It is a result tenants should avoid. However, a form of commercial lease used in practice of which the authors are aware adopted a solution on these lines.

None of the above three possibilities is an 'obvious' solution so a draftsman must decide which is appropriate and make provision accordingly. The outcome will certainly depend on the construction of the words of the lease. The authors prefer the first solution (ie restoring the rent on overriding review to its open market value even if lower) not only because it is best from the tenant's point of view but because it most closely accords with the results reached by a straightforward rent review. It must be borne in mind, however, that the fact of an annual increase through indexation in each year until the next review is a factor to be taken into account at each overriding rent review, unless there is a disregard of that factor.

(b) A rent subject to review with overriding indexation

This concept will only be appropriate in exceptional circumstances (for example, in the case of the sale and lease-back). The authors are aware of an example of a sale and lease-back for a term of 125 years subject to 7-year reviews to open market rent; but at the end of every 21 years there was overriding indexation to $3\frac{3}{4}$ per cent pa compound interest if this was higher than the then open market rent. The indexation was used as a means to secure a particular minimum financial return. There is, however, a potential stamp duty liability of massive proportions if the indexation formula allows the minimum rent at the 105th year to be calculated. Ad valorem duty will then be payable on this huge sum and not the fixed rent for the first 7 years (compare *Coventry City Council v Inland Revenue Commissioners* [1979] Ch 142).

(c) Indexation or rent review whichever is higher

A lessor in a strong bargaining position could choose to 'have his cake and eat it' or, in the words of Vinelott J get both 'belt and elastic braces'. Thus in *Bissett v Marwin Securities* [1987] 1 EGLR 115 the rent was to be reviewed to whichever one of four different ways of revalorisation produced the highest figure. One method was a standard review, two of the others were indexation, which in the circumstances produced higher figures. Lessees should firmly resist such clauses, for the lessor gets the higher rent if inflation lags behind rental values, but he also gets the higher increase when inflation is ahead of the rental value for his property. This will be so notwithstanding that in the real world the premises could not be let at the rent determined by the index which does not reflect the depreciation in the real value of the letting value of the premises.

6 Using index-linked rents

Parties considering the use of indexation to vary the rent reserved in a lease must be aware of its limitations and disadvantages when compared with the more standard rent review. On a practical level, an index-linked rent will change with each monthly, quarterly or annual adjustment in line with the index, and the effort in recalculating the sum due must not be underestimated. As Ross points out (*Drafting and Negotiating Commercial Leases* (3rd ed), para 6.64) a draftsman can mitigate constant changes, for example, by only altering the quantum of rent once the index varies by more than a certain percentage (or number of points) or by providing for a fixed rent with an annual statement showing any increase due as a result of change in the index. In particular, there is no guarantee that the rise alongside the index will closely accord with changes in property values, subject as they are to other factors, particularly localised ones (for example, changes in trading patterns caused by new shopping developments, the opening of a pedestrian precinct, or the disturbance caused by major road improvements or developments). This, in *Blumenthal v Gallery Five Ltd* (1971) 220 EG 31 a rent of £1,600 pa reserved in 1964 rose to some £2,048 by review by an indexation provision at the end of 7 years. However, had the rent been calculated by a review to open market value it would undoubtedly have been 'substantially higher' because rental values had at that time moved ahead of inflation. On the other hand, more recent experience, particularly of properties in other than 'prime locations', has shown that indexation provisions may result in tenants paying sums considerably higher than the market would otherwise justify. Where index-linked rents are substantially out of line one way or the other, the consequences are more than just a reduction in income for the lessor or financial burden to the tenant, important though these are. For the landlord who is receiving less than the market rent there is the difficulty of realising the full capital value of the investment should he decide to dispose of the reversion yet having the knowledge that the tenant will be able to assign his lease at a premium. In the reverse situation, where on paper the landlord is entitled to receive more rent than he would have obtained on review, he may, nevertheless, have to accommodate and renegotiate terms with a tenant who cannot carry the financial burden. Such a prospect may also reduce the willingness of a purchaser of the reversion to pay a price fully reflecting the index-linked return, and it is common experience that such reversions change hands at a market discount on their notional 'true value'. For the tenant seeking to escape from the situation by assignment (perhaps at a discount), there is the knowledge that he will remain liable on his covenant to pay rent whether as an original party to the lease or as an assignee who gave indemnity covenants to his assignor; and, though he will have taken indemnity covenants from his assignee, he may not always achieve full recovery thereon. Undoubtedly, there is no great enthusiasm for the indexed rent amongst landlords or tenants.

The above disadvantages of indexation of rents are only partly the result of the principle itself. They are magnified because commercial leases in the United Kingdom are dominated by the rent review structure. Should indexation ever become a recognised feature of industrial, commercial or office leases (and statutory renewals thereof) then the rents paid under such contracts would become a significant determining factor when rents of properties on the market fell to be determined and thus index-linked rents would not move so far out of line. Yet, even if there was an 'accepted rule' of indexation the danger would remain that the index (or indices) used would move out of line with property capital values, and there can be differences between the performance of one index and of another; see the figures given in the discussion of *Multiservice Bookbinding Ltd v Marden* [1979] Ch 84 at p 566, above. In such circumstances there would be the prospect of government intervention. At the present time, indexation of rents can only be recommended for consideration for leases for relatively short terms and even then for properties where the initial rent reserved is not large. In such circumstances the prospect of the rents paid becoming unrealistic is minimised, but the expense of review machinery, an important consideration when leasing the less valuable properties, is avoided. Perhaps the only practical methods of avoiding the long-term dangers of the process while securing its short-term benefits are as follows:

(1) A term of indexation (to the RPI or other indices) an overriding rent review, say, every 5 years.

(2) Indexing the rent in a short-term lease (say up to 5 years) which is subject to a joint application to the court to exclude the provision of the Landlord and Tenant Act 1954, Part II. At the expiry of the term, since no right to review arises, the landlord is free to re-offer the premises at the open market rent. If in such a case, the lessee is given a contractual option to renew, then machinery to establish the market rent in such a renewed term, with provision perhaps for further rent reviews, might be essential.

7 'Fundamental changes' in surrounding circumstances

Apart from the problems of possible divergence between a chosen index and property values and rents generally or even in a fairly restricted locality, there may be such a drastic alteration of circumstances in respect of a particular property, or even part of such a property, as to tempt one or other of the parties to invoke what may be termed the doctrine of 'quasi-frustration'. *Staffordshire Area Health Authority v South Staffordshire Waterworks Co* [1978] 1 WLR 1387 and *Pole Properties Ltd v Feinberg* (1980) 259 EG 417 are the two reported decisions from which the outlines or beginning of such a doctrine may be postulated, but its scope and possible application to the circumstances now under discussion remain to be settled. One contrary argument, paradoxically enough, could be that the indexation of the rent manifested an intention to divorce the level of rent from the attributes of the specific property and it was on an argument similar to this that an attempt to sustain a claim of frustration failed in *Bracknell Development Corporation v Greenlees Lennards Ltd* (1981) 260 EG 500 (see p 517, above). Nevertheless, the amounts sometimes at stake may justify litigation to resolve the issue just as so many other points have been litigated in the rent review field in recent years.

Chapter 21

Turnover and Equity Rents

Turnover and equity rents take many forms and exist under the guise of different names—'royalty rent', 'percentage lease' or 'equity sharing agreement'—sometimes reflecting the different purposes to which the idea may be adapted. The principle that unites them is that the variable nature of the rent received by the lessor depends upon the amount of turnover or income produced by the lessee from the demised premises. The lessor obtains indirect protection from the effects of inflation either as a consequence of the turnover of a business, which in real terms may remain constant, increasing in line with inflationary increases in the prices of goods sold or from the increase in the total rack rents obtained or obtainable by the mesne lessor being increased by rent review. The income produced by the premises is a sort of 'local index' to which the rent, or part thereof, is tied. Unlike indexation to some external set of figures, however, the rent will not be affected directly by factors extraneous to the premises; rather the performance of the tenant's business, the success of his enterprise or the management skill of the head lessee will have a significant effect on the (head) landlord's income from the property—and may have a greater impact than that of inflation.

A turnover rent is thus, at least in part, an investment in the tenant's business acumen; an equity rent in the future profitability of the development. This has the consequence that the concept is an ideal vehicle for schemes that are essentially a partnership in investment in development of the land, and the provisions in the lease for payment of rent are a form of equitable division of the proceeds of that investment. On the other hand, the tenant may well have the ability, to some extent, to control the amount of rent he pays, perhaps achieving a reduction in the rent by reducing or manipulating the turnover or income produced. To meet such contingencies, careful drafting is required with the landlord needing the right to receive details of the tenant's activities and an oversight, or perhaps even some control, of his affairs.

1   Scope of the concepts

Since the essential ingredient of a turnover rent is that the landlord is entitled to a sum as rent calculated upon the tenant's income from the land demised, there is plenty of scope for the use of such rents. In Chapter 3 (p 38) it was suggested that there is a close analogy to the ancient corn rents or royalty rents in mining leases, except that the idea is applied to business premises. The 'equity rent' is a further extension to commercial lettings where there is a particular element of partnership in development of the site and, unlike the turnover rent, it is applicable even if the end-users are not retailers of goods and services. Though the theoretical scope may be wide, reported examples of turnover rents in England are scarce, perhaps a reflection of the limited number of examples that are found in practice or an indication that those that do exist have not given rise to problems requiring litigation. Nevertheless, such examples are diverse, ranging from the lease of a cinema (*Bramhall Tudor Cinema Properties v Brennans Cinemas* (1955) *The Times*, 19 October) to that of the motorway service area (*Tucker v Granada Motorway Services Ltd* (1979) 1 WLR 87 and 683 and two of a cattle market (*Stride & Son v Chichester Corporation* (1960) 175 EG 315; *Naylor v Uttoxeter Urban District Council* (1974) 231 EG 619). It is notable that in the latter two cases the landlord might be said to have had a particular interest in the business of the premises that made a turnover rent especially appropriate (the Ministry of Transport in its motorway service areas; the local authority in its municipal livestock market). A few decisions deal with equity rents and these are discussed below.

In Canada and the United States, not only are reported examples of turnover rents and percentage leases found at an earlier date (eg *McAdam v Franklin* (1923) 1 DLR 1174, lease of a theatre in Nova Scotia) but also the current use of such rents is far more widespread. This is especially true of the United States where leases of stores and retail units (in particular) normally provide for a basic rent and, in addition, a percentage rent of anything between 1.5 per cent and 10 per cent of sales once turnover reaches a specified level. So widespread is the practice that commonly accepted percentage rates for the particular lessee's type of business are regularly published as guides. In contrast, 'revaluation' clauses are seen to give only periodic protection against inflation; and the valuation process, reflecting as it does the impact of various market factors on particular premises, is seen to be less advantageous than it is regarded in the United Kingdom, since it will not necessarily reflect inflationary trends.

Out of town shopping centres are the most obvious place where a turnover lease has attractions. Such rents are now well established in North American suburban shopping centres and in similar shopping malls in Australia and New Zealand.

2   The advantages and disadvantages of turnover rents

The North American preference for percentage leases, at least for retail premises, stems from a belief that they offer greater advantages for both parties than 'revaluation or reappraisal clauses' (the North American form of rent review). To what extent is this true?

(a)   Advantages for a lessee

From the lessee's point of view, since the amount of rent will vary (at least in part) with the income generated by his business, he will be better able to afford rent increases, yet should have some protection in times of depression or declining sales. He will face fewer fixed overheads and have a financial cushion in hard times. Indeed, the use of percentage leases in the United States was established in the Depression of the 1930s, partly on the insistence of tenants. Lessors were happy to agree where the alternative was a vacant unit (for unoccupied units in a development can have a depreciating effect on the letting value and prospects for other units). Moreover, a lessee will pay a rent reflecting his actual use of the land and not from a supervening theoretical better 'market' use—in other words, he can expect that his business can afford the new rent, which may not be the case for a conventional rent review. Finally, since a percentage lease gives a lessor an interest in the business conducted (say) from a shopping centre, the lessee(s) can be confident of a high level of management control. There will be a shared incentive to maintain lifts and common parts to a high standard, and a lessor may be willing to expend money on his own account in the expectation of a greater return from his share of the increased turnover. Tenants may feel that the arrangement will provide a direct incentive for the lessor, or some purchaser from him, to use his best efforts to establish and maintain the attractiveness and viability of the development. All in all, a turnover rent promises for the tenant, by necessity, greater co-operation from his landlord.

(b)   Advantages for a lessor

From the lessor's point of view, the minimum rent will secure a basic return and the percentage rent automatically and regularly increases the rent in times of inflation. He thereby gains an income which has the potential for annual growth; and in a successful scheme, he obtains the benefit of rental growth more or less immediately without waiting for the next rent review. Certainly, the percentage rent is primarily dependent upon the lessee's business success, but lessors should see this aspect as an investment in the productivity of the location of their premises. Indeed, percentage leases are especially used where the location of the premises is so important that the location itself is perceived as generating business profits in which the lessor can share. If, as is quite common, the minimum fixed rent is fairly high (as a proportion of the total) the basic return should be satisfactory. A greater control of use and assignment can be achieved and perhaps without the risk of a market rent at review below that generated by a fixed rent plus percentage. A lessor should be able to manage more effectively and gain immediate benefits from, say, timely investments in refurbishment works; the mutuality of interest should ensure less conflict with the tenant.

Percentage leases can also be used with advantage in uncertain locations in a manner not dissimilar to rent-free periods or pioneering rents. The tenant is attracted to accept the lease in the first place in the knowledge that if the business does not flourish, he will only have to pay a basic low minimum rent; the lessor obtains some income, at least, from the property instead of having the premises empty and an increased income if the business is successful. Moreover, if the lessor can, in this way, attract an initial key tenant to a development, prospects will be brighter for letting other units in the centre. A similar argument may lead to a swing towards turnover rents in times of restricted profitability in the general trading scene (as in the depressed United Kingdom market in 1990), the lessor securing a letting and an income, the hard-pressed retailer a reduction in overheads until the market recovers.

(c)   Disadvantages for a lessee

There are some obvious problems. The tenant is burdened with the provision of turnover information, which is not only a burdensome chore but also the tenant may be genuinely apprehensive about releasing facts which would assist its competitors if they fell into wrong hands. A tenant may actually prefer to operate with fixed rather than fluctuating overheads. Some trades may not easily fit into the scheme—for example, electrical shops where much of the trade is in renting equipment rather than sale. A particular problem is the belief that a tenant's success is dependent on his own efforts; the consumer interest is drawn by the tenant(s) and the goodwill and profit generated is theirs to enjoy. Unless that attitude is changed or dispelled, then the turnover rent will not achieve widespread acceptance. The ultimate test is the extent to which the lessor is prepared to shoulder a share of the risk—and institutional landlords tend to show a marked reluctance to abandon fixed returns and clear leases. If the base rent is approaching 100 per cent of the open market value, then one can be sure that the landlord is in a position to dictate terms and such turnover rents will only thrive where tenants are willing to take leases on any terms.

(d)   Disadvantages for a lessor

Just as with a tenant, the obvious problem relates to the calculation of turnover. The lessor does not have the knowledge; he must rely on the tenant's information and the provisions in the lease to check this.

Landlords may feel that a turnover rent may in some circumstances protect a weak tenant from the rigours of the market. The main impression, though, is fundamental—an unwillingness to accept the risk of a decline in rental income if turnover falls—even if 'decline' means merely a lower increase than a review to market rent would produce. This is a little surprising since the investors in property portfolios accept just such a risk in the stock market. Until lessors are willing to take a share of the risk, tenants will rightly resist the widespread use of such schemes.

Secondly, whilst greater involvement in the management of shopping centres, industrial business and science parks and other complexes is a general feature of landlord practice the need for expert management, at a local level, is more intense in relation to those let on turnover rents than with normal rent review. Such expertise is often provided on an in-house basis than delegated to managing agents and is not necessarily easy to secure.

(e) Conclusions

(i) Turnover rents

It is perhaps a matter of conjecture why greater use of percentage leases has not occurred in the United Kingdom beyond a relatively few shopping centre developments and the occasional specialist venue. The relative unpopularity of turnover rents may be the result of different market trends, the refinement and development of the rent review structure in a way that has not happened in North America, or the buoyancy of property values when compared with inflation. Other suggested factors have been the strength of the multiple retailers, who have largely resisted the idea as tenants (but who often franchise in store operations on a turnover basis) and the dominance of institutional landlords who, as investors, have placed a lower capital value on portfolios of properties let on turnover leases. It may also be the result of the complexities that such rents necessitate in drafting and accounting. Above all, it is suggested that it is the lack of the necessary mutuality—lessors fear the greater risks from trade deterioration while from the tenants' point of view a turnover rent is seen as the loss of part of a profit obtained from what is perceived to be their successful endeavours. Ironically, therefore, turnover rents are most likely to be used where one party is in a weak position; only if it is the only way to let (and the base rent will be low or non-existent) or (at the other end of the spectrum) the tenant is ready to accept any terms (where the base rent will be close to 100 per cent of the open market value) are such rents likely to be agreed. In such cases, there is an element of imposition; a widespread use of the rent requires a degree of partnership.

(ii) Equity rents

The forms of equity rent generally operate between a ground landlord and a developer whereas percentage or turnover leases are applicable between the developer or intermediate lessor and the trading tenant. In equity rent cases the landlord, perhaps a local authority, provides land to the tenant, a developer, and the agreed rent will be a percentage of the net income the developer receives or should receive. Significantly, however, the link between the two forms remains the continuing interest of the equity rent head lessor, who is frequently a local authority freeholder, in the development. The land may have been assembled by, or under the threat of, the use of compulsory powers or by a consortium including public bodies. A continuing equity involvement may have political as well as financial attractions. Local authorities, unlike private landowners, will have, in any event, an ongoing interest in a development in its area and a straight capital sale of the site may not have the same appeal when local authorities do not have the same freedom of disposal of capital receipts. A 'share in prosperity' argument may assist in political acceptance of the scheme. Equity rents and 'rentsharing' are then a creative element in funding responses in a changing financial climate.

The drafting of equity rents presents somewhat different problems from those of turnover rents and, consequently, will be considered separately. Other aspects of ground rent reviews generally are covered in Chapter 13.

In both cases, however, draftsmen may profit from the wisdom of North American experience and drafting suggestions made there (see, for example, Van Doren, (1951) 51 Col LR 186 and Hecht (1972) 72 Col LR 625). Several aspects of equity rents were helpfully reviewed by Wood and Finch in 'Side by Side Leases' (1983) 267 EG 229, 328. An examination of one specialised area is 'Rent Reviews in Shopping Developments' (1984) 271 EG 515 and 602, where the authors usefully compare the use of rent reviews, index-linked rents and turnover rents in modern shopping developments. More recent articles have appeared in (1987) 282 EG 550 and [1988] 13 EG 20.

3 Drafting turnover rents and percentage leases

Though some thought was been given at an early stage to drafting percentage leases in this country (Hargrove (1957) 21 Conv (NS) 265), relatively little has been published since the advent of the regular use of rent review clauses. A form of licence to occupy a 'Franchise Area' in a large store that includes a 'rent' based on turnover appears in Conveyancer Precedent 6–9, p 3040 (first published in 1978). This form only envisages a licence to occupy, however, and though some of the clauses included will find a counterpart in a turnover rent, the granting of a lease, as opposed to a licence, requires different treatment. Perhaps a sign of the slow growth of turnover leases in England, especially in new shopping centres, is the publication of precedents of two retail turnover rents in Vol 22 of EFP (5th ed) as Forms 139 and 140 at paras 1074 and 1076 respectively (though no precedents had appeared in the Additional Forms updating the 4th ed). The drafting of these new forms appears to owe something to the drafting advice below which appeared in modified form in the earlier editions of this book.

In presenting the following guide-lines, the authors acknowledge their indebtedness to the writers noted above who have drawn upon North American experience, and to contributors in the *Law Society's Gazette*—namely, Reeves (1979) 76 *Law Society's Gazette* 1218 and Aldridge (1980) 77 *Law Society's Gazette* 786 and the Blundell Memorial Lectures—to which the reader is referred.

(a) A minimum rent

Though by no means essential, it is usual for a minimum rent to be reserved, the amount of which will depend upon a number of factors—eg the parties' bargaining power, the type of business to be conducted on the premises, the projected volume of business or amount of sales, and the main motivation for the inclusion of a percentage rent. From the lessor's point of view, the minimum fixed rate ensures a certain income from which he can satisfy management expenses (to the extent these are not covered by service charges), and any interest charges, and be sure of at least some return on his capital. Without such a minimum sum a lessor, who will have no direct say in the management of the business, has no financial leverage to prevent a run-down of the concern, which will lead to a diminution of the rent paid. On the other hand, the lessee will wish the basic rent to be a sum he can afford to pay even in adverse trading conditions. Such factors may well result in the minimum rent being set at about 75 per cent of the open market value of the property, unlike 'dead rents' in mining or quarrying leases which are often nominal sums.

There may be situations where the minimum rent is fixed at or close to the current market value of the property, and the amount of the additional percentage rent reduced accordingly. Thus, perhaps, on renewal of a current lease, additional rent would only be paid when the turnover of the business exceeded the amount for the preceding year. In such circumstances, the aim of the percentage element of the rent is predominantly anti-inflationary and the benefit to a tenant of a percentage rent is much reduced.

The attractiveness of a turnover rent for a lessor may be increased if provision can be agreed for review of the minimum rent at intervals. This may take the form of a standard rent review with arbitration or valuation in default of agreement. Thus, if the minimum rent is set at 75 per cent of the open market rent, there could be a review to 75 per cent of the agreed or determined full value at the review date. Alternatively, the increase in the minimum rent could be based on the volume of business, being a set percentage of gross sales for a designated period prior to the review date. Such a scheme might be appropriate in a 'pioneering' situation where the low initial minimum rent reflects the uncertainty of the location or nature of the tenant's business.

It is important to clarify the relationship between the minimum rent and the percentage rent. Usually, it will be preferable to keep the two separate (as in EFP Forms 139 and 140), and the lessee's obligation will be to pay the combination of the two, the minimum rent and the percentage in addition. In other words, the minimum rent cannot be 'credited' against the percentage rent due. In such circumstances, the percentage rent will usually only be paid once sales reach a specified level. In the alternative (as in Form 140), the percentage rent payable will be 'such sum equivalent to the amount (if any) by which (x) per cent of the gross receipts exceeds the fixed minimum rent'. The minimum rent is credited against the percentage rent due, which is then more usually calculated upon the whole of the gross sales, and not only on the amount by which they exceed a specified level.

(b) The percentage rent

It is important to designate not only the percentage rate but the method of application to the selected base (eg gross sales).

The percentage rate will usually be an average to be applied to all sales. The amount will be a matter for bargain between the parties, though naturally it must be related to the size of the minimum rent. Unless the tenant is an established trader, much may depend upon predictions as to the volume of business. It is feasible to vary the percentage rate, either according to types of merchandise (which will necessitate more detailed accounting techniques) or to adopt a sliding scale or even fix a maximum total rent above which further turnover is ignored. A reduction in the amount levied as sales increase may encourage maximisation of sales but is dangerous to the lessor since in a time of inflation there will be a reduction in his return in real terms. On the other hand, provision for an increase in the percentage rate from an initial rather low figure once sales reach a certain level may enable the lessee to get established in a new venture and give him additional working capital in the earlier stages. In such circumstances, the lessor may wish to draft the clause to ensure that the higher percentage rate, once applied, continues even if sales subsequently fall below the specified amount, and additionally make the higher rate payable in any event at the expiration of a certain period from the grant of the lease. A lessee should beware of agreeing to a sliding scale that increases as sales increase, for if the increases that occur are largely inflationary without a comparable increase in real terms the percentage paid will become an increasing burden (cf *Tucker v Granada Motorway Services Ltd* [1979] 1 WLR 87 and 683); in that case the ratio of profit to turnover decreased, the business was increasingly uneconomic and the tenant had to seek renegotiation of the lease terms. The issue was complicated in that case by changes in taxation (an aspect considered at p 595, below).

It must be made clear to what the rate is to be applied. In retail businesses this will usually be to 'gross sales' and careful definition of such a base is needed (considered below). Whatever base is chosen, the percentage may be applied either to the total amount, or to the sum by which the sales exceed a specified amount (as discussed in (*a*) above).

(c)   The percentage base

From the drafting point of view, the most difficult and important section of the lease is the choice and definition of the base or formula to which the percentage is applied. The total volume of the business of the tenant may be adopted, and this is suitable to a wide variety of situations. For a retail business, the choice is usually 'gross turnover', 'gross sales', 'gross receipts' or 'gross takings' (*Tucker v Granada*), though it would be possible to use 'profits' or 'net sales'. It would be unusual for the percentage to be one of 'profits' (though this may appeal more to a tenant) since the base is more difficult to define, the accounting is more complex and the lessor is at a greater risk of facing a reduction in his income since profits fluctuate to a greater degree than turnover or gross rates and may be manipulated, perhaps for quite legitimate or fiscal reasons. A profits basis may place too great a reliance on the tenant's efficiency and though it has been suggested that tenants' advisers should relate the definition of turnover as closely as possible to actual profit (Lewison, *Drafting Business Leases*, p 65) it is not thought that such an approach is either feasible or acceptable to lessors. Nevertheless, in *Naylor v Uttoxeter Urban District Council* (1974) 231 EG 619, in a dispute as to the amount and terms of rent to be paid on statutory renewal of a lease of a cattle market, it was eventually agreed and approved by the judge that the rent should be a percentage of gross commission rather than of gross financial turnover since, in the judge's opinion, 'commission' was a more reasonable basis to reflect the financial success of the market. In that case, moreover, Brightman J (as he then was) drew attention to what is a major drawback of the turnover basis so far as the tenant is concerned. If the price of certain goods sold by the tenant increases more rapidly than the general cost of living, the trader may respond by taking a lower mark-up. Consequently, the rent, related to the total sale price, increases disproportionately to the tenant's profit margins. A similar result may come about where overheads, not least amongst them rates or service charges, rise at a velocity not capable of direct application to selling prices. There is a case to be considered for adjusting the tranches of gross turnover at which higher percentages (or indeed lower) become payable, to minimise the effect of inflation not reflected in comparable rises in even the arithmetical figures of profit.

Whatever the base chosen, and no matter how it is termed, it must be accurately and comprehensively defined in the lease. It is essential that contradictions and ambiguities be avoided to limit the scope for dispute and, as far as possible, the draftsman must state what is included in 'gross takings' and what is excluded. Thus, in *Bramhall Tudor Cinema Properties v Brennan's Cinemas* (1955) *The Times*, 19 October, the percentage rent was to be 'equal to 20 per cent of gross takings (less entertainment tax)'. The parties could not agree whether gross takings meant box office takings only or whether sales in the cinema of programmes, refreshments, etc were included. The Court of Appeal held that the term did not extend beyond box office takings. This may be contrasted with the Canadian case of *Lynn v Nathanson* (1931) 2 DLR 457 where a theatre lease, providing for a rent of 10 per cent of 'gross receipts from all sources whatsoever', did attempt to define gross receipts as 'all moneys taken in at the ticket office or otherwise'. Unfortunately, no provision was made for taxes; the Nova Scotia Supreme Court narrowly decided (3–2) that the amusement tax collected by the theatre for the government was not included in gross receipts.

These cases illustrate the importance of providing for all possible contingencies. Since the definition used will vary with the nature of the business and type of premises, it is only possible to indicate the most important factors to be borne in mind:

(i) Delimiting the formula

The draftsman will have to define exactly what constitutes his 'sales', 'receipts' or 'turnover', giving not only a definition but also expressly stating as far as possible what is to be included and what is to be excluded. The general approach will be to ensure that all payments, whether in cash, by credit or otherwise, and dealings with goods are included in 'gross sales' or 'receipts' for retail businesses, see clause 7.1 of EFP (5th ed) Form 140, Sched 3; where there is an element of rendering services the aim will be to include all payments or receipts resulting from the use of the premises. A tenant retailer will wish to ensure that only amounts actually received is included so that he is able to have sale items or special offers without penalty.

(ii) Items to be included

Where the lease is one of retail premises, it will be usual to make express provision to include receipts from conditional and credit sales and hire purchase, with agreement on whether such payments by instalments are to be credited at the time of the sale or only as they are received. Allowances may have to be made for the return of goods in default of payments, and for articles received in part exchange and the cost of servicing merchandise under guarantee. Where the business is one involving mail order sales, or includes orders received from agents or travelling salesmen, special provisions may be needed, with particular care if there are possibilities of substantial discount sales (which would reduce the turnover) to an associated company of the tenant. Thus Form 140, Sched 3, clause 7.1:1 includes a clause to cover orders made at the demised premises but delivered at or from a place elsewhere. Particularly important is provision for 'incidental receipts', like the refreshment sales in a cinema, or profits from vending machines. The issue may be complicated by the installation of such machines by a third party on a franchise basis. Unless the lease clearly provides for all these sources of income to be included in 'gross receipts', they may well be excluded (as in the *Bramhall Tudor Cinema* case) since they are not directly related to the tenant's business. All possible incidental sources of revenue should be covered or, at least, considered for inclusion. So Form 140 (clause 7.1:5 and 6) has provisions to cover grants, subsidies and fees of a revenue nature and (perhaps surprisingly) delivery and postal charges received.

(iii) Items to be excluded

Just as the lessor will wish to ensure that all proper receipts are included, a lessee will be concerned to see that payments of money passing through his hands that are really not part of his 'receipts' are excluded from the percentage base and excluded from the definition of gross sales or turnover. This will include discounts customarily allowed to employees, discounts properly and reasonably allowed to customers and allowances for defective or unsatisfactory goods. EFP (5th ed) Form 140 clause 7.3 contains a comprehensive list of such items which also includes (7.3:9) deduction of 'interest charges and credit account service charges'. It is suggested that this exclusion could be usefully expanded to cover all charges or commission paid on credit cards or any similar financial instrument. Direct payment cards whereby money is deducted direct from a customer's bank account are not true credit cards and with the pace of technological change, the definition should be comprehensive enough to exclude all commission paid by the retailer when goods are purchased by any kind of payment card or similar instrument.

The most important item to be considered will be the treatment of taxes and, particularly, VAT. When considering VAT, a clear distinction must be drawn between VAT chargeable on the tenant's goods and services (which the parties may agree to exclude from the computation of the turnover rent) and the VAT (if any) due upon the rent as so determined. Where no provision has been made in North American leases for sales taxes and the like, there has been a conflict of judicial opinion between those who view such taxes as merely money collected by the tenant-retailer on behalf of the state and, therefore, to be excluded from gross receipts, and those who view such taxes as revenue imposed on the trader and to be included in and paid out of gross receipts. The different approaches may be seen in *Lynn v Nathanson* (1931) 2 DLR 457 where the judges could declare the matter to be clear and straightforward yet reach opposite conclusions. The authors are not aware of any judicial guidance in this country in the following 70 years but prefer the view (of the minority in the *Lynn* case) that, without more, gross revenue or receipts includes any tax element. Express provision might provide for some taxes to be included and some excluded. (In the lease between the Minister of Transport and Granada Motorway Services, petrol duty was excluded but that on tobacco was included.) Generally, it seems right expressly to exclude all taxes and duties and EFP (5th ed) Forms 139 and 140 expressly so provide. The inclusion of taxes in gross turnover can give a false picture of business activity and later alterations in the amount of taxes levied may alter the amount of percentage rent received—perhaps to the disadvantage of the tenant as in *Tucker v Granada*. The parties should also consider exclusion of sales at cost, or without payment, of items customarily allowed to employees on which the tenant may make no profit, and perhaps allow the tenant to deduct bad debts—though it can be argued that the burden of a bad credit risk undertaken by a trader should not be shared with the landlord. Allowances are usually made for returns and refunds on items originally included in the gross sales. If the demised premises only constitute part of a tenant's business, careful apportionment of the turnover will be essential. Form 140, Sched 3, clause 7:3 provides a useful check-list of possible exclusions or deductions from the gross turnover.

(iv) Long stop provision

Since no draftsman can have the wisdom to anticipate every contingency it may be appropriate to include a clause whereby the parties agree that all receipts arising from the business on the demised premises that are not specifically excluded are deemed to be included in the percentage base. As an alternative, any disputes could be referred to some third party referee. In such a fallback provision, all that has been said in other places in this work on the desirability for clear criteria for such an independent judgment will apply.

(d) Rent periods

Greater attention than is usual must be given to times for payment of rent. The minimum or base rent may be treated in the usual way (eg by providing for quarterly payments in advance). A percentage rent poses greater difficulties when it is calculated, say, on annual or quarterly turnover or gross sales, for such figures can only be known at the end of the rent period to which they relate. It is unlikely that a lessor will be content to receive his rent in arrears, particularly if it is the greater or greatest proportion of the total rent due. Consequently, the lease will usually provide for instalment payments on account with a later reconciliation with what has actually been paid and an adjusted sum falling due for the last rental period of (say) the year. Reconciliation to the tenant's audited accounts may not be appropriate (for a host of reasons, eg different accounting period, or the inclusion of trade receipts from other premises) so separate final accounts will be needed. If the desired payment is for rent quarterly in arrears, then rent can be based on the actual 3–monthly figures with annual adjustments. Thus Hecht (1972) 2 Col LR 625 at 669 gives a typical North American example:

'. . . the rental will be computed and paid for the first three months. Three months later, the gross sales of the first quarter will be added to the gross sales of the second quarter and the percentage rate added to this total. The resulting figure is the percentage rental due for the two periods. The actual rent paid for the first quarter will be subtracted from the total rent due and the difference will be paid as the second quarter rental. The same process will be repeated for each successive period. At the end of the lease year the amount of rental paid will equal the annual rental.'

Adjustments to such a scheme may have to be made to allow for leases where the percentage rate only comes into operation when the turnover exceeds a certain sum; and if payments in advance are desired, as they usually will be, these will have to be based on 'preceding periods'. In such circumstances, excess payments may be made, and in the annual adjustment process, there should be provision either for refunding overpayments, perhaps with interest, or for carrying them forward against future payments. In the absence of such provisions, any excess may be recovered by action (*McAdam v Franklin* (1923) 1 DLR 1174) but that is hardly a recipe for harmonious landlord-tenant relationships.

In the published precedents, EFP (5th ed) Form 139 bases turnover rent instalments on the gross turnover for the preceding year so that payment 'in advance' can be made; in Form 140 the turnover rent is only due after a demand which in turn can only be issued in arrears after the tenant delivers his turnover certificate.

(e) Accounting

The lease should specify the details of the accounts to be kept and supplied by the lessee, requiring him to retain all sales receipts, vouchers etc and submit a certified statement of gross sales (or turnover etc). Either party should have the right to elect for an independent audit— the clause providing for the method of appointment, the incidence of the costs of the audit and declaring it to be binding on both parties.

Even with provision for such detailed accounting, the lessor must rely to some extent upon the lessee's good faith. Hargrove ((1957) 21 Conv (NS) 265 at 278) consequently suggests that the lessee's records should be subject to 'spot-checks' at any reasonable time without notice by an independent accountant. Such 'spot-checks' could be set in motion whenever the lessor so desired and he would bear the costs unless significant discrepancies were revealed between the actual sales and the audited records. The allowable discrepancies, perhaps a percentage, would have to be stated in the lease and it should be decided whether the allowable costs include the staff time of the lessee in collaborating with the auditor. The lessor should have rights of termination or compensation if the spot-check revealed deficiencies and the lessee would bear the costs of the check in such circumstances. The arbitration or other third party reference clause, a necessary feature of a lease containing a turnover or percentage rent, should be made to apply to such a clause should it be included. It might be feasible to incorporate the right to take 'spot-checks' with a more general right to enter and inspect (see below). Since the lessor will be given the right to careful perusal of the tenant's accounts, the lessee should insist on a covenant of secrecy and non-disclosure of the information so obtained.

Modern technology may supply more sophisticated checking methods. The tenant's computerised accounting machinery could be linked to the lessor's computer for a rapid calculation of the rent and check on turnover. Such a powerful intrusion into the tenant's activities might be resisted; a link to an independent party's computer could be an alternative. Even if such electronic eavesdropping could be established, precautions against evasion and fallback provisions in the case of computer failure would be needed and compatibility of cash and cheque handling facilities with both the original tenant and future assignees would be another factor.

It should be noted that the method of accounting is linked to the problem of rent periods, which has been alluded to previously. If the tenant's business is of such a nature that he has a measure of control over when receipts or sales are entered into his books, or if his trade is seasonal, relatively short rent periods (say, monthly or quarterly) may be inappropriate since (for example) receipts could be much higher in one period than in the others. In such cases longer rent periods (say, annually) may be an advantage.

(f) Provisions to protect the rent return

Perhaps the most intractable problem the lessor's draftsman faces is deciding exactly what measures are necessary to protect his client's return from the turnover rent and how they should be framed. His client will want him to ensure that the premises remain occupied by the tenant and that the business is conducted diligently with suitable provisions in default; but the tenant-entrepreneur will seek to limit the restrictions placed on his business operations. To achieve a balance between these conflicting objectives while maintaining clarity will demand a high degree of drafting skill.

Some or all of the following points will need to be covered:

(i)   Use and occupancy covenants

The basic requirement will be a covenant by the lessee to occupy the demised premises for the purpose of his business, and continuously operate the same, throughout the term of tenancy, with (probably) an additional covenant restricting the business to that agreed upon by the parties. This 'double' safeguard will both ensure that the tenant does not terminate his activities, nor substitute a business of a quite different type with (perhaps) a much lower turnover. An 'occupancy' clause should be relatively uncontentious, but it is nevertheless vital to the lessor to prevent a tenant vacating the premises and paying only the bare minimum rent. Occupancy may have even greater importance in a shopping centre where an empty unit can be detrimental to the centre as a whole. To meet this problem, a positive covenant to trade 'during the normal trading hours of the centre' (for example) will be required. This will be in addition to any covenant restrictive of use which would not of itself prevent cessation of trade. It should be noted that the lessors remedy for such breach of covenant will only be damages; a mandatory injunction is not available (*Braddon Towers v International Stores* (1979) [1987] 1 EGLR 209, *FW Woolworth plc v Charlwood Alliance Properties Ltd* [1987] 1 EGLR 53) though large damages claims may be possible for wrongful cessation.

Care must be taken if covenants either restrictive of the user of the premises or unduly restricting assignment are included, as the open market value of the property, relevant to any review of the minimum base rent, may be reduced thereby (as in *Plinth Properties Ltd v Mott, Hay and Anderson* (1978) 38 P & CR 361) unless the lease contains a direction that the use restriction is to be disregarded for that purpose. The phrasing of any use restriction, or limitation on the tenant's business activity, will ultimately depend upon the parties' respective bargaining powers. The lessor may seek detailed restrictions including (for retail premises) the items to be offered for sale, minimum opening hours and the manner of doing business, but he is really faced with a dilemma. A very 'general' user clause will give little control over variations in price range, or volume of goods stocked; but a detailed and specific clause may hinder a tenant in being able to react to market trends or eliminate unprofitable elements of his trade—to the disadvantage of both parties. United States' experience (see Hecht, pp 671–3) suggests the lease should specify the parties' intentions as far as possible; but this may only be essential in certain circumstances (eg where the lease is one of a unit in a shopping centre and competition between tenants in the one centre is to be restricted, or if the demised premises have a specialised use). In other circumstances a more general clause may suffice, provided the lessor is safeguarded by clauses covering certain contingencies which may adversely affect the tenant's business, and the arbitration clause is expressed to apply. Some care is also needed over any clause insisting on minimum opening hours, for a later shift in trading hours, for example, may reduce profitability.

(ii) Contingency clauses

Consideration should be given, where appropriate, to the inclusion of the following restrictions on the tenant, designed to encourage him to maintain his business at the demised premises: (1) a 'radius' clause, prohibiting the tenant from opening or operating a competing business within a specified distance; (2) a clause preventing transfer of all or (especially) part of the business to other locations (this may be linked to the occupancy clause (above) and will be particularly appropriate if the lessee has existing enterprises elsewhere); and (3) a clause whereby the tenant covenants not to alter substantially the manner of conducting his business. Each of these restrictions may be made subject to relaxation with consent of the lessor.

(iii) Assignment or sub-letting

Restrictions will be, or may be, required on assignment or sub-letting by the lessee, and the usual clauses will require modification. The simplest approach will be to restrict any assignment or sub-lease but even if this acceptable to the tenant express provision should be made for licences or concessions, particularly in large retail stores, so that sales or receipts of such concessions are deemed to be included in the lessees' gross sales. An alternative approach will be to permit assignment or sub-letting only with the lessor's consent so that he is able to approve the ability of the incoming tenant to maintain turnover. However, such consent cannot be unreasonably withheld (Landlord and Tenant Act 1927, s 19(2) and the onus of proof has now shifted to the landlord under the Landlord and Tenant Act 1988) and though the prospect of a diminution in rent should be reasonable grounds for refusing consent, each case will depend on its own circumstances. If the tenant is to be allowed to sub-let, this should be restricted to persons who will carry on the trade or business on the same or better terms, and the lessor must reserve the right to inspect the subtenant's accounts and require that any sub-lease contain these powers. From the tenant's point of view, the more complex the turnover provisions, the more detrimental it will be to the marketability of the lease, except in prime trading areas. EFP Form 140, in its Fourth Schedule, contains a complex scheme to cope with an assignment; to avoid the assignee paying rent on the outgoing tenant's turnover, the turnover rent is suspended for a period and the basic rent increased during the suspension until the turnover rent recommences. There is also provision to agree, or review by arbitration, the appropriate turnover percentage.

(iv) Right to enter

Leases commonly give the lessor the right to enter and view the demised premises but these are usually restricted to a limited number of times and for defined purposes. In percentage leases, however, the landlord's interests in the property and business are such that a right to enter the premises at reasonable times for the purpose of examination, or any other activity the lessor may deem necessary to protect his rights, may not be unreasonable.

(v) Dispute or arbitration clause

The arbitration clause in the lease should be made to apply to any disputes concerning the use of the premises, since arbitration (or expert determination) will be almost certainly preferable to direct recourse to the courts. A suitable compromise to such disputes may well be achieved by arbitration. If desired, and as an alternative to arbitration, disputes may be referred for settlement to a third party expert. Much of what has already been said elsewhere in this context (see Chapter 6) will apply. If determination by an expert is preferred, it may be necessary either to have separate clauses providing for different types of expert (eg valuer, accountant) according to the nature of the dispute or to allow the landlord at the time of the appointment to elect between the Presidents for the time being of the various professional bodies so that the appropriate President can appoint the expert from the ranks of his colleagues. In EFP (5th ed) Form 139, disputes as to the amount of gross turnover or the quantum of the turnover rent is referred to a member of the Institute of Chartered Accountants appointed by its President and acting as an expert. An accountant would seem to be appropriately qualified for this particular task, though the principal arbitration clause should be made to apply to all other disputes.

(vi) Provisions in default

The lessor must anticipate failure to observe the above, and expressly provide for default (eg failure to occupy the premises or furnish the certified accounts). One method would allow termination of the term, but (in England and Wales) this would be subject to the tenant's rights under the Landlord and Tenant Act 1954, Part II, though an application for a new tenancy could be resisted under s 30(1)(c)—namely, that there are substantial breaches of the tenant's obligations under the current tenancy. Since, however, the court has a discretion under s 30(1)(c) (namely, it may order a new tenancy if it considers it reasonable even if substantial breaches of the tenants' obligations are proved), an alternative solution might be to allow the lessor to serve a notice increasing the rent to the open market rent (with provisions for rent review in the normal manner thereafter), to be such sum as specified in the lessor's notice or, at the election of the tenant, to be determined by a third party referee. If a lessee failed to pay this sum, the lessor could terminate for non-payment of rent. An alternative protection suggested (EFP (5th ed) Vol 22, para 189) is to provide the lessor with the option of reverting to a conventional rent review in certain circumstances such as tenant default or the turnover falling below a specified figure.

(vii) No partnership clause

It may be appropriate in the interests of caution, to state expressly that the lessor and lessee do not intend to enter into partnership together and thereby ensure that the lessor is not liable for the lessee's losses, debts or torts. Such a clause is almost certainly unnecessary when the turnover rent is based on 'gross receipts' or 'gross turnover' since, by the Partnership Act 1890, s 2(2),'the sharing of gross returns does not of itself create a partnership'. Where the percentage base is net profit, such a clause may be helpful to ensure a partnership is not inadvertently created since a receipt of a share of profits is prima facie evidence of a partnership (s 2(3) of the 1890 Act). Even in the absence of such a clause, it is likely the landlord and tenant relationship will negative the prima facie assumption. If a joint venture is desired, though not common in this context, it is better created expressly in one or other of the accepted patterns.

4 Advantages of equity (or 'geared') rents

An equity rent (also known as 'gearing' or 'geared' rent) does not differ in principle from other forms of turnover rent, since the lessor still receives a percentage of the tenant's income, but in this case the percentage is based on the tenant's income from sub-letting the demised premises, often in smaller units. Almost invariably, it is not envisaged that the tenant will himself occupy any part of the premises at all (though suitable provision can and should be made for the eventuality of the tenant's occupation), indeed the lessor's income is linked to the tenant being successful in finding others who wish to occupy for their business. In Canada, at an early date, a lease reserving as a monthly rent a percentage of 'gross income' was upheld (*Trainshi v CPR* (1918) 2 WWR 1034) and it is but a short step to a lease giving an equity rent 'of one third of the rack rents which may be received by the lessees in respect of sub-lettings of the demised premises' as in *British Railways Board v Elgar House Ltd* (1969) 209 EG 1313.

Linking a head rent to the rental income of the tenant may have advantages in two situations. First, the determination of the open market rent for a large development which is wholly or largely sub-let at review involves difficulties both as to the assumptions and disregards (as in the *99 Bishopgate* case—see p 410, above) and in finding suitable comparables. An equity rent may avoid these difficulties. Secondly, as Aldridge observed ((1980) 77 *Law Society's Gazette* 786), equity rents are often employed as the best method of preserving the real value of ground rents, particularly those ground rents that reflect the continuing investment of the land owner (who may often be the 'land-assembler') in the development site on which the developer or even the occupying tenant has carried out the construction work. Such rents suffer from the impact of inflation as much as rack rents but it is more difficult periodically to review them in the manner usual for rack rents. There is the very real practical hurdle of obtaining evidence of the current value of ground rents when a review occurs, compounded by the notional assumption on which such a review will be based (namely, that the site is not built upon but is ripe for development); but the reality will be that the site is already developed, perhaps in a manner that planning regulations would no longer permit at the time of the review. Moreover, the larger the development the wider the geographical spread of comparables and the greater the variable elements in each comparator. A formula for statutory review of ground rents, based on letting value of the site, is found in the Leasehold Reform Act 1967, s 15, for residential ground rents. The rent for an extended lease under this Act is ascertained under a statutory formula based on the letting value of the notionally cleared site. Since it deals with residential ground rents, the use of the formula in commercial leases cannot be recommended.

Consequently, ground rents are often drafted in the form of an equity rent, so that the sum the mesne lessor pays to the head landlord is directly linked to the value of the open market rent or rents the lessor receives or should receive from the property as a whole. Certainly, a ground rent can be periodically reviewed based on the open market rent of the demised premises, so that a ground rent agreed at £5,000 in 1980 for a property with an open market rent of £100,000 might be reviewed at 5–year intervals to 5 per cent of the market rent at the review date. However, an equity rent may be more advantageous to both parties. The head landlord achieves a 'continuous review' since each quarterly or annual sum due will be the agreed percentage of the lessee's income as the sub-leases are subject to rent review (at least if they are staggered as may be wise), so the equity ground rent will increase accordingly, the head landlord gaining both protection from inflation and a return based on the ultimate letting value of his investment. To the extent that off-site improvements funded or prompted by the landlord enhances the attraction of the site, the return may be more immediate than with normal review of ground rents, especially if at fairly lengthy intervals. The lessee, on the other hand, will have the advantage that the ground rent will never be more than the agreed percentage of the income he receives (or should receive)—unlike a review of a ground rent to a percentage of the letting value of the premises as a whole, which might be more than the value of the premises, as subdivided between the existing tenants. The technique has much wider possibilities in the triple head lessor, mesne lessor and lessee relationship than in normal retail lettings. Ground rents are more fully discussed in Chapter 13 at p 459.

A valuable article by Reeves on leases embodying equity sharing appears at (1979) 76 *Law Socity's Gazette* 1218. Some salutary lessons can be learned from the case of *Freehold and Leasehold Shop Properties Ltd v Friends Provident Life Office* (1984) 271 EG 451.

5 Drafting equity rents

Many of the considerations relevant to drafting turnover rents outlined in the previous section of this chapter apply equally in the context of equity rents. Thus, there will often be a base minimum rent reserved (as in *BRB v Elgar House*); the equity rent may be based on the lessee's total income from sub-lettings or only on income in excess of a certain amount; thought must be given to rent periods, particularly if advance payments are desired, when the equity rent due may have to be based on the preceding rent periods applicable to the subtenancies; and the head landlord will need the lessee's covenant to disclose the necessary information and allow inspection of the relevant sub-leases and accounts.

It is perhaps worth stressing that there is a real difference between a true 'equity' rent—where the lessor's rental income is, in principle, only a mathematical calculation of a particular percentage of the lessees rental income at any given time (eg annually adjusted), and a rent review of the rent payable in the head lease by reference to that same income. The latter is really only a form of usual review, with a very different formula for ascertainment than a standard review. The *British Railways* case is an example of the former; the *Freehold and Leasehold Shop* decision and *Leigh v Certibilt Investments Ltd* [1988] 1 EGLR 116 contain examples of the latter.

The drafting concerns differ, as well as the structure of the clauses. In the former, the prime concern is ascertainment of the actual income received, with safeguards for voids, occupation by the tenant, concessions and to cover lettings at less than rack rent. In the latter, the focus is shifted to the market rental value of the sub-units, and the current income received may, or may not, represent that up-to-date value. The extent to which rental default by the occupying lessees does or does not affect the head-rent, or the gearing element in it, must be provided for, particularly in regard to whether or not there needs to be an incentive to the mesne lessor to be vigilant about taking swift action on arrears.

The distinction must be constantly borne in mind when assessing the following drafting concerns. The discussion is primarily directed to the 'true' equity rent but is also relevant to a rent review mechanism using the equity formula.

(a) Definition of the tenant's income

Just as the efficacy of a turnover percentage rent depends on the definition of 'gross sales' or 'receipts', so also detailed attention must be given to the definition of the tenant's income. As Reeves observes,

ultimately the ascertainment of the head lessor's income is no more than
a refined mathematical calculation (1979) 76 *Law Society's Gazette* 128)
in a true equity rent. This means that the definition of the tenant's income
must be as comprehensive as possible to remove or limit future disputes
between the parties. There are two principal features of such definition:
measuring the tenant's *gross* income and delimiting the allowable
expenses, outgoings and charges so as to arrive at the *net* income on
which the equity rent is based. If the equity rent is to be based solely
on gross income, then the tenant must ensure that the proportion of
the gross sum payable is fixed so as to reflect the management expenses
and costs he must pay from his share.

(b)   Gross income

The definition must ensure that all income and potential income from
the tenant's sub-letting or other exploitation of the demised premises
is included. This should extend to such items as fees for advertising
stations, licence fees for casual use or display areas, hiring out fees and
other payments for concessions. The main source of income will be from
the rack rents obtained from sub-leases, no doubt having rents subject
to review, and the aim of the draftsman will be to ensure that this income
is not diminished. To this end, it is essential that the head lease provides
that all sub-leases are at full open market rental value, and defines that
phrase (this was not done in the *Freehold and Leasehold Shop* case) and
provides that if a sub-lease is made at less than the open market rent,
the head lessor can substitute the full rack rent (as valued) for the purpose
of calculating his equity rent. (Where his bargaining position is strong,
the lessor might seek a power of veto in relation to sub-rents). An
alternative way of protection, at least where the letting is below the
maximum obtainable because a premium has been paid, is to stipulate
either that a proportion of the premium is to be paid to the head lessor
or to rentalise the premium for the equity rent calculation. The
identification of what constitutes a premium is another challenge to the
draftsman, one that has already faced the parliamentary draftsman in
relation to ss 34–39 of the Income and Corporation Taxes Act 1988,
and he must also steer clear of the prohibitions of s 144 of the Law
of Property Act 1925. Express provision for a specified proportion of
any later premium should avoid s 144. The lessee, the mesne landlord,
may wish to occupy all or part of the premises for his own purposes.
Though the court may be able, in the absence of express provision,
to construe the lease so that the rental value of the part so occupied
is taken into account (*British Railways Board v Elgar House Ltd* (1969)
209 EG 1313), it is important expressly to provide that the open market
rental value of the part so occupied is brought into account for the
computation of the equity rent. The basis of valuation of any property

so occupied must be stated (and can be linked to the similar valuation of vacant units).

Perhaps the most important contingency on which the parties must agree in advance is the treatment of vacant units. At the start of the term, the endeavours of the developer-lessee may be reflected in a peppercorn rent, and the equity rent may only become payable after a certain period. A more contentious area is the provision for later voids and a balance may have to be struck, for the lessee will be unhappy at the prospect of paying an equity rent on a unit empty because of difficulties in the property market, the lessor will not wish to lose income when the unit has been deliberately left unoccupied. The better solution may be to provide for a 'notional rent' for such empty premises equal to that obtainable in the open market for a hypothetical term (the details of which should be described in the lease)—and if the lessee can show that there are market difficulties, then these will be reflected in the notional open market rent. The lessee should consider bargaining for a reasonable 'rent free' period to allow for re-marketing of vacant units.

In all cases where a 'notional rent' is to be used as the basis, it will be necessary to provide for independent valuation (or arbitration) if the parties are unable to agree the relevant figure.

(c) Calculating the net income

The tenant will wish to deduct from the gross income all the costs of repairing, maintaining and managing the demised premises. Experience suggests, once again, that the prudent draftsman will attempt to cover the main areas of expense and thereby reduce the possibility of later disputes (see Reeves, loc cit). The definition of net income ought to cover insurance premiums, general and water rates, VAT (with provision for payment of taxes that may be levied in the future—eg local sales taxes), repair, maintenance and decoration costs and management expenses (where these are recovered by way of service charge on the occupying subtenants the service charge will have appeared as part of the gross income). Alternatively, those parts of service charges that are recoverable for the tenant may be deleted from gross income and consequently the costs of those services will not be an allowable deductible expense for the purposes of net income. Reasonable legal expenses, the cost of complying with statutory notices and the expense of re-letting vacant accommodation would also be appropriate deductions. A concluding clause may cover any items not expressly referred to by providing for deduction of expenditure that has the head lessor's prior written approval or is wholly, necessarily and exclusively expended in compliance with the covenants on the part of the tenant—with provision for arbitration or other third party reference on any matters which cannot be resolved within this framework.

Problems associated with calculation of net income are avoided if the lessor takes a percentage only of the gross income received; the proportion will, no doubt, be reduced to reflect management expenses and the risk of fluctuations in such costs is then borne entirely by the tenant. The experience of such formulae in the comparable field of turnover rents is not a happy omen for this approach.

(d)   Full information

As indicated, the head lessor will need the right to full information, as with retail percentage or turnover leases. In equity leases, consideration might be given to furnishing the head lessor with not only the right to information about the rent reviews of the sub-leases but also the right to be involved in the negotiations and review process, perhaps by allowing rights to be heard and to opt for third party reference if dissatisfied with any provisional agreement reached between mesne landlord and subtenant.

(e)   Terms of sub-leases

Since the head lessor's income will depend upon successful and secure occupation sub-leases, he will wish to have some control over the terms that may be agreed. Usual practice appears to be to agree standard forms in advance but obviously some machinery for later agreed variations should also be provided.

(f)   Problems with VAT

The regime where some but not all rents may be subject to VAT introduces a new drafting complication. Election or non-election to charge the tax can affect rent levels and merely eliminating the tax from the calculation is not sufficient since it will rarely serve to counter the consequence on the rent of the incidence of VAT (see Chapter 15, p 492). New leases with equity rents, or where the mesne lessor is subject to an equity rent, can deal with this expressly though there is a trend against multiplying artificialities of this kind. Earlier leases entered into before the introduction of the charge are unlikely to contain any express provision.

A new lease could bind the original lessee not to elect to charge VAT and thereby protect the level of the rent on which the equity rent in the head lease depends. It is doubtful whether such a covenant would bind assignees and even if it does potential assignees who have already elected in respect of the rest of their portfolio of holdings will be reluctant to purchase and thereby result in an argument for a rent discount on review of that rent.

(g) Rent periods

The amount of rent due may be recalculated continuously for each rent period, the sum payable being based on the occupation rents for a preceding period. Where, however, the equity rent is only received periodically, the head lessor will need to ensure that there is some control over the review periods in the sub-leases so as to prevent them having a review date just after the relevant time for determining the equity rent. Failure to cover such contingencies (as in the *Freehold and Leasehold Shop* case) may result in the sub rents used for calculation of the equity rent being substantially less than the current market rental value.

(h) Treatment of improvements

Since a frequent occasion for an equity rent is the provision of an assembled site by the ground landlord for development by the head lessee no question of disregard of the rental effect of initial improvements, ie the development, is appropriate. Frequently the sharing formula allows the head lessee a return on certified construction costs, or construction plus other specified development costs, before any sharing takes effect. However, consideration should be given to the treatment of later improvements by the head lessee, whether the original developer or its successor; these will often be designed to improve the sub-rents and a formula for eliminating the unfairness of simply permitting the head lessor to recoup his percentage of the enhanced sub-rents is desirable, and, from the head lessee's point of view, essential. Similarly where a sub-rent contains an element of reimbursement through rent of a head lessee's funding of work required by the occupying subtenants, machinery to identify, and authenticate, that element and eliminate it from the calculations should be included in the documentation. The sub-leases would, in contrast to the head leases, contain the usual disregard for voluntary improvements by subtenants, the form of which, as explained, will be of concern to the head lessor.

(i) No-partnership clause

The cautionary no-partnership clause (see p 601 above) is more worthy of inclusion in equity leases than in retail percentage agreements, for the parties are effectively sharing profits. Indeed the term 'partnership' is frequently adopted in relation to equity sharing, and provisions are sometimes inserted to share 'losses' incurred by a tenant as a result of actions by a head landlord who happens to be a local authority. Unless a full partnership in law is what is intended (which is unlikely) the no-partnership clause suggested above may be prudently inserted.

(j) Periodic review using the equity formula

Where the parties agree periodic review of the head lease but wish to use a percentage of the current income received by the tenant as a formula, then it may be appropriate to take the current income, or the current open market value of the sub-lettings, whichever is greater. (This may have been intended in the *Freehold and Leasehold Shop* case, but, if so, the draftsman failed in his purpose). A clear choice is required for the valuation basis of any hypothetical substitution for actual income between obtaining the value for a single letting of the whole of the premises or the basis of the aggregate rent of hypothetical lettings of the individual parts thereof. Failure to make this clear was at the root of the litigation in *Leigh v Certibilt*.

If the head lease review is to be tied to the actual income received, the head lessor will wish to ensure that the rent review periods in the sub-leases are consistent with that in the head lease so that they represent as far as possible the current rental value.

Provisions for voids and occupancy by the tenant will be similar to those required for true equity rents (above).

(k) Linking reviews in sub-leases

The 'reverse' of an equity rent occurs when the rent in a sub-lease is expressed as a percentage of the rent reserved in the head lease. Some problems of such rent reviews are discussed in Chapter 4, p 87, above.

(l) Development transactions

Sophisticated development transactions involving one or other variants of equity rent lie beyond the scope of this book. Some examples will be found in the precedent books but they do not exhaust the possibilities. The drafting of such development agreements can become quite complex, dealing with such matters as ascertainment of the allowable expenditure on which the developer is to receive his initial rent return (perhaps over and above a basic ground rent subject to review) the approval of subtenants, the period before the developer's guarantee of income becomes operative and machinery for extensions of that period and events of default. The involvement of a funder will further complicate the documentation. The paucity of reported cases may be as much a result of the large time scale involved in the revalorisation process as in the undoubted skill of the drafters.

6 Conclusion

There is a strong case for the adoption and continuing use of equity and turnover rents in certain particular commercial transactions, especially those involving shopping centres or large scale commercial developments whose participants find that they enable them to preserve a steady real income from their capital investment. The increasing involvement of foreign entities in the property and financial service industries may herald further use of these approaches at the expense of the insular, though highly developed, rent review regime.

Part Six

The RICS Guidance Notes

Part Six is the full text of the Guidance Notes for surveyors acting as arbitrators or as independent experts in rent reviews (Fourth Edition) produced by the Royal Institution of Chartered Surveyors and reproduced with permission.

Guidance Notes for Surveyors Acting as Arbitrators or as Independent Experts in Rent Reviews (Fourth Edition)

1-1 PART ONE: GENERAL INTRODUCTION

1.1.1. *Scope of Guidance Notes*

These Guidance Notes, together with a Commentary on them are printed in the Handbook of Rent Review by Bernstein and Reynolds (1985 Revision).

They are designed primarily to assist those who are appointed either by the President of the RICS, or directly by the parties to a dispute, to act as Arbitrators or as Independent Experts. They are also intended to assist the parties themselves and those acting for them by making them aware of the procedures likely to be followed, but these pages are not intended to be regarded as a treatise on the law and practice of arbitration generally. These Notes are based upon the law and practice in England and Wales; Scottish law and practice are somewhat different.

1.1.2. The majority of appointments made by the President are in Landlord and Tenant matters, notably rent review. Accordingly these Guidance notes were specifically prepared for rent review Arbitrations and Independent Expert appointments to determine rents. Some of the procedures included in the Notes, and the principles of natural justice, apply to all Arbitrations.

1.1.3 As regards agricultural holdings, however, it should be borne in mind that there are separate provisions to be found in the agricultural holdings legislation, concerning which the appropriate publications should be consulted.

1.1.4 While these Notes will provide adequate guidance for surveyors acting as Arbitrators in the great majority of cases it must be stressed that, in some cases, the surveyor Arbitrator will need to have a wider and deeper understanding of the law and procedure than it has been considered appropriate to provide in these pages. This is particularly so in construction industry arbitrations where the subject of the dispute is more likely to concern matters such as the necessity for or manner in which work should be carried out, or concerning the payment of a capital sum, for which it is unlikely that the 'written representation' procedure set out hereafter would be appropriate and an arbitration hearing conducted on more formal lines would probably apply.

Any surveyor likely to be appointed as Arbitrator in references which may involve issues of law and procedure outside his normal experience would be well advised to attend one of the courses conducted from time to time by the

RICS, the Chartered Institute of Arbitrators and the College of Estate Management.

The standard legal textbooks on the subject are *Russell on Arbitration* (published by Stevens and Sons); Mustill and Boyd, *Commercial Arbitrations* (published by Butterworths). *The Handbook of Arbitration Practice* (Sweet & Maxwell and the Chartered Institute of Arbitrators) contains inter alia a general section by Ronald Bernstein, QC, FCI Arb and a section on 'Practice in Rent Review Arbitrations by W G Nutley, BSc, FRICS.

Throughout these Guidance Notes, references to the masculine include the feminine.

1.1.5. *Comparison of arbitration with determination by Independent Expert*

The duties and suggested procedures for both Arbitrators and Independent Experts are in some respects the same. The differences as regards rent reviews may be summarised as follows:

Arbitrator

1. The Arbitrator acts (as does a judge) only on evidence and arguments submitted to him and bases his decision thereon. His Award must lie between the extremes contended for by the parties. He is however expected to use his expertise in assessing the relevance and quality of the evidence and arguments submitted to him—but see also paragraph 1.1.8.

2. The Arbitrator cannot decide without receiving evidence from the parties or (when proceeding *ex parte*) one of the parties.

3. The procedure for arbitration is regulated by the Arbitration Acts.

4. A party to an arbitration can (through the courts) compel disclosure of documents or the attendance of witnesses—see paragraph 3.6.3.

5. The Arbitrator's award may be enforceable as a judgment of the Court (This is not, however, of practical importance in rent review arbitrations. Enforcement of rent review Awards is by separate action for arrears of rent, or forfeiture or by distress).

Independent Expert

1. The Independent Expert has the duty of investigation to discover the facts and/or relevant transactions (though he may receive evidence of facts and/or transactions from the parties).

2. The Independent Expert must decide upon his own knowledge and investigations, but he may be required by the instrument under which he is appointed to receive submissions from the parties.

3. There is no legislation governing procedure for the Independent Expert.

4. The Independent Expert has no such powers.

5. The Independent Expert's determination cannot be enforced as such; a separate action must be brought based on it.

6. The Arbitrator's fees can be taxed by the Court under the Arbitration Acts—see Section 3.9.6.	6. There is no procedure for taxation of an Independent Expert's fees.
7. The Arbitrator is not liable for negligence (unless he is only nominally an arbitrator but is in truth an expert acting on his own investigations).	7. The Independent Expert, like any other valuer, is liable for negligence.
8. There is some (albeit limited) right of appeal against the Award of an Arbitrator on a point of law.	8. There is no right of appeal against the determination of an expert, though in some circumstances the Court might set it aside.

It is therefore essential that the parties and the person appointed should be absolutely clear which category of appointment is involved.

1.1.6. *Nature of appointment: interpretation of lease or agreement*

Where a lease or agreement, with reference to the appointment of a surveyor, mentions 'arbitrator' or 'arbitration' or the Arbitration Acts, even though it may also make reference to a 'valuer', 'independent valuer', 'expert', or other such term, it is generally treated as calling for the appointment of an Arbitrator, unless it is clear that the parties intended otherwise.

1.1.7 *Doubt as to nature of appointment*

The rent review clause will not always be clear as to whether the appointment is to be of an Arbitrator or an Independent Expert. The appointee should, therefore, ensure that the nature of the appointment is explicitly stated in the letter or other instrument of appointment. If it is not, he should clarify the point with the parties before he proceeds with his reference.

If there is any doubt as to the correct interpretation of the lease or other document giving rise to his appointment, the parties may agree which interpretation is correct. However, there is a danger that third parties (such as the original lessee, or a surety) will be able subsequently to dispute that agreed interpretation. In case of doubt, the parties may wish to have the question decided by the Court.

1.1.8. *Umpires*

By the Arbitration Act 1950, s 8, as amended by the Arbitration Act 1979, s 7, unless a contrary intention is expressed every arbitration agreement which provides for the appointment of two Arbitrators, one to be appointed by each party, shall be deemed to include a provision that the two Arbitrators may appoint an Umpire at any time after they are themselves appointed. If they fail to agree on their Award they must forthwith appoint an Umpire. The usual procedure is for the Arbitrators to attempt to agree on their Award, and if they fail they notify the Umpire in writing that they cannot agree, whereupon their functions as Arbitrators cease and the Umpire in effect becomes sole Arbitrator in their place. Moreover, once an Umpire has been appointed, the High Court may, on the application of either party and notwithstanding anything to the contrary in the arbitration agreement, order that the Umpire shall enter upon the reference in place of the arbitrators as if he were a sole Arbitrator. The appointment of an Umpire should be discussed with the parties as there could be advantages in appointing an Umpire at the beginning of the reference to avoid hearing evidence twice but this would involve the extra costs of the Umpire. In any event a stenographer should be employed if hearings take place.

The above refers to the appointment of an Umpire in its strict sense under the Arbitration Acts. In some leases however, the rent review clause provides that the new rent shall be determined by a 'surveyor acting as Umpire'. The effect of such wording is that normally the surveyor acts as Arbitrator, the word 'Umpire' in this context having no other meaning. There may be certain circumstances however where the use of the term Umpire may in fact mean to act in the capacity of an independent expert. This is a matter of interpretation of the lease.

Some old leases provide for a reference to two Arbitrators, one being appointed by each party, and in the event of their disagreeing upon a common award, to be determined by an Umpire. The two Arbitrators should consider themselves to be Arbitrators, not agents for the parties appointing them.

1.1.9. *The statutory framework: arbitration*

The principal Act governing the conduct of Arbitrators is the Arbitration Act of 1950 as amended by the Arbitration Act 1979. There is, of course, special legislation relating to agricultural holdings. The person appointed to act as Arbitrator must therefore have regard to the provisions of these Acts and, whatever his view may be as to the desirability of conducting the hearing with a greater or lesser degree of informality, it is important that he should be careful not to infringe any express provision of these Acts or of the arbitration agreement, lest his Award be set aside or remitted. (See paragraph 3.8.11, below).

1.1.10. *Independent Expert free to exercise his own judgment*

There is no legislation, and little case law, governing the appointment or conduct of a surveyor to act in this capacity; the person appointed must exercise his personal professional expertise and judgment. The notes in Part 4 of these Guidance Notes should afford general guidance.

1.1.11. *Fees and costs*

Sections 3–9 and 3–10 deal with fees and costs for Arbitrators and Independent Experts respectively.

2–1   PART TWO: APPOINTMENT AND ACCEPTANCE

2.1.1. *Application to the President for appointment*

Application to the President for the appointment of an Arbitrator or Independent Expert should be in writing and preferably made on the form obtainable on application to the RICS.

2.1.2 *Document(s) and fee on application*

The application will not be processed until the appropriate non-refundable fee, currently (1987) £80.50 including £10.50 VAT, has been received together with a copy of the lease or other document conferring on the President power to make the appointment.

2.1.3 *Appointee should study document under which appointment made*

Whether he has been appointed by the President or privately, the Arbitrator or Independent Expert should study in detail the lease or other document under which he is appointed so that he is clear as to the precise nature of the dispute and any special provisions that may apply.

2.1.4 *Responsibility and disqualifications*

The acceptance of an appointment as Arbitrator or Independent Expert carries with it heavy responsibility, and every effort is made by the President to select a person suitable for appointment in accordance with his current policy statement on conflict of interest.

A person considered suitable for appointment is then asked to confirm:
- (*a*)   that the matter falls within the scope of his own normal professional practice (not merely that of his firm);
- (*b*)   that he would be able to undertake the task with reasonable expedition;
- (*c*)   that there is no other reason why he should not accept the appointment

In deciding whether he should accept an appointment the prospective appointee should take into consideration all matters which might give rise to the possibility or appearance of bias. For example, if one of the parties is a company in which the appointee or his partners or his family have substantial shareholdings, bias would appear possible. If the appointee or his firm also acts for the landlords or tenants of a nearby property where rent reviews are due shortly, his decision might be thought to be influenced by the knowledge of the effect it will have on the imminent rent reviews. However, his general knowledge of a locality may well be to the advantage of the parties, rather than a ground for objection to his appointment.

The safe rule is that if there is any doubt as to whether a connection with the property, a party or a representative of a party might give rise to a conflict of interest, disclose it.

2.1.5 *When appointment takes effect*

The appointment takes effect from the date on which the President signs the appointment.

2.1.6. *After the appointment has been made*

Once the President has made an appointment, his jurisdiction in the matter is at an end unless the lease (or, in a relatively few cases, statute) itself provides to the contrary. If, therefore, after the appointment of the arbitrator or independent expert, a party should bring to the attention of the appointee a matter claimed to constitute a real pecuniary or other interest in the outcome of the dispute or to give rise to a real possibility of bias, the arbitrator or expert would be expected to:
- (*a*)   obtain full details of the objection in writing;
- (*b*)   notify the other party in writing and invite his comments;
- (*c*)   consider whether the matters disclosed might affect his mind in coming to a decision or would raise a real possibility of bias in the eyes of a reasonably-minded person;

(*d*) if the answer to either of these questions is yes, retire unless both parties agree in writing that he should continue;

(*e*) if the answer to each of these questions is no, continue.

Equally, if the arbitrator or independent expert should discover a matter which might affect his mind in coming to a decision, or would raise a real possibility of bias in the eyes of a reasonably-minded person, he would be expected immediately to disclose it to the parties and then proceed as in (*d*) or (*e*) above.

A Policy Statement on this subject has been issued by the President—see *Chartered Surveyor Weekly*, Vol 20, page 67 (10 September 1987).

2.1.7. *Acceptance of private appointments*

Some leases or other documents call for appointment of a surveyor (whether to act as an Arbitrator or an Independent Expert) by a person other than the President of the RICS. In such circumstances it is no less important that attention should be paid to the factors listed in paragraphs 1.1.7 and 2.1.4.

PART THREE: ARBITRATORS

3–1 POWERS AND DUTIES OF AN ARBITRATOR

3.1.1. *Deriving from contract*

Parties who include in any agreement a clause for settling by arbitration any dispute within the scope of that clause are thereby referring those disputes to private determination rather than to a court of law. Since in most cases the Arbitrator derives his authority from the contract between the parties they can also agree, as a matter of contract, the principles and procedure which he shall apply in any dispute which may arise, provided that these do not conflict with the Arbitration or other Acts. The first rule for the Arbitrator is therefore to look at the arbitration agreement and other sources of his authority to see what is provided.

3.1.2. *Other sources of powers and duties*

When the Arbitrator has been duly appointed, his powers and duties stem from the following:

(*a*) the Arbitration Act 1950 as amended by the Arbitration Act 1975 (which relates mainly to Foreign Arbitral Awards) and the Arbitration Act 1979;

(*b*) the provisions of any special legislation applying to the particular subject matter;

(*c*) the terms of the arbitration agreement (eg the rent review clause in the lease or the arbitration clause of a contract);

(*d*) the principles of natural justice.

Any problems arising in the arbitration that are not provided for expressly or implicitly in the arbitration agreement or the relevant Acts are matters for the Arbitrator's discretion. This must be exercised judicially, and in accordance with the rules of natural justice. Above all, it is the duty of an Arbitrator, as it is of a Judge, to hear both sides to the dispute (except when proceeding *ex parte*—see paragraph 3.6.11) and to decide it according to the evidence and to the law. These Notes are intended to indicate to surveyors, in relation to problems commonly arising in arbitrations, the principles on which this discretion should be exercised. In general, if there is nothing in the Acts or in the arbitration agreement to indicate the contrary, the Arbitrator should proceed in whatever way seems to him to be the fairest.

3.1.3 *Liquidators/receivers and guarantors*

Whilst the landlord and tenant are usually the parties in an arbitration, a properly appointed liquidator/receiver (for either the landlord or tenant) may take over the relevant role. A guarantor is not a party to the arbitration but he may be called as a witness or at the request of the relevant party act as his agent in pursuing the reference.

3.1.4. *The nature of arbitration*

Arbitration procedure, like civil litigation, is an adversarial procedure. Each party decides what evidence and what contentions he wishes to put before the Arbitrator, who then decides the issue upon that material. An Arbitrator, like a Judge, has no duty to make investigations, or to ensure that all relevant information has been put before him or to look beyond that information, but he may seek from the parties clarification of any evidence which he received. Nevertheless, since the surveyor has been appointed as Arbitrator because of his expertise and knowledge, if, during the hearing he considers that a party has overlooked a point of substance which in his opinion is material, or if there is some material fact (eg a comparable transaction) known to the Arbitrator of which the parties appear to be unaware, he should in the interests of justice specifically raise the point so as to give the parties an opportunity of commenting upon it, of calling other evidence, or seeking an adjournment for calling other evidence.

He must not however on any account decide the issue by ignoring the evidence presented to him and base his Award mainly on evidence within his own knowledge, without disclosing that personal knowledge to the parties or party so that it may be tested examined and debated before him (see *Fisher* v *P G Wellfair Ltd* (1982) 263 EG 589, 657).

3.1.5. *The Arbitrator must not award more than is sought by the claimant nor less than is submitted by the respondent*

Likewise he must not award more—or less—than is supported by the evidence put before him. He should, however, use his professional skill in assessing the relevance and quality of the evidence put before him.

3–2 ACTION BY THE ARBITRATOR ON BEING APPOINTED

3.2.1 *Informing the parties*

On appointment it is the Arbitrator's duty to proceed without delay. He should therefore notify the parties or their representatives of his appointment, and proceed with the arbitration unless requested by both parties to defer proceedings.

3.2.2. *Establishing the Arbitrator's fees or charges*

Unless already agreed at the time of accepting the appointment, the Arbitrator should at this stage state the amount of his fees or give an indication of the basis on which he intends to charge. Unless this is agreed, it might be subject to challenge by either party at a later stage. Where appropriate the fee should be expressed to be exclusive of disbursements, particularly any legal costs the Arbitrator may incur. See further as to fees, section 3.9 below, particularly paragraph 3.9.7 below.

3.2.3. *The possibility of compromise*

The Arbitrator should, at the outset, enquire of the parties whether there is any possibility of their reaching a negotiated settlement and, if so, whether they wish him to defer the arbitration. Either in the initial letter, or at the preliminary meeting if any, the parties should be reminded that they are at liberty to settle between themselves at any time prior to the award, but in this event will be liable for the Arbitrator's fees and disbursements to date.

3.2.4. *Award by consent*

If the parties compromise in the course of an arbitration their agreement may either be that their dispute is resolved upon the agreed terms, or that they will agree before the Arbitrator what award he should make. Technically, if the agreement is of the former nature its effect is to deprive the Arbitrator of his authority for there is no longer any dispute between the parties. Any award which he might subsequently make would be a nullity. In the latter case, the agreement is not technically a resolution of the dispute itself, but an agreement that the Arbitrator shall decide it in a particular way. In that case it will be an 'Award by Consent'. This distinction could be of importance if a question were to arise as to whether a third party was bound by an award. For this reason an award by consent is usually preferable to a compromise not incorporated in an award. An award by consent would be an award which incorporates the agreed terms of settlement and the apportionment between the parties of costs, including the fees and expenses of the Arbitrator.

Leases, being documents under seal, necessitate any amendments also being under seal. Many leases provide that a memorandum of any agreed review rent is to be endorsed on the lease and counterpart. Where however this provision does not occur, the parties may prefer that the agreed review rent is incorporated in an award by consent, since an award is a legally binding document. Such an award would avoid the (admittedly remote) possibility of future arguments between the parties and/or subsequent assignees which might arise if the agreed review rent was only incorporated in an exchange of letters.

3.2.5. *Choice between hearing or written representations*

If the parties agree, before or immediately after the appointment, that they wish to proceed by written representations without a hearing, the Arbitrator should write to each of them setting out the procedure he proposes to adopt and inviting them to agree, or to suggest different directions. otherwise, the Arbitrator should write asking the parties whether they wish him to proceed by way of written representations or by a hearing, pointing out that if one party so requires there must be a hearing.

However in most cases a preliminary meeting with the parties following his appointment should lead to more rapid identification and clarification of the matters which it is necessary for the Arbitrator to cover in his directions (see section 3–3).

Obviously both parties must be invited and should attend any such preliminary meeting—but see paragraphs 3.6.11 to 3.6.15 re proceeding *ex parte*.

The questions whether there is any issue of law between the parties, and if so how it is to be resolved, will often be material to the choice between a hearing and written representations only; see paragraphs 3.2.7 and 3.2.8.

3.2.6. *Written representation procedure often appropriate*

In view of the nature of the matters likely to concern surveyors, and their particular skill in the writing of reports, the written representation procedure is often more appropriate to a rent review dispute.

Even if this procedure is decided upon, the Arbitrator should reserve the right to call for a hearing. He may consider it necessary or desirable to have a hearing if matters of fact or evidence contained in the written representations require clarification, or if the difference between the parties' respective figures is so great as to require explanation. The prospect of an opinion expressed in writing being subjected to cross-examination under oath at a hearing may act as a deterrent to the inclusion of irresponsibly high (or low) figures.

3.2.7. *Disputes involving issues of law*

Although most rent review arbitrations involve mainly issues of valuation, they often also raise one or more points of law, such as the meaning of the rent review clause, or of parts of the lease, or the admissibility of evidence.

When a point of law is raised, the Arbitrator should require the party raising it to formulate it in writing and make sure he understands it. He should then consider with the parties how it should be dealt with. The following are the main possibilities:—

(*a*) The parties may enter into an 'exclusion agreement', thereby leaving the point for the sole decision of the Arbitrator without there being any possibility of a later appeal to the Court.

(*b*) The parties may authorise the Arbitrator to take legal advice on the point before making his award. It is desirable that the Arbitrator should seek to agree with the parties the wording of the question or questions on which he is to take legal advice.

(*c*) The Arbitrator may, with the parties' consent, appoint a legal assessor to sit with him and hear argument.

(*d*) A case may be stated jointly by the parties for the opinion of Counsel, the parties agreeing to be bound by that opinion. This would have the same effect as an 'exclusion agreement'.

(*e*) The point may be decided by the Court as a preliminary point of law—see paragraph 3.2.8.

(*f*) The point may be determined by the Arbitrator without prejudice to the right of appeal. If this course is adopted it is usually best for the Arbitrator to make an alternative Award stating what he would have awarded if he had decided the point of law the other way.

If the parties do not agree or consent to any of (*a*) to (*e*) above, the only course for the Arbitrator to adopt is to proceed as under (*f*).

The tendency of the Courts since the Arbitration Act 1979 to discourage appeals from Arbitrators, even on points of interpretation, places upon the Arbitrator who adopts procedure (*f*) a greatly increased responsibility. In cases of this kind the Arbitrator should refer to the Handbook of Rent Review, Part 10, and text books on Arbitration.

3.2.8. *The determination of a preliminary point of law*

It is sometimes convenient and economical to have a disputed question of interpretation of the lease decided as a preliminary point i.e. before any evidence on the valuation issues is called. This would be in the form of an interim award. Such cases are relatively rare because in most instances the issues of valuation and interpretation are inextricably interwoven.

Where such a request by one party is opposed by the other the Arbitrator should not grant the request unless he considers that the balance of advantage to the parties is overwhelming. In this respect he must consider the possibility that the Court may give leave to appeal against his decision on the point.

As an alternative to the preliminary point being decided by the Arbitrator, it may be decided by the Court under s 2 of the Arbitration Act 1979. This is only possible if (*a*) the Arbitrator or all the parties consent and (*b*) the High Court is satisfied that the determination might produce substantial savings in costs and that the point was one where leave to appeal would be likely to be given.

3.2.9. *Procedural differences between written representations and hearing procedure*

Once the choice has been made, the procedure thereafter will vary according to which has been chosen. Section 3–4 deals with procedure by written representations and section 3–5 with procedure by way of hearing. The remainder of section 3 (dealing with evidence, the award and fees and costs) is common to both procedures.

3.2.10 *Arbitrations on overlapping issues–powers and limitations*

Where the same or a substantially similar issue arises both under a contract between A and B and under a contract between B and C, and applications for the appointment of an arbitrator under each contract are made to the President at or about the same time, the President may decide to appoint the same person as arbitrator in both cases.

If he does so, the arbitrator should consider in consultation with all the parties whether a procedure can be devised which is acceptable to all of them.

There may be substantial benefits to the parties in terms of costs by arranging one combined hearing of the separate arbitrations.

If the arbitrator is appointed in two or more related cases:

(*a*) he must follow any procedural requirements laid down in any of the leases, even if these vary from lease to lease;

(*b*) he has no power to order combined hearings or submissions unless all parties consent, such consent to extend to agreeing that arbitrator may act in each case on all the evidence and submissions given at the combined hearing or contained in the combined submissions;

(*c*) if there are separate hearings or submissions, he must not act in one on evidence or argument not given in that arbitration. He may raise matters which have arisen in a previous arbitration or probe the evidence in the light of such knowledge, but he must not base his award on a point not argued before him (or present in submissions) in the arbitration to which his award relates;

(*d*) all cases, whether dealt with by written representations or hearings, must be given individual consideration and separate awards must be issued in respect of each.

Sometimes a party or parties may claim that the only fair way of dealing with related cases, particularly in headlease/sublease disputes on the same property, is to have combined hearings or submissions, whilst another party or parties take the opposite view. Since the arbitrator cannot order combined hearings against the wishes of one or more parties, he must decide whether he considers that the cases can fairly be dealt with separately. It is suggested that it will nearly always be possible to deal justly with such references separately if the principles listed at (a)–(d) are borne in mind.

3.2.11. *Arbitrations on overlapping issues–action on appointment*

When appointed the arbitrator should:
- (a) notify all parties in writing of all appointments;
- (b) call all the parties to a preliminary meeting;
- (c) give directions for the conduct of references bearing in mind the matters set out in paragraph 3.2.10.;
- (d) if one party claims that the only fair way to deal with related cases is to have combined hearings or submissions whilst another or others take the opposite view, the arbitrator must decide whether the cases can fairly be dealt with separately; since he cannot order combined hearings against the wishes of any parties;
- (e) the arbitrator should not attempt to withdraw from one or more references on the sole grounds that the parties are opposed on the question of having combined hearings, as this will not assist in the resolution of the disputes. If he were to withdraw, one or more replacement arbitrators would be faced with similar problems. The onus is on the party requesting combined hearings to apply to the Court for a declaration as to how the arbitrator should proceed, and the arbitrator would be wise to allow reasonable opportunity for such an application, but must be wary of delaying tactics.

3–3   PRELIMINARY MEETING

3.3.1. *Establishing the procedure*

In a relatively few cases, where it is clear that the sole issue is one of valuation and the parties have already agreed that the arbitration shall be conducted by written representations, the parties are able to agree upon a timetable and to agree also that a preliminary meeting is unnecessary, it is possible to dispense with a preliminary meeting. In most cases it is important to hold a preliminary meeting before issuing Directions. This enables the Arbitrator to establish (preferably by consent), the procedure to be followed, including many of the matters suggested in these Guidance Notes.

If either party intends to be represented at the hearing by a Solicitor or Counsel, it is highly desirable that the Solicitor be present at the preliminary meeting and (if it has been decided to instruct Counsel) that he discusses with Counsel before the meeting the nature of the directions desired. It is often helpful to the parties if the Arbitrator, when convening the meeting, sends to them a draft showing the directions that he is minded to give. In this way the attention of the parties will be drawn to the points that have to be considered and they may be able to agree all or most of the directions necessary to prepare for the hearing.

As a matter of courtesy and, more importantly, to avoid the costs and delay that would be caused by adjournments, a party who intends to be represented at the preliminary meeting by solicitor or counsel should notify the opposing party a sufficient time in advance to enable the opposing party, if so minded, to instruct solicitor or counsel.

3.3.2. *Request to defer proceedings*

If neither party wishes the Arbitrator to proceed, he should defer to their wish. He should inform the parties that he will proceed on the application of either party at any time.

3.3.3. *The unco-operative party*

It sometimes happens that one party (because he wants to delay or for some other reason) fails or refuses to co-operate in the holding of a preliminary meeting, or in discussions with the Arbitrator as to how the arbitration should notify both parties that unjustified delay in proceeding with the arbitration will be taken into account when he comes to consider the costs of the arbitration. If no immediately satisfactory solution can be reached, the arbitrator is advised to proceed as for a hearing (see paragraph 3–5).

3–4   PROCEDURE FOR WRITTEN REPRESENTATIONS

3.4.1. *Directions*

Whether or not a preliminary meeting is held, the Arbitrator should give directions dealing with the following matters;

    (*a*) The party who initiated the proceedings (usually the landlord) should be designated 'the Claimant' and the other party 'the Respondent'.

    (*b*) The parties should if possible agree by a specified date upon the description of the building, its services and amenities, net floor areas, planning use rights, lease use rights, and (if applicable) any tenant's improvements that are to be disregarded. The agreement should be recorded in a statement signed on behalf of each party.

    (*c*) If possible, the parties should also agree upon the like details with respect to each comparable property to which either party wishes to refer. As to agreeing facts generally, see paragraph 3.6.9.

    (*d*) Unless both parties otherwise agree, any 'without prejudice' negotiations or offers whether oral or contained in correspondence should not be referred to in any way in the representations.

    (*e*) Whether either party wishes to raise any point of law (eg as to the meaning of the rent review clause) affecting the dispute; if so, whether the parties wish the Arbitrator to decide the point after taking legal advice; if not, how the point is to be resolved. As to disputes involving issues of law see paragraph 3.2.7 and 3.2.8.

    (*f*) A date by which each party is to serve upon the Arbitrator two copies of his representations; when these have been lodged by each party the Arbitrator will send one copy to the opposing party (unless representations are to be exchanged in the Arbitrator's office). As a less favoured alternative, the Arbitrator may permit the parties to exchange submissions direct, sending the second copy of each to him. In either event the Arbitrator should state that he will allow a specified period, say five working days, to elapse before he examines the submissions, during which either party may object to the admissibility of any evidence. This gives each side the opportunity of checking the opposing side's representations to ensure that they do not disclose 'without prejudice' negotiations.

(g) Each representation should contain the valuer's honest opinion of the rental value of the subject premises in accordance with the terms of the lease.

(h) A date by which each party shall submit to the Arbitrator two copies of his representations in reply (commonly referred to as 'cross-representations'). Again, when these have been lodged by both parties the Arbitrator will send one copy to the opposing party unless they are to be exchanged in the Arbitrator's office. (*Note*: Cross-representations should not contain representations or evidence other than in rebuttal of points made in the opposing party's initial representations).

(i) The directions should specify whether the Award will be a final Award dealing with all matters in issue, including the costs of the Arbitration or an interim Award, final as to all matters except the costs of the Arbitration—see section 3.10.

(j) The Arbitrator's intentions and requirements for inspecting the subject property and comparables. (See paragraphs 3.6.16 and 3.6.17.)

(k) Confirmation of the amount of, or the basis for calculating, the Arbitrator's fee. This should be expressed to be exclusive or disbursements, and where appropriate of the cost of taking legal or other specialist advice—see section 3-9.

(l) Save in emergency, all communications with the Arbitrator should be in writing and a copy sent direct to the other party.

(m) The Arbitrator should expressly reserve the right to call for a hearing if at any time he considers it necessary; see for example paragraph 3.2.6.

3.4.2. *Directions to be confirmed in writing*

When the procedural matters outlined above have been decided (whether by agreement or by decision of the Arbitrator) the Arbitrator should confirm them in writing. If no preliminary meeting has been held prior to the Arbitrator's giving directions, he should invite the parties to suggest amendments to them within a specified time limit, but the final decision as to directions remains with the Arbitrator.

3.4.3. *The unco-operative party*

If the parties have agreed to written representations being the appropriate procedure but a party then fails or refuses to co-operate, the Arbitrator should notify the parties that he will proceed on the basis of the evidence submitted. He should however before making his award pass a copy of the single submission to the defaulting party for comment.

As to extending the power of the Arbitrator, see paragraph 3.6.12.

3–5   PROCEDURE WHERE THERE IS TO BE A HEARING

3.5.1. *Directions preliminary to a hearing*

(a) The party who initiated the proceedings (usually the landlord) should be designated 'the Claimant' and the other party 'the Respondent'.

(b) The parties should if possible agreed upon the description of the building, its services and amenities, net floor areas, planning use rights, lease use rights, and (if applicable) any tenant's improvements that are to be disregarded. The agreement should be recorded in a statement signed by or on behalf of each party.

(c) The parties should if possible agree upon the like details with respect to each comparable property to which either party wishes to refer. As to agreeing facts generally, see paragraph 3.6.9.

(d) If there is any issue as to tenant's improvements or other matters that are to be disregarded, directions should be given for identifying the issue and recording the contentions of each party upon it.

(e) If any issue of law is involved, directions should be given as to how to resolve it—see paragraph 3.2.7 and 3.2.8.

(f) A date should be specified by which each party is to serve upon the Arbitrator two copies of a statement of his case; when these have been lodged by each party, the Arbitrator will send one copy to the opposing party. (*Note*: In a relatively straightforward case, these statements may be full presentations of the case equivalent to written representations, but in others, particularly where the parties are to be legally represented, they may wish to omit matters of detail which will be covered by the expert witnesses in their proofs of evidence to be exchanged before the hearing). Unless both parties otherwise agree, any 'without prejudice' negotiations or offers whether oral or contained in correspondence should not be referred to in any way in the statements.

(g) A date should be specified by which each party shall submit to the Arbitrator two copies of his reply to the other party's statement. Again, when these have been lodged, the Arbitrator will send one copy to the opposing party. The Arbitrator should state that the cross representations should not contain representations or evidence other than in rebuttal of points made in the opposing party's initial representations.

(h) A date and procedure should be specified for the submission and exchange of proofs of evidence if applicable (eg when the initial statements do not constitute a full statement of the case).

(i) Each proof of evidence should contain the valuers honest opinion of the rental value of the subject premises in accordance with the terms of the lease.

(j) The directions should specify whether the Award will be a simple Award or if requested a reasoned Award (see paragraphs 3.8.8. and 3.8.9.) and that the Award will either be a Final Award dealing with all matters at issue, including the costs of the Arbitration, or will be an Interim Award, either on a preliminary point of law or final as to all matters except the costs of the Arbitration (see section 3–10).

(k) Save in emergency, all communications with the Arbitrator should be in writing and a copy sent direct to the other party.

(l) A date and place should be fixed for the hearing.

(m) The Arbitrator should state his intentions and requirements for inspecting the subject property and comparables—see paragraphs 3.6.16 and 3.6.17.

In particularly complicated cases it may be preferable instead of the directions outlined in (f) and (g) above to direct that the Claimant delivers points of claim by a specified date, that the Respondent delivers points of defence within a specified number of days thereafter, and that the Claimants deliver points of reply within a further specified period.

In one reported case (*Chapman* v *Charlwood Alliance* (1981) 260 EG 1041) determination of a preliminary point in a rent review arbitration was sought with the Arbitrator's consent but with the other party opposing. The Court refused to determine it because a substantial saving in costs was unlikely and the point was not one where leave to appeal would be likely to be given.

3–6   THE HEARING

3.6.1. *Hearing is Private*

An arbitration is a private tribunal, and the only persons entitled to attend are the parties themselves and those whose attendance is required in order to assist the parties in presenting their cases whether as advocates, advisers, or witnesses.

3.6.2. *Procedure*

The usual procedure at a hearing is set out below:
- (a) The Arbitrator opens the proceedings and announces the arrangements for the hearing.
- (b) The Claimant or his representative opens and presents his case and, where appropriate, his reply to any counter-claim, probably by summarising his case upon each.
- (c) The Claimant calls his first witness and examines him upon the evidence which he gives. (As to receiving written proofs of evidence see paragraph 3.7.7.)
- (d) The Respondent cross-examines the witness.
- (e) The Arbitrator questions if necessary. (see paragraph 3.6.4.)
- (f) The Claimant re-examines the witness by asking further questions, but only on matters arising out of stages (d) and (e) above.
- (g) Stages (c) to (f) are repeated for each subsequent witness.
- (h) The Respondent states his case if he wishes.
- (i) The Respondent calls his first witness.
- (j) The Claimant cross-examines.
- (k) The Arbitrator questions if necessary. (See paragraph 3.6.4.)
- (l) The Respondent re-examines only on matters arising out of stages (i) and (k) above.
- (m) Stages (i) and (l) are repeated for each subsequent witness.
- (n) The Respondent makes his final address.
- (o) The Claimant makes his final address.
- (p) The Arbitrator closes the hearing and makes arrangements to inspect.

3.6.3. *Witnesses*

The Arbitrator has no power to call a witness but he may re-call a witness if he thinks fit.

3.6.4. *Conduct by Arbitrator of the hearing*

When an advocate is making a submission, it is helpful to him and can considerably shorten the time if the Arbitrator indicates, as each point is made, whether or not he understands it and whether or not he provisionally agrees with it. But if he has 'stopped' the advocate on a point, by giving such an indication, he should not find against him on that point without giving him an opportunity of making further submissions on it—if necessary at a further hearing. The Arbitrator should always seek clarification of a point he does not understand. On the other hand, he should be careful not to interrupt the submission to such an extent that the advocate is prevented from putting a coherent case.

3.6.5. *Where a Surveyor is both advocate and witness*

A major difficulty for the Arbitrator may arise in a hearing where a party is represented by a surveyor acting both as witness and as advocate. The Arbitrator and the parties' surveyors must at all times seek to distinguish between the two roles and to establish in which capacity the Surveyor is acting at any one time. A Surveyor will be acting as an advocate when opening his case, summing up, or when he is cross-examining the expert surveyor acting for the other party, but he will be acting as an expert witness when giving evidence or expressing an opinion, and will be subject to cross-examination when doing so. It will help both him and the Arbitrator if the Surveyor occupies a different seat or position when giving evidence from that which he uses when making submissions.

3.6.6. *Note of evidence*

The Arbitrator must have a sufficiently full note of the evidence and arguments to enable him to make a reasoned Award dealing with the substance of the case made by each party.

The Arbitrator should either himself make a note of evidence and argument or (with both parties' consent) arrange for a shorthand typist familiar with property terminology to record the proceedings. In very substantial matters it may be desirable to have a note taken by professional Court Reporters. Although this is an expensive course, the delay involved in slowing down the proceedings so that the Arbitrator himself may take a note may be more expensive than the cost of employing Court Reporters.

Even when a complete transcript is being made the Arbitrator should still take sufficient notes to remind himself of any material points that need clarification during the hearing.

3.6.7. *Note of issues argued or agreed*

It is important that a precise note be made of any facts or propositions of law that may be agreed during the hearing. Similarly, if a point of law is being argued, the propositions contended for should be recorded in writing.

3.6.8. *Oath or affirmation*

Section 12(2) of the Arbitration Act 1950 provides that evidence shall be taken on oath or affirmation if the Arbitrator sees fit. The administration of the oath depends upon the religious beliefs of the witness, and before the hearing the Arbitrator should enquire whether it will be sufficient for him to have separate copies of the New Testament (for Christians) and the Old Testament (for Jews).

The witness should take the appropriate Testament in his uplifted hand and say or repeat after the Arbitrator.

> I swear by Almighty God that the evidence I shall give touching the matters in difference in this reference shall be the truth, the whole truth, and nothing but the truth.

If the witness has no religious belief, or if his religious beliefs prohibit the swearing of an oath in these circumstances, he is entitled to affirm. In such cases, he should say or repeat after the Arbitrator.

> I solemnly, sincerely and truly affirm and declare that I will true answers make to all such questions as shall be asked of me touching the matters in difference in this reference.

If other religions are involved, the Arbitrator should ask the party or his representative concerned to make appropriate arrangements in advance.

3.6.9. *Agreeing facts*

The presentation of oral evidence is time-consuming and therefore costly. Moreover, it may give rise to complex issues relating to the law of evidence. There are great advantages in persuading the parties at the preliminary meeting to agree facts, including the facts of comparables, to the greatest possible extent so that at the hearing the Arbitrator can concentrate on the presentation of argument and interpretation; see paragraph 3.7.5.

3.6.10. *Attendance of witnesses*

Under the Arbitration Act 1950, s 12(1), the Arbitrator has power, unless a contrary intention appears from the arbitration agreement, to make orders concerning the examination on oath of the parties, production of documents and other matters. Additionally, either party may apply to the High Court for a subpoena to compel witnesses to attend and to bring with them particular documents to be put in evidence—see s 12(4). Section 12(6) gives the Court wide powers to make orders in relation to the production of documents and other matters. Moreover, the Arbitration Act 1979, s 5 enables the High Court to confer on the Arbitrator the same power to continue after non-compliance with a direction as to the Court would have in similar circumstances—see paragraph 3.6.13., below. If a party persistently fails to comply with the direction of the Arbitrator, or with an order under s 12, legal advice should be sought.

3.6.11 *The unco-operative party*

If neither party wishes the Arbitrator to proceed, he should defer to their wishes. It sometimes happens that one of the parties has a motive for delay and fails or refuses to co-operate. If, despite receiving due notice of the hearing, a party fails to attend and gives no reason or gives a reason for non-attendance which the Arbitrator considers inadequate, the Arbitrator has the power to proceed *ex parte*, ie without the presence of the party or anyone representing him. However, if there is any doubt it would be wise to adjourn the hearing to a later date. Great care must be taken before proceeding *ex parte* and the Arbitrator must ensure that notification of the date for the adjourned hearing is given to the party concerned. This is particularly important if either of the parties is not professionally represented.

Prepaid recorded delivery to the appropriate address is desirable.

3.6.12. *Extending the Arbitrator's powers*

If a party fails to comply with a direction given by the Arbitrator, the opposing party or the Arbitrator himself may apply to the High Court under the Arbitration Act 1979, s 5, to have the Arbitrator's powers extended. If the High Court makes such an order, the Arbitrator will have power to continue with the reference notwithstanding the default of the party, in the same way as the Judge of the High Court could continue after non-compliance with an order of the Court.

3.6.13. *Proceeding ex parte*

Even when an order has been obtained under s 5 of the 1979 Act, or the hearing is continued *ex parte*, the Arbitrator must conduct the reference with the same fair and impartial regard to the evidence placed before him as if the defaulting party were present. Thus he must assess the value of evidence put before him notwithstanding the fact that the opposing party is not present.

Nevertheless it is not the Arbitrator's duty to represent the defaulting party who is not in attendance. If from his own experience and knowledge he doubts the value or accuracy of any of the evidence presented to him by the attending party, he should voice this doubt and give his reasons, so that the attending party has the opportunity to present evidence and/or argument to him on the view they take. See particularly *Fox/Fisher* v *P G Wellfair Ltd* (1982) 263 EG 589, 657.

The defaulting party does not lose any right he may have to ask for a reasoned Award or to challenge the Award on the ground of misconduct or on a question of law—see paragraphs 3.8.9. and 3.8.11.

3.6.14. *The raising of legal issues as a means to delay*

The Arbitrator should bear in mind when a point of law is raised, or when he is asked to give an Award containing reasons, that this may merely be an attempt to delay matters—see paragraph 3.8.8.

3.6.15. *Ex parte directions must be clear*

The unco-operative litigant is, almost by definition, particularly likely to seek to have an Award upset by the court in the event of *ex parte* proceedings. The Arbitrator in such a case should ensure that his directions are thorough, reasonable and clear, and that they are properly recorded and communicated.

3.6.16. *Inspections*

An Arbitrator will usually find it of advantage to make a brief preliminary inspection before the hearing (if any hearing is to be held). He should make a more detailed inspection after having received all evidence. The Arbitrator should inspect the subject property and the 'comparables' submitted to him (or at least those which he considers relevant and important) as soon as the hearing or the written representations have been concluded, so that the relevant evidence and submissions are still fresh in his mind when he inspects.

3.6.17. *Attendance at inspections*

The Arbitrator may often prefer and find it more convenient, with the agreement of the parties, to make inspections unaccompanied. Unless the Arbitrator is inspecting unaccompanied by the parties, inspections should be conducted in the presence of both parties or their representatives unless either party indicates in advance that he has no wish to be present and no objection to the inspection taking place in the presence of the other party. The inspection is not an appropriate occasion for re-opening the hearing.

It is unusual for the parties accompanying the Arbitrator on his inspection to address any comments to him. However if comments are made to the Arbitrator, they must be limited to drawing his attention during the inspection to factual matters covered in their evidence. Conversely the Arbitrator may put relevant questions to the parties during his inspection of any property.

3-7   EVIDENCE

3.7.1. *The rules of evidence*

Unless the parties have expressly or implicitly agreed to the contrary, an Arbitrator is bound by the same rules of evidence as the courts of law. Those rules are too lengthy to be included in these Notes. Further guidance is given in Part 7 of the Handbook of Rent Review (1985 Revision); and see paragraph 1.1.1. In practice the parties to an arbitration, like the parties to an action in court, will often agree to the admission of material which otherwise would not be strictly admissible as evidence, eg hearsay evidence of comparables. In commercial arbitrations, the court will often assume this even where no such agreement is specifically provided.

The recommendations in paragraphs 3.4.1. (*c*) and 3.5.1. (*c*) of these Guidance Notes are specifically included to enable the admission and presentation of what would otherwise be hearsay evidence of essential, valid, and material comparables, without incurring the sometimes considerable additional costs of calling the surveyors involved to give evidence of a particular transaction.

The following paragraphs attempt some guidance on points that often arise in rent review and other valuation arbitrations.

3.7.2. *Burden of proof*

The burden of proof of an assertion lies upon the party making the assertion.

3.7.3. *Hearsay evidence*

The rule against hearsay evidence can be stated as follows. A witness may give evidence only of matters within his own personal knowledge, and not of matters that he has been told either orally or by reading some document. The reason for this rule is practical rather than technical; for example, an apparently self contained arms length market transaction may well have been affected by the surrender of an existing lease or by family or by other personal relationships. Only a witness who has first hand personal knowledge of the transaction will be able to give full account of all relevant circumstances (see paragraph 3.7.10).

An Arbitrator like a judge, may have a discretion whether to allow hearsay evidence to be presented under the Civil Evidence Act 1968. But clearly he would have to consider very carefully what weight could be given to such evidence. He should beware of allowing hearsay evidence to be given of a matter which appears essential to his decision.

3.7.4. *Evidence of comparables*

In rent review arbitrations, the rule against hearsay evidence is most likely to be relevant to evidence of comparable transactions.

The subject of hearsay evidence in relation to comparables is fully dealt with in the judgment of Megarry J in *English Exporters (London) Ltd* v *Eldonwall Ltd* [1973] 1 All ER 726 (a case under the Landlord and Tenant Act 1954, Part II).

In that case the Judge said:—

(1) 'As an expert witness, the valuer is entitled to express his opinion about matters within his field of competence. In building up his opinions about values, he will no doubt have learned much from transactions in which he has himself been engaged and of which he could give first-hand evidence. But he will also have learned much from many other sources, including much of which he could give no first-hand evidence. Textbooks, journals, reports of auctions and other dealings, and information obtained from his professional brethren and others, some related to particular transactions and some more general and indefinite, will all have contributed their share ...... No question of giving hearsay evidence rises in such cases; the witness states his opinion from his general experience.'

(2) 'On the other hand, quite apart from merely expressing his opinion, the expert often is able to give factual evidence as well. If he has first-hand knowledge of a transaction, he can speak of that ...... Basically, the expert's factual evidence on matters of fact is in the same position as the factual evidence of any other witness. Further factual evidence that he cannot give himself is sometimes adduced in some other way, as by the testimony of some other witness who was himself concerned in the transaction in question, or by proving some document which carried the transaction through, or recorded it; and to the transaction thus established, like the transactions which the expert himself has proved, the expert may apply his experience and opinions, as tending to support or qualify his views.'

(3) 'That being so, it seems to me quite another matter when it is asserted that a valuer may give factual evidence of transactions of which he has no direct knowledge, whether per se or whether in the guise of giving reasons for his opinion as to value ... I know of no special rule giving expert valuation witnesses the right to give hearsay evidence of facts.'

(4) 'When a list of comparables is being prepared for the trial, as is usual and convenient, it is all too common to include in the list transactions upon which there will be no admissible evidence but only hearsay of a greater or lesser degree of reliability. If the parties exchange lists of comparables at an early date, often much time and money can be saved by the experts on each side agreeing such of the transactions in each list as, after any necessary enquiry, they feel they can accept as being reliably summarised; and in this way the additional expense of proving a favourable comparable not within an expert's own knowledge can be avoided. But if the other side will not accept the facts, then either the transaction must be proved by admissible evidence or it must be omitted as a comparable.'

3.7.5. *Agreeing facts of comparables*

As was suggested by Megarry J., in most cases, if particulars of the comparable transactions intended to be referred to by the witnesses are exchanged well before the hearing, so as to give the opposite party an opportunity of verifying the details given, the relevant facts can be admitted. First hand evidence of transactions in which the witnesses themselves have been involved is the most satisfactory. If this is not available then if the opposing party insists, particulars of the transaction must be proved by someone with personal knowledge of it, eg the agent who negotiated it, or by production of a document admissible in evidence, eg the original lease. If the parties are able to reach agreement, it is suggested that they should specifically set out in writing the facts which they agree under the following headings:—

(*a*) Age of the property.

(*b*) A brief description of the property and its construction.

(*c*) A brief description of the amenities and ancillary services.

(*d*) The agreed net floor areas.

(*e*) The nature of the comparable transactions *e.g.* whether it is a new letting or a rent review.

(*f*) The date of the lease in question, the date specified for commencement of the term, and the length of term.

(*g*) Full details of all terms and conditions in the lease which might have an effect on rental value.

(*h*) The rent review period or pattern, and the review valuation date.

(*i*) The names of the parties.

(*j*) The figure which has been agreed in the open market or upon rent review.

In all cases where comparables are being relied upon, they should be accompanied by a specific statement from a person having first-hand knowledge thereof as to whether there are, or are not, any special aspects of the transaction which might affect the weight to be attached to it as a comparable.

3.7.6. *Evidence of transactions occurring after the review date*

Evidence of transactions occurring after the review date is in general terms admissible. The weight to be given to such evidence is a matter for the arbitrator to assess in the light of his experience and knowledge of the relevant market. The longer the period between the valuation date and the date of the transaction, the less weight the evidence is likely to carry with the Arbitrator. If there has been some political or economic or local event which has significantly affected market values, this too will reduce—perhaps to zero—the weight to be attached to the evidence.

3.7.7. *Written proofs*

In valuation disputes it is usually convenient for an expert witness to present his evidence in written form, which he will read and which he may elaborate in response to questions from the party calling him. However, this procedure is liable to abuse, eg the proof may contain inadmissible material such as hearsay or reference to 'without prejudice' negotiations. For the procedure to work properly the proof should not contain such inadmissible matter. To safeguard against this a proof should not be placed before the Arbitrator (whether before or at the hearing) unless the opposing party has been given a copy and has said that he does not object to its being read. Directions for a hearing should specify a date for exchange of proofs intended to be placed before the Arbitrator.

3.7.8. *Duty when giving evidence of comparables*

A surveyor representing a party should remember that, when giving evidence of comparables, he is acting as an expert witness and not as an advocate. He must therefore disclose any relevant details of the transaction of which he is aware, whether such details assist his client's case or not. Failure to do so may be taken into account by the Arbitrator when considering his award as to costs. It could also amount to professional misconduct.

3.7.9. *Oral evidence as to the contents of a document*

Strictly speaking this is not acceptable; unless otherwise agreed, the original document or (in practice) what purports to be a photostat or certified copy of it, should be put in evidence.

3.7.10. *The Arbitrator's general approach to the strict rules of evidence*

Notwithstanding the points made above, the Arbitrator is in practice allowed considerable latitude in relation to the law of evidence. A submission to arbitration is a private judicial proceeding intended to be of a less formal nature than a court hearing. It will often be appropriate for the Arbitrator, with the agreement of the parties, to relax the strict rules of evidence. And the Arbitrator should not refuse to hear evidence tendered by one party unless the other party objects to it, in which case he must rule as to its admissibility. If the reason put forward is technically sound, but of no real merit, the Arbitrator may order the party taking the objection to pay the increased costs caused by the need to observe the technicalities.

3.7.11. *Hearsay and the Civil Evidence Act 1968*

It is open to the parties to take certain procedural steps under the Civil Evidence Act 1968 in order to make evidence of hearsay admissible.

A party who wishes to adduce hearsay evidence must serve notice on the other party, giving details of the hearsay statement. The party in receipt of the notice may serve a counternotice objecting to the hearsay and requiring direct evidence of the hearsay statement, but if no objection is made to the hearsay, it becomes admissible. Disputes regarding the admission of hearsay evidence should be settled by the Arbitrator before the hearing. The party wishing to call hearsay evidence may resist a counternotice requiring him to call direct evidence on certain statutory grounds, eg that the witness is dead, unfit to attend or cannot be found. If one of these grounds applies the Arbitrator must allow the admission of the hearsay evidence.

The Arbitrator has a discretion to admit hearsay evidence at the hearing, even though the requisite notices have not been served on the other party.

Further information is provided in section 7–7 of the *Handbook of Rent Review* (1985 Revision) by Bernstein and Reynolds.

3.7.12. *Discovery*

Discovery is an important feature of the English adversarial legal system and problems relating to it are probably the most difficult that an Arbitrator may have to face. These Guidance Notes can give only a bare outline of the process.

A full account can be found in *The Supreme Court Practice*. Part 7 of the *Handbook of Rent Review* (1985 Revision) deals with discovery in rent review arbitrations.

Discovery is the process by which one party to an arbitration is given access to documents in the possession power or control of the other party which may assist him in presenting his case. An example might be documents showing completed lettings of or attempts to let comparable properties known to one party only. If one party requests discovery, the Arbitrator should ask him to state his reasons and should then give the other party an opportunity to comment or object. The Arbitrator can order either:

(1) General Discovery. This requires a party to disclose all documents relating to matters in question in the arbitration.
(2) Specific Discovery. This requires a party to disclose specified documents or classes of documents.

In litigation general discovery is automatic. In arbitration it is discretionary, and in rent review arbitration it is suggested that the Arbitrator should not order general discovery unless he considers that for some reason an order for specific discovery would not meet the case.

The order for discovery should specify first a date by which a list of documents must be delivered and then a date by which the opposing party must be allowed to inspect and take copies.

3.7.13. *Privilege*

In some circumstances a document held by one of the parties is privileged from discovery. Correspondence between a client and his solicitor is almost always privileged. As a general rule an expert's report provided for a client will be privileged if it is provided with the primary purposes of assisting in the preparation of a contemplated arbitration, but not otherwise. Thus a valuation made for a proposed acquisition of a property may have to be disclosed in a subsequent rent review arbitration concerning that property. Once an arbitration reference has started, all discussions and correspondence concerned with the accumulation of evidence for the case are privileged, no matter between whom the communications take place. The Arbitrator may be asked to decide whether a document is privileged or not.

3.7.14. *Without prejudice correspondence and discussions*

Correspondence or discussions between the parties to a contemplated or pending arbitration will be privileged from discovery (whether before or at a hearing) if they concern an attempt to compromise the dispute. Such correspondence or discussions are said to have been 'without prejudice'. It cannot however automatically be assumed that a letter marked 'without prejudice' is privileged; it will only be so if it genuinely is part of negotiations pending with a view to achieving a compromise. Conversely, correspondence not marked 'without prejudice' may still be privileged if it is part of a genuine attempt to settle a dispute. A letter not itself marked 'without prejudice', which is part of continuing correspondence between the parties initially marked 'without prejudice', almost certainly would be privileged.

A Chartered Surveyor who intentionally submits 'without prejudice' information risks disciplinary action by the Professional Practice Committee of the Institution.

3–8   THE AWARD

3.8.1. *Award–time and minimum requirements*

The Award of an Arbitrator should be addressed to or otherwise refer to the parties to the dispute; as a minimum it should contain a clear finding on the subject of the dispute, directions as to costs and be signed and dated by the Arbitrator.

The arbitrator should proceed with his inspections and Award as soon as the hearing or the written representations have been concluded.

3.8.2. *Award–suggested contents*

For completeness, it is suggested that the Award should cover the following:
  (i)   a heading, naming the parties to the dispute and the subject property;
  (ii) reference to the Arbitrator's appointment, covering
        (a) the document containing the parties' agreement to submit to arbitration;
        (b) the date of appointment;
        (c) the method of appointment (eg whether by the President of the RICS or by the parties direct);
        (d) the instrument of appointment;
  (iii) the subject matter of the dispute;
  (iv) his decisions or findings on the subject matter of the dispute;
  (v)   his decision as to costs (or reservation to determine liability as to costs);
  (vi) signature and date.
It may also be desirable to include one or more of the following:
  (vii) a reference to the preliminary meeting, if held, and the procedures adopted;
  (viii) a reference to a statement of agreed facts, claimant's pleadings and the respondent's reply;
  (ix) the date and place of the hearing;
  (x)   the attendance of the parties or their representatives at the hearing, or the submission, in lieu of a hearing, of written representations and cross-representations;
  (xi) a reference to the Arbitrator's inspection of the subject matter and any 'comparables' submitted by the parties.

3.8.3. *Mistakes*

Except for the correction of slips, for which s 17 of the Arbitration Act 1950 provides, the Award once published cannot be altered.

3.8.4. *Splitting the difference*

The Arbitrator should in general avoid giving the false impression that the amount in his Award is determined by splitting the difference. To do so would be to fail in his duty to decide upon the evidence. If, however, after due consideration of the evidence, his view is that the figure lies exactly between the rival contentions of the parties, it is his duty so to find, notwithstanding that his Award might wrongly be thought to have been arrived at by splitting the difference.

3.8.5. *Issue of the award*

When the interim or final Award is ready for issue the Arbitrator should notify both parties that it is available to be taken up on payment of his total fee (including costs and VAT). If one party pays the full amount the Award should be issued to him and a signed and dated duplicate should be sent to the other party at the same time. This is important because there is a limited time during which to appeal (paragraph 3.7.11.). Thereafter either party has the right to obtain reimbursement in respect of costs in accordance with the terms of the Award by ordinary court proceedings. If the party who has paid the full fee in this way is not required by the terms of the Award to bear total responsibility for the Arbitrator's fee, he may obtain appropriate reimbursement in accordance with the terms of the Award. It frequently happens that the parties agree that, in order that the Award should be issued, each should pay half the fees subject to any necessary adjustment later. This practice is undesirable, for it causes complications in the publication of the award and in the running of time for appealing against the Award and in extreme cases a party may be shut out from appealing altogether. In the unlikely event that, having been advised that it is available, neither party takes up the Award within a reasonable time the Arbitrator should issue the Award to both parties and if eventually necessary, sue for recovery of his fees in accordance with the Award.

3.8.6. *Award not stating reasons*

Unless required by the terms of his appointment or by an order made under the Arbitration Act 1979 an Arbitrator is not obliged to give any reasons for his decision. In simple cases there will probably be no need for a 'speaking' Award (ie one that gives reasons) and an Award is binding and enforceable notwithstanding that it does not give reasons.

3.8.7. *Court's power to require reasons*

If the Arbitrator is asked to give an Award supported by reasons he should consider it in the light of the provisions of the Arbitration Act 1979, s 1. This section abolished the old 'special case' procedure (s 21 of the 1950 Act) and substituted a system of appeal 'on any question of law arising out of the Award'. It also gives the High Court a discretionary power to order an Arbitrator to 'state the reasons for his Award in sufficient detail to enable the Court, should an appeal be brought under this section, to consider any question of law arising out of the Award'. The High Court will make this order, on an application with the consent of both parties or failing such consent or agreement by leave of the High Court, only where:
  (i) it appears to the High Court that the Award does not set out any or any sufficient reasons for the Award, and
  (ii) either (a) at least one of the parties gave notice to the Arbitrator before the Award was made that he required a reasoned Award or (b) there is some special reason why notice was not given.

3.8.8. *When a reasoned award is requested*

It is suggested that the Arbitrator approach the question whether or not to give reasons in the following way:
  (1) If neither party asks him to give reasons he should not do so;

(2) If both parties request an Award supported by reasons the Arbitrator should comply;

(3) If one party asks him to give reasons and the other party is either silent or specifically requests that no reasons be given he should consider whether under the Arbitration Act 1979 the Courts would be likely to require a reasoned Award because a question of law is likely to arise out of his Award; whether the party asking for this is acting bona fide or is merely seeking to delay matters; and whether there are other circumstances making it desirable to give an Award supported by reasons (for example, because a point of principle not amounting to a point of law is involved which is likely to recur in future dealings between the parties). Unless he is satisfied that there is no justification for making an Award containing reasons he should normally accede to the request that he should give reasons.

(4) If the dispute concerns value only, with no legal issues or issues of principle arising, then a reasoned award is not justified.

3.8.9. *What a reasoned award should contain*

The requirements of a reasoned Award have been the subject of judicial guidance, set out in the case of *Westzucker* v *Bunge*, and may be summarised: The Arbitrator should

(a) explain why the arbitration came about;

(b) recount the facts as agreed between the parties;

(c) as regards the controversial issues, first set out the alternative versions both in relation to points of law and matters of fact and value;

(d) give his decision on each such issue, and the reasons why the alternatives have been rejected;

(e) end with his conclusion and his determination as to costs.

3.8.10. *Award must be final*

Although not all of the points mentioned in paragraphs 3.8.2. to 3.8.9. need to be covered in any Award, it is always essential that the Arbitrator makes an unequivocal decision on the amount of the rent. The wording of his findings and Award and his directions as to costs must therefore be clear and unambiguous. Where as suggested in paragraph 3.2.7.(f) the Arbitrator makes alternative findings, it is of course necessary to say which of the alternatives he accepts. As to Awards final on all matters except costs, see paragraph 3.10.7.

3.8.11. *Challenging or setting aside the Award*

The High Court has power to set aside, vary, or remit an Award if either there is an error of law which substantially affects the rights of one of the parties (Arbitration Act 1979, s. 1) or the Arbitrator has been guilty of 'misconduct' (Arbitration Act 1950, s. 23(2)). 'Misconduct' in this context is conduct which is not according to law and this can range from serious breaches such as accepting bribes to mere procedural error such as wrongly refusing to allow an adjournment, or by the Arbitrator using personal knowledge investigations or expertise without disclosing it or them to the parties (see *Fisher* v *P G Wellfair Ltd* (1982) EG 589, 657; *Top Shop Estates* v *Danino* (1985) 273 EG 197. The procedure for applying to the High Court is outside the scope of these Notes (see paragraph 1.1.1., above). However, it is important to note that an appeal against an award must be lodged within 21 days of the date of publication of the Award (or such other time as the Court may allow). The date of publication may be earlier than the date on which the Award is received by either party.

3–9 FEES

3.9.1. *Fees to be agreed or fixed by Arbitrator*

Unless the Arbitrator has agreed the amount of his fee (or more usually the basis on which it will be calculated), with the parties, the amount is a matter for his discretion subject to the right of either party to apply to the High Court for taxation of the fees under the Arbitration Act 1950, s 19(1). Thus it is prudent for the Arbitrator to agree in writing with the parties at an early stage following his appointment, the amount of his fee or the basis on which it is to be calculated. This is a matter which together with many other procedural matters could properly be settled at a preliminary meeting, and emphasises the advantages of holding a preliminary meeting. If there is to be no preliminary meeting the Arbitrator's intention as to fees should be notified in writing to the parties when he indicates his intended procedure and their written agreement should be obtained.

Where an Arbitrator has not agreed a lump sum fee or a fee which is a percentage of a fixed sum, he should from appointment onwards keep a full log of the time spent and disbursements so as to be able to justify his fees ultimately charged if either party challenges them. Once the Arbitrator has accepted the appointment, as a general rule he should not demand payment of fees in advance. But in exceptional circumstances it might be reasonable to call for security for his fees and/or disbursements.

3.9.2. *Percentage based fees*

Prior to the abolition of most of the RICS scale fees on 1 March 1982 following the investigation by the Monopolies Commisssion and discussions with the Office of Fair Trading, it was common practice for an Arbitrator to quote a bracket of percentages between which his fee would lie, eg 1/1½ or 1½/2 times the ad valorem RICS valuation scale charge.

While such a fee basis, because of its uncertainty, was not totally related to the amount of the Award, the RICS have been advised that any such fee basis might perhaps be capable of challenge in the Courts, and thereby might result in the Award being set aside.

This basis should not be used.

3.9.3. *The basis of charge*

In fixing his fee the Arbitrator may properly have regard to the complexity and importance of the matters in dispute, the degree of responsibility, skill and specialised knowledge involved the amount of time involved, the level of the representation and the amount or value in dispute. These are the criteria likely to be applied by the Taxing Masters if the Arbitrator's fees have to be taxed by the Court.

In many cases it will be impossible for him to name a precise fee at the outset though as stated in paragraph 3.2.2. he should give an indication as early as possible as to the basis he is going to adopt.

Where the amount or rental value of the subject property is small, a fee based on a normal hourly or daily rate of charging may be large in relation to the amount involved. In such cases it is common for the surveyor Arbitrator to charge a lower fee as part of the service that members of the RICS traditionally give to the public.

It is therefore suggested that the Arbitrator should

    (*a*) start with the hourly or daily rate that he would charge for routine professional work;

    (*b*) adjust this rate as he would in any case for the importance of the matters in dispute, the degree of responsibility, skill and specialised knowledge involved, the level of representation and the amount or value in dispute;

    (*c*) he should then look at the resultant figure and consider whether it is a fair amount to charge, having regard to the interests of the parties who have to pay it, and to the interests of the profession in providing the rent review service to the public;

    (*d*) the time rate will be applied to the time spent outside the hearing as well as in it, but the time spent must be reasonable;

    (*e*) the parties should be made aware that the shorter and clearer the submissions, the less will be the time required to peruse and understand them, with the consequent cost savings. Likewise, the smaller the number of comparables referred to, the less will be the time required;

    (*f*) the Arbitrator's fee may also vary according to whether or not a reasoned Award is required. The increase in the fee should reflect the amount of additional time taken to provide the reasoned Award.

3.9.4. *Fees where a negotiated settlement is reached before the Award is taken up*

Whilst it is impossible to make specific recommendations (because the appropriate fee must depend on the circumstances of each individual case) the following, read in conjunction with paragraphs 3.9.2., and 3.9.3. of these Notes, may provide some guidance.

Time of Settlement	*Appropriate Fee*
(*a*) After appointment and before (*b*) below.	Nominal charge, if any.
(*b*) After perusal of documents and/ or preliminary meeting and issue of directions, but before proceedings in accordance with those directions are commenced.	Quantum meruit (based on time) and disbursements.
(*c*) After action in (*b*) above together with submission of statement of agreed facts and delivery of pleadings, representations, and cross-representations, perusal by the Arbitrator, preliminary inspection and general preparation for the hearing.	A fee of ¼ to ½ of the full fee which would have been charged had the arbitration/expert valuation proceeded to finality.
(*d*) After action in (*b*), and (*c*) above, and holding the hearing, or giving detailed consideration to the representations and cross-submissions and	A fee of say two thirds to three quarters of the full fee as above.

detailed inspections of the subject
property and comparables, but before
preparation of the Award/Deter-
mination.

(e) After action in (b), (c) and (d)   The full fee.
above and completion of the Award/
Determination and notification to the
parties that it is available to be taken
up.

3.9.5. *Repetitive work*

Where an Arbitrator is appointed to determine a series of similar disputes,
eg several units in a parade of shops, or as regards the same premises, between
a head lessor, head lessee and under-lessee, or where the work is repetitive,
a fee on the previously mentioned basis might be appropriate for a selected
test unit, with reduced fees for the allied and subsequent arbitrations concerning
the adjacent properties or under-let parts of the property.

3.9.6. *Objections to the basis of charge*

If both parties object to the Arbitrator's proposed fee basis, and the matter
cannot be resolved by agreement, the Arbitrator can decline to act. In such
a case the Arbitrator should seek the parties' agreement to his resignation. The
procedure for replacement is as follows:
(a) The parties can agree upon a replacement Arbitrator or
(b) Either party may apply to the Court to appoint a replacement under
section 10 of the Arbitration Act 1950 or
(c) The parties may jointly apply to the President of the RICS to appoint
a replacement Arbitrator.
If the Arbitrator's fee basis remains unagreed he can proceed without any
agreement as to the basis of his charge. In this case he would be entitled to
receive a reasonable amount which, if the parties still do not agree it, would
be taxed by the High Court, upon the criteria mentioned in paragraph 3.9.3.
If one party only objects to the proposed basis of charge the Arbitrator may
obtain the agreement in writing of the other party to pay on the basis proposed.
Such an agreement will not deprive the objecting party of his right to have
the Arbitrator's charges taxed as between party and party. The result may be
that the party who pays the fees may be able to recover only part of the amount
paid, notwithstanding that the Award directs that the objecting party pay the
Arbitrator's charges.
It cannot be over emphasised that Presidential appointments as Arbitrators
are regarded as important matters carrying a high degree of responsibility on
the part of the member so appointed, whose ability to act with impartiality
is of paramount consideration. It is therefore unthinkable that an Arbitrator
would be prejudiced against a party because of an objection to the basis of
charge proposed by the Arbitrator.

3.9.7. *Fees–costs incurred by Arbitrator*

The Arbitrator's fees and disbursements will on occasion include also the
cost of taking legal or other specialist advice and these costs form part of the

costs of the reference. It will be wise for the Arbitrator to include these in his decision as to costs which forms part of his award.

However where such ancillary specialist costs seen likely to arise, the Arbitrator would be wise to obtain the parties' agreement to their payment at the outset and this is a matter which is best dealt with at the preliminary meeting.

3-10   COSTS

3.10.1. *Responsibilities for costs*

Under s 18 of the Arbitration Act 1950, any agreement entered into *before* a dispute has arisen to the effect that each party shall pay his own costs in arbitration proceedings is void. Thus the provision often found in leases and other arbitration agreements, stipulating an equal division between the parties of the costs of any arbitration proceedings, is void, but there is nothing to prevent the parties reaffirming their acceptance of this provision, *after* a dispute has arisen.

Unless an arbitration agreement contains valid provisions concerning division of costs (ie agreed after the dispute has arisen giving rise to the reference to arbitration) the Arbitrator has both power and the duty to include in his Award his decision as to how the costs of the arbitration are to be borne.

3.10.2. *Meaning of costs*

In many cases where the Award lies in between the parties submissions, the award as to costs will be limited to the Arbitrator's own fees and disbursements, including any fees for legal advice which he may have taken. However, the Arbitrator has a duty to deal in his award with the costs incurred by a party in preparing and presenting his case, including the fees of expert witnesses, Solicitors and Counsel. There is no clear authority on the circumstances in which a Judge or Arbitrator can award as part of the costs of the action or arbitration costs incurred before the commencement of the action or arbitration. It is suggested that in making an order for costs an arbitrator can, if so minded, order that the costs should include all costs that would have been incurred if the expert witness had been instructed for the first time at the moment when the arbitration commenced. Such costs would include costs of preparing an initial valuation, which would be the starting point of a proof of evidence.

Where the arbitration is conducted under the written representation procedure, the parties often request or agree, at the preliminary meeting, that the Arbitrator's Award as to fees and costs shall be limited to covering the Arbitrator's fees and costs only.

3.10.3. *Costs–the Award must include directions as to costs*

In the absence of any express provision to the contrary the costs of an arbitration are, under the Arbitration Act 1950, s 18 in the discretion of the Arbitrator who may direct to and by whom and in what manner those costs are to be paid, and may tax and settle the amount of them. If the parties have not agreed upon how the costs shall be borne and the Arbitrator fails to deal with the matter of costs in his final Award (see paragraphs 3.10.7. and 3.10.8. as to interim award excluding costs) the Award is defective for want of finality, and can be challenged by either party in court on that ground. In such an instance, if there were no other ground for challenging the Arbitrator's Award the court would probably refer the Award back to the Arbitrator for amendment by including in his Award his decision on the matter of costs.

Where the Arbitrator has omitted to deal with costs a more practical course is for either party to apply to the Arbitrator to amend his Award so as to deal with the question of costs. This application should be made within fourteen days (s 18(4)) of the publication of the Award, but the court has power to extend this time limit.

3.10.4. *Arbitrator–exercise of discretion as to costs*

The Arbitrator's discretion as to costs must be exercised judicially. That means it must be exercised according to the rules of reason and justice, not according to the private opinion of the Arbitrator nor from motives of (for example) benevolence, or sympathy, or annoyance.

Whilst there are many factors affecting the exercise of the discretion as to costs, one of the most important is whether it can fairly be said that one party or the other has 'won'.

It is the settled practice of the court that in the absence of special circumstances a successful litigant should receive his costs.

In rent review disputes, a party can be said to have 'been successful' if his figure is substantially nearer the Award than that of his opponent. In such a case in the absence of other factors it is open to the Arbitrator, if he thinks fit, to award him a substantial proportion or even the whole of his costs (including the Arbitrator's fees): see paragraph 3.10.2.

An Arbitrator must show reasons for any departure from these principles which could be supported in an appeal from his award. The following are examples where he might consider himself justified:

(a) One party or both parties have made an offer in the nature of a 'Calderbank' offer to settle the dispute; see paragraph 3.10.6. below.

(b) One of the parties has behaved in an obstructive or unco-operative manner and thereby increased the arbitration costs.

(c) One of the parties has produced an unnecessary volume of submissions of evidence having little or no bearing on the subject matter.

3.10.5. *Costs–where the truth lies in-between*

In rent review or other valuation disputes it is seldom that either party is wholly successful in that the Arbitrator awards one party the figure contended for. In such a case where neither party can be said in substance to have won it would be proper for the Arbitrator to award that there should be

... no order as to costs save that the Arbitrator's fees and disbursements shall be borne equally by the parties.

3.10.6. *'Calderbank' letters*

A party who wishes to protect himself against liability for costs, may send to the other party an unconditional written offer setting out the terms on which he is willing to settle the dispute. The offer should include a figure for the rent and also make provision for costs incurred up to the date of the offer. It is suggested that the appropriate provision for these costs will often be that each side should bear its own costs, plus half of the Arbitrator's fees and costs to the offer date.

Any such offer must be written 'Without Prejudice save as to Costs' so that it may be produced to the Arbitrator at the appropriate stage in the Arbitration proceedings, but not before (see paragraph 3.10.7. below).

Such an offer may be made by either or both parties, but assuming that the only offer is made by the landlord and that the tenant rejects the offer and the Arbitrator determines a rent equal to or higher than the landlord's offer then, in the absence of special circumstances, the landlord could properly expect the tenant to pay the Arbitrator's costs and the landlord's costs incurred after the date of the offer. If the rent determined is lower than the unaccepted offer, then the costs should be dealt with as though no offer had been made.

Such offers are commonly referred to as 'Calderbank' letters after the family law case *Calderbank* v *Calderbank;* (see also *Cutts* v *Head* [1984] 1 All ER 597).

3.10.7. *Award final on all matters except costs*

A party who has made such an offer should request the Arbitrator to issue his Award as an 'Award final on all matters save as to costs'.

After the issue of this Award the party or parties may, if they cannot agree, request the Arbitrator to issue a final Award dealing with the matter of costs, in the light of the 'Calderbank' offer or offers which are then submitted to the Arbitrator.

However, neither party may refer, without the consent of the other, to any discussion or letter written on a 'without prejudice' basis, where the right has not been expressly reserved to refer to it in connection with costs.

In his Final Award determining liability as to costs, in addition to the amount specified in any 'Calderbank' offers the Arbitrator may have regard to other factors; examples are whether either party has won or lost a distinct issue in the proceedings which ought to be dealt with separately in relation to costs, or whether a party has been obstructive, such as by refusing to comply with a notice to admit material facts which are later proved at the hearing, or by wasting time in the reference.

3.10.8. *Parties agreeing to disclosure of 'without prejudice' material*

As an alternative procedure the parties may agree at the preliminary meeting that the Arbitrator should issue an Interim Award as to the rent, and reserve the question of costs to be dealt with in a Final Award. With the parties' agreement, this Final Award could be based on a further hearing to enquire into the conduct of the negotiations, including 'without prejudice' offers and correspondence, notes of telephone calls etc.

3.10.9. *Where the above procedures have not been adopted*

If the alternative procedures in paragraphs 3.10.6., and 3.10.7. and 3.10.8. have not been adopted the Arbitrator must himself decide on what he considers to be a just Award as to the parties' respective liabilities for costs, which is likely to follow his decision as to the dispute and merits of the parties' submissions to him, and include that decision in his Award.

3.10.10. *Costs–determining the amount payable*

The Arbitrator should encourage the parties to agree costs between themselves. If the parties are unable to reach agreement, the Arbitrator should consider providing for the taxation of costs in one of the following ways:

    (*a*) If no lawyer is involved, the Arbitrator should tax costs himself as he is likely to be fully conversant with the costs of the surveyor experts employed by the parties.

(b) If lawyers are involved, the Arbitrator should give the parties a choice of

(i) taxation by the arbitrator with a costs assessor

(ii) taxation by the High Court or County Court.

3–11   OTHER MATTERS ARISING OUT OF THE AWARD

3.11.1. *Enforcement*

The Arbitration Act 1950, s 26, provides that an Award is enforceable, by leave of the High Court, in the same manner as a judgment or order of the High Court. However, this provision does not apply to the normal rent review arbitration because in such an arbitration the Arbitrator's powers extend only to determining the amount of the rent payable under the lease, and do not extend to ordering the payment by one party to the other of a sum of money. Accordingly once the Award has been made the remedy of the landlord whose tenant does not thereafter pay whatever sums may be due is to proceed for the recovery of arrears of rent in the usual way.

3.11.2. *Supplementary Award for amount due*

It is however open to the parties, if they so wish, to enter into a supplementary reference to arbitration conferring upon the Arbitrator who has been appointed under the rent review clause power to make an Award for the payment by the tenant to the landlord of any arrears of rent that may be payable at the date when the primary rent review Award is made. Such a supplementary Award can be enforced under s 26 of the Arbitration Act 1950 in the same manner as a judgment or order of the High Court.

3.11.3. *Award of interest on rent*

The usual form of rent review clause refers to the Arbitrator only the question of what should be the rent payable under the lease. Under such a clause the Arbitrator has no power to award interest.

Although modern leases often provide for the payment of interest where the review rent is determined after the date on which it is payable, they rarely confer power on an Arbitrator to make an order for payment of such interest. In the absence of such power the Arbitrator cannot make any order as to interest.

The new s 19A, inserted in the Arbitration Act 1950 by s 15 of and Sched 1 to the Administration of Justice Act 1982, does not apply to a determination of rent under a rent review clause.

4–1   PART FOUR: THE INDEPENDENT EXPERT

4.1.1. *The Independent Expert*

Where parties to a lease intend that disputes as to rental value shall be determined not by Arbitration but by a surveyor exercising his own professional expertise and judgment, they may call him 'independent valuer', 'independent surveyor', 'third surveyor' or even 'umpire'. In these notes the single expression

'Independent Expert' is used. There is no legislation, and little case law, governing the appointment or conduct of a surveyor acting in this capacity.

4.1.2. *To be distinguished from arbitrator*

Although surveyors appointed to act as 'Independent Experts' will find much that is of value to them in the earlier sections of these Notes, it is vital that they recognise that there are important differences between an Arbitrator and an Independent Expert. These are summarised in paragraph 1.1.5. but there are two which should be stressed again.

First an Independent Expert is appointed in order to provide an impartial rental valuation based on his own investigations, knowledge and experience.

Secondly, an Independent Expert may be liable in damages if either party is able to show that he has been negligent, either in the assembly of material relevant to the valuation or in the application of his professional skill and judgment to that material.

4.1.3. *The duty to assemble information*

The parties, through their surveyors or otherwise, may jointly agree to submit to the Independent Expert an agreed statement of facts covering, for example, such matters as floor areas, the existing use of the various parts of the premises, etc. Each party may also decide to send to the Independent Expert details of transactions of which they wish him to be aware, representations as to the matters which he should take into account, or even their own valuations. Nevertheless, it is still the duty of the Independent Expert to ensure that he has any additional information that is necessary for him to arrive at his own conclusions based on his own opinions and calculations. In a valuation dispute this may include data relating to planning restrictions, restrictive covenants, the condition of the premises as found and as they are to be valued under the terms of the lease, the adequacy and efficiency of the services and all allied matters.

4–2   CONDITIONS ATTACHED TO APPOINTMENTS

4.2.1. *Terms of reference*

It is essential that the Independent Expert establishes clearly his terms of reference and appointment, including the basis of his fee. His right to his fee may be at risk if he does not do so. The terms of the appointment of an Independent Expert may consist of nothing more than a direction that he is to carry out an independent valuation. However, particularly when he is privately appointed the appointment may include a variety of conditions. These may direct that he is to hold an enquiry or to receive representations from the parties' representatives. The Independent Expert may himself wish to establish conditions of engagement.

4.2.2. *Preliminary meeting*

A preliminary meeting is the best way of identifying the scope of the valuation, agreed matters, the procedures and format for submissions (if any) which the parties may wish to make including a timetable. Thus, unless all terms of his appointment have been clearly established in writing, or the parties agree between them that a preliminary meeting is not necessary, the Independent Expert should call the parties or their advisers to a preliminary meeting.

See section 4–4 in relation to fees and paragraph 4.5.3. in relation to points of law.

It is important that the Independent Expert's terms of engagement should provide for the parties to bear the costs of taking legal advice and for the possibility of the Independent Expert through no fault of his own being unable to proceed further. If no such provision has been made, he may have to bear such costs himself or face the prospect of an action for breach of contract for failing to complete the reference.

4.2.3. *Independent Expert not bound by representations*

Unless his terms of reference stipulate that the appropriate is both to receive and to be bound by written representations it follows from the nature of his task that he could be justified in finding a figure outside those which may have been put before him by the parties. If there is a direction in the lease that he is to be bound by written representations it is possible that he may be regarded by the Court as acting as an Arbitrator even if not described as such. In such circumstances, the appointed surveyor should seek to establish by agreement with the parties the nature of his appointment.

4.2.4. *Independent Expert–unconditional appointments*

In most appointments however, whether by the President of the RICS or by the parties themselves, there are no conditions laid down by the parties attaching to the appointment other than those that may be set out in the lease. In such cases, the appointee is free to agree with the parties his conditions of engagement (see paragraph 4.2.1.) and thereafter he may proceed wholly in accordance with his own judgment.

4–3 PROCEDURE AND CONDUCT FOR AN INDEPENDENT EXPERT

4.3.1. *At the preliminary meeting*

At the meeting, the Independent Expert will explain that its purpose is to settle procedural matters and emphasise that no negotiations must be mentioned at that meeting. The matters on which he will require confirmation or need to obtain decisions will include the following:

(*a*) The name of the present landlord and tenant and who is representing each.
(*b*) Confirmation that the lease documents provided to the Independent Expert are the relevant ones and that there are no supplemental Deeds of Variation etc.
(*c*) Confirmation that there is no dispute on the procedures relating to the notices/counter notices implementing the rent review and those leading to the appointment of the Independent Expert.
(*d*) Confirmation that he has been correctly appointed and that no objection is then raised.
(*e*) agreement on the rent review valuation date.
(*f*) Whether the parties want more time to negotiate a settlement. If so, he should record the request in his directions and should say that he will suspend the reference with liberty for either party to apply at any time for him to proceed.

    (*g*)   his terms of service and who will be responsible for his fees (see paragraph 4.4.2.).

    (*h*)   Whether or not the parties wish to make representations to the Independent Expert and, if so, agree the detailed procedure and timetable.

    (*i*)   Whether or not there appears to be any dispute on the interpretation of the lease or any other legal matter and if so, how they propose the Independent Expert should deal with this.

    (*j*)   Whether there are any other matters relevant to the valuation and if so, how they are to be dealt with.

Before closing the meeting, he should enquire whether the parties have any questions or further points to raise. All the above matters should be confirmed to the parties in writing.

4.3.2. *Receiving information and representation from the parties*

It is desirable to invite the parties to make available to the Independent Expert any relevant factual information known to them, as this may produce evidence of which the Independent Expert himself is not aware, and is often of assistance in difficult cases. Whether the Independent Expert should invite representations (that is to say, arguments) as distinct from factual information is a matter for his discretion. In some circumstances—for example where the parties are grossly unequal in financial or technical resources, and the weaker party assets that he does not wish to incur the expense of a professional valuation—it might be justifiable for him to invite factual information only, and to say that he will pay no attention to valuations, submissions or other representations. But he should not refuse to accept factual information that either party wishes to put before him. As to how far he should rely upon factual information put before him by an obviously interested party, this is a problem that may face any surveyor making a valuation, whether for a single client or as an Independent Expert, and it clearly calls for great caution in ensuring that the full facts have been disclosed to him and that they were wholly accurate eg seeing the correspondence and lease or agreed rent review confirmation concerning the comparable under discussion. This is because he has a duty to make his own investigations into details of all transactions which he considers might be relevant and all matters of fact affecting the rental value of the property.

In most cases, the parties themselves like the opportunity of submitting an agreed statement of facts and representations (and sometimes also cross-representations). The Independent Expert should appreciate that, subject to any special terms attached to his appointment, he is not constrained by the limits set by the parties' representations and must still carry out his own investigation and calculations as his final decision must be his own independent solution. There is no duty upon the Independent Expert to inspect all properties said to be comparable, if he does not consider them relevant.

He should not enter into correspondence with the parties on the merits or otherwise of their evidence other than to establish the correctness of the information presented. All correspondence from the Independent Expert should be sent to both parties, and a copy of any document received by the Independent Expert from one party should be sent to the other. He should as far as possible avoid any oral discussion with one party in the absence of the other.

4.3.3. *Representations by one party only*

If one party only wishes to accept an invitation to make representations or submit facts and the other party refuses or is silent, then (unless the terms of the lease plainly preclude them) the Independent Expert should make it plain he will still be prepared to receive representations. In this case, a copy should be sent to the other party to give him the opportunity to comment thereon. If he does so, then the party making the original representations should be offered an opportunity to respond. Thereafter no further representations should be allowed unless in response to a request by the Independent Expert.

If one party remains silent throughout, the Independent Expert must use great care in ensuring that any relevant facts disclosed to him by the other are both full and accurate. This may require him to see any correspondence relied upon, or to have confirmation of the rental evidence cited.

4.3.4. *Dual function*

Thus an Independent Expert has a dual function. In the first place, he must assemble all the information material to a decision on the issue in respect of which he has been appointed. In the second place, he must arrive at a determination upon that material by applying his own professional judgment.

4.3.5. *Evidence in determinations by an Independent Expert*

The rules of law as to the admissibility of evidence do not apply to determinations by an Independent Expert, and he can pay attention to any information he thinks relevant. But there is reason underlying most of them, and before flouting any rule he should ask himself whether it is sensible to do so.

4.3.6. *Disclosure of documents*

An Independent Expert has no power to direct any party to disclose documents. But he can of course request a party to supply documents or any other information. If his request is refused he can consider what inference can properly be drawn from the refusal.

4–4   FEES AND COSTS OF THE INDEPENDENT EXPERT

4.4.1. *General guidance*

The Independent Expert must decide his fee on the merits of each particular case. In view of his duty to assemble information and his potential liability in negligence, the Independent Expert may be justified in charging a fee higher than if he were acting as an Arbitrator. His fee should not be fixed as a percentage of his rental determination.

He has no authority to apportion the responsibility for his own fees and costs or the costs of the parties unless the terms of the lease or of his appointment expressly confer power on him to do this.

If he is required to deal with 'costs' or 'the costs of the determination' he should establish at a preliminary meeting (see paragraph 4.2.2.) whether this embraces only his own fees and disbursements or alternatively whether he is required to decide also on the division of responsibility for the parties' costs. In either case, the principles outlined in section 9.3–10 will usually prove helpful.

4.4.2. *Establishing the right to and amount of payment*

An Independent Expert who, after appointment, proceeds to a determination without any agreement of the parties (whether in the lease or separately) as to the payment of his fees and costs, may have a right in law to be paid a quantum meruit fee for work done at the implied request of both parties. However, he would be most unwise to proceed on this assumption. He should immediately upon appointment, or at latest at the preliminary meeting (if one is to be held), not only establish the basis of his fees and costs but also obtain an express agreement by one or both parties to pay them.

Current practice is for an Independent Expert to quote a fee higher than he would charge if acting as a valuer for either party alone.

The fee basis should be sufficiently flexible to cover disbursements for, eg legal advice.

4.4.3. *Fees where a negotiated settlement is reached before determination is issued*

It is impossible to make specific recommendations because the appropriate fee must depend on the circumstances of each individual case, but the following, read in conjunction with paragraph 4.4.2., may provide some guidance.

Time of Settlement	*Appropriate Fee*
(*a*) After appointment and/or perusal of documents and/or preliminary meetings and/or issue of directions but before the Independent Expert has done any further work.	No charge or if work has been done, a fee based on the amount of that work.
(*b*) After the steps in (*a*) above, and the receipt and perusal of representations but before the Independent Expert has done any further work.	A fee of ¼ to ½ of the full agreed feed.
(*c*) After the steps in (*a*) and (*b*) and the inspection of the premises, and assembly by an Independent Expert of his own material, and all further work except the completion and issue of the determination.	The full fee, subject to a reduction in respect of work not done.
(*d*) After the determination has been finalised and notification has been finalised and notification to the parties that it is available to be taken up.	The full fee.

4.4.4. *Excessive fees and costs*

As his fees and costs are not directly subject to the Court's control (as are those of an Arbitrator) the Independent Expert's fee and costs cannot be taxed. But a party who has paid would be entitled to bring an action to recoup an excessive payment if the amount or basis of the fee and costs has not been agreed and the payment has been made under protest.

4–5   THE DETERMINATION OF THE INDEPENDENT EXPERT

4.5.1. *The clarity of his decision*

When his determination on the matter is made, the Independent Expert should set it down clearly in writing and make it available to the parties once his fees have been paid.

It is suggested that the determination should cover the following:
- (i)   A heading, naming the parties to the dispute and subject property.
- (ii) Reference to the Independent Expert's appointment covering:
  - (*a*) the document (usually the lease) containing the parties' agreement to submit the dispute to an Independent Expert;
  - (*b*) the method of the appointment (eg whether by the President of the RICS or by the parties direct);
  - (*c*) the date of the appointment;
  - (*d*) the terms attaching to the appointment and any adopted procedure.
- (iii) The subject matter of the dispute.
- (iv) His decision on the subject matter of the dispute.
- (v)   Fees and costs if appropriate.
- (vi) His signature and date.

4.5.2. *Slips and clerical errors*

If the Independent Expert becomes aware of a slip or clerical error in his determination, he should rectify it and immediately inform both parties.

4.5.3. *A point of law*

If a point of law arises which is likely to affect his determination and which he considers to be a difficult one, the Independent Expert should ask the parties to consider whether:
- (i)   they will agree what is the correct answer to the point of law, or one of them will commence proceedings in the Courts to decide it, before he proceeds with his Determination;
- (ii) they would instead prefer him to take, and proceed on the basis of, legal advice on the point, which he incorporates in his Determination.
- (iii) he should continue to deal with the reference, but (by their written consent) as an Arbitrator, with or without a legal assessor.
- (iv) he should decide the point; state his decision and his Determination based upon it; and then state what his Determination would have been if he had decided the point differently.

If all these courses are rejected, it is suggested that the Independent Expert is entitled to refuse to proceed further in the matter.

4.5.4. *A request for reasoned determination*

A determination by an Independent Expert, unless required under the terms of his appointment, should not normally include reasons or the basis of calculations. Nor is there an obligation to respond to a later request for them. However, since the Independent Expert is liable in negligence, it will be prudent for him to make, and retain for an appropriate period, notes on the material that he has used in the course of arriving at his valuation.

5–1   GENERAL COMMENTS

5.1.1. The Chartered Surveyor may also be called upon by the parties to a lease or other similar agreement to determine other matters in dispute, such as the assessment of service charges or a valuation in connection with an option to purchase.

5.1.2. These notes are not intended to cover all such matters but in general terms the basic principles set out in the previous paragraphs of these Guidance Notes apply whether the reference is to Arbitrator or Independent Expert.

Part Seven

Precedents

Introduction

The collection of precedents contained in this Part is divided into sections.

Section One contains modern precedents of rent review clauses which may be adopted for use in new leases.

Section Two collects together some special forms of rent review and specialist clauses drafted to cover the impact of VAT.

Section Three includes a few older, now obsolete or obsolescent, forms of clause which are included because they appear to be the basis of many clauses in existing leases which will fall for review for some years to come.

Section Four contains rent review and indexation forms for residential tenancies which have been drafted by the authors and are designed for use in England and Wales in the light of the Housing Act 1988.

Section Five sets out clauses providing for indexation to the Retail Prices Index.

Section Six reproduces a short form of clause for a retail turnover rent.

Those precedents that were drafted as a form of rent review clause or indexation clause appear here in full (eg, The Model Forms, Conveyancer Precedent 5-5–57); but others (eg, EFP (5th ed Form 22)) are taken from precedents for complete leases.

The precedents in Section Three are now obsolete, obsolescent or have been superseded by redrafted variants but are included for reference purposes. They are included as first published.

The *Authors' Notes*, which include cross-references to the text, at the end of some of the precedents will pinpoint some of the amendments that may be desirable and refer the reader to some of the issues discussed in the text.

Acknowledgements

The Model Forms of Rent Review Clause (original 1979 version, revised 1980 version and revised 1985 version) are reproduced with the permission of the Joint Committee of the Law Society and the Royal Institution of Chartered Surveyors.

Conveyancer Precedents 5–57, 5–11, 5–11A, 5–99, 5–100, 5–103, 5–104 and 5–105 are reproduced with the permission of the publishers, Sweet and Maxwell Ltd.

Section One

Modern Precedents

1 RICS/LAW SOCIETY REVISED MODEL FORMS OF RENT REVIEW CLAUSE

[Revised 1985]

1985 Revised Model Forms of Rent Review Clauses Promulgated by Joint Working Party of the Law Society and the Royal Institution of Chartered Surveyors in Three Variants

(First published December 1985)

Introduction

The Law Society and the Royal Institution of Chartered Surveyors first published draft model forms of rent review clause relating to commercial leases in June 1979. Comments and criticisms from the professions and others were invited and received and recommended model forms and background notes relating thereto, which were published in March 1980, so far as possible took into account all the many points that had been made in correspondence to the Joint Committee set up to consider the matter.

The Joint Committee have revised the 1980 model forms of rent review clause in the light of recent case law and modern conveyancing practice and now publish a 1985 edition. The 1985 model forms supersede the 1980 model forms in their entirety. For greater convenience, these are set out in three principal variants, namely:

Variation A: determination in default of agreement by arbitration with alternative provisions for:
a. upwards only review; and
b. upwards or downwards review.

Variation B: determination in default of agreement by independent valuer acting as an expert with alternative provisions for:
a. upwards only review; and
b. upwards or downwards review.

Variation C: determination in default of agreement to be either by arbitration or by independent valuer acting as expert (at the landlord's option) with alternative provisions for:

a. upwards only review; and

b. upwards or downwards review.

In the model forms where words appear in italics, it denotes either that one or two alternatives is to be selected or that the inclusion is optional, and the notes applicable to the particular variation should be followed. The Joint Committee wish to emphasise that the model forms are published in order to assist those who possess professional expertise in the drafting of commercial leases. It will always be necessary to consider whether any of the variations set out below are appropriate to the particular case and, if considered to be so, what amendments may be required and which of the alternative clauses provided should be incorporated in the particular commercial lease. As these forms are designed to create specific legal rights and obligations, they are recommended for use only in accordance with the advice of somebody qualified as above.

MODEL FORM—VARIATION A

Determination in default of agreement by Arbitration with alternative provisions for (a) upwards only review, and (b) upwards or downwards review. [See *Introduction*]

...yielding and paying to the landlord yearly rents ascertained in accordance with the next four clauses hereof without any deduction by equal quarterly payments in advance on the usual quarter days the first payment (being an apportioned sum) to be made on the date hereof.

Clause 1: Definitions

In this lease 'review date' means the—day of——in the year 19— and in every ——year thereafter and 'review period' means the period starting with any review date up to the next review date or starting with the last review date up to the end of the term hereof

Clause 2

The yearly rent shall be:

(A) until the first review date the rent of £——and

[*Provisions for revision of rent in upwards only review*]
(B) during each successive review period a rent equal to the rent previously payable hereunder or such revised rent as may be ascertained as herein provided whichever be the greater

OR

[*For revision of rent in upwards or downwards review*]
(B)(i) during each successive review period such revised rent as may be ascertained as herein provided and
(B)(ii) in the event of a revised rent not being ascertained as herein provided the rent payable for the relevant review period shall be the rent payable immediately prior to the commencement of such period

Clause 3: Ascertainment of amount by arbitrator

Such revised rent for any review period may be agreed at any time between the landlord and the tenant or (in the absence of agreement) determined not earlier than the relevant review date by an arbitrator such arbitrator to be nominated in the absence of agreement by or on behalf of the President for the time being of the Royal Institution of Chartered Surveyors on the application of the landlord or the tenant made not earlier than six months before the relevant review date *but not later than the end of the relevant review period* and so that in the case of such arbitration the revised rent to be awarded by the arbitrator shall be such as he shall decide is the yearly rent at which the demised premises might reasonably be expected to be let at the relevant review date

[See Note 1]

(A) On the following assumptions at that date:
(i) That the demised premises:
  (a) are available to let on the open market without a fine or premium with vacant possession by a willing landlord to a willing tenant for a term of [10] years or the residue then unexpired of the term of this lease (whichever be the longer)
  (b) are to be let as a whole subject to the terms of this lease (other than the amount of the rent hereby reserved but including the provisions for review of that rent)
  (c) are fit and available for immediate occupation
  (d) may be used for any of the purposes permitted by this lease as varied or extended by any licence granted pursuant thereto

[See Note 2]

(ii) That the covenants herein contained on the part of *the landlord and* the tenant have been fully performed and observed

[See Note 3]

(iii) That no work has been carried out to the demised premises which has diminished the rental value and that in case the demised premises have been destroyed or damaged they have been fully restored.
(iv) That no reduction is to be made to take account of any rental concession which on a new letting with vacant possession might be granted to the incoming tenant for a period within which its fitting out works would take place

(B) But disregarding:
(i) any effect on rent of the fact that the tenant its sub-tenants or their respective predecessors in title have been in occupation of the demised premises
(ii) any goodwill attached to the demised premises by reason of the carrying on thereat of the business of the tenant its sub-tenant or their predecessors in title in their respective businesses and
(iii) any increase in rental value of the demised premises attributable to the existence at the relevant review date of any improvement to the demised premises or any part thereof carried out with consent where required otherwise than in pursuance of an obligation to the landlord or its predecessors in title except obligations requiring compliance with statutes or directions of Local Authorities or other bodies exercising powers under statute or Royal Charter either
  (a)   by the tenant its sub-tenant or their respective predecessors in title during

the said term or during any period of occupation prior thereto arising out of an agreement to grant such term or

(b) *by any tenant or sub-tenant of the demised premises before the commencement of the term hereby granted so long as the landlord or its predecessors in title have not since the improvement was carried out had vacant possession of the relevant part of the demised premises*

[See Notes 4 and 5]

Clause 4

IT IS HEREBY FURTHER PROVIDED in relation to the ascertainment and payment of revised rent as follows:

Further provisions as to Arbitration

(A) The arbitration shall be conducted in accordance with the Arbitration Acts 1950 and 1979 or any statutory modification or re-enactment thereof for the time being in force with the further provision that if the arbitrator nominated pursuant to Clause 3 hereof shall die or decline to act the President for the time being of the Royal Institution of Chartered Surveyors or the person acting on his behalf may on the application of either the landlord or the tenant by writing discharge the arbitrator and appoint another in his place

As to memoranda of ascertainment

(B) When the amount of any rent to be ascertained as hereinbefore provided shall have been so ascertained memoranda thereof shall thereupon be signed by or on behalf of the landlord and the tenant and annexed to his lease and the counterpart thereof and the landlord and the tenant shall bear their own costs in respect thereof

As to interim payments and final adjustments upwards only review

(C)(i) if the revised rent payable on and from any review date has not been agreed by that review date rent shall continue to be payable at the rate previously payable and forthwith opon the revised rent being ascertained the tenant shall pay to the landlord any shortfall between the rent and the revised rent payable up to and on the preceding quarter day together with interest on any shortfall at the seven day deposit rate of— Bank such interest to be calculated on a day to day basis from the relevant review date on which it would have been payable if the revised rent had then been ascertained to the date of actual payment of any shortfall and the interest so payable shall be recoverable in the same manner as rent in arrear

[See Note 6]

OR

Upwards or downwards review

(C)(i) if the revised rent payable on and from any review date has not been agreed by that review date rent shall continue to be payable at the rate previously payable and forthwith upon the revised rent being ascertained the tenant shall pay to the landlord any shortfall between the rent and the revised rent or as the case may be the landlord shall pay to the tenant any excess of the rent paid over the revised rent payable up to and on the preceding quarter day together with interest on any shortfall or as the case may be any excess at the seven day deposit rate of — Bank such interest to be calculated on a day to day basis from the relevant

*review date on which it would have been payable if the revised rent had then been
ascertained to the date of actual payment of any shortfall or any excess and the
interest so payable shall be recoverable in the same manner as rent in arrear or
as the case may be as a debt*

(ii) for the purposes of this proviso the revised rent shall be deemed to have
been ascertained on the date when the same has been agreed between the landlord
and the tenant or as the case may be the date of the award of the arbitrator

[See Note 6]

(D) If either the landlord or the tenant shall fail to pay any costs awarded
against it in an arbitration under the provisions hereof within twenty-one days
of the same being demanded by the arbitrator the other shall be entitled to
pay the same and the amount so paid shall be repaid by the party chargeable
on demand

Notes application to Variation A

1 See paragraph 3, background notes.
2 See paragraph 6, background notes.
3 See paragraphs 8 and 9, background notes.
4 See paragraph 10, background notes.
5 It should be considered in each case whether these words are relevant.
6 Insert name of bank and see paragraph 13, background notes.

MODEL FORM—VARIATION B

**Determination in default of agreement by independent valuer acting as an expert
with alternative provisions for (a) upwards only review and (b) upwards or downwards
review.** [*See Introduction*]

... yielding and paying to the landlord yearly rents ascertained in accordance
with the next four clauses hereof without any deduction by equal quarterly
payments in advance on the usual quarter days the first payment (being an
apportioned sum) to be made on the date hereof

Clause 1: Definitions

In this lease 'review date' means the — day of —— in the year 19— and
in every —— year thereafter and 'review period' means the period starting with
any review date up to the next review date or starting with the last review date
up to the end of the term hereof

Clause 2

The yearly rent shall be:
(A) until the first review date the rent of £—— and

[Provisions for revision of rent in upwards only review]
*(B) during each successive review period a rent equal to the rent previously payable
hereunder or such revised rent as may be ascertained as herein provided whichever
be the greater*

OR

[For revision of rent in upwards or downwards review]

(B)(i) during each successive review period such revised rent as may be ascertained as herein provided and
(B)(ii) in the event of a revised rent not being ascertained as herein provided the rent payable for the relevant review period shall be the rent payable immediately prior to the commencement of such period

Clause 3: Ascertainment of amount by independent valuer

Such revised rent for any review period may be agreed at any time between the landlord and the tenant or (in the absence of agreement) determined not earlier than the relevant review date by an independent valuer (acting as an expert and not as an arbitrator) such valuer to be nominated in the absence of agreement by or on behalf of the President for the time being of the Royal Institution of Chartered Surveyors on the application of the landlord or the tenant made not earlier than six months before the relevant review date *but not later than the end of the relevant review period* and so that in the case of such valuation the revised rent to be determined by the valuer shall be such as he shall decide is the yearly rent at which the demised premises might reasonably be expected to be let at the relevant review date

[See Note 1]

(A) On the following assumptions at that date:
(i) That the demised premises:
   (a)   are available to let on the open market without a fine or premium with vacant possession by a willing landlord to a willing tenant for a term of [10] years or the residue then unexpired of the term of this lease (whichever be the longer)

[See Note 2]

   (b)   are to be let as a whole subject to the terms of this lease (other than the amount of the rent hereby reserved but including the provisions for review of that rent)
   (c)   are fit and available for immediate occupation
   (d)   may be used for any of the purposes permitted by this lease as varied or extended by any licence granted pursuant thereto
(ii) That the covenants herein contained on the part of *the landlord and* the tenant have been fully performed and observed

[See Note 3]

(iii) That no work has been carried out to the demised premises which has diminished the rental value and that in case the demised premises have been destroyed or damaged they have been fully restored
(iv) That no reduction is to be made to take account of any rental concession which on a new letting with vacant possession might be granted to the incoming tenant for a period within which its fitting out works would take place

(B) But disregarding:
(i) any effect on rent of the fact that the tenant its sub-tenant or their respective predecessors in title have been in occupation of the demised premises
(ii) any goodwill attached to the demised premises by reason of the carrying on thereat of the business of the tenant its sub-tenants or their predecessors in title in their respective businesses and
(iii) any increase in rental value of the demised premises attributable to the

existence at the relevant review date of any improvement to the demised premises or any part thereof carried out with consent where required otherwise than in pursuance of an obligation to the landlord or its predecessors in title except obligations requiring compliance with statutes or directions of Local Authorities or other bodies exercising powers under statute or Royal Charter either

[See Note 4]

(a) by the tenant its sub-tenants or their respective predecessors in title during the said term or during any period of occupation prior thereto arising out of an agreement to grant such term or

(b) by any tenant or sub-tenant of the demised premises before the commencement of the term hereby granted so long as the landlord or its predecessors in title have not since the improvement was carried out had vacant possession of the relevant part of the demised premises

[See Note 5]

Clause 4

IT IS HEREBY FURTHER PROVIDED in relation to the ascertainment and payment of revised rent as follows:

As to independent valuation

(A)(i) the fees and expenses of the valuer including the cost of his nomination shall be borne equally by the landlord and the tenant who shall otherwise bear their own costs and

(ii) the valuer shall afford the landlord and the tenant an opportunity to make representations to him and

(iii) if the valuer nominated pursuant to Clause 3 hereof shall die, delay or become unwilling, unfit or incapable of acting or if for any reason the President for the time being of the Royal Institution of Chartered Surveyors or the person acting on his behalf shall in his absolute discretion think fit he may on the application of either the landlord or the tenant by writing discharge the valuer and appoint another in his place.

As to memoranda of ascertainment

(B) When the amount of any rent to be ascertained as hereinbefore provided shall have been so ascertained memoranda thereof shall thereupon be signed by or on behalf of the landlord and the tenant and annexed to this lease and the counterpart thereof and the landlord and the tenant shall bear their own costs in respect thereof

Provisions as to interim payments final adjustments upwards only review

(C)(i) If the revised rent payable on and from any review date has not been agreed by that review date rent shall continue to be payable at the rate previously payable and forthwith upon the revised rent being ascertained the tenant shall pay to the landlord any shortfall between the rent and the revised rent payable up to and on the preceding quarter day together with interest on any shortfall at the seven day deposit rate of — Bank such interest to be calculated on a day-to-day basis from the relevant review date on which it would have been payable if the revised rent had then been ascertained to the date of actual payment of any shortfall and the interest so payable shall be recoverable in the same manner as rent in arrear

[See Note 6]

OR

Upwards or downwards review

(C)(i) if the revised rent payable on and from any review date has not been agreed by that review date rent shall continue to be payable at the rate previously payable and forthwith upon the revised rent being ascertained the tenant shall pay to the landlord any shortfall between the rent and the revised rent or as the case may be the landlord shall pay to the tenant any excess of the rent paid over the revised rent payable up to and on the preceding quarter day together with interest on any shortfall or as the case may be any excess at the seven day deposit rate of —— Bank such interest to be calculated on a day to day basis from the relevant review date on which it would have been payable if the revised rent had then been ascertained to the date of actual payment of any shortfall or any excess and the interest so payable shall be recoverable in the same manner as rent in arrear or as the case may be as a debt

[See Note 6]

(ii) for the purposes of this proviso the revised rent shall be deemed to have been ascertained on the date when the same has been agreed between the landlord and the tenant or as the case may be the date of the determination by the valuer

(D) If either the landlord or the tenant shall fail to pay the moiety of the fees and expenses of the valuer under the provisions hereof within twenty-one days of the same being demanded by the valuer, the other shall be entitled to pay the same and the amount so paid shall be repaid by the party chargeable on demand

Notes applicable to Variation B

1 See paragraph 3, background notes.
2 See paragraph 6, background notes.
3 See paragraph 8 and 9, background notes.
4 See paragraph 10, background notes.
5 It should be considered in each case whether these words are relevant.
6 Insert name of bank and see paragraph 13, background notes.

MODEL FORM—VARIATION C

Determination in default of agreement to be either by arbitration or by independent valuer acting as expert (at the landlord's option) with alternative provisions for (a) upwards only review and (b) upwards and downwards review. [*See Introduction*]

... yielding and paying to the landlord yearly rents ascertained in accordance with the next four clauses hereof without any deduction by equal quarterly payments in advance on the usual quarter days the first payment (being an apportioned sum) to be made on the date hereof

Clause 1: Definitions

In this lease 'review date' means the —— day of —— in the year 19— and in every —— year thereafter and 'review period' means the period starting with any review date up to the next review date or starting with the last review date up to the end of the term hereof

Clause 2

The yearly rent shall be:
(A) until the first review date the rent of £—— and

[Provisions for revision of rent in upwards only review]

(B) during each successive review period a rent equal to the rent previously payable hereunder or such revised rent as may be ascertained as herein provided whichever be the greater

OR

[For revision of rent in upwards or downwards review]

(B)(i) during each successive review period such revised rent as may be ascertained as herein provided and
(B)(ii) in the event of a revised rent not being ascertained as herein provided the rent payable for the relevant review period shall be the rent payable immediately prior to the commencement of such period

Clause 3: Ascertainment of amount by arbitrator or by independent valuer at the landlord's option

[See Note 7]

Such revised rent for any review period may be agreed at any time between the landlord and the tenant or (in the absence of agreement) determined not earlier than the relevant review date at the option of the landlord either by an arbitrator or by an independent valuer (acting as an expert and not as an arbitrator) such arbitrator or valuer to be nominated in the absence of agreement by or on behalf of the President for the time being of the Royal Institution of Chartered Surveyors on the application of the landlord (in exercise of the said option) made not earlier than six months before the relevant review date *but not later than the end of the relevant review period* and so that in the case of such arbitration or valuation the revised rent to be awarded or determined by the arbitrator or valuer shall be such as he shall decide is the yearly rent at which the demised premises might reasonably be expected to be let at the relevant review date

[See Note 1]

(A) On the following assumptions at that date:
(i) That the demised premises:

[See Note 2]

(a) are available to let on the open market without a fine or premium with vacant possession by a willing landlord to a willing tenant for a term of [10] years or the residue then unexpired of the term of this lease (whichever be the longer)

[See Note 2]

(b) are to be let as a whole subject to the terms of this lease (other than the amount of the rent hereby reserved but including the provisions for review of that rent)

(c) are fit and available for immediate occupation

(d) may be used for any of the purposes permitted by this lease as varied or extended by any licence granted pursuant thereto

(ii) That the covenants herein contained on the part of *the landlord and* the tenant have been fully performed and observed

[See Note 3]

(iii) That no work has been carried out to the demised premises which has diminished the rental value and that in case the demised premises have been destroyed or damaged they have been fully restored

(iv) That no reduction is to be made to take account of any rental concession which on a new letting with vacant possession might be granted to the incoming tenant for a period within which its fitting out works would take place

(B) But disregarding:

(i) any effect on rent of the fact that the tenant its sub-tenants or their respective predecessors in title have been in occupation of the demised premises

(ii) any goodwill attached to the demised premises by reason of the carrying on thereat of the business of the tenant its sub-tenants or their predecessors in title in their respective businesses and

[See Note 4]

(iii) any increase in rental value of the demised premises attributable to the existence at the relevant review date of any improvement to the demised premises or any part thereof carried out with consent where required otherwise than in pursuance of an obligation to the landlord or its predecessors in title except obligations requiring compliance with statutes or directions of Local Authorities or other bodies exercising powers under statute or Royal Charter either

[See Note 4]

(a) by the tenant its sub-tenants or their respective predecessors in title during the said term or during any period of occupation prior thereto arising out of an agreement to grant such term or

[See Note 5]

(b) *by any tenant or sub-tenant of the demised premises before the commencement of the term hereby granted so long as the landlord or its predecessors in title have not since the improvement was carried out had vacant possession of the relevant part of the demised premises*

[See Note 5]

Clause 4

IT IS HEREBY FURTHER PROVIDED in relation to the ascertainment and payment of revised rent as follows:

Further provisions as to arbitration

(A) (In the case of arbitration) the arbitration shall be conducted in accordance with the Arbitration Acts 1950 and 1979 or any statutory modification or re-enactment thereof for the time being in force with the further provision that if the arbitrator nominated pursuant to Clause 3 hereof shall die or decline to act the President for the time being of the Royal Institution of Chartered

Surveyors or the person acting on his behalf may on the application of either the landlord or the tenant by writing discharge the arbitrator and appoint another in his place

As to independent valuation

(B) (In the case of determination by a valuer)
(i) the fees and expenses of the valuer including the cost of his nomination shall be borne equally by the landlord and the tenant who shall otherwise each bear their own costs and
(ii) the valuer shall afford the landlord and the tenant an opportunity to make representations to him and
(iii) if the valuer nominated pursuant to Clause 3 hereof shall die, delay or become unwilling, unfit or incapable of acting or if for any other reason the President for the time being of the Royal Institution of Chartered Surveyors or the person acting on his behalf shall in his absolute discretion think fit he may on the application of either the landlord or the tenant by writing discharge the valuer and appoint another in his place

As to memoranda of ascertainment

(C) When the amount of any rent to be ascertained as hereinbefore provided shall have been so ascertained memoranda thereof shall thereupon be signed by or on behalf of the landlord and the tenant and annexed to this lease and the counterpart thereof and the landlord and the tenant shall bear their own costs in respect thereof

As to interim payments and final adjustments upwards only review

(D)(i) If the revised rent payable on and from any review date has not been agreed by that review date rent shall continue to be payable at the rate previously payable and forthwith upon the revised rent being ascertained, the tenant shall pay to the landlord any shortfall between the rent and the revised rent payable up to and on the preceding quarter day together with interest on any shortfall at the seven day deposit rate of -- Bank such interest to be calculated on a day to day basis from the relevant review date on which it would have been payable if the revised rent had then been ascertained to the date of actual payment of any shortfall and the interest so payable shall be recoverable in the same manner as rent in arrear

[See Note 6]

OR

Upwards or downwards review

(D)(i) If the revised rent payable on and from any review date has not been agreed by that review date rent shall continue to be payable at the rate previously payable and forthwith upon the revised rent being ascertained the tenant shall pay to the landlord any shortfall between the rent and the revised rent or as the case may be the landlord shall pay to the tenant any excess of the rent paid over the revised rent payable up to and on the preceding quarter day together with interest on any shortfall or as the case may be any excess at the seven day deposit rate of -- Bank such interest to be calculated on a day to day basis from the relevant review date on which it would have been payable if the revised rent had then been ascertained to the date of actual payment of any shortfall or any excess and the interest so payable shall be recoverable in the same manner as rent in arrear or as the case may be as a debt

[*See Note 6*]

(ii) for the purpose of this proviso the revised rent shall be deemed to have been ascertained on the date when the same has been agreed between the landlord and the tenant or as the case may be the date of the award of the arbitrator or of the determination by the valuer

(E) If either the landlord or the tenant shall fail to pay any costs awarded against it in the case of an arbitration or the moiety of the fees and expenses of the valuer under the provisions hereof within twenty one days of the same being demanded by the arbitrator or the valuer (as the case may be) the other shall be entitled to pay the same and the amount so paid shall be repaid by the party chargeable on demand.

As to notice by the tenant to trigger landlord's application

(F) *Whenever a revised rent in respect of any review period has not been agreed between the landlord and the tenant before the relevant review date and where no agreement has been reached as to the appointment of an arbitrator or valuer nor has the landlord made any application to the President for the time being of the Royal Institution of Chartered Surveyors as hereinbefore provided the tenant may serve on the landlord notice in writing referring to this provision and containing a proposal as to the amount of such revised rent (which shall not be less than the rent payable immediately before the commencement of the relevant review period) and the amount so proposed shall be deemed to have been agreed by the landlord and the tenant as the revised rent for the relevant review period and sub-clause (D)(i) hereof shall apply accordingly unless the landlord shall make such application as aforesaid within three months after service of such notice by the tenant. Time shall be of the essence in respect of this provision.*

[*See Notes 7 and 8*]

Notes applicable to Variation C

1 See paragraph 3, background notes.
2 See paragraph 6, background notes.
3 See paragraphs 8 and 9, background notes.
4 See paragraph 10, background notes.
5 It should be considered in each case whether these words are relevant.
6 Insert name of bank and see paragraph 13, background notes.
7 See paragraph 2(b), background notes.
8 The words in parenthesis should only be included if the review provision is upwards only.

Background Notes (published by the sponsor)

The following brief notes have been produced to provide information as to the background reasoning which led to the many variations included in the revised published rent review clauses and as to the phraseology used in them, the need for some of the different provisions, and to explain why some of the revisions have been found necessary.
1 The clauses were drafted to embrace the widest range of business premises, varying from poor quality multi-tenanted buildings to lettings to single tenants of large and modern properties with sophisticated services and facilities.
2 In making revisions to the 1980 Edition, the Joint Committee remained

of the view that the revised model clauses should be able to reflect the market conditions prevailing at the time when the letting is negotiated. Thus, the following alternatives contained in the 1980 Edition remain:

(a) Provisions which cover 'upwards only' and 'upwards/downwards' rent reviews;

(b)(i) Provision for the landlord to choose between an arbitrator and a valuer acting as an expert. In this case, it follows from the drafting that the landlord will also control the initiation of the review. Clause 4(F) of Variation C is therefore included to protect the tenant in the situation where he needs to avoid uncertainty or wants to assign after a rent review date and the landlord has not applied for the nomination of an arbitrator or valuer;

(ii) Pre-determined type of appointment, coupled with the more balanced right for either party to initiate the review.

3 In the light of the Burnley and Cheapside decisions (*United Scientific Holdings Limited v Burnley Borough Council* and *Cheapside Land Development Company Limited v Messels Service Company* [1978] AC 904), the Joint Committee have continued to avoid, as far as possible, strict time limits and notices, in order to give effect to the contract between the parties (ie a letting for a term of years with rent reviews at specified intervals) and remove the risk of that contract being frustrated by human error. There is, however, provision, as an alternative, for a time limit after which a review can no longer be initiated.

4 The Joint Committee also remained of the view that, in an inflationary economy and in often rapidly changing market conditions, it is wrong to expect a valuer or arbitrator to determine the rent in advance of a review date. Hence, the referral process enables the appointment to take place prior to the review date, but requires that the revised rent may not be determined until the review date (save of course by mutual agreement).

5 Amendments contained in the 1985 Edition make it abundantly clear that the revised rent to be determined is in respect of a hypothetical letting of the premises actually demised at the relevant review date on certain assumptions and disregarding certain factors. The 1980 Edition was on the same basis despite any appearances to the contrary.

6 The Joint Committee have made significant revisions to the assumptions to be made in respect of the hypothetical lease to be considered when the revised rent is ascertained. As to the length of the hypothetical lease to be considered, recent market experience has suggested that neither 'the unexpired term' nor 'a term equivalent to the original term' is entirely satisfactory. If the unexpired term is to be assumed, then at the later review dates a very limited unexpired length of term could depress the rent unfairly. However, the alternative assumption of a term equivalent to the original term of a long lease could equally be regarded as having a depreciating effect on rental value if obsolescence is thereby ignored. The Joint Committee were of the view that the unexpired term, subject to a minimum term (suggested to be ten years or a figure closest thereto which represents a multiple of the 'review period'), was the most appropriate compromise.

7 Assumptions that in the hypothetical letting the premises are to be let 'on the open market', 'with vacant possession' and 'as a whole' have all been retained. However, there may be occasional circumstances, such as when there are existing sub-tenancies at the start of the lease, where this should not necessarily apply. Furthermore, the original drafting of the 1980 Edition

would appear to cover more than adequately the problems raised in the case of *National Westminster Bank plc v Arthur Young McLelland Moores & Co* (1984) 273 EG 402, where it was held that if the revised rent were to be assessed on the basis of the provisions of the actual lease 'other than the rent...reserved', the provisions relating to rent review are also to be disregarded.

8   The assumption of landlord's covenants being fulfilled on review is included as an option in view of the uncertain position in law and the injustices which can occur either way. The Joint Committee were particularly concerned as to whether or not it should be assumed that the landlord had complied with his repairing obligations. If disrepair is recognised in assessing the rent, subsequent fulfilment of obligations by the landlord may be inhibited or he may conversely incur unnecessary expense (recoverable from the tenant) to avoid that situation. Conversely, assumption of repair can disadvantage a tenant, notwithstanding any legal rights of redress. Unless therefore a review clause is specifically drafted to provide for a differential rent in the event of disrepair, the assumption to form the basis of valuation must remain a matter to be agreed by the parties in the circumstances.

9   The Joint Committee considered it appropriate, in the light of difficulties arising from rent-free concessions in vacant possession lettings, to include an entirely new assumption that no account should be taken of any fitting-out period which might be allowed to a hypothetical tenant on a new letting. It was considered that if such a period were to be granted specifically for that purpose in the open market, it was a 'once-off' concession made by the landlord to the tenant in respect of the full term of the lease and was not therefore a benefit that should be granted to the tenant at subsequent rent reviews.

10 The disregards, referred to in Clause 3(B), include and extend the disregards, referred to in s 34 of the Landlord and Tenant Act 1954 as amended. The Joint Committee gave extensive consideration to Clause 3(B)(iii) which deals with the disregard in respect of tenants' improvements. The basis adopted in the 1980 Edition has been retained, subject only to minor variation. The alternative, as recommended by the ISVA, of undertaking a valuation 'rebus sic stantibus' thereafter making a 'fair allowance' to the tenant in respect of any alteration or improvement undertaken, was considered but rejected. Provision is now made for the landlord not to take the benefit of any increase in rental value resulting from obligations placed upon the tenant requiring compliance with enactments or directions of Government or Local Authorities. Furthermore, the provisions go beyond the Landlord and Tenant Act 1954 in protecting tenants against being charged rent on the improvements of their sub-tenants or predecessors in title. It is no longer suggested that the value of tenants' improvements over twenty one years old may be taken into account by the landlord.

11 In an arbitration, the parties have the right to appearance and the arbitrator must adjudicate. The independent valuer, however appointed, is not bound by the rules and procedures laid down by the Arbitration Acts and, unless the lease provides that he shall do so, may decline to receive any statement of facts or evidence from either of the parties to the dispute. In the 1985 Edition of the model clauses, where reference is to an independent valuer, the Joint Committee have included a provision instead of an option which appeared in the 1980 Edition that the valuer shall afford to each of the parties an opportunity to make representations.

12   If in the case of determination by arbitration, the arbitrator shall die or
     decline to act, the revised model clauses provide that the President of the
     RICS may appoint another in his place. This should enable a further
     appointment to be made more quickly than by following the procedures
     laid down by the Arbitration Acts.

13   In making revisions to the 1980 Edition, the Joint Committee decided that
     it was now common practice for interest payments on arrears of increased
     rents to be included and as a result there has been an appropriate addition
     to the model clauses. In the view of the Joint Committee, the interest rate
     to be selected should equate to a deposit rate.

14   Finally, Clause 4 provides for memoranda to be signed by or on behalf
     of the landlord and the tenant recording the amount of any reviewed rent
     ascertained. The form of memorandum recommended as published with
     the 1980 Edition and is reprinted below for ease of reference.

MEMORANDUM

Lease dated: Premises: Parties

BY THIS MEMORANDUM dated the —— day of —— 19——
——(as Landlord) and —— (as Tenant) desire to record the fact that the rent
payable under the above-mentioned lease has been reviewed under the provisions
of Clause —— thereof and fixed in accordance with those provisions of £ —
— per year from the —— 19— to the —— 19—

For and on behalf of the (Landlord) (Tenant)

Note

  The above Notes and Clauses are published by kind permission of the
sponsoring bodies.

2   ISVA FORMS

Clauses for Rent Review to Open Market Rent Promulgated by Incorporated Society of Valuers and Auctioneers[1]

(First published December 1984)

FORM A

The Reservation of Rent

  YIELDING AND PAYING therefor FIRST the Principal Rent ascertained in
accordance with [Clause] [Schedule] on the dates and in the manner there specified
and ...

The [Clause] [Schedule] specifying the ascertainment of the Principal Rent

1. In this [Clause] [Schedule]:—
1.1 'Review Date' means the —— in the years —— and —— and includes
any other date that becomes a Review Date pursuant to paragraph 7

1.2 'Rent Period' means:—

(A)   each period of the Term beginning on a Review Date and ending on the day before the new Review Date

(B)   the period of the Term commencing on the last Review Date and ending on the expiry of the Term

1.3 'Rental Value' means the yearly rent at which the Demised Premises might reasonably be expected to be let on the open market with vacant possession on the relevant Review Date by a willing landlord to a willing tenant for a term of [10][3] years or a term equal to the residue then unexpired of the Term (whichever is the longer) but otherwise on the terms of this lease.

ASSUMING:—

(A)   that the Demised Premises had been fully fitted out and equipped so as to be ready for immediate occupation and use by such willing tenant for the use permitted by this Lease and by any licence given by the Landlord at the request of the Tenant before the relevant Review Date[4]

(B)   that all the Tenant's covenants herein had been complied with

(C)   that even if compliance with the Tenant's covenants herein did not so require any destruction of or damage to the Demised Premises had been made good before the relevant Review Date

(D)   that the benefit of any planning or other consent current at the relevant Review Date[5] is available also for such willing tenant

but DISREGARDING:—

(E)   any effect on rent of the occupation of the Demised Premises by the Tenant or by any predecessor in title of the Tenant

(F)   any goodwill attached to the Demised Premises by reason of the user thereof by the Tenant

and MAKING:—

(G)   a fair allowance[6] to the Tenant in respect of any alteration or improvement to the Demised Premises made (otherwise than pursuant to any obligation of the Tenant to carry out such work) by the Tenant [during the Term] [during the last 21 years immediately before the relevant Review date][7] with any necessary prior consent of the Landlord

and PROVIDING:

(H)   that for the avoidance of doubt no value shall be attributed to the equipment and other property of the Tenant in the Demised Premises;

(I)   that in paragraphs (E) (F) and (G) only references to the Tenant shall be deemed to include references to any permitted undertenant

1.4 'Principle Rent' means:—

(A)   until the first Review Date the rent reserved in Clause 1

(B)   during each Rent Period the yearly rent ascertained in accordance with the following provisions of this [Clause] [Schedule]

1.5 'President' meant the President for the time being of the Incorporated Society of Valuers and Auctioneers (or any body for the time being performing the functions of the Incorporated Society as successor to it) or the person for the time being authorised to act on his behalf

1.6 'Valuer' means a valuer agreed between the Landlord and the Tenant or in default of such agreement appointed by the President

1.7 'Act' means any Act of Parliament now or hereafter to be passed and includes any statutory instrument made under any Act

2 From each Review Date the Principal Rent shall be such amount either as may at any time be agreed between the Landlord and the Tenant as the Principal

Rent payable from that Review Date or (in default of such agreement) whichever is the greater of:—

(A)   the Rental Value or

(B)   the Principal Rent contractually payable immediately before that Review Date

3 If [by a date 3 months][8] before a Review Date the Principal Rent payable from that Review Date has not been agreed the Landlord and the Tenant may agree upon a Valuer to determine the Rental Value but in default of such agreement the Landlord or the Tenant may at any time apply to the President to appoint a Valuer to determine the Rental Value

4 Unless the Landlord and the Tenant shall have otherwise agreed before the Valuer shall have accepted appointment the Valuer shall act as an arbitrator and the provisions of the Arbitration Acts 1950 and 1979 shall apply.[9]

5 If the Valuer whether appointed as arbitrator or expert refuses to act or is incapable of acting or dies the Landlord or the Tenant may apply to the President for the further appointment of a Valuer to act in the same capacity

6 If by a Review Date the Principal Rent payable from that Review Date has not been ascertained the Tenant shall continue to pay the Principal Rent at the rate previously payable and [on the quarter day next] [within 7 days] after such ascertainment the Tenant shall pay to the Landlord the amount of the difference between the Principal Rent paid and the Principal Rent ascertained for the period of the Term commencing on such Review Date and ending on that quarter day [together with interest thereon calculated from day to day at the rate of the Base Lending Rate of —— Bank[10] Limited prevailing from time to time]

7 If at any time there is by virtue of any Act a restriction upon the Landlord's right to review the Principal Rent or upon the right of the Landlord to recover the Principal Rent otherwise payable then upon the ending removal or modification of such restriction the Landlord may at any time thereafter give to the Tenant notice requiring an additional rent review as at a quarter day specified therein which quarter day shall be not earlier than 3 months after the giving of the notice and shall for the purposes of this [Clause] [Schedule] be a Review Date

8 The Principal Rent shall be paid without deduction by four equal payments in advance on the usual quarter days and the first payment thereof of £—— shall be made on the —— in respect of the period ending on the ——

9 The amount of any increase Principal Rent ascertained in accordance with this Schedule shall within 28 days of such ascertainment be [endorsed on this Lease and the Counterpart thereof at the expense of the Tenant and the Landlord respectively] [entered in the Table below

Table of Principal Rent Review Date	Principal Rent payable from that Review Date
. . . .	. . . .]

10 Within 14 days of a written request therefore the Landlord or the Tenant as the case may be shall serve upon the other a copy of [the endorsement] [the Table] certified as correct by a solicitor

Published Notes

1 The Society states, in its Notes:
'this Form is best suited to a lease of commercial premises where the tenant has not paid a premium and where it is intended to reserve a rack rent—as opposed to a ground rent.'
Copies of the form with an Introduction and Notes can be purchased from ISVA at 3 Cadogan Gate, London, SW1.
     The following Notes are those issued by the Society (the headings being supplied).

2 Here as elsewhere in the Form, one alternative should be consistently deleted.

Notional Term

3 This valuation holds the balance fairly between the interests of landlord and tenant on the occasion of the last rent review. Where the reviews are at intervals other than five years, the figure '10' should be adjusted to the figure nearest to 10 which is divisible by the interval between reviews, eg 9 for three-year reviews, 14 for seven-year reviews.

Notional Use

4 This ensures that changes of use which are permitted by the landlord's licence are taken account of but unilateral attempts by the landlord to widen restrictive user clauses will still be ineffectual (so that the effect of such clauses will remain as is illustrated in *Plinth Property Investments Ltd* v *Mott, Hay & Anderson* (1978) 38 P & CR 361).

Assumption on Planning Permission

5 This assumption prevents premises which are actually being used by the tenant for a use, for which he has a personal planning consent, having to be valued as if that use were not an established use by reason of the 'disregard' of the effect on rent of the occupation of the actual tenant, so that only the other use is the established use.

Treatment of Improvements

6 'A fair allowance'. This method avoids the difficulties which arise in respect of the 'disregard' of the effect on rent of tenant's improvements, eg the problems of fitting out time or of works paid for partly by the landlord and partly by the tenant. Improvements can now be treated in a commonsense way.

7 Delete one or other alternative. The second alternative is only appropriate if the lease is a renewal to a former tenant or undertenant. Note that if the tenant is to carry out work to the demised premises before the execution of the lease (eg under an agreement for lease) then whether those works are to be the subject of the fair allowance requires to be specifically agreed, and provided for in the review clause. This can be done most easily either by providing that works done pursuant to the agreement for lease shall or shall not be included in the relevant works or that only specifically designated works carried out before the date of the lease shall be included.

Appointment of Valuer

8 Delete words in square brackets if it is desired that application for the appointment of a Valuer may only be made after the review date. Delete

only the square brackets if it is desired that the application can be made before the review date, and amend '3 months' to a longer period if so desired.

Arbitration Act

9   The 1950 Act does not apply to Scotland and Northern Ireland and the 1979 Act does not apply to Scotland; where appropriate drafting changes should be made.

Bank

10   Specify the agreed clearing Bank.

Additional Notes

See full commentaries on the Form by Finch at (1984) 272 EG 57; (1984) 81 LS Gaz 3020, by Freedman and Fogel at (1984) 272 EG 496 and 618 (and (1984) 81 LS Gaz 3169) and by Finch at (1984) 272 EG 1274 (and (1985) 82 LS Gaz 110), which, incidentally, suggests one possible minor amendment.

Principal Rent

There is at present a risk of circularity, because the reddendum refers to the Principal Rent as a sum ascertained by reference to something in the Schedule and the Schedule (paragraph 1.4) to that reserved by Clause 1. Doubtless this possible trap will be removed in any second edition, adverted to in the final article cited in the last note.

Clauses for Rent Review to Return on Freehold Value Promulgated by Incorporated Society of Valuers and Auctioneers[1]

(First published December 1984)

FORM B

The Reservation of Rent

YIELDING AND PAYING therefor FIRST the Principal Rent ascertained in accordance with [Clause] [Schedule] on the dates and in the manner there specified
...

The [Clause] [Schedule] specifying the ascertainment of the Principal Rent

1. In this [Clause] [Schedule]:[2]—
1.1 'Review Date' means the —— in the years —— and —— and includes any other date that becomes a Review Date pursuant to paragraph 7
1.2 'Rent Period' means:—
    (A)   each period of the Term beginning on a Review Date and ending on the day before the next Review Date
    (B)   the period of the Term commencing on the last Review Date and ending on the expiry of the Term
1.3 'Rental Value' means a sum equal of ——[3] per cent of the price which the Demised Premises might reasonably be expected to realise if sold in the open market by a willing vendor at the relevant Review Date freehold and with vacant possession assuming:—

(A)   that the Demised Premises have been fully fitted out and equipped for immediate occupation and use by the purchaser for the use permitted by this Lease and by any lience given by the Landlord at the request of the Tenant before the relevant Review Date[4]

(B)   that all the Tenant's covenants herein had been complied with

(C)   that even if compliance with the Tenant's covenants herein did not so require any destruction of or damage to the Demised Premises had been made good before the relevant Review Date[5]

(D)   that the benefit of any planning or other consent current at the relevant Review Date is available to the purchaser[6]

PROVIDING:—

(E)   that for the avoidance of doubt no value shall be attributed to the equipment and other property of the Tenant in the Demised Premises

1.4 'Principal Rent' means:—

(A)   until the first Review Date the rent reserved in Clause 1

(B)   during each Rent Period the yearly rent ascertained in accordance with the following provisions of this [Clause] [Schedule]

1.5 'President' means the President for the time being of the Incorporated Society of Valuers and Auctioneers (or any body for the time being performing the functions of the Incorporated Society as successor to it) or the person for the time being authorised to act on his behalf

1.6 'Valuer' means a valuer agreed between the Landlord and the Tenant or in default of such agreement appointed by the President

1.7 'Act' means act Act of Parliament now or hereafter to be passed and includes any statutory instrument made under any Act

2 From each Review Date the Principal Rent shall be such amount either as may at any time be agreed between the Landlord and the Tenant as the Principal Rent payable from that Review Date or (in default of such agreement) whichever is the greater of:—

(A)   the Rental Value or

(B)   The Principal Rent contractually payable immediately before that Review Date

3 If [by a date 3 months][7] before a Review Date the Principal Rent payable from that Review Date has not been agreed the Landlord and the Tenant may agree upon a Valuer to determine the Rental Value but in default of such agreement the Landlord or the Tenant may at any time apply to the President to appoint a Valuer to determine the Rental Value

4 Unless the Landlord and the Tenant shall have otherwise agreed before the Valuer shall have accepted appointment the Valuer shall act as an arbitrator and the provisions of the Arbitration Acts 1950 and 1979 shall apply[8]

5 If the Valuer whether appointed as arbitrator or expert refuses to act or is incapable of acting or dies the Landlord or the Tenant may apply to the President for the further appointment of a Valuer to act in the same capacity

6 If by a Review Date the Principal Rent payable from that Review Date has not been ascertained the Tenant shall continue to pay the Principal Rent at the rate previously payable and [on the quarter day next] [within 7 days] after such ascertainment the Tenant shall pay to the Landlord the amount of the difference between the Principal Rent paid and the Principal Rent ascertained for the period of the Term commencing on such Review Date and ending on that quarter day [together with interest thereon calculated from day to day at the rate of the Base Lending Rate of ——[9] Bank Limited prevailing from time to time]

7 If at any time there is by virtue of any Act a restriction upon the Landlord's
right to review the Principal Rent or upon the right of the Landlord to recover
the Principal Rent otherwise payable then upon the ending removal or
modification of such restriction the Landlord may at any time thereafter give
to the Tenant notice requiring an additional rent review as at a quarter day
specified therein which quarter day shall be not earlier than 3 months after
the giving of the notice and shall for the purposes of this [Clause] [Schedule]
be a Review Date

8 The Principal Rent shall be paid without deduction by four equal payments
in advance on the usual quarter days and the first payment thereof of £——
shall be made on the —— in respect of the period ending on the ——

9 The amount of any increased Principal Rent ascertained in accordance with
this Schedule shall within 28 days of such ascertainment be [endorsed on this
Lease and the Counterpart thereof at the expense of the Tenant and the Landlord
respectively] [entered in the Table below

Table of Principal Rent Review Date	Principal Rent payable from that Review Date
. . . .	. . . .]

10 Within 14 days of a written request therefor the Landlord or the Tenant
as the case may be shall serve upon the other a copy of [the endorsement]
[the Table] certified as correct by a solicitor

Published Notes

1   The Incorporated Society states in its Notes:
    'This Form is best suited to a lease of residential premises, but can be
    used in the case of commercial premises if a premium has been paid or
    if the lease is (or resembles) a building lease, so that a ground rent is to
    be paid.'
      Copies of the Form can be purchased from ISVA at 3 Cadogan Gate,
    London, SW1, with an introduction and Notes. The latter are produced
    below, with headings added.

2   Here, as elsewhere in the Form, one alternative should be consistently deleted.

Rent Review Formula

3   If the Principal rent is to be a reviewable ground rent, the percentage to
    be inserted must reflect both the reasonable return on the value of the
    premises and the proportion which is to be taken as the ground rent, eg
    if 15 per cent is agreed as the reasonable return and if the site value is
    30 per cent of the total cost of development (the balance of 70 per cent
    representing the development cost borne by the tenant) the percentage would
    be

$$15 \times \frac{30}{100} = 4.5\%.$$

Notional Use

4   This ensures that changes of use which are permitted by the landlord's licence are taken account of; but unilateral attempts by the landlord to widen restrictive user clauses will still be ineffectual (so that the effect of such clauses will remain as is illustrated in *Plinth Property Investments Ltd v Mott, Hay & Anderson* (1978) 38 P & CR 361).

Disregards

5   The disregards in Form A are not appropriate, but it may be desired (especially if the lease is a long lease) to include a provision whereby the tenant is given a fair allowance in respect of improvements carried out after the initial development or fitting out has been completed. Alternatively, that possibility can be reflected in the percentage used in Clause 1.4 to quantify the ground rent.

Planning Assumption

6   The assumption prevents premises which are actually being used by the tenant for a use for which he has a personal planning consent, having to be valued as if that use were not an established use by reason of the 'disregard' of the effect on rent of the occupation of the actual tenant, so that the other use is the established use.

Appointment of Valuer

7   Delete words in square brackets if it is desired that application for the appointment of a Valuer may only be made after the review date. Delete only the square brackets if it is desired that the application can be made before the review date, and amend '3 months' to a longer period if so desired.

Arbitration Acts

8   The 1950 Act does not apply to Scotland and Northern Ireland and the 1979 Act does not apply to Scotland, where appropriate drafting changes should be made.

Bank

9   Specify the agreed clearing bank.

Additional Notes

To the extent that the same clauses appear in the two forms, the commentaries mentioned in the Additional Notes to the preceding Form apply also to this Form.

3   EFP (5th ed) FORM 22

Authors' Note: Only the Rent Review Schedule to this Form, a Lease of a Lock-up Shop, is printed below.

Encyclopaedia of Forms and Precedents (5th ed) Volume 22, Form 22

(First published 1986)

SECOND SCHEDULE
Rent and rent review

1 *Definitions*

1.1   The terms defined in this paragraph shall for all purposes of this schedule
       have the meanings specified

1.2   'Review Period' means the period between any Review Date and the day
       prior to the next Review Date (inclusive) or between the lst Review Date
       and the expiry of the Term (inclusive)

1.3   'the Assumptions' means the following assumptions at the relevant Review
       Date:

    1.3:1   that no work has been carried out on the Premises by the Tenant
       [its] subtenants or their predecessors in title during the Term
       which has diminished the rental value of the Premises [other than
       work carried out in compliance with clause _____][1]

    1.3:2   that if the Premises have been destroyed or damaged they have
       been fully restored[2]

    1.3:3   that the covenants contained in this lease on the part of the
       [Landlord and the] Tenant have been fully performed and
       observed[3]

    1.3:4   that the Premises are available to let by a willing landlord to
       a willing tenant[4] by one lease without a premium being paid
       by either party and with vacant possession[5]

    1.3:5   that the Premises are ready for and fitting out and equipped
       for immediate occupation and use for the purpose or purposes
       required by the willing tenant referred to in paragraph 1.3:4 and
       that all the services required for such occupation and use are
       connected to the Premises[6]

    1.3:6   that the lease referred to in paragraph 1.3:4 contains the same
       terms as this lease except the amount of the Initial Rent and
       any rent free period allowed to the Tenant for fitting out the
       Premises for [its] occupation and use at the commencement of
       the Term but including the provisions for rent review on the
       Review Dates and at similar intervals after the last Review Date[7]
       and except as set out in paragraph 1.3:7

    1.3:7   that the term of the lease referred to in paragraph 1.3:4 is equal
       in length to [the Contractual Term *or* the Contractual Term
       remaining unexpired at the relevant Review Date *or* the
       Contractual Term remaining unexpired at the relevant Review
       Date or a period of [15] years whichever is the greater][8] and
       that such term begins on the relevant Review Date and that the
       rent shall commence to be payable from that date and that the
       years during which the tenant covenants to decorate the Premises
       are at similar intervals after the beginning of the term of such
       lease as those specified in this lease

    1.3:8   that the lease referred to in paragraph 1.3:4 will be renewed at
       the expiry of its term under the provisions of the 1954 Act][9]

1.4   'the Disregarded Matters' means:

    1.4:1   any effect on rent of the fact that the Tenant [its] subtenants or their respective predecessors in title have been in occupation of the Premises[10]

1.4:2   any goodwill[11] attached to the Premises by reason of the carrying on at the Premises of the business of the Tenant [its] subtenants or their predecessors in title in their respective businesses

1.4:3   any increase in rental value of the Premises attributable to the existence at the relevant Review Date of any improvement[12] to the Premises carried out with consent where required otherwise than in pursuance of an obligation [except an obligation contained in clause   ][1] to the Landlord or [its] predecessors in title either:

     1.4:3.1   by the Tenant [its] subtenants or their respective predecessors in title [or by any lawful occupiers] during the Term or during any period of occupation prior to the Term arising out of an agreement to grant or

1.4:3.2   by any tenant or subtenant of the Premises [or by any lawful occupiers] before the commencement of the Term so long as the Landlord or [its] predecessors in title have not since the improvement was carried out had vacant possession of the relevant part of the Premises

1.5   'the President' means the President for the time being of the Royal Institution of Chartered Surveyors the duly appointed deputy of the President or any person authorised by the President to make appointments on his behalf

1.6   'the Arbitrator'[13] means a person appointed by agreement between the parties or in the absence of agreement within [14] days[14] of one party giving notice to the other of [its] nomination or nominations nominated by the President on the application of either party made not earlier than [6] months before the relevant Review Date or at any time afterwards

2   Ascertaining the Rent

2.1   The Rent shall be:

     2.1:1   until the first Review Date the Initial Rent and

     2.1:2   during each successive review Period a rent equal to the greater[15] of:

     2.1:2.1   the Rent payable immediately prior to the relevant Review Date or if payment of Rent has been suspended pursuant to the proviso to that effect contained in this lease the Rent which would have been payable had there been no such suspension or

     2.1:2.2   such Rent as may be ascertained in accordance with this schedule

2.2   Such revised Rent for any Review Period may be agreed in writing at any time between the parties or (in the absence of agreement) will be determined [not earlier than the relevant Review Date] by the Arbitrator[16]

2.3   The revised Rent to be determined by the Arbitrator[13] shall be such as he shall decide to be the rent at which the Premises might reasonably be expected to be let on the open market at the relevant Review Date making the Assumptions but disregarding the Disregarded Matters

2.4   The arbitration[13] shall be conducted in accordance with the Arbitration Acts 1950 to 1979 except that if the Arbitrator nominated pursuant to paragraph 1.6 shall die or decline to act the President may on the application of either party discharge the Arbitrator and appoint another in his place

2.5	Whenever the Rent shall have been ascertained in accordance with this schedule memoranda to this effect shall be signed by or on behalf of the parties and annexed to this lease and its counterpart and the parties shall bear their own costs in this respect

### 3	Arrangements pending ascertainment of revised Rent

3.1	If the revised Rent payable during any Review Period has not been ascertained by the relevant Review Date Rent shall continue to be payable at the rate previously payable such payments being on account of the Rent for that Review Period

3.2	If one party shall upon publication of the Arbitrator's award pay all the Arbitrator's fees and expenses such party shall be entitled to recover [(in default of payment within [21] days of a demand to that effect in the case of the Landlord as Rent in arrears or in the case of the Tenant by deduction from Rent)] such proportion of them (if any) as the Arbitrator shall award against the other party

### 4	Payment of revised Rent

4.1	If the revised Rent shall be ascertained on or before the relevant Review Date and that date is not a quarter day the Tenant shall on that Review Date pay to the Landlord the amount by which one quarter's Rent at the rent payable on the immediately preceding quarter day is less than one quarter's Rent at the rate of the revised rent apportioned on a daily basis for that part of the quarter during which the revised Rent is payable

4.2	If the revised Rent payable during any Review Period has not been ascertained by the relevant Review Date then immediately after the date when the same has been agreed between the parties or the date upon which the Arbitrator's award shall be received by one party the Tenant shall pay to the Landlord:

	4.2:1	any shortfall between the Rent which would have been paid on the Review Date and on any subsequent quarter days had the revised rent been ascertained on or before the relevant Review Date and the payments made by the Tenant on account and

	4.2:2	interest at the base lending rate of the bank referred to in or nominated pursuant to clause 1.7 prevailing on the day upon which the shortfall is paid in respect of each instalment of Rent due on or after the Review Date on the amount by which the instalment of revised Rent which would have been paid on the relevant Review Date or such quarter day exceeds the amount paid on account and such interest shall be payable for the period from the date upon which the instalment was due up to the date of payment of the shortfall[17]

### 5	Arrangements when increasing Rent prevented etc

5.1	If at any of the Review Dates there shall be in force a statute which shall prevent restrict or modify the Landlord's right to review the Rent in accordance with this Lease and/or to recover any increase in the Rent the Landlord shall when such restriction or modification is removed relaxed or modified be entitled (but without prejudice to [its] rights (if any) to recover any Rent the payment of which has only been deferred by law) on giving not less than [one] month's nor more than [3] months' notice in writing to the Tenant [at any time within [6] months (time being of the essence of the contract) of the restriction or modification being removed relaxed or modified][18] to invoke the provisions of paragraph 5.2

5.2   Upon the service of a notice pursuant to paragraph 5.1 the Landlord shall be entitled:

5.2:1   to proceed with any review of the Rent which may have been prevented or further to review the Rent in respect of any review where the Landlord's right was restricted or modified and the date of expiry of such notice shall be deemed for the purposes of this lease to be a Review Date (provided that without prejudice to the operation of this paragraph nothing in this paragraph shall be construed as varying any subsequent Review Dates

5.2:2   to recover any increase in Rent with effect from the earliest date permitted by law

Authors' Notes

1   See p 421 (Page cross-references are to pages in the text of this book.) The exception in square brackets is a reference to Clause 5.7:1 of the full precedent which requires the tenant to comply with statutory requirements at the tenants' expense.

2   See p 422.

3   See p 413.

4   See p 393.

5   See p 406.

6   See p 418.

7   See p 329, 333.

8   See p 396.

9   See p 403. This makes express provision that the valuer is to assume the tenancy will be renewed and strengthens the general rule that a valuer is entitled to take account of the possibility of renewal: see *Secretary of State for the Environment* v *Pivot Properties Ltd* (1980) 256 EG 1176.

10   See p 454.

11   See p 452.

12   See p 427.

13   For amendment for determination by an expert see EFP (5th ed) Form 119, p 681, below.

14   The published footnote reads:
It seems desirable to provide a mechanism so that it can easily be determined if the parties have not agreed (and are not still considering the matter) and thus an application can be made.

15   Ie upwards only.

16   This closely follows the Model Forms. The published footnote reads:
A criticism has been made that there is nothing specified in order to get the process of rent review started ie service of notice. This was clearly prompted by the wish not to have time of the essence (or even arguably of the essence) but if the parties feel that it is helpful, there is no objection to inserting a provision to serve as a reminder to start the process eg '6 months before each Review Date (time not being of the essence of the contract) the Landlord and the Tenant shall explore the possibility of [open negotiations with a view to] reaching agreement in writing between them as to the revised rent

for the following Review Period and such revised rent may be
agreed . . .'

17   The published footnote reads:
        The tenant's solicitor needs to ensure that the provision for interest
        on shortfall is not drafted in such a way that interest would be payable
        on the total shortfall from the review date up to the date of payment.
        This is clearly unfair where several rent days have elapsed since the
        review date before the revised rent is determined. The interest should
        be on the shortfall on each instalment from the date that instalment
        was due up to the date the shortfall is paid; and see p 81.

18   The published footnote reads:
        The words in square brackets should be proposed by the tenant
        otherwise the landlord could have this right throughout the residue
        of the term and could wait for a convenient moment, perhaps years
        later, before exercising it. The tenant could perhaps go further and
        provide that the right may not be exercised within one year of the
        next Review Date.

4   EFP (5th ed) FORM 119

**Authors' Note: This Form is designed to be incorporated in and vary Form 22
above**

**Encyclopaedia of Forms and Precedents (5th ed)
Volume 22, Form 119**

(First published 1986)

DETERMINATION BY AN EXPERT[1]

SECOND SCHEDULE

1.6   (*continue as in Form 22 second schedule paragraph 1.6 substituting 'Expert'
       for 'Arbitrator' and 'an independent valuer'[2] for 'a person'*)
2.2   (*continue as in Form 22 second schedule paragraph 2.2 substituting 'Expert'
       for 'Arbitrator'*)
2.3   (*continue as in Form 22 second schedule paragraph 2.3 substituting 'Expert'
       for 'Arbitrator' and inserting '(acting as an expert and not as an arbitrator
       or quasi-arbitrator[3])' after 'decide'*)
        2.4:1   The fees and expenses of the Expert including the cost of his
                 appointment shall be borne equally by the parties who shall
                 otherwise each bear their own costs[4]
        2.4:2   The Expert will afford each of the parties an opportunity to make
                 written representations to him[5] [and also an opportunity to make
                 written counter-representations[5] on any representations made to
                 him by the other party[6]] but will not be in any way limited or
                 fettered by such representations [and counter-representations] and
                 will be entitled to rely on his own judgment and opinion

2.4:3   If the Expert dies or refuses to act or becomes incapable of acting [or if he fails to publish his determination within [4] months of the date upon which he accepted the appointment] either party may apply to the President to discharge the Expert and appoint another in his place[7]

3.2   *(continue as in Form 22 second schedule paragraph 3.2 substituting 'Expert's determination' for 'Arbitrator's award', 'Expert's' for 'Arbitrator's' and deleting all words from and including 'such proportion ...' and substituting 'half of them from the other party')*

4.2   *(continue as in Form 22 second schedule paragraph 4.2 substituting 'Expert's determination' for 'Arbitrator's award')*

Published Footnotes (authors' amendments and additions in square brackets)

1   This Form is designed to be incorporated in Form 22 second schedule, and the paragraphs set out in this Form should be substituted and/or added where appropriate. Those paragraphs to which no references are made in this Form should be set out in full as they appear in Form 22
[As to the distinction between arbitration and expert determination generally see p 188.]

2   In the interests of certainty the parties may prefer to stipulate that the expert is to be either an Associate or Fellow of the Royal Institution of Chartered Surveyors or the Incorporated Society of Valuers and Auctioneers.

3   As to the liability of an expert in negligence to the parties and the nature of quasi-arbitration see [p 216 and] *Palacath Ltd* v *Flanagan* [1985] 2 All ER 161.

4   An expert has no inherent jurisdiction towards costs unless he is specifically given it. If the expert is to be given this quasi-judicial function, it may give weight to the argument that he is in fact a quasi-arbitrator [but see the authors' views in the text at p 218]. See *Palacath Ltd* v *Flanagan* [1985] 2 All ER 161. Paragraph 2.4 as it appears in Form 22 should be deleted.

5   Without these provisions the parties will have no right to make representations to the expert or comment upon the representations made by the other party, unless the expert so asks them. Including such a provision does tend to make an expert determination resemble a simple arbitration carried out by written representations without a hearing but avoids placing the parties in the frustrating position of not being able to make any case at all and so potentially depriving the expert of some evidence or information of which he would otherwise be unaware.

6   As to the question of whether or not the expert should be given more powers [see p 177, 186].

7   In the strictest sense the expert is not appointed by the President. He is appointed by the parties on the nomination of the President. The wording is, however, commonly used and understood.

5   EFP (5th ed) FORM 127

Authors' Note: This Form is designed to be incorporated in and amend Form 22, above. It is a modern version of the once prevalent 'notice and counternotice' form of rent review (see p 703 and the older precedents in Section Three, below).

Encyclopaedia of Forms and Precedents (5th ed)
Volume 22, Form 127

(First published 1986)

PROVISIONS for rent review notices and counter-notices[1]

1.6 'the Arbitrator' means a person appointed by agreement between the parties within the period of [21] days [(or such longer period as the parties may agree in writing)][2] after the date of service[3] of the Tenant's counter-notice referred to in paragraph 2.2:3 below or in default of agreement within such period [(or longer period)[2]] by the President on the application of either party

2.2 Such revised rent for any Review Period shall be either:

2.2:1   specified in a notice[4] in writing given by the Landlord to the Tenant at any time[5] [not earlier than [6] months before the Review Date to which it relates] ('the Review Notice') or

2.2:2   agreed[6] between the parties in writing within [3] months after the date of service of the Review Notice in substitution for the sum specified in the Review Notice or

2.2:3   determined at the election of the Tenant[7] by the Arbitrator[8] (such election to be made in and by a written counter-notice[9] served on the Landlord within [3] months after the date of service of the Review Notice

and time shall be of the essence in relation to all stipulations as to time in this paragraph[10]

Published Notes (authors' amendments and additions in square brackets)

1   This Form provides what has become commonly known as a 'trigger notice' clause: [see p 124]. This Form is designed to be incorporated in Form 22 second schedule and the paragraphs set out in this Form should be substituted and/or added where appropriate. Those paragraphs to which no reference is made in this Form should be set out as they appear in Form 22.

2   Either both or neither of these amendments in square brackets must be used.

3   As to date of service [see p 131] but attention should be paid to any notice provisions in the lease in question.

4   For a form of such a notice see Form 128 [not reproduced].

5   Thus time is not of the essence so far as service of the Review Notice is concerned: [see pp 92 and 169].

6   [See p 59 and Ch 8].

7   The fact that the landlord cannot so elect does not prevent such a rent review schedule constituting a valid agreement to submit a future dispute (as to revised rent) to arbitration: *Pittalis* v *Sherefettin* [1986] QB 868, CA.

8   If the review is determined by an expert, amendments will be required similar to those set out in Form 119, above.

9   For a form of such a notice see Form 129 [not reproduced].

10   [See p 95].

6   CONVEYANCER PRECEDENT 5–57

RENT REVIEW CLAUSE PROVIDING FOR THE VARIATION OF RENT BY REFERENCE TO MARKET RENTAL VALUES: OPTION FOR REFERENCE TO ARBITRATOR OR VALUER

Precedents for the Conveyancer, Form 5–57

(First published August 1977 incorporating all subsequent amendments, most recently October 1990)[1]

(a) In this clause
'review date' means [(subject to the provisions of sub-clause (k))] every fifth anniversary of the commencement date of the said term namely the — day of —— 19—, 19— and 19— [or as the case may be][2]
'review period' means the period between one review date and the ensuring review date or the end of the said term (as the case may be)
'current rental value' means such rent as would be obtainable on the relevant review date for the demised premises[3] let as a whole[4] without premium upon the open market between a willing landlord and a willing tenant[5] on the assumptions of a letting with vacant possession[6] for a term equal to the original length of the said term running from the relevant review date[7] on the basis that all covenants and conditions of this Lease have been fully complied with[8] and upon all the covenants and conditions of this Lease (other than that as to the original rent but including this present clause) but disregarding:—[EITHER]
(i) Any effect on rent of the fact that the Lessee (or any person lawfully deriving title under the Lessee) has been in occupation of the demised premises[9] or of any goodwill attaching to the demised premises by reason of the Lessee (or any person lawfully deriving title under the Lessee) having carried on business on the demised premises[10] and
(ii) Any effect on rent of any improvement to the demised premises carried out by the Lessee (or any person lawfully deriving title under the Lessee)[11] during the said term or under the agreement preceding it otherwise than in pursuance of an obligation except an obligation to observe statutory obligations arising under this Lease[12] or under the agreement preceding it[13] [or to the cost of which the Lessee shall (or but for having done the work would otherwise) have been required to contribute by reason of Clause—[the service charge provision]]
[OR]
[where disregards are also to reflect earlier leases]
(i) any effect on rent . . . [as above] . . . or of any goodwill attaching to the demised premises by reason of the Lessee or its predecessors in title to the business carried on by the Lessee at the review date having carried on business on the demised premises [during a period not exceeding [21] years before the relevant review date] and
(ii) any effect on rent of any improvement to the demised premises carried out by the Lessee or any person deriving title under the Lessee or their respective predecessors in title and completed within the period of [21] years before the relevant review date and not carried out in pursuance of an obligation (except an obligation to observe statutory obligations) arising under this Lease or any agreement or Lease preceding it or to the cost of which the Lessee or its

predecessors in title shall (or but for having done the work would otherwise) have been required to contribute by reason of Clause ____ [*the service charge provision*] or the equivalent provision in any earlier Lease.

(b) The rent payable in respect of any review period shall be ascertained in the following manner:—

(1) [14]the Lessor by notice in writing served upon the Lessee at any time not earlier than 6 months before a review date may specify a substituted rent in respect of the ensuing review period and in the event of absence of agreement on a different sum under (ii) below or determination of a different sum under (iii) below such sum so specified shall be the substituted rent payable throughout the ensuing review period.

(ii) [15]the parties may agree in writing not later than 3 months (time to be of the essence[17]) after service of the notice under (i) upon the substituted rent payable throughout the relevant review period.

(iii) [16]the Lessee not later than 3 months (time to be of the essence)[17] after the service of the notice under (i) by counter-notice in writing served upon the Lessor may require the substituted rent to be determined under the following sub-clauses (c) to (g) (inclusive) and the sum so determined shall be the substituted rent payable throughout the relevant review period.

(iv) [18]if there shall not have been any service of a notice under (i) by any review date the Lessee may serve upon the Lessor a notice in writing specifying a sum to be the substituted rent in respect of the then current review period and thereupon the provisions of (ii) and (iii) above shall apply (save that any counter-notice under (iii) requiring determination of the substituted rent shall be given by the Lessor) as if the Lessee's notice had in fact been a Lessor's notice under (i) and in the absence of agreement on a different sum under (ii) above or determination of a different sum under (iii) above such sum specified in the Lessee's notice shall be the substituted rent payable throughout the current review period.

(c) The determination of a substituted rent consequent upon the service of a counter-notice under (iii) of the foregoing sub-clause shall be effected by a referee agreed on by the parties or if not agreed on by them within one month from the nomination in writing or a referee by one party to the other appointed on the application of either party by the President for the time being of the Royal Institution of Chartered Surveyors (or of some other officer of that body if the President be unable to act).

(d) [19]The referee agreed upon or appointed under sub-clause (c) shall act as an arbitrator pursuant to the Arbitration Act for the time being in force (save as modified by the provisions of this Clause) if the Lessor shall so stipulate by notice in writing served upon the Lessee within one month (time to be of the essence) of service of the counter-notice under (iii) or (iv) of sub-clause (b) but shall otherwise act as an expert and not as an arbitrator

(e) If any such referee as aforesaid acts as an expert he shall afford each party the opportunity to make such written and (at the option of either party) oral representations to him as they wish subject to such reasonable time and other limits as he may prescribe and he shall have regard to any such representations but not be bound thereby

(f) (i) The referee shall notify in writing to the parties such sum as he shall determine to be the current rental value of the demised premises at the review date and such sums shall be the substituted rent payable throughout the relevant review period.

(ii) The award of the referee shall also provide for the manner in which the

costs of the determination shall be borne and may also provide for the payment
of costs by one party to the other and in settling upon such matters the referee
may have regard to the contents of any notice served any offers made by either
party to the other (whether 'without prejudice' or not) and the nature and content
of any representation made to him by or on behalf of the parties.

(g) Under no circumstances shall the substituted rent for any review period
be less than the rent payable for the period prior to the commencement of
such period[20].

(h) During any period that any substituted rent payable under the preceding
sub-clause of this Clause has not been ascertained the Lessee shall continue
to pay rent of the amount previously payable but within 14 days of such
ascertainment the Lessee shall pay to the Lessor any difference between the
amounts actually paid and the amounts payable as a result of such ascertainment
(such sum not to bear interest unless the referee in his award under sub-clause
(f) shall provide for the payment of interest for such period and at such rate
as he may specify because of delay by the Lessee in or about the determination
of the substituted rent)[21]

(j) During any period that any substituted rent ascertained under this Clause
shall not be recoverable in whole or party by virtue of any statute regulation
instrument or order the Lessee shall pay rent at the highest level from time
to time recoverable under the restrictions and shall pay the full amount of the
substituted rent as soon as the restrictions shall cease to be effective[22].

(k) If at or following any review date any statute regulation instrument or
order shall prevent the exercise of the process of ascertainment of a substituted
rent provided for in this Clause neither party shall be able to serve any notice
specified in (i) or (iv) of sub-clause (b) until such prohibition be repealed or
so released or modified as to permit such step to be taken[23] [and the review
date shall be such date not earlier than [one month] nor later than [three months]
after service of the notice as shall be specified therein.[24]

(l) After the ascertainment of any substituted rent under this Clause a
memorandum recording the amount of the same signed by or on behalf of the
parties shall forthwith be attached to this Lease and the Counterpart thereof.

Authors' Notes

1   The precedent incorporates minor amendments made subsequently to its
    publication, the latest in August 1987. Readers using this precedent may
    also wish to refer to the notes and discussion appended to the form in
    Precedents for the Conveyancer pp 2914ff.
2   Specifying the anniversary dates avoids the problem of the meaning of 'the
    commencement date'—see p 143.
3   See p 318.
4   For the significance of including the words 'as a whole' see p 411.
5   For the significance of the parties being willing see p 343.
6   See p 406.
7   See p 396. In the light of recent decisions, the words 'running from the
    relevant review date' ensure that the notional lease is for a term of years
    equal to the original terms.
8   See p 413.
9   See discussion at p 454.
10 See discussion at p 452.
11 See pp 427 and 436. This disregard covers persons deriving title under the
    Lessee thus avoiding the 'trap' that the Lessee might have to pay a rent

partly reflecting a subtenant's improvements which would have to be disregarded in settling the new rent under the sublease.

12   See discussion on pp 437–441.

13   The reference to obligations arising under the agreement for the Lease, avoids the problems illustrated by the decision in *Euston Centre Properties Ltd* v *H & J Wilson Ltd* (1981) – see p 443.

14   See p 124.

15   See p 59.

16   See p128.

17   See p 95.

18   The wording of clause b (iv) may be compared to that of the 1985 Model Forms Variation C, clause 4(f)—see p 666.

19   The wording of clause (d) may be compared to that of the Variation A of clause 3 of the 1985 Model Forms (p 657).

20   The inclusion of this clause prevents a downwards review (p 50).

21   See p 81.

22   See generally Chapter 19.

23   This subclause is discussed in Chapter 19, p 554.

24   The optional phrase in square brackets (with a consequential amendment to the definition of 'review date' in subclause (a)) means that the review date is not a past review date but a date after service of the review notice.

7   KELLY'S DRAFTSMAN FORMS 14 AND 15

Kelly's Draftsman (15th ed)—Lease and Tenancy Agreements—Form 14, p 367-9

(Published 1986)

14.   *Rent-variation if rent subject to review or linked to Retail Prices Index*[1] Paying (in advance by equal monthly instalments on the [first] day of every month [*or* equal quarterly instalments on each 31 March, 30 June, 30 September and 31 December [*or* the usual quarter days]] in advance the first payment (calculated on a daily basis) to be made on the date of this deed for the period from the commencement of the term to the first due date of payment) the yearly rent of £—— [during the first year of the term and of £—— during the second year thereof and £—— during etc].

or (a) where the rent is subject to periodic review
the yearly rent ascertained in accordance with the provisions contained in the [second] schedule to this lease

or (b) where index linked
the yearly rent during the first period of one year from the commencement of the term of £—— and during each succeeding period of one year the greater of the sum of £—— and that sum multiplied by the Index of Retail Prices maintained by the Department of Employment on the [January] immediately preceding the end of each such period of one year and divided by the amount of the said index on the 1 [January] 19——[2] namely ——[3]

or (c) where index linked, another version
the yearly rent during the first period of one year from the commencement of the term of £—— and during such succeeding period of one year the sum increased by the sum of £—— for each point by which the Index of Retail Prices maintained by the Department of Employment has on the 1 [January] immediately preceding the end of each such period of one year increased over the amount of the said index on the 1 [January] 19——[2] namely ——[3]

15. *Schedule to lease using form 14 (a) for period review of rent*

THE [SECOND] SCHEDULE

Provisions for ascertaining the yearly rent payable under this lease.

1. During the period from the commencement of the term to [Ladyday] 19[90] the year rent shall be £——

2. During each of the respective periods of [five] years from [Ladyday] 19[90] and 19[95], 20[00] and 20[05] [*or as the case may be*] ('the Review Dates' or in the case of any of them 'the Review Date') the yearly rent shall be the greater of the yearly rent payable immediately before each respective Review Date and either

(a)   such sum as not less than [three] months prior to each respective Review Date is agreed in writing[4] between the parties or if agreement is not reached not less than [two] months prior to the Review Date

(b)   such sum as is certified in writing by a valuer (to be appointed by the parties or if they do not agree upon a valuer not less than [one] month prior to the Review Date to be appointed by the [President for the time being of the Royal Institution of Chartered Surveyors] on the application of the first of the parties hereto to apply to him) as the fair market rent[5] of the Demised Premises [*disregarding the value of any improvements or additions thereto effected by the Tenant with the licence of the Landlord*][6] with vacant possession[7] between a willing lessor and a willing lessee[8] at each respective Review Date[9] but disregarding any effect on it of the considerations specified in paragraphs (a) (b) and (c) of section 34 (1) of the Landlord and Tenant Act 1954 as amended by the Law of Property Act 1969[10]

3. If the amount of the yearly rent in respect of any period is not so agreed or certified until after the commencement of that period the Tenant shall pay to the Landlord on the next day on which a payment of rent falls due after the amount of it has been agreed or certified such sum if any as is equal to the excess of the rent so agreed or certified over that which has been paid for so much of the period as has then elapsed.

4. The valuer appointed under paragraph 2:2 of this schedule shall act as [an expert and not as] an arbitrator [and the Arbitration Acts 1950 and 1979 shall apply].

5. The costs of any valuer appointed under this schedule shall be borne by the parties in equal shares.

6. Time shall [not] be of the essence in respect of the provisions of this schedule[11]

Authors' Notes

1   The published footnote at this point reads:
'This clause cannot be used in the case of lettings within the Rent Act 1977 if its operation would increase the rent above the limits imposed by

the Rent Act. Two figures are published by the Government. The Retail
Prices Index published monthly by the Department of Employment and
Productivity and which is generally noted in the press, and the Consumers'
Price Index published by the Central Statistical Office which takes into
account many other matters besides retail prices'
On which generally see Chapters 17 and 20.

2   The published footnote at this point reads:
'The base month selected should be not less than two months before the
start of the term, to allow for delay in the publication of the index when
the time comes to increase the rent'
On which see p 570.

3   The published footnote at this point reads:
'Whilst it is not essential to do so, doubt will be avoided if the base figure
of the index is inserted'.

4   See pp 570–572.

5   It may be preferable to refer to the 'open market rent' at this point; a
'fair market rent' may have a different meaning not dissimilar to that of
'fair rent' or 'reasonable rent'—see p 386 and *Ponsford* v *HMS Aerosols
Ltd* [1979] AC 63. The published footnote to the form assumes the *Ponsford*
case applies to a 'fair market rent' but this may not be true.

6   The words italicised in square brackets appeared in this Form in the 14th
ed (1979) but not in the 15th ed. See generally p 437.

7   See p 406.

8   See p 392.

9   This form may be defective in that it does not clearly state the notional
period of letting for which the rent is to be calculated at review. An express
indication of the desired period is recommended at this point, but in the
absence of any addition, the notional term is likely to be a period equivalent
to the residue of the term at the relevant review date.

10   See p 441; and the device of incorporation by reference is better avoided
(p 446).

11   The published footnote at this point reads:
'In the absence of certain indications, the presumption is that, in the
completion of the various stages for determining the rent, time is not of
the essence. Hence this paragraph is not strictly necessary, but if time is
to be of the essence the word "not" may be omitted'.
See generally Chapter 5; and if the word is not omitted, time will be of
the essence for all stages of the review process.

Section Two

Special Forms of Rent Review

Introduction: This section collects together some special forms of rent review and specialist clauses drafted to cover the impact of VAT.

1 EFP (5th ed) FORM 120
RENT REVIEW ON BASIS OF A VACANT SITE (GROUND RENT REVIEW)

Encyclopaedia of Forms and Precedents (5th ed) Volume 22, Form 120

(First published 1986)

REVISED RENT to be that for a vacant site without buildings which have been or are to be erected on it[1]

SECOND SCHEDULE

1.1–1.2 (*continue as in Form 22 second schedule paragraphs 1.1 to 1.2 above*)

1.3 'the Assumptions' means the following assumptions at the relevant Review Date:

    1.3:1   that the Premises consist of a vacant site upon which no buildings or works of any kind have been erected or carried out [in the condition shown by the schedule of condition annexed to this lease[2]]

    1.3:2   that the Premises have the benefit of the Planning Permission[3] and that the Planning Permission bears the same date as the relevant Review Date and not the actual date shown on it[4]

    1.3:3   (*continue as in Form 22 second schedule paragraph 1.3:4 above*)[5]

    1.3:4   (*continue as in Form 22 second schedule paragraph 1.3:6 above substituting paragraph '1.3:3' for paragraph '1.3:4' and paragraph '1.3:5' for paragraph '1.3:7'*)

    1.3:5   (*continue as in Form 22 second schedule paragraph 1.3:7 above substituting paragraph '1.3:3' for paragraph '1.3:4'*)[6]

    1.3:6   (*continue as in Form 22 second schedule paragraph 1.3:8 above substituting paragraph '1.3:3' for paragraph '1.3:4'*)

1.4:1–1.4:2 (*continue as in Form 22 second schedule paragraphs 1.4:1 to 1.4:2
            above*)

1.4:3   the effect of any statutes enacted after today's date which would
            have the effect of preventing or delaying the erection of [the
            Building] in accordance with the Planning Permission despite the
            actual and/or assumed existence of the Planning Permission[7]

1.4:4   any possibility that the Premises may be either used for a purpose
            or developed in a way otherwise than in accordance with the
            Planning Permission[8]

1.5–1.6 (*continue as in Form 22 second schedule paragraphs 1.4:1 to 1.4:2 above*)

1.7 'the Planning Permission'[9] means the planning permission of which a copy
     is (together with copies of the application for and the plans and
     documentation which accompanied such application) annexed to this lease[10]

2.1–5.2:2 (*continue as in Form 22 second schedule paragraphs 2.1 to 5.2:2 above*)

Published Footnotes

1   This Form is designed to be incorporated in Form 22 second schedule,
     and the paragraphs set out in this Form should be substituted and/or added
     as appropriate.
        This form of review provision is likely to suit the circumstances where
     the tenant has been granted a building lease and is obliged at its own expense
     to construct a building. The landlord is to receive a reviewable 'ground
     rent'. Use of this form may assist in avoiding valuation arguments over
     the correct method of disregarding the tenant's expenditure on the
     improvement which the building will constitute. See *GREA Real Property
     Investments Ltd* v *Williams* (1979) 250 EG 651 and [see p 255].

2   There may be a considerable difference between the ground rent for a cleared
     and level site and an uncleared site. Rather than refer to the state of the
     site before the lease was granted it seems preferable to provide a schedule
     of condition (if possible with photographs) so as to remind the parties and
     their successors in title and any arbitrator or expert what the state of the
     site was before the tenant erected any buildings. Additionally, the landlord
     may have provided infrastructure works and describing these may well be
     simpler in a schedule of condition.

3   If the landlord is letting the site with the benefit of a planning permission
     obtained before the agreement for lease or lease was entered into it ought
     presumably to have the rental benefit ensuing from it.

4   The planning permission will inevitably contain a time limit condition under
     the Town and Country Planning Act 1971 s 41 (46 Halsbury's Statutes (4th
     Edn) TOWN AND COUNTRY PLANNING). This provision avoids the
     argument by the tenant that the actual planning permission will have expired
     (as the result of the condition imposed under ibid s 41), since hypothetically
     no building will have been built within the time limit in the actual permission.

5   Consideration should be given to the hypothetical terms of the lease since
     it may be appropriate to vary the terms of the hypothetical lease.

6   It seems likely that the question of whether or not the tenant has complied
     with its covenants under the lease will be irrelevant to valuation of a vacant
     site. There may, however, be circumstances where some of the tenant's
     obligations are relevant.

7   It would be inequitable for the tenant to be able to argue at review that
     hypothetically no building could be built as a result of the hypothetical
     planning permission because of intervening legislation eg a restoration of

the legislation which provided for Office Development Permits and Industrial Development Certificates. The tenant has not suffered under such legislation since the building has in fact been erected.

8   This disregard is included in order to prevent the landlord arguing, when the review takes place, that the hypothetically vacant site has development potential for a use other than that contemplated in the Planning Permission which produces a higher ground rental than is produced as a result of the actual Planning Permission, as was the case in *Rushmoor Borough Council v Goacher* [1985] EGLR 140. Clearly the user and alteration clause in the hypothetical lease will also be relevant in relation to such an argument.

9   Identifying the planning permission is crucial.

10 Most planning permissions are phrased so as to permit the development for which the applicant applied in accordance with the plans and specifications which accompanied the application. These documents are therefore as important as the actual permission in identifying what was permitted. It would presumably also be prudent to add, if necessary, any other permissions which were required in the same way eg consents from those entitled to the benefit of restrictive covenants.

2   EFP (5th ed) FORM 130
RENT REVIEW WITH 'FLIP FLOP' VALUATION

Encyclopaedia of Forms and Precedents (5th ed), Volume 22, Form 130

DETERMINATION OF REVISED RENT to be by an expert with restricted discretion[1]

(First published 1986)

1.6 'the Expert' means a Fellow or Associate of the Royal Institution of Chartered Surveyors[2] appointed by agreement between the parties or in the absence of agreement within [14] days of one party giving notice to the other of [its] nomination or nominations nominated by the President on the application of either party made not earlier than [6] months before the relevant Review Date or at any time after that date

1.7 'Review Commencement Date' means in relation to any Review Period the day occurring [3] months before the Review Date upon which such Review Period begins

2.2 Such revised rent for any Review Period may be agreed in writing at any time between the parties or (in the absence of agreement[3] by the relevant Review Commencement Date) will be determined in accordance with paragraph 2.3 below

2.3:1   The Landlord and the Tenant shall each prepare a written submission stating the rent at which in that party's opinion the Premises might reasonably be expected to be let in the open market at the relevant Review Date making the Assumptions but disregarding the Disregarded Matters ('Rental Opinion') (accompanied if desired by reasons and supporting evidence)[4] and shall deliver the same to the Expert (and a complete copy to the other party) no later than either

[6] weeks after the Review Commencement Date or (if the Expert has not notified the parties in writing that he has accepted appointment within [2] weeks after the Review Commencement Date) [4] weeks after the Expert has so notified the parties[5]

2.3:2　Time shall be of the essence[6] in respect of the time limits for delivery of the submissions to the Expert and accordingly:

　　2.3:2.1　if one party fails to deliver a submission to the Expert within those time limits the revised rent for the relevant Review Period shall be the rent specified in the submission which has been delivered by the other party or

　　2.3:2.2　if both parties fail to deliver submissions to the Expert within those time limits the revised rent for the relevant Review Period shall be the Rent payable during the preceding Review Period

and in either case the Expert shall so notify the parties in writing

2.3:3　If both parties shall have delivered submissions to the Expert within those time limits the Expert will:

　　2.3:3.1　immediately so notify both parties in writing and

　　2.3:3.2　as soon as is reasonably possible subsequently notify the parties in writing which of the submissions he shall in his opinion determine contains the correct or more correct statement of the rent at which the Premises might reasonably be expected to be let in the open market at the relevant Review Date making the Assumptions but disregarding the Disregarded Matters and the Expert shall not be entitled to determine that both submissions are equally correct[7]

and the revised rent for the relevant Review Period shall be the rent specified in that submission of Rental Opinion and the Expert's written notice shall so state and shall be conclusive and binding on the parties

2.4:1　The fees and expenses of the Expert including the cost (if any) of his appointment shall be borne equally by the parties who shall otherwise bear their own costs

2.4:2　The Expert may consider the reasons and supporting evidence (if any) contained in the submissions but (subject to paragraph 2.3:2 above) shall not be in any way limited or fettered by such reasons and supporting evidence and in determining which submission in his opinion contains the correct or more correct opinion of revised rent shall be entitled to rely on his own judgment and opinion and shall make his determination as an expert and not as an arbitrator or quasi-arbitrator[8]

2.4:3　If the Expert dies or refuses to act or becomes incapable of acting [or if he fails to notify the parties of his determination within [2] months after the receiving the last submission delivered to him] either party may apply to the President to discharge the Expert and appoint another in his place[9]

3.2　(*continue as in Form 22 second schedule paragraph 3.2 above substituting 'Expert's determination' for 'Arbitrator's award', 'Expert's' for 'Arbitrator's' and deleting all words from and including 'such proportion' and inserting 'half of them from the other party'*)

4.2　(*continue as in Form 22 second schedule paragraph 4.2 above substituting 'Expert's determination' for 'Arbitrator's award'*)

Published Notes (Authors amendments and additions in square brackets)

1   This Form is designed to be incorporated in Form 22 second schedule and the paragraphs set out in this Form should be substituted and/or added where appropriate. Those paragraphs to which no reference is made in this Form should be set out in full as they appear in Form 22.

Rent review provisions of this kind have been called 'flip flop' review provisions: see eg *Henry Smith's Charity Trustees* v *AWADA Trading and Promotion Services Ltd* (1983) 269 EG 729, CA). Effectively, under these provisions, the expert can only decide which of the parties' valuations is correct or at least more correct. The provisions do not give the expert power to decide that neither is correct or more correct. The intention behind such a provision is to encourage the parties to be reasonable with a view to settling the review by agreement without reference to an expert. These provisions give the parties an incentive to do so because it is likely that the expert's own opinion of rental value will fall between those expressed by the landlord and the tenant. Accordingly, it is probable that the landlord will tend to revise his valuation downwards and the tenant tends to review his upwards into the hope of brining their respective valuations into a position where they are, as a result, more likely to be found correct, or at least more correct by the expert. Because of their relative lack of sophistication, these provisions are unlikely to be suitable for inclusion in leases of unusual or large premises or premises which may for any reason be difficult to value. They are, however, suitable for inclusion in leases of small premises in circumstances where there is always likely to be a large supply of suitable comparable rental evidence. [See also p 68]

2   The words 'or of the Incorporated Society of Valuers and Auctioneers' might be added.

3   [See p 59].

4   There is no reason why such supporting evidence should not include a valuation carried out by a qualified valuer. References to valuation have been excluded, since the 'flip flop' review is suitable for use where the demised premises are relatively small and consequently either party may feel that the expense of valuation fees is unjustified.

5   Alternatively, the lease may provide that the expert will, as soon as he has accepted appointment, specify a reasonable period (perhaps with a minimum) within which the parties must submit their valuations to him. For a suitable form of words see Form 131 para 2.5:1 [below].

6   The object of having a 'flip flop' review clause is to provide for an expeditious review and therefore the parties should be made aware of the fact that, once the Review Commencement Date has passed, events may occur swiftly and that failure to provide a valuation in time may be extremely disadvantageous. [See p 68]

7   At first sight this may appear Draconian but the whole intention of the paragraph (see note 1 above) is defeated if the Expert is entitled to adopt a mid-way position.

8   See *Palacath Ltd* v *Flanagan* [1985] 2 All ER 161.

9   See Form 119 note 9 above.

3   EFP (5th ed) FORM 131
RENT REVIEW WITH A 'BASEBALL' BASIS OF VALUATION

Encyclopaedia of Forms and Precedents (5th ed) Volume 22, Form 131

(First published 1986)

REVISED RENT to be determined by averaging the two closest of three valuations;

SECOND SCHEDULE

1.6 'Valuer' means an Associate or Fellow of either the Royal Institution of
Chartered Surveyors and/or the Incorporated Society of Valuers and
Auctioneers and no person shall be appointed as a Valuer by either the
Landlord or the Tenant or as Third Valuer who is not either an Associate
or Fellow of either the above Institution or the above Society [having at
least [10] years' experience prior to appointment in valuation of [offices
or shops *or* industrial premises *or as appropriate*] in [the United Kingdom
or the County of ...]][2]

1.7 'Review Commencement Date' means in relation to any Review Period the
day occurring [3] months before the Review Date upon which such Review
Period begins

2.2 (*continue as in Form 22 second schedule paragraph 2.2 above substituting
'by valuation in accordance with the provisions of this schedule' for '[not earlier
than the relevant Review Date] by the Arbitrator'*)

  2.3:1   At any time on or after the Review Commencement Date either
the Landlord or the Tenant may elect by written notice ('the Notice
of Election') given to the other to have the revised rent for the
relevant Review Period determined by valuation in accordance with
the provisions of this schedule and the Notice of Election shall specify
the name and address of the Valuer appointed by the party giving
the Notice of Election ('the First Valuer')

  2.3:2   Within [21] days after the service of the Notice of Election the other
party shall serve a written notice ('Counter-notice') on the party
who served the Notice of Election specifying the name and address
of the Valuer appointed by the party serving the Counter-notice
('the Second Valuer') and time shall be of the essence[3] in relation
to the service of the Counter-notice and accordingly no Counter-
notice shall be served out of time and no valuation shall be prepared
and served by or on behalf of the party who failed to serve a Counter-
notice in time

  2.3:3   Within [30] days of the Notice of Election
    2.3:3.1 where no valid counter-notice has been served the First Valuer
shall prepare and serve on the other party or
    2.3:3.2 where a valid counter-notice has been served each Valuer
shall prepare and serve on the other Valuer
  a written valuation specifying the rent at which in the respective
opinions of such Valuers (or Valuer as the case may be) the Premises
might reasonably be expected to be let in the open market at the
relevant Review Date making the Assumptions but disregarding the
Disregarded Matters and time shall be of the essence[3] in relation

to the preparation and service of the valuation (or valuations) and accordingly no valuation shall be prepared and served out of time

2.4   If the parties shall not have agreed upon the revised Rent for the relevant Review Period [in writing] within [60] days of the service of the Notice of Election then (whether or not a valid Counter-notice has been served) a third Valuer ('the Third Valuer') shall be appointed either by agreement between the parties or (in the absence of such agreement within [14] days after either party shall first have proposed in writing one or more candidates for appointment as Third Valuer to the other party) by the President on the application of either party[4]

2.5:1   The Third Valuer shall as soon as he accepts the appointment so notify the parties in writing and within [7] days of such notice the First Valuer and the Second Valuer (or the First Valuer only if no Counter-notice was served in time) shall each submit to him a copy of his or their written valuation prepared in accordance with paragraph 2.3:3[5]

2.5:2   Time shall be of the essence[3] in relation to the submission of valuations to the Third Valuer and accordingly any valuation submitted out of time shall be disregarded for the purposes of this schedule[6]

2.5:3   The Third Valuer shall as soon as may [reasonably] be possible after accepting appointment prepare his own valuation[5] specifying the rent at which in his opinion the Premises might reasonably be expected to be let in the open market at the relevant Review Date making the Assumptions but disregarding the Disregarded Matters and immediately after the closing date for submission of valuations to him he shall simultaneously supply both parties with copies of his valuation and any valuations which were properly submitted to him in time by the First and Second Valuers

2.6:1   If both the First Valuer and the Second Valuer have properly and in time prepared and served valuations in accordance with paragraphs 2.3:3 and 2.5:1 the revised rent for the relevant Review Period shall be the average of whichever 2 of the 3 valuations are closest in rental value

2.6:2   If only one valuation has been properly and in time prepared and served in accordance with paragraphs 2.3:3 and 2.5:1 the revised rent for the relevant Review Period shall be the average of that valuation and the Third Valuer's valuation

2.6:3   If either:

2.6:3.1   no valuations have been properly and in time prepared and served in accordance with paragraphs 2.3:3 and 2.5:1 or

2.6:3.2   both the First Valuer and the Second Valuer have properly and in time prepared and served valuations in accordance with paragraphs 2.3:3 and 2.5:1 and the Third Valuer's valuation is the average of the valuations submitted by the First and Second Valuers[6] then

the revised rent for the relevant Review Period shall be the rent specified in the Third Valuer's valuation

2.6:4   The Third Valuer shall append to his valuation a statement of the amount of the revised rent for the relevant Review Period and which of the circumstances specified in paragraphs 2.6:1, 2.6:2, 2.6:3.1 or 2.6:3.2 applies

2.7:1 The Third Valuer shall be entitled at any time to request either or both of the parties or the Valuers to furnish him in writing with such information as to matters of fact or copy documents[7] as he may [reasonably] request and the parties shall comply with such requests as soon as is [reasonably] practicable

2.7:2 The fees and expenses of the Third Valuer including the cost of his appointment shall be borne equally by the parties who shall otherwise bear their own costs[8]

2.7:3 The Third Valuer shall not be in any way limited or fettered by the valuation evidence if any contained either in the First Valuer's and/or Second Valuer's valuations or in the information or documents submitted to him under paragraph 2.7:1 above but shall be entitled to rely entirely on his own judgment and opinion and shall act as an expert valuer and not as an arbitrator or quasi-arbitrator[9]

2.7:4 If the Third Valuer dies or refuses to act or becomes incapable of acting [or if he shall fail to publish his valuation within [4] months of the date upon which he accepted the appointment] either party may apply to the President to discharge the Third Valuer and appoint another in his place

2.8 *(continue as in Form 22 second schedule paragraph 2.5 above)*

3.2 *(continue as in Form 22 second schedule paragraph 3.2 above substituting 'Third Valuer's valuation' and 'Third Valuer's' for 'Arbitrator's Award' and 'Arbitrator's' respectively and deleting all words from and including 'such proportion' and substituting 'half of them from the other party')*

4.2 *(continue as in Form 22 second schedule paragraph 4.2 above substituting 'Third Valuer's valuation' for 'Arbitrator's Award')*

Published Footnotes (authors' amendments or additions in square brackets)

1 This Form is designed to be incorporated in Form 22 second schedule above and the paragraphs set out in this Form should be substituted and/or added where appropriate. Those paragraphs to which no reference is made in this Form should be set out in full as they appear in Form 22 above [see p 676].

This method of determining a rent review in the event of disagreement is widely used in the United States where it is known as a 'baseball' review since the method was first used to determine baseball contract disputes. Like the 'flip flop' review (see Form 130 [above]) it is designed to encourage the parties to be reasonable in the first place with a view to avoiding the necessity of a reference to a third party. In this Form, if the parties are unable to agree upon a reviewed rent, 3 valuations are prepared, one each by valuers appointed by the landlord and the tenant and one by an independent third valuer. The reviewed rent is the result of averaging whichever 2 valuations are closest. Since the third valuer's opinion of rent is likely to be somewhere between the figure provided by the landlord's valuer and that provided by the tenant's valuer, the parties are given the incentive to adjust their valuations (downwards in the case of the landlord and upwards in the case of the tenant) in the hope of being closer to the rental valuation opinion of the third valuer. This form of determination has another advantage in that it makes a so called 'robust' award ie an arbitrator's award or an expert's determination, which is almost or exactly equidistant between the landlord's and the tenant's figures regardless of the respective merits of either case almost impossible. Further, the unfortunate position where an expert's figure is either less than the tenant's figure or more than the landlord's figure is also mitigated. Its sophistication is such that it can be much more widely used than a 'flip flop' review provision, but even so its suitability may be limited to lettings where there are unlikely to be legal issues having a significant effect at rent review.

2   Widely differing views are held amongst valuers and solicitors as to the advantages and disadvantages of including such restrictions.

3   One of the objects of using a 'baseball' review is to ensure that the review is prosecuted expeditiously. It therefore seems reasonable to suppose that the parties should be aware that the Review Commencement Date is impending and that once it has passed events may occur quite swiftly. They should similarly be made aware that the consequence of failure to act in good time in relation to any step under this form of review provision will almost certainly be extremely disadvantageous.

4   Even if a party has failed to serve a Counter-notice it can still apply for a presidential appointment of a third valuer. His position is not hopeless since the third valuer's valuation will almost certainly have a mitigating effect on the valuation prepared by the other party's valuer.

5   On balance there appears to be no conclusive argument for providing that the third valuer shall be unaware of the contents of the first and second valuers' valuations when preparing his own valuation. They will be of assistance to him in respect of matters of fact and may well be so on matters of valuation. However, if desired such provision might be inserted here.

6   Clearly provision must be made for the unlikely event that the third valuer's rental figure is equidistant from the landlord's and the tenant's figures.

7   The third valuer must be entitled to see a copy of the lease and other title or licence deeds etc. Further, the first and second valuers' valuations may not supply him with all information as to matters of fact that he feels he needs.

8   Since the valuer is probably not acting in any quasi-judicial manner, it would be inappropriate to give him a discretion as to costs.

9   See *Palacath Ltd* v *Flanagan* [1985] 2 All ER 161.

4   CONVEYANCER PRECEDENT VAT CLAUSES FOR LEASES
5–105

Precedents for the conveyancer, Form 5–105

(First published June 1989)

I

Clause in a new lease designed to ensure that rent (or any other taxable supply which is capable of bearing VAT) is deemed to be exclusive of VAT and that the tenant is bound to pay that VAT

All sums payable under or in connection with this Lease in respect of rent payable, or taxable supplies received, by the Tenant shall be deemed to be exclusive of Value Added Tax (or any similar tax which shall replace Value Added Tax) and upon the production by the Landlord to the Tenant of an invoice appropriate to that tax the Tenant shall pay such tax in addition to those sums and the Landlord shall have the same remedies for non-payment of the tax as if the tax were part of the rent or the supply

Notes to Part I

The issues arising from the new VAT regime in respect of rent are discussed in an article by the draftsman (Steven Fogel, Solicitor) and Mr Plumbe at [1989] 16 EG 76.

The words 'upon the production by the Landlord to the tenant of an invoice appropriate for the purposes of that tax' have two functions. First, it is plainly important for the tenant to pay tax against a proper VAT invoice and thereby keep proper VAT records. Secondly, the quoted words are designed to protect the landlord against a claim by the tenant that, as otherwise drafted, the clause represents a strong implication that the landlord will exercise the option to tax.

It appears that if a new lease says nothing about VAT, and the parties have reached no agreement about VAT, then the landlord will still be able to add VAT to the rent, etc, as long as a new lease is granted at a time when there is no election to tax in force.

II

Requirement by landlord that rent should be reviewed on a basis which seeks to adjust evidence of rents passing under leases to tenants with disadvantaged tax statutes

If the Landlord or Tenant shall offer to any person determining the revised rent evidence of the rental value of other property which property is reasonably comparable to the demised premises and which is let to a lessee who is, or may be, disadvantaged by reason of any actual or potential election by the reversioner of that property to waive exemption in respect of Value Added Tax (or any similar tax which shall replace Value Added Tax) so far as concerns rent or any other taxable supply received by that lessee under or in connection with that letting, then the person determining the revised rent shall, for the purposes of the determination of the revised rent, assume that the rental value of that property is instead a higher value based upon the amount which the lessee would reasonably have paid if suffering no such disadvantage.

Notes of Part II

Most rents are determined by reference to 'comparables', the rental value of other property. A landlord who fears the development of a 'two-tier market', a market in which similar buildings attract different rental values for reasons connected with VAT, may wish to vet these comparables. One approach would be simply to disqualify as a comparable any property where the tenant pays less rent than would otherwise be obtainable for a VAT-connected reason, eg its own status in relation to the tax. The difficulty in this approach is that it may involve the rejection of a perfect comparable in a market where genuine comparables are scarce, or the rejection of a comparable which would favour the landlord if only it were adjusted to exclude the VAT factor.

The above precedent represents an attempt to require the independent valuer (or arbitrator) to accept that relevant comparables should be adjusted upwards before they are applied as an indicator of the correct rent for the subject property. The precedent should be treated with caution: it should be pointed out to any landlord who requires a provision of this nature that the referee might regard it as impertinent for the landlord to inspire a clause which tells the valuer to do what he might do anyway, which is intelligently to analyse a comparable and make any necessary adjustment.

A clause which is a reverse mutation of the above might just as well be demanded by a tenant whose concern goes the opposite way and who is in a bargaining position to demand the adjustment. He would want to ensure, even if it runs contrary to what the valuer would otherwise wish to do, that comparables of rents paid by VAT-disadvantaged tenants are *not* adjusted upwards.

III

Rent review assumption to protect landlord against adverse VAT valuation factors affecting the current tenant or arising from the terms of the lease

The rent shall be reviewed on the following assumptions at the relevant date:—
[........]

that the willing lessee and its potential assignees or underlessees of the demised premises suffer no disadvantage at the relevant review date or at any time during the term arising from an actual or potential election by the Landlord to waive exemption in respect of Value Added Tax so far as concerns rent or any other taxable supply received by the Tenant under or in connection with this Lease.

Notes to Part III

In many situations it may be considered adequate simply to add an assumption that the person bidding for the premises in the open market, the 'willing lessee' (who may well be the actual tenant), has a VAT status which enables full recovery by that tenant of tax paid to the landlord. However, this may not be an end of the matter. The willing lessee, albeit with a real or assumed favourable tax status, would prefer to take the property knowing that it is possible to dispose to someone who is not going to require compensation for the fact that the current or any future landlord has the unfettered right to decide whether to add VAT. One therefore needs to design a provision to take away the ability of the tenant to say 'Yes, I see that in my capacity of 'willing lessee' I am deemed to be a person who can pass on the burden if VAT, even although in reality I cannot. However, the notional lease which I am deemed to take on review contains a rent review clause identical to that which is now being operated. That clause contains artificial assumptions about VAT which would deter willing lessees such as me. I am therefore entitled to lower my rental bid to compensate me for having to take such an unusual lease.'

One way to design a provision to neutralise this argument would be to draft an additional assumption to the effect that, contrary to reality, the review clause omits any reference to the tenants assumed tax status and to the consequent ability of the willing lessee to recover VAT. It would be logical for such an assumption to refer also to the direction to the valuer set out in Part II. However, an 'assumption that there is no assumption' is inelegant and the form which it would have to take almost demands a hostile response from the tenant.

The drafting method chosen in the clause set out above is a little unusual because it refers not only to the willing lessee, but also its successors. The aim is to leave the hypothetical lease unedited but to stop the willing lessee claiming that the lease could be disadvantageous to an assignee, etc., because both the willing lessee and the assignee are assumed never to be disadvantaged on VAT grounds.

IV

Tenant's stipulation of landlord's covenant for itself and its successors not to elect to add VAT to rent and other taxable supplies

1. The Landlord covenants not
1.1 to charge to the Tenant Value Added Tax (or any similar tax which shall replace Value Added Tax) in respect of any rent payable or taxable supply received by the tenant under or in connection with this Lease;
1.2 to make any election to waive exemption in respect of such tax so far as concerns rent or other payments receivable in connection with the demised premises;
1.3 to assure the reversion to the demised premises (or any part of it) without ensuring that:
1.3.1. the new reversioner has given the Tenant a direct covenant to observe the provisions of this clause (including this sub-clause) such covenant to take effect from the date of transfer of ownership to the new reversioner and to be given or sent to the Tenant on or immediately after that date and
1.3.2. the assurance, in the case of registered property, contains a request by the parties to HM Land Registry to enter or perserve a note upon the registers of the title to the effect that no transfer of ownership of the demised premises, any part of them or the demised premises and other property, shall be registered unless the application for registration is accompanied by a solicitor's certificate to the effect that this clause (including this subclause) has been complied with.
2. If the Tenant shall at any time so require of the Landlord by giving notice in writing to the Landlord referring to this clause, the Landlord shall as soon as practicable properly elect to waive the exemption in respect of Value Added Tax so far as concerns rent or other payments receivable in connection with the demised premises and with effect from the making of that election the preceding clause shall cease to have effect.

Notes to Part IV

Again, the tenant's ability to obtain this covenant depends upon its bargaining strength and the landlord must think particularly hard on the possible dampening effect on a sale of the reversion of the limitation on succession.

Although it will not be possible to elect for only part of a building to be subject to VAT on rents, the benefit of the restriction on part disposals would arise if the whole later came into one ownership or if the demised premises comprise more than one building.

V

Rent review assumption to protect tenant against adverse VAT valuation factors arising from the terms of the lease

The rent shall be reviewed on the following assumptions at the relevant review date:— [....]

that the demised premises are available for letting on the terms of this lease other than the amount of the rent reserved by this lease (including all the provisions for the review of that rent) as if clause [   ] were omitted.

Notes to Part V

Similar comments as to the tenant's ability to obtain this concession apply.

Section Three

Obsolete or Obsolescent Forms of Rent Review

Introduction: The first three forms reproduced here are no longer recommended as the basis of rent review in a lease. They are included because clauses in many existing leases are based upon them. They were originally published in the *Encyclopaedia of Forms and Precedents* (4th ed).

The last two forms in this section are the original, 1979, version of the Model Forms and the First Revision published in 1980.

1   EFP (4th ed) FORM 8:1[1]

Encyclopaedia of Forms and Precedents (4th ed) Volume 12, Form 8–1

(First published 1966).

[*Note:* Only the clauses of the Form relating to rent review are set out.
See also the revision of this clause below in EFP Additional Form 76]

TO HOLD the demised premises unto the tenant from the ... day of ... for the term of [twenty-one] years thence next ensuring (that is to say until the ... day of ...) subject nevertheless to the proviso for re-entry hereinafter contained yielding and paying therefor during the said term yearly and proportionately for any fraction of a year the rents hereunder set out:

(A)   For the first [fourteen] years of the said term the rent of £ ... (hereinafter when specifically referred to called the first reserved rent)

(B)   For the residue of the said term (hereinafter called the review period) a rent to be determined in accordance with the provision in that behalf contained in clause 3 hereof (hereinafter when specifically referred to called the reviewed rent)

(C)   Throughout the said term the further and additional rent in clause 2 (2) herein described.

and the first reserved rent and the reviewed rent shall in all cases be paid by equal quarterly payments [in advance] on the usual quarter days [*or state days of payment*] in every year without any deduction whatsoever except as authorised by any statutory enactment for the time being in force the first payment apportioned in respect of the period from the ... day of ... to the quarter day [*or* ... day of ...] next thereafter to be paid on the execution hereof and also paying in addition throughout the said term by way of further rent from time to time a sum or sums of money equal to the amount (if any) that may be demanded by the insurance company referred to in clause 4 hereof in respect of increased premiums occasioned by the nature of the occupation or business of the tenant (which amount the lessor may at its absolute discretion decide shall be wholly borne and paid by the tenant) the same to be paid without deduction on the quarter day next ensuing after expenditure thereof by the lessor.

2. The tenant hereby covenants with the lessor to the intent that the obligations may continue throughout the said term as follows:
  (1)   To pay during the said term the said reserved rents and the further and additional rent hereinafter mentioned at the times and in manner herein provided without any deduction except as aforesaid; ...

3. The reviewed rent (payable by the tenant during the review period as hereinbefore provided) shall be determined in manner following that is to say it shall be whichever shall be the higher of the first reserved rent and the open market rental value of the demised premises for the review period PROVIDED that and it is hereby agreed as follows:
  (1)   The expression the open market rental value as aforesaid means a sum in relation to the review period determined in manner hereinafter provided as being at the time of such determination the annual rental value of the demised premises in the open market on a lease for a term of [seven] years certain (consisting of the review period) with vacant possession at the commencement of the term but upon the supposition (if not a fact) that the tenant has complied with the obligations as to repair and decorate herein imposed on the tenant such lease being on the same terms and conditions other than as to the amount of rent and the length of the term as are herein contained without the payment of any fine or premium and disregarding (if applicable) those matters set out in paragraphs (a) (b) and (c) of section 34 of the Landlord and Tenant Act 1954;
  (2) The said open market rental value shall be determined as follows:
  (a)   it shall be such sum as shall be specified in a notice in writing by the lessor to the tenant at any time before the expiration of the period of [thirteen and a half] years after the commencement of the term hereby granted; or
  (b)   as shall within three months after such notice be agreed between the parties in writing in substitution for the said sum; or
  (c)   it shall be determined at the election of the tenant by counter-notice in writing to the lessor not later than three months after the lessor's said notice (time to be of the essence hereof) by an independent surveyor appointed for that purpose by the parties jointly in writing or upon their failure to agree upon such appointment within one month after the date of the said counter-notice then by an independent surveyor appointed for that purpose by the President for the time being of the Royal Institution of Chartered Surveyors and every such determination shall be made in accordance (so far as not inconsistent herewith) with the provisions of the Arbitration Act 1950 or any statutory modification

or re-enactment thereof for the time being in force and shall be subject to the further provisions of the next succeeding sub-clause hereof;

(3) In the event of the determination by such independent surveyor not having been made and communicated to both parties hereto prior to the commencement of the review period for any reason whatever then in respect of the period of time (hereinafter called 'the said interval') beginning with the said commencement and ending on the quarter day immediately following the date on which such determination shall have been made and communicated as aforesaid the rent payable hereunder shall continue to be paid at the rate of the first reserved rent PROVIDED that at the expiration of the said interval there shall be due as additional rent payable by the tenant to the lessor on demand a sum of money equal to the amount whereby the reviewed rent shall exceed the first reserved rent but duly apportioned in respect of the said interval.

2   EFP (4th ed) ADDITIONAL FORM 76

Encyclopaedia of Forms and Precedents (4th ed) Additional Form 76 (Service, Section [62] p 184).

[*Note:*   The clause set out here is a revised version of EFP Form 8:1.]

TO HOLD the demised premises unto the tenant from the ... day of ... for the term of [fourteen] years thence next ensuing (that is to say until the ... day of ...) subject nevertheless to the proviso for re-entry hereinafter contained yielding and paying therefor during the said term yearly and proportionately for any fraction of a year the rents hereunder set out:

(a)   For the first [seven] years of the said term the rent of £... (hereinafter when specifically referred to called the first reserved rent)

(b)   For the residue of the said term (hereinafter called the review period) a rent to be determined in accordance with the provision in that behalf contained in clause [2] hereof (hereinafter when specifically referred to called the reviewed rent)

[(c)   *Provision as to service charges or other payments as required*]

and the first reserved rent and the reviewed rent shall in all cases be paid by equal quarterly payments [in advance] on the usual quarter days [*or state days of payment*] in every year without any deduction whatsoever except as authorised by any statutory enactment for the time being in force the first payment apportioned in respect of the period from the ... day of ... to the quarter day [*or* ...day of ...] next thereafter to be paid on the execution hereof.

[2]. The reviewed rent (payable by the tenant during the review period as hereinbefore provided) shall be determined in manner following that is to say it shall be whichever shall be the higher of the first reserved rent and the open market rental value of the demised premises for the review period PROVIDED that and it is hereby agreed as follows:

(1) The expression the open market rental value as aforesaid means a sum in relation to the review period determined in manner hereinafter provided as being at the time of such determination the annual rental value of the demised premises in the open market on a lease for a term of [seven] years certain (consisting of the review period) with vacant possession at the commencement of the term but upon the supposition (if not a fact) that the tenant has complied with the

obligations as to repair and decoration herein imposed on the tenant) such lease being on the same terms and conditions other than as to the amount of rent and the length of the term as are herein contained without the payment of any fine or premium and disregarding (if applicable) those matters set out in paragraphs (a), (b) and (c) of section 34 of the Landlord and Tenant Act 1954 (as amended);

(2) The said open market rental value shall be determined as follows.

(a)   it shall be such sum as shall be specified in a notice in writing by the lessor to the tenant at any time before the expiration of the period of [six and a half] years after the commencement of the term hereby granted; or

(b)   as shall within three months after such notice be agreed between the parties in writing in substitution for the said sum; or

(c)   it shall be determined at the election of the tenant by counter-notice in writing to the lessor not later than three months after the lessor's said notice (time to be of the essence hereof) by an independent surveyor appointed for that purpose by the parties jointly in writing or upon their failure to agree upon such appointment within one month after the date of the said counter-notice then by an independent surveyor appointed for that purpose by the President for the time being of the Royal Institution of Chartered Surveyors and every such determination shall be made in accordance (so far as not inconsistent herewith) with the provisions of the Arbitration Act 1950 or any statutory modification or re-enactment thereof for the time being in force and shall be subject to the further provisions of the next succeeding sub-clause hereof;

(3) In the event of the determination by such independent surveyor not having been made and communicated to both parties hereto prior to the commencement of the review period for any reason whatever then in respect of the period of time (hereinafter called 'the said interval') beginning with the said commencement and ending on the quarter day immediately following the date on which such determination shall have been made and communicated as aforesaid the rent payable hereunder shall continue to be paid at the rate of the first reserved rent PROVIDED that at the expiration of the said interval there shall be due as additional rent payable by the tenant to the lessor on demand a sum of money equal to the amount whereby the reviewed rent shall exceed the first reserved rent but duly apportioned in respect of the said interval.

(4) Time shall not be of the essence as regards the service of notice by the lessor under paragraph (a) of sub-clause (2) of this clause and if for any reason whatsoever the lessor fails to give notice under that paragraph before the expiration of the time therein specified but gives such a notice at any time thereafter [but within [one year] of the commencement of the review period] the foregoing provisions of this clause shall have effect for the purposes of determining the open market rental for the review period as if the said paragraph (a) required the notice to be served by the lessor at the time when it was in fact served and if the determination of the open market rental value by an independent surveyor under paragraph (c) of his sub-clause is made after the commencement of the review period it shall notwithstanding anything in sub-clause (1) of this clause be made on the basis of values prevailing at the commencement of that period and not those prevailing at the time of determination and sub-clause (1) shall apply in relation to the valuation subject to that modification.

3   EFP (4th ed) FORM 7:1

Encyclopaedia of Forms and Precedents (4th ed) Volume 12, Form 7:1

(First published 1966).

[*Note:* Only the clauses relating to rent review are set out.]

TO HOLD the demised premises unto the tenant from the ... day of ... for the term of ... years [(less ... days)] thence next ensuing that is to say until the ... day of ... subject nevertheless to the provisos for determination hereinafter contained paying therefor during the said term yearly and proportionately for any fraction of a year the rents hereunder set out:

(A)   For the first ... years of the said term the yearly rent of £ ...

(B)   For the next ... years of the said term either the yearly rent reserved in sub-clause (A) hereof or the open market rental value of the demised premises at the review date whichever is the higher and in either case the same shall remain constant during the whole period referred to in this sub-clause

(C)   For the next ... years of the said term either the yearly rent reserved in sub-clause (A) hereof or that in sub-clause (B) hereof or the open market rental value of the demised premises at the review date whichever is the higher and in any case the same shall remain constant during the whole period referred to in this sub-clause.

And the said rents shall in all cases be paid by equal payments in advance on the usual quarter days in every year without any deduction whatsoever except as authorised notwithstanding any agreement between the parties by any statutory enactment relating to income tax for the time being in force the first payment apportioned in respect of the period from the ... day of ... to the quarter day next hereafter to be paid on the execution hereof

PROVIDED that for the purposes of sub-clauses (B) and (C) hereof it is hereby agreed that the following definitions and provisions shall apply namely:

(1)   The expression 'open market rental value' means the annual rental value of the demised premises in the open market which might reasonably be demanded by a willing landlord on a lease for a term of years certain equivalent in length to the residue unexpired at the review date of the term of years hereby granted with vacant possession at the commencement of the term but upon the supposition (if not a fact) that the tenant has complied with all the obligations as to repair and decoration herein imposed on the tenant (but without prejudice to any rights or remedies of the lessor in regard thereto) and there being disregarded (if applicable) those matters set out in paragraphs (a), (b) and (c) of section 34 of the Landlord and Tenant Act 1954 and there being disregarded (so far as may be permitted by law) all restrictions whatsoever relating to rent or to security of tenure contained in any statute or orders rules or regulations thereunder and any directions thereby given relating to any method of determination of rent such lease being on the same terms and conditions (other than as to amount of rent and length of term) as this present demise without the payment of any fine or premium;

(2)   The expression 'review date' means the expiration of the ... year of the
      said term or the expiration of the ... year of the said term as the context
      requires for the purpose of ascertainment of the open market rental value
      under sub-clause (B) or sub-clause (C) hereof respectively;
(3)   The open market rental value shall be determined in manner following
      that is to say it shall be such annual sum as shall be:
      (a) specified in a notice in writing signed by or on behalf of the lessor
           and posted by recorded delivery post in a pre-paid envelope addressed
           to the tenant at the demised premises at any time before the beginning
           of a clear period of two quarters of a year (commencing on one
           of the usual quarter days hereinbefore mentioned) immediately
           preceding the review date (and such notice shall be conclusively
           deemed to have been received by the tenant in due course of post)
           or
      (b) agreed between the parties before the expiration of three months
           immediately after the date of posting of such notice as aforesaid
           in substitution for the said sum or
      (c) determined at the election of the tenant (to be made by counter-
           notice in writing served by the tenant upon the lessor not later than
           the expiration of the said three months) by an independent surveyor
           appointed for that purpose by the parties jointly in writing or upon
           their failure to agree upon such appointment within one month
           immediately after the date of service of the said counter-notice then
           by an independent surveyor appointed for that purpose on the
           application of either party alone by the President for the time being
           of the Royal Institution of Chartered Surveyors and in either case
           in accordance with the provisions of the Arbitraton Act 1950:

(4)   In the event of the determination of such independent surveyor not having
      been published prior to the review date for any reason whatever then
      in respect of the period of time (hereinafter called the said interval)
      beginning with the review date and ending on the quarter day immediately
      following the date on which such determination shall have been published
      the tenant shall pay to the lessor in manner hereinbefore provided rent
      at the yearly rate payable immediately before the review date PROVIDED
      that at the expiration of the said interval there shall be due as a debt
      payable by the tenant to the lessor on demand a sum of money equal
      to the amount whereby the yearly rent determined by such independent
      surveyor shall exceed the yearly rent at the yearly rate aforesaid but
      duly apportioned on a daily basis in respect of the said interval;
(5)   All stipulations as to time in the foregoing sub-clauses numbered (1)
      (2) (3) and (4) shall be of the essence of the contract and shall not be
      capable of enlargement save as agreed in writing by the parties;
And also paying in addition throughout the said term by way of further (insurance)
rent from time to time a sum or sums of money equal to the amount which
the lessor may expend in effecting or maintaining the insurance of the demised
premises against loss or damage by fire and such other risks as the lessor may
deem desirable or expedient (including loss of rent hereunder for such number
of years as the lessor may deem appropriate and architects' and surveyors' fees
and demolition clearance and similar expenses) together with all sums that may
be demanded by the insurance company in respect of increased premiums
occasioned by the nature of the occupation or business of the tenant such further
rent to be paid without any deduction on the quarter day next ensuing after

the said expenditure and to be recoverable by distress in the same way as rent in arrear.

4   RICS/LAW SOCIETY MODEL FORMS OF RENT REVIEW CLAUSE
[ORIGINAL (1979) VERSION]

Model Forms of Rent Review Clause Published by the Joint Working Party of the Royal Institution of Chartered Surveyors and the Law Society

Original (1979) Version—for 1985 Revised Model Forms, see p 655 above)

Introductory Note

1. The Law Society and the Royal Institution of Chartered Surveyors believe that it would be in the interests of the respective professions and of their clients that some degree of standardisation of clauses in leases should be made possible. They have accordingly set in motion joint studies of such clauses with the object of producing outlines of the clauses, which would assist practitioners in the professions in considering points relevant to such clauses, and in negotiating and drafting such clauses to suit the particular circumstances of the case.

2. One of the clauses now most commonly found in business leases is a clause providing for rent reviews at stated intervals. This type of clause has been the subject of much argument in recent years, and of important judicial decisions—notably that of the House of Lords in the case of *United Scientific Holdings Ltd* v *Burnley Borough Council* [1978] AC 904. Attention has first been directed to this type of clause; and there will be found below a model form of rent review clause, showing various alternatives, and with accompanying notes.

3. The Law Society and the Royal Institution of Chartered Surveyors wish to recommend to their respective members that they should adopt this lay-out as the basis for rent review clauses in business leases to the greatest possible extent. There will be situations where modifications are required. No attempt has been made, for example, to deal with interest on unpaid rent, nor to allow for other factors such as an unusual length of term or where the age of the building is a significant factor. Neither does it take into account any need for a change in the existing rent review pattern.

4. There is also set out below a model form of memorandum recording a change in the rent following a review. Use of the memorandum, which will be signed before being annexed in the lease and counterpart, avoids the need for the original deeds to be circulated for signature. Normally the memorandum need not be under seal and need not be signed by a guarantor, but this will depend on the terms of the lease which might, for example, restrict the guarantor's liability to the amount of the original rent.

Model Forms of Rent Review Clause

... yielding and paying therefore unto the landlord the yearly rent hereinafter mentioned without any deduction by equal quarterly payments in advance on the usual quarter days the first payment (*being an apportioned sum*) to be made on the execution of this lease.

The yearly rent payable hereunder shall be as follows—

Clause 1: Provisions for revision of rent

(A) until the —— day of —— 19— the rent of £——

(B)1. from the —— day of —— 19— to the —— day of —— 19— *the rent of £ —— or* such revised rent as may be agreed or determined as hereinafter provided (*whichever be the greater*).

Sub-clauses for leases containing not more than two rent reviews. (See Notes 1, 2, and 4.)

(C) and during the residue of the said term *a rent equal to the rent previously payable hereunder or* such revised rent as may be agreed or determined as hereinafter provided (*whichever be the greater*)

Equivalent sub-clause for lease containing more than two rent reviews. (See Notes 3 and 5.)

(B)2. and during each of the successive periods of —— years of which the first begins on the said day of —— 19— and during the residue of the said term beginning on the —— day of 19— *a rent equal to the rent previously payable hereunder or* such revised rent as may be agreed or determined as hereinafter provided (*whichever be the greater*).

Additional sub-clause for upwards/downwards reviews only. (See Notes 4 and 5.)

(D) and in the event of a rent not being agreed or determined as herein provided the rent payable for the relevant period shall be the rent payable immediately prior to the commencement of such period.

Notes

1   If there is to be only one rent review, Clause 1 will consist of paras A and C alone. See also Note 4 below.

2   If there are to be two reviews, Clause 1 will consist of paras A, B1 and C. See also Note 4 below.

3   If there are to be more than two reviews, Clause 1 will consist of paras A and B2. See also Note 5 below.

4   If there are to be one or two reviews 'upwards only,' paras B1 (where relevant) and C should contain the italicised words. If the reviews are to be 'upwards/ downwards' those italicised words should be omitted, but para D should be added.

5   If there are to be more than two reviews 'upwards only,' para B2 should contain the italicised words. If the reviews are to be 'upwards/downwards' those italicised words should be omitted, but para C should be added.

Clause 2(1): Ascertainment of amount

Alternative commencing provisions–(1) At landlord's option by arbitrator or by valuer acting as expert. (See Notes 6 and 7.)

Such revised rent hereinbefore referred to may be agreed at any time between the landlord and the tenant or (in the absence of agreement) determined not earlier than the commencement of the period to which it relates at the option of the landlord either by an arbitrator or by a valuer (acting as an expert and not as arbitrator) such arbitrator or valuer to be nominated in the absence of agreement by the President for the time being of the Royal Institution of Chartered

Surveyors on the application of the landlord made not more than six months
before or at any time after the commencement of the relevant period and so
that in case of such arbitration or valuation the revised rent to be determined
by the arbitrator or valuer shall be such as in his opinion should be the yearly
rent for the demised premises let as a whole:—

—OR—

Clause 2(2)

(2) By arbitrator by either party. (See Notes 6 and 7.)

Such revised rent hereinbefore referred to may be agreed at any time between
the landlord and the tenant or (in the absence of agreement) determined not
earlier than the commencement of the period to which it relates by an arbitrator
such arbitrator to be nominated in the absence of agreement by the President
for the time being of the Royal Institution of Chartered Surveyors on the
application of the landlord or the tenant made not more than six months before
or at any time after the commencement of the relevant period and so that in
case of such arbitration the revised rent to be determined by the arbitrator shall
be such as in his opinion should be the yearly rent for the demised premises
let as a whole:—

—OR—

Clause 2(3)

(3) By valuer acting as expert by either party. (See Notes 6 and 7.)

Such revised rent hereinbefore referred to may be agreed at any time between
the landlord and the tenant or (in the absence of agreement) determined not
earlier than the commencement of the period to which it relates by a valuer
(acting as an expert and not as an arbitrator) such valuer to be nominated
in the absence of agreement by the President for the time being of the Royal
Institution of Chartered Surveyors on the application of the landlord or the
tenant made not more than six months before or at any time after the
commencement of the relevant period and so that in case of such valuation
the revised rent to be determined by the valuer shall be such as in his opinion
should be the yearly rent for the demised premises let as a whole:—

Notes

6   Only one of the three alternatives in Clause 2 may be included, the essential
     differences being:
     Clause 2(1) gives to the landlord alone the right to opt for arbitration or
     independent expert valuation, and to initiate either process, in which case
     the tenant has the protection of Clause 3(6); under Clause 2(2) either party
     has the right to initiate the reference process, which is specified as being
     to arbitration only.
     Under Clause 2(3), again either party has the right to initiate the reference
     process which under this Clause is to a valuer acting as an expert.

Provisions applicable in all cases

(i) on the basis that at the commencement of the relevant period they are
fit for immediate occupation and use and that no work has been carried out
thereon by the tenant or its predecessors in title during the said term which

has diminished the rental value of the demised premises and that in case the demised premises have been destroyed or damaged they have been fully restored.

(ii) having regard to market rental values current at the commencement of the relevant period for property let without a premium with vacant possession and subject to the provisions of this Lease (other than the amount of the rent hereby reserved but including the provisions for rent review) for a term equal to the original term of this Lease by a willing landlord to a willing tenant.

(iii) on the assumption that the covenants herein contained have been fully performed and observed until the commencement of the relevant period[2] but disregarding:

(a) any effect on rent of the fact that the tenant or its predecessors in title[3] has been in occupation of the demised premises and any goodwill attached to the demised premises by reason of the carrying on thereat of the business of the tenant or its predecessors in title in that business and

(b) any increase in rental value of the demised premises attributable to the existence at the commencement of the relevant period of any improvement to the demised premises or any part thereof (shown to be such by the tenant) carried out (i) by the tenant or its predecessors in title or a sub-tenant during the said term or during any period of occupation prior thereto arising out of an agreement to grant such term or (ii) by any previous tenant of the demised premises before the commencement of the term hereby granted (provided it did not quit) otherwise than in pursuance of an obligation to the tenant's or such previous tenant's immediate landlord to the extent that any such improvement as aforesaid shall have been carried out without liability on the part of such immediate landlord to reimburse the cost thereof and that the improvement was carried out with the written consent of such immediate landlord (where required) and completed not more than twenty one years before the commencement of the relevant period.

Clause 3

Further provisos

IT IS HEREBY FURTHER PROVIDED in relation to the said revised rents as follows:—

As to arbitration (See Note 7)

(1) in the case of an arbitration the arbitration shall be conducted in accordance with the Arbitration Act 1950 or any statutory modification or re-enactment thereof for the time being in force.

As to references to a valuer acting as expert (See Note 7)

(2) in the case of reference to a valuer (a) the costs of the reference shall be in the award of the valuer whose decision shall be final and binding on the parties hereto (b) *the valuer shall afford to each of the parties hereto an opportunity to make representations to him and* (c) if he shall die delay or become unwilling or incapable of acting or if for any other reason the President for the time being of the Royal Institution of Chartered Surveyors shall in his absolute discretion think fit the said President may by writing discharge him and appoint another valuer in his place.

As to memoranda of ascertainment (See Note 7)

(3) when the amount of any rent to be ascertained as hereinbefore provided shall have been so ascertained memoranda thereof shall thereupon be signed

by or on behalf of the landlord and the tenant and annexed to this Lease and Counterpart thereof and the parties shall bear their own costs in respect thereof.

As to interim payments (See Note 7)

(4) if and so often as a revised rent in respect of any period has not been ascertained pursuant to the foregoing provisions before the first day hereby appointed for payment of rent for the relevant period rent shall continue to be payable during that period at the rate equal to the rent payable immediately before the commencement of the relevant period until the first day of payment of rent after that revised rent has been ascertained or until the expiration of that period (whichever shall first happen).

Notes

7   If Clause 2(1) above is used, Clauses 3(1) and 3 (2) *both* apply.
     If Clause 2(2) above is used, omit Clauses 3(2) *and* 3 (6).
     If Clause 2(3) above is used, omit Clauses 3(1) *and* 3 (6).

Note: the words in italics in Clause 3(2) are optional, but if they are omitted insert 'and (b)'.

As to final adjustments (See Note 8)

(5) on the first day for payment of rent after the revised rent has been ascertained there shall be payable by the tenant to the landlord by way of rent (in addition to the amount of rent otherwise due on that day) the aggregate of the amounts by which the instalments of rent payable in respect of that period in accordance with proviso (4) hereof fall short of the amounts which would have been payable if the revised rent had been ascertained before the first day for payment of rent for the relevant period [*or (as the case may be) there shall be deducted from such payment and where necessary from subsequent payments the aggregate of the amounts by which such instalments exceed the amounts which would have been so payable*]

Notes

8   The words in italics in Clause 3(5) should be omitted if the reviews are 'upwards only.'

As to notice by tenant where appointment of arbitrator or expert is at landlord's option (See Notes 7 and 9)

(6) if and so often as a revised rent in respect of any period has not been agreed between the landlord and the tenant before the first day hereby appointed for payment of the rent for the relevant period and the landlord has not before that day made any application to the President for the time being of the Royal Institution of Chartered Surveyors as hereinbefore provided the tenant may at any time thereafter serve on the landlord notice in writing containing a proposal as to the amount of such revised rent *not being less than the rent payable immediately before the commencement of the relevant period* and the amount so proposed shall be the revised rent for the relevant period unless the landlord shall make such application as aforesaid within three months after service of such notice and proviso (5) hereof shall apply accordingly upon the first day for payment of rent after the expiration of such three months unless such application has been made within such three months.

Notes

9   The words in italics in Clause 3(6) should be included if the reviews are 'upwards only.'

5   RICS/LAW SOCIETY REVISED MODEL FORMS OF RENT REVIEW CLAUSE
[REVISED 1980]

Revised Model Forms of Rent Review Clauses promulgated by Joint Working Party of the Law Society and the Royal Institution of Chartered Surveyors

Revised 1980—for 1985 Revised Model Forms, see p 655, above)

Background Notes

The following brief notes have been produced to provide information as to the background reasoning which led to the many variations included in the published rent review clause and as to phraseology used in it and the need for some of the differing provisions.

1. The clause was drafted to embrace the widest range of business premises, varying from poor quality multi-tenanted buildings to letting to a single tenant of large and modern properties with sophisticated services and facilities.

2. The Joint Committee had to take into account various lengths of lease which could range from as little as five years or less, up to (say) 25 years.

3. A most important consideration was that the model clause should be able to reflect the market conditions prevailing at the time when the letting was negotiated. Thus there are variations which cover 'upwards only' and 'upwards/downwards' rent reviews:

(a)   There are provisions which might apply in a Landlord's market where the Landlord has the sole right to initiate the review process and to choose either arbitration or reference to a valuer acting as an expert. In this case, clause 4(E) was included to protect the tenant in the situation where he needs to avoid uncertainty or wants to assign after a rent review date and the Landlord has not applied for the appointment of an arbitrator or valuer.

(b)   There is also provision which might apply in a Tenant's market for either party to be able to initiate the review procedure where the choice as to arbitration or reference to an independent valuer is fixed at the outset.

4. In the light of the *Burnley* and *Cheapside* decisions (*United Scientific Holdings Limited v Burnley Council* and *Cheapside Land Development Co. Limited v Messels Service Company* [1978] AC 904) the Joint Committee sought to avoid, as far as possible, strict time limits and notices, in order to give effect to the contract between the parties (ie a letting for a term of years with rent reviews at specified intervals) and remove the risk of that contract being frustrated by human error.

5. The Joint Committee decided that, in an inflationary economy and in often rapidly changing market conditions, it is wrong to expect a valuer or an arbitrator to determine the rent in advance of the review date. Hence the referral process enables the appointment to take place prior to the review date, but requires

that the reviewed rent may not be determined until the review date (save of course by mutual agreement).

6. There are really two alternatives as to the length of the hypothetical lease to be considered when the review rent is assessed:

(i) The unexpired term

(ii) A term equivalent to the original term

If the unexpired term is to be assumed, then at the later review dates in a lease of what in the local market might be considered a large demise, a very limited unexpired length of term could affect the rental dramatically as continued occupation after expiry cannot be assumed, eg a lease of a very large factory or office building with only five or perhaps two or three years to run on the lease. The alternative assumption of a term equivalent to the original term of lease avoids this false temporary reduced rental situation and temporary reduction of investment value and, in the Joint Committee's view, would not normally prejudice the tenant's interest.

7. The Joint Committee set out to produce a basic clause with variations to cover the prime situations resulting from changes dictated by market forces and, though they considered other variations (such as those mentioned above), they did not feel it appropriate to include more than they have done. One topic of concern was whether to provide for interest payments on arrears of increased rents, but it was thought that this was a matter for which general provision for interest on all unpaid rent etc should be made elsewhere in the lease, if this accorded with market practice at the time when the lease was granted.

8. Where the President of a professional or learned society is required to appoint an arbitrator, this method of appointment is specified because the person so appointed should have (and under arbitration law is expected to utilise) his specialised professional skills in adjudicating upon the matter in dispute, which includes in particular his ability to distinguish between the quality, relevance and value of the evidence presented to him. In any RICS Presidential appointments, in order to ensure impartiality, enquiries are made of possible appointees to ensure that neither they nor their firm or partners have had any previous business or social connections with either of the parties to the dispute, or the subject property, or for any other reason are likely to be held to be biased, are able to deal with the subject of the dispute expeditiously, and finally that the subject matter of the dispute falls within their normal sphere of everyday professional work.

Thus whether a Presidential appointment or 'appointment by agreement between the parties' arises, any valuer so instructed would normally decline the appointment, unless he can satisfy these conditions. In an arbitration, the parties at least have the right to appearance and the valuer must adjudicate. The independent valuer, however appointed, is not bound by the rules and procedures laid down by the Arbitration Acts and may, unless the lease provides that he shall do so, properly decline to receive any statement of facts or evidence from either of the parties to the dispute. On balance the Joint Committee consider that reference to an arbitrator is more appropriate in most cases than reference to an independent valuer.

9. 'Provisions applicable in all cases' include and extend matters referred to in section 34 of the Landlord and Tenant Act 1954 to cover contingencies which in the experience of the Joint Committee do arise from time to time and should in fairness be included. This has the added advantage of avoiding the need to refer to statue which, in any event, can be amended. In clause 3(A) the arbitrator or valuer is to assume open market rental values at the review date. The Joint

Committee were asked to reconsider the expression 'market value' as a number of correspondents felt that 'open market value' would be clearer. Although it was felt that market value must be that in an open market, it was decided to include the word 'open'. This would include vacant possession lettings and also reviews and renewals, provided they are settled on a similar basis. The premises are assumed to be let 'as a whole' without a premium and with vacant possession. There may be occasional circumstances such as when there are existing subtenancies at the start of the lease, where this should not necessarily apply.

In clause 3 (B) (iii) the value of tenant's improvement over 21 years old may be taken into account. In the case of longer leases where rent reviews might fall outside the 21 year period during the currency of the lease, a modification may be called for by the tenant to avoid the tenant being assessed for rent on his own improvement. Unauthorised improvement will not be disregarded.

The provisions go further than the Landlord and Tenant Act 1954 in protecting tenants against being charged rent on the improvements of their subtenants or predecessors in title. It was felt important that as tenant's improvements were excluded from the assessment of rent so far as the Landlord was concerned, this benefit should also be extended to subtenant's improvements, as it would be unreasonable to allow the Landlord to have an unfair advantage over the tenant with a subtenant, merely because of the wording of the lease. This does not alter the position as between tenant and subtenant, and there may be similar rights over improvements between these two, to which the landlord is not a party and from which he should derive no benefit. The landlord's investment is protected by the time limit of 21 years, after which tenant's improvements would be taken into account, unless this period is altered or the limit omitted entirely.

Habendum

... yielding and paying to the Landlord yearly rents ascertained in accordance with the next four clauses hereof without any deduction by equal quarterly payments in advance on the usual quarterdays the first payment (being an apportioned sum) to be made on the date hereof.

Clause 1.

Definitions

In this deed 'Review Date' means the —— day of —— in the year 19— and in every —— year thereafter and 'Review Period' means the period starting with any Review Date up to the next Review Date or starting with the last Review Date up to the end of the term hereof.

Clause 2.

Provisions for revision of rent (See Note 1)

The yearly rent shall be: (A) until the first Review Date the rent of £—— and (B) during each successive Review Period *a rent equal to the rent previously payable hereunder or* such revised rent as may be ascertained as herein provided *whichever be the*

Additional Sub-Clause for upwards/downwards reviews only

greater and
(C) in the event of a revised rent not being ascertained as herein provided the rent payable for the relevant Review Period shall be the rent payable immediately prior to the commencement of such period

NOTE 1. If the reviews are to be 'upwards/downwards' the words in italics should be omitted and paragraph (C) should be added.

Clause 3.
Ascertainment of amount at Landlord's option by arbitrator or independent valuer
(see Notes 2 and 3)

Such revised rent for any Review Period may be agreed at any time between the Landlord and the Tenant or (in the absence of agreement) determined not earlier than the relevant Review Date at the option of the Landlord either by an arbitrator or by an independent valuer (acting as an expert and not as an arbitrator) such arbitrator or valuer to be nominated in the absence of agreement by or on behalf of the President for the time being of the Royal Institution of Chartered Surveyors on the application of the Landlord made not earlier than six months before the relevant Review Date *but not later than the end of the relevant Review Period* and so that in the case of such arbitration or valuation the revised rent to be awarded or determined by the arbitrator or valuer shall be such as he shall decide should be the yearly rent at the relevant Review Date for the demised premises.
(A) On the following assumptions at that date:—

OR

Clause 3.
Ascertainment of amount by arbitrator (see Notes 2 and 3)

Such revised rent for any Review Period may be agreed at any time between the Landlord and the Tenant or (in the absence of agreement) determined not earlier than the relevant Review Date by an arbitrator such arbitrator to be nominated in the absence of agreement by or on behalf of the President for the time being of the Royal Institution of Chartered Surveyors on the application of the

Landlord or the Tenant made not
earlier than six months before the
relevant Review Date *but not later than
the end of the relevant Review Period*
and so that in the case of such
arbitration the revised rent to be
awarded by the arbitrator shall be such
as he shall decide should be the yearly
rent at the relevant Review Date for
the demised premises
(A) On the following assumptions at
that date:—

OR

Clause 3.
Ascertainment of amount
by independent valuer
(see Notes 2 and 3)

Such revised rent for any Review
Period may be agreed at any time
between the Landlord and the Tenant
or (in the absence of agreement)
determined not earlier than the
relevant Review Date by an
independent valuer (acting as an expert
and not as an arbitrator) such valuer
to be nominated in the absence of
agreement by or on behalf of the
President for the time being of the
Royal Institution of Chartered
Surveyors on the application of the
Landlord or the Tenant made not
earlier than six months before the
relevant Review Date *but not later than
the end of the relevant Review Period*
and so that in the case of such
valuation the revised rent to be
determined by the valuer shall be such
as he shall decide should be the yearly
rent at the relevant Review Date for
the demised premises

Provisions applicable
in all cases

(A) On the following assumptions at
that date:—
(i)   that the demised premises are fit
        for immediate occupation and
        use and that no work has been
        carried out thereon by the
        Tenant its sub-tenants or their
        predecessors in title during the
        said term which has diminished
        the rental value of the demised
        premises and that in case the
        demised premises have been
        destroyed or damaged they have

been fully restored.
(ii)   that the demised premises are available to let by a willing landlord to a willing tenant as a whole without a premium but with vacant possession and subject to the provisions of this lease (other than the amount of the rent hereby reserved but including the provisions for rent review) for a term equal to the original term of this lease
(iii)   that the covenants herein contained on the part of the Tenant have been fully performed and observed

AND having regard to open market rental values current at the relevant Review Date

(B) But disregarding:—
(i)   any effect on rent of the fact that the Tenant its sub-tenants or their respective predecessors in title have been in occupation of the demised premises.
(ii)   any goodwill attached to the demised premises by reason of the carrying on thereat of the business of the Tenant its sub-tenants or their predecessors in title in their respective businesses and
(iii)   any increase in rental value of the demised premises attributable to the existence of the relevant Review Date of any improvement to the demised premises or any part thereof carried out with consent where required otherwise than in pursuance of an obligation to the Landlord or its predecessors in title
either (a) by the Tenant its sub-tenants or their respective predecessors in title during the said term or during any period of occupation prior thereto arising out of an agreement to grant such term
or (b) *by any tenant or sub-tenant*

of the demised premises before the
commencement of the term hereby
granted so long as the Landlord or
its predecessors in title have not
since the improvement was carried
out had vacant possession of the
relevant part of the demised
premises [AND *the improvement*
was completed not more than
twenty-one years before the
relevant Review Date]

NOTE 2. Only one of the three commencing paragraphs given for Clause 3 should be used. The essential differences are that the first gives the Landlord alone the right to opt for arbitration or independent valuation. The second and third provide respectively for arbitration only and for independent valuation only but both allow either the Landlord or the Tenant to initiate the process.

If the words in italics are included in the commencing paragraph there will be a time limit after which a review can no longer be initiated.

NOTE 3. Paragraph B (iii) (b) may be applicable only on a renewal. Additionally the words in square brackets may be omitted or amended if the 21-year period is not appropriate.

Clause 4.
Further provisions
As to Arbitration
(see Note 4)

IT IS HEREBY FURTHER PROVIDED in relation to the said revised rent as follows:—

(A) (*in the case of arbitration*) the arbitration shall be conducted in accordance with the Arbitration Act 1950 or any statutory modification or re-enactment thereof for the time being in force

As to independent
valuation
(see Note 4)

(B) (*in the case of determination by a valuer*)

(i) the fees and expenses of the valuer including the cost of his appointment shall be borne equally by the Landlord and the Tenant who shall otherwise each bear their own costs and

(ii) *the valuer shall afford to each of the parties hereto an opportunity to make representations to him and*

(iii) if the valuer shall die delay or become unwilling or incapable of acting or if for any other reason the President for the time being

of the Royal Institution of
Chartered Surveyors or the
person acting on his behalf shall
in his absolute discretion think
fit he may by writing discharge
the valuer and appoint another
in his place

**As to memoranda
of ascertainment**

(C) When the amount of any rent to be
ascertained as hereinbefore provided shall
have been so ascertained memoranda
thereof shall thereupon be signed by or on
behalf of the Landlord and the Tenant
and annexed to this lease and counterpart
thereof and the parties shall bear their
own costs in respect thereof

**As to interim
payments and
final adjustments
(see Note 5)**

(D) (i) if the revised rent payable on and
from any Review Date has not been
agreed by that Review Date rent shall
continue to be payable at the rate
previously payable and forthwith upon the
revised rent being ascertained the Tenant
shall pay to the Landlord any shortfall
between the rent and the revised rent *or as
the case may be the Landlord shall pay to
the Tenant any excess of the rent paid over
the revised rent* payable up to and on the
preceding quarter day
(ii) for the purposes of this proviso the
revised rent shall be deemed to have been
ascertained on the date when the same has
been agreed between the parties or as the
case may be the date of the award of the
arbitrator or of the determination by the
valuer

**As to notice by the
Tenant where
appointment of
Arbitrator or
independent valuer
is at the Landlord's
option
(see Note 6)**

(E) Whenever a revised rent in respect of
any Review Period has not been agreed
between the Landlord and the Tenant
before the relevant Review Date and the
Landlord has not made any application to
the President for the time being of the
Royal Institution of Chartered Surveyors
as hereinbefore provided the Tenant may
serve on the Landlord notice in writing
containing a proposal as to the amount of
such revised rent *not being less than the
rent payable immediately before the
commencement of the relevant Review
Period* and the amount so proposed shall
be deemed to have been agreed by the

parties as the revised rent for the relevant
Review Period and sub-clause (D) (i)
hereof shall apply accordingly unless the
Landlord shall make such application as
aforesaid within three months after service
of such notice by the Tenant.

NOTE 4. If the first version of Clause 3 is used (arbitrator or valuer) both
(A) and (B) apply. If the second version (arbitrator) is used (B) should be omitted
and if the third version (independent valuer) is used (A) should be omitted.
(b) (ii) is optional as regards an independent valuer.

NOTE 5. The words in italics should be omitted if the reviews are 'upwards
only'.

NOTE 6. The words in italics should be included if the reviews are 'upwards
only'.

Section Four

Rent Review and Indexation Forms for Residential Tenancies

Introduction: These forms are drafted by the authors and are designed for use in England and Wales in the light of the Housing Act 1988

1   CONVEYANCER PRECEDENT 5–99
INDEXATION OF RENT CLAUSE FOR ASSURED TENANCY

Precedents for the Conveyancer, Form 5–99

(First published December 1988)

a. On every anniversary of this tenancy the rent will be revised.

b. If the base date for the Retail Prices Index has not changed from the current base date the rent will be the initial rent increased by the same proportion as the RPI last published before the relevant anniversary has increased over the RPI last published before the date of this agreement [which figure is noted below].

c. If the base date for the RPI has changed the rent will be increased to the figure of the revised rent at the date of the change increased by the same proportion as the RPI last published before the relevant anniversary has increased over 100.

d. The process in (c) will apply after the second or later change in the base date.

[e. All revised rents will be rounded up or down to the nearest figure that gives a monthly payment in full pounds without pence.]

Notes

The issues of the effect on rents linked to the Retail Prices Index of a change in the base date are discussed in the Notes for Form 5–11.[1] The clause does not provide for the eventuality of abandonment of the RPI, in the interests of brevity. Should that happen then, in the absence of agreement, the Landlord could offer the Tenant a new tenancy of the premises on identical terms except for the basis of rental adjustment and seek possession on the suitable alternative accommodation ground if the Tenant declines. Alternatively the Landlord could invoke the jurisdiction of the court demonstrated in *Pole Properties Ltd* v *Feinberg*

723

(1981) 41 P & CR 121 to rewrite the contract to reflect a fundamental change of circumstances.

Authors' Note

1   See p 728.

2   CONVEYANCER PRECEDENT 5–100
RENT REVIEW PROVISION FOR ASSURED TENANCY

Precedents for the Conveyancer, Form 5–100

(First published December 1988)

a. The landlord may serve a notice stating a revised rent to take effect not less than four weeks after service and not earlier than one year from the later of the start of the tenancy or the last revision date. The revised rent stated in that notice is 'the Landlord's Figure'.

b. The tenant within two weeks of service of the landlord's notice may serve a counter notice stating a different revised rent. The revised rent stated in that notice is 'the Tenant's Figure'.

c. If the tenant does not serve a counter notice the landlord's notice takes effect at the revision date stated in it to revise the rent to the Landlord's Figure. If the landlord accepts the Tenant's Figure the tenant's counter-notice takes effect at the revision date stated in the landlord's notice to revise the rent to the Tenant's Figure.

d. If the Tenant's Figure has not been accepted by the revision date either party may refer the issue of the revised rent to the decision of the Nominated Valuer. The Nominated Valuer is the valuer named in the landlord's notice or, if none is named in that notice, named in the tenant's counter-notice but if a different valuer is named in both the notice and the counter-notice a valuer shall be appointed at the request of either party by the senior officer of the local [Law Society] [branch of the RICS]. The Nominated Valuer must invite each party to make written representations in support of their respective Figures and must then notify the parties which of the Landlord's Figure and Tenant's Figure is in his opinion as an expert the nearer to the market rent for the premises (assuming full performance of the Tenant's obligations) in the light of the terms of this agreement at the revision date and the figure so chosen is the revised rent from the revision date. The parties must each pay one half of the Valuer's fees [unless the Valuer decides that one party has acted unreasonably in not agreeing the other party's figure when he may decide the former must meet the whole fees].

e. Pending the notification of the Nominated Valuer's decision the Tenant must pay rent at a figure half-way between the Landlord's Figure and the Tenant's Figure. On the next rent day after notification the payment must reflect the amount due to either party as a consequence of the decision in the light of the interim payments.

f. All time limits in this clause must be strictly observed.

Notes

If an assured tenancy contains provisions for adjustment of the rent the provisions of the Housing Act 1988, ss 13 and 14 for service of a rent revision notice and the tenant's right to refer it to a Rent Assessment Committee do not apply.

Although the third party is to act as an expert and not an arbitrator, the process to be followed is based on the notion of the so-called 'flip flop' or 'pendulum' arbitration whereby the referee chooses between the two figures put forward, so reducing the cost of the decision and putting each party under pressure to put forward a realistic figure. The optional provision at the end of sub-clause (d) will be a further sanction, if it is included, against putting in a figure too low or too high to an unreasonable extent.

Form 5–104 provides for a more usual formula for valuation in default of agreement, and its approach of reference to a third party only after failure to agree may be combined with this Form.

3   CONVEYANCER PRECEDENT 5–103
RENT REVIEW CLAUSE FOR AN ASSURED TENANCY BY LESSORS
UNILATERAL NOTICE

Precedents for the Conveyancer, Form 5–103

(First published April 1989)

(a) The landlord may by written notice (a 'Rent Revision Notice') served on the tenant revise the rent payable under this agreement.

(b) The Rent Revision Notice shall specify the [monthly] [weekly] rent which is to become payable and the date on which it is to take effect (the 'Rent Revision Date').

(c) The Rent Revision Date so specified in the Rent Revision Notice for the new rent to become payable shall in no event be earlier than the anniversary of the start of the tenancy or the last Rent Revision Date, as the case may be; it must also be at least four weeks after the service of the Rent Revision Notice.

[(d) In the four week period following the service of the Rent Revision Notice, the tenant may serve on the landlord a four weeks notice to quit and if the tenant so terminates the tenancy, the Rent Revision Notice shall be of no effect].

Notes

Use of this Form avoids the expense and delay of (possible) reference to a third party.

The validity of varying a rent by unilateral notice was upheld by the Court of Appeal in *Greater London Council* v *Connelly* [1970] 2 QB 100.

This Form seeks to ensure that a landlord can give notice of an annual increase of rent. A retrospective increase is not possible; there is no obstacle to revision more frequently than once a year, but that might create 'consumer resistance'.

The inclusion (especially in a fixed term tenancy) of sub-clause (d), allowing a tenant to quit is recommended. A court might shrink from allowing a tenant to be burdened with a unilaterally imposed increase in a situation where he is left without the option of leaving.

4   CONVEYANCER PRECEDENT 5–104
RENT REVIEW CLAUSE FOR AN ASSURED TENANCY BY AGREEMENT BETWEEN THE PARTIES, WITH INDEPENDENT VALUATION IN DEFAULT

Precedents for the Conveyancer, Form 5–104

(First published April 1989)

    (a) The Rent Revision Date shall be —— 19— and every anniversary thereafter.

    (b) On each Rent Revision Date the rent may be revised to such sum as is agreed [in writing] between the parties. [Any sum so agreed shall be endorsed on this tenancy agreement].

    (c) If the parties fail to agree on the rent payable from any Rent Revision Date then either party may refer the issue of the revised rent to the decision of the Nominated Valuer.

    (d) The Nominated Valuer shall be a valuer agreed upon by the parties or, in default of agreement, appointed on the application of either party by the President or senior officer of the local [Law Society] [branch of the RICS].

    (e) The Nominated Valuer shall determine the revised rent at that at which he considers the [property] might reasonably be expected to be let in the open market by a willing landlord under an assured [shorthold] tenancy—

    (i)   which is a tenancy of the same fixed term or having the same periods as this tenancy;

    (ii) which begins on the Rent Revision Date;

    (iii) the terms of which (other than relating to the amount of the rent) are the same as those of this tenancy;

but disregarding those matters set out in sections 14(2) and 14(3) of the Housing Act 1988.

    (f) The revised rent as so agreed or so determined shall take effect from the Rent Revision Date [save that if the reference to an agreed Nominated Valuer, or application for appointment of a Nominated Valuer, occurs more than [three] months after the Rent Revision Date then the revised rent shall take effect at the first rent date following such reference or application].

    (g) The [Nominated Valuer shall have power to provide for the payment of his fees by only one party if he considers that that party has acted unreasonably in not agreeing a rent proposed by the other party but otherwise the] fees of the Nominated Valuer shall be borne equally by the parties.

Notes

    It is anticipated that the Form will be used primarily in fixed term assured tenancies. Periodic tenancies may have the rent revised under section 13 of the Housing Act 1988, but those provisions, with the possible intervention of the Rent Assessment Committee, do not apply where the tenancy agreement itself provides for variation and there is no objection in principle to such a provision in a periodic tenancy.

The Form avoids notices and is designed to encourage rent revision by informal agreement. Where reference to a valuer is necessary, the basis of valuation is designed to mirror the statutory formula set out in section 14 of the Housing Act. The disregards referred to in clause (e) may be set out in full if it is so desired.

Reference should be made to the Notes to Form 5–100.

Section Five

Clauses providing for Indexation to the Retail Prices Index

1   CONVEYANCER PRECEDENT 5–11
VARIABLE RENT CLAUSE PROVIDING FOR THE VARIATION OF RENT (AT SPECIFIED POINTS) ACCORDING TO THE INDEX OF RETAIL PRICES

Precedents for the Conveyancer, Form 5–11

(First published April 1971. Withdrawn and republished August 1988)

Yielding and Paying Therefor

1. For the period from and including the date of this Lease to and including the —— day of —— 19— the Initial Rent defined in the Schedule.
2. For each successive Rental Period as defined in the Schedule the Adjusted Rent as defined in the Schedule.

THE SCHEDULE
1. In this Schedule
'the Adjusted Rent' means the Initial Rent multiplied by the Variable Factor
'Adjustment Date' means the first day of each Rental Period
'the Index' means the Index of Retail Prices published by the Department of Employment or by any other Department Ministry or other body upon which the duties in connection with the Index devolves
'Index Date' means the base date of the Index
'the Initial Rent' means the yearly rent of £......
'New Index Date' has the meaning given in paragraph 2
'Rental Period' means the successive periods of [5 years] commencing on —— — 19— and on every [fifth] anniversary of that date
'the Variable Factor' means
(i)   if the Index Date remains January 13 1987 the fraction of which the denominator is —— [*the selected base figure, eg the Index figure last published, that last published of the preceding quarter day or as the case may be*] and the numerator is the average figure of the twelve Indices last published prior to the Adjustment Date
(ii) if the Index Date does not remain January 13 1987 the composite fraction calculated under paragraph 2.
2. If the Index Date does not remain January 13 1987

728

(i) the 'New Index Date' means the Index Date last fixed

(ii) the Variable Factor shall be calculated by ascertaining what the Variable Factor would have been had the New Index Date been an Adjustment Date and at the next Adjustment Date multiplying that fraction by a second fraction of which the denominator is 100 and the numerator is the average figure of the twelve Indices last published since the New Index Date and prior to the Adjustment Date or of those Indices published since the New Index Date and prior to the Adjustment Date if fewer than twelve

(iii) the calculation specified in (ii) shall be repeated on the occasion of each successive change in the Index Date.

3. A memorandum of each calculation of a Variable Factor under paragraph 1 and of a notional Variable Factor at a New Index Date and each following Variable Factor under paragraph 2 and of each Adjusted Rent shall be signed by or on behalf of the Landlord and the Tenant and attached to this Lease and the counter-part Lease and shall thereafter be binding on both parties.

4. Notwithstanding anything hereinbefore otherwise contained where the rent in relation to a Rental Period would (apart from this provision) not be greater than the yearly rent payable immediately before the commencement of such Rental Period then the Adjusted Rent for such Rental Period shall be the same as the amount of the yearly rent payable for the period immediately proceeding such Rental Period.

5. If any dispute difference or question arises between the Landlord and the Tenant as to the amount of rent payable or the construction or effect of this Schedule or if Her Majesty's Government ceases to publish any Index of Retail Prices or if it becomes impossible or impracticable to implement the above provisions for calculating rent then the question as to the amount of the rent payable for any Rental Period shall be referred for determination by a single arbitrator [in accordance with the provisions of the Arbitration Act 1950]

(i) the arbitrator shall determine the rent payable for the Rental Period in question on the basis of the amount of yearly rent which as between a willing landlord and a willing tenant might in the market conditions prevailing at the commencement of the Rental Period in question ('the Relevant Date') have been expected to be obtainable for the demised premises on the footing that the same were being let on lease with vacant possession without a fine for a term corresponding to the unexpired residue of the term at the Relevant Date and on the hypothesis that all the Tenant's covenants have been duly performed and observed down to the Relevant Date and that the covenants and provisions to be inserted in the lease are those contained in this Lease except those for the calculation of rent under paragraphs (1) and (2) but including this present paragraph for ascertaining the rent for each following Rental Period and the rent ascertained under this paragraph shall be deemed the Adjusted Rent

(ii) if and so long as after the commencement of any Rental Period the rent payable for that period shall not have been determined then provided the Tenant shall continue to pay rent on the basis of the yearly rent payable during the immediately preceding period and shall pay on the quarter day next following the date on which the rent for the said Rental Period shall have been determined the amount of any accrued additional rent which shall be found to be payable together with interest thereon at the rate of [   ] payable from the date upon which such accrued additional rent shall have been found to have been payable then the Tenant shall not in relation to the period between the commencement of the said Rental Period and the said quarter day be considered as being in arrear with the payment of rent hereunder but shall otherwise be considered as being in arrear (in whole or in part as the case may be) with such payment.

Publishers Notes

1   The original notes in April 1971 read:
'Doubts have, from time to time, been cast upon the validity of variable rent clauses as a matter of principle (as opposed to questions of uncertainty of language) but they are now well-established in the leasehold world and have now been recognised by statute (see section 2 of the Law of Property Act 1969). See also *Beachway Management Ltd* v *Wisewell* [1970] 3 WLR 1118. For some of the basic problems concerning such clauses, see an article by B Hargrove in (1957) 21 Conv (NS) 265–279.
The present form contemplates a series of rental periods and gears the rent payable in all but the first of these periods to the "Cost of Living" Index and adopts the average monthly figure for the preceding twelve-month period as the criterion rather than the monthly figure for the preceding month. The reason for this is that the latter may fluctuate seasonally and produce an exaggerated result (either way) in relation to the trend of prices generally.'

2   *General*

The validity of a variable rent linked to the Retail Prices Index was clearly accepted in *Blumenthal* v *Gallery Five Ltd* [1971] EGD 820.

3   *1988 Revisions*

The original wording has been recast in a more modern style and to clarify the effect of any adjustment in the base date of the RPI, as has happened since first publication. Various changes have also been made to bring what is, in effect, the alternative 'rent review' more closely in line with modern drafting practice. Other elements of rent review formulas, eg disregard of rental effect of voluntary improvements, goodwill or the tenant occupation could be added, if desired.

4   *Adjustments to Index other than Base Date*

Attempts have been made to cater for adjustments to the make-up; one such provision was litigated in *Cumshaw Ltd* v *Bowen* (1987) 281 EG 68 and the minor changes were held not to trigger the abandonment of indexation.

5   *Arbitration*

The optional phrase in Clause 5 is unnecessary as by s 32 of the 1950 Act it applies to all written arbitration agreements.

Authors' Note

This form is discussed in Chapter 20; see especially pp 568–576.

2   CONVEYANCER PRECEDENT 5–11A
VARIATION OF LAST FORM—ANNUAL ADJUSTMENTS

Precedents for the Conveyancer, Form 5–11A

(First published August 1980. Withdrawn and republished October 1988)

Yielding and Paying therefor
1. For the year starting on the date of this Lease the Initial Rent stated in the Schedule
2. For each successive year the Adjusted Rent as defined in the Schedule

THE SCHEDULE

1. In this Schedule
'the Adjusted Rent' means [*continue as in Form 5–11*]
'Adjustment Date' means the —— —— in each year
'the Index' means [*continue as in Form 5–11*]
'Index Date' means [*continue as in Form 5–11*]
'the Initial Rent' is £——
'New Index Date' has the meaning given in paragraph 2
'the Variable Factor' means
(a) if the Index Date remains January 13, 1987 the fraction of which the denominator is —— [*the selected base figure*] and the numerator is the Index figure last published before the Adjustment Date.
(b) if the Index Date does not remain January 13, 1987 the composite fraction calculated under paragraph 2.
2. If the Index Date does not remain January 13, 1987
(a) 'New Index Date' means the Index Date last fixed
(b) 'the Variable Factor' shall be calculated by ascertaining what the Variable Factor would have been had the New Index Date been an Adjustment Date and at the next Adjustment Date multiplying that factor by a second fraction of which the denominator is 100 and the numerator is the Index figure last published before that Adjustment Date
(c) [*as paragraph 2(iii) in Form 5–11*]
3. [*as in Form 5–11*]

OR

3. Within [14 days] after each Adjustment Date the Landlord must serve on the Tenant a notice showing how the Adjusted Rent has been calculated for the year then current and the Tenant may only challenge such calculations by serving on the Landlord a notice specifying any objections to the calculation within [21 days] after service of the Landlord's notice.
4. [*as in Form 5–11 but altering* 'Rental Period' *to* 'year' *throughout*]
5. [*as in Form 5–11 but altering* 'Rental Period' *to* 'year' *throughout*]

Publisher's Notes

The major differences between this Form and Form 5–11 is that it provides for annual adjustments and uses the Index last published before each anniversary, despite the problems of arbitrariness that may create as referred to in the Notes to Form 5–11.

The alternative form of paragraph 3 avoids the possibly unwieldy machinery of a yearly addition to the attached Memoranda.

Form 5–99 is an alternative formulation for annual indexation (see p 723).

Section Six

Short Form of Clause for a Retail Turnover Rent

Introduction: This section contains Form 139 from the *Encyclopaedia of Forms and Precedents* (5th ed). Form 140 is a longer form and is not reproduced here.

EFP (5th ed) FORM 139

Encyclopaedia of Forms and Precedents (5th ed) Volume 22, Form 139

PROVISIONS where rent is linked to tenant's turnover—short form¡

(First published 1986)

1.11 'Turnover Rent Percentage' means ...%
1.12 'Turnover Period' means each period of one year commencing on the ... day of ...
2.10 'Turnover Rent' means rent ascertained in accordance with the fifth schedule
2.11 'Rent' means the Initial Rent and rent ascertained in accordance with the second schedule and such term includes neither the Insurance Rent nor the Turnover Rent but the terms 'rents' includes the Rent the Insurance and the Turnover Rent
2.12–2.13 *(continue as in Form 22 clauses 2.11 and 2.12)*
4 *(continue as in Form 22 clause 4 but add '4.3 By way of further rent the Turnover Rent payable in accordance with the fifth schedule')*

SECOND SCHEDULE

(continue as in Form 22 second schedule making the following amendments:
- *paragraph 1.3:6 to conclude 'except as set out in paragraphs 1.3:7 and 1.3:9'*
- *paragraph 1.3:7 to begin 'that the lease referred to in paragraph 1.3:4 does not include the reservation of the Turnover Rent and that the only rents reserved by that lease are the Initial Rent and rent ascertained in accordance with the second schedule and the Insurance Rent (there being no references in the lease to Turnover Rent Percentage Turnover Period or Turnover Rent) and that the term of the lease ...'*
(continue as in Form 22 second schedule paragraph 1.3:7)

- *add as paragraph 1.3:9 'that [75]% of is deleted from paragraph 2.3 of the second schedule to the lease referred to in paragraph 1.3:4'*
- *insert in paragraph 2.3 '[75]% of' after 'he shall decide to be' and before 'the rent at which'*

FIFTH SCHEDULE

1 Gross Turnover

'Gross Turnover'[2] means the aggregate of all sums:
1.1   received or receivable for all goods sold leased hired or otherwise disposed of or for services rendered at in from or upon the Premises by the Tenant or any other person and
1.2   received or receivable by the Tenant for the use and/or occupation of the Premises or any part of the Premises by any other person
but excluding:
1.3   VAT purchase tax and any similar sales or excise tax imposed directly on the Tenant in respect of the supply of goods or services and actually paid or accounted for by the Tenant to the taxing authorities and
1.4   any sum refunded or credit given to [its] customers in respect of defective or unsatisfactory goods or services provided that such sum or credit shall not exceed the sale price of the goods or the charge for the services included in the Gross Turnover and
1.5   ...% of any sum received by the Tenant for services performed otherwise than at the Premises but where the orders are received at the Premises

2 Turnover Rent

The Turnover Rent for a Turnover Period shall be the Turnover Rent Percentage of the Gross Turnover for the year immediately preceding that Turnover Period

3 Certificate

Within [30] days after the end of a Turnover Period the Tenant shall deliver to the Landlord a certificate signed by a professionally qualified accountant appointed by the Tenant certifying the amount of the Gross Turnover during such Turnover Period PROVIDED that if:
3.1   the Tenant fails to supply a certificate under the provisions of this paragraph or
3.2   any dispute arises between the parties as to the amount of the Gross Turnover or the Turnover Rent
the Gross Turnover and the Turnover Rent shall be determined by a member of the Institute of Chartered Accountants in England and Wales appointed by the President of such Institute acting as an expert and not as an arbitrator whose decision shall be binding on both parties

4 Inspection of accounts etc

The Tenant shall make available for inspection at all reasonable times by the Landlord or [its] agent duly authorised for that purpose in writing the Tenant's books documents and records which are or in the opinion of the Landlord ought to be kept by the Tenant for purpose of ascertaining and verifying the Gross Turnover or which in the opinion of the Landlord are or may be relevant for such purpose and the Tenant shall bear the cost of such inspection if any material discrepancy is discovered

5 Payment and interim provisions

5.1 The Turnover Rent shall be payable without deduction by equal quarterly payments in advance on the usual quarter days

5.2 If the Turnover Rent has not been determined for a Turnover Period on or before the first quarter day during that Turnover Period the Tenant shall pay to the Landlord on that and any subsequent quarter days prior to the determination of the Turnover Rent a sum on account of the Turnover Rent equal to the amount of Turnover Rent that was payable on the quarter day immediately preceding the beginning of that Turnover Period ('Sum on Account')

5.3 Upon determination of the Turnover Rent there shall be payable [immediately *or* upon the next quarter day] the difference between the Sum on Account and what would have been payable had the Turnover Rent been determined on or before the first quarter day of the Turnover Period ('Actual Sum')

[5.4 Where the Sum on Account exceeds the Actual Sum the Tenant shall be entitled to deduct the difference from the Rent due on the next quarter day]

[5.5 If the Turnover Rent is determined in accordance with paragraphs 3.1 or 3.2 and if the Actual Sum exceeds the Sum on Account the Tenant shall pay Interest on the difference between each instalment of the Sum on Account and what would have been payable on each quarter day had the Turnover Rent for that Turnover Period been determined for the period from the quarter day upon which the instalment was due up to the date of payment]

Published Notes [Authors changes in square brackets]

1 This Form is designed to be incorporated in Form 22 second schedule [above p 681] and the clauses and paragraphs set out in this Form should be substituted and/or added where appropriate. The clauses and paragraphs to which no reference is made in this Form should be set out in full as they appear in Form 22. As to rents linked to turnover generally [see p 584]. This Form contemplates that a basic rent will also be reserved [see p 590]. This will be a defined percentage of the open market rent and will be reviewed in the normal way. The landlord might like to give itself the right to vary the lease by deleting the turnover rent provisions so that the rent reverts to the full open market rent. For more sophisticated provisions see Form 140 [not printed in this book].

2 For a more detailed definition of Gross Turnover see Form 140.

Index

737